Lomas : The First One Hundred Years

1894-1993

18 94	18 95	18 96	18 97	18 98	18 99	19 00	19 01	19 02	19 03
19 04	19 05	19 06	19 07	19 08	19 09	19 10	19 11	19 12	19 13
19 14	19 15	19 16	19 17	19 18	19 19	19 20	19 21	19 22	19 23
19 24	19 25	19 26	19 27	19 28	19 29	19 30	19 31	19 32	19 33
19 34	19 35	19 36	19 37	19 38	19 39	19 40	19 41	19 42	19 43
19 44	19 45	19 46	19 47	19 48	19 49	19 50	19 51	19 52	19 53
19 54	19 55	19 56	19 57	19 58	19 59	19 60	19 61	19 62	19 63
19 64	19 65	19 66	19 67	19 68	19 69	19 70	19 71	19 72	19 73
19 74	19 75	19 76	19 77	19 78	19 79	19 80	19 81	19 82	19 83
19 84	19 85	19 86	19 87	19 88	19 89	19 90	19 91	19 92	19 93

L O M A S

THE FIRST ONE HUNDRED YEARS

A
History of
The Lomas Financial Group

By
William R. Simon

Pictorial research by
James A. Ledbetter

This publication was written, designed, and produced by commission
for Lomas Financial Corporation, Dallas, Texas.

First edition, 1994.

Lomas Financial Corporation
1600 Viceroy Drive
Dallas, Texas 75235

ISBN 0-9640427-0-3
Library of Congress Catalogue Card number 94-75268

Designed and produced by James A. Ledbetter, Dallas, Texas.

Printed and bound in Hong Kong by South China Printing Company.

LOMAS

COVER
Corporate offices of the Lomas Financial Group.

FRONTISPIECE
Lobby/atrium of Lomas Mortgage USA building.

CONTENTS

For any company to reach the 100-year mark defies all odds. For one involved in the real estate industry to last that long nearly defies imagination.

The very fact that so few businesses, whatever their industry, achieve this remarkable milestone stands as a tribute to the companies that do. More than that, it is a tribute to the men and women who lead them. We have had the privilege of being witnesses to, and in small ways participants in, three decades in the extraordinary history of one of those rare companies. We can attest that the story of Lomas' rise to national stature is a dramatic and inspiring one, peopled with characters well worth knowing—and none more so than our friend Jess Hay, whose vision and character have been the backbone of Lomas during its most challenging years.

That is our eyewitness perspective. Yet as we review the whole of Lomas' first century, it is obvious that we have been acquainted with merely the latest generation of strong leadership. At any given time in any industry, a company's operating environment may be more or less sunny, and the consequences of management decisions may be more or less favorable. Yet even in the most turbulent of industries, Lomas has always found individuals whose cool heads and sound principles would anchor the company in prosperous times and pull it through calamitous ones. (That they have sometimes, as in Jess' case, had to arrive on the scene for eleventh-hour heroics only makes the story better.)

In the history of Lomas we see a company that started right, with sound thinking and strong ethics, and has always managed, come what might, to keep its principles straight. The way Lomas reached this centennial year is truly an American success story. We are grateful to have seen firsthand how great a company can become when it is built on a solid foundation, and as heads of companies ourselves we are inspired by Lomas' example.

Gene H. Bishop
Chairman and Chief Executive Officer,
Life Partners Group, Inc.
Dallas, Texas

Stan Richards
Principal,
The Richards Group
Dallas, Texas

ACKNOWLEDGMENTS

Many people helped in the preparation of this history. I owe special thanks to Lomas Financial Corporation chairman and CEO Jess Hay, whose initiative launched this project in 1988 in anticipation of Lomas Mortgage USA's approaching 100th anniversary.

I also owe a debt of gratitude to the members of Mr. Hay's staff, whose exceptional professionalism facilitated the book's progress: Joy Weldon, Judy Justice, Rebecca Reed, Kevin McGarry, Barbara Deborah, Valerie Masters, Carol Forsberg, and Betty Watson. Senior vice president and secretary Ramona Taylor deserves special recognition for her superb management of the thousand and one details that a project of this complexity requires, and for the remarkable attention to detail that she applied to the task of editing and proofreading. Lorraine Grant's outstanding audio tape transcriptions and morale-boosting notes and observations provided another source of support for which I am grateful.

I wish to express my appreciation to the scores of individuals I interviewed. Without their contribution, this book would have been impossible to write.

Jim Ledbetter—colleague, cohort, and graphic designer par excellence—was a constant source of inspiration. His relentless pursuit of graphic material led to the discovery of a number of remarkable archival treasures, including the 1878 personal diary of Lomas founder John E. Lomas. Matthew Abbate, who edited the manuscript and prepared the index, made many notable improvements to the book.

The Farmers Branch Manske Library was an invaluable resource, and I am indebted to assistant library director and head of public services Karel Tabor and all the other staff members for their assistance and courtesy.

My earliest preparation for authorship began on board the *Pequod*, and I am deeply grateful to my mother, Florence Simon, whose introduction to that and other adventures nurtured an interest in reading and storytelling that continues to this day. And I must certainly thank my wife Elaine, whose fine editorial eye saved me from myself on numerous occasions. Her support and patience were indispensable. I am also indebted to my daughter Rebecca, whose enthusiasm for turning off my computer never waned, and who has given me a new understanding of the word adoration.

William R. Simon
Dallas, Texas

INTRODUCTION

With the conclusion of 1993, the Lomas Financial Group celebrated 100 years as a continuous business enterprise. The company's overriding goal during this period has been constant: to provide products and services for the mortgage banking industry. Over 600,000 homeowners in 50 states rely on Lomas' mortgage servicing to collect their mortgage payments, maintain their escrow accounts for real estate taxes and mortgage insurance, and distribute those payments to institutional investors. The fees the company collects for this service are small, but thanks to the benefit of scale it has quietly used those predictable, recurring revenues to build the second largest independent mortgage banking company in the nation.

Lasting success in business is rare. One of the qualities that enables a firm to thrive, decade after decade, is entrepreneurship. Lomas encourages managers to behave as entrepreneurs. Michael Patrick, chief financial officer and president of Lomas Mortgage USA and Lomas Information Systems, calls that trait "the spirit of Lomas—the willingness to let people within the organization go to bat and swing." People at Lomas have been stepping up to the plate and swinging throughout its history. The company has long valued what Franklin Roosevelt called "bold, persistent experimentation."

Like that of many corporations of substantial size, Lomas' growth has not been all internal. Acquisitions have played a major role in its expansion. The story of Lomas is also the story of companies that made separate contributions to the mortgage banking industry before uniting under the Lomas name. The company welcomed the dynamism and creativity they brought with them, but the challenge of integrating diverse corporate cultures was not easy. Disputes within the Lomas family were, at times, contentious.

For the past 29 years, chairman and CEO Jess Hay has shouldered the responsibility for harnessing the company's disparate parts. The driving force behind his leadership has been the certain knowledge of where the company was going and how it should get there. "Successful CEOs see themselves as leaders, not managers," says Warren Bennis, noted author, teacher, and former university president. Visionary leadership is the hallmark of Hay's professional career. John Naisbitt and Patricia Aburdene in their book *Reinventing the Corporation* identified "vision" as the critical component for a successful business philosophy. "By envisioning the future you want, you can more easily achieve your goal. Vision is the link between dream and action. . . . Intellectual strategies alone will not motivate people. Only a company with a real mission or sense of purpose that comes out of an intuitive or spiritual dimension will capture people's hearts. And you must have people's hearts to inspire the hard work required to realize a vision." Hay's ability to formulate visions and inspire others to realize them is strongly connected to spirituality. At the core of his philosophy is a set of Christian values and an absolute belief in integrity. "Profit with honor" became the corporate credo that continues to permeate the organization under his leadership.

It was during the company's darkest hour following its filing under Chapter 11 in 1989 that this writer witnessed a small but telling example of Lomas honor in action. Price Waterhouse, the accounting firm for the creditors committee in the bankruptcy proceedings, had recently arrived at Lomas' Dallas operations. Complaints about the PW representatives' aggressive, intrusive behavior and the disruption it caused ultimately reached the desk of former Lomas Administrative Services president Buddy Miller. In an interview at the time, Miller explained how he was going to fix up an unused area the company leased at Bryan Tower, its corporate headquarters, for the accountants' exclusive use. It would of course contain the essentials: phones, desks, chairs, and file cabinets. But Miller kept emphasizing how *nice* it was going to be. It would be more than a bare bones work space; he intended to provide a pleasant working environment. At the end of his recitation of its aesthetic enhancements, he turned to me and said, "After all, they're people, too." Buddy Miller's simple assertion of humanity glittered like a rare jewel in an atmosphere rife with recrimination, anger, and resentment.

Profit is the other half of the Lomas credo. Like all institutions that succeed over time, the company understands that profits come from meeting customers' needs, which are ever changing. The Lomas Financial Group's ability to identify and meet changes head on has allowed it to build its position of leadership as the most efficient provider of mortgage banking services. Lomas' continued commitment to entrepreneurship is the source of corporate strength that calls forth new responses to the opportunities of the present and to those still hidden in the future.

Viewed from a larger perspective, this book represents more than the history of a successful business enterprise. Lomas is a company connected to the way Americans live. We are reminded of those ties each time we enter an office building, shopping center, school, hospital, church, apartment, or home. The product of Lomas' services shapes the landscape of our lives in ways that touch us directly and personally. What follows is the story of the Lomas Financial Group and its contribution to the building of America.

PROLOGUE

When Wallace Properties, Inc., opened for business on April 1, 1960, in Dallas, Texas, the earth did not move. In fact, the organizers of the company considered their real estate venture little more than a means of diversifying nonessential capital. Most had larger and hotter irons in other financial fires. It was only later, after the company had evolved into Lomas & Nettleton Financial Corporation, that what began as a sideshow, unnoticed by most, became a multi-billion-dollar main event, with every corporate move scrutinized by security analysts up and down Wall Street. Despite the company's modest entry into the business world, there was a consensus among its investors on at least one point—Wallace Properties was a dead-certain cinch to cash in on the real estate boom.

Their confidence came from 15 years of explosive economic growth. Beginning at the end of World War II, converging supply and demand propelled the American economy toward unprecedented prosperity. The record-breaking levels of production that had won the war went on to break new records trying to meet America's postwar expectations for a better life. After a brief grinding of gears for retooling, the economy climbed, then soared. The pent-up demand for consumer goods was overwhelming. The goods and services people couldn't afford during the Depression and couldn't obtain during the war were a fading memory everyone wanted to forget.

Americans were ready for a buying binge: and they had the money to pay for it. The income they had accumulated during the war meant substantial postwar purchasing power. From 1946 to 1949 annual purchases of consumer durable goods more than doubled over the rate of the previous 15 years, and housing produc-

Returning veterans from World War II brought home with them a desire for a better world and a better life. National Archives, Washington, D.C.

tion tripled. One Korean War veteran returning home to Hastings, Nebraska, in 1950 was astonished at what he found: "Man, I never saw anything like it. This town is just one big boom." That same year New York state had so few unemployment claims that it fired five hundred people in its compensation division. Long-established brokerage firms like Ira Haupt & Co. were now setting up tent exhibits at places like the Mineola, Long Island, County Fair. "Money has changed hands," said Ernest E. Ruppe, the Haupt man assigned to the fair. "The people who used to have it don't. The workingman does. One of my best customers is a potato farmer in Hicksville; I've sold him nineteen thousand dollars worth of mutual funds."

The best barometer for measuring postwar economic vitality was the housing industry. During the thirties, lack of funds and uncertainty had cut deeply into construction and housing starts. Homebuilding further declined during the war when strict federal controls redirected materials and industry toward war production. With hostilities concluded, an already critical housing shortage intensified as the government initiated a rapid "wanna-go-home" demobilization of its 16 million servicemen. For many vets the return to civilian life meant marriage. And that meant children—lots of them.

Almost before anybody could say Dr. Spock, the United States had another boom on its hands. By 1947 six million families were doubling up with family or friends. Two thousand people answered an ad for one apartment in Atlanta. In Chicago, 250 former trolley cars were sold as homes. Surplus grain bins in North

The lack of housing for growing families was a pressing need for millions of Americans. Many types of shelter became homes, such as this converted trailer. National Archives, Washington, D.C.

Dakota were turned into apartments. In Omaha a newspaper advertisement proposed: "Big Ice Box 7 x 17 feet, could be fixed up to live in." In New York City a newlywed couple set up housekeeping for two days in a department store window in hopes that the publicity would help them find an apartment. One of the strongest advocates for housing was Senator Glen Taylor, a cowboy singer sent to the capital by the people of Idaho primarily on the strength of his skill with a banjo. Standing on the Capitol steps with his wife and children, he sang:

Oh, give me a home near the Capitol dome,
With a yard where little children can play.
Just one room or two, any old thing will do,
Oh, we cain't find a pla-ace to stay.

To make matters worse, the housing industry didn't have the ability to respond to the shortage. Residential construction was dominated by small, poorly organized builders. It would take a miracle to accomplish what one government study claimed was needed: a ten-year program that would erect 1.5 million homes a year.

The miracle turned out to be an ex-Navy Seabee by the name of William J. Levitt. He answered the prayers of millions by transforming a cottage industry into a major manufacturing process. Through the use of prefabricated and assembly line techniques, Levitt performed production miracles that rivaled anything accomplished during the war. He proudly referred to his family company, Levitt and Sons, as "the General Motors of the housing industry."

The housing industry didn't have the answer to the shortage in residential construction. However, William Levitt did. Levittown Public Library Photograph Collection.

"I remember," says William Levitt, "sitting out in Pearl Harbor with a couple of fellow officers. I was in the Seabees, and all of us, of course, were associated one way or another with building. And I said to them, 'Do you fellows realize that for five years, the year before the war and four more for us, there's been literally no housing built for people. Some defense housing, but that's all. And when we get home, there's going to be a mad rush.'"

Levitt started the rush in a Long Island potato field. Land was cheap and Levitt didn't care much for cities anyway. Here, in 1949, he built Levittown and revolutionized residential construction. "It was the reverse of the automobile assembly line," Levitt explains. "The product stood still and the workmen moved. Very specialized crews came in one by one and built parts of the house. For instance, one carpenter crew did only framing. Another did only trimming. Another did only roofing.

"It was just a question of trying to build as fast as you could. And we were building at the rate of 18 houses in the morning and 18 in the afternoon, every day, five days a week."

Despite their best efforts, the frantic building pace couldn't keep up with demand. "We ran an ad," says Levitt, "saying that Monday morning the [show] house will open and we'll take deposits, a hundred dollars down. On Wednesday night, crowds began to gather on the lawn . . . and across the road. By Monday morning the line was as far as your eye could see. We drew up 1,100 contracts in one day."

The people who moved into the development were pioneers, too. "The thing that was different here," says Clare Worthing, an original Levittown resident, "is we started from potato fields; there was no community when we moved in. We were all new, so we were all facing the same things. [Many] homes didn't have telephones initially, so we had to know which neighbors had phones in case of emergencies. Lawns were seeded, so we had to live through the mud and all the problems of getting established."

A field of dreams. Long Island potato fields before being developed into Levittown, c. 1947. Nassau County Museum Reference Library.

Levittown after construction, c. 1949. Nassau County Museum Reference Library.

Levittown also launched the beginning of a new American lifestyle. The "good life" postwar America yearned for meant a house of one's own with grass and trees, a place for children to play and grow. For millions of Americans home ownership and suburban living represented freedom, independence, and security. By 1950 homeowners exceeded renters for the first time since census information became available in 1890.

Sandy and Rita Holzsweig were typical of those who found satisfaction in suburbia. A struggling young family with two babies, they remember their first new home in a Levitt-like development in Pleasant Hill, Pennsylvania, outside of Pittsburgh. "It was just a plain box," Rita Holzsweig recalls. "No frills. None at all. Everything was white. There was no wallpaper. We later wallpapered the bathroom.

"But it was brand new. And spanking clean. It was such a thrill to move into a new house of our own. It wasn't even finished. The builder added the brick veneer to the house after we moved in. I remember the Italian workmen singing opera for two days while they laid the brick."

House selection was limited. Buyers could choose either ranch style or split-level. But, like Levittown, it was very affordable. "The house cost $15,000," says Sandy Holzsweig, then working as an engineer for

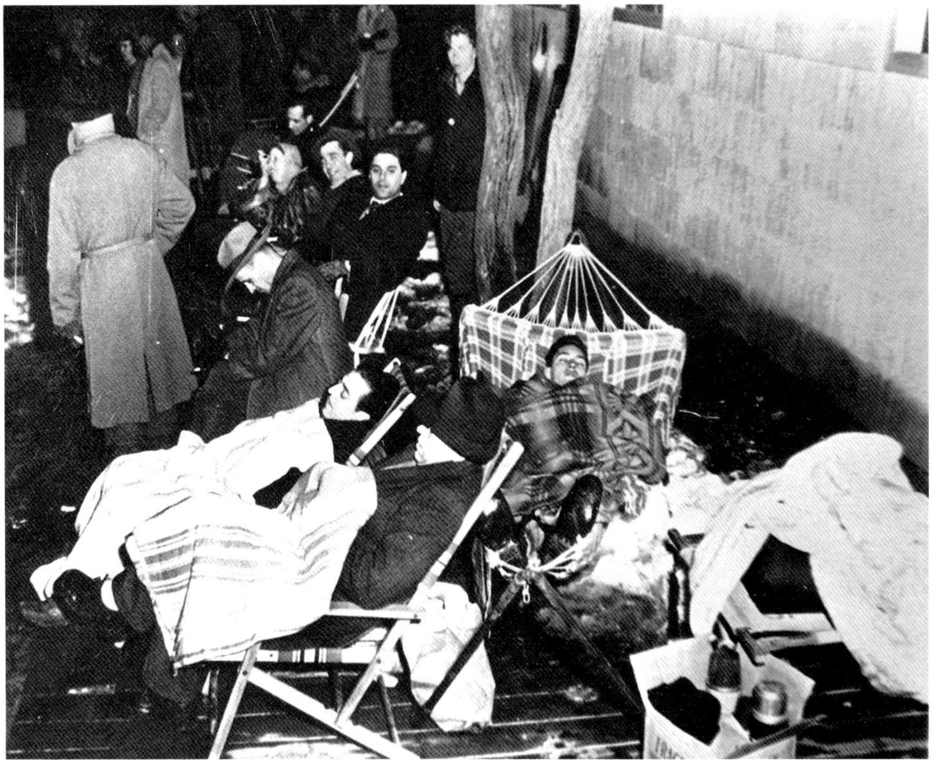

After a newspaper notice appeared, returning veterans and ordinary civilians lined up and camped out waiting to sign up to buy a Levitt house. Levittown Public Library Photograph Collection.

Workers finishing a row of ranch style houses worked hard to keep pace with the demand for the new American lifestyle started at Levittown. Levittown Public Library Photograph Collection.

For many, the "good life" started in this finished section of Cape Cod style houses, c. 1947–48. Levittown Public Library Photograph Collection.

Westinghouse. "I was an ex-serviceman; so we borrowed the full amount and financed it at four and a half percent. Our payments were a hundred dollars a month."

Levitt's potato field dreams became part of the American dream. His revolutionary building techniques paved the way for affordable suburban housing. "There were people," says Levittown homeowner Jerry Worthing, "that were really grateful—everybody was grateful—to have some sort of place to live. William Levitt was a hero."

Besides accolades, Levitt's company earned hefty profits. Real estate development and construction became a high stakes arena that attracted a new breed of developer. They were men who dreamed large dreams and subscribed to William Levitt's business philosophy: "You have to have nerve. You have to think big."

Dallas' post–World War II growth, much of it generated by its outstanding businessmen, was reflected in the ever-changing skyline, seen in this 1945 photograph. From the collections of the Texas/Dallas History and Archives Division, Dallas Public Library.

CHAPTER 1

BIRTH OF A BUSINESS

Dallas, Texas, had no shortage of businessmen who dreamed large dreams. Much of the credit for the city's determined march toward postwar prosperity belonged to the visionary business ethic that guided civic affairs. A nod of national recognition for the success of that ethic came from *Fortune* magazine in 1949: "There Dallas stands—its skyscrapers soaring abruptly up from the black land like Maxfield Parrish castles. . . . It is the Athens of the Southwest, the undisputed leader of finance, insurance, distribution, culture and fashion for this land of the super-Americans. It is one of the cleanest, best policed, best managed cities in the country and one of the fastest growing."

Still on a red-hot roll in the late fifties, the Dallas real estate market attracted the attention of private investors like Edmund M. Hoffman. "It occurred to me," says Hoffman, "that there were a lot of people who wanted to invest in real estate, but they didn't have the opportunity." Hoffman recognized that by pooling capital through a syndicate, investors would have access to larger and more profitable transactions. In 1958 he laid the groundwork for just such an organization. "We had a group that was ready to go," Hoffman says. "The problem was we couldn't agree on the management, and that prevented it from coming together."

A year later Trammell Crow and his friend and business associate Eugene M. Locke, senior partner for the law firm Locke, Purnell, Boren, Laney & Neely, made a similar attempt. Their initiative led to the organization of Wallace Properties, Inc., the first link in the chain that became Lomas Financial Corporation.

By 1959 Trammell Crow already had an impressive string of real estate projects to his credit. His understanding of the Dallas real estate market and keen

Dallas investor Ed Hoffman attempted to organize a real estate investment syndicate.

Developer Trammell Crow was a founding member of the investment group that became Wallace Properties, Inc. Trammell Crow Company Archives.

instinct for commercial development led him to the Trinity Industrial District near downtown Dallas in the late 1940s. There he erected his first speculative warehouse and proceeded to build America's largest private real estate firm—the Trammell Crow Company, with more than $5 billion in assets.

. . . there were a lot of people who wanted to invest in real estate, but they didn't have the opportunity.

Organization of Locke and Crow's company was based on finding investors willing to contribute income-producing property in exchange for stock. Additional capital would come from a public offering and access to bank credit lines.

Following their initial discussions, Crow and Locke invited Ed Hoffman to participate. Gradually, the circle expanded to include Hoffman's uncle Jerome K. Crossman, chairman of the board and president of Ryan Consolidated Petroleum Co., and Henry C. Beck, Jr., president of the Henry C. Beck Company. Joe B. Hutchison, a Beck Company executive vice president and prominent Atlanta developer, also joined the board.

Besides sizable property contributions, Henry Beck, Jr., brought to the venture a national reputation for commercial construction. His company's projects list from the 1950s included a $2 million aircraft hangar at the Jacksonville, Florida, Naval Air Station, a $7 million 20-story office building for the National Bank of Commerce in San Antonio, a United States post office and courthouse in Illinois, NIKE guided missile facilities near Rapid City, South Dakota, and a $42 million jet aircraft engine plant for Pratt & Whitney near West Palm Beach, Florida.

During this early phase of organization, E. E. (Gene) Wallace, Jr., joined the investment group. Hoffman and Locke interviewed Wallace shortly after

Left: Eugene Locke, senior partner for the law firm of Locke, Purnell, Boren, Laney & Neely, cofounded and actively organized the investment group. Locke Purnell Rain Harrell Archives.

Right: The investment group expanded to include Henry Beck, contractor. Henry C. Beck Company Archives.

Below: Gene Wallace at the testimonial banquet of his close friend and business associate Ira Rupley. Frances Eason Archives.

his resignation as Republic National Bank's senior vice president in charge of the real estate division. His rags-to-riches track record at the bank was impressive. Beginning with a tiny two-man operation after the war, Wallace built a national real estate loan portfolio that represented 30 percent of Republic Bank's earnings on a continuous basis.

His qualifications and availability also solved the management problem that had stymied Hoffman's earlier effort. The principals asked Gene Wallace to join the board and serve as president at an annual salary of $75,000. In deference to his national banking reputation and real estate connections, they also agreed to name the company Wallace Properties, Inc.

He immediately made his presence felt by adding several business associates to the board of directors. John F. Austin, Jr., president of the Houston-based T. J. Bettes Company, the country's largest mortgage

Personal friendships and professional associations were much in evidence at the Ira L. Rupley Testimonial Banquet. From left to right: Tom Lively, Ira Rupley, and A. B. Cass, Jr. Frances Eason Archives.

company, gave the new company additional national prestige. Closer to home the board included A. B. Cass, Jr., president of Genell Diversified Properties, a development and apartment management company, and Tom Lively, president of Centex Construction Company, a national homebuilding firm with a controlling interest held by Dallas financier Clint Murchison, Jr., and Ira L. Rupley, cofounder of both Centex and Genell.

The personal friendships and professional association of Rupley, Lively, Cass, and Wallace in many ways typified the close-knit, aggressive, entrepreneurial spirit of the Dallas real estate industry. In terms of both age and experience, Ira Rupley was the mentor of the group. Reputed to have made and lost two fortunes before moving to Dallas in 1936, he entered the real estate market in the early 1940s by forming the Ruplex Development Co. In 1946 at the age of 66, Rupley cofounded the Rupley-Lively Construction Co. along with a young, energetic developer named Tom Lively. The insatiable demand for housing convinced the builders that a large-scale operation was justified. Rupley and Lively expanded their partnership in 1950 to include Fletcher Lippett, a former associate of Texas hotel builder Leo Corrigan. The infusion of capital from Lippett launched the firm, now called Centex Construction Company, toward national prominence.

Like William Levitt, the principal owners of Centex weren't afraid to dream large dreams. They thought in terms of national markets. Centex projects soon stretched across the country as far as California, Idaho, and Illinois. In their fifth year of operation, the company captured first place honors as the largest homebuilder in the nation. A year later *House and Home Magazine* recognized Centex as "the first and probably only truly national home building company." By 1961, Lively averaged 100,000 air miles of travel per year in order to keep track of building projects in 14 states—including Alaska and Hawaii as well as Puerto Rico.

The largest and most ambitious Centex project

during the 1950s was Elk Grove Village. The company borrowed a page from William Levitt's pioneering approach to residential development by designing and executing the construction of a totally planned community. The Texans began buying 1,500 acres of unincorporated farmland 20 miles northwest of Chicago's Loop beginning in 1954. Half of the acreage was allocated for single-family homes and half for an industrial park, whose projected contribution to the town's tax base was especially appealing to prospective homebuyers. When the adjacent O'Hare International Airport opened for commercial traffic in 1955, the value of the industrial park property increased substantially. The concept worked. At Elk Grove's twentieth anniversary in 1976, the industrial park generated 60 percent of the township's taxes.

Centex built a wall in front of the property in 1956 to conceal construction of the model homes and generate interest. The billboard-style message announced the imminent arrival of "Elk Grove Village—CHICAGOLAND'S SMARTEST NEW SUBURB." Opening day festivities at the development in the

The most ambitious project for Centex was Elk Grove Village in Illinois. Rudy's Tavern at the intersection of Route 72 and Higgins Road shows the rural character of the land in 1952 before development into a planned community. Mary McCarthy Archives.

Half of the purchased land was for single-family houses. This aerial view shows construction of the site with curving streets. In the grove of trees at left of center, middle distance, is Rudy's Tavern. The open space at the far right became the first fire station. Mary McCarthy Archives.

Finished houses in Elk Grove Village with Ira L. Rupley Elementary School in the background. Mary McCarthy Archives.

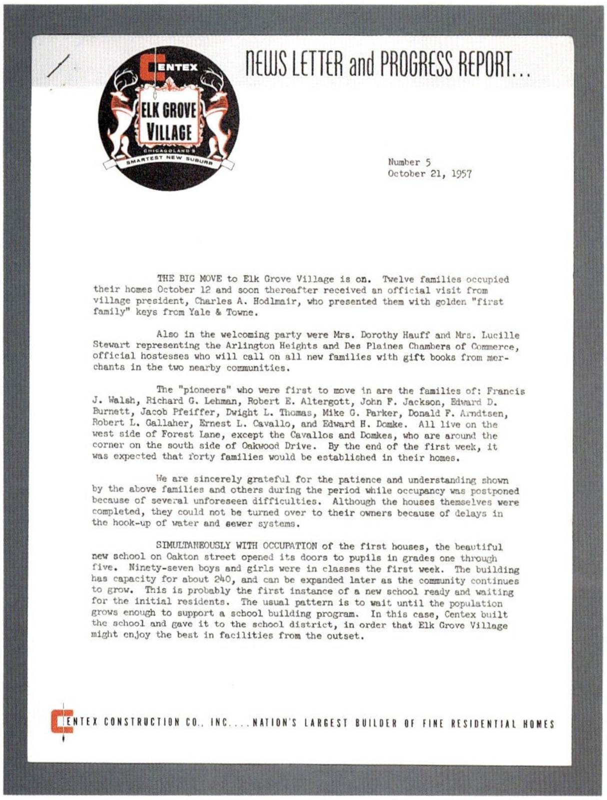

CENTEX
ELK GROVE VILLAGE
CHICAGOLAND'S SMARTEST NEW SUBURB

NEWS LETTER and PROGRESS REPORT...

Number 5
October 21, 1957

THE BIG MOVE to Elk Grove Village is on. Twelve families occupied their homes October 12 and soon thereafter received an official visit from village president, Charles A. Hodlmair, who presented them with golden "first family" keys from Yale & Towne.

Also in the welcoming party were Mrs. Dorothy Hauff and Mrs. Lucille Stewart representing the Arlington Heights and Des Plaines Chambers of Commerce, official hostesses who will call on all new families with gift books from merchants in the two nearby communities.

The "pioneers" who were first to move in are the families of: Francis J. Walsh, Richard G. Lehman, Robert E. Altergott, John F. Jackson, Edward D. Burnett, Jacob Pfeiffer, Dwight L. Thomas, Mike G. Parker, Donald F. Arndtsen, Robert L. Gallaher, Ernest L. Cavallo, and Edward H. Domke. All live on the west side of Forest Lane, except the Cavallos and Domkes, who are around the corner on the south side of Oakwood Drive. By the end of the first week, it was expected that forty families would be established in their homes.

We are sincerely grateful for the patience and understanding shown by the above families and others during the period while occupancy was postponed because of several unforeseen difficulties. Although the houses themselves were completed, they could not be turned over to their owners because of delays in the hook-up of water and sewer systems.

SIMULTANEOUSLY WITH OCCUPATION of the first houses, the beautiful new school on Oakton street opened its doors to pupils in grades one through five. Ninety-seven boys and girls were in classes the first week. The building has capacity for about 240, and can be expanded later as the community continues to grow. This is probably the first instance of a new school ready and waiting for the initial residents. The usual pattern is to wait until the population grows enough to support a school building program. In this case, Centex built the school and gave it to the school district, in order that Elk Grove Village might enjoy the best in facilities from the outset.

CENTEX CONSTRUCTION CO., INC.... NATION'S LARGEST BUILDER OF FINE RESIDENTIAL HOMES

The Elk Grove Village "News Letter and Progress Report" of October 21, 1957, opened with "THE BIG MOVE to Elk Grove Village is on." Opening day for Elk Grove Village was in the spring of 1957. On October 12, 1957, the first twelve families moved in. Mary McCarthy Archives.

The success of Elk Grove Village is reflected in the 1959 road sign before its first census as an incorporated village. Mary McCarthy Archives.

spring of 1957 brought a turnout estimated at 15,000 persons. The firm reported 312 sales, of which 75 percent were made with "GI financing." A story in the *Chicago Daily News* on April 5 praised the gutsy Texans with headlines that read: "The Eyes of Texas Are Upon Us—Lone Star dynamos start 6,000 homes in Elk Grove." The caption under a photograph of Lively and Centex vice president Frank M. Crossen emphasized their drive and determination: "Imaginative Texans map plans for 6,000 homes in Elk Grove development in big invasion of Chicago housing market."

A. B. Cass, Jr., was another real estate entrepreneur on a fast track. He won a certain amount of local celebrity in 1946 and 1947 when as a brash 26-year-old he put together a strip shopping center development on Lovers Lane that he called "The Miracle Mile." "He had great ideas, and he wasn't afraid to take a risk," says Doris Cass, his former wife. "He'd try anything. Lovers Lane was nothing. Lovers Lane was just a lover's lane, literally. But he made friends easily. Everybody liked him, and he liked everybody. He was very charismatic. He could sell anybody anything." Persistence and a flair for promotion enabled Cass to obtain the property needed for development from 15 landowners and successfully complete the shopping center.

That project gave Cass the momentum and connections he needed to tackle larger real estate ventures. His friendships with Rupley, Lively, and Republic National Bank senior vice president E. E. Wallace, Jr., led the four men to start Genell, Inc., in 1954. Later called Genell Diversified Properties, the new venture concentrated on land development and apartment development and management. As president of Genell, Cass' status as a "major Dallas real estate developer" was acknowledged in 1956 by no less an authority than *The Wall Street Journal*. Not even an overbuilt apartment market, the subject of the article, dampened the developer's confidence. According to the *Journal* story, Cass overcame that obstacle with characteristic brio:

> "Dallas is learning now what the rest of the country will soon learn—that you need good management and good merchandising in the apartment business just like in any other business," says A. B. Cass, Jr., a major Dallas real estate developer. Mr. Cass and partners recently took over the Westwood Apartments which were running about 50% vacant, and invested about $250,000 in a swimming pool, landscaping, remodeling, air conditioning and a promotion campaign. "We've got a waiting list now," he notes, thumping his desk.

A. B. Cass, Jr., developed Dallas' "Miracle Mile" on Lover's Lane in 1946–1947. He was a cofounder of Genell, Inc., later Genell Diversified Properties, and a founding director of Wallace Properties. To the right is J. Liener Temerlin, Glenn Advertising account executive for Genell, Inc., who was responsible for the arrangements of the Rupley tribute. Cass Archives.

Genell also enjoyed considerable success with land development. One of its largest and most profitable ventures was the purchase of a 50-acre tract at the corner of Northwest Highway and Preston Road just north of "the exclusive Preston Center shopping area." A newspaper article at the time noted that the sales price of $12,500+ an acre was believed to be the highest price ever paid "for undeveloped acreage in Dallas."

Despite their own real estate savvy, Cass, Lively, and Wallace relied heavily on Ira Rupley's expertise. Former Genell secretary Frances Eason believes that trust was well placed: "Mr. Rupley had a lot of vision when it came to real estate." Doris Cass, who sometimes accompanied her husband and Rupley when they went out to look at land, agrees: "Mr. Rupley was a genius at picking the right spots for development. He could study a piece of raw land and tell you in about a half hour whether or not it would be profitable to develop. He studied the land, made notes, and then he'd give you the reasons why it was or was not a good location. He was an amazing man. And he was a good man for two young men starting out after the war. Tom was like A. B. He'd take a chance on anything. Mr. Rupley was the one that kept them under control. He was the one that held the reins."

Appreciation of Rupley's real estate accomplishments took a public turn in 1958 when Lively, Cass, and Wallace organized an elaborate tribute dinner for their partner and colleague. According to one newspaper account: "More than 700 persons jammed into the candle-lit, flower-decked Grand Ballroom of the Statler Hilton Hotel Friday night to pay tribute to Ira Lee Rupley, civic leader and founder of one of the biggest home building corporations in the United States.

Tom Lively, right, was cofounder and first president of Centex Construction Company and one of the founding directors of Wallace Properties, Inc. He is talking with Dave Fox, a principal of the Fox & Jacobs Construction Company of Dallas, at the Rupley banquet. Cass Archives.

At the Rupley banquet, A. B. Cass, Jr., left, talks with Ward Wilcox, president and chairman of Glenn Advertising Agency. Cass Archives.

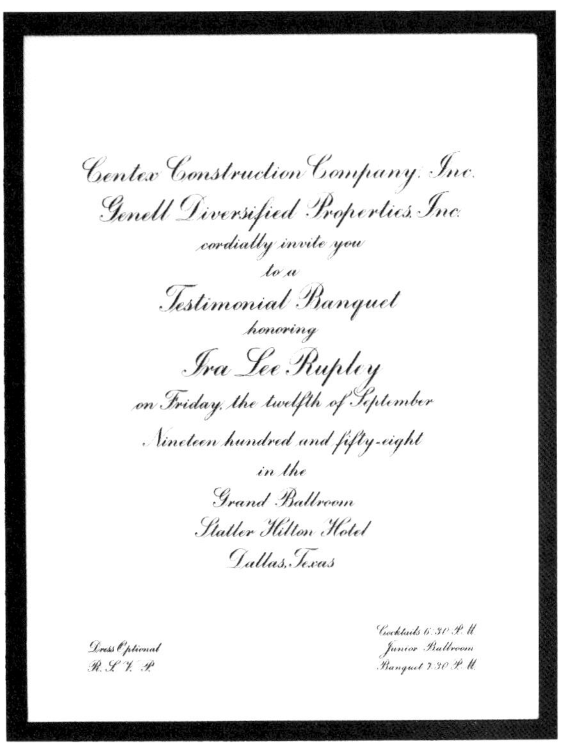

Centex Construction Company, Inc.
Genell Diversified Properties, Inc.
cordially invite you
to a
Testimonial Banquet
honoring
Ira Lee Rupley
on Friday, the twelfth of September
Nineteen hundred and fifty-eight
in the
Grand Ballroom
Statler Hilton Hotel
Dallas, Texas

Dress Optional
R.S.V.P.

Cocktails 6:30 P.M.
Junior Ballroom
Banquet 7:30 P.M.

Invitation for the Ira L. Rupley Testimonial Banquet. Frances Eason Archives.

The centerpiece for the occasion was a five-tiered cake. Cass Archives.

"The 78-year-old realtor and land developer received commendations, gifts and thunderous applause as Master of Ceremonies Art Gilmore, network radio and television announcer, narrated and illustrated with slides the high points of the life of the honor guest."

Fred Florence, chairman of the board of Republic National Bank, took Gene Wallace as a protege.

Gene Wallace was as accomplished in real estate finance as his partners were in land development, and no less ambitious. His fast-track career path from bank runner to senior vice president was pure Horatio Alger. Centex Corporation vice chairman Frank Crossen remembers Wallace in the early postwar years as "a hard-charging, ambitious, aggressive young man" and very much the protege of Republic National Bank president Fred Florence. "Gene was very personable," says former Republic National Bank president James Aston, "a great salesman. He was a wheeler-dealer. There wasn't anything too big for him to undertake. Nothing scared him."

Gene Wallace was a wheeler - dealer.

Republic National Bank president James Aston considered Wallace "a great salesman." Courtesy Southwestern Medical Foundation.

He certainly wasn't afraid to break banking's traditional reluctance to make construction loans. Conventional banking wisdom at the time considered them fraught with risk. Builders may or may not make correct estimates, pay their bills, or even know what to do with projects once they're completed. Wallace was one of the first bankers in the country to minimize those risks by using take-out commitments. A take-out was a third-party agreement, purchased for a fee usually from a savings association or insurance company, that guaranteed payment to the short-term lender in the event the borrower failed to meet his loan obligations. These agreements eliminated much of the bank's risk in interim lending and enabled Republic Bank to build a national lending program that financed the construction of homes, apartments, and office buildings. The short-term feature of construction loans had the added advantage of rapid rollover and reinvestment, which accelerated bank earnings.

Wallace was just as comfortable breaking down geographic boundaries. Traditionally, Republic Bank marketed its services on a local and regional basis; anything beyond the Southwest was considered terra incognita. The senior vice president, on the other hand, thought in terms of national markets.

Those who wanted to mine real estate's richest bonanza went west—to California. Gene Wallace seized the opportunity and made a major commitment to single-family construction loans in Southern California. "We pioneered the effort in California," says Walter Brogdon, former Republic Bank vice president who worked with Wallace, "especially when developers started building in Orange County. I guess we financed 90 percent of the housing built in Orange County at that time. It wasn't uncommon for us to have $50 or $75 million outstanding in California at one time. We had more loans there than Bank of America or any other California bank."

Wallace's performance lifted the real estate division out of obscurity and into the limelight. Republic National Bank led the Southwest in interim construction lending. "The real estate division," says James Aston, "was the largest and most active lender in the bank. For example, it completely overshadowed our oil department. It was probably the most profitable, too. It just blossomed after the war." As the real estate division expanded, so did its clientele. By the mid-fifties some of the largest builders in the country considered themselves Republic National Bank customers.

The growth of the division also enhanced Wallace's reputation. But it was a reputation that had little in common with mainstream banking. His lending style was too unconventional for that. "Gene Wallace was a maverick and an entrepreneur in construction financing and commercial real estate," says a former banking colleague. "He wasn't a credit analyst as much as a seat-of-the-pants type lender."

Wallace's independent approach to banking meshed well with his flamboyant personal style. Ignoring the conformity of the gray-flannel fifties and his profession's conservative tradition, he cultivated the image of a high roller. Whenever attending banking or homebuilding conventions, the real estate vice president stayed in the largest rooms at the most expensive hotels. Word spread quickly among conventioneers that they could expect lavish hospitality and a place to party far into the night at the Wallace suite. He always kept a roll of money in his pockets for tips. Reportedly, whenever he took a taxi in New York City, Gene peeled off a ten dollar bill for each green light the driver made. One former Republic Bank executive remembers a business meeting in New York where Wallace handled the arrangements. When the bank executives stepped off the plane they were met by a chauffeured limousine flying an American flag on one fender and a Texas flag on the other. Instead of going out to a restaurant that evening, Wallace arranged to have dinner served in their suite by a retinue of waiters wearing black tuxedos with white serving cloths draped across their arms. "His attitude," says Walter Brogdon, "was that if Republic Bank was going to do something, it should be done first class with no holds barred. If the bank attended a meeting, it should sit at the head of the table, so to speak." Others thought Wallace's extravagance reflected the insecurity of a poor boy without an education who had worked his way up from bank messenger to senior vice president of one of the country's largest banks. "I believe at the heart of it," James Aston says, "Gene Wallace felt insecure and compensated with a big ego and [by] playing the big shot."

Besides personal expertise, Gene Wallace brought with him the management skills of individuals from Genell Diversified Properties. Among the Genell staff that operated Wallace Properties and figured significantly in the company's future history were M. D. Wommack, later executive vice president at Lomas Financial Corporation, Lanelle Latendresse, later execu-

The Genell Diversified Properties management staff that came to Wallace Properties included, left to right, DeWayne Wommack, Lanelle Latendresse, and John Sexton.

tive vice president at Lomas Management, Inc., and John F. Sexton, later executive vice president at Lomas Financial Corporation.

Other members of the board for Wallace Properties included notable Dallas business leaders Felix Harris, a partner at Felix Harris & Company (general insurance agents), and H. Neil Mallon, chairman of the board of Dresser Industries, Inc. The youngest and least prominent board member was a 29-year-old attorney from Locke, Purnell, Boren, Laney & Neely named Jess Hay. Despite his junior status, Eugene Locke tapped him to handle the company's legal work and serve as corporate secretary. The young attorney's impressive performance since graduating from Southern Methodist University's law school and joining the firm five years earlier was a source of pride for Locke.

By the end of 1959 the organizers of Wallace Properties agreed that the company would operate in three principal areas. One would be the management of the income-producing properties. Other property would be added when opportunities were favorable.

Short-term real estate lending was considered the company's most profitable activity. These loans would finance the acquisition and development of property as well as the construction of residential, commercial, and industrial projects. In conjunction with these lending activities, the company planned to participate in some of the most promising ventures.

The company also acquired raw land suitable for residential subdivision. Besides generating profits from sales, the land would create a built-in demand for construction loans. By early 1960 the company obtained an option on two tracts of prime acreage. The largest, later called Woodland Hills, was 2,373 acres located near Los Angeles in the San Fernando Valley some eight miles from Beverly Hills. The other was a 1,154-acre tract called Canyon Creek, located in Richardson, one of Dallas' most desirable suburban locations. In 1959 Richardson accounted for one-third of all residential

...a company in formation with no history and no track record.

construction in Dallas County.

Wallace Properties, Inc., formally opened the doors of its office in Suite 1111 of the Hartford Building on April 1, 1960. A month later, based on the appraisal of Henry S. Miller, Jr., the company acquired title to the 29 income-producing properties in exchange for 1,737,163 shares of its common stock. According to the appraisal, the properties had an aggregate value of $10,422,978. The investors also made cash contributions totaling $285,000.

The first priority for the company was raising the capital needed to conduct business. An investment banking friend of Gene Locke's who worked for Mutual of New York recommended a New York firm, Harriman Ripley & Co., to organize and sell the public underwriting.

Stuart Silloway, president of Harriman Ripley, agreed to handle the account and asked for an earnings projection to determine how much money they could raise. Silloway looked at the figures presented by Gene Locke, Ed Hoffman, Gene Wallace, A. B. Cass, Jr., and Jess Hay at a meeting in early 1960 and told them Harriman Ripley couldn't sell the issue based on those earnings. "So, we go back to the hotel," explains Ed Hoffman, "and increase the earnings on the same assets, primarily by selling land at a faster rate. At Harriman Ripley the next day Silloway says we still don't have enough. We go back to the hotel and accelerate our earnings again. Finally, on the fourth or fifth projection Silloway says he thought we would come in with not less than $1 a share. We go back to the hotel, rework the assets again and come up with $1.04 a share. That made the underwriting saleable in Silloway's mind."

Even with dollar a share earnings, the $25 million Wallace Properties hoped to raise died a quick death in

Among members of the board of directors for Wallace Properties was H. Neil Mallon, chairman of the board of Dresser Industries, Inc. Dresser Industries Archives.

Jess Hay was the youngest board member and served as corporate secretary. Betty Jo and Jess Hay Archives.

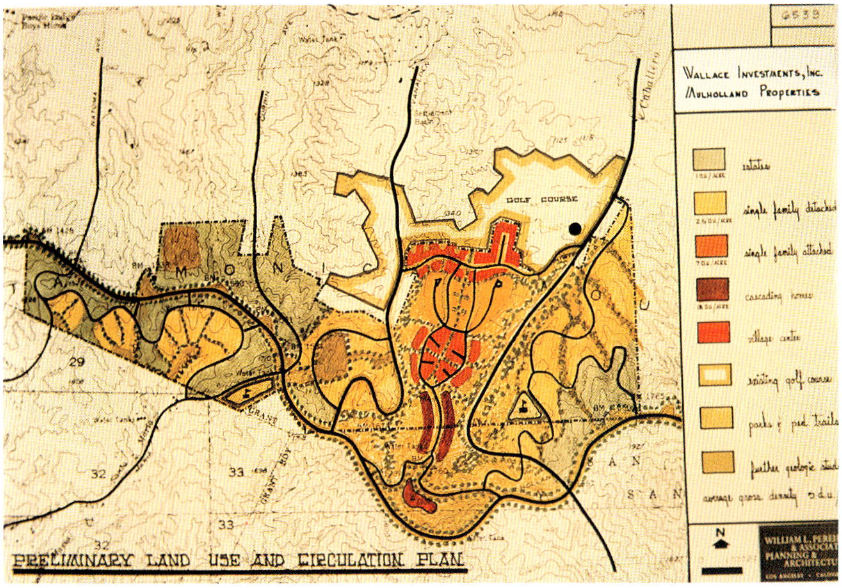

Wallace Properties acquired Mulholland Properties in the Los Angeles area for a residential subdivision.

Left: Canyon Creek was Wallace Properties' first planned development. The swimming pool at the Canyon Creek Country Club was a featured amenity. Vice presidents John Sexton (left) and Pete Scarbrough review the plat of the community in the lower picture.

Above: Canyon Creek did not build homes. Rather, it developed residential lots and sold them to builders. The development was planned for families with children.

Wallace Properties, Inc., opened for business in the Hartford Building in downtown Dallas on April 1, 1960. Courtesy Prentiss Properties Limited, Inc.

New York. Harriman Ripley said they would be fortunate to raise $15 million.

Then, just as the Dallas company was ready to file notice of the sale with the Securities and Exchange Commission, there was more bad news. Uris Brothers, a large New York real estate company, filed with the SEC one day before Wallace Properties. "That put a lot of pressure on us," says Ed Hoffman, "because Uris Brothers was well known among the Wall Street crowd. They had a familiar name and familiar management. We didn't. We were strangers, a company in formation with no history and no track record."

Nothing about the underwriting was easy. M. D. Wommack, who worked as chief accountant for Genell and then as treasurer for Wallace Properties, recalls the long hours at the Dallas office and the leadership role of Jess Hay: "During the period just before the company went public, I worked with Gene Wallace and Jess Hay putting together the numbers, projections, and memorandums concerning the operation of the company. A lot of what I did was respond to questions and run numbers for Jess, who structured the documents relating to the underwriting of the first issue of stock in subordinated debentures. We spent a great deal of time on that project." Lanelle Latendresse, an accounting assistant first for Genell and then for Wallace Properties, describes Hay as "kind of a central cruise director. He assigned duties and told us what we needed to do. Most of it involved working on financial and operating statements."

Making sales presentations on the road wasn't any easier. "We had a hell of a hard time selling it," says Hoffman. "For the first six months of 1960 Harriman Ripley scheduled meetings for us with prospective underwriting groups. We called on insurance investors, pension fund investors, and everything else. We were on the road an awful long time.

"Harriman Ripley had extreme difficulty getting underwriters to line up. Finally, the week before the issue sold at the end of June, we went back to New York, and Silloway said he couldn't guarantee our underwriting and wanted us to agree to a 'best efforts' deal. We refused, and one week later they put together a firm commitment."

On June 30, 1960, the hard work finally paid off. The result was an underwritten sale of $12 million of 6 ½ percent convertible debentures and 360,000 shares of common stock, which netted the company $13,704,000 after commission and expenses.

To celebrate the occasion and show his appreciation for the extraordinary effort of his staff and legal team, Wallace paid for the spouses of those involved in the underwriting effort to join them in New York for the closing of the sale. Senior executive vice president, Lomas Insurance Services Ned R. Harris, who had arranged a $2 million SEC liability policy for Wallace Properties at the time as an independent agent, remembers the festivities as one of the high points in his life. No one could have been more surprised when he and Jess Hay walked into the Pierre Hotel suite Wallace had reserved for them. "My God," Harris says, "the entry hall was as big as my office. The living room was huge. The bedrooms were fabulous. The dining room and kitchen were unbelievable. And the patio overlooking Central Park—God almighty! We were in tall cotton." For several days the Wallace entourage made the rounds of the top Broadway shows, four-star restaurants, and most elegant nightclubs. One of Harris' most vivid memories of Gene Wallace's grand style was arriving at the Pierre Hotel's crowded nightclub one evening and watching in amazement as waiters carried tables over their heads and set them up on the dance floor for the Wallace party.

Shortly after the underwriting sale, Wallace Properties exercised its options and purchased the large tracts of land in Los Angeles and Dallas. The company also moved immediately into development and construction lending. They made their first large loan to real estate guru William Zeckendorf, the man *Time* magazine called "the biggest of the big-time developers, the premier impresario of the real estate world." His national celebrity was based on what he called making "bananas out of peanuts." One of his first and

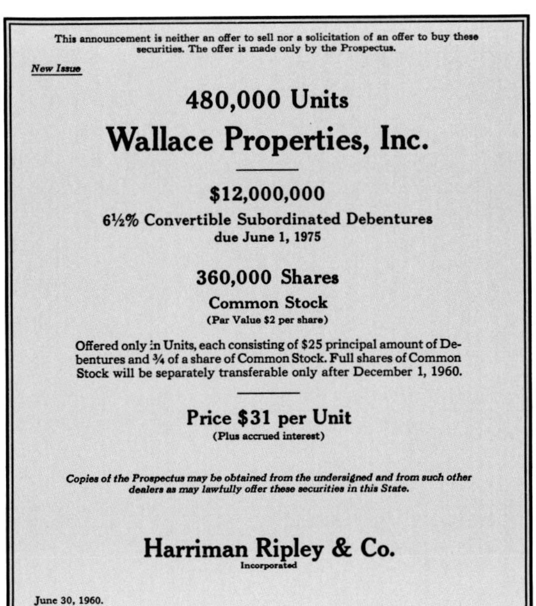
This announcement is neither an offer to sell nor a solicitation of an offer to buy these securities. The offer is made only by the Prospectus.

New Issue

480,000 Units

Wallace Properties, Inc.

$12,000,000

6½% Convertible Subordinated Debentures

due June 1, 1975

360,000 Shares

Common Stock

(Par Value $2 per share)

Offered only in Units, each consisting of $25 principal amount of Debentures and ¾ of a share of Common Stock. Full shares of Common Stock will be separately transferable only after December 1, 1960.

Price $31 per Unit

(Plus accrued interest)

Copies of the Prospectus may be obtained from the undersigned and from such other dealers as may lawfully offer these securities in this State.

Harriman Ripley & Co.

Incorporated

June 30, 1960.

Announcement and check for the successful sale of convertible debentures and 360,000 shares of common stock by Harriman Ripley & Company.

Common stock certificate for Wallace Properties, Inc.

Ned Harris arranged an SEC liability policy for Wallace Properties.

most famous ventures began with the purchase of a particularly unpleasant Manhattan peanut, eight acres of cattle pens, packing plants, and stomach-turning stench. But Zeckendorf was a persuasive visionary. He convinced the United Nations that the property made an ideal location for its international headquarters. Zeckendorf was also famous for a notoriously poor cash position, prompting the following real estate industry joke, an exchange between William Zeckendorf and his son William, Jr.: Zeckendorf, Jr., pointing to a New York building: "Dad, there's a hotel we can buy for only $15 million." Zeckendorf, Sr., sadly: "I know, son, but they want $5,000 in cash."

With typical Zeckendorf panache, the developer made a commitment in 1960 to build the largest office building in Canada, a $60 million complex in Montreal called Place Ville Marie. Although he had both the interim construction money and permanent financing lined up, a delay in the final arrangements forced him to begin construction with temporary money. Zeckendorf contacted Wallace Properties through an introduction from Stuart Silloway. After reviewing the project in Montreal, Wallace met with the developer in New York. Accompanying Wallace was assistant vice president John Sexton, a bright but inexperienced Harvard M.B.A. "It was the first construction loan I ever worked on," says Sexton. "I was just a kid that didn't know a damned thing about any of this and Wallace kind of took me under his arm. I remember Zeckendorf saying, 'Gene, I'm willing to pay a lot of money for this loan because I really need it.'"

In exchange for the $6 million loan, Zeckendorf agreed to pay a fee of two percent above the prime rate for each month he used the money. The astronomically high interest rate matched the freewheeling developer's borrowing philosophy: "I'd rather be alive at 18 percent than dead at the prime." Three months later Zeckendorf paid off the loan, and Wallace Properties

Wallace had a lot of pressure to report profits.

walked away with a half million dollar fee.

The unusually profitable Zeckendorf loan may have been a happy accident, but the company needed many more of them if it was to meet its goals for growth. Pressured by the souped-up projections the company used to sell the public offering, Gene Wallace embarked on a race for earnings. He realized after a few months that the company's diversified approach wouldn't take them where he wanted to go. Despite some initial activity from land sales, the real profitability for those ventures was clearly long-term.

Most disappointing of all were the income-producing properties. Originally intended to service the debt on the debentures, they never produced a significant cash flow. By December 1960, Wallace decided short-term lending was the fast track to corporate growth, and he began selling the properties and using the money for construction loans. The company sold six properties in the spring of 1961. The remaining 23 properties were sold to the Futterman Corporation in September. At the time of the final sale the board of directors endorsed the shift in corporate direction by changing the company name to Wallace Investments, Inc.

Although the directors' confidence in the company's president was strong, it wasn't universal. An exam-

Wallace Properties made its first large loan to William Zeckendorf, Sr., a New York-based developer. Zeckendorf Company, Inc. Photograph by Bachrach.

The Zeckendorf loan was for the Place Ville Marie project in Montreal. I. M. Pei & Partners, Architects and Planners. Photograph by George Cserna.

By December 1960, Wallace decided to sell certain properties. The remaining 23 properties were sold to the Futterman Corporation in September 1961. Bob Futterman (left) hands Gene Wallace a check to finalize the transaction.

ination of several loans Gene Wallace bought from Republic Bank, loans he had made for the bank before his resignation, led Trammell Crow to seriously question the chief executive's judgment. Crow believed continued leadership under Gene Wallace would lead the company to "a disaster."

Most members of the board either didn't share Crow's view or were unwilling to disturb things just when the enterprise seemed to be picking up steam. In August 1961, after selling a large portion of his stock, Trammell Crow resigned from the board of directors. His departure was considered an unfortunate glitch, more a personality conflict than a cause for serious corporate concern.

The decision to concentrate on construction lending made Wallace take a long, hard look at the servicing side of long-term lending. In December 1960 the company acquired Institutional Mortgage Company, a firm that originated and serviced the mortgage loans of single-family and multifamily residential properties. Like the Woodland Hills land purchase, the acquisition of Institutional Mortgage was a product of Gene Wallace's close business relationship with Herbert Heftler, a well-known Florida developer. The addition of the mortgage company strengthened Wallace's lending activities by providing access to permanent financing. This gave the company an edge in attracting clients who wanted full-service financing. Institutional serviced about $300 million in mortgages for fifty institutional investors. Ninety percent of these were government-guaranteed FHA or VA loans. Geographically, Institutional's offices were located in what

The principals of Wallace Investments, Inc., were present at the September 1961 sale. Seated left to right: Lanelle Latendresse, Jess Hay, Morris Jaffee, unidentified man, Bob Futterman, Gene Wallace, Howard Cordray, and unidentified man. Standing left to right: Jim Laney, Joe Stalcup, M. D. Wommack, unidentified man, Carl Wilson, Henry Miller, Jr., Ben Walker, Louis Hexter, and Neil O'Brien.

Wallace considered important real estate hot spots—California, Arizona, Florida, Colorado, and Puerto Rico.

Besides $3,216,000 in servicing revenues, Institutional Mortgage also brought a reputation for fast, reliable servicing of government-backed loans that snarled most mortgage companies in bureaucratic red tape. "Processing those loans," says George Hayes, a former vice president at Institutional Mortgage, "took a ton of work. But Institutional was organized to efficiently process the loan applications and conduct the credit research and the verifications and all the things that make up the FHA and VA loan application packages so the builder could close his sale. The quicker a builder got his money, the more apt he was to make a profit. Processing and service on a volume basis to developers was Institutional Mortgage Company's forte."

The chase for construction loan earnings precipitated a parallel pursuit of capital to finance the company's expanding loan portfolio. In June 1961 the company sold $10 million in 6 percent notes to ten institutional investors. Six months later Wallace Investments sold an additional $7 million in 6 percent notes to other investors. Even more significant was the operating capital that became available when Gene Wallace used his connections to open a series of unsecured credit lines with Republic, First National, and Mercantile banks in Dallas and other banks across the country. By 1963 the company had access to $37.5 million in bank credit lines.

Since the cost of money for Wallace Investments

fell at or near the prime rate, the company's most profitable loans came from borrowers who couldn't qualify for bank loans and were willing to pay higher interest rates for the money they needed. It was a hazardous niche that forced the company toward more liberal lending policies and exposed them to greater risk.

Besides generous lending practices, Wallace Investments offered the kind of rapid response for which many developers were glad to pay a premium. One example was a loan made to a group of Houston investors who were considered close personal friends of then Vice President Lyndon Johnson. Whether from inside information, as some claim, or clairvoyance, the businessmen had signed an option to buy what became a valuable tract of land in southeast Houston. Turned down by Houston banks, which at the time considered loans for raw land too risky, the syndicate turned to Wallace Investments.

Gene Wallace asked former executive vice president James R. Stanley to check it out. The report he sent back crackled like exploding firecrackers. A few weeks earlier NASA had announced that a space center would be built where the investors' optioned land was located. Nearby land was already selling for $7,000 and $8,000 an acre. The investors' option was for $3,000 an acre. Wallace agreed to make the $2.5 million loan, but time was running out. The option expired at 5:00 Monday afternoon. Stanley called attorney Jim Laney at Locke, Purnell on Thursday and asked him to fly to Houston the next day. "We worked our fannies off getting that loan approved," says Jim Stanley. The two men worked all day Friday in Houston, flew to Dallas and worked all weekend drawing up papers. On Monday morning they flew back to Houston with the papers and a cashier's check for $2.5 million. Most of that business day was spent rewriting documents to reflect changes in prepayment, payment, and release provisions. Then, with the clock nearing 5:00 p.m. and the papers ready for signing, the owner of the land announced he wanted the payment in cash. Since the banks were closed there was no way he could be paid in cash, and he considered the option contract null and void. "One of the investors ran and got the cashier's check real quick," says Jim Stanley. "And he said, 'Look, here's a cashier's check, we'll just endorse it over to you.' The owner said that's not cash, and the discussion became heated. Even the landowner's attorney assured his client that his objection wouldn't dance and the cashier's check was the equivalent of cash.

"Still, the owner refused to sign. Finally, he said, 'Well, I don't know if that check is good but my lawyer tells me it is. Meet me at the teller's window at First City Bank at 9:00 a.m. tomorrow morning and give me a deposit slip that says the bank accepts this check, and I'll sign the deed right there.' And that's the way we closed the deal." The owner's anger and frustration at having to sell his land for $3,000 an acre probably didn't improve right away. According to Stanley, within three or four weeks of the closing, adjacent property was selling for "fifteen, twenty, and fifty thousand dollars an acre."

One way a lender could either make good loans better or shore up weak loans was by purchasing take-out commitments. These agreements guaranteed payment to the lender from a third party if the borrower had a problem repaying the loan. Wallace had used these effectively at Republic National Bank and continued the practice to a large extent at Wallace Investments. Besides being a safe lending practice, take-out commitments were required by many of the banks he borrowed from for certain land development loans.

Jim Stanley negotiated one such agreement with Stewart Morris, who owned a chain of title companies. The loan Wallace Investments wanted to make was for a condominium development overlooking Del Mar race track near San Diego, but the deal hinged on whether or not Wallace Investments could line up a take-out commitment. "Stewart Morris was a horse trader," says Stanley, recalling their negotiations at a posh San Diego hotel. "We were up in my room trying to make a deal but getting nowhere and Stewart said, 'You know,

The undeveloped ranchland that became the future site of the Manned Spacecraft Center (March 1962 photo). Wallace Investments made the loan to a group of Houston investors who had signed an option to buy the valuable tract.
National Aeronautics and Space Administration.

A July 1989 aerial view of the developed Lyndon B. Johnson Space Center near Houston.
National Aeronautics and Space Administration.

you're awful hard to deal with.' And I said, 'Let's take a break.' Now, I don't drink and I don't smoke and Stewart Morris was a good Baptist and complete teetotaler. I said, 'Why don't we call down to room service. They've got some of the best banana splits you've ever tasted.' I ordered two banana splits, and boy they were good. After we finished our ice cream, he said, 'I never thought I'd be snookered into a deal because of a banana split, but let's do it.' We called that the banana split loan."

The early loans were, for the most part, good loans that according to Stanley "paid off like a slot machine." Unfortunately, reliability and safety meant lower profit margins, and Gene Wallace decided the company couldn't afford that. "Wallace had a lot of pressure to report profits," says M. D. Wommack. "The investors who contributed property and got stock back were counting their gains every day the stock went up. They were always calling to find out what was going on . . . like kids with a new toy. And the stock was going up. We were making money—paper money."

Marginal people, marginal projects

The pressure to meet projected earnings forced the company to accept loans that generated higher profits and greater risks. "The chase for profits got so strong," remembers John Sexton, "that Wallace took on projects that weren't viable. They involved marginal people, with marginal projects, under marginal circumstances."

Despite the risky nature of some of the company's loans, Wallace demonstrated a remarkable ability to structure deals that produced impressive paper profits. Former board member A. B. Cass recalled one occasion when a loan agreement was signed and the company immediately booked a $1 million profit. "But it was all paper," Cass explained. "The company kept two sets of books, a cash set and an accrued set. So, in the accrued set of books the company picked up $1 million for that quarter.

"But you don't make a damn thing if nothing moves. Sooner or later you've got to convert that paper to money. At some point you've got to start unwinding those deals."

The problem was that several loans involving "marginal people" wouldn't unwind. Jim Stanley refers to some of these as "Cadillac loans" because when he inspected the development site after the first loan advance, the man who borrowed the money often drove up in a brand new Cadillac. "As a result of our loans," says John Sexton, "some developers thought they were rich. They went out and bought a new car, a new house, a new wife . . ."

W. A. (Pete) Scarbrough, a Wallace Investments vice president who specialized in property management, remembers a million dollar deal that turned sour. When Scarbrough was called into Gene Wallace's office one day, he found Wallace standing behind his desk staring out the window, hands clenched behind his back. Without turning around Wallace said, "Pete, we've got a major problem with a loan in Maryland. Go take care of it."

Scarbrough found the residential development in "terrible shape." "The major problem," he says, "was the three men we loaned the money to. They had never done a development before and didn't know how much money they had drawn or how much they were going to use. There were no progress reports, no anything. But they all had big houses and big cars."

Scarbrough acted immediately. By exercising the company's loan agreements, he took control of the development and initiated an audit to find out what was going on. "I worked with that deal about two years," says Scarbrough. "We didn't make any money. But I believe we negated, to a great extent, major losses.

"In my opinion, deals like that were put together for purposes other than making money out of the real estate. They were made for purposes of enhancing stock values."

To compound matters, a downturn in the economy in late 1962 meant the real estate market was almost as marginal as some of the company's loans. Wallace responded in most cases to the troubled loans by granting extensions. Those with more serious problems required workouts like the one Pete Scarbrough handled in Maryland.

Slow paybacks, loan extensions, and major workouts didn't shake Wallace's faith in short-term lending, but it redirected his attention to the company's other activities. In early July 1963, Wallace Investments purchased the James N. Tardy Mortgage Company, a small Dallas firm "acquired for its personnel, mortgage servicing portfolio, and its important correspondent relationships." Later that month the company changed the name of Institutional Mortgage Company to Wallace Realty Mortgage Company, and then merged the Tardy operation under the new name.

a shift toward mortgage banking

The company also strengthened its insurance capability by acquiring three insurance agencies and one company. Admiral Fire Insurance Company, purchased from T. J. Bettes for $2.5 million, was a ten-year-old firm operating in 12 states. Wallace considered competitive insurance a profitable adjunct to the company's lending activities.

But it was the acquisition of The Lomas & Nettleton Company on August 22, 1963, for $5 million that put real muscle behind the company's mortgage banking operations. In one bold move, Wallace Investments doubled its servicing portfolio to about $700 million, which made it the eighth largest mortgage operation in the nation.

Gene Wallace's banking connections provided the opportunity. A friend of his at United California Bank in Los Angeles learned that The Lomas & Nettleton Company was looking for a buyer and arranged the introduction.

Wallace liked what he saw. Lomas & Nettleton was an old New Haven, Connecticut, company with an excellent reputation. Safe, conservative, and profitable were the words most often used by industry experts to describe the company. Although it was based in New England, the largest percentage of its servicing was in California, still considered the country's hottest residential real estate market. Lomas & Nettleton brought with it blue-chip institutional investors like Metropolitan Life Insurance Company, the kind of industry giant that could easily accommodate future mortgage loan growth.

Financial leverage was another reason for increasing the company's servicing portfolio. Access to additional operating capital was always a concern at Wallace Investments. Lomas & Nettleton provided a powerful new weapon to wield. "Most of the loan agreements," says Jim Stanley, "between mortgage companies and banks were worked out because the mortgage companies control the disposition of the escrow funds generated by the loans they service. And those damn things add up to a hell of a lot of money.

"If you've got $5 million in funds that you control, a mortgage company could go to a bank and say, 'We want to increase our credit line, or we're going to move our escrow funds somewhere else.' Not quite as blunt as that, but that's the idea."

The August 1963 acquisition of The Lomas & Nettleton Company marked the brightest spot in an increasingly difficult period for Wallace Investments. The new subsidiary would prove its resiliency through even darker days ahead. More importantly, from within its ranks emerged part of the leadership needed to guide the company toward a new future.

The earliest known photograph of John Ellsworth Lomas, taken in 1865 when he was two and a half years old. Beatrice Lomas Gould Archive.

CHAPTER II

THE COMPANY WITH A PROUD PAST

The Lomas & Nettleton Company was no stranger to difficult business conditions. In fact, an economic calamity from another era had precipitated its formation.

When it struck, the Panic of 1893 sent devastating shock waves across the country. The stock exchange collapsed on May 3. The next day the National Cordage Company was in the hands of receivers, and three Wall Street brokerage houses failed. In Chicago, wheat sold at its lowest price in 30 years. Near year's end, New York police counted almost 70,000 unemployed and 20,000 homeless and vagrant. By December, Samuel Gompers of the American Federation of Labor estimated the number of unemployed at three million. Coxey's Army, led by wealthy quarry owner Jacob S. Coxey of Masillon, Ohio, marched on Washington, D.C., in the spring of 1894 to support legislation to create jobs. "Everyone is in a blue fit of terror," observed American historian Henry Adams, "and each individual thinks himself more ruined than his neighbor." Almost 16,000 businesses failed by the end of 1893. Among them was a Cleveland furniture store owned by John E. Lomas.

John Ellsworth Lomas was born in Bridgeport, Connecticut, in 1862, the son of John R. Lomas and Jane Meloy Lomas. He grew up in solidly middle class surroundings. When the family moved to West Haven in 1869, they had sufficient means to build an unpretentious two-story house on Elm Street, in a comfortable though not affluent neighborhood. Lomas was a product of the historical and cultural forces that shaped his world. The Industrial Revolution that dominated the nineteenth century unleashed powerful social forces

The J. R. Lomas residence at 72 Elm Street, West Haven, Connecticut, was built in 1869 when the family moved from Bridgeport. The street address was later changed from 72 to 95 Elm Street. Beatrice Lomas Gould Archive.

that propelled the middle class toward prosperity and ascendence.

John R. Lomas was employed by the B. Shoninger Piano and Organ Company in neighboring New Haven, where for many years he held the position of factory superintendent. Shoninger's apparent satisfaction with his management was demonstrated on one occasion in 1878. When the company selected a small delegation of individuals from senior management to attend an industrial exposition in Paris that summer, Lomas was one of the firm's representatives. On his way to the Paris exposition, during a brief stopover in London, he made a point of visiting the Crystal Palace, one of the principal icons of the Industrial Revolution. Originally built in London for the Great Exposition of 1851, the first commercial and industrial world's fair, the 19-acre glass and steel extravaganza had become an emblem of the social, commercial, and industrial achievements of its time. Belief in progress represented by industry and science became a nineteenth-century obsession. Almost as obsessive was the Victorian notion of social progress. A system of middle class values that

Left: John Richard Lomas, father of John E. Lomas. Beatrice Lomas Gould Archive.

Right: Jane Richards Meloy Lomas, mother of John E. Lomas. Beatrice Lomas Gould Archive.

worshipped success and respectability dominated the popular culture.

The most vivid and personal glimpse into the formation of John E. Lomas' character came from a journal he kept in 1878 and 1879, when he was 15 and 16 years old. His youthful enthusiasm for *John Halifax, Gentleman*, a popular Victorian novel written in 1856 by Dinah Mulock Craik, underscored his strong identification with the values of his age. The sixteen-year-old's journal entry on October 27, 1878, mentioned an upcoming writing assignment for school: "Our next subject for a composition is 'the character in fiction that I most admire.' I think I shall take John Halifax for my character." A second reading of the novel a week later did nothing to diminish his admiration. "Tomorrow I write my composition on John Halifax," Lomas noted. "I have finished the book of that title and like it as much as ever. I think it is just splendid."

I think I shall take John Halifax for my character.

A literary *Cyclopedia of Principal Characters* described John Halifax as "an orphan who has an honest face and wants only a chance to prove himself. He is given a chance by Abel Fletcher and proceeds to rise in the world by his efforts, honest dealings, and gentlemanly behavior. He wins the hand of a wealthy heiress, becomes a behind-the-scenes political power and a wealthy manufacturer. He is a good husband and father, rearing a fine family before he dies peacefully in his sleep."

As one critic put it, Ms. Craik "celebrates the moral and domestic pieties of the new middle class. In *John Halifax, Gentleman* we are unashamedly offered the hero as Victorian businessman and paterfamilias." Particularly prominent in the novel was the Victorian idea of self-help. The book championed the values of achievement over those of birth and station. Halifax's initiative, resourcefulness, and "indomitable will" triumphed over every obstacle he encountered. "We are in the world of self-help," another critic observed, "where character is destiny and God helps those who help themselves. 'I am what God made me,' John Halifax declares at the outset of his career, 'and what with His blessing, I will make myself.'"

The novel gave dramatic form to the heroic myth of the middle class: "It expressed faith in continued progress, offered respect to business, said that poverty was not a disgrace but rather a necessary spur to industry and that economic success was a laudable goal. It showed the rewards of hard work and self-help and proclaimed that any practical occupation was valuable."

The book, in fact, hit just the right note for tens of thousands of readers who made it something of a nineteenth-century bestseller. Those who believed in it elevated it to the status of a social force. For some readers, it became a kind of testament, a personal gospel to be compared with *Pilgrim's Progress* and *The Imitation of Christ*.

John Lomas appeared to embrace *John Halifax, Gentleman* as his personal gospel. Clearly, it struck a responsive chord within him and reflected deeply held beliefs. Fifty-two years later, at the time of Lomas' death, the portrait painted by a newspaper obituary bore a striking resemblance to the fictional character John Halifax: "John Ellsworth Lomas, president of The Lomas & Nettleton Company, passed away at his home in Huntington Street after an illness of many months. . . . A self-made man of sterling character, he possessed a keen judgment in all matters pertaining to his business. His friendly nature endeared him to all who really knew him, and he was always ready with unfailing sympathy for those in trouble. His greatest joy was in his home life with his wife, children and grandchildren."

Occasionally John's journal entries reflected Halifaxian admonitions to self-improvement. After one report card, Lomas wrote: "Greek and Latin are my drawbacks and I must learn to master them." Lomas learned at another grading period that several of his friends made higher scores than he did. He voiced displeasure at his performance with the scolding comment: "That won't do, John!"

Lomas needed no such exhortation when it came to literature. He was an avid and voracious reader. The only impediment to that pursuit was physical. A childhood case of measles had left him with weakened eyesight; difficulty with his eyes would plague him throughout his life.

Toward the end of his sophomore year at Hillhouse High School in New Haven, John's father suffered a professional setback: "Father came home feeling pretty badly tonight, for he has been cut down $500, his wages now being $1,500 per year. I expect I shall have to go to work soon."

Whether or not the younger Lomas had to leave school for financial reasons isn't clear, but when the school year ended in April 1879 so did his formal education. Apparently, it wasn't uncommon for boys his age without professional goals to leave school and begin their work careers. Among John's friends who followed that path, one went "to work for Tuttle, Morehouse & Taylor, the great printers in New Haven @ $4 a week. . . . Rol Hine is working in New Haven at Mallet's hardware store." Another boy was "a shipping clerk in the rubber factory." Hal Nettleton and his older brother "Eddie Lee" worked for their father in West Haven. The Nettleton family owned a grocery store, one of the town's principal businesses at the time.

John Lomas, however, aspired to something more than a menial position. Diligence and persistence eventually paid off, but in mid-July the difficulty of the search took some of the edge off his optimism: "I have been trying for about a month to get a place to work in New Haven but without success yet. Mr. Jas. Graham and Rev. Mr. Brooks have let me refer to them. I have written a letter to Bunnell & Scranton [a small banker/broker office] but I do not expect any answer now."

Besides being supportive of his son, John's father had an inventive, entrepreneurial streak that John wrote about on August 5: "Father has got something for me to do now. He has got up a new thing called a 'blow-tube attachment' for the use of dentists and jewelers and he expects me to travel around and get orders for him. I may commence it tomorrow."

> *I* have a very responsible position . . .

Fate intervened the next day, however, and John now had the opportunity to move in the direction he originally intended: Bunnell & Scranton offered him a position. After a break in his journal of almost four months, he resumed his entries on November 28, 1879: "The principal event of the interim is the event of my 'finding a place.' Said event happened August 6 and consists of a clerkship in the office of Bunnell & Scranton, Bankers and Brokers, 216 & 218 Chapel St. New Haven. My pay is $3 a week for the first year and my hours are from quarter past seven in the morning to, on average, quarter to six at night. I have a very responsible position but am endeavoring to do the best I can. Besides Mr. Bunnell & Mr. Scranton there is no one in the office but Mr. Newton, the bookkeeper. . . . This morning and afternoon I've been very busy adding up and writing off interest tickets for the various depositors and helping Newton on the accounts."

John E. Lomas applied himself to his work and appeared to enjoy the challenges it offered. Five days later he had the opportunity to exercise some initiative in an unsupervised office transaction. "Before anyone came to the office," John wrote, "a young fellow representing H. K. Pease & Son came and wanted to deposit some money as he wished to leave on the 8:05 train, so I took it and gave him a receipt for it. I afterwards handed it over to Mr. Bunnell. This morning went like a 'streak o' lightning.' I helped Mr. Newton on accounts & chalked quotations on the blackboard."

The fast-paced office environment seemed to agree with young Lomas: "This morning I had a busy time of it getting off a mess of foreign drafts. . . . " A week later he wrote, "This morning I had my hands just jam full sorting out and filing away a years worth of checks and deposit tickets. It took me till about two in the afternoon and I helped Mr. Newton nearly all the rest of the day. Mr. Scranton has gone up to Boston on the five o'clock train tonight and may not be back for several days. So I shall be quite busy for a while."

Despite its small size, Bunnell & Scranton was a busy place responsible for a wide variety of financial transactions. "Yesterday, Friday night Mr. Bunnell being in New York, I was busy all day long, our chief event was the selling of 7500 Hartford bonds to the New Haven Savings Bank. . . . Today I kept busy putting on quotations and getting out interest slips." John's commitment to his work was evident from a journal entry he made on December 18: "I brought home a book tonight entitled 'Laws of business.'" John E. Lomas' employment at the firm continued for at least five years. The lessons he learned there made a deep impression. When he opened a mortgage banking and financial services business in 1894, he modeled the venture after Bunnell & Scranton.

The other major event in John Lomas' life was the beginning of an emotional attachment to Marinda (Rinnie) Belle Crane. By December, his journal indicated that John and "Rin" saw each other several times

John Lomas and Marinda (Rinnie) Belle Crane were married Tuesday evening, June 9, 1885, at the Methodist Episcopal Church in Bristol, Connecticut. Beatrice Lomas Gould Archive.

a week. John's personable and gregarious personality appeared to mesh well with Rinnie's fun-loving nature. One Sunday evening after attending a Methodist Young People's Meeting, John walked her home. Arriving at the Cranes' house, John wrote, "Rinnie told me one of the greatest jokes I ever heard in my life about a dream and I can't even trust these pages with it. I just leaned up against the grape arbor and roared." These two major threads in his life continued to develop over the next five years. On June 9, 1885, John E. Lomas, now promoted to teller at Bunnell & Scranton, married Marinda Crane.

Soon after the marriage, Lomas' weak eyesight deteriorated further. Doctors diagnosed the problem as detached retinas. The condition made reading difficult. There was no cure at the time, and the best medical advice his physician could offer was the suggestion to move to Cleveland, Ohio. It was thought that that city's overcast skies would help relieve the strain on his eyes.

John and Rinnie moved to Cleveland in 1887. He opened a furniture business and later took his father into partnership with him. It wasn't clear why Lomas chose to retail furniture for his first business venture. The association with his father, however, provided among other things an outlet for Shoninger pianos and organs. A son, Russell E. Lomas, was born in August 1893. The happy event was overshadowed to some extent by the crippling economic conditions of the Panic and the impending demise of the furniture store. The end came in early 1894. John and his family moved back to West Haven that spring. It was a major setback; it required several years of effort to clear the wreckage from that business debacle. Two years later,

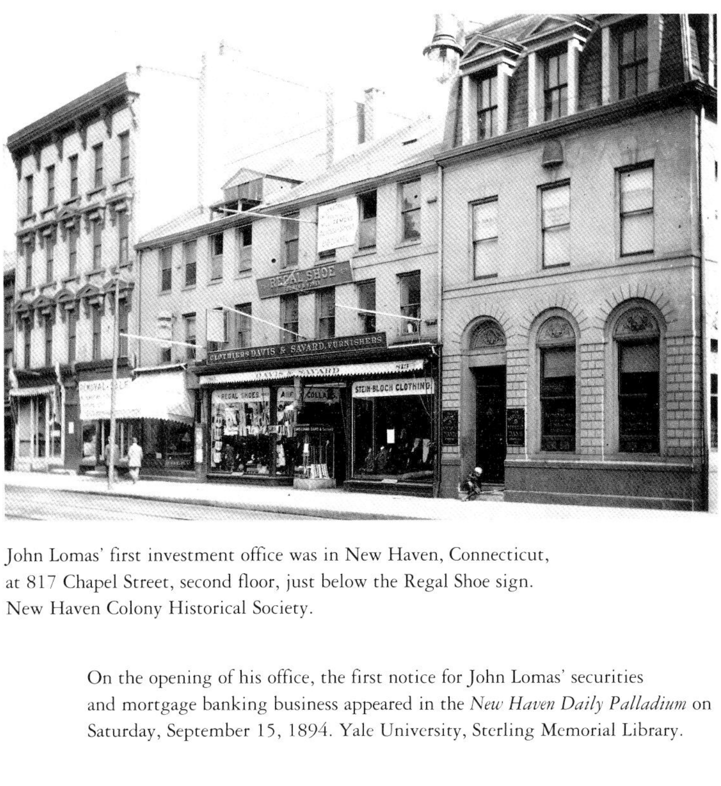

John Lomas' first investment office was in New Haven, Connecticut, at 817 Chapel Street, second floor, just below the Regal Shoe sign. New Haven Colony Historical Society.

SATURDAY SEPTEMBER 15 1894

HOME.

ful Explorers k.

ery drunk on ge Thursday S. Jackson sisted fiercely he abdomen. nd got to the 1. He was rt yesterday with being officer. He o but it was n court this n dollars for ail for thirty

elligent looking years of age t the Starin waiting for York. They icer on duty to do so at- He tried to nes and when at he wanted The officer two of the aping. The

FINANCIAL

SECURITIES FOR SALE.

$1,000 City of New Haven 4 per cent. School Bonds.
$10,000 City of Waterbury, Conn., 4 per cent. Bonds.
$5,000 City of Jacksonville, Fla., 5 per cent. Bonds,
9 shares Swift & Co., Stock
12 shares Connecticut Fire Insurance Co. Stock.
50 shares Pequonnoch National Bank of Bridgeport.
5 and 6 per cent. Loans on Real Estate in New Haven and vicinity.

J. E. LOMAS,

817 Chapel Street, New Haven, Conn.

MONEY MADE

EASILY, RAPIDLY. LEGITIMATELY,

BY OUR PLAN OF

SYNDICATE SPECULATION

In Stocks, Bonds, Etc.

AUGUST DIVIDEND 100 PER CENT

On the opening of his office, the first notice for John Lomas' securities and mortgage banking business appeared in the *New Haven Daily Palladium* on Saturday, September 15, 1894. Yale University, Sterling Memorial Library.

A southeast view of New Haven and part of the harbor in 1786, the earliest surviving view. The woodcut was used as the masthead for the *New Haven Chronicle*. New Haven Colony Historical Society.

Lomas and his father were still attempting to collect outstanding receivables "for pianoes [*sic*] and organs . . . and other accounts" by entering into an agreement with a Cleveland attorney who specialized in difficult collections.

The failure in Cleveland didn't keep Lomas down long. He turned to what was familiar—financial services. On September 15, 1894, John E. Lomas, 32, started a mortgage and general investment business at 817 Chapel Street in the heart of New Haven's financial district.

The New Haven Green, c. 1871. The building on the left is the First Congregational Church, known as Center Church, and the building on the right is the United Church, known as North Church. The Edward Nettleton family were members of North Church. New Haven Colony Historical Society.

New Haven had been settled by Europeans in 1638. The small colony of 500 zealous Puritans and their dogmatic leaders, John Davenport and Theophilus Eaton, attempted to lay the foundation for a spiritual utopia as well as a commercial empire that controlled the Long Island Sound. Blessed with a good harbor and a fertile river valley, the colony prospered.

Over the next two hundred years New Haven evolved from a Puritan village into a Yankee city.

When the focus of local life moved from the waterfront to the New Haven Green, the city's historical center, it reflected a decisive change from maritime trade to an industrial economy. A strong, diversified manufacturing base brought the city sustained economic growth from the 1870s to the 1920s.

John E. Lomas, Investment Securities

Industrial expansion created a demand for capital. Connecticut's most famous financial service, the insurance industry, began in Hartford when a group of colonial investors agreed to cover shipowners' losses if their vessels were lost at sea. As shipping declined in the nineteenth century, the market shifted from marine to fire insurance. One incident in particular solidified Connecticut's reputation in the industry. On October 31, 1835, a fire broke out in New York City, destroying more than 600 buildings. The enormous number of claims filed forced many New York insurance firms into bankruptcy; however, on a snowy night the president of the Hartford Fire Insurance Company traveled to New York to assure his policyholders that their claims would be honored. The reputable record of Connecticut's insurance and banking industry was part of the business environment when Lomas opened his office. It complemented the strong sense of personal integrity that he brought to his new venture.

By necessity it was a low-overhead operation, with a rolltop desk, brass teller's cage, gas lamps, and one employee. The one-room, walk-up office had few amenities. Even something as basic as drinking water required a trip to the New Haven Green to fill a couple of pitchers at the public water fountain.

One of the most important ledgers was the one that kept track of business expenses. There Lomas recorded in detail the cost of doing business at the turn of the century: monthly office rent, $14.00; weekly

Where it all began. The account book for John Lomas' business and the Expenses and Profits pages for January 1895.
Beatrice Lomas Gould Archive.

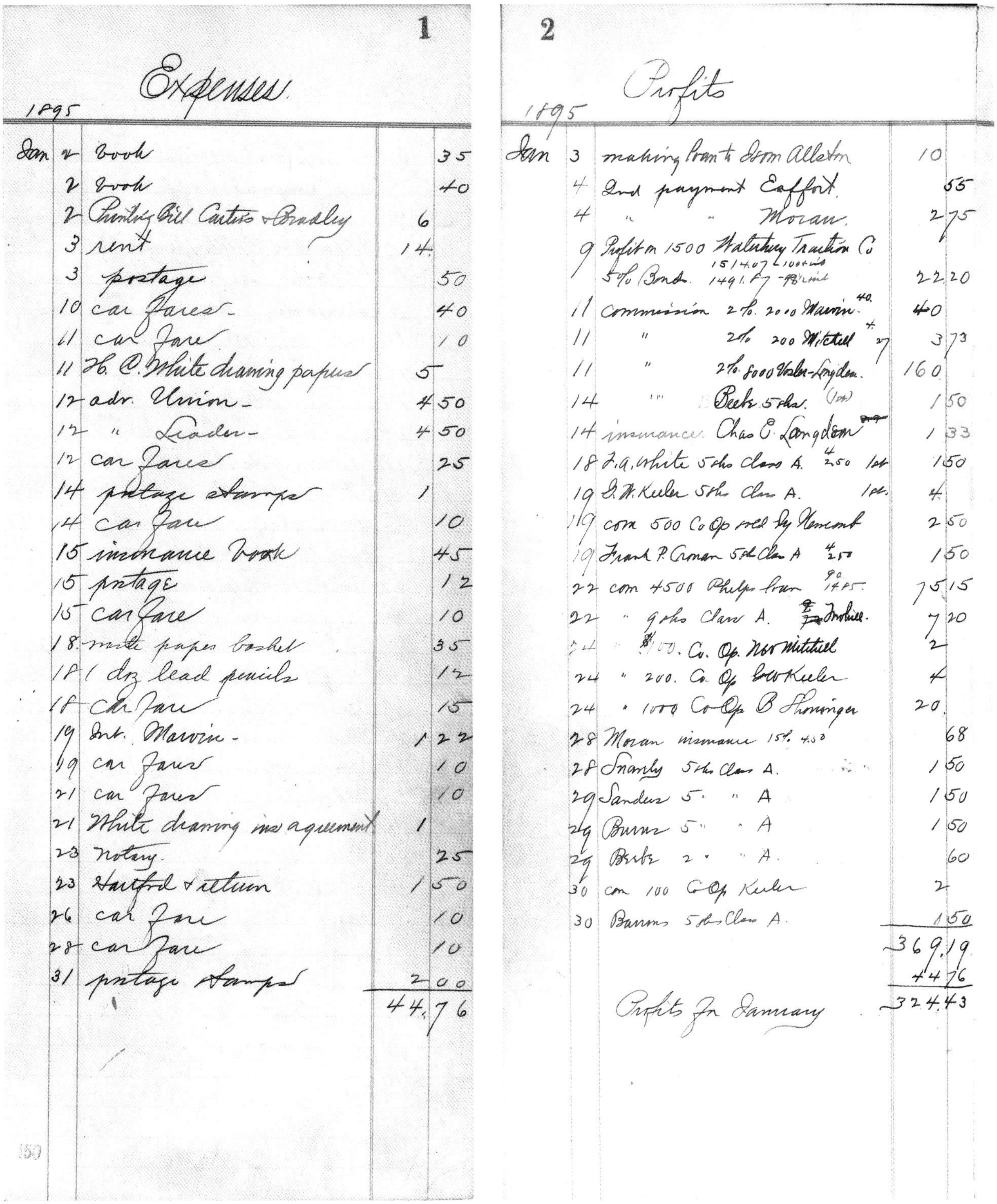

1

Expenses

1895				
Jan	2	book		35
	2	book		40
	2	Printing Bill Carters & Bradley	6	
	3	rent	14.	
	3	postage		50
	10	car fares		40
	11	car fare		10
	11	H. C. White drawing papers	5	
	12	adv. Union	4	50
	12	" Leader	4	50
	12	car fares		25
	14	postage stamps	1	
	14	car fare		10
	15	insurance book		45
	15	postage		12
	15	car fare		10
	18	waste paper basket		35
	18	1 doz lead pencils		12
	18	car fare		15
	19	Int. Marvin	1	22
	19	car fares		10
	21	car fares		10
	21	White drawing ins agreement	1	
	23	notary		25
	23	Hartford & return	1	50
	26	car fare		10
	28	car fare		10
	31	postage stamps	2	00
			44.	76

2

Profits

1895				
Jan	3	making loan to Isom Allston	10	
	4	2nd payment Eafford		55
	4	" " Moran	2	75
	9	Profit on 1500 Waterbury Traction Co 5% Bonds 1514.07 1491.87	22	20
	11	commission 2%. 2000 Marvin	40	
	11	" 2% 200 Mitchell	3	73
	11	" 2% 8000 Vosler-Langdon	160	
	14	" Beebe 5 shs.	1	50
	14	insurance Chas E. Langdon	1	33
	18	F. A. White 5 shs Class A.	1	50
	19	G. W. Keeler 5 shs Class A.	4	
	19	com 500 Co Op sold by Newcomb	2	50
	19	Frank P. Crozman 5 sh Class A	1	50
	22	com 4500 Phelps loan	75	15
	22	" 9 shs Class A.	7	20
	24	" $100. Co. Op. Nor Mitchell	2	
	24	" 200. Co Op Geo Keeler	4	
	24	" 1000 Co Op B Shonnger	20	
	28	Moran insurance 15% 4.50		68
	28	Snanly 5 shs Class A.	1	50
	29	Sanders 5 " A	1	50
	29	Burns 5 " A	1	50
	29	Beebe 2 " A.		60
	30	com 100 Co Op Keeler	2	
	30	Barnes 5 shs Class A.	1	50
			369	19
			44	76
		Profits for January	324	43

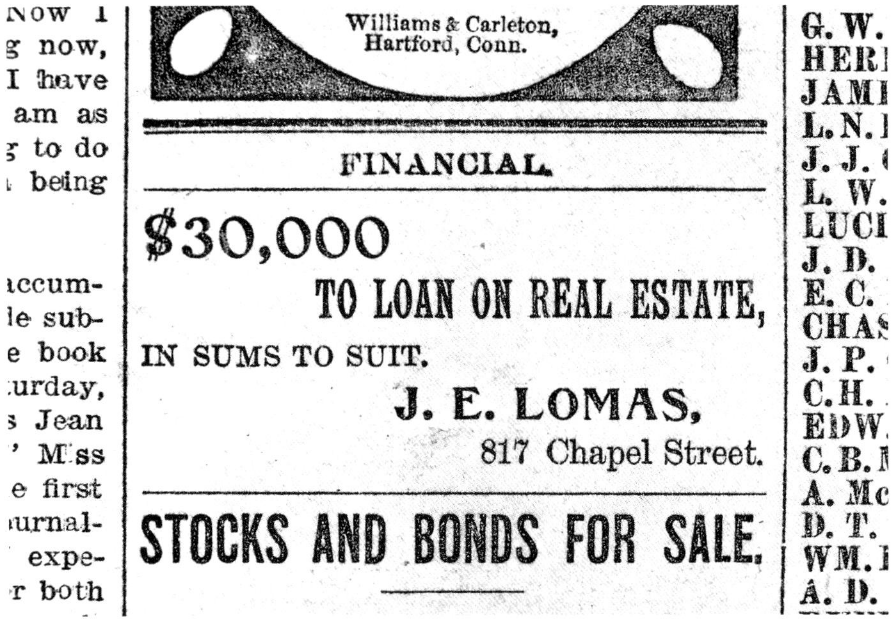
Williams & Carleton,
Hartford, Conn.

FINANCIAL.

$30,000

TO LOAN ON REAL ESTATE,

IN SUMS TO SUIT.

J. E. LOMAS,

817 Chapel Street.

STOCKS AND BONDS FOR SALE.

Left: On Saturday, January 12, 1895, John Lomas placed an ad in *The Evening Leader* and entered the transaction in his account book. The following Monday, January 14, 1895, the ad appeared in the financial section of the newspaper. See item entered on Expenses page of account book, tenth line from top: "1895, Jan 12, adv Leader, 4.50." Yale University, Sterling Memorial Library.

Below: John Lomas placed two ads in the 1895 New Haven City Directory. One was in the Fire Insurance section and this ad was in the Investment Bankers and Brokers section. Above the Lomas ad is one for the Scranton Company, where Lomas had gotten his introduction to the investment business (when it was known as Bunnell & Scranton). New Haven Colony Historical Society.

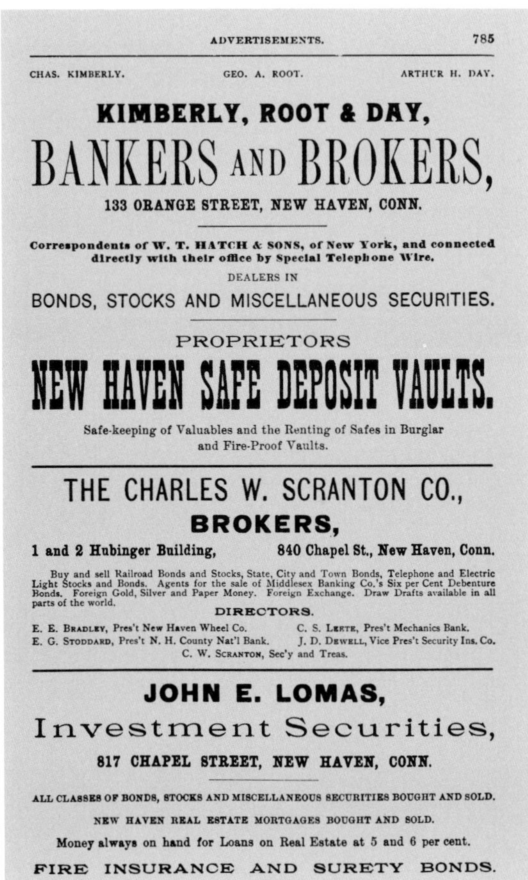
ADVERTISEMENTS. 785

CHAS. KIMBERLY. GEO. A. ROOT. ARTHUR H. DAY.

KIMBERLY, ROOT & DAY,

BANKERS AND BROKERS,

133 ORANGE STREET, NEW HAVEN, CONN.

Correspondents of W. T. HATCH & SONS, of New York, and connected directly with their office by Special Telephone Wire.

DEALERS IN

BONDS, STOCKS AND MISCELLANEOUS SECURITIES.

PROPRIETORS

NEW HAVEN SAFE DEPOSIT VAULTS.

Safe-keeping of Valuables and the Renting of Safes in Burglar and Fire-Proof Vaults.

THE CHARLES W. SCRANTON CO.,

BROKERS,

1 and 2 Hubinger Building, 840 Chapel St., New Haven, Conn.

Buy and sell Railroad Bonds and Stocks, State, City and Town Bonds, Telephone and Electric Light Stocks and Bonds. Agents for the sale of Middlesex Banking Co.'s Six per Cent Debenture Bonds. Foreign Gold, Silver and Paper Money. Foreign Exchange. Draw Drafts available in all parts of the world.

DIRECTORS.

E. E. BRADLEY, Pres't New Haven Wheel Co. C. S. LEETE, Pres't Mechanics Bank.
E. G. STODDARD, Pres't N. H. County Nat'l Bank. J. D. DEWELL, Vice Pres't Security Ins. Co.
C. W. SCRANTON, Sec'y and Treas.

JOHN E. LOMAS,

Investment Securities,

817 CHAPEL STREET, NEW HAVEN, CONN.

ALL CLASSES OF BONDS, STOCKS AND MISCELLANEOUS SECURITIES BOUGHT AND SOLD.

NEW HAVEN REAL ESTATE MORTGAGES BOUGHT AND SOLD.

Money always on hand for Loans on Real Estate at 5 and 6 per cent.

FIRE INSURANCE AND SURETY BONDS.

salary for clerk, $4.00; real estate appraisal, $2.50; notarizing a document, 25¢; cleaning office, 50¢; trolley fare from West Haven to New Haven, 10¢.

Survival was Lomas' first concern. He hedged his bets by offering a variety of investments and financial services. The heading in an 1895 advertisement announced: "Investment Securities: All classes of bonds." But the heart of the ad revealed an early emphasis on mortgage banking: "New Haven Real Estate Mortgages Bought and Sold. Money always on hand for Loans on Real Estate at 5 and 6 percent."

The first few months in business were a break-even proposition at best. For the month of February 1895, Lomas' account book showed an income of $55.72 and expenses of $65.03. A month later the black ink indicated a $9.40 profit.

Once he cleared the hurdle of the initial start-up, however, the ledger showed a consistent profit. Diligence and an aptitude for the business began to pay off. By November 1896, a major purchase like a Remington typewriter for $40.00 was easily absorbed within that month's profit of $480.29. Lomas generated $1,850.24 worth of business in his first year and earned a respectable net profit of $1,062.06. A year later net profits topped $1,700. In 1899 he took home almost $1,900.

The turn of the century marked an important milestone for John Lomas' enterprise. Increasing business volume required a move to a larger office space at 850 Chapel Street. Even more important for the future of the company was his decision to ask his boyhood friend, Edward L. Nettleton, to join the business. Nettleton accepted, although it meant stepping down as the head of an established West Haven grocery business that his father had built. With a capital investment of $3,000, Edward Nettleton became an equal partner in 1900.

The chemistry of the partnership was so successful that by 1903 they had to relocate to a more spacious office at 137 Orange Street. At the end of their second full year together in 1902, they earned $5,058 in net profits, providing each partner with an annual salary of $2,500. Their advertisements still offered the same variety of financial services, but the ads now read, "Lomas & Nettleton—Bankers and Brokers." In 1903 Lomas and Nettleton became members of the American Bankers Association. There were no restrictions on opening a private bank in those days. "All you had to do," Kenneth Nettleton later wrote in his 1954 company history, "was paint the sign 'Bankers' on the front window.

"Our main banking business was in checking accounts. Deposits were made as with any commercial bank. Entries were made in deposit books bearing the

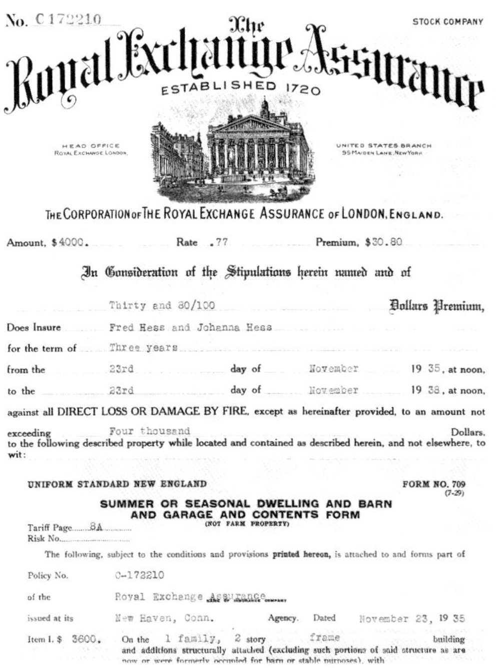

No. C172210 STOCK COMPANY

The Royal Exchange Assurance

ESTABLISHED 1720

THE CORPORATION OF THE ROYAL EXCHANGE ASSURANCE OF LONDON, ENGLAND.

Amount, $4000. Rate .77 Premium, $30.80

In Consideration of the Stipulations herein named and of

Thirty and 80/100 Dollars Premium,

Does Insure Fred Hess and Johanna Hess

for the term of Three years

from the 23rd day of November 19 35, at noon,

to the 23rd day of November 19 38, at noon,

against all DIRECT LOSS OR DAMAGE BY FIRE, except as hereinafter provided, to an amount not exceeding Four thousand Dollars, to the following described property while located and contained as described herein, and not elsewhere, to wit:

UNIFORM STANDARD NEW ENGLAND FORM NO. 709

SUMMER OR SEASONAL DWELLING AND BARN AND GARAGE AND CONTENTS FORM

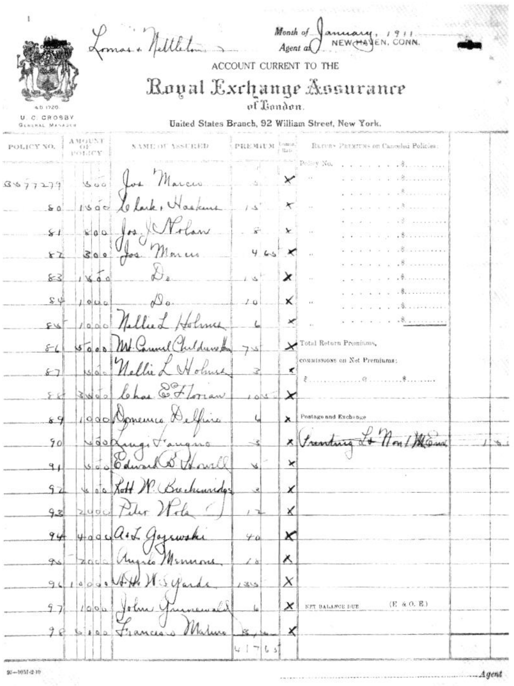

Month of January, 1911

Agent at NEW HAVEN, CONN.

ACCOUNT CURRENT TO THE

Royal Exchange Assurance of London.

United States Branch, 92 William Street, New York.

From the time John Lomas opened his business in 1894, he sold fire insurance as an agent of The Royal Exchange Assurance Corporation of London. On the left is a contract from 1935, and on the right an accounts list from 1911. Beatrice Lomas Gould Archive.

Lomas & Nettleton name. Checkbooks had checks with Lomas & Nettleton named as the banker."

The direction of the business, however, moved toward mortgage banking. On October 23, 1907, John E. Lomas wrote a check from Lomas & Nettleton Bankers for $6,200 to help underwrite a second mortgage lending venture—Lenox Realty Company. Mortgage banking, still a relatively new industry at the turn of the century, proved the most lucrative financial service Lomas & Nettleton offered. Each partner at the end of 1907 earned over $4,000.

Lomas & Nettleton, Bankers and Brokers

Mortgage banking is a business that originates, markets, and services long-term loans secured by real property. The mortgage itself is a legal document that pledges real property as security for the payment of a loan. In the 1800s most mortgage or real estate loans were secured by farm property. By the early twentieth century, the concentration of industrial labor spurred the demand for new housing and stimulated real estate development. A typical residential loan at that time was for three to five years and required a down payment of 40 to 50 percent. Mortgage payments were usually for interest only, payable semiannually. Since these loans weren't amortized over their term, a large lump sum payment was usually due at the end of the loan. Typically, lenders renewed these loans for another three- to five-year period.

Lomas & Nettleton was a middleman operation in the truest sense. It brought together borrowers and lenders for the benefit of both. This relationship generated two primary sources of income. The partnership earned a fee for loan originations, which meant taking applications from borrowers and processing them. Servicing the loan, however, generated the most profits. In exchange for a fee based on a small percentage of the

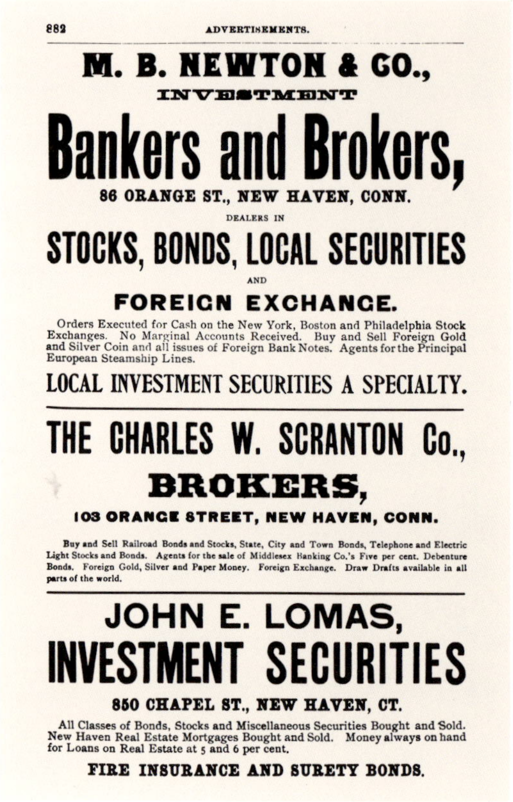

In 1900, after five years in the same location, John Lomas moved his investment business to 850 Chapel Street and a larger office with an eye to the future and expansion. This ad appeared in the 1900 New Haven City Directory. New Haven Colony Historical Society.

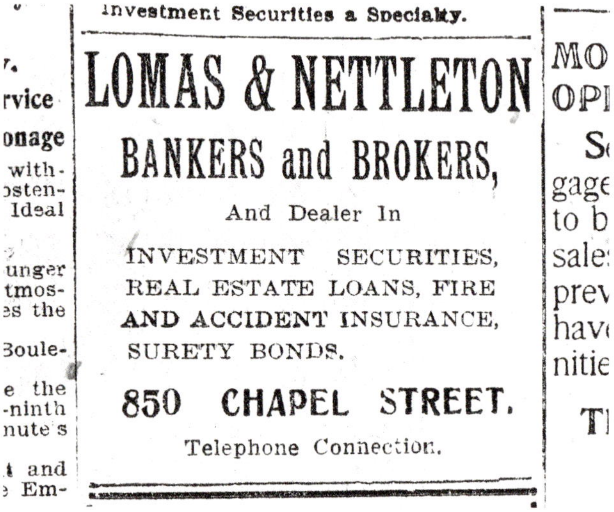

Edward Nettleton joined John Lomas in December 1900. The first public announcement of the new firm of Lomas & Nettleton appeared in a newspaper ad in *The New Haven Daily Palladium* on Thursday, December 13, 1900. Yale University, Sterling Memorial Library.

The Lomas family in 1900, about the time Nettleton joined the business. From left to right: John Ellsworth Lomas, Russell Ellsworth Lomas, Beatrice Elizabeth Lomas, and Marinda Crane Lomas. A third child, John Crane Lomas, had died in infancy in 1891 at Cleveland, Ohio. Photograph courtesy Barbara Townshend.

The Nettleton family in 1899, Edward's last year managing the family grocery business. From left to right: Edward Lee Nettleton, Donald Edward Nettleton, Kenneth Elwood Nettleton, Elwood Thomas Nettleton, and Eva Thomas Nettleton. John Edward Nettleton Archive.

Interior of the 1900, second-floor office of Lomas & Nettleton at 850 Chapel Street. From left to right: John E. Lomas behind desk, Amanda Donovan, secretary, Edward L. Nettleton, and Clarence V. Smith, bookkeeper, behind grille. Kenneth Elwood Nettleton Archive.

On February 1, 1896, Edward Nettleton took over the family grocery business, located in West Haven, Connecticut, from his father Hezekiah Edward Nettleton. He operated the store until 1900 when he went into business with John Lomas. Kenneth Elwood Nettleton Archive.

Left: Hezekiah Edward Nettleton, father of Edward L. Nettleton. John Edward Nettleton Archive.

Right: Emma Smith Nettleton, mother of Edward L. Nettleton. John Edward Nettleton Archive.

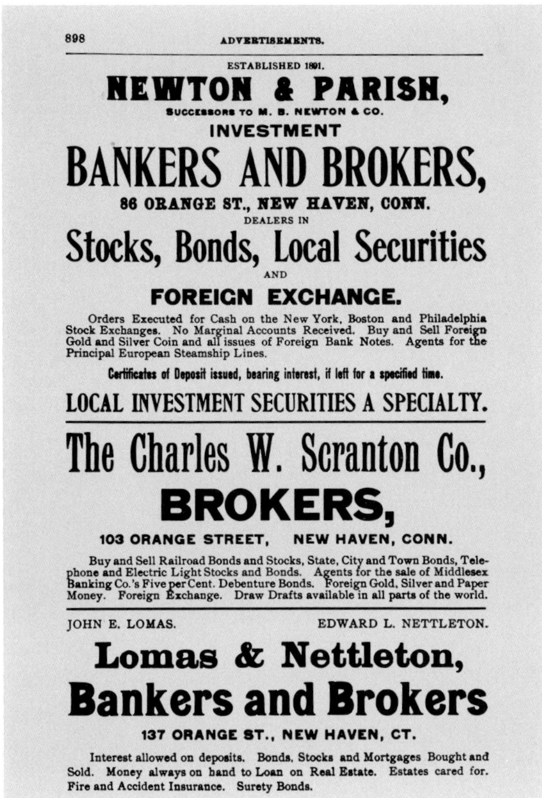

898 ADVERTISEMENTS.

ESTABLISHED 1891.

NEWTON & PARISH,

SUCCESSORS TO M. B. NEWTON & CO.

INVESTMENT

BANKERS AND BROKERS,

86 ORANGE ST., NEW HAVEN, CONN.

DEALERS IN

Stocks, Bonds, Local Securities

AND

FOREIGN EXCHANGE.

Orders Executed for Cash on the New York, Boston and Philadelphia Stock Exchanges. No Marginal Accounts Received. Buy and Sell Foreign Gold and Silver Coin and all issues of Foreign Bank Notes. Agents for the Principal European Steamship Lines.

Certificates of Deposit issued, bearing interest, if left for a specified time.

LOCAL INVESTMENT SECURITIES A SPECIALTY.

The Charles W. Scranton Co.,

BROKERS,

103 ORANGE STREET, NEW HAVEN, CONN.

Buy and Sell Railroad Bonds and Stocks, State, City and Town Bonds, Telephone and Electric Light Stocks and Bonds. Agents for the sale of Middlesex Banking Co.'s Five per Cent. Debenture Bonds. Foreign Gold, Silver and Paper Money. Foreign Exchange. Draw Drafts available in all parts of the world.

JOHN E. LOMAS. EDWARD L. NETTLETON.

Lomas & Nettleton,

Bankers and Brokers

137 ORANGE ST., NEW HAVEN, CT.

Interest allowed on deposits. Bonds, Stocks and Mortgages Bought and Sold. Money always on hand to Loan on Real Estate. Estates cared for. Fire and Accident Insurance. Surety Bonds.

By 1903 business had outgrown 850 Chapel Street, and Lomas & Nettleton moved to larger quarters on the ground floor at 137 Orange Street in the Palladium Building. Notice from the 1903 New Haven City Directory. New Haven Colony Historical Society.

loan amount, Lomas & Nettleton collected payments and remitted the principal and interest to the respective investors, handled delinquency problems, and, later, accumulated escrow funds for insurance and property taxes and disbursed them when they came due.

Lomas & Nettleton's interest rates and responsive customer service attracted many investors. "Lomas & Nettleton paid five, five and a half percent interest when the banks were only paying four," says former L&N vice president Harold Whitcher, who joined the company in 1927. "Percentage-wise our investors were getting a 25 percent higher return on their money than they would in a savings bank." Customers either invested in single mortgages or bought participation notes. A $10,000 mortgage, for example, might be divided among 20 investors, with each taking a $500 participation.

For sales purposes, the company divided the state of Connecticut into territories. Harold Whitcher remembers one of the top salesmen, Edwin Kirschner, who earned the princely sum of $125 a week: "He was our best salesman. I thought he was a millionaire. But

A very rare document from the corporate archives is this check drawn on the Lomas & Nettleton bank to fund the Lenox Realty Company and signed by John E. Lomas. This is the only document extant from the banking business. Beatrice Lomas Gould Archive.

Above: A photograph of the 137 Orange Street office some years after the 1903 move, perhaps Friday, June 26, 1914. From left to right: Madelle Flynn, John Wilson, unidentified woman, Levi Shew, unidentified woman, Jacob C. Edwards (?), and Clarence Smith. Kenneth Elwood Nettleton Archive.

Left: On August 5, 1907, Lomas & Nettleton expanded their office space at 137 Orange Street by adding the next-door space at 141. This photograph was taken at the same time as the preceding one. From left to right, standing: John E. Lomas, Hermine Roth Clouse, Mildred Bogart Parker (?), and John Parker, with Edward L. Nettleton seated in back office. Kenneth Elwood Nettleton Archive.

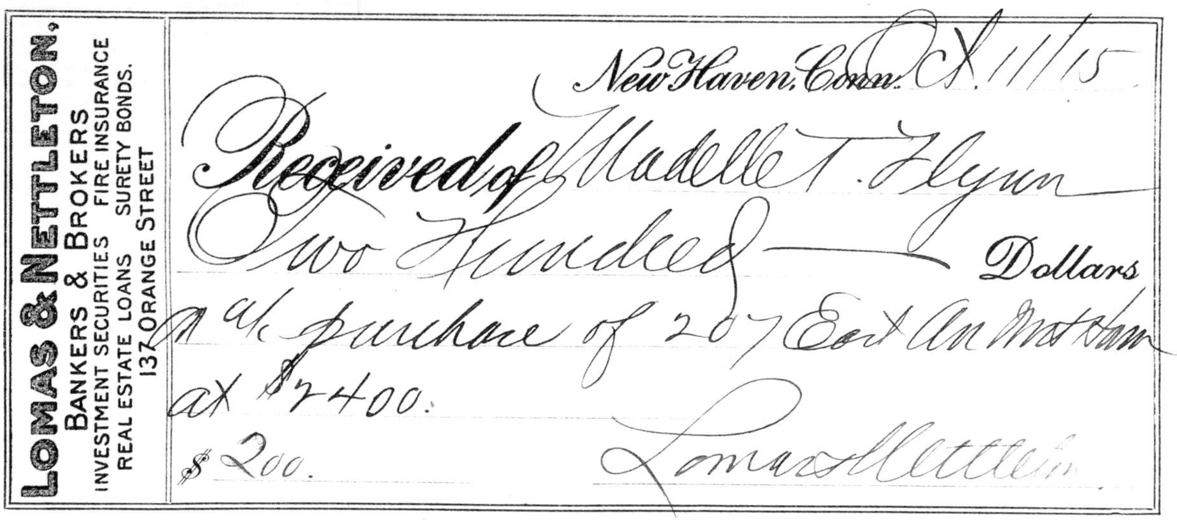
Lomas & Nettleton,
Bankers & Brokers
Investment Securities Fire Insurance
Real Estate Loans Surety Bonds.
137 Orange Street

New Haven, Conn. Oct. 11/15.
Received of Madelle T. Flynn
Two Hundred — Dollars
a/c purchase of 207 East Av
at $2400.
$200.
Lomas & Nettleton

A receipt taken by Madelle Flynn on October 11, 1915.

he was a down-to-earth person who got your confidence first and then sold you something later."

Once the partnership established itself, selling participations was not difficult. Rarely were investors in short supply. During the prosperous 1920s, investment money often exceeded the number of available mortgages.

The successful division of management by the partners contributed to the company's growth. Edward Nettleton developed an expertise in appraising property and making safe loans. "By real estate and banking authorities throughout the state of Connecticut," read a corporate tribute following Nettleton's death, "Edward Nettleton was considered one of the best judges of real estate—always keen and alert, with an active mind and body, with intuitive insight in business, and a judgment which could not be swayed by the lesser knowledge of others." Although Nettleton was less outgoing than his partner, former L&N vice president Edmund L. Stoddard remembered him taking the time to teach him the fundamentals of real estate appraisal. On one of their first trips together, Nettleton stopped in front of a house and Stoddard immediately jumped out of the car and began taking measurements: "'Wait a minute,' Nettleton said. 'Stand up here on the front porch and look around. I want you to see what the homeowner is going to see every day when he walks out of his house. There are three things to remember about real estate—location, location, location.'" Stoddard described him as "a gentleman of the old school . . . severe-looking, proper, and definitely not someone who would joke around." Alida Grava, John Lomas' secretary from 1919 to 1930, remembered Nettleton as an "austere, dignified gentleman who always made his sons wear their coats to the dinner table no matter how hot it was."

Lomas, on the other hand, was much less formal. "John Lomas," says Harold Whitcher, "would come up to you, shake hands, and say, 'My name is John Lomas, glad to meet you.' But Edward would sit there with his hands in his lap and say, 'It certainly is nice to have you drop in and see us.'" It wasn't uncommon, according to Stoddard, to find the more relaxed John Lomas leaning back in his chair with one foot up on his rolltop desk reading documents with a magnifying glass.

With one exception, Lomas never permitted his visual impairment to interfere with supervision of the partnership. Balancing the books on December 31 was the most important event of the business year and usually meant extended hours for both management and staff. "I know one thing," said Alida Grava. "Those books had to be balanced at the end of the year before we could go home. My husband and I never made plans for New Year's Eve because the books came first." It was a long, tedious operation, one that Harold Whitcher says had to balance "down to the penny." John Lomas' daughter Beatrice Lomas Gould, born in 1900, recalled one of her father's favorite sayings: "It takes a blind man to find things." Armed with a magnifying glass and thick reading glasses, he pored over the ledgers, personally correcting many of the accounting errors.

There are three things to remember about real estate . . .

"He hewed a very narrow path, with his attentions focused on his family and his work," read the company tribute to John Lomas following his death. "He loved the mortgage banking business and gave it a consuming interest . . . one of the few fortunate men in the world for whom his work was both his hobby and delight."

Even on vacations with his family to Twin Lake Villa, a New Hampshire resort hotel, Lomas managed to incorporate "his hobby." His outgoing nature made it easy for him to meet other hotel guests. He invited those with money to invest on long, leisurely drives through the White Mountains in his chauffeur-driven Packard. One former employee credits those car tours with the sale of thousands of dollars of mortgage notes.

His ability to reach out wasn't confined to sales. During the summers of 1924–1926, Harold Whitcher, then a student at Colby Academy in New London, New Hampshire, worked as a bellhop at Twin Lake Villa. "That's where I met John E. Lomas," says Whitcher. "White hair, white moustache, glasses, and friendly to everyone. Mrs. Lomas was not well at the time, and had to have her breakfast brought to her room. Fortunately for me I'm the one that brought it up, and Mr. Lomas was always there." Toward the end of Whitcher's last summer at Twin Lake, Lomas told the young man he would help him find a job in New Haven when he graduated. Whitcher accepted the offer in 1927, but was surprised by the warmth of the reception when he arrived. John Lomas made arrangements to meet the former bellhop personally at the train station and drive him to the Lomas home for dinner. The next day Lomas took him to several companies offering jobs. But Whitcher made it clear that he was only interested in working for L&N: "So he took me back to Lomas & Nettleton, and I stayed there 46 years."

Edmund Stoddard was another who benefited from Lomas' desire to reach out and help others. Hired as an office boy in 1922 at a salary of $12.00 a week, Stoddard told Lomas his only regret was not being able to afford a college education. "'Well, you stick with me, and I'll see you get the equivalent of a college education,'" Stoddard remembered Lomas telling him. "'When you're filing I want you to read every letter and document before you file it, just to get the gist of it. If you don't understand it, bring it to me and I'll explain it to you.'" The instruction didn't end there. Every Wednesday afternoon for many months Stoddard studied the general statutes of Connecticut and read law with John Lomas. Looking back from the vantage point of his retirement, Stoddard remarked: "How many senior executives do you know that would take the time to train an entry-level employee?"

The active involvement of a second generation of

Twin Lake Villa near New London, New Hampshire, was the Lomas family's favorite vacation destination. Beatrice Lomas Gould Archive.

Harold Whitcher, August 1990. Photograph by James A. Ledbetter.

Edmund Stoddard, August 1990, shortly before his death. Photograph by James A. Ledbetter.

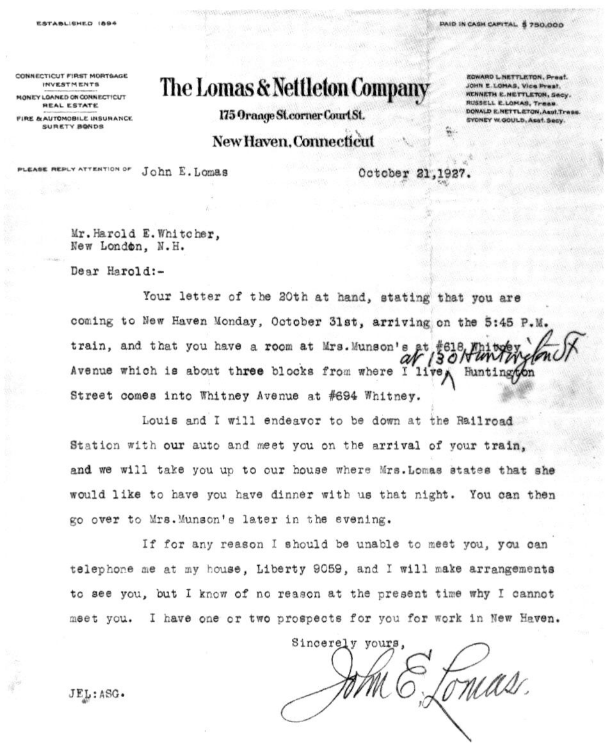

ESTABLISHED 1894 PAID IN CASH CAPITAL $750,000

CONNECTICUT FIRST MORTGAGE INVESTMENTS
MONEY LOANED ON CONNECTICUT REAL ESTATE
FIRE & AUTOMOBILE INSURANCE SURETY BONDS

The Lomas & Nettleton Company
175 Orange St. corner Court St.
New Haven, Connecticut

EDWARD L. NETTLETON, Prest.
JOHN E. LOMAS, Vice Prest.
KENNETH E. NETTLETON, Secy.
RUSSELL E. LOMAS, Treas.
DONALD E. NETTLETON, Asst. Treas.
SYDNEY W. GOULD, Asst. Secy.

PLEASE REPLY ATTENTION OF John E. Lomas October 21, 1927.

Mr. Harold E. Whitcher,
New London, N.H.

Dear Harold:-

Your letter of the 20th at hand, stating that you are coming to New Haven Monday, October 31st, arriving on the 5:45 P.M. train, and that you have a room at Mrs. Munson's at #618 Whitney Avenue which is about three blocks from where I live. Huntington Street comes into Whitney Avenue at #694 Whitney.

Louis and I will endeavor to be down at the Railroad Station with our auto and meet you on the arrival of your train, and we will take you up to our house where Mrs. Lomas states that she would like to have you have dinner with us that night. You can then go over to Mrs. Munson's later in the evening.

If for any reason I should be unable to meet you, you can telephone me at my house, Liberty 9059, and I will make arrangements to see you, but I know of no reason at the present time why I cannot meet you. I have one or two prospects for you for work in New Haven.

Sincerely yours,
John E. Lomas.

JEL:ASG.

The letter John Lomas wrote to Harold Whitcher explaining the arrangements for his arrival in New Haven.
Courtesy Harold Whitcher.

family management toward the end of the partnership's second decade prompted John Lomas and Edward Nettleton to restructure. Kenneth Nettleton, Edward's oldest son, joined the firm in 1912 after graduating from Yale Law School in 1911. Russell Lomas came into the business following his graduation from Yale Law School in 1916. Kenneth's younger brother, Donald, who attended Yale but never graduated, joined the company in 1919. To protect and accommodate their interests, Lomas & Nettleton incorporated the business on July 11, 1917, under a slightly altered name—The Lomas & Nettleton Company. The company continued to solidify its focus on mortgage banking by dropping its private banking business after incorporation.

John Lomas suffered a major medical event in 1916 that underscored the fragility of the partnership structure and increased the urgency for change. Serious impairment of his vision required almost a year's absence from the business. In a letter to a friend a number of years later, Lomas described the trouble in the following way: "I am all right except that I had serious trouble with my eyes about twelve years ago so that my sight is quite a little impaired, but I am going right along and attending to business just the same as usual and not worrying about it." At the time, however, it wasn't clear that Lomas could continue his leading role. When the business incorporated in 1917, Edward L. Nettleton became president and John E. Lomas vice president.

The new corporation was a privately held company governed by a board of directors made up of family members. Besides John Lomas and Edward Nettleton, the new board included Kenneth Nettleton and Russell Lomas. A few years later Donald Nettleton and John Lomas' son-in-law, Sydney W. Gould, were added to the board. Originally from Canton, Ohio, Gould graduated from West Point in the engineering corps with the "war class" of 1918. The armistice was signed just before he reached Europe. When he returned to the United States the government sent him to MIT to

Left: Kenneth Nettleton in 1911, his graduation year from Yale Law School. He joined Lomas & Nettleton in the fall of 1912 in the mortgage sales department with John Lomas. Kenneth Elwood Nettleton Archive.

Right: Russell Lomas in his freshman year at Yale University, academic class of 1914, law class of 1916. After graduation in 1916 he entered Edward Nettleton's department in the fall. Beatrice Lomas Gould Archive.

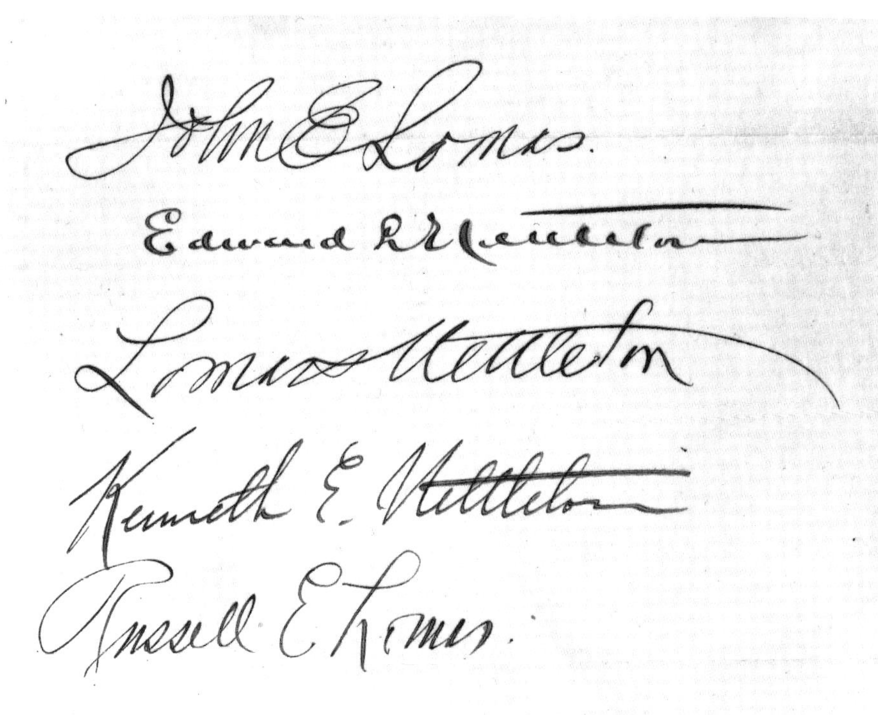

A business of fathers and sons. The signatures of John E. Lomas and Edward L. Nettleton, fathers, and their sons Kenneth E. Nettleton and Russell E. Lomas. Taken from the 1917 instrument of incorporation.

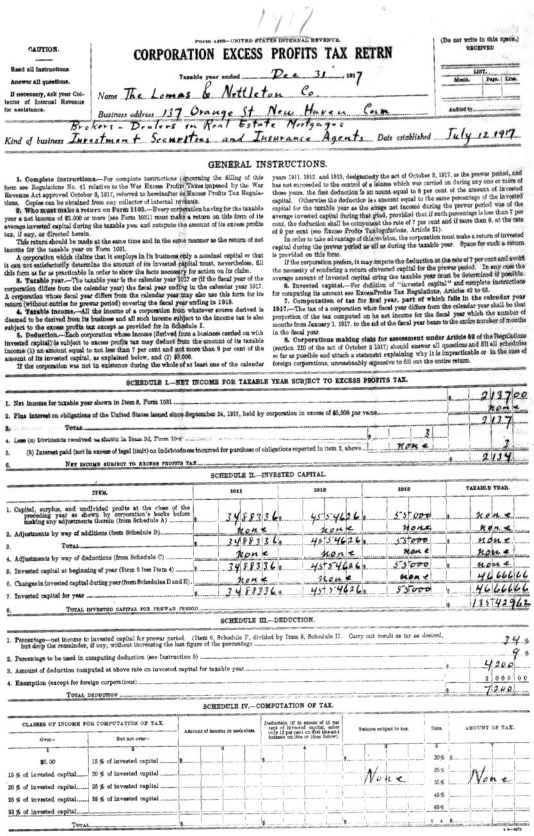
1917

CORPORATION EXCESS PROFITS TAX RETRN

Taxable year ended Dec. 31, 1917

Name The Lomas & Nettleton Co.

Business address 137 Orange St. New Haven Conn

Kind of business Brokers – Dealers in Real Estate Mortgages Investment Securities and Insurance Agents

Date established July 12 1917

GENERAL INSTRUCTIONS.

SCHEDULE I.—NET INCOME FOR TAXABLE YEAR SUBJECT TO EXCESS PROFITS TAX.

SCHEDULE II.—INVESTED CAPITAL.

SCHEDULE III.—DEDUCTION.

SCHEDULE IV.—COMPUTATION OF TAX.

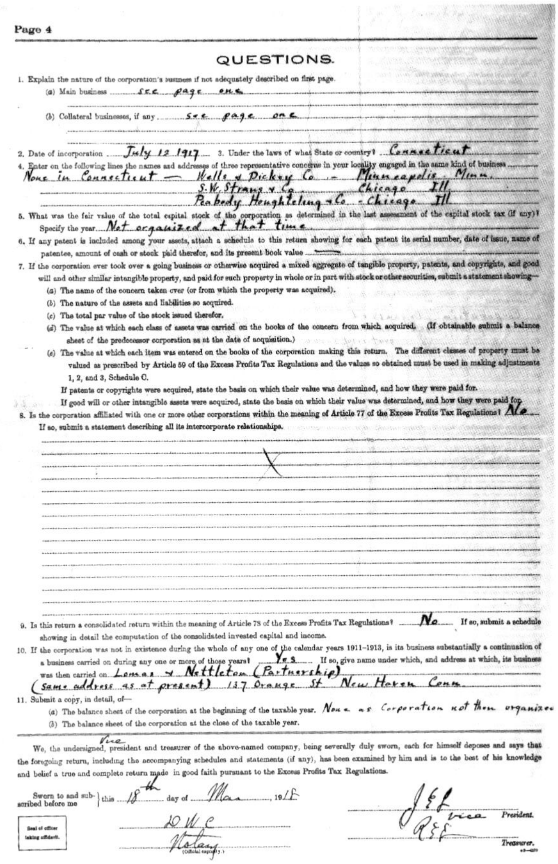
Page 4

QUESTIONS.

1. Explain the nature of the corporation's business if not adequately described on first page.
(a) Main business see page one
(b) Collateral businesses, if any see page one

2. Date of incorporation July 12 1917 3. Under the laws of what State or country? Connecticut

4. Enter on the following lines the names and addresses of three representative concerns in your locality engaged in the same kind of business.
None in Connecticut — Wells & Dickey Co. – Minneapolis, Minn.
S.W. Straus & Co. Chicago Ill
Peabody Houghteling & Co. – Chicago Ill

5. Specify the year Not organized at that time.

8. Is the corporation affiliated with one or more other corporations within the meaning of Article 77 of the Excess Profits Tax Regulations? No

9. Is this return a consolidated return within the meaning of Article 78 of the Excess Profits Tax Regulations? No

10. ... Yes ... Lomas & Nettleton (Partnership) (Same address as at present) 137 Orange St. New Haven Conn.

11. ... None as Corporation not then organized

Balance Sheet of The Lomas & Nettleton Co.
at close of business December 31, 1917.

Assets		Liabilities	
Due from Banks	42,182.65	Capital	100,000.
Accounts due	9,379.08	Surplus	557.37
First Mortgages on Real Estate	349,750.	Due Banks on Collateral Notes	123,300.
Bills Receivable	6,125.	Bills Payable	36,895.70
Bonds	9,060.	Clients Accounts Drawing Interest	59,636.14
Stocks	500.	Clients Accounts No Interest	4,992.20
Cash on hand	2,439.71	Balances Due on Uncompleted Buildings	98,397.42
Automobile	1,000.		
Furniture & Fixtures	3,342.39		
	423,778.83		423,778.83

Above: The working copy, front and back, of the Corporation Excess Profits Tax Return for the taxable year ended December 31, 1917, showing the altered name of The Lomas & Nettleton Company. Beatrice Lomas Gould Archive.

Left: The working balance sheet from the 1917 tax return showing the company's assets and liabilities. Beatrice Lomas Gould Archive.

obtain a special degree. Although Beatrice Lomas attended Vassar, she met Sydney Gould while enrolled at Harvard's summer school. They took their meals at the same boarding house. "It seems to have been a case of love at first sight," John Lomas wrote in a letter eight years later, "for it was all we could do to get them to wait for a year before getting married. . . . I needed him in my business and Beatrice and Sydney were both pleased to come back to New Haven in 1922. They have two children, Sydney Ward Gould, Jr. and Arleen, and they also live about three or four blocks from us. So, we are blessed by having our children and grandchildren living near us so that we see them nearly every day, and I also have two fine business helpers to carry on for me." When it came to organization and technology Gould was brilliant. The contributions he made during the Great Depression helped the company survive when the question of survival was very much in doubt. His personal skills, however, were less well developed. The authoritarian, military approach he brought to the workplace was not well received. Former Lomas employee Helen Sloan recalls Gould's intimidating style: "I used to watch people going into Sydney's office and you could hear him shouting at them. Irving Rhodes was the secretary of our company and a graduate of Yale. He was a very quiet, mild person. And I remember one time when he came back to his desk after a session with Sydney and his face was red. Then it turned white, and he just held his head in his hands. I was worried about him. Later, when I was called up to take work to Sydney's office I screwed up my courage and told him that I didn't think much of the way he treated people, and the way he treated Mr. Rhodes was not right. I remember he looked at me and said, 'You have no right to speak to me like that. My wife doesn't even talk to me like that.' And I said to him, 'Well, I'm not your wife. I'm your secretary, and I don't think it's right for you to treat people like that.'

"The next day he called Mr. Rhodes up the first thing in the morning and apologized to him. And when I came up to his office later he said, 'I hope you're

Bankers and Brokers

NEW HAVEN (1917) DIRECTORY 41

Edward L. Nettleton, President
John E. Lomas, Vice-President

Kenneth E. Nettleton, Secretary
Russell E. Lomas, Treasurer

Lomas & Nettleton Co.

First Mortgage
Real Estate Loans

Investment Securities, Insurance and Surety Bonds. Money to Loan on Real Estate

137-141 Orange Street **New Haven, Conn.**

Le Roy Sargent, President
William J. Townsend, Sales Manager

Sargent & Company, Inc.

Investment Securities
High Grade Securities Only
Branches in all principal cities of the United States

111 Broadway **New York**
New Haven Office, (400 and 401) 902 Chapel Street

Maps of New Haven

For Sale at the Directory Office
246 Meadow Street

Price 25 Cents Each

The 1917 New Haven City Directory reflects Edward Nettleton becoming president and the emergence of the second generation of family members into the business. New Haven Colony Historical Society.

Sydney Ward Gould, John Lomas' son-in-law, was graduated from the United States Military Academy, West Point, New York, in the Corps of Engineers with the "war class of 1918." Beatrice Lomas Gould Archives.

happy and satisfied. I apologized to Irv.' And when I asked him why he treated Mr. Rhodes like that, he said it was because he's so meek."

The company further solidified its position in 1920 by constructing an office that still stands at the corner of Orange and Court Streets. Although not elaborate, the structure was imposing. Framed above the columned entrance, the corporate name carved in limestone projected security and confidence. Three years later, The Lomas & Nettleton Company opened its first branch office in Hartford.

The good times ended on Black Thursday, October 24, 1929, when the stock market began its plunge toward disaster. Five days later it crashed, leaving investors with a staggering $8 billion in losses and the nation stunned. It was only the beginning. Within three years the Great Depression would shatter the entire economy.

It was hard times.

Marian Whitcher, who worked for the Mechanics Bank and Trust Company in New Haven, remembered the panic that gripped depositors when they made a run on the bank: "That morning when we opened our doors a large crowd was standing in line waiting to get in. The mayor, a short, round-shouldered man, stood on one of the tables in the middle of the bank lobby begging people not to withdraw their money. But no one listened to him. The bank lasted until three o'clock that afternoon. It had enough money to get through the day. Then it closed its doors and never opened them again."

Every section of the country felt the effects of economic devastation. Albert N. Rohnstedt, a key figure in the history of both L&N and Lomas Financial Corporation, remembered the early Depression in Sioux City, Iowa, where he worked for a finance company. When the bottom fell out in that part of the farm belt, his company had to repossess 500 juke boxes. "During the Depression, people didn't have the nickels to put in them," Rohnstedt said. "I couldn't give the machines away, and warehouse storage was expensive. I finally had them carted to the city dump.

"One thing I'll never forget. There was a milk strike on. Farmers brought in truckloads of milk in five-gallon cans and dumped them in the gutters downtown. I saw that and thought to myself, 'My God! What a waste.' But the farmers couldn't sell their milk. It was hard times. Very hard. You almost had to see it to believe it."

Preparation for the new Lomas & Nettleton building, left, and construction, right, at 175 Orange Street at the corner of Court Street, 1920.

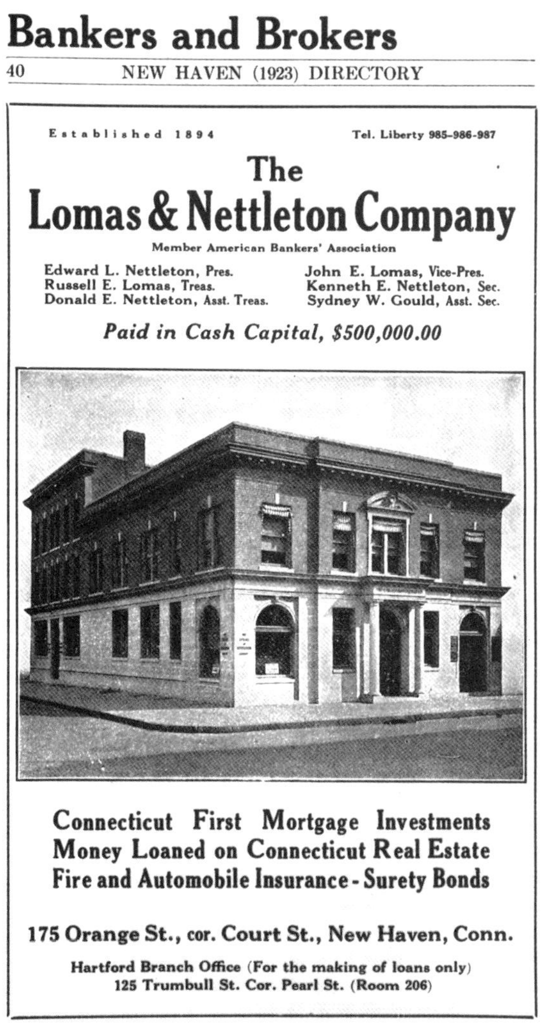

Bankers and Brokers

40 NEW HAVEN (1923) DIRECTORY

Established 1894 Tel. Liberty 985-986-987

The Lomas & Nettleton Company

Member American Bankers' Association

Edward L. Nettleton, Pres. John E. Lomas, Vice-Pres.
Russell E. Lomas, Treas. Kenneth E. Nettleton, Sec.
Donald E. Nettleton, Asst. Treas. Sydney W. Gould, Asst. Sec.

Paid in Cash Capital, $500,000.00

Connecticut First Mortgage Investments
Money Loaned on Connecticut Real Estate
Fire and Automobile Insurance - Surety Bonds

175 Orange St., cor. Court St., New Haven, Conn.

Hartford Branch Office (For the making of loans only)
125 Trumbull St. Cor. Pearl St. (Room 206)

The 1923 full-page directory notice evidenced more changes for the expanding company. Prominently displayed is the picture of the newly completed building and the names of two additional second-generation family members. Donald E. Nettleton, son of Edward Nettleton, joined in 1919. Sydney W. Gould started in 1922. Also listed is the branch office in Hartford. The New Haven Colony Historical Society.

Among the Depression's wreckage lay the housing industry and the homeowner. Between 1928 and 1933, the construction of residential property fell by 95 percent, and home repair expenditures fell by 90 percent. Taking 1926 as a typical pre-Depression year, about 68,000 homes were foreclosed in the United States. In 1930, 150,000 residential households lost their property through foreclosure. The number rose to 200,000 in 1931 and 250,000 in 1932. By the spring of 1933, half of all home mortgages in the country were technically in default, and the home-financing system drifted toward complete collapse.

These economic changes coincided with changes in leadership at The Lomas & Nettleton Company. Edward L. Nettleton died in 1928, followed two years later by John E. Lomas. Kenneth E. Nettleton became president of the company in 1930.

But it was the past judgment of the deceased founders that saved the company from the initial economic cataclysm. Their refusal to guarantee mortgages was the dike that prevented L&N from drowning in a flood of foreclosures. One mortgage banking competitor, Parker & Smith, attracted customers with a large sign at the corner of Church and Chapel Streets that read: "Six and a half percent and safety. We guarantee our mortgages." When hard times hit and foreclosures swept through New Haven, the sign became the company's epitaph in 1929. The Colonial Bond and Mortgage Company failed in May 1930. The Connecticut Mortgage Title and Guarantee Company failed in August 1930.

It was one thing to watch competitors fall and quite another to deal with the individual agony of your own clients. So unsettling were the pleas of anguish

Wall Street in panic on October 24, 1929, Black Thursday. New York Times Paris File, National Archives, Washington, D.C.

Left: On Saturday, May 5, 1928, Edward L. Nettleton died at 69 years of age at Mount Eva, the family country estate.

Right: On Thursday, June 26, 1930, John E. Lomas, age 67, died at his Huntington Street home in New Haven.

Russell Lomas, left, and Kenneth Nettleton, right, about 1930, when the second generation of the two families was assuming leadership of the company and Kenneth Nettleton became president. Kenneth E. Nettleton Archive.

from those losing their homes and property at L&N that Kenneth Nettleton insulated the walls of his office. Russell Lomas also found the suffering difficult to bear. "All day long we had people come in whose property we had foreclosed," says former assistant secretary Helen Sloan, "and they begged Russell Lomas to please arrange something so they wouldn't lose their homes. He often stayed at the office late at night writing letters, trying to find a way to help our mortgagors. I think that was what really killed him." Russell Lomas died of a heart attack in 1932. He was 39 years old.

Lomas & Nettleton wasn't immune to trauma inspired by its own imprudence. The practice of advancing several hundred thousand dollars of interest payments to investors created serious problems for the company. The challenge of recovering that deficit lasted several years.

But the greatest threat to investors came from taxes. "The real estate world went to hell," said Sydney Gould in a letter he wrote in 1951. "About a million dollars in back taxes existed. These had to be paid first, and in the meantime the noteholders were not receiving interest. The situation was pregnant with trouble. It was a ticklish period."

In a "General Letter To Our Investors" dated May 1933, The Lomas & Nettleton Company explained the action it took regarding taxes: "Taxes at present constitute one of the greatest factors delaying interest payments. Our policy of stopping all interest payments until taxes are paid has seemed to some investors very severe, but the reason for this policy is that taxes are a first lien against the property, and in order to preserve the first mortgage equity of the investor in the premises it is vitally important that taxes be paid."

General economic devastation brought radical change to the real estate market. At Lomas & Nettleton that meant a shift in focus from mortgage lending and mortgage investment to property management. Sydney Gould concluded that in the face of an avalanche of distressed properties the only realistic way to improve their value was through the strict supervision of diminished income and rising costs.

Gould addressed the issue with both zeal and imagination. He assumed responsibility for organizing and managing the newly created property management department. "When things went sour," says retired General Luke Finlay, a former part-time L&N employee who worked for Gould in 1933, "Sydney decided the company had to study those properties and see if it couldn't improve their financial results. So, he established a cost accounting system. I believe Sydney was the first person in the mortgage investment business to develop an accounting system for following real estate properties." Esther Johnson, personally hired by Donald Nettleton in 1932, was a key figure in the start up and successful operation of the new department. Through detailed tracking of operating expenses and fixed expenses against income, L&N improved the condition of the properties under its supervision. Even more importantly, it protected most investors from major losses.

> Sydney decided the company had to study those properties . . .

The company also improved its bottom line. It now had two new sources of income to help offset what it lost in loan revenues: a trustee fee paid by noteholders of one-half percent "per annum on the face amount of the mortgage, or foreclosed mortgage," and a 5 percent property management fee.

As the number of distressed and foreclosed properties increased, so did the property management department's workload. The stream of paperwork became a flood. Gould later claimed to have personally supervised the foreclosure of 1,000 home loans and 225 apartment loans. In 1933, Sydney Gould turned to a small, relatively unknown company called International Business Machines to help automate L&N's

rent bills, tax listings, and management reports. He plunged into the world of early data processing with the enthusiasm of a born technocrat. The Lomas & Nettleton Company had an automated punch card system up and running by January 1, 1934. "Our I.B.M. set-up consisted primarily of three sets of machines," wrote Kenneth Nettleton in his 1954 history of the company, "typewriter-like machines for punching the tabulating cards, which were fairly noisy; a sorter for sorting cards, which had a somewhat pleasant whir; a printer which sounded like a battery of die-punches in a machine shop. When the machines were running, no office conversation was possible without shouting.

"All these machines were costly. They were not purchased but were leased from I.B.M."

Despite the rudimentary nature of the early technology, it was light-years ahead of the handwritten system. "When we ran monthly property reports," said Harold Whitcher, "we completed 50 to 100 reports using the IBM equipment in the time it took to write one report by hand."

Supported by the most sophisticated technology available, L&N actively solicited property management business. "As we became proficient in our tabulating operation, we began receiving requests from outside property owners to manage their properties," says Helen Sloan. "It was not unusual for us to work six days a week in that growing department . . . sometimes, even on Sunday." To keep pace with the increased demand, property management offices opened in Stamford, Bristol, Bridgeport, New Britain, and Norwalk in 1933. A Waterbury office opened in 1934. Chicago Title and Trust Company, New York Life, and several savings and loan institutions entrusted their Connecticut properties to L&N's efficient new management service. "Lomas & Nettleton became one of the largest landlords in Connecticut," says Robert E. Nettleton, a former Lomas vice president and son of Donald Nettleton, "managing about 50 percent of the apartment houses in the state. And that's what carried the company through the Depression."

In 1933, Sydney W. Gould went to International Business Machines to help solve the workload produced by the endless stream of paper in the new property management department.
Beatrice Lomas Gould Archive.

Above left: By early 1934 Sydney Gould had The Lomas & Nettleton Company operating with an automated punch card system on three different machines. The IBM 032 Alpha Printing Punch was one of the new machines. International Business Machines Corporation Archives.

Above right: After the punch cards were formatted they were sorted by the IBM 80 Horizontal Sorter. International Business Machines Corporation Archives.

Left: The IBM 30 Alphabetic Duplicating Punch was part of the new technology. International Business Machines Corporation Archives.

Helen Sloan began her career with L&N in February 1930 as a temporary file clerk and lasted long enough to retire after 46 years of service to the company. She worked closely with Gould and his new IBM machines. Photograph by James A. Ledbetter.

Unfortunately, the clerical and management staff required by the new department offset much of its profitability. "The company never lost money [after 1932]," says former L&N secretary-treasurer Irving L. Rhodes, "but it didn't make much either. Holding your own was considered good in those days."

The Lomas & Nettleton Company suffered small losses in 1931 and 1932 of $5,198 and $3,209, respectively. At the end of the first full year of property management in 1933, the company showed a profit of $1,257. In 1934, after one year of IBM automated tabulation, L&N showed a profit of $12,647. A report from a Lomas & Nettleton stockholders' meeting in 1932 gave a bleak financial picture: "With existing conditions as they are, any operating profits for the company could not be hoped for, and therefore only one-half of the May 1st preferred dividend was paid. . . . The holders of the common stock have received no dividends for the last several years." A year later there was reason for slightly more optimism. "Although dividends were not paid to the stockholders during the year 1933," Kenneth Nettleton wrote in his president's report, "there was a slight operating profit for the company. . . . This, at least, is a hopeful sign."

Nowhere did the winds of hope blow stronger than in Washington, D.C. Immediately following his inauguration in 1933, President Franklin D. Roosevelt launched the New Deal, an activist approach to the national crisis based on government intervention. Roosevelt quickly declared the protection of home ownership part of his national policy. In June 1933, he signed a law creating the Home Owners Loan Corporation (HOLC). It was an emergency measure that refinanced tens of thousands of mortgages in danger of default and foreclosure. It even granted low interest loans permitting owners to recover homes lost through forced sale. Between 1933 and 1935 alone, the HOLC supplied over $3 billion for over one million mortgages.

I thought FHA was about the only thing that made sense in the mortgage business.

But it was the Federal Housing Administration (FHA) that had the most profound and lasting effect on home ownership in America. It was created in June 1934 "to encourage improvement in housing standards and conditions, to facilitate sound home financing on reasonable terms, and to exert a stabilizing influence on the mortgage market." The President instructed his staff to come up with a program that would stimulate construction without government spending. The FHA met those requirements by insuring long-term, amortizing mortgage loans made by private lenders for home construction and sale. The agency would collect premiums, set up reserves for losses, and indemnify the lender in the

In March 1933, newly inaugurated President Franklin Delano Roosevelt signed into law New Deal legislation with Secretary of the Treasury William Woodin at his side. New York Times Paris File, National Archives, Washington, D.C.

event of default on a mortgage. It would not build houses or lend money itself. By insuring mortgage loans backed by the full weight of the United States Treasury, it reasoned, FHA loans would attract lenders who had money to invest in residential mortgages.

The impact of FHA loan guidelines on the home finance industry was considerable. Prior to 1934, a prospective homebuyer needed a down payment of at least 30 percent to close a loan. FHA-secured loans required down payments of no more than 10 percent. FHA also extended the repayment period to 25 or 30 years and required their loans to be fully amortized during the primary term. And with decreased risk to the lender because of the government guarantee, interest rates fell by two or three percentage points. Smaller down payments, low monthly payments, and lower interest rates opened the door to home ownership for thousands and later millions of Americans who never could have met the conventional loan requirements. The new housing policy and gradually improving economic conditions had a positive effect on construction starts, which increased to 332,000 in 1937, 399,000 in 1938, 485,000 in 1939, and 530,000 in 1940.

Albert Rohnstedt, who joined Lomas & Nettleton in 1934, recognized the importance of FHA-guaranteed mortgage loans. His ability to persuade others that FHA would benefit both borrowers and lenders gave the company an early lead in the new market. Besides having business ability, Rohnstedt inspired confidence. Several coworkers attributed much of his success to determination and force of personality. Helen Sloan remembers him as dynamic, outgoing, and extremely knowledgeable. Edmund Stoddard described him as: "Very tall. Very impressive. And very persuasive. He had the ability to make people instinctively trust him. He had the ability to convince people that he was someone they could depend on."

On May 29, 1935, The Lomas & Nettleton

Albert N. Rohnstedt joined Lomas & Nettleton in May 1934.

Company became the first Connecticut-approved FHA mortgagee. "I thought FHA was about the only thing that made sense in the mortgage business," said Rohnstedt. At first, FHA seemed to make more sense to borrowers than to lenders. The Depression knocked out L&N's old, private investor system. Now the company had the task of building a network of institutional investors. Trying to sell banks on FHA mortgages, Rohnstedt said, "was like climbing a very high wall. They told me they didn't want a damn thing to do with the government."

National Life Insurance Company of Vermont had no such qualms and became L&N's first corporate investor. "Douglas Meredith of National Life knew a hell of a lot about FHA," said Rohnstedt. "He wasn't hard to sell. He was half sold before I talked to him." National Life's acceptance opened the door to other Vermont insurance companies and banks.

It wasn't unusual for many of these companies to send representatives to inspect the properties firsthand. On one such tour, Edmund Stoddard showed mortgages to the chairman, president, and senior vice president of a bank in rural Vermont, a region noted for its livestock. As he drove through the New Haven neighborhoods, Stoddard gave what he thought was an upbeat, reassuring spiel: "I told them that Lomas & Nettleton was happy to be servicing this property for them, servicing that property for them, and so on." Instead of a calming effect, however, the bankers became increasingly uneasy. Finally, the chairman spoke up: "Young man, I wish you'd be more careful about the words you use. Where we come from, when someone talks about 'servicing' that means something is getting screwed."

Despite rural sensibilities, "servicing" was a difficult word for Lomas & Nettleton to avoid now that its mortgage loan department began to benefit from the increasing popularity of FHA loans and the infusion of investment dollars from private companies. The policy that scored the most points with investors and gave L&N an edge over many competitors was the decision to sell only completed loans. Many mortgage companies sold loans before they were closed. "We used our own money to close the loans we made," said Al Rohnstedt. "It was our loan, and then we sold it. When investors bought it, they bought a completed loan. There wasn't anything missing, and there weren't any last-minute problems." That kind of thoroughness contributed to the company's largest and most prestigious investor breakthrough. In 1937, Metropolitan Life Insurance Company designated Lomas & Nettleton as its sole mortgage loan correspondent in Connecticut.

The company continued to improve during World War II, only now the real estate market was war-related. Kenneth Nettleton's report for 1943 noted that "an encouraging entry has been made into the field of man-

★ *Members of* ★

THE LOMAS & NETTLETON COMPANY

Staff who entered the Armed Forces

ALBERT P. BLOIS
GEORGE E. DILLON, JR.
JOHN E. FIELD
ARTHUR GOODMAN
SYDNEY W. GOULD
GEORGE GUNNING
HAYES JONES
JOHN W. LOMAS
EDWARD MCKENNA★
ALBERT N. ROHNSTEDT
REMORE B. ROSS
RUSSELL A. WERME
WARREN WIBERG
HARRIET E. WINKELMANN
WILLIAM L. YUSTIS

In addition to the former members of our office staff now in Service, many of our building superintendents have joined the Armed Forces.

★

The present personnel of the Company volunteered in many war services here at home.

Five volunteered with the Aircraft Warning Service
Fourteen as Air Raid Wardens
One with the American Women's Voluntary Service
Four as Auxiliary Police
Three at Civilian Defense Control Centers
Two with Ration Boards
Two as Red Cross Gray Ladies
One with the Red Cross Home Service
Two with the Red Cross Home Nursing
One as Red Cross Nurses Aide
Two as members of Salvage Committees
Two with the United States Coast Guard Auxiliary
Seven with the United Service Organizations
One with the War Emergency Radio Service
Three on War Bond Drive Committees.
One with the War Relief Children's Clothing Exchange
One with the Women's Land Army Corps.
Thirteen completed Red Cross First Aid Courses.

Many have also contributed as Blood Donors and have given time on Red Cross and other community drives.

agement of war housing properties." He also said that "practically all mortgages made by our Mortgage Loan Department have been FHA Title II or Title VI [military housing] loans."

The company confronted war conditions and the temporary loss of male staff by training women to fill many of the supervisory functions. War hysteria contributed to a breach in the protection of civil liberties that cost one L&N employee his job and, briefly, his freedom. "William Ohlms, manager of our Bristol office," wrote Kenneth Nettleton, "who had been an officer in the German cavalry in World War I, was rounded up with certain other former German citizens living in Connecticut, and for a short time held in custody." Lomas & Nettleton made one concession to the prospect of hostilities on American soil. As a precautionary measure, they photographed all the important corporate records and stored them in an underground heat- and moisture-controlled vault in the mountains of New Hampshire. "If New Haven were bombed and our records destroyed," said Stoddard, "we had a duplicate set up in the mountains." It was also during the

Above: The Second World War was a trying time for Lomas & Nettleton what with government controls and important personnel leaving for military service. This list commemorates staff members who served in the armed forces and those who volunteered war services at home. Beatrice Lomas Gould Archive.

Right: The Lomas & Nettleton office in April 1943 reflects the loss of male staff during the war. Kenneth Nettleton is the tallest man standing, back row, center.

PAGE TEN NEW HAVEN EVENING REGISTER, FRIDAY, SEPTEMBER 22, 1944

Fifty Years of REAL ESTATE

Mortgages · Insurance · Property Management & Sales

September 1894 to September 1944

The Lomas & Nettleton Company

New Haven, Connecticut

The Founders of The Lomas & Nettleton Co.

JOHN E. LOMAS

EDWARD L. NETTLETON

Present Officers of The Lomas & Nettleton Company

KENNETH E. NETTLETON, President

DONALD E. NETTLETON, Vice-President and Treasurer

IRVING L. RHODES, Ass't Treasurer

MINOTT A. DAVIS, Secretary

NELSON E. KNAPP, Ass't Secretary

The Lomas & Nettleton Co's Offices Then and Now!

Early offices at 850 Chapel St. (Second Floor)

The Lomas & Nettleton Co.'s Building at 175 Orange St.

Looking Backward 50 Years

– or do you remember when?

1894–John E. Lomas Started business 817 Chapel St., New Haven
1895
1896
1897
1898

Show Place HOUSES POPULAR

Trolleys Developed Suburbs

Battleship MAINE Blown Up, 1898

1899–Edward L. Nettleton Joined John E. Lomas *in partnership*
1900
1901
1902
1903

1901 Yale Bi-Centennial

First Airplane Flight, by Wright Brothers

1904
1905
1906
1907
1908

Franklin Elm Church and Chapel Cut Down . . Planted by James Hillhouse

San Francisco Fire and Earthquake, 1906

1909
1910
1911
1912
1913

Give!

The FEDERAL INCOME TAX STARTED

Two-family Houses in Vogue

1914
1915
1916
1917–Lomas & Nettleton
1918 *incorporates*

World War I Begins

Garages become a home necessity

New Railroad Station Built, 1917

1919
1920–Office Moves
1921 to 175 Orange St.
1922
1923–Hartford Office *opened*

Post-war Prohibition

Westville joins N. H. 1921

Building BOOM Many apartment houses built

1924
1925
1926
1927
1928

SUN'S ECLIPSE IN 1924

Lindberg flew the Atlantic

ONE DAY *Governor* 1925

1929
1930
1931
1932
1933–Stamford and Bristol offices open

Market crashed

Bank Holidays

1930 Sterling Library Built

Many foreclosures

1934
1935–Company was Approved
1936 to make F.H.A. mortgages
1937–Lomas & Nettleton Approved
1938 Mortgage Loan Correspondent in Conn. for Metropolitan Life Ins. Co.

H. O. L. C. slowed foreclosures

F.H.A. Set up to Finance Homes

Edward VIII abdicates

Seymour new Pres. of YALE. 1937

1938, New Haven's 300th. Anniv.

1939
1940
1941
1942
1943

U. S. Territory Attacked enters World War II

New Construction limited to War Housing

1944 One-half Century of Business

One bright event during the dark war years was the fiftieth anniversary celebration in September 1944. A full-page newspaper announcement heralded prominent events marked along the way. Beatrice Lomas Gould Archive.

war that The Lomas & Nettleton Company celebrated its fiftieth anniversary. Because of the conflict, the 1944 event lacked the fanfare it might otherwise have attracted. Publicity was limited to a newspaper advertisement.

Two years later there was greater cause for celebration. The war was over and Lomas & Nettleton already felt the effects of a surge in the economy. "Operating costs have increased substantially," read a report about L&N's progress in 1946, "but these have been more than offset by increases in revenue, particularly from property sales, mortgage fees, and insurance commissions, all three of these accounts showing large gains over the previous year."

Harold Whitcher developed one innovative postwar insurance program in 1947. It protected homeowners and their families from foreclosure in the event of disability or death. "I was in the collection department before I was in the insurance department," says Whitcher, "and I saw so many people who couldn't make their monthly payments when they became disabled. From personal experience I could tell there was a need. And when I moved into the insurance department, I was able to do something about it." Whitcher created the Home Mortgage Security Plan, a group insurance plan that paid the homeowner's monthly mortgage payment in the event of disability caused by either accident or illness and paid off the mortgage in the event of death. Turned down at first by two national insurance companies, Whitcher finally placed the plan with a Connecticut firm, Commercial Travelers Insurance Company. The new policy sold well among Lomas & Nettleton customers. It proved so popular over the next five years that Whitcher sold it to 26 Connecticut savings banks and savings and loan associations.

Harold Whitcher developed an insurance program that protected homeowners and their families from foreclosure in the event of disability or death.

The most difficult postwar question for Al Rohnstedt was whether or not to stay with the company. Rohnstedt wanted to test himself in a wider arena. When New York Life offered him a correspondency in Connecticut, it turned his head. "I wasn't unhappy with L&N," said Rohnstedt, in an interview after his retirement from Lomas. "They were fine people, but I felt I had greater opportunity somewhere else, maybe even a piece of the action." Unwilling to lose their key executive, L&N's top management countered with an offer Rohnstedt "couldn't refuse." After 16 years as president, Kenneth Nettleton decided to retire. Donald Nettleton arranged for Rohnstedt to buy Kenneth's interest in the company. When his brother stepped down in 1946, Donald Nettleton became president and Albert Rohnstedt found himself on the board of directors with a 25 percent piece of the action.

Absence did not make the heart grow fonder when it came to Sydney Gould. His return to Lomas & Nettleton, following his military service at a Pentagon staff job, created turmoil among the staff. Donald Nettleton in particular found Gould's martinet style and outbursts of anger increasingly unacceptable.

Kenneth Nettleton, with Hermine Roth Clouse, at Nettleton's retirement dinner in 1946. He was president for 16 years. In his last years, she became his main support in the mortgage sales department at Lomas & Nettleton and stayed until her retirement in 1950, after 40 years of service with the company. Photograph courtesy Marjorie M. Beecher.

Helen Sloan remembers loud arguments between Donald Nettleton and Gould after he returned from the war: "They {Kenneth and Donald Nettleton} didn't have much love for Sydney at all. Neither one. Donald especially. They constantly argued. The general feeling at the office was that nobody liked him {Gould}, because he was so abrasive to everybody." The axe finally fell at a board meeting in July 1951 when it voted to sever Gould from the management of the company. "The following morning the telephone rang, and it was Mr. Gould," Helen Sloan recalls. "He asked me to collect all the things in the file cabinets and desk drawers that belonged to him and bring them out to his house. But he never mentioned anything about being let go. And so I took all the items to him, and we sat on his porch. He sat down and began to cry. 'I'm not going to be there any longer.' That's all he could say. Finally, he said, 'I can't talk to you. I'll have to tell Bea to come out and discuss this with you.' Then he got up and walked inside the house."

With a freer hand to make the company grow, Rohnstedt began looking at mortgage banking beyond Connecticut. He liked what he saw in Texas and California, states that could generate a volume business. "There weren't any volume builders in Connecticut," said Rohnstedt. "If a Connecticut builder put up 50 houses, he was considered a big builder. Developers in California were putting up 500 houses."

I had a hell of a time convincing them to try California.

Management, however, hesitated to move beyond the safe and familiar. "Lomas & Nettleton was a very old and conservative house," said Rohnstedt. "I had a hell of a time convincing them to try California." Rohnstedt met with little success at first. His proposal went against the grain of a board whose vision of the future was shaped by a Puritan tradition of conservative principles and frugality.

As it turned out, it was the needs of L&N's institutional investors that convinced the company to branch out. Connecticut passed a law in the early 1950s requiring savings banks to place 80 percent of their assets in mortgages. Since the Connecticut housing market couldn't supply enough mortgages, the banks were forced to invest their money outside the state. It was a major change for institutions unaccustomed to doing business over great distances. Anxiety prompted them to turn to someone they trusted. "A number of Connecticut Savings Banks," read the minutes from a May 1954 L&N board meeting, "have manifested their intention of buying mortgage loans outside of Connecticut, and have in numerous instances expressed a willingness to have such business transacted and serviced for them by The Lomas & Nettleton Company."

At that same meeting, the board approved Rohnstedt's request to transact business in California.

Although Rohnstedt went to the West Coast with the board's blessing, the $25,000 budget it authorized wasn't enough to open a full service operation. That didn't deter Rohnstedt: "I rented an office and hired a manager and a few other employees. That pretty well ate up the $25,000." He planned to use the skeleton office staff to originate mortgage loans, then arranged for one of the large California banks to service them temporarily. It wasn't an easy deal to sell. "I finally convinced Hal Menden, executive vice president of the United California Bank," said Rohnstedt. "I said, 'Look. It isn't going to cost you anything, and you'll be earning the servicing fee. You're already servicing loans now. You would just be adding these loans to your portfolio. The only thing is you've got to let them go when I tell you to let them go. Also, you're going to get a good customer who will give you a lot of future business.' They agreed to service our loans with the stipulation that the total didn't exceed $25 million.

"And that's what we did. By the time we reached $25 million, we had enough volume to put together a servicing staff and make it pay for itself."

In March 1956, The Lomas & Nettleton Company opened a full service branch in Los Angeles at 510 South Spring Street. It didn't take long for the California office to generate the kind of volume Al

While the company was expanding in California, it was business as usual in Connecticut. These two ads, from the August 1955 issue of the *National Real Estate and Building Journal*, were created by E. J. Lush, Inc., a New Haven advertising agency. The ads ran in the Sunday newspapers, one preceding the grand opening of the Ridgeland project. They emphasized easy financing arrangements and sales features, pointing out the excellent sales record.

Lomas & Nettleton opened a full service branch office in Los Angeles, California in March 1956 at 510 South Spring Street.

The Lomas & Nettleton board of directors in 1956. From left to right: Edmund L. Stoddard, John W. Lomas, Remore B. Ross, Donald E. Nettleton, Albert N. Rohnstedt, Harold C. Whitcher, and Irving L. Rhodes.

Rohnstedt had predicted. At its peak, California produced five times as many originations as all of Connecticut. The company opened another branch office in San Francisco in 1961.

Former L&N vice chairman of the board Remore B. Ross and former executive vice president F. Peter Gaffey marketed the loans to institutional investors. Gaffey attributes much of their success to a quality product: "Remore Ross and I handled the national marketing at the time. We checked the credit reports on all the loans. The ones we didn't like we shipped back and said, 'Don't make these loans.' We had to sell those loans to investors, and we made sure they got the cream. We had some investors that never had a foreclosure for years."

The infusion of business from California added fresh authority to Lomas & Nettleton's reputation. Under the leadership of Donald Nettleton and Albert Rohnstedt, the company's servicing portfolio increased from $13 million in 1946 to $240 million in 1961. That achievement prompted a company press release to note in early 1962: "This puts the concern in the position of being the leading mortgage banking company in New England and among the foremost in the nation." The company celebrated its regional and national standing that year by adding 5,700 square feet of office space to its New Haven headquarters and updating its data processing equipment. At a board meeting in January 1962, Donald Nettleton became chairman of the board and Al Rohnstedt moved from first vice president to president.

But it was Donald Nettleton's increasing concern for the future welfare of his family that abruptly changed the company's direction. Now in his sixties, Nettleton decided that the best way to ensure a comfortable retirement and protect the estate he had accumulated was to sell his interest in Lomas & Nettleton. From a practical standpoint that meant selling the company. "I didn't want to sell," said Rohnstedt, who

In January 1962, Lomas & Nettleton announced that the board of directors had promoted Donald Nettleton, seated right, from president to chairman of the board, and Albert Rohnstedt, seated left, from first vice president to president. Other promotions included four new assistant vice presidents. Standing left to right are George S. Harkins, Alan E. Marshall, and Richard W. Shields. F. Peter Gaffey, the fourth of the group, was not present when the picture was taken.

. . . the leading mortgage banking company in New England and among the foremost in the nation.

owned a quarter interest in L&N, "but I didn't want to stand in the way of any of the principals. They had a right to do what they wanted with their investment. I told Donald that I'd like to buy him out, but I couldn't afford it."

Metropolitan Life Insurance Company expressed an interest in buying the company when Rohnstedt approached them. But Metropolitan's legal department blocked the proposal, claiming a conflict of interest might cause it future problems. Donald Nettleton talked to a company in Philadelphia. They offered to buy Lomas & Nettleton, but only on the condition that Al Rohnstedt stayed with the company. "I wouldn't agree to that," said Rohnstedt. "I agreed not to stand in the way of their selling the company, but I didn't say they could sell me.

"Finally, I talked to Hal Menden at United California Bank about buying us, but they weren't in a position to do it at that time. I was going back to Connecticut that night. When I got to the airport, there was a message for me to call Menden at his home. He said, 'I've got someone who wants to talk to you about buying the company.' I said, 'Hal, my flight leaves in a few minutes.' He said, 'That's okay. This guy is in New York.' So, I agreed to see Gene Wallace in New York. Gene and I talked for a half hour at the most when he said, 'I'll buy it. Give me a couple of days to write up a contract.'

"Sure enough. A few days later, we received a contract. And it was a good contract. We made one or two small changes and signed it. That's how we got into Wallace Investments. It didn't take long."

One reason the transaction didn't take long was because Gene Wallace agreed to buy the company for about $5 million, a price both sides regarded as fair. Wallace asked Rohnstedt to stay on as president. The addition of L&N to Wallace Realty Mortgage Company made the combined servicing portfolio the eighth largest in the country and broadened its geographical range. Wallace also promised a large infusion of capital for construction loans.

What those associated with The Lomas & Nettleton Company didn't realize was that Gene Wallace's grandiose plans for a mortgage banking empire stood on very shaky financial ground. His acquisition of Lomas & Nettleton was both a failure and a success. It failed in the short term because its purchase helped propel the parent company toward financial crisis. On the other hand, Lomas & Nettleton became a critical piece of the foundation upon which the company later rebuilt itself.

CITY EDITION

The New Haven Register

WEATHER
TODAY—Hot and Humid
TOMORROW—Cloudy, Warm
Full Details—Page 2

151ST YEAR—NO. 206 ★ ★ NEW HAVEN 3, CONN., SUNDAY, JULY 28, 1963 PHONE 562-1121 25 CENTS

Harriman Calls Test Ban No Barrier To Atomic War

Associated Press Photo

Under Secretary of State W. Averell Harriman pulls jacket over plain white shirt as he arrives for press conference in Hyannis, Mass., after talk with President Kennedy.

Leaders Plug A-Pact; GOP Urges Study

Associated Press Photo

The world's first atomic explosion creates weird scene over the desert in shattering blast July 16, 1945, at Alamogordo, New Mexico.

Reaction To Treaty

HYANNIS PORT, Mass. (AP)—The White House said that telegrams on President Kennedy's speech on the nuclear test ban agreement were running about 40-1 in favor of the President's position.

* * *

MADRAS, India (AP)—Prime Minister Nehru hailed the test ban and said "The United States, Soviet Russia and Great Britain deserve all our congratulations."

* * *

LONDON (AP)—Lord Hailsham came home from Moscow Saturday, describing the test ban treaty "as an opportunity not to be missed." The British negotiator at the Moscow talks said he believed East and West must now look for further solutions to cold war issues.

* * *

PARIS (UPI)—President Charles deGaulle apparently is resolved to "go-it-alone" again on nuclear testing and a possible East-West non-aggression pact. DeGaulle meets the press Monday. According to purportedly "inside" information, DeGaulle will: Reject firmly all appeals both by his allies and the Russians to join the Moscow nuclear test ban agreement. He will emphasize he is determined to push ahead with France's nuclear force and not to sign any test pact until his nuclear force is ready and unless there is simultaneous agreement to destroy all existing nuclear stockpiles and the vehicles for delivering them.

* * *

BERKELEY, Calif. (AP)—Dr. Edward Teller, famed nuclear physicist, said Friday "there are serious reasons to be concerned" about the proposed test ban treaty. "I feel that prompt ratification or prompt rejection by the Senate would be a grave mistake," Dr. Teller told the Associated Press. "I hope that the matter will receive the most careful consideration from every angle before definite action is taken." One can think of a ban which, I believe, would be thoroughly acceptable. We would agree to limit the release of radioactivity into the atmosphere to a level equal to the amount that each year decays by natural causes. This would permit the Russians and the United States each to put into the atmosphere a 1,000 kiloton equivalent of fission products each year and still leave something over for other nations. Such an agreement of limitation would elimi-

(Please Turn to Page 2)

Briefs JFK On Sessions With Nikita

Senators Ask 'Serious' Try For Rail Pact

WASHINGTON (AP)—The Senate Commerce Committee cut short a hearing Saturday on President Kennedy's rail labor legislation with a plea that both sides get down to serious collective bargaining.

In recessing the hearing until Monday, Acting Chairman John O. Pastore, D-R.I., said he thinks "a better purpose would be served" by giving the carriers and the brotherhoods time to negotiate.

Secretary of Labor W. Willard Wirtz announced in advance that as soon as the hearing was over he would resume meetings begun Friday night in a renewed effort to work out an agreement.

The only witness the committee heard was H. E. Gilbert, president of the Brotherhood of Locomotive Firemen and Enginemen (AFL-

(Please Turn to Page 2)

Texas Firm Buying Lomas & Nettleton

A Texas corporation is buying the Lomas & Nettleton Co. for $5 million in the largest financial transaction in recent New Haven history.

The real estate mortgage concern, with executive offices at Orange and Court Streets, is being purchased by Wallace Investments, Inc., of Dallas.

Wallace is buying all the common stock of Lomas & Nettleton. The transaction is expected to be completed shortly, according to Donald E. Nettleton, chairman of the board of directors of Lomas & Nettleton.

The corporate and physical status of Lomas & Nettleton will not be changed, Nettleton said. The affiliation with Wallace Investments may result in geographical expansion in the future, he added.

Lomas & Nettleton services about $350 million in mortgages for the Metropolitan Life Insurance Co. and for savings banks in Connecticut, New York, California and Nevada.

It also deals in insurance, but this is a relatively small part of the business.

Lomas & Nettleton has nearly 200 employes. Of this total, 115 are assigned to the company's headquarters office at 175 Orange St. The others are located in branch offices in Hartford, Stamford, Los Angeles and San Francisco.

Founded In 1894

The firm was founded here in 1894 by John E. Lomas and Edward L. Nettleton. Donald Nettleton is a son of one of the founders. The president and chief executive officer is Albert N. Rohnstedt.

Wallace Investments, in addition to purchasing Lomas & Nettleton, has contracted to purchase the Admiral Fire Insurance Co. of Houston for $2.5 million.

Ex-Yale President Makes Disclosure

1919 Wilson-House Rift Explained

Col. Edward M. House and Woodrow Wilson in 1917.

The Earth Still Trembles

Relief Sped To Quake Zone

In Today's Register

Missing Express Safe After Quake

182 PAGES

UPI Telephoto

Yugoslavia's President Tito (right), walks through the streets of earth-wracked Skopje, Yugoslavia. A "minor-tremor" rocked the center of the city as Tito arrived.

The negotiated purchase of Lomas & Nettleton by Wallace Investments in June 1963 was announced on the front page, second column, of *The New Haven Register* on Sunday, July 28. Beatrice Lomas Gould Archive.

CHAPTER III

CRISIS

By the time Gene Wallace negotiated the purchase of Lomas & Nettleton in June 1963, the real estate crunch had already taken its toll on Wallace Investments. As the market skidded downward, so did the value of the company's notes and collateral. Deals stalled. Revenue slowed, and in some cases dried up. More and more loans had to be extended. Those extensions, observes former board member Ed Hoffman, placed the company in the uneconomic position of "using short-term money to finance long-term deals."

The hope that Lomas & Nettleton's profitable operation and reliable revenues would offset the company's lending problems was unrealistic. The mortgage company wasn't large enough. It was a case of too little, too late.

No one was more deeply affected by the company's trauma than Gene Wallace. The real estate bubble upon which his career rested had finally burst. For the first time in his professional life, he faced a situation over which he had no control; brilliant deals, charismatic charm, and important contacts couldn't compensate for a down market.

To escape the stress, Gene Wallace turned to alcohol. By early 1963, alcohol abuse began to impair his judgment and job performance. Wallace's dependency increased as the year progressed. Ed Hoffman first realized the extent of the problem in January when the two traveled to New York on business. On that occasion, Hoffman remembers that Wallace started drinking about 11:00 a.m. in the Admiral's Club at Love Field. Then on their noon flight, Wallace had two complimentary cocktails as well as Hoffman's two. When they arrived at the company's Carlyle Hotel apartment suite

Wallace began drinking in earnest. "Gene," says Hoffman, "was drinking vodka he had stashed all over the dadburned apartment. He'd gulp it down and pass out for a couple of hours. Then he'd wake up and start drinking again." Hoffman couldn't do anything with Wallace. Neither could anyone on the hotel staff or even the male nurse Hoffman hired to stay with him. Finally, Hoffman contacted Wallace's doctor in Dallas. The physician flew to New York and managed to get him in good enough shape to board a plane and fly back to Dallas.

It was a tough era.

Executive vice president Jim Stanley helped Wallace in similar circumstances. "I remember," says Stanley, "one time when Herb Heftler was in New York with Wallace, Herb called and asked me to come up there and help him with Gene. So I flew up, and the first thing I did was pour out all the vodka Gene kept in the deep freeze, the toilet water tank, and everywhere else. I got rid of them and was trying to sober him up when the doorbell rang. It was the bell captain. Gene had called him and ordered more bottles of vodka. I canceled the order. Gene looked at me and said, 'You son-of-a-bitch, you're fired.' And I said, 'That's fine, because I don't want to work for no drunk anyway.' I remember Herb Heftler called me aside and said, 'Jim, he's firing you.' I said, 'Oh hell, he isn't firing me. He's just mad and needs to get home.' I got him on a plane, took him back to Dallas, and drove him out to his house. He put his arm around me and thanked me. The next day I got a raise and everything was hunky-dory.

"Gene Wallace had a tremendous inferiority complex. Some people didn't see that in him, but I damn sure saw it. He had so much pressure on him to make profits and make deals. He knew some of the deals he made were bad. The pressure just got to him. He couldn't handle it."

Wallace Investments' executive vice president Jim Stanley was experienced in helping Gene Wallace in many ways.

Jim Stanley also recalls how Wallace's drinking interfered more directly with the management of the company: "Once when Jess and I were up in New York with Gene for a meeting with a group of investment bankers, he was so drunk he couldn't talk. Jess had to give the speech for him."

Later that summer, after the Lomas & Nettleton acquisition, Al Rohnstedt also witnessed how far Wallace's illness had progressed: "We both stayed in the Drake Hotel because Wallace Investments' New York office was right around the corner. I remember going to a coffee shop across the street at eight o'clock in the morning, and there was Gene drinking a cup of coffee, except it wasn't coffee.

"When he was sober, he was a hell of a businessman. A brilliant, brilliant guy in real estate. No question about it. Of course, when he was drunk it was a different set of facts. Unfortunately, he was drunk most of the time."

Board members gradually learned about Wallace's alcohol problem and its effect on the management of the company. "I became concerned," says Atlanta developer and former board member Joe B. Hutchison, "about the lack of routine corporate discipline. The Miami office spent huge sums of money on entertaining that, in my opinion, had no relation to bringing the company business. I'm talking about big-time parties, chartered yachts, Caribbean trips, and all that stuff. When I saw the income figures that were being produced in Miami and the amount of goddamn money they were spending, it scared the hell out of me. That's when I first realized the company was not being run right and someone had to start monitoring it."

"It was a very confusing time," says Ed Hoffman. "One problem was that Gene Wallace would make deals over the telephone at night when he was drunk. It was a tough era. I can tell you that."

Although Wallace demonstrated an increasing inability to lead effectively, the board of directors was just as lax in its supervision of management. Most of the directors had primary responsibilities elsewhere and little time to devote to Wallace Investments. Several board members were Gene Wallace's friends and close business associates. The good-old-boy network that normally enhanced business relationships in this case prevented the board from recognizing the problems, and later from taking effective measures to correct them. "Many of those on the board," says Ed Hoffman, "had been involved with Gene over a period of years. They felt obligated to him. They didn't want to hurt him."

By the summer of 1963, the company's financial problems finally began to surface. According to the terms of a new bank loan agreement that gave Wallace Investments a $46 million line of credit, the company's executive committee had to review all assets and send a written report to the banks. For four long days in June the executive committee, made up of Gene Locke, Ed Hoffman, Henry C. Beck, Jr., and Tom Lively, studied every asset and liability in the company. They concluded that Gene Wallace's projections were too optimistic. "After we reviewed the assets," says Ed Hoffman, "we reversed a lot of the profitability. We took reserves for losses, because we knew we hadn't made the dadburned money, and because we knew we had loans that were questionable." After the review, the executive committee instructed the treasurer "to write off certain assets of the company." The committee also increased the allowance for possible losses from $1,750,000 to $2,300,000.

Feeling some heat from the executive committee because of the problems uncovered during their review, Gene Wallace requested special assistance from board member and corporate secretary Jess Hay. Hay's law firm agreed to give the young attorney a 90-day leave of absence to work exclusively on the problems at Wallace Investments. But if asking for help was intended as a public relations gesture by Wallace, that wasn't Jess Hay's understanding. He plunged into the assignment with the intensity and seriousness the situation demanded. On July 20, in a confidential memorandum to Gene Wallace, Hay wrote, "the primary problem is not one of underlying value, but rather one of liquidity." Based on his research, Hay concluded that 80 percent of the company's resources was tied up in nonliquid assets. He proposed two strategies to correct the problem:

> Jess was the first person to openly admit the company was in trouble.

(1) To do whatever is necessary to reduce the amount of non-liquid assets of the Company,

> through sales or other means, to 60% of the Company's usable resources within 90 days, and to 50% thereof within one year;
>
> (2) To make no new loans or other commitments, . . . until the Company's investment in non-liquid assets has been reduced to below 50% of the Company's usable resources.

These proposals were followed by detailed procedures for liquidating the company's nonliquid assets. Then, on page seven of the nine-page document, Hay summarized in one sentence the heart of the problem at Wallace Investments: "however, the specific means selected is not nearly as important, in my judgment, as is the decision that the Company needs to frontally attack the problem and adopt some plan of action reasonably calculated to bring the Company to a strong working capital condition."

To dramatize the importance of the report, Hay asked executive vice president and treasurer M. D. Wommack and executive vice president Jim Stanley to accompany him to New York and personally deliver the memorandum to Gene Wallace. Wommack calls this a crucial moment in the company's history because "Jess was the first person to openly admit the company was in trouble, and he was the first person that tried to convince Wallace.

"When we walked into Wallace's hotel suite, Gene gave Hay a Rolex watch and said, 'Jess, I want you to have this.' Then, as Jess handed the report to Gene, he said, 'You can have the watch back, but I've got to give you this.'"

For former Lomas executive vice president Lanelle Latendresse, who helped research some of the information used in the report, it was Hay's courage and integrity that made a lasting impression. "As far as I know," says Latendresse, "this was the first time anybody stood up and said these loans and these deals are not like they should be. And that's a pretty tall order for a young attorney to take on. None of the rest of us were courageous enough to do that."

Two days later, in a 19-page memorandum, Gene Wallace responded to Hay's recommendations by denying the seriousness of the situation. "We do not feel," wrote Wallace in conclusion, "that the Company is in an alarming financial condition." Despite the evidence, the president had refused to face reality. "I felt," says Wommack, "that Wallace knew things were reaching a crisis point. But he didn't want to deal with it, couldn't deal with it, and hid from it via the alcohol."

Two incidents in particular convinced the executive committee and the rest of the board that their confidence in Gene Wallace was misplaced. At a board meeting on July 8, despite Wallace's strong recommendation, the board considered the purchase of Admiral Fire Insurance Company from T. J. Bettes for $2.5 million a poor investment and refused to approve it. Wallace then asked the board for the authority to investigate "the matter further and then report back to the Executive Committee or the Board for future action . . . if additional facts . . . are developed by such investigation." On July 27, in clear violation of his instructions from the board, Gene Wallace issued a press release to Dallas newspapers announcing that Wallace Investments had agreed to purchase Admiral Fire Insurance Company from T. J. Bettes for $2.5 million. No one on the board was notified prior to this public announcement.

> We had given Gene Wallace specific instructions not to proceed.

The challenge to their authority caught the executive committee's attention like a slap across the face. On August 9, the committee wrote a strongly worded letter of reprimand to Gene Wallace and came very close to rescinding the purchase agreement. "We were very upset," says Ed Hoffman, a member of the executive committee. "We had given Gene Wallace specific instructions not to proceed."

In contrast, when it came time to finance the acquisition of Lomas & Nettleton and Admiral Fire, Gene Wallace displayed little initiative or leadership. By early August, the time allotted for purchasing the two companies was running out. At that critical moment, in what Wommack calls a "classic event" in the company's history, Wallace and his wife boarded a ship and sailed to Europe for a vacation. He had been drinking heavily at the time and according to close associates had to be carried on the boat. "His last statement to me before leaving," says Jess Hay, "was, 'I've done all I can. I'm going to leave it with you. I just ask one favor. Close these two transactions for me.' Well, hell, we were $7.5 million away from closing."

Astonished by their departing president's request, Wommack recalls senior management's response to the challenge: "Hay, Stanley, and I and a couple of others were in New York at the time, and we just looked at each other and asked, 'How are we going to do this?' We understood the difficulty of the task. At that period in our history, it looked pretty hopeless, but no one was giving up. So we started pounding the pavement. It was just a matter of going from bank to bank and putting together a group that would make the loan."

Most board members realized by now that something had to be done about the company's leadership. The problem was that Wallace still commanded the obligation and friendship of important stockholders. "Gene Locke, Henry Beck, and I," says Ed Hoffman, "represented about 20 percent of the stock. We did not trust Gene Wallace. But we didn't want to have a head-on collision in terminating him at that point because he had too many friends who owned stock that he could manipulate. For instance, we didn't know what position Murchison would take. We didn't know what Tom Lively would do. We didn't know what Herb Heftler, another large stockholder, would do. So we were trying to figure out how to keep the company from going downhill and ultimately replace Gene Wallace. Our first step was to bring in Jim Cumby, the number two man at Republic Bank."

The arrival of James Cumby was noted in the 1963 annual report: "On July 8, 1963, the company was pleased to announce the addition of James M. Cumby, Vice Chairman of the Board of Directors of the Republic National Bank of Dallas, to the company's management and Board of Directors. Mr. Cumby has agreed to take an active part in our operations as an officer of the Company and was elected to the position of Chairman of the Board to be effective October 8, 1963."

Hoffman and the other board members who feared the direction in which Wallace was leading the company hoped Cumby would help stabilize management. He never got the chance. Within days of his taking over as chairman, disaster struck. Republic National Bank and Continental Illinois National Bank, representing a total of 12 banks, declared Wallace Investments in technical default of its loan agreement and called for the collateral needed to secure the loan.

It wasn't a monetary default because the company was still able to pay its principal and interest. The violation involved technical procedures. According to the terms of the bank loan, the company's construction loans had to be paid back within a certain time period. The company's extensions pushed the loans beyond their legal limit and into default. As the lead bank in charge of monitoring the loan, Republic National Bank discovered the violations, which triggered the call for collateral and the transfer of company assets to the banks.

M. D. Wommack remembers the shock he felt when the telegram demanding collateral arrived at corporate headquarters. He realized it either meant bankruptcy or a long, slow, difficult workout. If Gene Wallace was disturbed, he concealed it under a cloak of anger. "Gene was infuriated," says Wommack. "He didn't think there was any reason for the banks to take that action. He believed the notes we were extending were still qualifiers, that they were still good in their particular categories. But it was stretching a point. It wasn't exactly a lie, but it wasn't telling the whole story either.

"His first instructions to Lanelle Latendresse and me were to drag our feet. He said he was going to try to resolve the problem without ever having to assign the collateral to the banks."

Not surprisingly, Gene Wallace, the consummate dealmaker, tried to wheel and deal his way out of the crisis. His efforts, however, were directed more toward buying time than looking for real solutions. Near the end of October, he entered into discussions with the Bank of America to loan Wallace Investments $50 million to replace the company's current bank loan. "That was probably Wallace's last gasp at trying to stave this thing off," says Wommack. "He kept saying, 'I'm going to get those damn banks out.'"

The board of directors, on the other hand, acknowledged the crisis and began to grapple with it. Still smarting from Wallace's insubordination over the Admiral Fire Insurance Company acquisition, the board asserted its authority by approving the following resolution a few days after the call for collateral: "RESOLVED, that the Company shall not enter into new agreements, consummate new loans or close new land transactions, without prior approval of the Executive Committee." A few weeks later, when the board learned about Wallace's Bank of America negotiations, they passed resolutions requiring prior executive committee approval for any changes in the company's banking arrangements.

Republic National Bank's reputation for killing its own snakes was about to be tested. The Wallace loan was especially embarrassing for the competitive, image-conscious bank. To a large extent, Republic's sponsorship had attracted the participation of the eleven other blue-chip banks. And a major selling point must surely have been Wallace's reputation as Republic's former real estate genius. Then there was the loan amount. At the time, a $34 million workout qualified as more than a minor headache.

Republic Bank responded by placing the problem in the veteran hands of general vice president and executive committee member DeWitt T. Ray, Sr. In his mid-sixties, with over forty years of banking experience, the lean, irascible executive had little patience for public relations. "Mr. Ray was a dear man," says Robert M. Baumgartner, a former Republic Bank assistant vice president. "I had very warm feelings for him. At the time, maybe some of them were not so warm. He was a taskmaster, and he had an expression that was part of his philosophy. He used to say, 'Once you've got a son-of-a-bitch by the balls, don't ever let go for a better hold.' He was a conservative banker and a good watchdog.

> **Mr. Ray minced no words.**

"He wanted to take control of the assets, to police the company very closely, but permit them to go forward and work out their problems. Part of that may have had to do with the fact that Wallace Investments was a home-grown company sponsored by Republic Bank. The bank's reputation was at stake. It wasn't prepared to see the company go under."

Art Blanchard, an attorney representing Republic Bank at the time, remembers DeWitt Ray's scrupulous attention to detail. He made sure an attorney signed off on all important documents. "He always said, 'Write it here, lawyer-man . . . in black ink.' Those were the days when photocopy machines couldn't pick up blue ink.

"He was very, very experienced in the corporate game and not the gentlest fellow in the world to work with. But very smart and very able. And the ideal man to lead a difficult workout."

At a get-acquainted meeting with Republic Bank

Republic National Bank placed the problem of Wallace Investments' technical default of its loan agreement in the care of DeWitt Ray, an all-business, no-nonsense type of person.

representatives in Wallace Investments' boardroom, Lanelle Latendresse recalls the strong impression Ray made as he informed them about the bank's new role. "Mr. Ray," says Latendresse, "minced no words. He told us he and his staff had been appointed to review our assets in detail. He was impressive. A very forceful man."

Dick Drake, who worked for Continental Illinois National Bank's real estate division, was another member of Ray's staff: "My function was to work with John Stuart and Bob Baumgartner and evaluate the collateral to be pledged. By using the company's files, we picked apart each deal and tried to write a coherent assessment of its collectibility.

"In terms of even trying to get an understanding of the deals, it was very, very difficult. The files were in complete disarray, which typified the way in which Wallace did business near the end. He was the only guy that really knew what the hell was going on, and it's very tough if you've got an incoherent deal originator making deals.

"You'd look for an appraisal and you may or may not find one. And if you did, it may or may not relate to what appeared to be the collateral. It was very difficult to find out what you really had a security position on."

What they discovered after slogging through the

John Stuart of Republic National Bank worked with Continental Illinois National Bank's real estate division to evaluate the collateral to be pledged. He would later become president of First RepublicBank, Dallas.

company's loan files was not reassuring. "We found out," says former First RepublicBank, Dallas president John Stuart, a former credit analyst who worked for Mr. Ray, "that the loan quality was not what had been reported. There were some good assets, and there were some dogs. Most of the assets were highly illiquid. It was difficult to see how they could provide the company with any cash flow."

By mid-November, Ray had enough information to call a meeting of bank creditors to determine what action should be taken against Wallace Investments. Two opposing views had already emerged. The hardliners, led by Continental Illinois senior vice president Jim Johnson, described by one colleague as "a great big, gruff-looking fellow and very experienced banker," wanted to stick to the letter of the loan agreement, which provided for the immediate collection of the debt. DeWitt Ray and J. D. Francis, president of Mercantile National Bank, took a more conciliatory view. They wanted to restructure the loan and help the company work through its debt problems.

This moderate approach was bolstered by their confidence in the company's new chairman, James Cumby. Besides Cumby's friendship with DeWitt Ray and close professional ties to Republic Bank, he had a "soothing" personality and "a lot of bedside manner." Above all, he gave the company stability. "Cumby," says Art Blanchard, "was responsible for the thing changing from a wild mess to something that began to have some direction.

"The critical factor was the friendship between Cumby and Ray. They had confidence in each other. Typically, workouts fail because the creditors don't believe the information they're getting. Cumby settled things down and began to get a handle on the information and reassure the banks about the people who worked for Gene Wallace. He developed confidence in people like Wommack and Lanelle Latendresse. That these were good people you could trust. Cumby established a trustful relationship with the creditors when it

The banks were comforted about the people who worked for Wallace, like DeWayne Wommack, left, and Lanelle Latendresse, right.

was absolutely crucial for the survival of the company."

When the creditors finally met in Dallas at Republic National Bank on November 22, 1963, fear and tension dominated the event. According to a participant, one New York bank arrived with a tough, East Coast attitude: "'You guys can do whatever you want, but we're going to put this outfit into bankruptcy, immediately.'"

The meeting also represented the first time the banks had an opportunity to confront Gene Wallace. "The problem was," says John Stuart, "Wallace didn't show up that morning because he got drunk and went on one of his toots."

Wallace's absence fueled an already volatile situation. DeWitt Ray spoke in favor of a gradual workout, but his words didn't impress the emotionally charged bankers. "I told them," says Ray, who moderated the meeting, "that if we handle it right and don't get excited and work with the people who borrowed the money, I don't think there's any question that we can get everyone out without loss."

Ray's plea for moderation was difficult to hear. "The banks," says Stuart, "were really mad at the way this company had been run. They were really up in arms that Gene Wallace hadn't been responsive and wasn't trying to work with them. They were ready to put the company in bankruptcy. That was the mood of the meeting. I was just a young guy sitting there. And I remember thinking, 'Gee, this is going to get tough.'"

The anger, frustration, and strident voices flung across Republic National Bank's conference room that day didn't bode well for the company's survival. The moment of truth, however, never arrived. At 12:30, from the sixth-floor window of the Texas Schoolbook Depository Building nine blocks away, deliverance came from the barrel of an Italian 6.5mm Mannlicher-Carcano rifle and the fatal wounding of President John F. Kennedy.

News of the event ended the bank meeting. "I'll never forget it," says Art Blanchard. "DeWitt came through the door and said, 'Gentlemen, the President has just been shot.' Everybody was stunned. One of the bankers from First National of Boston broke down and cried. I suppose he banked for the Kennedys and knew the family personally. The meeting just piffled out."

Everything kind of stopped. It was awesome.

John Stuart remembers the effect of the assassination on the bankers: "Everything kind of stopped. It was awesome. These guys just shut their briefcases and left." It was also a moment of tragic irony. The President's death meant life for Wallace Investments. "November 22, 1963," says Stuart, "was probably the most significant day in the history of the company. You could put a stake in the ground and say that was the key moment. It created a cooling off period. When the bankers met again a week or two later, they sat down and worked it out."

Survival, however, was costly. Creditors demanded the removal of Gene Wallace from management and the approval of restrictive amendments to the loan agreement. In a letter dated November 25, Gene Wallace requested a leave of absence of indefinite duration because of his "physical condition." On December 14, he formally resigned as president and executive committee member, but remained on the board. The amendments to the loan agreements tightened the banks' control over the company and the way it operated. "Any monies," says M. D. Wommack, "that were advanced under the loan agreement had to go through the offices of Republic Bank with Mr. Ray and his staff reviewing everything we did.

"If we needed to make an advance on some loans that we were committed to, we had to prepare a request and submit it to the bank, and they would verify what we were using the money for and approve the disburse-

Jess Hay was active in the presidential campaign to elect John F. Kennedy and was waiting at the Trade Mart to honor him with a luncheon when he was shot. At the same time, the creditors met in Dallas at Republic National Bank on November 22, 1963. Betty Jo and Jess Hay Archives.

ment. And if any money came in, we passed it back to them. They were the conduit through which we operated for quite some time."

The new restrictions and controls didn't sway Jim Cumby, now chief executive officer following Wallace's departure, from his commitment to an orderly workout. In an address to the board on December 14, using the lofty rhetoric of an older generation, he spoke of the hardships ahead and asked for cooperation: "I must say to you that solemn problems lie ahead. It is not a time for recrimination, blame or vilification. I ask you not to indulge in it. It is a time for sober evaluation and estimation. . . . I am not a stranger to affluence or austerity. The Company will invoke retrenchment and trim its fat without loss of efficiency. I am not unmindful of the need for competing and the Company will adjust as needed. Prompt decisions will be made when appropriate, but democratic policy will prevail."

Despite the "solemn problems," there were a few board members like Eugene Locke and Jess Hay who never lost their faith in the company. "Many of us," says Henry C. Beck, Jr., "thought that Wallace Investments would certainly have to fold. It was Eugene Locke and Jess Hay who really felt they could make it go. They were gung-ho for making it work." Art Blanchard remembers a rousing speech Jess Hay made to a group of bankers at the time: "By George! It was just like a jury summation or a sermon. 'This company is sound. It's going to make it. Don't sell this company short.' That kind of thing. It was really well done, and it had an impact. And I think it probably had an impact on Jess' career because it took him out of the realm of just being the secretary and put him into play as a real personality who might be worthy of consideration for something else."

Jim Cumby made it clear that his stay at Wallace Investments was to be a limited one. After a long and distinguished banking career, he looked forward to a well-earned retirement. In December, Eugene Locke and major stockholder Clint Murchison, Jr., assumed responsibility for finding a new president and hired the services of an executive search company.

Those who thought Gene Wallace's departure from management closed the curtain on his influence, however, underestimated his reluctance to leave center stage, his penchant for intrigue, and the loyalty of his friends. The former president found it difficult to accept the fact that he no longer controlled the company that bore his name. And with a pocketful of I.O.U.s from directors and stockholders who owed Wallace much of their financial success, there was little incentive for him to make a final bow.

THE DALLAS TIMES HERALD FINAL EDITION
CONTINUOUSLY PUBLISHED FOR 87 YEARS THE TIMES 1876 THE HERALD 1886 CONSOLIDATED 1888
87th Year—No. 292 DALLAS, TEXAS, FRIDAY EVENING, NOVEMBER 22, 1963 3 Parts Price Five Cents

Suspect Arrested

PRESIDENT DEAD, CONNALLY SHOT

Johnson Assumes Office

President John F. Kennedy was assassinated by a sniper's bullet in Dallas Friday.

He died at 1 p.m. in Parkland Hospital—31 minutes after an ambush bullet struck his head near Houston and Elm.

Gov. John Connally, riding at his side in the open convertible, was shot in the back. He was in surgery in mid-afternoon. His condition was satisfactory.

The President was waving to sidewalk throngs near the Triple Underpass when gunfire erupted—apparently from the Schoolbook Depository building at 411 Elm.

He clutched his chest and fell into his wife's arms.

Gov. Connally was shot in the back. He fell to the floor at his wife's feet. The two wives, sobbing, huddled over their husbands.

Lee Oswald, 24, a 30-day employe of the Texas School Book Depository, from whose building the assassin's bullet was believed fired, was arrested several minutes later, as a suspect in the fatal shooting of a policeman in Oak Cliff.

Oswald, a resident of Irving whose job at the depository firm was filling orders and wrapping, was seen in the building about noon.

Ochus V. Campbell, vice president of the firm, said the sixth floor of the building, where the rifle was found, would have been easily accessible to Oswald.

"Shortly after the shooting, we raced back into the building and saw him in a small storage room on the ground floor," Mr. Campbell said. "Then, we noticed he was gone. He didn't have permission to leave and we haven't seen him since."

Vice President Lyndon B. Johnson was sworn in as President of the United States by U.S. Dist. Judge Sarah T. Hughes aboard the presidential jet at Love Field.

Shortly before 3 p.m., Mr. Johnson raised his right hand and said: "I do solemnly swear that I will faithfully execute the office of President of the United States, and will to the best of my ability, preserve, protect and defend the Constitution of the United States."

Mr. Johnson was to leave immediately after for Washington.

Photographer Bob Jackson of The Times Herald heard one shot and then two more rapid shots. From his vantage point in an open convertible, the eighth car in the procession, Jackson saw two men peering from the building window on the fifth floor.

They were looking directly above their heads. Jackson saw a rifle being drawn back into a sixth floor window.

It disappeared quickly and he saw no more. The stock appeared to be dark brown, Jackson said.

Secret Service agents ordered the motorcade to proceed at high speed to Parkland Hospital.

—Staff Photo by William Allen

This picture was taken at Love Field on the President's arrival.

President Kennedy, still cradled in his wife's arms, was rushed to emergency. Blood transfusions of B positive blood were administered.

Shortly before 1 p.m. two Catholic priests entered emergency. Several minutes later they emerged and announced the President was dead.

White House assistant press secretary Malcolm Kilduff said at 1:30 p.m.:

"President John F. Kennedy died at approximately 1 o'clock Central Standard Time. He died of a gunshot wound in the brain."

Mr. Kilduff said Gov. Connally was hit once in the left side and once in the wrist. Vice President Johnson escaped injury.

An Oneal Funeral Home hearse took the President's body from Parkland Hospital at 2:08 p.m. His body was to be flown to Washington.

Mrs. Kennedy left Parkland Hospital surrounded by police officers shortly after the body of her husband was placed in the hearse. She spoke briefly to an Air Force officer and then left in the hearse.

Gov. Connally's Austin office, in contact with Parkland Hospital by a "hot line," had reported the governor's condition at 1:41 p.m. as "serious." This was later changed to satisfactory.

Press secretary George Christian said the governor was hit in the right chest, front and back; had a fracture of the radius and a minor leg wound.

He said X-rays were just taken and the governor was prepared for surgery.

"All the vital signs are good—pulse normal, blood pressure good, color good. He is in great pain but calm and has been conscious the whole time," Christian reported.

As FBI Director J. Edgar Hoovered ordered Dallas FBI men into the extensive search for the assassin, investigators reported finding the rifle thought to have fired the fatal shots.

The gun, described as a high-powered World War II surplus weapon with a telescopic sight, was uncovered in the northwest corner of the sixth floor of the book depository building.

LYNDON JOHNSON
Succeeds Kennedy

The weapon with a shell still in it was found half hidden under stacks of school and religious books.

In front of an open window, Police Sgt. Jerry Hill said, three expended rifle shells were discovered. By the window were remnants of fried chicken.

A wall of book boxes had been erected and three boxes in front of the window were believed to have been used by the sniper to steady his aim.

There were unconfirmed reports that a Secret Service agent was also killed by gunfire.

A spokesman at the Secret Service headquarters at Dallas said could not confirm or deny the report.

"All I've heard," he told newsmen, "is the same reports you've heard."

Sheriff Bill Decker reported his investigators had picked up two eye-witnesses to the shooting who had seen a man with a rifle.

"I couldn't question them here on the street. They claim they can identify the person with the rifle if they see him," the sheriff said.

Squad cars and motorcycles with sirens wailing sped through the downtown Dallas area moments after the shooting as all available officers were

See ASSASSINATION on Page 19

Front page of *The Dallas Times Herald*, Friday, November 22, 1963. Reprinted with permission of *The Dallas Morning News*.

Night of the Soul
A shocked city numbly grieves—See editorial on Page 2-A

THE DALLAS TIMES HERALD

FINAL EDITION

CONTINUOUSLY PUBLISHED FOR 87 YEARS THE TIMES 1876 THE HERALD 1886 CONSOLIDATED 1888

[illegible] ★★★ DALLAS, TEXAS, MONDAY EVENING, NOVEMBER 25, 1963 Telephones [illegible] 3 Parts Price Five Cents

Sad Nation Bids Kennedy Farewell

FBI Tipped Oswald Would Be Killed

Copyright, 1963, The Dallas Times Herald—Staff Photo by Bob Jackson

The President's accused killer as executioner's bullet pierces body.

Anonymous Call Forecast Slaying During Transfer

The self-appointed executioner of President Kennedy's accused assassin was the materialization of a blunt warning issued police hours earlier, The Times Herald learned Monday.

An anonymous telephone call to Federal Bureau of Investigation headquarters at 2:15 a.m. warned that Lee Harvey Oswald would be killed during his transfer from the city lockup to county jail.

The FBI immediately relayed the warning to police and the sheriff's office.

Oswald, notwithstanding the warning and dozens of pistol-armed policemen, was fatally wounded in the basement of the police and courts building at 11:20 a.m. as officers prepared to place him in an armored car for the short ride to the courthouse.

Jack Ruby, nightclub operator and physical culture addict, darted from a crowd of newsmen with cat-like speed, rammed a .38 revolver into Oswald's body and triggered a shot witnessed by the world.

Police stood helpless. One managed only to swear in the split second that added a second explosive chapter in the President's assassination.

Meanwhile, Ruby was transferred from city to county jail without incident about noon Monday.

Savings in Mercantile Bank on deposit a year or more at interest paying date, earn 4% interest. Member F.D.I.C.—(Adv.)

The transfer took place so casually that neither newsmen covering the county court and records building nor the crowds outside had an inkling of the action.

Nearly an hour after Ruby's transfer Monday, Sheriff Bill Decker held a press conference to inform the news representatives that Ruby had been transferred but he would not reveal which jail cell was used.

The Times Herald learned Monday afternoon that Ruby was with John Holbrook, a Dallas psychiatrist often used by the district attorney's office to determine the sanity of criminal suspects.

Ruby's attorney, Tom Howard, has indicated his client may plead

See OSWALD on Page 24

History Recorded

The historic photograph above was made by Bob Jackson, staff photographer of The Times Herald, from a few feet. It was caught at the precise moment the bullet from Jack Ruby's pistol entered the body of Lee Harvey Oswald, accused assassin of President Kennedy.

Note outstretched arm at right attempting to thwart the killer. Photographer Jackson has recorded for history one of its most bizarre and dramatic moments.

SIX FLAGS OVER TEXAS
Only 1 more weekend!
Sat & Sun 10 a.m.-8 p.m. (Adv.)

GRIEVING WORLD WEEPS

Nation Buries Its Chief

WASHINGTON (AP) — Amid pangs of sorrow and with solemn rites, America and world statesmen bade farewell today to John Fitzgerald Kennedy as a grieving world wept.

Following the martyred President closely every inch of travel to the grave in Arlington National Cemetery was his young widow, Jacqueline, bravely bearing up.

Her beautiful face partly obscured in a long veil, she went part of the tragic way on foot—from the White House to St. Matthew's Cathedral for the requiem mass.

So also did one of the greatest arrays of foreign statesmen ever assembled — they came from 53 nations and included 26 heads of state or government.

At the mass, Richard Cardinal Cushing of Boston, old friend of the Kennedy family, offered up the holy eucharist, and prayed:

"Almighty God, may this sacrifice cleanse from sin the soul of your servant, John, who has gone from this world, and so may he receive forgiveness and everlasting rest from you."

Near the flag-enveloped coffin, Mrs. Kennedy knelt before the high altar and received the cardinal's hand the wafer of communion — the wafer which in the Roman Catholic faith had been converted into the flesh of Christ.

Grieving in the cathedral were the new President, Lyndon B. Johnson, and his wife, Lady Bird. They too rode and walked in the procession that took the body from the Capitol, past the White House, to the cathedral, and then to Arlington, across the Potomac River in Virginia.

The Kennedy children, Caroline and John, with whom their father loved to play, were at the great church to say their own goodbye.

When the services ended, Cardinal Cushing stooped and kissed Caroline.

Mrs. Kennedy, her veil floating in the cool breeze, took Caroline and John by their hands. They walked down the cathedral steps behind the casket.

As servicemen put the casket back on the caisson for the three-mile journey to Arlington, John put his hand up in salute.

Little John, 3 years old today, seemed a little bewildered. He turned his head to the side, and looked behind him. Caroline, who will be 6 on Wednesday, was composed but pale.

The church bells tolled. The muffled drums beat.

Mrs. Kennedy and the others rode to Arlington in limousines.

See NATION on Page 26

The events from both the creditors' meeting and the Kennedy assassination from the previous Friday carried over to the following Monday. Gene Wallace requested a leave of absence and Jack Ruby shot Lee Harvey Oswald. Reprinted with permission of *The Dallas Morning News.*

Eugene Locke was one of the principal opponents of Wallace and his supporters. Although financial considerations played a role in his opposition, so did pride. "Gene Locke was a leading citizen in Dallas," says a former member of senior management. "He was honorable, and he had a lot of friends in the company. And he'd been telling everybody how damn good things were going when the stock went from eight to twenty-two during the early days when the company was making all those goofy loans that never paid off. He had a lot of pride, ego, and money invested. And he wanted to get the company straightened out and make more money. I've never met a Texan that didn't want more money than he had and also have something he could hold his head up and be proud of.

We walked into the middle of a hornet's nest.

"Locke was a political animal with an outgoing personality. He was, in my view, sort of the archetype of a back room politician. He wore the rumpled suit, smoked the big cigar, had the John L. Lewis eyebrows, and always wanted to cut the right deal."

Those who sided with Locke included public-minded board members like H. Neil Mallon, the seasoned senior executive from Dresser Industries. Directors like Mallon acted in the long-term best interest of the company. They considered Gene Wallace irresponsible and a threat to the corporation.

Another director who played a key role in this crisis was Jess Hay, corporate attorney and protege of Locke. Although personally low-key, he made a dynamic contribution to the resolution of the conflict. His commitment to the company and ability as a mediator proved invaluable. "Jess," says Robert L. Kinney, a former Wallace Investments vice president, "had a very unique capacity to stay calm at all times and communicate with everybody, even those that didn't share his viewpoint. He never ranted and raved or talked a lot, but he was very persuasive when he did talk. Jess is the kind of guy that sits back and listens and lets the parties bicker back and forth and then comes up with the right thing to do."

The divided loyalties, hidden agendas, and behind-the-scenes maneuvering finally burst into open conflict in January over the hiring of Richard M. Wartes as president. Opposition to the selection of Wartes by pro-Wallace directors didn't prevent his appointment, but it won them two concessions. They were able to limit the president's role on the executive committee by designating him an ex officio member without the right to vote. A second concession permitted them to fill the company's second highest management position. They chose Jim Stanley, a staunch Wallace loyalist whose personal and professional dislike for Wartes was already well known. Earlier that month Locke had asked Stanley and Wommack to stop in Phoenix on their way back from a California business trip and meet Dick Wartes, vice president in charge of commercial development for the Del E. Webb Corporation. Not surprisingly, Stanley, who was the Wallace faction's choice for president, was unimpressed with Wartes. "He and I clashed from the word go," says Jim Stanley. "He was bragging about all the things he'd done and how smart he was. But to me, he was just a four-flusher type. He wore alligator shoes with tassels and one of those string ties with jade on it. He took us out to his house; I remember he had a swimming pool in his bedroom.

"Anyway, when we got back to Dallas, we went to see Gene Locke. He asked me what I thought about Wartes. I told him I thought he was full of shit. Then he looked at me and said, 'Well now, Jim, whether you like it or not, he's going to be president.' I said, 'Then you don't need to know what I think about him, do you?' And that was the end of that conversation."

Wartes learned just how difficult his job was going to be a week after he made the commitment to become

In January 1964, Dick Wartes, vice president in charge of commercial development for the Del E. Webb Corporation of Phoenix, Arizona, was hired as president of Wallace Investments. Wartes, second from left, at the March 1962 construction site of the Del Webb Building. Courtesy Del E. Webb Corporation.

president. "The board was split when we came in," says a former Wallace executive who joined the company from Del Webb to assist Dick Wartes. "After Wartes had been hired and named president of the company, and while we were still in Arizona, the board appointed an executive vice president without even consulting him. That's a poor start if you're coming in with a new management team and all of a sudden the board picks your number two guy. It was just another manifestation of a very split board of directors. The guys that had the upper hand picked the number one man, and the opposition picked the number two man. It was a very bad situation right from the beginning. We walked into the middle of a hornet's nest."

But there were those besides Wallace supporters who questioned the new president's ability. "Wartes was a nice enough guy," says Al Rohnstedt, "but he had ideas of grandeur for himself, frankly. And he wasn't a mortgage banker and never would be. He was more of a developer kind of guy."

By the time Dick Wartes made his first appearance before the board as president on March 6, most of the corporate news was bad. The allowance for possible losses had been increased from $2.3 million to $6.8 million. The company sustained over $3 million in after-tax operating losses as of December 31, 1963. The bank debt stood at $27 million. And the company remained in a condition of default under the terms of both its bank loan agreement and 6½ percent notes.

The Wallace faction greeted the new president and

the board with a merger proposal that was in essence a vote of no confidence for new management and a declaration of war for control of the company. Having lost the battle for the presidency, they changed tactics. Now their strategy called for taking control of the company from the outside. "Mr. Henry C. Beck, Jr.," reads a portion of the minutes from the March 6 board meeting, "reported that he and Messrs. E. E. Wallace, Jr. and Tom Lively during the last several weeks had been exploring on a very preliminary basis with Messrs. John F. Austin [president of T. J. Bettes] and William Keesler [chairman of T. J. Bettes] the possibility of merging the company with two other corporations; namely, T. J. Bettes and Cabot, Cabot & Forbes." Because of Wallace's close friendships with Austin and Keesler, most directors considered the Bettes offer a thinly disguised attempt to return Wallace to power. The board approved the formation of a special committee made up of Beck, Lively, and Wallace to continue merger discussions.

John Austin, president of T. J. Bettes, and Wallace were close friends and shared many business interests.

With the merger gauntlet thrown down, internal strife escalated into what one observer describes as "all kinds of backbiting, factionalism, and various and sundry forms of mischief." Jim Cumby tried to close the rift by strengthening the hand of management. In a March 31 address to the board, he offered support for Dick Wartes: "His [Wartes'] four short weeks with us have impressed me favorably and I feel sure that the entire Board will unselfishly extend its offer of cooperation and encouragement to him. I do now recommend and propose that the new President be designated Chief Executive Officer." The board approved Cumby's recommendation.

Internal strife notwithstanding, management's first priority was to take the company out of default. At a May 1 executive committee meeting, Jim Cumby, Dick Wartes, and Jess Hay discussed their informal meetings with the company's senior noteholders and reported that "the noteholders were satisfied as to the safety of their principal and generally pleased with the progress the Company has made in reducing its bank debt." The committee also emphasized the importance "of solidifying the Dallas Banks in support of our prime banking objective of getting the Company out of default." In May, the twelve banks agreed to extend the company's loan agreement until December 31.

On May 20, T. J. Bettes backed off from its initial merger proposal and offered instead a management

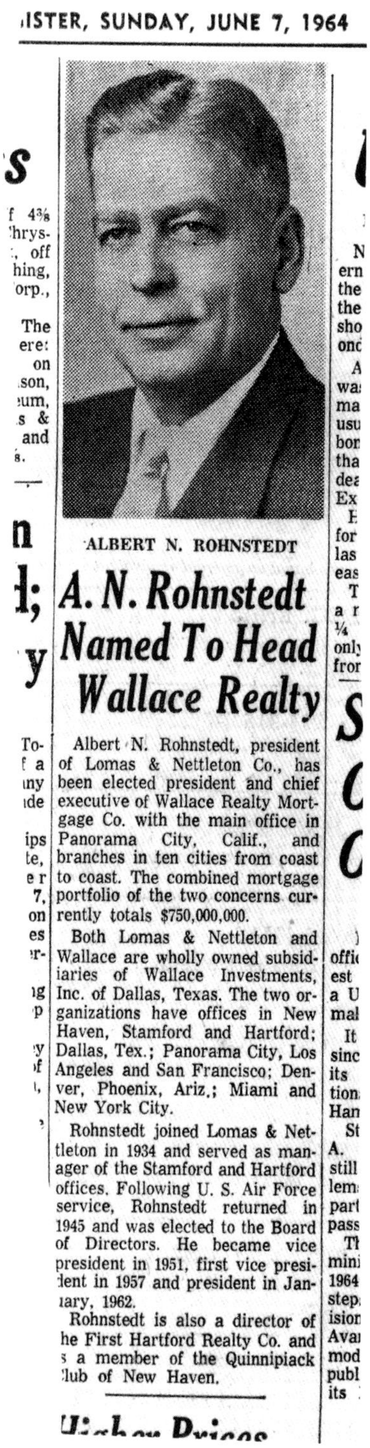

ISTER, SUNDAY, JUNE 7, 1964

ALBERT N. ROHNSTEDT

A. N. Rohnstedt Named To Head Wallace Realty

Albert N. Rohnstedt, president of Lomas & Nettleton Co., has been elected president and chief executive of Wallace Realty Mortgage Co. with the main office in Panorama City, Calif., and branches in ten cities from coast to coast. The combined mortgage portfolio of the two concerns currently totals $750,000,000.

Both Lomas & Nettleton and Wallace are wholly owned subsidiaries of Wallace Investments, Inc. of Dallas, Texas. The two organizations have offices in New Haven, Stamford and Hartford; Dallas, Tex.; Panorama City, Los Angeles and San Francisco; Denver, Phoenix, Ariz.; Miami and New York City.

Rohnstedt joined Lomas & Nettleton in 1934 and served as manager of the Stamford and Hartford offices. Following U. S. Air Force service, Rohnstedt returned in 1945 and was elected to the Board of Directors. He became vice president in 1951, first vice president in 1957 and president in January, 1962.

Rohnstedt is also a director of the First Hartford Realty Co. and is a member of the Quinnipiack Club of New Haven.

At the time negotiations were under way for a merger between T. J. Bettes and Wallace, Albert Rohnstedt, president of The Lomas & Nettleton Company, was elected president and chief executive officer of Wallace Realty Mortgage Company. Beatrice Lomas Gould Archive. Reprinted with permission of *The New Haven Register*.

contract along with a two-year option for Bettes to buy a controlling interest in the company based on a price of $8 a share. Once again the board agreed to consider the proposal. At that same meeting, the anti-Wallace faction strengthened its hand by making Dick Wartes a voting member of the executive committee.

The company learned on June 14 that Bettes was unable to fulfill its offer to acquire control at $8 per share. But the suitor continued to express interest in managing the company. Jess Hay cautioned the executive committee about the need to protect the company and its stockholders and expressed concern that interlocking management with Bettes could leave the company holding "marginal assets and/or servicing contracts." Besides having a basic distrust of the offer, Hay reported that the fallout from the merger talks hurt the company's relationship with its noteholders, who were "increasingly concerned as to who is really running the Company and what progress is being made toward restoring its financial condition."

The creditor nervousness materialized at the end of June when the noteholders demanded the company protect their position by giving them a second lien on the collateral the banks held. Sensitive to the increasing perception of instability, the executive committee imposed a July 15 presentation deadline on Bettes.

By the end of June, the T. J. Bettes Company's white knight image had begun to fade. Besides the tarnished motives suggested by Hay and others, there appeared to be significant chinks in the Houston-based company's financial armor. When Wallace Investments told Bettes they intended to exercise their take-out commitment guaranteeing a loan that had run into trouble, Bettes informed Wallace Investments that they were unable to honor that commitment and requested an extension. Several board members suspected T. J. Bettes might be in worse financial shape than the Dallas company.

Sensing a cooling of merger enthusiasm, Wartes mounted a modest counteroffensive with a memorandum demanding a decision from the board about the company's direction: "Our creditors are becoming very restive. . . . They want a program that has the solid backing of the Board which they have heard is very seriously split. They want to know who is going to administer the program and bring this Company back into a position of strength—the recently installed management or the T. J. Bettes interests."

Pressure from Wartes or anyone else proved unnecessary. Tom Lively informed the executive committee on July 15 that the T. J. Bettes Company was unable to arrange the necessary financing for their merger proposal. The committee immediately passed a resolution supporting the company "as an independent operating Company under the direction of the present management" and that the company refrain from negotiations with other companies until it was financially secure. The next day, at a board meeting, the anti-Wallace forces consolidated their victory by passing a resolution aimed at rogue directors and stockholders: ". . . no Director or stockholder of the Company is authorized to pursue any such [merger] discussions . . . except upon request of the President of the Company."

Gene Wallace, however, was nothing if not persistent. At the October 30 board meeting, he and his partisans mounted what turned out to be the final offensive for control of the board. Ignoring the board's decision to end discussions with other companies, Tom Lively presented still another offer from the T. J. Bettes Company. This proposal included the purchase of Wallace Realty Mortgage Company and The Lomas & Nettleton Company as well as an option to buy from stockholders 51 percent of their shares. The deal also proposed a management arrangement under John Austin and William Keesler.

It was a last-gasp effort that never had a chance. By now, a majority of the board believed the company could probably work out of its problems. And even if it couldn't, they realized that T. J. Bettes wasn't the answer. They also understood the damage that negotiations like this were causing the company. The proposal triggered angry denunciations from several board members. One director couldn't understand why the board should give the company away when the prospects for full recovery under present management were so favorable. Jerome Crossman considered it a "terrible deal that made absolutely no sense, viewed solely from the company's point of view." H. Neil Mallon thought the proposal was absurd, and "had never been connected with a company that had tried to commit suicide so many times." Eugene Locke said he was absolutely opposed to the deal and would not vote for it under any circumstances. Disgusted with the turmoil and efforts to undermine new management, Jess Hay spoke against the proposal to a board that increasingly valued his opinion: "On one day the Directors and major stockholders join in telling the Banks and Noteholders we are behind this management, we believe in it and we urge you to place your confidence in it; and on the next day we talk about radical changes in the management and the whole thrust of the Company. What are the creditors to believe? What is our management to believe? Dick Wartes and his staff deserve better support than they have had. We certainly should not 'pull the rug' from under him again by acting as though confidence in the Company and its management is lacking."

> Dick Wartes and his staff deserve better support than they have had.

Hay then suggested a resolution to defer action until T. J. Bettes submitted its proposal to the company's noteholders, who had the right of approval. The unanimously accepted resolution was in fact a death sentence. Eastman, Dillon, Union Securities & Co., hired by the company in September to supervise noteholder relationships as well as normal investment banking functions, already indicated that the noteholders would not agree to the proposal.

Faced with overwhelming opposition, T. J. Bettes withdrew its offer. On November 4, 1964, Gene Wallace resigned from the board, severing his connection to the company on something of a philosophical note: "I have many fond and many unpleasant memories as it regards Wallace Investments, Inc., but such is life."

Wallace's resignation ended the battle for control of the board. There was, however, little cause for celebration. The company's survival was still in doubt. Saddled with large debts and restrictive bank covenants that prevented the company from making loans, the healing process for Wallace Investments promised to be long and difficult. For the fiscal year ending June 30, 1964, the company suffered an operating loss of almost $5 million. There was also the anxiety of knowing that the company's creditors could demand payment at any moment. But at least with the dust settling in the boardroom, management was finally able to focus its full attention on recovery.

The Mercantile National Bank rescued Wallace Investments with a more liberal credit line, whereas Dallas' two largest banks, First National and Republic, refused. Courtesy Bank One, Texas N.A., Dallas.

CHAPTER IV

RECOVERY

The end of the internal power struggle permitted the company to move toward recovery. The most formidable obstacle to that process was the banks and noteholders, whose restrictions effectively prevented the company from generating profits and assets.

Discussions with creditors failed to produce flexibility. In December 1964 the banks agreed to extend the bank loan debt to March 31, 1965, but refused to loosen restrictions against the company. It was clear by then that although the creditors weren't going to pull the plug on the company, they weren't going to cut it any slack either.

According to a former Wallace Investments senior executive, the majority of the twelve participating banks "wanted to kick the company in the butt, get their money, and get the hell out of town." It was a harsh regime that confirmed a basic lack of confidence in the company. "For all practical purposes," says Jess Hay, "the company was under a severe, almost receivership-type supervision by its line banks. They had no confidence in our future and therefore were very restrictive and negative in their approach to the credit."

Pursuit of a more liberal bank credit line became the company's top priority. After refusals from Dallas' two largest banks, First National and Republic, Wallace Investments finally found the knight in shining armor it desperately needed. J. D. Francis, former president and later chairman and CEO of Mercantile National Bank, the smallest of Dallas' three major banks, rescued the company with a new credit line that "gave it room to move and grow and do new things," says Hay. "That was the first major step in the recovery process."

"J. D. Francis," says former director Ed Hoffman, "was the most knowledgeable banking officer in the Southwest, especially in real estate. He commanded a tremendous amount of respect. The banking community knew him to be a man of integrity, and they knew he knew real estate." Francis' career climb to president had, in fact, taken him through the ranks of Mercantile's real estate division. It was that expertise that gave him the confidence to back Wallace Investments. Unlike the other bankers, J. D. Francis was able to look beyond the problems and debt and see a viable company.

J. D. Francis put together a new bank credit line, and we stayed in business.

His judgment was based on firsthand knowledge. Of the twelve creditor banks, Mercantile was the only one to physically inspect the company's collateral and assets. True to his management style, Francis conducted the evaluation personally. "That was really the way he ran the bank," says Jess Hay. "Mercantile was an institution at that time with assets of about $1.1 or $1.2 billion, and he literally looked at every single loan transaction at the bank. He had to have a certain level of personal confidence. That's the kind of hands-on banker he was."

"J. D. Francis," says Hoffman, "went to all the major projects the company was financing. When he finished, he said there was significant equity in the company. . . . That meant, in effect, that the loan could be paid off and the stockholders would have something left. And because of that, J. D. Francis put together a new bank credit line, and we stayed in business."

Another problem with the existing credit line, Francis believed, was the fact that too many banks, each with its own agenda, were involved. He thought a smaller, more homogeneous group would enhance communication.

J. D. Francis, president of Mercantile National Bank.
Courtesy Bank One, Texas N.A., Dallas.

The difficulty in putting together a credit group of any kind became clear at a bank meeting organized by Mercantile National Bank. "J. D. Francis," says former vice president Robert L. Kinney, "had a meeting with all these New York and Chicago bankers and said, 'We're going to put together a new banking group, and we welcome your participation in this. We think the company has to move forward, and if you're not willing to stay in, we want to take you out.' And everybody ran for the woods."

Not quite everybody. United California Bank and First National Bank of Boston agreed to participate. Both were strong real estate lenders and had close, personal friendships with J. D. Francis. Besides those connections, both banks enjoyed strong historical ties to

The Lomas & Nettleton Company. Later, a fourth financial institution, Irving Trust Company, joined the others. Above all, it was Francis' reputation and personality that welded the group together. Dick Wartes announced at the January 15, 1965, board meeting "that Mr. J. D. Francis, president of Mercantile National Bank of Dallas, had obtained the commitment of First National Bank of Boston and United California Bank to participate with Mercantile in underwriting the Company's bank line in the initial aggregate amount of $20 million." The board responded to this news by warmly congratulating Wartes and voting to increase his annual salary from $50,000 to $62,500.

One obstacle remained. The company was still in default with its senior noteholders, and they imposed restrictions as harsh as the banks'. Implementation of the new bank line now hinged on negotiations to modify the notes. "Initially," says Jess Hay, "the noteholders played hardball, in effect wanting out. But they didn't realize, and this is incredible, that they were subordinate to the bank loan. Once that realization came fully home, they were much more cooperative." Even so, the "heavily lawyered" proceedings required months of tedious negotiations. Five months later a final draft was written and sent to the noteholders for review, where it hit another snag. Guardian Life Insurance Company expressed dissatisfaction with the proposal and refused to sign it. Once again, J. D. Francis came riding to the rescue. He told Guardian Life that Mercantile's trust department would purchase their note. It was a $1 million vote of confidence that impressed the remaining noteholders, who quickly approved the final agreement.

Although at the time many considered the bank's belief in Wallace Investments an act of courage, Mercantile's president was not among them. In fact, Francis never regarded the bank's loan to the company as anything except a good banking decision. "I never felt," says J. D. Francis, "after making the loan that we had any jeopardy in the thing. I never made loans that I worried about after I made them. I did all my worrying beforehand."

On June 11, 1965, eight days before the celebration of Juneteenth, the traditional Texas holiday commemorating the abolition of slavery, the board of directors declared their financial emancipation by voting unanimous approval of both the new bank credit and the amended noteholder agreement. For the first time in over a year and a half, the company was free of operating restrictions and defaults. Once again, Jess Hay had played a prominent role. In a letter included in board meeting minutes, Dick Wartes singled out Hay for special commendation: "With the successful conclusion of our credit documents last week, our Company truly achieved a momentous milestone. This achievement needed the help of many people not one of whom was more essential than your good self. Your contribution of invaluable historical knowledge coupled to an enviable combination of tact, patience, diplomacy and perspicacity all contributed so vitally that without your unique talents success would have evaded us."

Despite less restrictive credit, the corporate picture was generally gloomy, with one shining exception. The

Al Rohnstedt continued to operate Lomas & Nettleton at a profit when Wallace Investments went into default.

mortgage banking business under the strong leadership of Al Rohnstedt continued to operate at a profit. When the parent company skidded into default in the fall of 1963, Rohnstedt, president of The Lomas & Nettleton Company and a Wallace Investments senior vice president, reported "that substantial economies were being effected by consolidating parts of the operations of our two mortgage companies," with current earnings of $125,000 per month and a projected increase to $150,000 within the year. In early 1964, Rohnstedt became chief executive officer of the consolidated operations of the two mortgage companies, even though both continued to maintain separate corporate identities. Impressed by Rohnstedt's ability and performance, the board made him a director on March 31, 1964.

Rohnstedt consolidates mortgage banking

The partial merging of operations brought to light serious problems at Wallace Realty Mortgage Company. Poor servicing and a cash flow problem caused the most concern. According to Rohnstedt, "putting out fires at Wallace Realty Mortgage Company" demanded most of his time. He responded quickly. The first cuts came from payroll and office space reductions. Next, he sold unprofitable portions of Wallace Realty Mortgage Company. These measures worked, but Rohnstedt believed that the most substantial, long-term economies would be realized through its complete merger into The Lomas & Nettleton Company. A company study estimated a savings of $300,000 to $500,000 per year without sacrificing efficiency. "This savings occurs by reason of reduction in payroll and employee expense costs, I.B.M. rentals, legal and accounting fees, rental costs, and improved personnel utilization." The board approved the consolidation in July 1964. And now, as president and CEO of both mortgage companies, Rohnstedt had the authority he needed to accomplish the merger.

First, he upgraded the computer operation at New Haven headquarters. In October 1964 *The New Haven Register* reported the completion of a new IBM magnetic tape system at The Lomas & Nettleton Company. "The opening of new offices throughout the country," said Al Rohnstedt in the news story, "and the planned centralization of servicing operations in the New Haven office necessitated the establishment of the new enlarged data processing center."

The actual transfer of computer servicing was a gradual, office-by-office process requiring eight months to complete. By January 1965, with the centralized data center in place and the transfer of servicing under way, Al Rohnstedt began consolidating the company's various insurance operations into a single department within Lomas & Nettleton. Finally, on June 11, the board of directors approved the legal act required to complete the merger. Rohnstedt's skillful consolidation of the company's mortgage banking and insurance operations was a major contribution to the recovery process. His intervention in Wallace Realty Mortgage Company resulted in the timely rescue of that troubled operation. The stability and efficiency that had long been a Lomas & Nettleton trademark now included the company's entire mortgage banking operation. Despite heavy nonrecurring expenses due to the merger, The Lomas & Nettleton Company on June 30, 1965, showed a 48 percent increase in pretax earnings over the previous fiscal year.

The most important reorganization decision that the parent company faced during the first half of 1965 was choosing a name. "Wallace Investments, Inc." had, to say the least, outlived its usefulness. "Janus Corporation" was one of several suggestions by senior management, but the board of directors favored using some derivation of their subsidiary, The Lomas & Nettleton Company. Besides its status as the company's outstanding asset, Lomas & Nettleton had a 71-year national reputation for integrity and customer service.

As president and CEO of the consolidated Wallace Realty Mortgage Company and The Lomas & Nettleton Company, Al Rohnstedt in 1964 upgraded the computer operation at the New Haven headquarters' new data processing center, at right. At the far left is 175 Orange Street, the headquarters building. The second floor housed the outside insurance, tax, and clerical departments. The third floor had the employee cafeteria, administrative offices, and executive suites.

A portion of the main department in the Lomas & Nettleton data processing center. Shown left to right are Joseph Romano summarizing information from the daily disbursement journal; Marshall Chiaraluce supervising a daily tax analysis on the IBM 1402 Card Read Punch unit; and Bernard Doyle, administrative supervisor, operating the IBM 1403 Printer. Other electronic equipment shown are the IBM #85 Collator and the #1401 Computer Processing Unit.

A reverse view of the main department of the Lomas & Nettleton data processing center.

Part of the new equipment included four IBM 7330 Tape Drives and an IBM 1009 Transceiver Unit, in corner, which gave the New Haven office a direct link to California.

Anticipating a greater volume of business, the company installed an IBM magnetic tape system with advanced reporting and tabulating capabilities. The new facilities were air conditioned and moisture controlled to obtain the greatest efficiency from the high-speed equipment.

The punch card department of the new data processing center was located on the street level, with access to the second- and third-floor mortgage departments.

The key punch department and supervisor's control room of The Lomas & Nettleton Company's data processing center. It handled 50,000 mortgage loans monthly involving 15 operations each and totaling $400 million in mortgages annually.

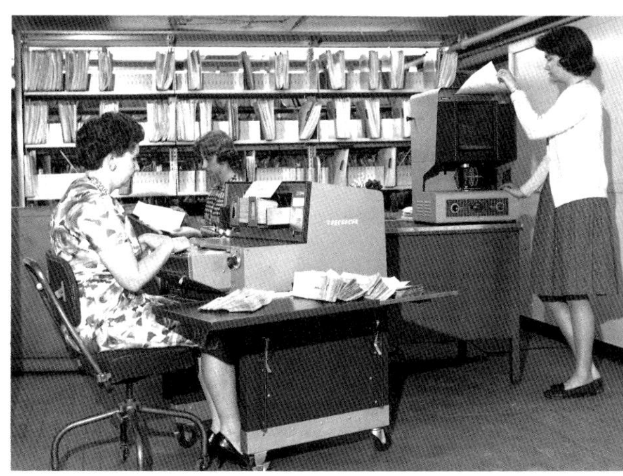

The microfilming department kept the records of the expanded operations in a smaller and more concise format.

It counted among its investors companies like Metropolitan Life Insurance Co. with reputations as impeccable as its own. "The objective," says Jess Hay, "was to appropriate the goodwill and financially conservative reputation of The Lomas & Nettleton Company, particularly among Eastern banks and savings institutions." One suggestion was to change the company's name to The Lomas & Nettleton Corporation. But the similarity of that to its mortgage banking subsidiary was confusing. Al Rohnstedt recommended renaming the parent company Lomas & Nettleton Financial Corporation. The board agreed. Their approval on June 11 finally shed the company of its most visible connection to the Wallace period.

The company further enhanced its reputation in January 1965 when Trammell Crow agreed to rejoin the corporate board. His association provided a vote of confidence that helped boost corporate morale. DeWitt Ray, another familiar face, was elected chairman of the board on June 11, 1965, shortly after his retirement from Republic National Bank. Ray's leadership reinforced the company's commitment to financial responsibility and strong banking relationships. By the middle of 1965, Dick Wartes claimed in a president's message that "the Company's financial agreements have solved its core problems," and said it was now time for management to turn its attention toward reinvestment and the conversion of its nonperforming assets into cash.

His assessment ignored one major obstacle to the company's moving forward: the problem of leadership. Despite his ability as a salesman and promoter, Dick Wartes didn't have the temperament or background to solve the financial problems at Lomas & Nettleton Financial Corporation. "I don't think Wartes ever really had a recovery program," says former director Frank M. Crossen. "That was one of the problems. I think he was trying to be a wheeler-dealer. That had been the history of the company, but that wasn't what it needed. Wallace and Wartes were looking for the big deals that would bail them out. And, of course, that just got them into worse trouble."

Besides the large number of problem deals from the Wallace era, M. D. Wommack recalls at least two major loans made by the Wartes administration that had to be added to the list of workouts. The CEO also had trouble getting a handle on the heavy administrative expenses inherited from Gene Wallace. Instead of deep cuts, he gingerly attacked the problem with 10 percent salary reductions. As a result of the failures on these two fronts, the company continued to lose money. Most board members recognized that Wartes was unable to cope with the company's problems. The board asked for his resignation, effective September 23,

The name Wallace Investments, Inc., had outlived its usefulness. Logo and logotype of Wallace Investments in 1965.

1965.

On September 27, 1965, the board elected Jess Hay president and chief executive officer of Lomas & Nettleton Financial Corporation. The company now had the leadership it needed. "When Jess Hay took over," says former board member Trammell Crow, "you could *feel* things change. It was just like morning broke, and the sun slowly rose."

It was just like morning broke, and the sun slowly rose.

For those who knew him, there was no question about Hay's ability. Even at the relatively youthful age of 34, his life was footnoted with accomplishments that pointed toward a distinguished future. What few realized was how much his life bore the imprint of a childhood shaped by traditional values.

Born on January 22, 1931, in Forney, Texas, 18 miles east of Dallas, Jess Thomas Hay was a child of the Depression. Although George and Myrtle Hay's material circumstances were modest, Jess drew a lifelong strength from his upbringing. "I always felt warmly nurtured by my family," he says, "and I count that as probably the overriding blessing and grace in my life. My mother and grandmother, Nettie Fleming Roddy, were the affirming influences of my childhood days, and my father was the one who consistently challenged me to do better."

Adherence to a strong work ethic and strict religious code was the central fact of their family life. Credit for the lasting strength of those values belongs as much to the messengers as the message. George Hay, in particular, possessed a quiet dignity that expressed both conviction and commitment. "Our father never raised his voice," says Patsy Harlow, Jess Hay's sister. "He would never rant or rave. To my knowledge, I never heard him say a cuss word. He was the most even-

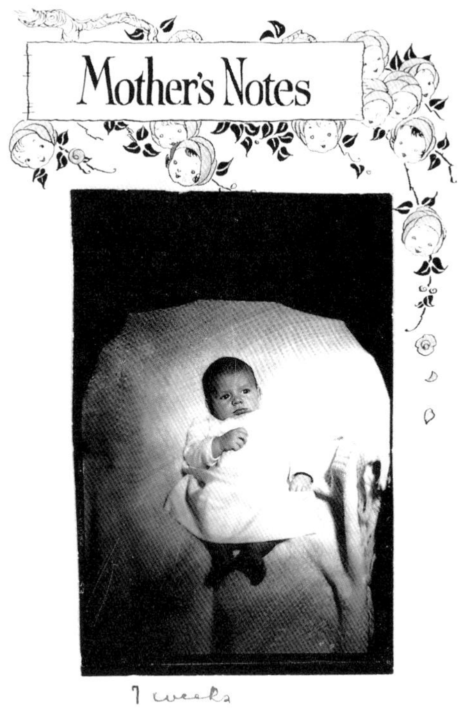

Jess Thomas Hay was born on January 22, 1931, in the North Texas town of Forney. The photograph was taken at seven weeks. Myrtle Roddy Hay Archive.

Jess' mother, Myrtle Roddy Hay, holding Jess when he was six months. Myrtle Roddy Hay Archive.

Top left: The family of Jess Hay's mother. From left to right: Jesse J. Roddy, Jess' grandfather, Myrtle Roddy, mother, Nettie Fleming Roddy, grandmother, Nora Roddy, aunt, and Ray Roddy, uncle. Betty Jo and Jess Hay Archives.

Top right: Jess at 18 months and one week, with "Mammy," his grandmother, Nettie Fleming Roddy. There was a strong, loving relationship between Jess and his grandmother. Myrtle Roddy Hay Archive.

Left: Jess Thomas and his sister Patsy at approximately eight and four years. Myrtle Roddy Hay Archive.

tempered person you'd ever meet. If you did something wrong, he didn't get all excited. He sat down and talked to you about it."

When parental duty required it, he could be a taskmaster and disciplinarian. For someone as fun-loving and outgoing as Hubert (Sprad) Spradling, Jess' best buddy in high school, George Hay imposed a harsh regime. Spradling recalls Mr. Hay as "a prudish fellow. Very stuffy. Always correcting Jess. A very strict parent who demanded excellence. He was continually on Jess and me—'What are you boys doing out there playing? Why aren't you inside studying?'" Spradling remembers Myrtle Hay, on the other hand, as "lovable . . . the kind of mother everyone would like to have." She also helped bail the boys out when the going got rough. "She took George aside and talked to him. I don't know what she said, but whatever it was it had an effect." Jack McClendon, a younger classmate who worked on the school yearbook staff with Jess, also remembers George Hay: "Mr. Hay seemed to be very quiet and not possessing a lot of energy. He seemed to be sitting and thinking most of the time. He read. He had a very soft voice. I never saw him without a suit and tie and a hat. My father only wore a suit when he went to church or to the movies. And Mrs. Hay always dressed as if she were going somewhere. She always wore pearls and earrings and had her hair curled."

It was George Hay's view that parental guidance also meant active involvement. He provided opportunities for Jess to test himself. Although a county health inspector by profession, Hay had an entrepreneur's eye for money-making ventures. The Hay family moved to Orange, Texas, in 1942 at the beginning of an economic boom. George Hay saw the opportunities there and showed Jess how he could profit from them.

Orange was a sleepy little town, and then it became a boomtown.

George Hay had a profound effect on the young and impressionable Jess Hay with his conviction and his commitment to forthrightness. Betty Jo and Jess Hay Archives.

Orange is located on the eastern boundary of East Texas, tucked into a bend of the Sabine River 28 miles above the Gulf of Mexico. The town's deepest cultural roots spring from the soil of the Old South. Prior to World War II, the people there had more in common with Louisiana than with most of Texas. Topography provides another connection to the neighboring state. Orange is surrounded by coastal and inland marshes, wetlands, and a labyrinth of sluggish bayous and sloughs that snake their way through land choked with vegetation. Orange's seven thousand residents lived the kind of drowsy, undisturbed existence familiar to Southern backwater towns in 1940. When asked to

The Hay family's strong grounding in religion is seen in Jess' "My Record of Promotion" from the beginner to primary levels of the Methodist Sunday School in Forney, Texas. Myrtle Roddy Hay Archive.

describe Orange then, one resident invoked the fictional image of Maycomb, Alabama, Harper Lee's indestructible archetype of a sleepy, Depression-era Southern hamlet in her novel *To Kill a Mockingbird*.

Japanese bombs fell on Hawaii in 1941 and changed all that. The following year the federal government selected Orange as a shipbuilding center to help supply the Navy with destroyers and destroyer escorts. The liberal infusion of federal aid facilitated the town's transformation into an industrial complex. "Orange was a sleepy little town, and then it became a boomtown," recalls Haskell M. Monroe, Jr., Professor of History at the University of Missouri-Columbia and former president of The University of Texas at El Paso. His family moved to Orange in 1942, where he graduated with Jess Hay from Stark High School in 1948. "The town's population exploded from 7,000 to 60,000 in 24 months. I remember how crowded everything was. There were three shipyards. My dad worked for Consolidated Steel Corp., Ltd., the largest shipbuilding company in Orange. It employed 16,000 workers, a veritable horde of people, most of whom had come from Southwest Louisiana and East Texas.

"Housing was horribly inadequate and folks like us lived in a trailer house. Then the federal government came in with special funding, and they pumped sand out of the Sabine River in what had been a big swamp just northeast of Orange. They built a huge housing development on top of the sand and called it Riverside. That's where Jess' family and my family lived. The houses were one-story duplexes and fourplexes and two-story eightplexes. It was thoroughly adequate housing, particularly after what we had been accustomed to during the Depression.

"In the seventh grade I remember we didn't even have a lunchroom because they held classes in the cafeteria. You brought your lunch and ate in your classroom. Classes were held in the hallway on the third floor. I remember literally standing in line to use the restroom." A year later federal aid helped build a new school, Lutcher Stark Senior High School, named after one of Orange's wealthiest citizens whose interest in

Haskell Monroe and his family moved to Orange about the same time as the Hay family. From the 1948 *Orange Peel*.

education extended primarily to the boys' marching band and the girls' drum and bugle corps.

The crowded classrooms also exposed middle class youngsters like Monroe and Hay to the reality of American diversity. The most extreme examples came from across the river. Jack McClendon recalls their harsh living conditions: "They came out of the swamps of Louisiana to work in the shipyards. Many of these people had never seen the light of day. They didn't speak much English. They couldn't read. And some of their children literally came to school barefoot." Norma Scott Johnson, a former Stark High School English teacher, remembers a female student who lived on a houseboat in the Sabine River with her father and two younger brothers: "He was a fisherman. They were Cajuns. She would tell me how difficult it was providing clothing for them because it was so hard getting anything dry. She'd wash their clothes and hang them out on the boat, but it was so damp and humid that it

The intersection of Fifth and Front streets in Orange, Texas, during Jess Hay's high school period. From the 1948 *Orange Peel*.

Orange, Texas, had been selected as a shipbuilding and ship repairing center to supply the Navy with destroyers and destroyer escorts. One hundred and thirty ships of the United States Navy were assigned to the Orange Basin. These ships ranged in size from 15,000-ton destroyer tenders to smaller ships of 700 tons. By 1948 they were deactivated. From the 1948 *Orange Peel*.

Riverside housing development was built in Orange, Texas, during World War II to help meet the demands for wartime housing. Jess Hay and his family moved to Orange in 1942 and later lived on Destroyer Drive. Courtesy Howard C. Williams, M.D.

took days and days for anything to dry.

"The girl was very, very bright and made perfect grades on the tests I gave her. But she absolutely butchered the English language when she spoke. After I'd worked with her a couple of years I asked her why she used such bad grammar when she obviously knew how to speak correctly. She looked at me real hard and said, 'You don't understand. I couldn't stay at home if I talks like you talk. If I talked that high-faluting English in front of my daddy, he'd run me off.' She had to speak like her people spoke in order to survive."

Families who came from the East Texas piney woods weren't much better off. Johnson remembers another female student whose father worked at a lumber mill before they moved to Orange: "They were living in very desperate circumstances. When she came to Orange and started to school her total wardrobe consisted of two dresses. She'd wear one dress and then come home and wash it after school. The next morning she ironed her other dress and wore it to school. A year or two later when the girl told me this story she was so happy because now she had a different dress to wear—every day! She thought she was on top of the world because she owned five dresses. That tells you something about living conditions in those days."

To help Jess and his friend Sprad earn spending money, George Hay guided the boys toward the marketing of consumable food items, a lucrative business in any boomtown, especially so in war-rationed Orange. Mr. Hay's work as a health inspector brought him in contact with food producers. One such producer owned a remote, backwoods poultry farm. Hay arranged for the owner to ship three cases of eggs to Orange by railroad express, which the boys picked up at the train station in a car borrowed from Sprad's father. They sold the eggs in Riverside on Saturday morning. "We had two red wagons," says Spradling. "We started knocking on doors early, around 7:30 or 8:00 in the morning. Normally, we could peddle a case of eggs in one hour. The duplex doors were right next to each other. You could knock on four doors in five minutes. We made about $10.00 an hour when most men were making 98¢ to $1.19 per hour. We felt like we were millionaires. That was our first business venture." The two friends continued with their business and developed a regular clientele that knew them by their first names.

We felt like we were millionaires.

Mr. Hay's quick response when a freight train passing through Orange broke down led to another entrepreneurial coup. He helped Jess and Hubert buy a carload of unrefrigerated tomatoes. Spradling recalls the frantic race for sales before their inventory spoiled: "We worked day and night selling tomatoes to restaurants, hospitals, families—anywhere we could. We used a wagon for a lot of the door-to-door peddling. Over half the tomatoes went bad on us, but we still made a 50 percent profit."

George Hay also assisted the boys with their most successful venture, a summer watermelon stand. Through an acquaintance of his, Mr. Hay found out when the first shipment of melons from the Rio Grande Valley would arrive and staked the youngsters the $200 to $300 needed to buy a truckload. For at least two summers the boys' watermelon stand was a summer fixture along heavily traveled Highway 90. "We'd rent the front yard of a pretty nice home for a dollar a day, $30 a month. That was our biggest overhead. Back then, everybody passed up and down Highway 90. They'd see our lights, our stacks of melons, our coolers, and they'd pull off the road and buy watermelons from us.

"We kept our own set of books, and Jess' father taught us about debits and credits. We also learned about markup. For each watermelon we sold as is, we made a 25 percent profit. We earned a 50 percent profit by cooling them. But then we had to deduct the cost of the ice, which we bought in 300-pound blocks."

It wasn't unusual for each boy to show a net profit of several hundred dollars by summer's end. Much of the money went for clothes, the kind of clothes that

Lutcher Stark Senior High School, Orange, Texas was built in 1942 with federal assistance. From the 1946 *Orange Peel.*

made a parent like George Hay cringe. After the boys proudly displayed the results from one such clothes-buying spree, Mr. Hay claimed they looked like "a couple of gamblers."

These early business experiences instilled a successful formula for achieving goals. The discovery that imagination, hard work, and sharply focused attention opened the door to accomplishment made a deep and lasting impression on Jess Hay. Those qualities became the tools he relied on to shape his world.

Both college-educated, George and Myrtle Hay also encouraged scholastic excellence. "Some fathers like their sons to be football players, and some fathers like their sons to be scholars," says Spradling. "Jess was directed toward learning." He responded by applying himself to school. In seventh grade, "an unusually gifted teacher" encouraged his interest in history and

ORANGE STEWARDS—The junior board of stewards of the First Methodist church of Orange, includes the following youths: Front row, left to right, Bobby Jones, chairman; Preston Prince, secretary; R. L. Norris, Jr., treasurer; Jess Hay, Hubert Spradling and Tony Crutchfield. Second row, left to right, Don Perry, Cecil Cleveland, Dick Sells, George Sells, Sime Peeples, Carl Miller and Donald Bates. Others not in the picture are: Jack Forrest, Billy Bell, Allen Smith and Elvis Davis. Rev. Walton B. Gardner is pastor of the church.

Jess Hay at approximately 15 years, about the time George Hay assisted Jess and Hubert Spradling in the watermelon business. Myrtle Roddy Hay Archive.

Jess Hay and Hubert Spradling were close friends. One of their many mutual interests was the First Methodist Church of Orange, where they served on the junior board of stewards. Myrtle Roddy Hay Archive. Reprinted with permission of the *Beaumont Enterprise*.

Clothes were important to Jess and Hubert, who had similar tastes. The matching sweaters indicated that they were best buddies. The photograph is from the *Orange Peel* of 1948, when Jess was editor. From left to right: Carroll Graham, Mary Everheart, sponsor, Howard Chenoweth, Jess Hay, and Hubert Spradling.

debate. Those subjects meshed well with his early decision to pursue a career in law. "Whenever Jess and I talked about the future," says Monroe, "he always talked about going to SMU and becoming a lawyer. That was my earliest recollection of what Jess wanted to do after high school—go to SMU and be a lawyer."

Jess did enough homework to get the facts and win.

Among the characteristics that made an impression on those that knew young Hay was the importance he placed on preparation. It was the key, according to Spradling, to his success on the debate team: "I'd go listen to him, and I thought I'd like to do that because I love to argue. But you had to have the facts to back you up. Jess did enough homework to get the facts and win."

Another trait that distinguished Jess from other students was an awareness of and interest in the world beyond school. A pattern of concern for larger issues began to emerge toward the end of high school. But awareness wasn't sufficient. Jess sought meaningful participation, and the key to that was power.

The most obvious arena was the political process, and it became a consuming interest. His passion for politics would last a lifetime. In his sophomore year he was elected vice president of his class. But the office had little meaning, and his interest in student government waned. Two years later he was ready to tackle the real thing. No doubt influenced by his father's admiration for Franklin Roosevelt and Harry Truman, Jess Hay raised his banner for Lyndon Baines Johnson, a young Texas congressman who was running for the United States Senate. Johnson's youth, staunch New Deal philosophy, and underdog status appealed to Jess. On his own initiative Jess wrote to the Johnson campaign headquarters for the graphic material to make posters. Jack McClendon remembers Jess spending money that he earned from his watermelon business to print a large stack of posters to put up around town. One day Jack got a call for help from his older friend Jess. "To me, Jess was really like an uncle," says McClendon. "I thought he was just a wonderful person. Whatever he said, I would do.

In Jess' sophomore year of high school he was elected vice president of his class. Jess is seen with the class officers, standing on the stairs, hand on railing. From the 1946 *Orange Peel*.

"The posters were printed in black ink on a sort of gray cardboard. They had a picture of Lyndon Johnson and some words. Jess had a couple of hammers and two big sacks of big, broad-headed roofing tacks. We put the posters and nails in our bicycle baskets and every time we came to a utility pole or tree we'd put up a poster. Two or three hours later, after we'd put about half of them up, we came back by and they had been torn off. I asked Jess why. He said, 'Certain people don't like Johnson, and they don't want him to win so they tear them down. That's why we're going to put some more up with even more nails.'" On primary election night, McClendon recalls the two boys on their bikes racing back and forth between the courthouse where the local votes were tallied and the newspaper office where the results of the state race came off the teletype. "It was a long, long night." The dispute that arose from the primary runoff election results was settled in Johnson's favor by a margin of 87 votes. Besides a

As a junior, Jess was assistant business manager and sports editor of the 1947 *Orange Peel*, which prepared him for his senior year as editor of the annual. Jess is seated, second from left. From the 1947 *Orange Peel*.

paper-thin victory, the new junior senator from Texas also won the moniker "Landslide Lyndon."

It was in his senior year as editor of the school annual, the 1948 *Orange Peel*, that Jess found an opportunity to wield power. The project enabled him to display an emerging talent for organization and leadership. His appointment to the top position was no fluke. As a junior, he had labored long and hard down in the trenches learning the ropes of annual publication and carrying the titles assistant business manager and sports editor to prove it.

But Jess Hay brought something more to the position than experience. He had a vision. In keeping with a growing interest in the world beyond his immediate sphere, Jess chose industry in Orange as the theme for the 1948 annual. He and the staff presented that theme in the book's foreword: "On the pages of our yearbook are revealed many of the phases of industrial development in our community and the stages in our training as furture [*sic*] citizens who plan to do our part in building a 'Bigger and Better Orange.'"

"I remember Jess," says Mary (Everheart) Gibbert, former Stark High School English teacher and annual staff sponsor. "Jess was very creative and original. He was a marvelous editor of the yearbook because he had so many good ideas. It was his idea to use local industry as the theme for the yearbook in 1948. He worked well with the rest of the staff—in making assignments and getting them organized." Jack McClendon, two years younger than Jess, remembers him as "a very authoritative person who knew what he wanted . . . and was confident about achieving it."

Hay also showed confidence in recruiting the staff he needed. One day while McClendon was in his junior high art class an older boy walked into the classroom and asked the teacher who could draw. She pointed to McClendon. The boy walked over and asked Jack if he would like to make some drawings for the yearbook. Flattered, McClendon agreed. "He asked me to come over to the high school that afternoon. I did, and that's when I found out he was Jess Hay. He explained that he

Besides serving as yearbook editor during his senior year, Jess was a member of the Quill and Scroll, the high school's literary club. Jess is top row, third from left. From the 1948 *Orange Peel*.

wanted to invent a character for the yearbook that would represent the industrial spirit of Orange. I would say he pretty much had the whole project in his mind, and he knew how to delegate the tasks that needed to be done."

Hay's aptitude for persuasion contributed to the successful delegation of yearbook assignments. "Jess was very talented at that," recalls Spradling, recruited by Hay to serve as business manager. "He'd say, 'Hubert, would you do this for me.' Knowing it was exactly the opposite of what I wanted to do. And I'd say, 'Well, certainly, I'll do that for you.'"

The special friendship between yearbook sponsor Mary Everheart and Jess and Sprad was the catalyst that made the boys' hard work on the annual so rewarding. Jack McClendon refers to them at that time as the "queen bee and the two knights."

"I adored her," says McClendon. "I think everybody did. Mary Everheart was always cheerful. She had a twinkle in her eye. She liked to come down to the yearbook office and see what we were doing, but she gave us a free rein." Part of her popularity with adoles-

Jess Thomas Hay's high school graduation photograph. Betty Jo and Jess Hay Archives.

cent students, especially the restless ones, stemmed from her refusal to bow to the strict conformity demanded by the community. For an individual who was intelligent and somewhat progressive, the atmosphere in Orange could be as suffocating as the humidity. "Mary Everheart smoked at a time when teachers were not supposed to smoke," says Monroe. "After normal teaching hours, she sometimes came back to the school building dressed in slacks. And it was reported that sometimes she was seen in the company of enlisted sailors." "I liked to go out, and I liked to dance," says Gibbert, "and I probably raised a few eyebrows in Orange. I was not a stereotypical English teacher."

Friendship with Everheart gave Jess a window on the outside world and a connection to a larger life beyond Orange. "I was very fond of Jess and Hubert," says Gibbert. "We worked closely together on the yearbook. We worked a lot after school, and we had a close relationship—a friendship." "She [Everheart] lived just a few blocks from the school in an apartment," says Spradling. "Jess and I might drop by her house at seven or eight o'clock at night and go in and have a cup of coffee with her. Or, she might cook up some bacon and eggs. We considered her a friend."

By the end of Jess' senior year, his interest in public affairs was reflected in almost every aspect of his life. It could be seen in his work on the *Orange Peel*, at the First Methodist Church where he served on the junior board of stewards, in politics as a campaign worker, and in his decision to become an attorney. But active participation didn't necessarily mean cavalry-charging leadership. Hay preferred to work behind the scenes. "Jess was not an elected school power," says Monroe, "but through hard work he acquired influence. And I believe that explains, in part, the way he is today.

. . . through work he acquired influence.

"When [Dolph] Briscoe was finishing his term as governor, I was teaching at Texas A&M, and I said, 'Jess, if you plan to run for governor please let me know and I'll do anything I possibly can to help. I believe you are the kind of decent, honorable person who would be good for this state.' And he said, 'No, I don't believe I will. I think I can do more good behind the scenes helping good people get elected and bringing support to them.'"

One of the last photographs of Jess Hay in Orange was taken by Sprad at the end of a visit during Jess' freshman year at Southern Methodist University. The image of young Hay standing beside an empty stretch of highway, thumb out, holding a hitchhiking sign suggests a separation from family and friends more profound than simply one of miles. The road to SMU led to a new life.

Jess Hay enrolled at Southern Methodist University in the fall of 1948. His strongest interest besides academics was politics, both on and off campus. He helped organize a political action group of SMU students called the Youth Council For Better Government. After thoughtful consideration, the Youth Council selected candidates, then rolled up its sleeves and joined the political fray as campaign workers. Dallas attorney Bill E. Brice, a personal friend of Hay's and former member of the Youth Council, remembers campaigning for Henry Wade in his first successful run for district attorney in 1950. The large contingent of SMU student volunteers made an important contribution to Wade's election.

Goodbye Orange, hello Dallas and Southern Methodist University. When Jess' friend Sprad took this photograph, he captured a major transition in the life of a person on his way upward. Courtesy Hubert Spradling.

Later, in law school, Jess Hay became Brice's campaign manager when he ran for SMU student body president. Always comfortable with coalition, Hay organized the Better Candidates' Association. The Association was an alliance of campus groups that endorsed a slate of candidates, with Bill Brice at the top of the ticket. The strategy worked. On election day, BCA candidates swept the field.

There wasn't anything political, however, about Hay's interest in the assertive coed he got to know in English class and on the debate team. Betty Jo Peacock, who Jess Hay describes as "a reasonably feisty person who expresses her feelings very directly," was equally impressed with Hay. They married in 1951 just before their senior year. A year later the first of two daughters was born.

When Hay entered SMU law school in 1953, he confronted the responsibilities of a family and heavy academic load with characteristic vigor. Dallas attorney Lewis T. Sweet, Jr., a close friend and law school classmate, recalls Hay's impressive capacity for work. "There were times," says Sweet, "when we studied together at night, and I'd fall asleep with my head on the typewriter. When I woke up an hour or two later, there was Jess still going strong. He had enormous stamina. He could work all night and be just as bright and sharp and brilliant the next morning as if he had had a good night's sleep."

That kind of intensity paid off. Sweet remembers a law professor's comment about an exam Hay had taken. The professor claimed it was the finest, most comprehensive examination he'd ever read. No student had ever scored a grade higher than 85 in his class. Jess took home a 90.

The struggle to make ends meet also required unusual effort by the young couple. During the week, Jess managed the SMU student center. For three hours a night, he worked at the Science Library. And on weekends, he sold clothes for Jas. K. Wilson. Betty Jo worked as a typist in the geography department, sometimes with their daughter Debby parked in a stroller

Left: The photograph that accompanied Jess Hay's application to law school. Courtesy Southern Methodist University Law School.

Dallas attorney Bill Brice was Hay's friend at SMU and shared an interest in politics. Shown is Brice's application photograph to law school. Courtesy Southern Methodist University Law School.

beside her.

The semester before he graduated *magna cum laude* and number one in his class, Jess Hay was already working part-time for the law firm Locke, Purnell, Boren, Laney & Neely. Small, prestigious, and absolutely blue chip, the firm had built its reputation representing Dallas banks and insurance companies beginning in the 1890s.

Senior partner Gene Locke liked what he saw in Hay and personally took the initiative in hiring him. It was the beginning of a close professional and personal friendship. An attorney who knew both Locke and Hay believes their rapport was based on several shared characteristics. Both men had great powers of concentration and the ability to absorb large amounts of information. Their mental attitude was positive; "no" and "it can't be done" weren't part of their vocabulary.

One early interaction in particular helped cement their mutual respect. Locke asked Hay to help him prepare an appeal to the Texas Supreme Court. "Jess and Gene," says Lewis Sweet, "sat for hours bouncing theories back and forth. Both had extremely creative minds. Finally, they decided on what legal route to take, worked together on the brief, and were successful. It was a great piece of legal work. From that point forward, I'm sure Gene had total confidence in Jess."

Hay also won the respect of Charles G. Purnell. As general counsel for the Dallas/Fort Worth Turnpike Authority, the firm was responsible for acquiring the land needed to build the 30-mile turnpike between the two cities. Purnell headed the effort with the help of Hay, who had just graduated from law school. For over two years, the attorneys drew up deeds and contracts, worked with title companies, and negotiated sales agreements in order to obtain 500 pieces of land. Despite his lack of experience, Jess learned quickly. "I recognized right away," says Purnell, "that Jess was a tremendous worker and had great ability. Very soon

Top left: Betty Jo Peacock in her sophomore year at Southern Methodist University. Betty Jo and Jess Hay Archives.

Top right: Not all of Jess Hay's student days at SMU were serious and political. Betty Jo and Jess Hay Archives.

Left: During Jess' junior year in 1951, he and Betty Jo were members of the university's Debate Club. Jess is front row, second from left. Betty Jo, secretary of the club, is front row, fourth from left. From the 1951 SMU annual, *Rotunda*.

Betty Jo Peacock and Jess Hay married in the summer of 1951. Betty Jo and Jess Hay Archives.

The union of the families Peacock and Hay. From left to right: Duncan and Kathryn Peacock, Jess Hay, Betty Jo Hay, and George and Myrtle Hay. Betty Jo and Jess Hay Archives.

after he came to work with me I felt comfortable letting him handle anything that needed to be done." Later, Hay broadened his experience by representing landowners in condemnation suits. Hay's value to the law firm grew rapidly; in 1961, the senior attorneys offered him a partnership.

When asked to become president of Lomas & Nettleton Financial Corporation four years later, he accepted with the understanding that at the end of the first year he could return to the law firm if he wished. The transition from corporate attorney to CEO required almost no learning curve. Intimately involved with the company since its founding, Hay was already familiar with most aspects of the business.

Although many of the goals that Wartes talked

about didn't change significantly, Jess Hay's leadership and execution were dramatically different. "Jess," says former board member Ed Hoffman, "brought a level of confidence and a level of soundness that had not been there. You knew he was straightforward. You knew there wasn't any double-talk, and that made a significant difference."

Jess Hay got his arms around LNFC and began to change the nature of the company.

"Jess Hay got his arms around Lomas & Nettleton Financial Corporation," says Frank Crossen, "and began to change the nature of the company."

Hay lost no time in revealing his character and intentions. Within days of taking over, he announced a new corporate objective: "To achieve profit with honor." Unlike the pragmatists before him, Jess Hay saw another dimension to the bottom line. The path to profits was as important as profitability itself.

His view of the corporate world had a "moral squint" not unlike that of Sir Thomas More in the play *A Man for All Seasons*. "I believe," says More, "when statesmen forsake their own private conscience for the sake of their public duties . . . they lead their country by a short route to chaos." Substitute corporation for government and More's credo bears a striking similarity to Jess Hay's concept of honor. In a staff meeting speech a few years later, Hay reemphasized the connection between private conscience and corporate responsibility:

> But in our concentration on profit, we should not forget the other and *more subtle* side of our stated objective: the achievement of an honored place in the financial community of which we are a part. . . . Respect is intangible, and honor is an accolade earned over a long period. However, *of this you can be certain*, honor and respect certainly will accrue to the Company and to you each time you confront the community with integrity, with responsibility, and with pride in your work and in the Company you serve. *Equally certain* is the fact that each time we compromise our own integrity; each time we seek to take unfair advantage of those with whom we deal; . . . each time we permit our own character to fail, a little of the Company's character is eroded away. . .

Jess Hay in 1956, early in his practice of law with Locke, Purnell, Boren, Laney & Neely of Dallas. Betty Jo and Jess Hay Archives.

Thus, I encourage each of you to remember that it is important that each transaction not only yield a profit, but that it also contribute to our reputation as a sound and fair institution.

Because of his long association with Jess Hay, M. D. Wommack appreciates the importance of character for the company and its leader: "Jess has always included integrity as a key word in his dealings with the staff. He communicates that from the top so that the company's transactions are done in that manner.

"I believe it comes from his own Christian ethic, which he feels should be reflected both in business and in his personal life."

But honor without action was meaningless for a company with as many problems as LNFC. Hay immediately implemented his recovery program. "The very first decision I made internally," he says, "was that at all

Top: Eugene Locke, senior law partner, saw much potential in Jess Hay and personally hired him. Eugene M. Locke Archives.

Left: Charles Purnell, fourth from left, a member of the law firm Locke, Purnell, Boren, Laney & Neely, was general counsel for the Dallas/Fort Worth Turnpike Authority. Jess Hay, at Purnell's side, third from left, is photographed with members of the Authority. Betty Jo and Jess Hay Archives.

The Hay family in 1960, one year before Jess was offered a partnership in the law firm. From left to right: Patty, Jess, Debby, and Betty Jo. Betty Jo and Jess Hay Archives.

costs we were going to protect the mortgage banking unit of Lomas & Nettleton and make that the cornerstone of our continuing operations. It was clear to me that mortgage banking was the one operation we had that was solid and fundamentally sound as a business. I think that was a decision I made in my own mind even before I was asked to become president.

"We didn't yield to the easy temptation of selling the mortgage banking operation, which could have been done and could have provided significant financial relief. But then we wouldn't have had anything left to build on."

Hay's program called for immediate reductions in general and administrative expenses, including personnel. It also placed a priority on increasing the yield of existing assets. The personnel and administrative cost reductions were part of an effort to stop losses and bring about "a quick restitution of the break-even."

"General and administrative expenses," says Hay, "were reduced in a very harsh manner starting almost the day I got here. We reduced our work force by about 50 percent. I didn't like it, but we had to do it. It wasn't pleasant."

The smaller staff responded by taking on greater responsibilities. "Those of us who stayed," says Betty Watson, former vice president for training, "had to take up the slack. I was hired as Mr. Wommack's secretary, but during the cutback I handled the insurance administrative duties, which included enrolling employees and filing claims." And when the company's bookkeeper left, Wommack gave Watson a crash course in operating the bookkeeping machine.

Divesting the company of the expensive trappings and costly fringe benefits that supported the high-roller image of the Wallace and to some extent Wartes eras was the most visible sign of change at corporate headquarters. A fleet of cars maintained for the use of officers was eliminated. The company kept only one automobile for banking and courier errands.

Austerity meant, quite literally, no more free lunches served on fine china and lace tablecloths. Less elaborate stationery replaced the embossed pattern. The breakroom pantry no longer furnished fruit, food, cigarettes, Cokes, malts, and milkshakes. "Mr. Hay," says Robert E. Price, former assistant vice president for office services, "made it known that when that food ran out, that was it for that service." Instead of several photocopying machines scattered around the offices, employees used a single, centrally located machine. New mailroom restrictions on stamps and postage saved the company hundreds of dollars a month. "It is very interesting," says Price, "to look back on how everybody pulled together as a team. We felt Mr. Hay had a sense of purpose, and he was going to turn it around some kind of way. We all felt that, and we all rallied around what we believed."

Hay's fiscal discipline worked. The company trimmed its general and administrative costs 33 percent in 1966 and another 30 percent the following year. From expenses of more than $1.1 million in 1965, the chief executive's decisive action reduced costs to a lean

$547,330 by 1967.

Hay demonstrated equal resolution in attacking the company's troubled assets. Stalled deals, floundering workouts, and low-yielding assets represented another major obstacle in the drive toward financial stability. "When Jess came over," says M. D. Wommack, "he immediately got into the nitty-gritty of reviewing every asset to determine what was earning and what was nonearning. Our goal was to turn the nonearning assets around and put them in an earning position.

"Many of our notes receivable weren't paying any interest. We tried to work with the borrowers in order to get the notes back to an earning position. We spent an awful lot of time in that effort, working with the notes receivable and the real estate."

Every step the company took that contributed to incremental income meant something. Although LNFC was no longer interested in rental property, it still owned a handful of older apartments that represented a serious cash drain. "Someone suggested," says Warren F. Caldwell, senior vice president and treasurer, "that we start our own interior decorating firm to gain access to the Furniture Mart. It saved us a lot of money. There's a heck of a markup on furniture. If you're talking about a $100 chair, for example, we were able to buy it direct from the manufacturer for $50. We saved hundreds of thousands of dollars on drapes, lamps, carpet, the whole schmear." Even with those savings, the apartments couldn't compete profitably with the newer complexes, and losses continued until the last two apartments were finally sold in 1968.

One major liquidation involved a tract of land near Los Angeles called Woodland Hills. It was purchased

Although Jess was deep in work and highly committed to the company, he found time for his passion of politics. He is seen here with Betty Jo at a tribute in Dallas in 1965 for her uncle, Carl Albert, former Speaker of the United States House of Representatives. Betty Jo and Jess Hay Archives.

Braemar's landscape with winding canyons and steep hillsides was along the lower slopes of the Santa Monica Mountains.

The spectacular views of Braemar came with breathtaking costs. Along with clearing the land, it had to be reshaped.

by the company during the formation of Wallace Properties, Inc., in 1960. After Hay took over, about half the 1,200 acres was sold for cash to developer Herbert Heftler. The remaining 585 acres became part of a joint venture residential development named Braemar. Sidney Dinow and Lewis Maler provided the homebuilding expertise for the deal, and Metropolitan Life Insurance Company and the Weyerhaeuser Company financed the development loan.

Braemar's winding canyons and steep hillsides along the lower slopes of the Santa Monica Mountains offered spectacular views and breathtaking costs. "Development costs," says Richard H. Bramblett, former LNFC vice president assigned to monitor the subdivision, "were horrendous. Besides clearing the land, you also had to reshape it. We moved over two million cubic yards of dirt just to prepare the first 130 lots." When Jess Hay arranged for a group of bankers and LNFC directors to visit the property for Braemar's opening in the fall of 1967, the attractive model home compound stood in sharp contrast to the rest of the heavily bulldozed development site. Mercantile Bank president J. D. Francis' observation after surveying the subdivision was characteristically blunt: "I've never seen so much dad-gum starting and so little finishing in all my life." Despite the slow start, sales quickly moved past the first-year projection of $6.1 million to $8.9 million by July 31, 1968.

The deep cuts and aggressive workouts had a positive effect both immediately and long-term. For the half-year ending in December 1965, the company suffered losses of over $1.6 million. Six months later, in the second half of fiscal 1966, Hay's stringent program wrought a modest miracle, $161,230 in net income—the company's first profit in more than three years. Despite a loss of $1.5 million for the year, the company had turned an important corner. For 1967, LNFC recorded a net income of $545,334, its first profitable year since the beginning of the financial crisis. A year later the figure was $944,649. With this successful two-year track record, Jess Hay commented in the

Top: map of the Los Angeles area showing the location of Braemar. Bottom: senior vice president DeWayne Wommack, right, with vice presidents Lanelle Latendresse and Robert Kinney, worked on the Woodland Hills real estate development of Braemar from their Dallas offices. From the 1967 Lomas & Nettleton annual report.

Vice president Richard Bramblett, center, discusses development plans for the Braemar project with Los Angeles builders Lewis Maler and Sidney Dinow. From the 1967 Lomas & Nettleton annual report.

The party in Los Angeles celebrating the opening of Braemar, May 1968. Third from left is Sidney Dinow, executive vice president of Galaxy Homes, standing next to Lewis Maler, president of Galaxy Homes. On the extreme right is Jess Hay, standing next to J. D. Francis, chairman and CEO of Mercantile National Bank at Dallas. Betty Jo and Jess Hay Archives.

Braemar principals were, from left to right, Sidney Dinow, executive vice president of Galaxy Homes, Jess Hay, president of Lomas & Nettleton Financial Corporation, and Lewis Maler, Galaxy president.

The Braemar land investment by Lomas & Nettleton evolved into a successful residential development. The project was a joint venture between Lomas & Nettleton and Galaxy Homes of Southern California. Braemar offered sweeping views of Los Angeles' San Fernando Valley and a rolling foothill golf course, in the background.

1968 annual report: "The Company has survived. It has 'turned around.' It now operates within the context of an economically sound foundation and its momentum is such that the favorable earnings trend should be sustained in future periods."

While LNFC scratched and clawed its way toward financial stability, the company's mortgage banking operation, ranked eighth largest in the nation, soared high overhead among the eagles of its industry. Al Rohnstedt's consolidation and data processing expansion in 1964 and 1965 took a year to crank into gear. Those operating efficiencies made a major contribution to The Lomas & Nettleton Company's 1967 record-breaking income of $1,537,680, up from $211,536 in the previous year. Mortgage operations contributed earnings of $1,937,546 in fiscal 1968, another record. This growing strength reinforced management's decision to make mortgage banking the company's cornerstone.

Much like its low-key president, the company's recovery produced little in the way of drama. Cutting

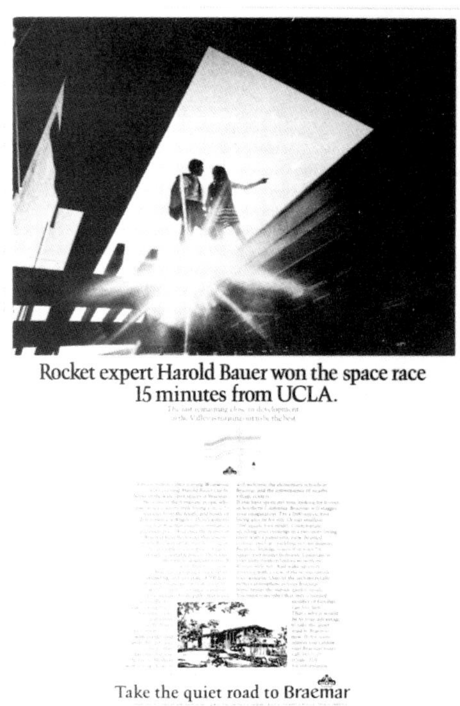

An advertisement contrasted the din of the city to the "quiet road" that led to Braemar.

expenses and upgrading assets could hardly be called innovative. The program's effectiveness came from its simplicity and reliance on fundamental principles of fiscal responsibility and integrity. Applying those principles to a lean, efficient work force together with aggressive workouts produced enough cash to further reduce the company's bank debt and fund the working capital needed for future growth.

Less tangible but equally important, the recovery "rekindled external and internal confidence." By 1968, that feeling of self-assurance encouraged LNFC to seize an opportunity that profoundly altered the company's future. The T. J. Bettes Company, whose shaky financial position had prevented a merger attempt with Wallace Investments four years earlier, now offered the Dallas company an acquisition opportunity that was hard to resist. The mortgage banking giant's financial position had eroded to the point that its principal creditor, First City National Bank of Houston, was close to declaring it bankrupt. "First City Bank," says Jim Stanley, who worked for T. J. Bettes at the time, "was on the verge of taking over, and I called John Sexton and Jess Hay and told them that the bank was getting ready to steal this thing. I said you better get down here, and they did. They came down and made a deal."

Stanley's phone call was par-

. . . an opportunity presented itself, and we were in a position to appropriate that opportunity.

In 1967, LNFC recorded its first profitable year since the beginning of the financial crisis. Board chairman DeWitt Ray and president Jess Hay, right, review the company's financial position. From the 1967 Lomas & Nettleton annual report.

Al Rohnstedt, left, was in favor of the purchase of the T. J. Bettes Company of Houston and bolstered the confidence of Jess Hay, seated at right. From the 1968 Lomas & Nettleton annual report.

E
EVE NHVN 7/11 NL *56*

VICE-PRESIᴛENT
RICHARᴛ GLYNN ^ THE LO''AS ANᴛ NETTLETON CO. ~~NO~~ 1 CONSTITUTION
PLAZA HARTFORᴛ CONN

JOHN W. LOMAS VICE-PRESIᴛENT THE LO''AS ANᴛ NETTLETON CO.
441 SU'''ER ST. STA''FORᴛ CONN

NOR''AN HALL SENIOR VICE-PRESIᴛENT THE LO''AS ANᴛ NETTLETON CO
8155 VAN NUYS BLVᴛ. PANORA''A CITY CALIF

HUGH H. TEBAULT VICE-PRESIᴛENT THE LO''AS ANᴛ NETTLETON CO
120 ''ONTGO''ERY ST. SFRAN

RICHARᴛ ᴛANLEY VICE-PRESIᴛENT THE LO''AS ANᴛ NETTLETON CO
1111 HARTFORᴛ BLᴛG ᴛALLAS TEXAS

''RS. SHIRLEY ROBERTSON ASST. SECRETARY THE LO''AS ANᴛ NETTLETON CO
1860 LINCOLN ST. ᴛVR

PAUL LOW VICE-PRESIᴛENT THE LO''AS ANᴛ NETTLETON CO.
ᴛUPONT PLAZA CENTER ''IA''I FLORIᴛA

FREᴛ BRUNN VICE-PRESIᴛENT THE LO''AS ANᴛ NETTLETON CO.
111 WEST OSBORN ROAᴛ PHOENIX ARIZONA

LO''AS ANᴛ NETTLETON FINANCIAL CORP. HAS ENTEREᴛ INTO A CONTRACT TO PURCHASE THE CO''BINEᴛ ''ORTGAGE SERVICING PORTFOLIO ANᴛ INSURANCE AGENCIES OF THE T.J. BETTES CO. OF HOUSTON TEXAS ANᴛ T.J. BETTES CO. OF CALIFORNIA. THE TRANSACTION WHICH IS SUBJECT TO INVESTOR APPROVAL IS SCHEᴛULEᴛ FOR CLOSING IN AUGUST.

ALBERT N. ROHNSTEᴛT CHAIR''AN OF THE BOARᴛ
LO''AS ANᴛ NETTLETON CO. 175 ORANGE ST
NEW HAVEN CONN

865-4171 COPY FURN COPY ~~TO~~ ATTN ~~MR~~ ''ISS SLOAN

The July 11, 1968, telegram that Al Rohnstedt sent to key company personnel throughout the country (listed before message), stating Lomas & Nettleton Financial Corporation's intent to purchase the T. J. Bettes Companies of Houston and California.

28 THE NEW HAVEN REGISTER, WEDNESDAY, JULY 17, 1968

Register Photo by Art Diello

City Headquarters Of New Biggest U.S. Mortgage Firm

This unimposing building at Orange and Court Streets is the headquarters of what will be the biggest mortgage banking company in the United States. The Lomas & Nettleton Co., and affiliated firms will have a mortgage portfolio of $2.4 billion. The city will take the No. 1 title by buying the mortgage-servicing business of the T. J. Bettes Co. of California, and the T. J. Bettes Co. of Houston. Besides the corner building, Lomas & Nettleton also occupies a portion of the structure at right. The Southern New England Telephone Co.'s Court Street building rises in background.

On the announcement of the Lomas & Nettleton acquisition of the T. J. Bettes Companies, *The New Haven Register* published a picture of the Orange Street headquarters and an eye-catching caption. Reprinted with permission of *The New Haven Register.*

ticularly timely. By the summer of 1968, with two and a half years of recovery under its belt, LNFC was a survivor with just enough financial muscle to put a deal together. "I knew," says Jess Hay, "that the perception in the minds of at least the Dallas banks was that we had turned the corner, and our survival was no longer in question. That gave us the capacity to generate the required funding. If we hadn't had that modest recovery by that time, I doubt we would have moved with as much confidence and as decisively as we did."

Al Rohnstedt, four-square in favor of the purchase, bolstered Hay's confidence by reassuring the CEO that The Lomas & Nettleton Company had the depth of personnel to manage the new acquisition even if large numbers of Bettes resignations made that necessary. In retrospect, this assurance was probably inaccurate. Fortunately, the company never had to test it; over 90 percent of the Bettes employees stayed with LNFC. In fact, they turned out to be the acquisition's hidden benefit, providing the company with a leadership core of mortgage banking personnel that lasted 15 years.

LNFC management believed they could run the Bettes operation regardless of staffing problems. More importantly, their bankers believed they could. "He [Rohnstedt] gave me the confidence," says Hay, "that this was an undertaking which we could handle operationally. Al Rohnstedt lent great credibility to our capacity to handle the transaction. He lent credibility not only to me but to the banks that finally financed it. We *wouldn't* have done it without him."

But it was diligent homework on Hay's part that gave the company an edge in negotiations. He knew that besides normal unsecured lines of credit First City National Bank also provided Bettes with several million dollars in overdrafts. This placed the bank's loan involvement with Bettes well beyond the regulatory limits for a single customer. Forcing T. J. Bettes into bankruptcy was the last thing the bank wanted. "It was a moment in time," says Hay, "when an opportunity presented itself, and that has been one of our fundamental strategies. We were in a position to move very quickly and appropriate that opportunity." Hay made it clear that the company was only interested in buying mortgage servicing. Negotiations between the two companies began by telephone. When Jess Hay and Al Rohnstedt flew to Houston for the final face-to-face discussions with First City and Bettes representatives, the meeting lasted less than three hours. The final offer was $16 million for a mortgage servicing portfolio that totaled $1.5 billion. "When their lawyer asked how we were going to pay for it," says Al Rohnstedt, "Jess hesitated, and I piped up and said, 'cash.' I knew they had to have cash. A bunch of notes wouldn't do them any good.

"Later, on our way back to Dallas, Jess asked what the hell we were going to use for money. I said, 'I don't know, Jess. That's your job.'"

It wasn't difficult. First, Hay got a loan commitment from Gene Bishop, senior credit officer for First National Bank of Dallas, with the understanding that LNFC first had to offer the loan to Mercantile National Bank. Lomas & Nettleton Financial Corporation never got an opportunity to exercise Bishop's commitment. Mercantile's J. D. Francis, now chairman and CEO, enthusiastically assured Hay that the bank would handle his company's financing. "Lomas & Nettleton West, Inc.," read the company's 1968 annual report announcement, "a wholly-owned subsidiary of Lomas & Nettleton Financial Corporation, on August 1, 1968, purchased the combined mortgage servicing portfolios of the T. J. Bettes Companies of Houston and California."

The acquisition had a profound effect on LNFC. "Bettes," says Al Rohnstedt, "had been the largest mortgage banking company in the world, and that made us the largest in 1968." The company's dream of expanding mortgage banking into a national operation suddenly had substance. "It gave us a broader geographic spread and a broader base to work from," says Hay. "It was the most significant and best mortgage banking acquisition we've ever made—in terms of price, in terms of preserving the organization, and in terms of serving as the catalyst for the aggressive pursuit of other acquisitions."

Spindletop and the adjacent oil fields brought a new era to Texas with their treasure of black gold. The Lucas Gusher at Spindletop blew in about 10:00 a.m., January 10, 1901. Beaumont Heritage Society, Beaumont, Texas.

CHAPTER V

THE T. J. BETTES COMPANY

It isn't surprising that Texas produced a mortgage banking colossus like T. J. Bettes. It's even less surprising that the company found a home in Houston. In a state where achievement is typically measured by size and wealth, the city of Houston stands as a monument to both.

The "Bayou City" made its first claim to prosperity at the beginning of the century when the discovery of oil in 1901 on Spindletop Hill, 60 miles from Houston, opened the floodgates that drenched South Texas in a river of black gold. Three years later oil strikes in Harris County established Houston as the state's petroleum capital, ruled by a collection of ruthless oil barons who confirmed J. Paul Getty's observation: "The meek shall inherit the earth, but not its mineral rights."

Houston's greatest resource, in fact, turned out to be a core of shrewd, aggressive businessmen who dug out a place for their city along the flat Gulf coastal plain. City fathers floated a bond issue shortly after the turn of the century to create a channel from the Gulf of Mexico to Houston, 50 miles inland. When Eastern financiers refused to invest in the reckless scheme, a group of Houston bankers put up the money themselves. Within 25 years, the Port of Houston ranked third in the United States in total cargo tonnage. One famous example of civic largesse occurred when Jesse Holman Jones, the city's leading banker, brought the Democratic National Convention to Houston in 1928 by literally handing the political party a blank check. And during the darkest days of the Depression, city bankers pooled their assets and gave aid to ailing banks, making Houston the only city in the nation to survive the crisis without a bank failure.

Prosperity turned to boom after World War II. On Main Street, lots sold for $2,000 per front inch. According to one 1950 study, Houston led the nation in industrial construction. Bulldozers had waiting lists. Secretaries stuffed cotton in their ears before descending to the street for lunch because of the noise from downtown construction projects. It was a city where boosters claimed: "A fellow can make ten million dollars if he wants to run after it. He can make one million dollars just by standing still."

A fellow can make ten million dollars if he wants to run after it. He can make one million dollars just by standing still.

There were few restraints among the Houston business community, least of all on the God-given right to accumulate and spend money. It was an era when both excess and vulgarity were applauded. One millionaire indulged his wife's passion for interior decorating by buying a hotel and assigning her to redo it. He also stocked his ranch with exotic game and rode to the hunt on half-tracks mounted with machine guns. One oilman appeared at public gatherings with a hundred-dollar bill serving as his bow tie, and if the evening went well, he would rip it off and throw it to the nearest attractive woman, and clip on another. A man wrote to Picasso in the south of France and sought to buy ten paintings. He specified no color or subject preference, only the dimensions of his room. One millionaire's wife always purchased two extra first-class airplane tickets for travels to New York and Paris. Where else would she put her matched poodles with jeweled collars and chinchilla sweaters? Another Houston woman wrote to the Smithsonian inquiring if the Hope Diamond was for sale. One man spent $50,000 vainly trying to keep penguins alive in a refrigerated room of his home; another rode lions bareback to greet the mailman. A furrier who knew the tastes of his Houston customers sent out a letter: "I am taking bids from several people on a mink bedspread. . . . The bidding will start at ten thousand dollars if you desire the bedspread to be the only one in Texas, or at twenty-five thousand if you desire the bedspread to be the only one in existence."

Houston's carnival of wealth and glittering opportunity proved an irresistible magnet. Thousands of people poured in to stake their claim to a piece of the action. The city's metropolitan population jumped

The underground riches from the oil fields around Spindletop produced a skyline of derricks, which translated into another kind of skyline in Houston. Beaumont Heritage Society, Beaumont, Texas.

Soon after the opening of Spindletop, Houston showed its new-found prosperity. A 1910 view of downtown Houston at the intersection of Main and Capitol streets. Houston Metropolitan Research Center, Houston Public Library.

from 500,000 in 1940 to 1,250,000 by 1960, the largest increase anywhere in the country.

With that kind of growth in population, a successful mortgage company might not be unexpected. Even so, bright, aggressive management pushed Houston's T. J. Bettes Company to an unprecedented level of success within its industry. By the mid-forties, T. J. Bettes was the largest mortgage banking company in Texas. By the mid-fifties, it was the largest in the United States.

Torrey James Bettes, the guiding hand behind the enterprise, was born in Grand Rapids, Michigan, on September 29, 1888. His father, Chalmers Bettes, was a Grand Rapids fruit grower originally from Ontario, Canada. T. J. Bettes graduated from Michigan State College with a degree in engineering. At the age of 23, he entered the mortgage banking business in Atlanta. By 1923 Bettes had moved to Dallas, where he formed a partnership and served as general manager of the Investment and Securities Company of Texas.

The turning point in his career came not long after his marriage in 1927 to Ruth Rogers, the daughter of

An 1894 view of the Houston channel before turn-of-the-century construction and expansion. Houston Metropolitan Research Center, Houston Public Library.

Jesse Holman Jones was Houston's leading banker. He is shown at his desk in this 1928 photograph, the same year he brought the Democratic National Convention to Houston. On either side of his desk are souvenirs of the convention. Houston Metropolitan Research Center, Houston Public Library.

Hall interior at the 1928 Democratic National Convention, held in Houston. Houston Metropolitan Research Center, Houston Public Library.

a wealthy Brownwood ranching and banking family. Increasing disagreements between Bettes and his co-owner ended their partnership. Bettes moved to Houston in 1928, where he became associated with Ross Sterling, a prominent Houston business and political figure who was elected governor of Texas in 1931. In the late twenties, Sterling's mortgage banking company, The Trust Company of Texas, ran into financial problems, and Sterling asked Torrey Bettes to liquidate the company's assets. Apparently, he did a good job. Sterling turned the corporate shell over to Bettes and paid him for his services with three or four pieces of property that included a fourplex apartment and a warehouse. For the first time, T. J. Bettes exercised control over his own business.

Bettes' years of mortgage experience enabled him to build a modest conventional loan business, which included among other investors the Prudential Life Insurance Company. "T. J. Bettes," says former Lomas

& Nettleton senior executive vice president Everett Mattson, who joined the Bettes Company in 1945, "was one of the greatest salesmen I've ever known. He developed relationships with investors like nobody has since. Whatever he said he'd do, he did it. He gave them excellent service." That kind of attention to investor relationships paid off. Mattson remembers that once, when the company had accumulated $300,000 in uncommitted conventional loans, he listened while Bettes telephoned an investor and asked him to buy the mortgages. Within minutes, the investor agreed to purchase the entire package: "Mr. Bettes hung up the phone, turned to me and said, 'That's how you sell loans.' None of the rest of us could have done that, but Bettes could."

T. J. was a very sharp guy. He had a lot of vision. He could see things coming.

After World War II, construction in downtown Houston was busy, with bulldozers digging basements and outlines of buildings reaching for the sky. Houston Metropolitan Research Center, Houston Public Library.

A 1950 study showed that Houston led the nation in industrial construction, with much of the activity at the Port of Houston and along the ship channel. Houston Metropolitan Research Center, Houston Public Library.

Torrey James Bettes founded a mortgage banking company that was the largest in Texas by the mid-forties and the largest in the nation by the mid-fifties.

T. J. Bettes of the Trust Company of Texas, first row second from left, acted as agent in making the first FHA-approved mortgage in Houston. This photograph appeared in *The Houston Press* on March 22, 1935.

Ross Sterling, c. 1920s. Sterling, a business associate of T. J. Bettes, was chairman of the Houston Port Commission, a prominent mortgage banker, and later governor of Texas. Houston Metropolitan Research Center, Houston Public Library.

T. J. Bettes also had the ability to catch industry trends early and make them work for the company. "T. J. was a very sharp guy," says former Lomas & Nettleton senior vice president John R. Butler, who joined the Bettes Company in 1941. "He had a lot of vision. He could see things coming." The first trend he caught was the Federal Housing Administration's federally insured loan program. On March 22, 1935, Bettes made mortgage banking history in Houston by originating a $5,800 loan on a two-story brick veneer residence at 1825 South Boulevard in Houston. It was the first FHA-approved loan in the district. "The loan," read an article in *The Houston Press*, "was made to the Realty Servicing Corporation, builder of the house, by the Indianapolis Life Insurance Company. It was made through T. J. Bettes of the Trust Company of Texas, who said he was acting personally as agent in this particular loan."

The early response to FHA loans in Houston must have been encouraging. On March 23, 1936, with assets from the Trust Company of Texas and, it is rumored, a substantial contribution from his wife,

Ruth, Torrey Bettes organized the T. J. Bettes Company with a $100,000 capitalization, the minimum needed to become an FHA mortgagee. Mrs. Elva Nelson, secretary to T. J. Bettes, remembered the company's first location: "a small, two-room office with a five-employee staff including Mr. Bettes. We were located then in what was known as the Post Dispatch Building, now the Shell Building." A few years later the company moved to larger quarters at 616 Fannin Street.

The corporate goals Bettes envisioned went beyond Houston's city limits. He opened the company's first branch office in Fort Worth in April 1936. A second branch later opened in San Antonio. But it was the network of branch representatives acting as agents for the company that gave Bettes complete coverage throughout the state. Less than five years after its incorporation, the T. J. Bettes Company serviced $29 million in mortgage loans and established itself as the largest mortgage banker in Texas.

Gathering war clouds in Europe and the Pacific suggested a shift in priorities for the homebuilding industry, and Bettes was ready. "When the war came along," says John Butler, "Torrey Bettes saw the FHA program peter out because of war-related building restrictions. So he jumped into the Title VI program of FHA with both feet. The Title VI business was what made the Bettes Company."

Title VI was a war housing program that encouraged volume residential construction for approved locations near war-related industry and military facilities. The Houston area with its petroleum and chemical industries was an indispensable part of the war effort and a prime Title VI location. Along with its two

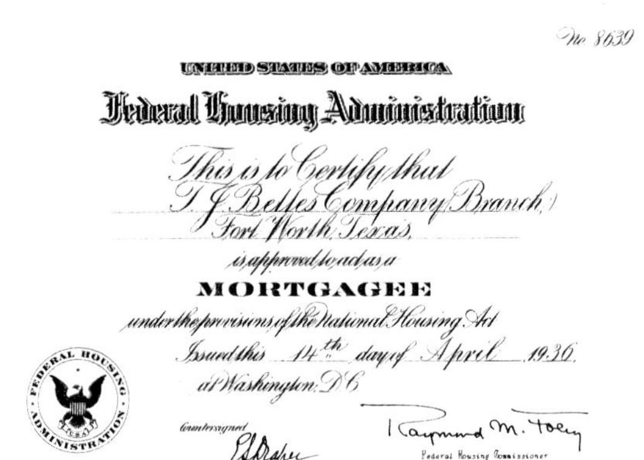

No. 8639

UNITED STATES OF AMERICA

Federal Housing Administration

This is to Certify that T. J. Bettes Company (Branch) Fort Worth, Texas, is approved to act as a

MORTGAGEE

under the provisions of the National Housing Act

Issued this 14th day of April 1936, at Washington, D.C.

Countersigned

Deputy Commissioner

Raymond M. Foley
Federal Housing Commissioner

The T. J. Bettes Company opened its first branch office in Fort Worth in April 1936, the same time as the Federal Housing Administration approved the branch as mortgagee.

The T. J. Bettes Company was first located in a two-room office with five employees in the Post Dispatch Building. Houston Metropolitan Research Center, Houston Public Library.

LOANS AND INVESTMENTS 126

CLINE MORTGAGE & TRUST COMPANY

Capital, Surplus and Reserves Over $75,000.00

LOANS ON
—Residences
—Duplexes
—Apartments
—Community Centers
—Business Properties

ATTRACTIVE TERMS
LOW INTEREST RATES
NO BROKERAGE

OFFICERS
A. R. CLINE, President-Treasurer
R. L. JACOBE, Vice-President
I. O. LILJEROS, Loan Officer

DIRECTORS
W. B. Bates
G. M. Cline
Leon H. Curtin
R. L. Jacobe
A. R. Cline

General Counsel
FULBRIGHT, CROOKER & FREEMAN

SECOND NATIONAL BANK BLDG. PHONE CAPITOL 5141

FOR REFINANCE OR NEW CONSTRUCTION

T. J. BETTES COMPANY

RESIDENCE — APARTMENTS — BUSINESS

Interest Rates as Low as 5% Without Brokerage
Terms: Payable Monthly or Yearly or Can Place Your Loan Through FHA
(25 Years Mortgage Loan Service)

1509 STERLING BUILDING FAX. 8144

INVESTORS SYNDICATE

ESTABLISHED 1894
Roy Kiesling, Manager Houston Office Phone Fairfax 2738
509 GULF BUILDING
Investors Syndicate Agency Offices in 152 Leading Cities, Including:
Dallas — San Antonio
New York† — Baltimore — Richmond — Memphis — New Orleans — Chicago
Indianapolis — Des Moines — Oklahoma City — Salt Lake City — Los Angeles — Portland — Montreal* — Toronto* — Winnipeg
Home Office: Minneapolis, Minn.
†Office Investors Syndicate Title and Guaranty Co.
*Office Investors Syndicate, Ltd., Canada
THESE COMPANIES ARE AFFILIATES OF INVESTORS SYNDICATE

Left: The Bettes Company expanded from the building on Fannin Street into the Sterling Building, where it eventually leased three floors. Houston Metropolitan Research Center, Houston Public Library, and The Greater Houston Partnership.

Right: The first notice for the T. J. Bettes Company appeared in the 1937–1938 Houston City Directory. It shows the company's new location in the Sterling Building. Houston Metropolitan Research Center, Houston Public Library.

Below: In July of 1940, T. J. Bettes, second row center, was elected president of the Houston Mortgage Bankers Association.

branch offices and branch representative network, the company was able to respond to the large Title VI construction projects springing up all over Texas. "The company took off in 1941 and 1942 when all the war housing came along," says Everett Mattson. "There was a lot of building in Houston, Texas City, and all along the ship channel. There was a lot of activity in Texarkana because of the Red River Arsenal and even out in West Texas near Pampa where there was a big carbon black plant." The company also moved into Little Rock, Arkansas, and Shreveport and Alexandria, Louisiana.

Expansion was balanced with a concern for servicing details. John Butler remembers wrestling with a problem involving escrow fund shortages. The tax rates

MEMBERS OF THE
HOUSTON MORTGAGE BANKERS ASSOCIATION
HOUSTON, TEXAS
Taken in front of Houston City Hall, July 1940

OFFICERS
T. J. Bettes, President
L. K. Busch, Vice-President
Lee M. Duggan, Vice-President
Dan McCrary, Secretary-Treasurer

DIRECTORS
Burke Baker
T. J. Bettes
L. K. Busch
Allyn R. Cline
Lee M. Duggan
I. Friedlander
R. N. Gay
J. C. Leonard
C. M. Malone
I. B. McFarland
Dan McCrary
R. D. Buck Walton
C. L. Westcott

Back Row: Nat U. Collier, manager, Hermann Hospital Estates; Paul Kowalski, associate of Hugh Ritchie; Fred Hester, department manager, San Jacinto National Bank; Frank C. Olmsted, district manager, Mortgage Investment Corporation; B. B. Yeager, assistant secretary, Gulf Coast Investment Corporation; I. Lee Campbell, mortgage loans; C. N. Peck, agent, Farm & Home Savings & Loan Association; G. L. Seger, Second National Bank; T. J. Bettes, president, T. J. Bettes Company; Burke Baker, president, Seaboard Life Insurance Company; C. M. Malone, president, Guardian Trust Company; John W. Painter, vice-president, T. J. Bettes Company; I. Friedlander, president, Gibraltar Savings & Building Association; I. B. McFarland, president, Houston First Federal Savings & Loan Association; Charles Tips, president, Texas Industrial Investment Company; R. N. Gay, R. N. Gay & Company; Presley E. Vinson, loan manager, Farm & Home Savings & Loan Association.

Front Row: Elmo Corbell, vice-president, Gulf Coast Investment Corporation; L. K. Busch, vice-president, J. E. Foster & Son, Inc.; C. L. Westcott, president, Southland Mortgage Company; W. Cecil Sisson, W. Cecil Sisson Mortgage Company; H. A. Crabb, Crabb & Trotter; Dan McCrary, Guardian Trust Company; B. Sparks, chief underwriter, Federal Housing Administration; C. H. DeBell, C. H. DeBell Mortgage Company; Henry L. Hodell, Jr., loan correspondent, Union Central Life Insurance Company.

Members not shown: J. H. Barker, assistant secretary-treasurer, Great Southern Life Insurance Company; B. C. Burchfield, president, Burchfield Development Company; A. R. Cline, president, Cline Mortgage & Trust Company; Harry Copeland, vice-president, Texas Mortgage Company; Lee Duggan, district manager, Pacific Mutual Life Insurance Company; A. C. Ford, district director, Federal Housing Administration; J. C. Leonard, president, J. C. Leonard Company; Lester J. Peterson, manager, Guaranty Federal Savings & Loan Association; Harry Richards, manager real estate department, Second National Bank; Hugh Ritchie, loan correspondent, General American Life Insurance Company; H. Russell Smith, manager, Jefferson Standard Life Insurance Company; R. D. Buck Walton, vice-president, American General Investment Corporation; F. E. Wood, loan correspondent, Pan-American Life Insurance Company.

Honolulu Star-Bulletin 1st EXTRA

Evening Bulletin, Est. 1882, No. 11287
Hawaiian Star, Vol. XLVIII No. 15359

HONOLULU, TERRITORY OF HAWAII, U. S. A., SUNDAY, DECEMBER 7, 1941

★ PRICE FIVE CENTS

WAR!

(Associated Press by Transpacific Telephone)

SAN FRANCISCO, Dec. 7.—President Roosevelt announced this morning that Japanese planes had attacked Manila and Pearl Harbor.

OAHU BOMBED BY JAPANESE PLANES

SIX KNOWN DEAD, 21 INJURED, AT EMERGENCY HOSPITAL

Attack Made On Island's Defense Areas

By UNITED PRESS

WASHINGTON, Dec. 7. —Text of a White House announcement detai ling the attack on the Hawaiian islands is:

"The Japanese attacked Pearl Harbor from the air and all naval and military activities on the island of Oahu, principal American base in the Hawaiian islands."

Oahu was attacked at 7:55 this morning by Japanese planes.

The Rising Sun, emblem of Japan, was seen on plane wing tips.

Wave after wave of bombers streamed through the clouded morning sky from the southwest and flung their missiles on a city resting in peaceful Sabbath calm.

According to an unconfirmed report received at the governor's office, the Japanese force that attacked Oahu reached island waters aboard two small airplane carriers.

It was also reported that at the governor's office either an attempt had been made to bomb the USS Lexington, or that it had been bombed.

CITY IN UPROAR

Within 10 minutes the city was in an uproar. As bombs fell in many parts of the city, and in defense areas the defenders of the islands went into quick action.

Army intelligence officers at Ft. Shafter announced officially shortly after 9 a. m. the fact of the bombardment by an enemy but long previous army and navy had taken immediate measures in defense.

"Oahu is under a sporadic air raid," the announcement said.

"Civilians are ordered to stay off the streets until further notice."

CIVILIANS ORDERED OFF STREETS

The army has ordered that all civilians stay off the streets and highways and not use telephones.

Evidence that the Japanese attack has registered some hits was shown by three billowing pillars of smoke in the Pearl Harbor and Hickam field area.

All navy personnel and civilian defense workers, with the exception of women, have been ordered to duty at Pearl Harbor.

The Pearl Harbor highway was immediately a mass of racing cars.

A trickling stream of injured people began pouring into the city emergency hospital a few minutes after the bombardment started.

Thousands of telephone calls almost swamped the Mutual Telephone Co., which put extra operators on duty.

At The Star-Bulletin office the phone calls deluged the single operator and it was impossible for this newspaper, for sometime, to handle the flood of calls. Here also an emergency operator was called.

HOUR OF ATTACK—7:55 A. M.

An official army report from department headquarters, made public shortly before 11, is that the first attack was at 7:55 a. m.

Witnesses said they saw at least 50 airplanes over Pearl Harbor.

The attack centered in the Pearl Harbor, Army authorities said:

"The rising sun was seen on the wing tips of the airplanes."

Although martial law has not been declared officially, the city of Honolulu was operating under M-Day conditions.

It is reliably reported that enemy objectives under attack were Wheeler field Hickam field, Kaneohe bay and naval air station and Pearl Harbor.

Some enemy planes were reported short shot down.

The body of the pilot was seen in a plane burning at Wahiawa.

Oahu appeared to be taking calmly after the first uproar of queries.

ANTIAIRCRAFT GUNS IN ACTION

First indication of the raid came shodtly before 8 this morning when antiaircraft guns around Pearl Habor began sending up a thunderous barrage.

At the same time a vast cloud of black smoke arose from the naval base and also from Hickam field where flames could be seen.

BOMB NEAR GOVERNOR'S MANSION

Shortly before 9:30 a bomb fell near Washington Place, the residence of the governor. Governor Poindexter and Secretary Charles M, Hite were there.

It was reported that the bomb killed an unidentified Chinese man across the street in front of the Schuman Carriage Co. where windows were broken.

C. E. Daniels, a welder, found a fragment of shell or bomb at South and Queen Sts. which he brought into the City Hall. This fragrent weighed about a pound.

At 10:05 a. m. today Governor Poindexter telephoned to The Star-Bulletin announcing he has declared a state of emergency for the entire territory.

He announced that Edouard L. Doty, executive secretary of t he major disaster council, has been appointed director under the M-Day law's provisions.

Governor Poindexter urged all residents of Honolulu to remain off the street, and the people of the territory to remain calm.

Mr. Doty reported that all major disaster council wardens and medical units were on duty within a half hour of the time the alarm was given.

Workers employed at Pearl Harbor were ordered at 10:10 a. m. not to report at Pearl Harbor.

The mayor's major disaster council was to meet at the city hall at about 10:30 this morning

At least two Japanese planes were reported at Hawaiian department headquarters to have been shot down.

One of the planes was shot down at Ft. Kamehameha and the other back of the Wa-

Turn to Page 2, Column 1

Hundreds See City Bombed

Hundreds of Honolulans who hurried to the top of Punchbowl soon after bombs began to fall, saw spread out before them the whole panaroma of surprise attack and defense.

Far off over Pearl Harbor the white sky was polka-dotted with anti-aircraft smoke.

Rolling away from the navy base were billowing clouds of ugly black smoke. Sometimes a burst of flame reddened the black sources of the smoke.

Out from the silver-surfaced mouth of the harbor a flotilla of destroyers streamed to battle, smoke pouring from their stacks.

Turn to Page 2, Column 3

Names of Dead and Injured

The city emergency hospital reported at 10:30 a list of 6 killed and 21 injured.

The complete list will be carried later. Here is a partial list:

Peter Lopes, 34, of 3641 Kamanaiki St., was reported at 9:30 a. m. to be in serious condition from wounds in the upper abdomen.

Bernice Gouveia, 12, 1768 Kalihi St., is suffering from a mangled thigh, lacerations on the right leg and left arm.

A Portuguese girl, unidentified, 16 years old, died on arrival from puncture wounds.

Another victim who died on arrival was Frank Ohashi, 29, 1768 Kamanaiki St., from puncture wounds in the chest.

Cecelia Broadly, 35, Moanalua gardens, was released from the hospital after treatment for lacerations.

Three were reported injured and one reported killed from the bomb that fell at Fort and School Sts.

Schools Closed

All schools on Oahu, both public and private, will remain closed until further notice, Edouard L. Doty, territorial director of civilian defense, announced at 11 a. m. today. This does not apply elsewhere in the territory.

Editorial

HAWAII MEETS THE CRISIS

Honolulu and Hawaii will meet the emergency of war today as Honolulu and Hawaii have met emergencies in the past—coolly, calmly and with immediate and complete support of the officials, officers and troops who are in charge.

Governor Poindexter and the army and navy leaders have called upon the public to remain calm; for civilians who have no essential business on the streets to stay off; and for every man and woman to do his duty.

That request, coupled with the measures promptly taken to meet the situation that has suddenly and terribly developed, will be needed.

Hawaii will do its part—as a loyal American territory.

In this crisis, every difference of race, creed and color will be submerged in the one desire and determination to play the part that Americans always play in crisis.

BULLETIN

Additional Star-Bulletin extras today will cover the latest developments in this war move.

With the attack on Pearl Harbor by the Japanese, the T. J. Bettes Company expanded by directing its efforts toward the Title VI war-related housing program. Reprinted with permission of the *Honolulu Star-Bulletin*.

frequently changed during the first year on new construction, and no one was monitoring the changes. "We worked down there," says Butler, "night after night during the war with all the help we could find." The service department solved the problem by introducing a "graduated up-payment" to correct the shortages.

The Houston company also broke new ground by requiring escrow funds for conventional loans. When they discovered that some of their conventional mortgagors in Houston hadn't paid taxes for two or three years, it caught their attention since tax liability served as a prior lien to a mortgage. "We started putting them on escrow funds," says Butler, "and that became general practice during the mid-forties when all the insurance companies started requiring it."

We made a ton of VA loans.

With the surrender of Germany in May 1945 and the defeat of Japan only three months away, Torrey Bettes prepared for still another shift in business strategy. The pent-up demand for civilian housing would unleash a homebuilding boom, and he knew FHA would play a leading role along with a frisky young upstart called VA. The newcomer was a product of the Serviceman's Readjustment Act passed by Congress in 1944, which provided for a Veterans Administration mortgage loan program similar to FHA. This new law gave official endorsement to the view that the 16 million GI's of World War II should return to civilian life with a home of their own.

"Bettes," says John Butler, "saw what was going to happen when the VA loan program came into effect. It was going to be the coming thing because there was no down payment and because veterans had no trouble getting credit approval. Our company made the first VA loan in Houston. We made a ton of VA loans. It turned out to be a godsend. Our insurance investors were buying both FHA and VA loans as fast as we could process them. It was strictly a volume business."

The volume came from builders who were putting up hundreds of houses a year. "Everybody was building houses like gangbusters," says Henry P. Winkler, a former Lomas & Nettleton vice president and senior insurance executive. "People were buying them right off the slab."

"It was right after the war ended," recalls former escrow accounts analyst Gerhard H. Spence, who joined T. J. Bettes in 1946, "and all the servicemen came back and had to have houses to live in. The builders back then were building those crackerbox houses, four rooms and a bath. The building industry was flooded with that stuff. And the Bettes Company was financing 80 percent of it in the Houston area. It seemed to me that we doubled our size in two years' time."

The Bettes Company also captured a substantial share of the market in other cities. The company's size and reputation for quality servicing played a major role in attracting the largest developers. "We were the largest mortgage loan company in Houston and the state," says Everett Mattson. "And we were the largest producers of FHA and VA loans in Texas. Most of our builders were putting up between three and five hundred houses a year."

The Dallas branch office, which opened in 1946 and faced stiff competition from well-established savings and loan associations, served as a model for the company's entry into new markets. Former Lomas Mortgage USA chairman James M. Wooten, who first joined the Bettes Company's Dallas branch in 1946, responded to their underdog status by going after the people who sold the houses—the realtors and builders. "It was simply a matter of cultivating realtor sources and builder sources," says Wooten, "and providing a service for them. I went out and knocked on doors and persuaded them that we could handle it. It was pure sales effort. Plus, once we got in we smothered their buyers with kindness. We stayed in close contact. It was Saturdays and Sundays and nights. I knew this business better than any other mortgage banker or any savings and loan person."

The Dallas branch under the leadership of Everett Mattson and later Jim Wooten was one of the most innovative and entrepreneurial in the Bettes organization. By the mid-fifties, Wooten's knowledge and confidence in the Dallas housing market encouraged him to commit the Bettes Company to partnerships with the city's three largest builders: "We were 50-50 partners—buying the land, financing it, building the houses, selling them, and splitting the profits. And, of course, our branch handled all the mortgage loans. We made a bucketful of money. Sometimes our branch made more money than the rest of the company put together."

Dallas may have been a top producer, but it was only a matter of degree. It was hard to find a branch in the Bettes organization that wasn't breaking new production records. The avalanche of new business pouring into the Houston office forced the company to increase its staff and office space. "We didn't have to go out and solicit loans," says Porter E. Morris, a former Lomas & Nettleton vice president and branch manager of Corpus Christi who joined T. J. Bettes in 1946. "We were so well established that builders came to us. I was in banking and shipping at the time, and we were making so many VA loans that we had a backlog in a row of file cabinets four feet high and twenty feet long. We worked until eight or nine o'clock at night to clear them out." Henry Winkler, who joined the Bettes Company in 1946, remembers the long customer lines and his temporary recruitment into the loan application process even though he was hired to work in insurance: "I didn't know much about the mortgage business, but John Butler wanted me to help process mortgage applications. He gave me a ten-minute how-to course, and I stayed there until midnight completing those damned mortgage applications. It was hot and heavy like that for about four years. We just kept getting bigger and bigger."

The Bettes Christmas party of 1944 was a time of celebration. First row, left to right: Mr. and Mrs. McConnell, Mr. and Mrs. T. J. Bettes, Mrs. Elva Nelson, secretary to T. J. Bettes. Second row, left to right: Henry and Hazel DuPre, Mr. and Mrs. Garner, unidentified man, Mr. Campbell, unidentified lady, Mrs. Campbell, Mr. and Mrs. John L. Leonard, and John Butler.

The Dallas branch office opened in 1946 under the leadership of Everett Mattson.

Later Jim Wooten became Dallas branch manager. Shown are Tom McDonald, vice president at Bettes headquarters, seated at left; Jim Wooten, Dallas branch manager, standing; and Austin Tatum, manager of the Fort Worth office, right.

Homer R. Riley, the former president of the L&N Employees Credit Union who also joined the company in 1946, remembers the frequent rearrangement of departments in order to accommodate new staff: "It was rather frustrating for me. I'd go home on the weekend and come back Monday morning, and my desk would be gone."

But shifting departments and shuffling desks offered little relief for the company's growing work force. "Every time you turned around," says Gerhard Spence, "we needed more space. From the second-floor office building on Fannin Street, we expanded into the Sterling Building and eventually leased three floors there. Even so, they had to move the insurance department all the way down to Texas Avenue about six or eight blocks away. We just didn't have room for them."

Despite the crowded conditions and hectic work pace, morale was high. T. J. Bettes demonstrated the same heartfelt concern for employees as he did for investors. "One day when I had my head down, working like hell," Henry Winkler recalls, "I felt a hand on my shoulder. I looked up, and there was Mr. Bettes. He just stopped by to say hello and ask how I was doing." Bettes' concern often went beyond everyday pleasantries. "I had just gotten married," Winkler explains, "and I was working my tail off, and my nerves weren't in too good a shape. Mr. Bettes found out about it and called me in his office and said, 'Mr. Winkler, I'm going to give you some cash, and I want you and your wife to go to Florida on vacation and stay down there for at least ten days.' I asked, 'What for?' And he said, 'Because you need a rest.' So, my wife and I went to Florida and spent ten days at Key Biscayne. That's the kind of thoughtful individual Mr. Bettes was."

By the mid-fifties, the Bettes Company was in partnership with Dallas' three largest homebuilders. One of the three was Fox & Jacobs, whose principals are pictured in this 1959 photograph. Ike Jacobs is on the left and Dave Fox on the right, with Jim Wooten at center.

T. J. Bettes lavished the same kind of attention on the branch offices. Jim Wooten describes the deep impression that his first meeting with Torrey Bettes made on him: "I was taking a loan application from a fellow wearing overalls who looked like he might have been an auto mechanic. He had come in to get a GI loan to buy a house. Mr. Bettes walked in and stopped at a desk near me to shake hands with the employee there. Then, he came straight over to the man at my desk and said, 'I'm Torrey Bettes, and I'm delighted you're doing business with me. If there's anything I can do to help you, give me a call. I appreciate your being here.' Then, he introduced himself to me.

"He was in our office four or five times after that, and he never left without shaking hands and visiting with each employee."

As the mortgage loan business accelerated, so did the opportunities in related ventures where the company could use its captive, large-volume customer base to its best advantage. One of the most successful was an FHA program called Title I. It was a federally insured home improvement loan program designed to help homeowners maintain their property with relatively inexpensive financing. In September 1946, Charles H. Underwood was hired to start up a Title I loan program known at the T. J. Bettes Company as the consumer credit department. Working from a list of Title I–approved contractors or dealers who owned fence, lumber, siding, and roofing companies, the new department cultivated relationships that led to direct referrals. Consumer credit also used direct mail solicitation to reach the company's mortgage customers. Two investors supplied the funding for the loans; the larger of the two, the First National Bank of St. Louis, eventually provided a $20 million line of credit. The department's aggressive sale of installment insurance, which in the event of death or disability either paid off the loan or made the monthly payments, added another source of income. At its peak, Bettes ranked eighth in the nation among the 5,500 companies handling Title I lending.

The popularity of Title I loans and the growing expertise of the department's staff encouraged Charles Underwood to invent a more profitable product. The Green Plan, so named because all the forms, approvals, and documents were printed on green stationery, was a conventional home improvement loan program. "Those loans," says former Lomas & Nettleton Company vice president Sidney L. Kelley, a former Bettes consumer credit employee, "started out at $3,500, and we just kept moving up as our experience got stronger until we made many loans at $5,000. We weren't limited by FHA restrictions. Our initial interest rates on those loans were 7 or 7½ percent, whereas the FHA rate was 5 percent. So, we had higher interest rates, larger loans, and larger insurance premiums. The Green Plan was really much more profitable to us than the FHA side of it. In fact, the conventional plan became so attractive that we stopped soliciting FHA Title I loans." At its peak, the consumer credit department's portfolio contained 35,000 loans valued at $20 million.

Another stream of profits flowed from an insurance operation closely connected to the mortgage loan business. Once again, it was the Bettes Company's rapport with the large builders that made insurance sales so successful. "We went to builders," says Henry Winkler, "all over Texas and Arkansas, and signed them up as agents. Nobody was fighting you for the insurance at that time. So we got a double dip. We got the mortgage loan, and the insurance, too." Like Wooten in Dallas, the company's general insurance agency built its business through the salesmanship of men like Winkler: "The mortgage people would tell me they were getting a bunch of loans in from Texarkana, for example, and I'd haul my butt up there and tell the builder I was going to show him how he could make more money." To attract builders who were uncomfortable with the complexities of the insurance business, the Bettes insurance agency set up accounting systems and recommended individuals who could run the builders' insurance operations. The Bettes general agency received a 10 percent override on each agent's commission. "We probably had 450 agents all over the state of Texas," says Winkler.

The efficiency of the Bettes Company's servicing matched their strong sales effort. "The company recognized," says former Lomas & Nettleton executive vice president Hugh S. (Dee) DeWitt, "that all we really had to offer was service. I maintained some charts on mortgage delinquency ratios for about ten years beginning in 1955, and by far we were the national leader in controlling delinquencies.

"We had our past due notices out to delinquent mortgagors at least by the tenth of every month and were calling them by the fifteenth. Most of our competitors didn't bother to send their first notice until the fifteenth, which is when the penalty became due."

Beginning in the 1960s, former senior vice president Carl F. Geiser, Jr., and former vice president Andrew (Hap) Roberts guided Bettes' servicing operation. "Bettes had a reputation for servicing," says DeWitt. "Carl Geiser was as good a servicing administrator as anyone in the country." "He [Geiser] ran a tight, disciplined, accurately handled operation," says Jim Wooten. "He knew the business, but he was stubborn. Once he decided how something ought to be, he was about as flexible as a tire tool. He wouldn't budge a half-inch." Those who knew both men say Roberts was as capable as Geiser and broadened the leadership needed to run a first-rate organization.

Geiser and Roberts' service was especially critical in winning and maintaining strong builder relationships. The large volume of mortgage loans that fed the company's portfolio depended on it. John Butler describes one innovation that gave the Bettes Company an important edge over competitors: "We were probably the first company in the country that preapproved loans. Most mortgage companies had to send their loans to an investor for approval before they could make the permanent loan. This caused the builders and realtors a great deal of delay, which cost them money. But our customers knew as soon as Bettes got a loan approved by FHA or VA that we would immediately give them our commitment for it. We called it 'same-day service.' That's the way we met a lot of our competition."

John Austin was the guy who supplied the money to really make this thing go.

But preapproved loans also presented a problem. It took approximately two months from the time Bettes closed a loan until it received the money from an investor. This forced the Bettes Company to temporarily fund the loans themselves with borrowed bank money, a procedure known in mortgage banking as warehousing. The difficulty was that Bettes' bank credit lines weren't large enough to keep up with the increase in mortgage volume. With individual borrowers clamoring for mortgage loans and a long list of eager investors willing to pay premiums for FHA and VA loans, insufficient short-term bank credit was a potential bottleneck that could keep the company from cashing in on a bonanza. Using his finely tuned instinct for what the company needed, Torrey Bettes hired John F. Austin, Jr., as executive vice president in 1948. "Mr. Bettes realized," says former Lomas & Nettleton executive vice president E. G. Bray, "that in order to keep things going he had to find somebody who had connections in financial circles. And that was John Austin. John Austin was the guy who supplied the money to really make this thing go."

Born in Frankston, Texas, Austin came from a fam-

The men of Bettes, c. 1948, with Torrey James Bettes seated center. The photograph was taken a year before his death in May 1949.

T. J. Bettes hired John Austin as executive vice president in 1948.

John Austin became president after T. J. Bettes died. Shown with Austin are Ruth Bettes and Donald McGregor, c. 1950.

Austin was known as an outgoing person and a "good time Charlie." In this 1950s photograph, he enjoyed being a part of the Bettes Christmas program.

ily of bankers. There was little doubt about his choice of careers. After graduating from The University of Texas and the Graduate School of Banking at Rutgers University, he began his career at the First State Bank of Frankston. Later, Austin served as senior bank examiner for the Federal Reserve Bank in Dallas. By the mid-forties, he was a senior executive for South Texas National Bank in Houston.

John Austin wasted no time using his professional connections to secure additional credit lines for the Bettes Company. "Through John Austin," says E. G. Bray, "we got into the Dallas banks. Dallas was where you went to get money. We went from a $6 million credit line to a $100 million credit line. By 1955, with Republic National Bank alone, we were getting $70 million worth of paper."

In fact, the mortgage volume had grown so large by the mid-fifties that the Bettes Company found itself knocking on New York bank doors. "Most of the commercial banks," says Jim Wooten, "were not sophisti-

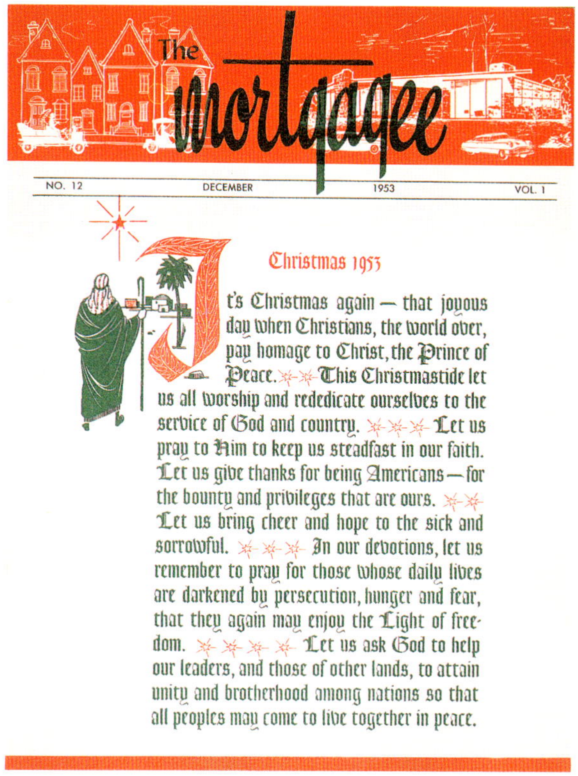

The mortgagee

NO. 12 | DECEMBER | 1953 | VOL. 1

Christmas 1953

It's Christmas again — that joyous day when Christians, the world over, pay homage to Christ, the Prince of Peace. This Christmastide let us all worship and rededicate ourselves to the service of God and country. Let us pray to Him to keep us steadfast in our faith. Let us give thanks for being Americans — for the bounty and privileges that are ours. Let us bring cheer and hope to the sick and sorrowful. In our devotions, let us remember to pray for those whose daily lives are darkened by persecution, hunger and fear, that they again may enjoy the Light of freedom. Let us ask God to help our leaders, and those of other lands, to attain unity and brotherhood among nations so that all peoples may come to live together in peace.

One of Austin's ideas for the rapidly expanding company was *The Mortgagee*, an in-house publication instituted to help unify T. J. Bettes. The December 1953 issue celebrated the first anniversary of its publication.

cated in warehousing mortgages for mortgage bankers, so you had to kind of educate them. I remember going to New York in 1954 or 1955 with a bundle of loans to what is now Citibank, putting those loans in their bank, and going home with two or three million dollars. It was the first time they had ever warehoused mortgage loans. I did the same thing at J. P. Morgan. It was their first time, too."

Torrey James Bettes never lived to see the company benefit from the expanded credit lines. He died in May 1949 at the age of 62. Still, he had the satisfaction of building the company from a two-room office into a regional giant that at the time of his death claimed to be the largest privately owned mortgage company in the country. According to the book *Men of Achievement*, published a year before his death, the T. J. Bettes Company operated seven branch offices in Texas, Louisiana, and Arkansas and employed 300 persons and 150 representatives and agents. It serviced over 50,000 accounts for individual customers, which represented a servicing portfolio of $125 million. The company's investors included 230 life insurance companies, banks, and institutional investors.

But the numbers reflected only one measure of achievement. At the center of those statistics was the vision of T. J. Bettes, a man who seized opportunities and made them profitable. For 13 years he guided a company that excelled in both sales and servicing, and made Bettes a respected name in mortgage banking.

It was a foregone conclusion that John Austin would follow T. J. Bettes as president. Even before his death, Bettes had turned a substantial portion of the company's management over to the new executive vice president. Torrey Bettes' widow, Ruth, became chairman of the board, but her supervision was minimal. The ambitious Austin had a free hand in charting the company's course toward greater growth. "John Austin," says Bray, "was a very outgoing person. He was one of those 'good time Charlies.' And there's no question he built the Bettes organization." Others who worked with Austin describe him as having been quick-minded and extremely bright as well as self-focused and greedy.

Confident about his goals for expansion, Austin's first major decision was to automate the company's accounting system in 1950. The manual system, struggling to keep up with current levels of production, was hopelessly inadequate to handle additional volume. A mortgage banking company in Jacksonville, Florida, pointed to the future by becoming one of the first in the nation to automate. Austin's friendship with a principal in that company provided the Bettes Company with the opportunity for a closer look at the new technology. Austin liked what he saw. Less than a year after the fact-finding trip to Florida, the T. J. Bettes Company tossed out its manual ledger system and converted to IBM punch cards. "That was a period of time," says John Butler, "when we were making loans left and right. We never could have handled the volume of servicing that we got into without the computer. It was our right arm."

The company continued to rely on the latest technology to maintain its edge in servicing. The first programmable computer, an IBM 650, was installed in 1959. But the big leap forward was in 1963, when the company bought an NCR 315. This machine's ability to store data on magnetic strips made the punch card system obsolete. Equally significant was the system's remote inquiry capability, which gave Bettes' branch offices, now expanded into California and Oklahoma, direct access to the computer. "We had a branch in Oklahoma City and a branch in Los Angeles," says E. G. Bray, who was vice president and manager of data processing at the time, "and both of those offices were tied into the system. This was the first time, as far as I know, that any mortgage company had ever had remote access to a data base. We also had a device that took branch payment cards, read the data, and transmitted the information to Houston. I believe that was the first time that was ever done by a mortgage company."

The data processing department was preparing in 1962 for the advanced technology that was to come to the company in 1963 with an NCR 315 computer, which made the punch card system obsolete.

The company organized T. J. Bettes of California to take advantage of the rapidly expanding residential construction in Southern California. One day there would be citrus groves to the edge of the mountains, and a few days later they were bulldozed away.

It was the entrepreneurially oriented Dallas branch in 1952 that set the stage for the company's greatest expansion. One of Dallas' largest builders, Centex, put together a large construction project in San Diego and asked the Bettes Company to handle the mortgage loan business. The Dallas branch manager, Everett Mattson, agreed to participate for what he thought would be a temporary, one-shot deal. As a precautionary measure, a separate company called T. J. Bettes of California was organized. "We didn't know if the California venture was going to work out," says John Butler, "and we didn't want to jeopardize the main Bettes Company if it didn't."

Initially it was strictly a makeshift operation. According to Jim Wooten, "we had no office or facilities in San Diego. So, we took all the plats and plans and filled out all the applications at our Dallas branch and got all that ready to take back and file with the San Diego FHA office, so we could get commitments before starting construction." The demand for housing exceeded all expectations. In one two-week period, Centex sold 325 houses. "Residential construction in Southern California," says Henry Winkler, "was going like crazy. I used to go out there around Anaheim and one day you'd see all these orange groves. Two days later they'd be gone, bulldozed down to make way for a new subdivision. That's how fast it was developing. And we were in on it."

The Southern California building frenzy prompted T. J. Bettes of California to open a Los Angeles office in January 1954. Jack L. Lee, a Dallas branch executive who helped run the San Diego project, was named vice president and branch manager. Another reason the California market proved so lucrative was that Gene Wallace, real estate vice president for Republic Bank, was "lending bucketsful of construction money to big, sophisticated developers. With unlimited construction money from Republic Bank," says E. G. Bray, "there was no way in the world we could fail. We just had to find builders. And everybody was building tract housing."

In 1955, T. J. Bettes of California solidified its position by purchasing Pacific Mortgage Company, a small Los Angeles company that gave Bettes increased

Encouraged by early success, T. J. Bettes Company of California expanded west in 1955 to Hawaii. The Honolulu office prepared an elaborate publication, spiral-bound with original photographs, to promote the sale of the islands' real estate.

There was a great deal of expansion going on in every direction.

access to builders and investors. "We were newcomers," says Bray. "Other than the fact we had Republic's money, we didn't have much else going for us. But buying an old, established company brought along certain relationships." At a branch managers' meeting in March 1955, Jack Lee reported that according to the records of the Los Angeles VA office, Bettes of California made more GI loans in the state than any other mortgage company. Max Bates, branch manager for the recently opened San Francisco office, said his main problem was lack of space, and he planned to move to "larger quarters and also open a sub-office in Redwood City to facilitate loan processing in that area." After only three years of operation, the California venture claimed more than 30,000 mortgages in its servicing portfolio.

Spurred by this early burst of success, T. J. Bettes Company of California initiated a concerted expansion program. Besides San Diego, Los Angeles, and San Francisco, they opened branches in Bakersfield, Fresno, Sacramento, and Santa Ana. In 1955, Bettes expanded west to Honolulu, Hawaii, and then east to Phoenix and Tucson, Arizona.

The Houston-based T. J. Bettes Company was also growing. In 1953, it bought W. R. Johnston & Co., the largest mortgage banker in Oklahoma. Bettes also opened branches in New Orleans, Louisiana, and Albuquerque, New Mexico.

The Texas branches, however, were the ones that made the largest contribution to the company's growing loan portfolio. One deal in particular demonstrated the strength of the Houston economy and that city's flair for dramatic dealmaking. In a state where project size and ego size are often closely connected, developer Frank W. Sharp organized Sharpstown, a subdivision in southwest Houston guaranteed to satisfy both. The development called for a capital investment of $400 million and the participation of 60 homebuilders to construct 25,000 houses. At a preliminary meeting for the builders in 1955, Bettes Company vice president

Certificate No. 1
For - 8 - Shares
Issued to THOMAS B. WARD
Dated May 4, 1961
From whom transferred
Dated 19
No. Original Certificate | No. Original Shares | No. of Shares Transferred
Received Certificate No. for Shares this day of 19

INCORPORATED UNDER THE LAWS OF THE STATE OF ARIZONA
1
- 8 -
BETTES INSURANCE AGENCY
CAPITAL STOCK $1,000,000.00 • 10,000 SHARES • PAR VALUE $100.00 EACH
This Certifies that THOMAS B. WARD is the owner of - - EIGHT - - Shares of the Capital Stock of BETTES INSURANCE AGENCY transferable only on the books of the Corporation in person or by duly authorized Attorney upon surrender of this Certificate properly endorsed.
Witness the Seal of the Corporation and the signatures of its duly authorized officers
Dated May 4, 1961
SECRETARY PRESIDENT

Certificate No. 2
For - 2 - Shares
Issued to WILLIAM A. HAMLIN
Dated May 4, 1961
From whom transferred
Dated 19
No. Original Certificate | No. Original Shares | No. of Shares Transferred
Received Certificate No. for Shares this day of 19

INCORPORATED UNDER THE LAWS OF THE STATE OF ARIZONA
2
- 2 -
BETTES INSURANCE AGENCY
CAPITAL STOCK $1,000,000.00 • 10,000 SHARES • PAR VALUE $100.00 EACH
This Certifies that WILLIAM A. HAMLIN is the owner of - - TWO - - Shares of the Capital Stock of BETTES INSURANCE AGENCY transferable only on the books of the Corporation in person or by duly authorized Attorney upon surrender of this Certificate properly endorsed.
Witness the Seal of the Corporation and the signatures of its duly authorized officers
Dated May 4, 1961
SECRETARY PRESIDENT

With the westward expansion of the mortgage banking business, the insurance business also expanded. Certificates no. 1 and no. 2 reflect the western organization of the Bettes Insurance Agency.

B. B. Adkins was invited to discuss mortgage financing for the project.

The T. J. Bettes Company finally confronted its need for office space in 1956 by purchasing an eight-story building from First City National Bank. Located at 201 Main Street, the historic structure represented an imposing part of Houston's past. The first section was built in 1907, with a later addition constructed in 1923. The grandeur of the lobby, lined with two rows of ornate Corinthian columns, must have fit John Austin's vision of the company, which by now was the country's largest mortgage banker. The company spent 12 months and $500,000 before moving into its spacious new headquarters, renamed the Bettes Building. For the first time in many years, the T. J. Bettes Company was consolidated under one roof. "It had a two-story lobby with a balcony," says John Butler, who worked on the building's renovation. "It was quite impressive entering this massive room with its two rows of columns. We put in overhead lighting to enhance its effectiveness and show off the cornice and other fine architectural detailing. It was a beautifully built building."

The Bettes newsletter, *The Mortgagee*, first published in 1953, offered another source of prestige and visibility for the company. As the magazine's second editor, former vice president William H. Laird communicated the corporate message with flair and enthusiasm. Former executive vice president James W. Pickup remembers Laird later, in the early 1970s, as "a

Sharpstown Center under construction. Houston Metropolitan Research Center, Houston Public Library.

Developer Frank Sharp organized Sharpstown in southwest Houston in the mid-1950s. Houston Metropolitan Research Center, Houston Public Library.

quiet, reserved fellow who practically ran a one-man show. He wrote for the magazine prolifically and published it religiously."

The company gained additional prominence in 1956 when the Mortgage Bankers Association elected John F. Austin national president at its 43rd annual convention in Chicago. His election marked the beginning of a strong Association presence for the company. Two more individuals from the Bettes organization, Everett Mattson and Jim Wooten, eventually served as national presidents.

The First National Bank Building, shown in this 1924 photograph, was purchased by the T. J. Bettes Company in 1956 for much-needed office space. The site and building had a long and illustrious association with Houston banking. Houston Metropolitan Research Center, Houston Public Library.

A

A. The corner at Main and Franklin, seen in this turn-of-the-century photograph, was in the key business section of Houston. The remodeled structure was occupied by First National Bank from 1883 to 1904; it was the forerunner of the building T. J. Bettes bought. The building to the right contained the private bank of T. W. House and Company.

B

B. The steel framework in the background is that of the eight-story building for First National Bank. A temporary building had been erected just behind at Fannin and Franklin streets.

C

C. The impressive new building, only 25 feet wide, was completed in 1905. The building's long facade is on Franklin Street from Main to Fannin.

D

D. A 1909 view southward on Main Street shows, at left, work in progress to enlarge the narrow, original bank building by 50 feet of new frontage. The steel structures in the distance are those of the Scanlan Building at Preston Avenue and the Goggan Building.

E

E. The First National Bank Building as it appeared after construction of the addition was completed. Over a 50-year period the building was enlarged three times. It had much of its original looks when the Bettes Company purchased it from First City National Bank in 1956.

The main floor of the old First National Bank Building was what John Austin envisioned as a proper place to conduct business for the Bettes Company, by that time the country's largest mortgage banker.

Bettes' leaders were always prominent at mortgage bankers' meetings. Under the "Welcome" sign at the Houston Mortgage Bankers' open house of 1958 are, from left to right, Henry DuPre, E. G. Bray, and Henry Winkler.

By the end of the 1950s, mortgage banking no longer offered the challenges that John Austin needed. Full of restless energy, he shifted his primary business interest to real estate development. "You always want to get bigger," says E. G. Bray, "and there's always another opportunity. I guess that's the driving force of all entrepreneurs."

There were, however, other traits that influenced John Austin. "I always felt John liked brinkmanship," says Jim Wooten. "He liked to get into tight places and see if he could extricate himself. Plus, I think he got into a midlife crisis and started chasing girls and spending money and being a big shot. I think he got a lot of power and a lot of recognition awfully fast, and it became difficult for him to handle."

As the company grew in size, Ruth Bettes conceded more and more authority to John Austin, who was able to provide her with an income that kept pace with her increasingly lavish lifestyle. Now a doting grandmother, she reportedly added a $35,000 nursery to her River Oaks home. She also bought a ranch stocked with fine show horses to indulge her oldest granddaughter's equestrian passion. One Bettes executive described her corporate involvement this way: "The company was prospering and making enough money for her to spend, so why mess with a goose that keeps laying golden eggs."

John Austin's course was set.

Unfortunately, the eggs laid by the Bettes Company's real estate investments in the early sixties were anything but golden. The economic downturn that crippled Wallace Investments hit T. J. Bettes equally hard. "We were financing builders, subdivisions, and land," says E. G. Bray, "with short-term money. We sold lots and tracts to builders at low interest rates. Then our cost of money suddenly started going up, and that put us in a double squeeze. That's what kills you. We had all these assets and stuff sold to builders, and they couldn't perform. The next thing you know we had a lot of liability. We probably had $100 million worth of stuff tied up in questionable assets, mainly real estate. It just wasn't moving."

This, in turn, put the squeeze on the company's cash flow requirements, a burden the profitable mortgage banking operation was unable to meet. To help relieve the demand for cash, T. J. Bettes sold the Admiral Fire Insurance Company in 1963 to Wallace Investments for $2.5 million.

Still another, more dramatic reversal in the company's fortunes was the sale of the Bettes Building that same year to a New York real estate investment trust for $3 million. After only seven years of ownership, the T. J. Bettes Company suffered the indignity of leasing

Ruth Bettes conceded more authority to John Austin as the company grew. Here he presents her a scroll making her a member of "The Royal Order of Well-wishers."

Ruth's Silhouette

Ruth, granddaughter of Mrs. T. J. Bettes and the daughter of Mrs. Roger (Bette Bettes) Daily, in her first year of training and one of the younger riders in the Thoroughbred Horse Show Circuit. She is shown riding Silhouette, owned by Mrs. Bettes. This photograph was reproduced in the Bettes corporate magazine *The Mortgagee*.

office space in the building that once symbolized its power and prestige.

Excessive demands for cash were felt throughout the company. The Dallas branch, for example, had to sell several tracts of land before they had an opportunity to become profitable. "John pressured me into selling off a corner to somebody for $75,000," says Jim Wooten recalling one piece of property that he was forced to sell. "I practically begged him not to do it, but he said we had to have the money. The person who bought that corner turned around six or seven months later and sold it to Exxon for $200,000. And that became a pattern."

Wooten, now a senior executive reporting directly to Austin, considered the company's business problems a personal challenge. Twenty years of successful management experience led him to believe that he could reverse the company's destructive direction. But his efforts to put "realism" into the corporate leadership failed. When Wooten realized individual discussions with John Austin weren't working, he enlisted the aid of William F. Keesler, the former senior vice president of the First National Bank of Boston, elected to the board of directors of the Bettes companies in 1963.

Jim Wooten, rising in the Bettes organization, is seen in this 1960 photograph with Dallas homebuilder George Chapman, center, and Bettes vice president Bernie Snoddy, right.

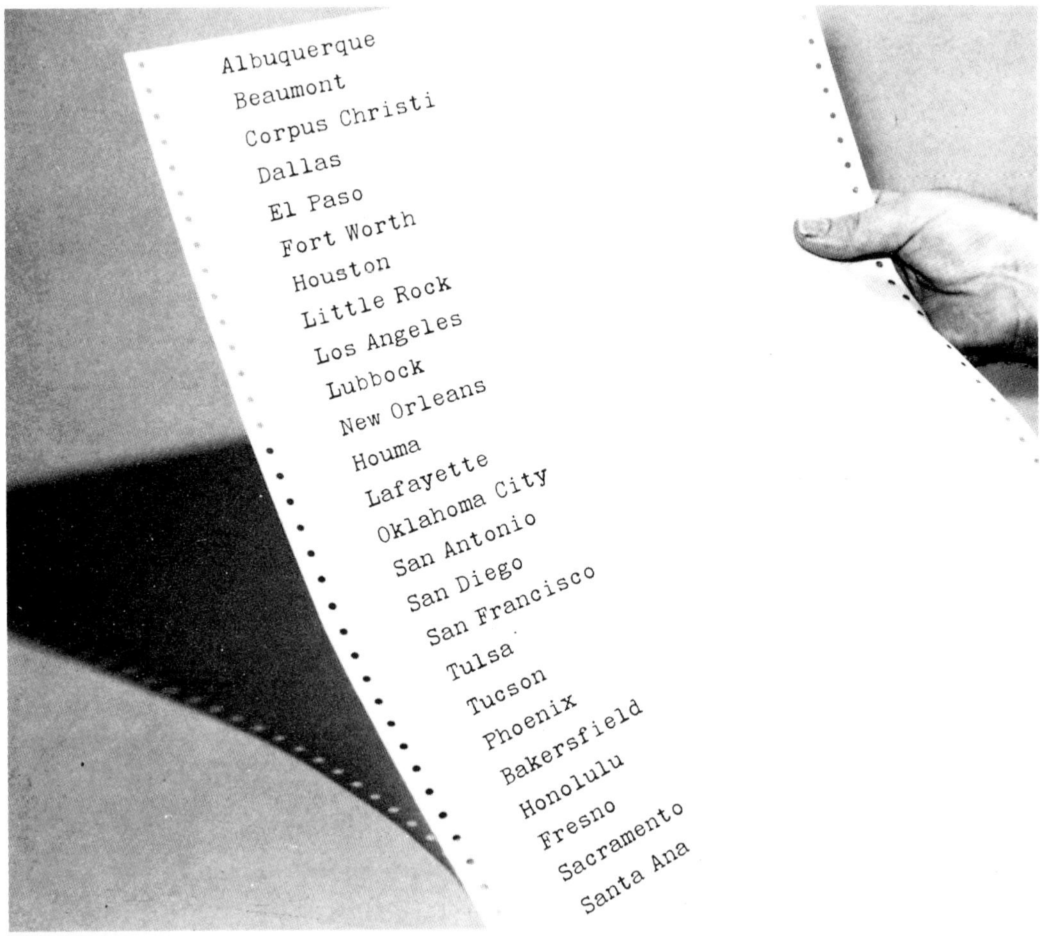

TWENTY-FIVE REASONS

why Bettes excels as a mortgage loan correspondent

Offices in 25 major cities in eight states . . . important reasons why Bettes excels as a mortgage loan correspondent. Competent Bettes loan production personnel have both the ability and the judgment to outline projects realistically and with authority. And every Bettes office has aggressive, knowledgeable management and a staff that can give you an honest, accurate representation of loan prospects with the advantages of loan diversification in the nation's big growth areas.

Bettes' professional mortgage servicing specialists have experienced a most favorable delinquency ratio over the years. Advanced electronic equipment (with remote inquiry) and a full-time technical systems staff let Bettes provide the information you need **faster!** So, for a dependable mortgage loan correspondent, consult Bettes — the world's most experienced company in the Mortgage Field.

T. J. BETTES COMPANY

THE BETTES BUILDING, 201 MAIN STREET • FINANCING COMMUNITY DEVELOPMENT

The back cover ad of the September 1964 *Mortgagee* was boastful. However, "twenty-five reasons" were not enough to help John Austin keep the company going.

Taking an early retirement from the bank in 1965, Keesler was elected vice chairman of the board, a member of the executive committee, and a full-time consultant to the companies. Titles notwithstanding, Keesler's attempts to redirect Austin were also unsuccessful. "John Austin's course was set," says Jim Wooten. "He was the captain of the ship, and there was no way to turn the bow around." Ruth Bettes, who theoretically held the reins of power as chairman of the board and principal stockholder, also failed to alter Austin's direction.

The fact that Austin kept the company going as long as he did was a tribute to his considerable skill at juggling cash, credit, and assets. But ultimately the company couldn't borrow any more money, and the performance abruptly ended. As in the case of Wallace Investments, it was a bank that dropped the final curtain. "John Austin," says John Butler, "was quite a buddy of Judge Elkins, who was the head of First City National Bank. Because of that friendship, the bank

May Become No. 1

Lomas & Nettleton Co. Buying California Firm

The Lomas & Nettleton Co. today is expected to announce the purchase of a California firm which will make Lomas & Nettleton the biggest mortgage banking concern in the nation.

Lomas & Nettleton is acquiring the T. J. Bettes Co. Details of the transaction were not available at Lomas & Nettleton headquarters here.

With the acquisition, Lomas & Nettleton will have a mortgage portfolio of approximately $1.5 billion.

Lomas & Nettleton services mortgages throughout the United States for the Metropolitan Life Insurance Co. and various savings banks. Metropolitan Life is by far its biggest client.

Lomas & Nettleton, which has its headquarters at Orange and Court Streets, was founded here in 1894.

Prior to the acquisition being announced today, it was the sixth biggest mortgage banking company in the nation.

Kidney Recipients Are 'Satsfactory' At Yale-New Haven

Connecticut's two newest kidney transplant recipients were

Lake Is Searched In New Hampshire For West Havener

MEREDITH, N.H. (UPI)—A search was underway today at Lake Waukewan in Meredith for Anthony Ciaffe, 56, of 45 Hillside Ave., West Haven, Conn.

Ciaffe was knocked from a boat Sunday night in a collision.

He was a passenger in the boat of Joseph Miller of Branford, Conn., which reportedly collided with a boat driven by William Fairbanks, 18, of Natick, Mass.

This article in a New Haven newspaper anticipates that Lomas & Nettleton would take advantage of the rare business opportunity and buy the combined servicing portfolios of the T. J. Bettes companies. Reprinted with permission of *The New Haven Register*.

Shortly after the acquisition of the T. J. Bettes companies' servicing portfolios, the Lomas & Nettleton sign was erected atop the Bettes Building in Houston.

The data processing staff of the world's largest mortgage banking operation, the T. J. Bettes Company, at the time of its acquisition by Lomas & Nettleton in 1968.

lent us more money than they should have. They used as poor judgment as did Mr. Austin." In fact, the bank had honored several million dollars in overdrafts before it decided to take action against the company. In 1967 it assigned one of its officers to physically move into Bettes headquarters to oversee operating procedures and generally act as trustee. Their objective was to prevent the company from filing for bankruptcy, which would jeopardize its primary asset, the mortgage loan portfolio. They succeeded. A year later, Lomas & Nettleton Financial Corporation took advantage of a rare business opportunity and bought the combined servicing portfolio of the Bettes Texas and California companies. On August 1, 1968, the world's largest and most efficient mortgage banking operation, unscathed by the Bettes companies' other financial problems, was safely in the hands of Al Rohnstedt and Jess Hay.

46

Tops In Nation

Lomas & Nettleton Co. To Be Mortgage Leader

A New Haven-based company is going to become the biggest mortgage banking firm in the nation.

The Lomas & Nettleton Co. confirmed Monday afternoon that it is purchasing the mortgage-servicing portfolios of the T. J. Bettes Co. of California and the T. J. Bettes Co. of Houston. The purchase price was not revealed, but is expected to be in the range of $10 to $15 million.

$2.4 Billion

The acquisition will give Lomas & Nettleton a mortgage portfolio of approximately $2.4 billion. It currently has a portfolio of over $800 million, making it the eighth largest real estate financing concern in the country, while the Bettes companies rank No. 1, with a portfolio in excess of $1.5 billion.

Lomas & Nettleton, which has its headquarters at Orange and Court Streets, is making the purchase through an affiliated company, the Lomas & Nettleton Financial Corp., of Dallas.

The transaction is expected to be closed next month. The combined companies will have 900 employes and offices in Connecticut, Texas, California, Colorado, Arizona, Florida, New Mexico, Oklahoma, Arkansas and Louisiana.

The Bettes portfolios will be managed by a new company, Lomas & Nettleton West, which will have its headquarters in Houston. Albert N. Rohnstedt, chairman of the board and chief executive officer of Lomas & Nettleton, will hold these titles in Lomas & Nettleton West.

Acquire Agencies

In addition to buying the mortgage portfolios of the Bettes companies, Lomas & Nettleton will also acquire their insurance agencies.

The sale has been approved by all of the companies involved, and is now subject to invest or approval.

The acquisition was announced in a joint statment by Rohnstedt, who lives in Greenwich; Jess Hay, president of the Lomas & Nettletown Financial Corp., and Everett Mattson, president of the two Bettes companies.

Lomas & Nettleton was founded in New Haven in 1894. It services mortgages throughout the United States for the nation's biggest insurance companies, including Metropolitan Life and Aetna, and for banks.

Lomas & Nettleton stock, traded over the counter, has more than doubled recently, going from a 1968 low of $4.50 per share to Monday's closing price of 9⅝ bid and 9¾ asked Monday's bid price was up ¼.

An article from the New Haven newspaper asserted that, with the acquisition of T. J. Bettes Company's mortgage servicing portfolios of Houston and California, Lomas & Nettleton became the largest mortgage banking organization in the nation. Beatrice Lomas Gould Archive. Reprinted with permission of *The New Haven Register*.

CHAPTER VI

BIGGER IS BETTER

The acquisition of T. J. Bettes' servicing portfolios signaled the first step toward the company's goal of building a truly national mortgage banking operation. At the annual shareholders meeting in September 1968, Jess Hay publicly declared that intention: "We want to service mortgage banking needs on a nationwide basis, and we are well on our way to realizing this aim." He also announced a 73 percent increase in net income, up from $545,334 in 1967 to $944,649 in 1968.

The turnaround and the Bettes purchase also garnered well-deserved recognition for Hay in the national press. *Fortune* magazine acknowledged his achievement in its October 1968 issue:

> In dire straits three years ago, Lomas & Nettleton Financial Corp., a Dallas-based mortgage-banking and real-estate company, asked Jess Hay, [34], to take over as president. The young lawyer, who had a bookkeeper's job while working his way through S.M.U. Law School (first in his class), quickly unloaded $26 million in low-yielding assets, cut overhead costs in half, and refinanced the company's debt. From a $1,500,000 loss in its 1966 fiscal year, L&N posted a $945,000 profit this year. Now Hay, seeking new horizons, has bought the mortgage-servicing portfolios of the T. J. Bettes companies, making L&N the biggest mortgage-banking firm in the world (servicing more than $2 billion in loans). Next target: expanding operations in the Southeast and Northwest.

Lomas & Nettleton Financial Corporation's sudden leap toward mortgage banking prominence and increased profitability didn't go unnoticed at home, either. On March 3, 1969, the directors of both First National Bank in Dallas and LNFC approved a merger proposal that called for the purchase of 80 percent of LNFC's common stock for about $66 million. "The price was attractive relative to the market," says John Sexton. "The board looked favorably on the deal in view of all the problems the company had had up to that point. There was a history of dissatisfaction, and I'm sure there were several directors who looked at it as a way out. The bank was a great bank, and their offer was a great out.

"From management's standpoint, it made sense, but it was not a 'do-or-die' deal. From the bank's viewpoint it was pretty exciting. They approached us."

But the transaction, "contingent on all necessary approvals by appropriate authorities," failed to obtain government approval and was called off three months later. In a joint communique on June 10, First National Chairman Robert H. Stewart III and Jess Hay said that "delays in getting a decision from the United States Department of Justice and {the imposition of} certain regulatory requirements left no reasonable alternative."

The deal may have died, but the bank's confidence in Lomas & Nettleton did not. Intense scrutiny of the company and its operations during the merger attempt convinced First National that L&N was the kind of investment that should be added to their portfolio. Through their affiliated securities company, First

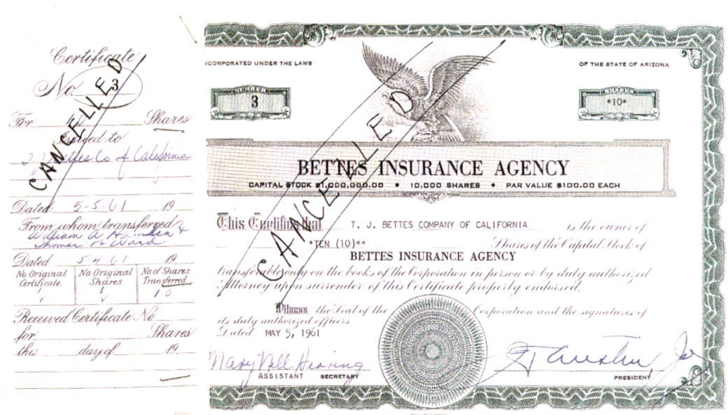

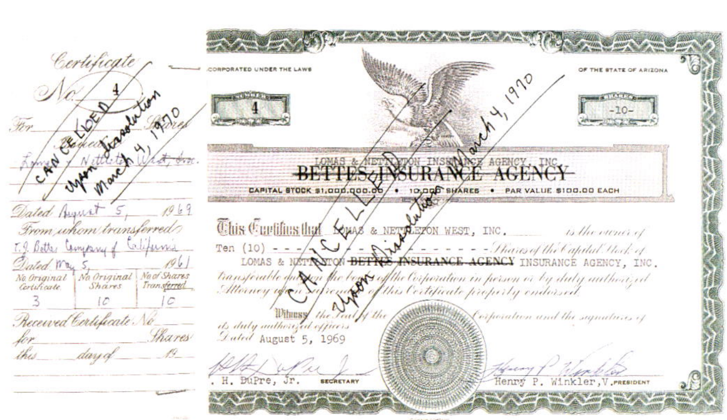

In addition to purchasing the mortgage portfolios of the Bettes companies, Lomas & Nettleton also acquired their insurance agencies. Certificate 3 shows that T. J. Bettes Company of California owned ten shares of the Bettes Insurance Agency. Certificate 4 shows the acquisition of those shares by Lomas & Nettleton West, Inc., on August 5, 1969, with the Bettes Insurance Agency showing acquisition by the Lomas & Nettleton Insurance Agency, Inc. Later, on March 4, 1970, Lomas & Nettleton West, Inc., was dissolved.

Adventures in Banking

Hay of Lomas & Nettleton

In dire straits three years ago, Lomas & Nettleton Financial Corp., a Dallas-based mortgage-banking and real-estate company, asked **Jess Hay,** 37, to take over as president. The young lawyer, who had a bookkeeper's job while working his way through S.M.U. Law School (first in his class), quickly unloaded $26 million in low-yielding assets, cut overhead costs in half, and refinanced the company's debt. From a $1,500,000 loss in its 1966 fiscal year, L. & N. posted a $945,000 profit this year. Now Hay, seeking new horizons, has bought the mortgage-servicing portfolios of the T. J. Bettes companies, making L. & N. the biggest mortgage-banking firm in the world (servicing more than $2 billion in loans). Next target: expanding operations in the Southeast and Northwest.

In October 1968, *Fortune* magazine profiled Jess Hay in its "Businessman in the News" section. The article highlighted the financial turnaround at Lomas & Nettleton and the acquisition of the T. J. Bettes companies' mortgage servicing portfolios. Reprinted with permission of *Fortune.*

National purchased approximately 7.5 percent of LNFC's outstanding common stock, making it the largest single owner of L&N stock.

ties, airports, utilities and com- ministrative, recreational and

Lomas & Nettleton Buying Control Of Computer Firm

Jan 8, 1969

The Lomas & Nettleton Finance Corp., of Dallas, announced today an agreement to acquire approximately 60 per cent of the capital stock of National Computer Service, Inc. (NCS), also of Dallas, for $350,000 in cash and 40,000 shares of Lomas & Nettleton common stock.

According to Lomas & Nettleton President Jess Hay, Lomas & Nettleton has also agreed to purchase $600,000 principal amount of NCS convertible subordinated debentures.

Lomas & Nettleton Financial Corp., with its two subsidiaries, the Lomas & Nettleton Co. of New Haven and Lomas & Nettleton West of Houston, is the nation's largest mortgage banking institution and is also engaged in other real estate, finance, and development activities.

NCS provides computer software services and was formed in April, 1968. Its present management group would continue as principal executive officers and directors of NCS.

A wholly owned subsidiary of NCS, Lomas & Nettleton Computer Serivce, Inc. is to enter into a contract to provide all data-processing services necessary for Lomas & Nettleton's banking activities.

Personnel of Lomas & Nettleton now engaged in data processing would be employed by this subsidiary.

Subject to obtaining requisite consents and compliance with applicable security laws, Lomas & Nettleton intends to distribute approximately 20 per cent of the capital stock of NCS to Lomas & Nettleton stockholders as a dividend. The distribution, if approved. would occur in March.

It was also announced that Lomas & Nettleton was considering the redemption in February of all its outstanding 6½ per cent convertible subordinated debentures due 1975.

In addition, Lomas & Nettleton intends to file a registration statement with the Securities and Exchange Commission (SEC) during the first quarter of 1969 for the purpose of registering an issue of convertible subordinated debentures of public offering.

The proceeds of this issue would be used to retire a substantial portion of Lomas and Nettleton's -32 million indebtedness excluding borrowings related to its mortgage banking operation.

In January 1969, Lomas & Nettleton Financial Corporation acquired National Computer Service, Inc., which would aid the parent company's data processing department as well as mark an early attempt to diversify. Beatrice Lomas Gould Archive. Reprinted with permission of *The New Haven Register*.

Withdrawal of the bank's offer permitted LNFC to focus its attention on growth. Unlike the erratic, shoot-from-the-hip push for profits that had characterized the Wallace years, Jess Hay carefully guided the company toward an orderly expansion. "The plan," says John Sexton, "was to make mortgage banking our principal business. Capitalization was the first big step that gave us the wherewithal to pursue that objective. Expanding our capital base really postured us to get more and more into mortgage banking through acquisition."

It put $20 million of additional permanent capitalization into our picture.

The company initiated a financial restructuring in January 1969 by redeeming its 6½ percent subordinated debentures due June 1, 1975, and converting most of them into common stock. In July, the company raised $20 million through a public offering of 6¾ percent convertible subordinated debentures due July 15, 1989. These two events made a substantial contribution to the company's financial strength. "It put," says Jess Hay, "$20 million of additional permanent capital into our picture, and it gave us a capital base of $47 million instead of $27 million."

The capital base wasn't the only part of the company that needed strengthening. Realizing that his skeletal management staff was inadequate to direct the expansion, Hay reached out to those he knew and trusted. Hay's association and friendship with Gene H. Bishop, executive vice president at First National Bank, had begun in the late fifties when he became Hay's personal banker. Well aware of Bishop's financial

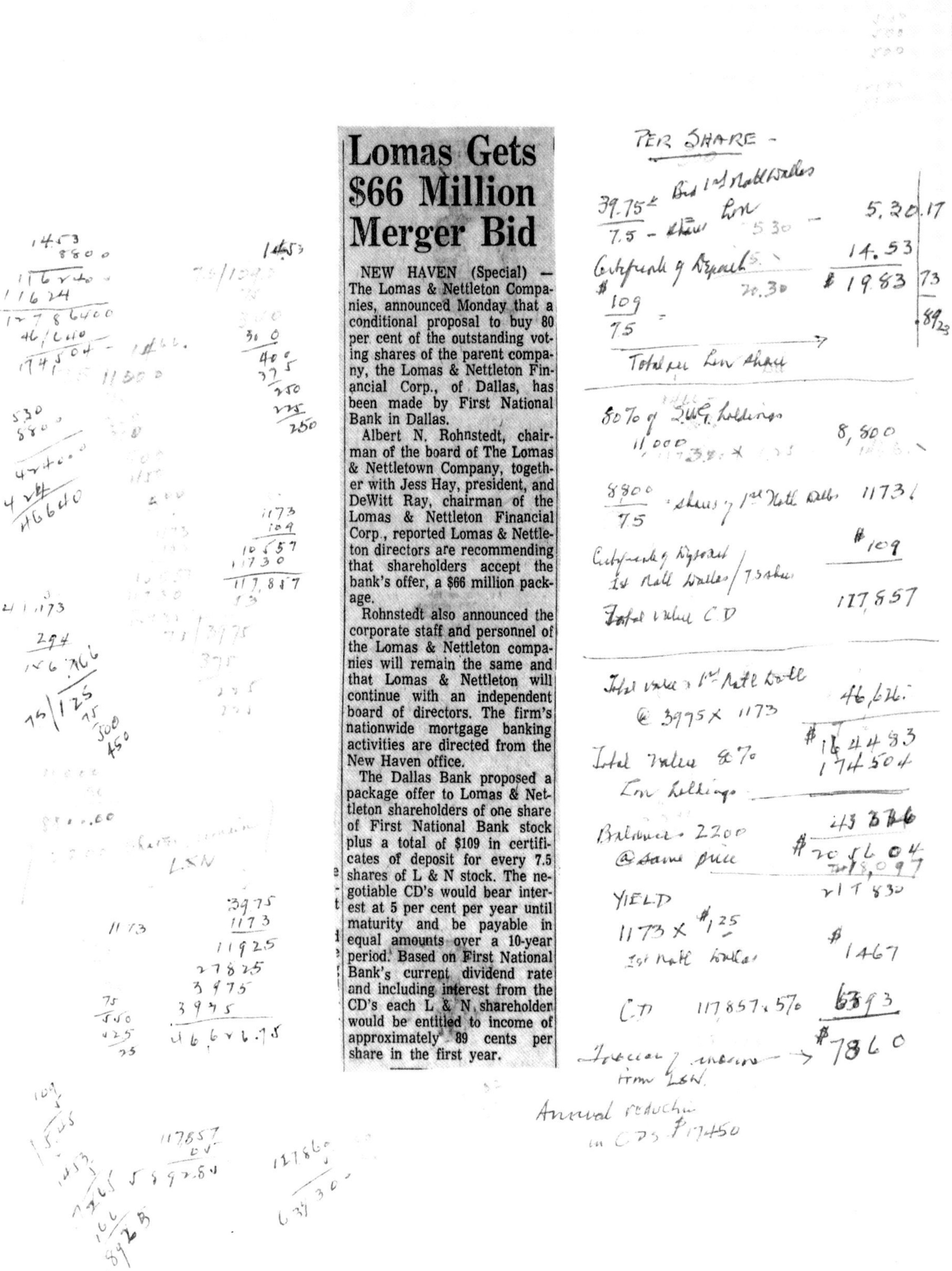

Lomas Gets $66 Million Merger Bid

NEW HAVEN (Special) — The Lomas & Nettleton Companies, announced Monday that a conditional proposal to buy 80 per cent of the outstanding voting shares of the parent company, the Lomas & Nettleton Financial Corp., of Dallas, has been made by First National Bank in Dallas.

Albert N. Rohnstedt, chairman of the board of The Lomas & Nettletown Company, together with Jess Hay, president, and DeWitt Ray, chairman of the Lomas & Nettleton Financial Corp., reported Lomas & Nettleton directors are recommending that shareholders accept the bank's offer, a $66 million package.

Rohnstedt also announced the corporate staff and personnel of the Lomas & Nettleton companies will remain the same and that Lomas & Nettleton will continue with an independent board of directors. The firm's nationwide mortgage banking activities are directed from the New Haven office.

The Dallas Bank proposed a package offer to Lomas & Nettleton shareholders of one share of First National Bank stock plus a total of $109 in certificates of deposit for every 7.5 shares of L & N stock. The negotiable CD's would bear interest at 5 per cent per year until maturity and be payable in equal amounts over a 10-year period. Based on First National Bank's current dividend rate and including interest from the CD's each L & N shareholder would be entitled to income of approximately .89 cents per share in the first year.

With the company's dramatic strides toward mortgage banking prominence, the directors of First National Bank in Dallas offered Lomas & Nettleton Financial Corporation a merger proposal. The notations are by Sydney Gould, who had an ever-ready pencil for figures. Beatrice Lomas Gould Archive. Reprinted with permission of *The New Haven Register.*

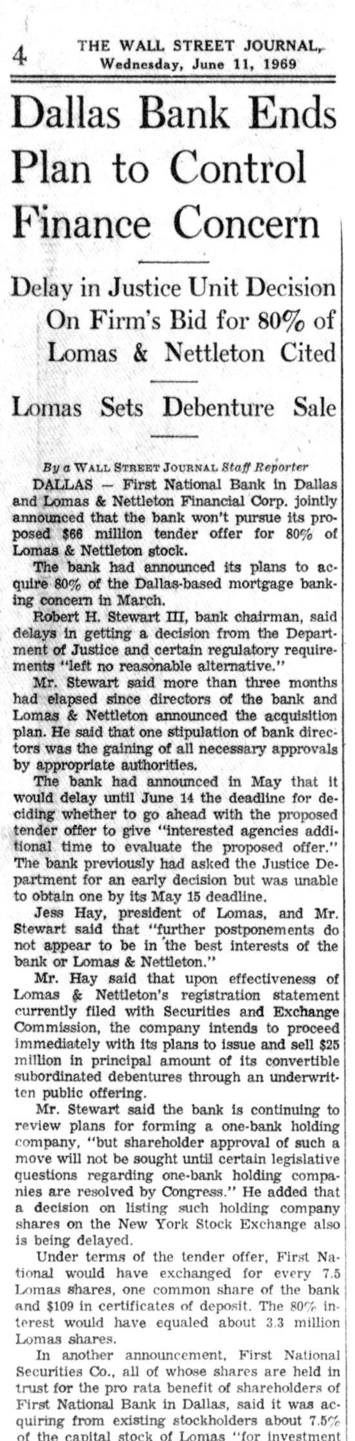

4 THE WALL STREET JOURNAL, Wednesday, June 11, 1969

Dallas Bank Ends Plan to Control Finance Concern

Delay in Justice Unit Decision On Firm's Bid for 80% of Lomas & Nettleton Cited

Lomas Sets Debenture Sale

By a WALL STREET JOURNAL *Staff Reporter*

DALLAS — First National Bank in Dallas and Lomas & Nettleton Financial Corp. jointly announced that the bank won't pursue its proposed $66 million tender offer for 80% of Lomas & Nettleton stock.

The bank had announced its plans to acquire 80% of the Dallas-based mortgage banking concern in March.

Robert H. Stewart III, bank chairman, said delays in getting a decision from the Department of Justice and certain regulatory requirements "left no reasonable alternative."

Mr. Stewart said more than three months had elapsed since directors of the bank and Lomas & Nettleton announced the acquisition plan. He said that one stipulation of bank directors was the gaining of all necessary approvals by appropriate authorities.

The bank had announced in May that it would delay until June 14 the deadline for deciding whether to go ahead with the proposed tender offer to give "interested agencies additional time to evaluate the proposed offer." The bank previously had asked the Justice Department for an early decision but was unable to obtain one by its May 15 deadline.

Jess Hay, president of Lomas, and Mr. Stewart said that "further postponements do not appear to be in the best interests of the bank or Lomas & Nettleton."

Mr. Hay said that upon effectiveness of Lomas & Nettleton's registration statement currently filed with Securities and Exchange Commission, the company intends to proceed immediately with its plans to issue and sell $25 million in principal amount of its convertible subordinated debentures through an underwritten public offering.

Mr. Stewart said the bank is continuing to review plans for forming a one-bank holding company, "but shareholder approval of such a move will not be sought until certain legislative questions regarding one-bank holding companies are resolved by Congress." He added that a decision on listing such holding company shares on the New York Stock Exchange also is being delayed.

Under terms of the tender offer, First National would have exchanged for every 7.5 Lomas shares, one common share of the bank and $109 in certificates of deposit. The 80% interest would have equaled about 3.3 million Lomas shares.

In another announcement, First National Securities Co., all of whose shares are held in trust for the pro rata benefit of shareholders of First National Bank in Dallas, said it was acquiring from existing stockholders about 7.5% of the capital stock of Lomas "for investment purposes."

The headline from *The Wall Street Journal* article said it all. The merger proposal was halted. Beatrice Lomas Gould Archive. Reprinted with permission of *The Wall Street Journal.*

talent, Hay was further impressed by the administrative ability he had demonstrated in planning the proposed integration of the two companies. "We needed Gene's strengths," says Hay, "and we were able to provide him with a challenge that we probably could not have offered him earlier. So, it was a happy coincidence."

Jess Hay had served as a mentor to R. Ted Enloe III much as Gene Locke had earlier to Hay. After graduating first in his class from SMU Law School in June 1964, Ted Enloe joined the law firm of Locke, Purnell, Boren, Laney & Neely; on his first day at the office, he wound up working for Hay. A year and a half later, when Hay left the law firm to become president of LNFC, he selected Enloe to succeed him as the compa-

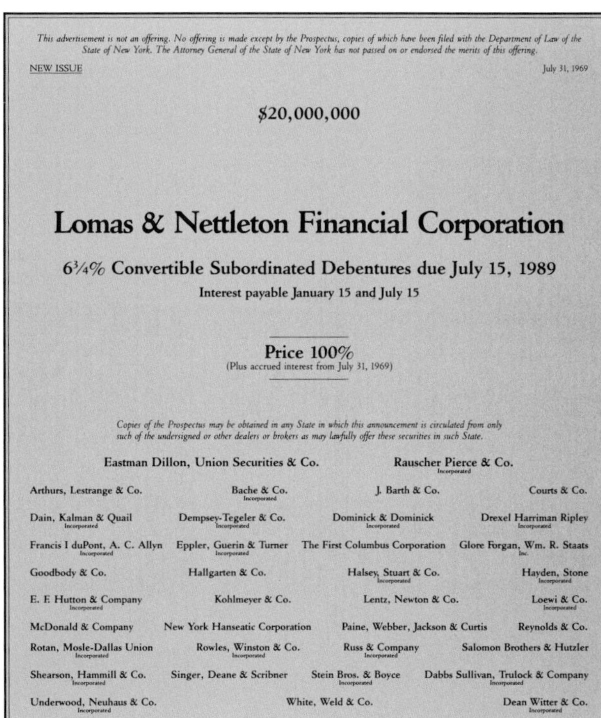

The advertisement for the $20 million raised through a public offering in 1969, part of the financial restructuring that expanded the company's capital base.

The photograph Ted Enloe submitted with his application to law school. Courtesy Southern Methodist University Law School.

ny's corporate secretary. It was clear from the beginning that Hay recognized Enloe's outstanding ability and his capacity for work. H. H. (Buddy) Miller, Jr., former senior executive vice president at L&N Management, Inc., and a friend and close associate of both men, noted several characteristics they shared: "Ted Enloe has a tremendous mind. He compares very favorably with Hay to the extent that he can grasp and understand a problem about as quick as any man I've met. His memory is phenomenal. He can remember numbers and events that took place 15 years ago. Ted is a hard-working, intensely competitive guy who, like Hay, can probably get fourteen hours' work out of a ten-hour day."

On October 7, 1969, Lomas & Nettleton announced the reorganization of its executive structure. Jess Hay was named chairman and retained his post as chief executive officer. Gene H. Bishop was elected president and Ted Enloe executive vice president. Former chairman DeWitt T. Ray, Sr., became chairman of the executive committee. Albert N. Rohnstedt, who continued as head of mortgage banking operations, was given the additional title of vice chairman of the board.

Lomas & Nettleton Mortgage Investors

The executive reorganization was timed to coincide with the beginning of the company's renewed interest in short-term lending. It also marked the beginning of expansion into businesses that contributed to LNFC's goal of becoming a national leader in real estate financial services. "The real estate investment trust [REIT]," says Jess Hay, "under existing tax laws was a vehicle ideally suited for the accumulation of capital to provide short-term financing to builders, developers, and real estate investors.

"We created Lomas & Nettleton Mortgage Investors in 1969 for the purpose of making short-term construction and development loans, thereby broadening our capacity to serve the financial needs of major real estate developers. The idea was that the developer could come to us, and we could provide his short-term requirements. We could also handle his need for permanent financing and through that process attract more business at both ends." It was ideal for generating additional profits from both new and established customers and expanding a financial service closely connected to mortgage banking. "We felt it would be synergistic with our other businesses," says Ted Enloe. "One would tend to feed the other, and it would give our developers one-stop shopping."

The vehicle that made short-term lending so pop-

In October 1969, Ted Enloe, left, and Gene Bishop, right, joined Jess Hay at Lomas & Nettleton.
Betty Jo and Jess Hay Archives.

ular in the late 1960s was a relatively new entity known as the real estate investment trust. According to a law passed in 1960, a REIT that distributed at least 90 percent of its income to its shareholders was not required to pay taxes on that income. To qualify for this treatment, 75 percent of the trust's gross income had to come from real estate sources. But it was the tight money crunch in 1968 and 1969 that made REITs blossom. Commercial banks, the traditional source for short-term real estate financing, had little money available. About the same time, security analysts discovered that the two largest trusts had been growing at compounded annual rates of more than 20 percent. Both were selling at better than two and a half times their book value. The surge in prices and tight money conditions encouraged a rush of new underwritings. "Everybody jumped on the bandwagon," says John Sexton. "The real estate investment trust became the darling of Wall Street. Billions of dollars were raised. It fit us very well because we were in that kind of lending, but a lot of those who jumped into it didn't have any idea what the hell they were doing."

The withdrawal of First National Bank's acquisition offer cleared the way for Lomas & Nettleton to put together a real estate trust. On June 26, 1969, Lomas & Nettleton Mortgage Investors (LNMI) was organized as a Massachusetts business trust. Dominick & Dominick and Rauscher Pierce & Co. were selected to manage the initial public offering of the trust's shares of beneficial interest.

One of the REITs' most troublesome features, and an area of great concern for Jess Hay and Dominick & Dominick vice president James Callery, was the lack of responsibility for investments on the part of the trust's management.

"Ours was different," says John Sexton. "The first thing we did was devise a formula for sharing the risk. LNFC would retain at least 10 percent and no more

On October 7, 1969, Lomas & Nettleton announced an executive restructuring. Seated, left to right: R. Ted Enloe III, executive vice president; Jess Hay, chairman and chief executive officer; Gene H. Bishop, president. Standing, left to right: DeWitt T. Ray, Sr., chairman of the executive committee; Albert N. Rohnstedt, continuing as head of mortgage banking and now also vice chairman of the board.
Betty Jo and Jess Hay Archives.

than one-third of each loan and would participate the balance to the trust. That's a significant difference because the manager, under the stated formula, shared the risk involved in each investment. I don't believe any other trust did that. We didn't select good assets for the Financial Corp. and put the turkeys in the trust."

Despite LNMI's formula for accountability and emphasis on conservative loan policies, investors were difficult to find. To a large extent, the problem was timing. "If we had gotten there sooner," says Ted Enloe, "when things were really hot it would have been easier, but we were all tied up with the First National transaction. So, we were late to the party. By the time we got there, the market was flooded with new trusts."

There was another disadvantage over which L&N had more control but which it refused to change because it went to the heart of their low-risk loan philosophy. The moderate growth projected by LNMI's conservative lending policies had trouble competing against the earning projections of the fast-track trusts. "A lot of other REITs," says Enloe, "were promising much faster growth. They were leveraging five, six, and seven to one. We said we aren't going to leverage more than two or three to one. We were criticized for that, for being stodgy and too conservative. Of course, history proved us to be right. But at the time, all the analysts told us we didn't know what we were doing. They said, 'You've got to get with it, got to get more swing.' It was a tough sell."

The underwriting sales team ended their first tour of 30 to 40 financial institutions without a single sale. This was followed by other tours and more disappointment. Then the underwriters shifted sales strategy, opting to sell a smaller number of shares over a larger market. The bulk of these retail sales came from what James Callery calls the "widows-and-orphans income-oriented trusts," sold primarily through Dominick &

Dominick branch offices and their elderly sales staff. "Boston and Buffalo," says Callery, "had typical Dominick & Dominick offices, a lot of elderly brokers who really knew the game. I remember walking into the Boston office, and the first thing that greeted you was the cane rack, because a lot of these men were in their sixties and seventies. But they knew their clients. Most of them held a virtual proxy for what their clients would or would not buy. If they said they would sell it, you could forget it. It was done." The underwriters' extensive national branch and correspondent network produced a total sale of $27 million. On October 14, 1969, LNMI began its short-term lending operation with public offering net proceeds of $24,586,915.

The deviation from recognized lending practices that had brought down Wallace Investments strengthened Jess Hay's resolve to pursue sound lending principles. "There was never any question in my mind," says Hay, "that this was an extremely good business. What happened during the Wallace years was a complete departure from traditional short-term lending concepts. Gene Wallace moved away from those and into the more speculative land-type deals. You can call them 18-month loans if you wish. But if it is going to take 15 or 20 years to develop the property, you really are in a different kind of business. The main contribution that earlier period made to our reentry was to develop some very rigid . . . loan administration policies that really did separate LNMI from all other trusts. . . . These policies related to the type of lending we would do, the type of leverage we would employ, the type of rigid documentation required going into the transaction, and the strict administrative procedures we would follow after the loan started. If you do all those things well, you may occasionally lose some money, but you're not going to get hurt real bad."

. . . *a* very well-controlled operation.

Insights drawn from the company's early years led Hay to mandate and the trustees of LNMI to adopt

In Boston on June 26, 1969, Lomas & Nettleton Mortgage Investors was created for the purpose of making short-term construction and development loans. Left to right. Seated: Al Rohnstedt, Jess Hay, J. D. Francis, and Helmer Johnson. Standing: Dick Danley, David Kelly, Carroll (Buzz) Bennett, James Callery, Gene Bishop, Preston Breed, unidentified man, Joe French, and unidentified man.

three policies that drove and disciplined the trust's operations since 1969. Responsibility for implementing these directives fell to the trust's manager, L&N Management, Inc., a subsidiary of LNFC. The first policy related to investments. Emphasis was placed on short-term construction and development loans with terms of nine to 24 months with the real prospect of repayment within those stated terms. Faithful adherence to this policy produced for LNMI the highest liquidity ratios in the real estate finance industry. The second policy related to financial discipline. The trust's debt-to-capital ratio was limited to 300 percent, though many competitors were employing much higher leverage ratios. The third fundamental policy related to staffing and operations. From its inception, L&N Management, Inc., gave equal weight to underwriting, documentation, and loan administration. This balanced approach—which placed simultaneous, independent, and coordinated emphasis on risk selection, contractual structures, and asset management—was a key contributor to the trust's success in good times and bad. To assure that each leg of the tripod was firmly in place and maintained, Hay relied on Bishop and Enloe to oversee investment decisions, Lanelle Latendresse to oversee loan documentation, closings, and servicing, and H. H. (Buddy) Miller to organize and supervise loan administration.

L&N Management's centralized administration provided the framework for controlling procedures. "Every loan we make," says John Sexton, "we make out of corporate headquarters. We don't let our offices around the country make loans. We don't let franchises make loans for us. We don't let people who don't work for us send loans into the system. We control it very tightly. We inspect every loan we make once a month. It's a very well-controlled operation."

The problems confronting L&N Management's first two employees, Richard E. Danley and Lanelle Latendresse, were daunting. "It was a busy time for us," says Latendresse. "We had to invent how we were going to organize it, just like we did when we started the company." In response to the policy directives of the trustees, three principal areas of responsibility evolved: production and underwriting (risk selection), documentation (making certain that the risk underwritten coincided with the risk actually assumed), and loan administration (making sure that the risk was not increased during the construction or development process). The underwriting department was responsible for producing quality loans for the trust. Its recommendations, supported by detailed financial analyses and appraisals and by cost and physical analyses provided by the loan administration staff, became the basis for loan approvals. Finding developers and builders who needed short-term construction loans was the least of the trust's problems, according to former L&N vice president Richard Danley. When word of LNMI's successful public offering went out, it was all Danley could do to wade through the flood of loan offers coming into the office. Former executive vice president Lanelle Latendresse was responsible for the documentation and servicing of the loans after their approval. The loan administration department physically monitored the progress of construction or development work related to each loan, a task often considered secondary in importance by other lenders but clearly affirmed by LNMI as a function of equal stature to the initial underwriting. Former senior executive vice president Buddy Miller supervised loan administration from the early seventies. His previous experience as the owner of a construction company gave him an edge in tracking loan projects. "If we're going to lend money to developers," said Miller, "we wanted inspection personnel that spoke their language. We should know what our developers' needs are and how to satisfy them. On the other side of the coin, we should

> ...We had to start from scratch.

Buddy Miller organized and supervised loan administration in the company's short-term lending division, which managed LNMI.

also know all the tricks of the trade. That falls under the old adage: 'It takes a thief to know one.'

"Our policy is to make a monthly check of each construction project. I have 18 men who 'have-suitcase-will-travel.' They are gone at least two, maybe three weeks a month. We don't lend money on any project that we don't physically look at every month. If the builder says there's $400,000 worth of work done, we want to see that there's $400,000 worth of work done."

Keeping tabs on construction projects became a vital part of incremental releases of loan money. As in most other areas of the new venture, procedures for releasing that money had to be invented. Miller assumed that all he had to do was copy the formats their line banks used. He was surprised to find an absence of procedures. At one of Dallas' largest banks, draw requests were casually scribbled on the backs of manila envelopes whenever clients dropped by to pick up their next cash advance. It was an example of what Miller called the good-old-boy method: "But we wouldn't operate that way. So we had to start from scratch."

The administrative procedures that gradually evolved over the first year or two proved themselves over a span of almost 20 years. Just how well those policies served LNMI was reflected in a loan commitment level in 1988 of about $3 billion with nonearning assets of only about $60 million. By way of extreme comparison, the former FirstRepublic Bank had a $3 billion real estate loan portfolio with nonearning assets of $1.2 to 1.5 billion. "Sure we're proud," Miller put it. "The policy decisions that were put in place 20 years ago have served us well."

John Sexton also credits the policies and their administration for the trust's success. "We've loaned about ten billion dollars since 1969," said Sexton in 1988, "and we've recovered it all with a loss ratio of less than one-half percent. No other short-term lender in the country can say that. It has been a hell of a business and is today."

Jess Hay credits Gene Bishop, who joined the company as president in October 1969, with a major role in shaping the trust's operations to conform to its stated investment, financial, and operating policies. Bishop's extensive experience as a senior executive and chief credit officer for First National Bank in Dallas contributed immeasurably to the successful launching of the trust. "Gene," says Hay, "is a man who combines, as effectively as anyone I know, sound judgment, aggressive spirit, impeccable integrity, and superlative interpersonal skills. He is a leader who motivates others to do their very best. We were fortunate, indeed, to have had him with us for the five critical years during which we formed LNMI and consolidated our mortgage banking operations."

The difficulty in selling the public offering contrasted sharply with the trust's growth after it began operations. Favorable economic conditions during the first two years played an important role. "At the time we formed the trust," says Ted Enloe, "we were in a tight money crunch, and there was very little money available at any price. Our first loans, for example, were to high-quality developers like Trammell Crow, and we charged 6 percent over prime for construction loans with Metropolitan Life takeouts. For that kind of loan today, you'd be fortunate to get 1 percent over prime."

Formulating procedures during the first nine months of its operation didn't detract from the trust's performance. Short-term loan production of almost $28 million in 1969 jumped to $165 million by June 1970. The 1970 contribution in gross income of $3,312,000 represented an increase of 139 percent over fiscal 1969. Through a series of public offerings, LNMI increased its capitalization so that by 1973 its capital base exceeded $122 million. In 1971, gross income from short-term lending surpassed $5 million and loan production increased 78 percent to over $294 million. LNMI also realized a significant increase in its management fees, $1,450,236 million in 1971 compared to $332,446 for the previous year. The trust also began to find a national market. The 117 loans in its portfolio at the end of fiscal 1971 were spread among 23 states coast to coast. By the end of fiscal 1973, short-term loan production for the year reached a record $614 million and contributed $10,908,352 in gross income, up from $7,239,003 in the previous year. Management fees reached $4,505,046, compared to $2,690,925 in fiscal 1972. By 1973, Lomas & Nettleton Mortgage Investors had established itself as a national leader in short-term lending.

The company's mortgage banking commercial loan division was transformed when Fred Morrison became president of The Lomas & Nettleton Company in 1967. He moved his operation from the New Haven office to the Dallas headquarters.

Short-term lending wasn't the only business activity that underwent revitalization at Lomas & Nettleton. Mortgage banking's commercial loan division experienced a dramatic transformation under the leadership of Fred B. Morrison, who became president of The Lomas & Nettleton Company in 1967. Personally recruited by Al Rohnstedt, Morrison brought 13 years of financial experience to L&N. As a former mortgage investment vice president for Metropolitan Life Insurance Company, Morrison was well connected to the largest and most prestigious institutional investors.

Shortly after his arrival, Morrison characterized commercial lending at L&N as "embryonic." Commercial loan production at the company's Dallas, Phoenix, Miami, and Connecticut offices was moderately active, at best. In keeping with the overall corporate goal of building strong financial services, the new president proceeded to expand the division into a 20-office national organization, the largest of its kind in the country. "Fred Morrison's lasting monument at L&N," says Jess Hay, "is that he moved us into the commercial loan business. He really built it."

Noted for his marketing and customer savvy, Morrison displayed those skills at a mortgage bankers' convention in Dallas soon after joining the company. Ignoring the convention itself, he organized real estate tours for savings bank and insurance company investors. To their surprise, they discovered that Dallas had some of the most sophisticated and imaginatively designed apartments anywhere in the country. "It was a brand new world for them," says Morrison. "We walked them through apartments and introduced them to developers and really gave them a flavor of what we had. I was hardly at the convention because we were so busy shuttling these guys around."

The commercial loan division generated big income.

Morrison's enthusiasm matched that of his audience. Because of changes in the industry, banks and insurance companies were as eager to hear L&N's commercial lending pitch as the company was to give it. Recent state legislation permitted New York and New England savings banks to make commercial loans throughout the country. More importantly, single-family mortgages had lost much of their appeal among investors, who now favored commercial mortgages because they were easier to process and more profitable. "When I started with Metropolitan Life in 1957," says Morrison, "Metropolitan did $500 million worth of business that year and 95 percent of it was single-family. Ten years later when I left, they were doing a billion and a half a year and 95 percent of it was commercial. There was a major revolution that took place in this business. The insurance companies, who had been the largest source of single-family money, made the transition almost entirely into commercial."

Before L&N could fully participate in this new investment preference, Morrison first had to find a way to break down the geographic restrictions imposed by the insurance industry's correspondent system. L&N faced the challenge head-on. "We broke that wall down," says Morrison, "through sheer persistence. By producing business and banging away at them. By being energetic and showing them we were a good source of business. And by a lot of politicking." Correspondent relationships with Metropolitan Life, for example, increased from one in Connecticut to an additional three in the important Sunbelt states of Texas, California, and Arizona. The benefits from these relationships were significant. Insurance company correspondents automatically handled the servicing for the loans they originated, which represented a highly profitable stream of income.

The commercial loan division also enjoyed the advantages of its national network. Morrison made a practice of hiring only managers who were experts in the territories they were responsible for. "We were leaders," says Morrison, "in the sense that we had more offices with a wider geographic distribution than anyone else, and we reaped the harvest of that advantage. If John Hancock dropped their rates in order to be more competitive and get more business, we could notify 20 offices in 20 different markets. We could stimulate business by focusing our personnel. That made a difference. They were delighted to have somebody who could respond in that fashion."

Investors showed their appreciation in ways that contributed to L&N's bottom line. Instead of requiring borrowers to put up cash for good faith deposits, for example, they could instead substitute letters of credit "which made life a little easier and gave us a competitive advantage."

Geographic diversity also gave commercial lending the ability to minimize the effects of regional economic downturns. When a market became overbuilt, L&N intensified its efforts in other areas. This flexibility enabled the division to maintain a consistency of earnings.

One of the most important internal innovations was the establishment of a compensation program that attracted highly skilled commercial loan personnel. The norm within the industry at the time was a salary and arbitrary bonus. "We had," says Morrison, "the first incentive compensation system for commercial loan men. We actually put our people on a P&L [profit and loss] basis, and they earned a percentage of the profit they produced for their office. So, a man could plan and look at the numbers and know what he was going to get. That's the way we attracted the best people. And by attracting the best people we were able to get high-quality business. They worked their asses off because they were compensated. It doesn't sound like much in today's world, but at the time it was revolutionary."

By the end of fiscal 1970, the impact of a revitalized commercial loan division began to be felt. The division produced $106,652,000 in total loan amount, a substantial increase over the previous year's total of $30,765,000. It also claimed a nation-wide organization, with 12 regional offices that produced a volume of business ranking Lomas & Nettleton among the top six mortgage bankers and brokers in the country.

A new section of the 1968 Housing Act provided the company with one of its most profitable commercial loan ventures. It was known as Section 242, a federally insured FHA program designed to encourage hospital expansion. Paul M. Low, the manager of Lomas & Nettleton's Florida operation in 1970 and later president of L&N, had a reputation for building new business opportunities. During the sixties, Low developed an expertise in commercial multifamily FHA lending. When Section 242 came along, he pegged it as a potential moneymaker and became an expert in its application. The incorporation of the Florida operation into L&N's new Southeast Region freed Low from the responsibilities of day-to-day management and enabled him to concentrate on commercial loans.

In early 1970, Fred Morrison contacted Low about the difficulties St. Anthony Hospital was having in Oklahoma City. Halfway through the construction of an 800-patient addition, the hospital's financing fell apart. Most lenders avoided loans with problems as serious as that. Paul Low looked it over and saw how he could make it work. "It was a messy deal," said Low, "but we handled it with a great deal of professionalism and speed. I knew what I was doing, and I trusted the contractor. I was very confident." The company shared Low's confidence and courage by taking a substantial lending risk, since the loan wouldn't be insured until the building was completed. Paul Low successfully negotiated with the FHA, paid off the bonds committed to fund the construction, "and everybody lived happily ever after."

It was a tour de force beyond belief.

Proud of commercial lending's new success, the company heralded its achievement on the back cover of the Spring 1970 issue of the *Mortgagee*. Under a drawing of St. Anthony Hospital's new annex and the heading "bigger is better," the ad announced the following loan highlights: "Lomas & Nettleton has put together the largest mortgage loan in the history of Oklahoma—$21.7 million under FHA Section 242 for St. Anthony Hospital in Oklahoma City. This is only the fourth such loan under the federal program inaugurated in 1968. L&N experience and know-how provided the interim financing on this project." The St. Anthony Hospital loan marked the beginning of what Morrison called "a tour de force beyond belief."

Morrison and Low followed up their Oklahoma City success with a Section 242 training program for all their commercial loan men. Low's understanding of the

A $21.7 million loan for St. Anthony Hospital in Oklahoma City was made by Lomas & Nettleton West, Inc., through the 1968 Federal Housing Administration Act, Section 242. The loan picked up all indebtedness of the hospital, including debts already incurred on equipment, parking, and power plant. It was only the fourth loan of its type under the FHA Act and the first to pick up financing of a project under construction. Present at the signing ceremonies, seated left to right, are Sister Louise Hirner, Mother Rosina Higgs, and Sister Bernadette Hardesty. Standing, Larry Wilson, left, and Paul Low, right, both represent Lomas & Nettleton. The man in the center is unidentified.

Proud of the commercial lending division's success in the St. Anthony Hospital project, the company devoted the back cover of the Spring 1970 issue of the *Mortgagee* to a full-page announcement.

system and its procedures gave their staff access to valuable leads. Before a hospital could expand, it first had to receive a certificate of need from the government. Filing for these certificates was a matter of public record, and they became a primary resource for identifying hospitals that were planning expansion projects.

Several of Low's leads came from within L&N's increasingly motivated staff. Executive vice president Gary H. Kell, the manager of L&N's Little Rock office at the time, read an article in the *Mortgagee* about Paul Low and hospital finance. One afternoon not long afterward, Kell was having a beer with a real estate friend who told him about the trouble Baptist Medical Hospital was having finding a lender for a proposed expansion project. Kell's friend told him whom to contact. "I called the hospital administrator," says Kell, "but he wouldn't see me. Then, I found out the chairman of the board for the hospital owned the building that I had my office in. I knew he would see me because he's my landlord. I went to see him and showed him the article in the *Mortgagee* about our ability to do hospital financing. He read the article and immediately set me up a meeting with the hospital administrator. I called Paul Low on a Tuesday. He told me what information he needed in order to put together a proposal. I called him back with that information Wednesday afternoon. Paul flew into Little Rock Friday evening with a bound proposal. He made the presentation to the hospital board on Saturday. The following Tuesday L&N was named financing agent."

Finding an investor for the Baptist Medical Hospital loan was no problem for Low: "The hospital wanted to borrow $20 million, and it had $15 million in cash. It was a slam-dunk deal."

Paul Low's expert knowledge and rapid response gave L&N a dominant position in the hospital finance market. At one point, Section 242 loans represented 50 percent of the commercial loan division's annual business. Within a span of two years, Low financed four hospitals in Miami and became known among commercial lending circles as "Mr. Hospital."

Low also accepted the responsibility that he believed went with L&N's leadership role. He pursued an open-door loan policy that enhanced Lomas & Nettleton's guiding principle—profit with honor. "We financed a little hospital in Culpeper, Virginia," says Low, "a two million dollar loan, because nobody else would help them. And, frankly, we could have used our time more profitably elsewhere. I took the view that that was not the way we were going to run our business. We would take them all."

We are committed to mortgage banking as the core of our operations and as the springboard for our future growth.

By 1973, the commercial loan division produced $347,843,000 in loans, up from $278,695,000 in 1972. It couldn't compete in size with residential mortgages, but it made a hefty contribution to L&N profits. "The commercial loan division" says Fred Morrison, "generated big income. We never became the big muscle in the organization, but we made a significant contribution, and we contributed to the overall reputation of the company."

Single-family residential mortgages wielded the most muscle at L&N. Already the largest single-family mortgage banking operation in the country, LNFC implemented an expansion program that made it even larger. But size was not an end in itself. Jess Hay directed the mortgage banking expansion with national objectives that had nothing to do with growth for growth's sake. As Al Rohnstedt later explained: "The acquisitions that we've made have not been for the sake of bigness, but for the sake of viability—a place in the national economy." An L&N advertising campaign at the time, using the headline "Bigger Is Better," underscored the fact that corporate expansion was the best means for achieving the benefits of national scale for their customers. In fact, LNFC formulated its national approach to mortgage banking in response to fundamental industry changes. On October 29, 1970, in a speech to the New York Society of Security Analysts, Jess Hay outlined the company's goals:

> We are committed to mortgage banking as the core of our operations and as the springboard for our future growth. . . . This objective is not merely for the purpose of becoming bigger. Rather it is based on the notion that the character of mortgage banking should be reflective of the character of the real estate industry itself. Just as the real estate industry increasingly is dominated by large developers doing business on a national scale, so mortgage banking, if it is to serve its builder-developer customers and investors adequately, must break out of the localized and fragmented patterns inherited from the past.

The company's plan for expansion appeared prominently in its 1970 annual report: "Our objective is to become the first truly national mortgage banking operation, the first actively engaged in every major marketing area of the country. To achieve our aim . . . we hope to penetrate within the next two to three years, by acquisition or otherwise, the Southeast, the Midwest and the Pacific Northwest." LNFC management considered acquisition the fastest, most efficient strategy for achieving their goal. As J. Peter Grace, chairman of

W. R. Grace & Company and something of an expert on acquisition and diversification, once observed: "If there's a way to get big without buying companies, I haven't found it yet."

Most of the preparations for the expansion were completed by mid-1970. Increased capitalization from the previous year gave L&N the financial strength to proceed, and the addition of Gene Bishop and Ted Enloe bolstered management.

The proposed expansion also required reorganization of the mortgage banking division. For two years, The Lomas & Nettleton Company, based in New Haven, operated separately from Houston-based Lomas & Nettleton West, Inc., formerly the T. J. Bettes Company. An in-house study at the end of 1969 recommended consolidating the two companies' portfolios in Houston because of its larger, more advanced data processing capability. A low-grade rivalry that had been smoldering for a year and a half between New Haven and Houston finally surfaced as a result of the report's finding. "That document," says E. G. Bray, L&N's former data processing specialist and a member of the committee that prepared the report, "didn't sit too well with Mr. Rohnstedt. He didn't like the Houston organization to begin with, and he obviously was more comfortable with the people in New Haven." But the discrepancy in size between the two servicing portfolios weighed heavily in Houston's favor. New Haven's 60,000 loans contrasted sharply with Houston's 140,000. As Bray noted, "it was a lot easier putting 60 into 140 than 140 into 60."

The company's 1970 annual report featured the plan for future expansion. The cover pictured a street scene with a crowd of determined people heading for their destinations, symbolizing burgeoning new markets.

Further restructuring led to the development of a regional system with enough flexibility to accommodate immediate expansion and, ultimately, a national network. Jim Wooten, the entrepreneurially adept former Bettes executive, pressed for a decentralized regional system. He contended that semiautonomous regions would produce the most innovation and the greatest number of loans. After all, Wooten argued, the people already there knew their regions better than anyone in Dallas. What emerged was an inspired blend of decentralized and centralized management. It preserved the aggressive, entrepreneurial side of mortgage banking production that characterized the best of the L&N and Bettes companies. At the same time, the benefits of a consolidated loan administration were substantial in terms of cost reductions and improved efficiency.

On July 1, 1970, LNFC's two mortgage banking subsidiaries merged under the banner of The Lomas & Nettleton Company. New Haven was designated the location for corporate headquarters and Houston for national loan administration. The four operational areas

Al Rohnstedt, on the left with Jess Hay, did not like the 1969 study that recommended the consolidation in Houston of the two mortgage banking portfolios. Betty Jo and Jess Hay Archives.

included the Western Region with a central office in Los Angeles, the Southwest Region with headquarters in Phoenix, the Central Region administered in Dallas, and the Eastern Region with a main office in New Haven.

Three months later, LNFC purchased United Mortgagee Servicing Corporation and several other mortgage servicing companies from U.I.P. Corporation of Milwaukee for just over $10 million. The acquisition increased Lomas & Nettleton's servicing portfolio by $707 million and added 38 offices in 14 states. Most importantly, it gave the company an entree into the southeastern United States, including a substantial presence in Virginia, Georgia, Tennessee, Kentucky, North Carolina, and South Carolina. With its headquarters in Virginia Beach, Virginia, the new acquisition was designated the Southeast Region. This addition to the new system forced the Eastern Region to become the Northeast Region and adjust its boundaries accordingly.

The United Mortgagee purchase, like that of T. J. Bettes and future acquisitions, shared a common characteristic. The companies that owned them were all financially troubled. U.I.P. Corporation was a prime example. "U.I.P. had delusions of grandeur," says former L&N executive vice president James W. Pickup, who had joined United Mortgagee as vice president for loan administration in 1965. "They were going to become a miniconglomerate. They had a boat company that made catamarans, and they had a foundry that produced some kind of iron works. They got into all kinds of stuff. Grossly undercapitalized. To make a long story short, they started going down the tubes. We realized how bad it had gotten when they started calling George Wilson almost daily to send them money as fast as we were getting it in. We knew it was only a matter of time before they were going to have to sell in order to survive. And that's how we got sold to The Lomas & Nettleton Company."

Many at United Mortgagee believed L&N had

saved them from a difficult if not fatal relationship with U.I.P. Corporation. Their gratitude was reciprocated by Al Rohnstedt. He looked at United Mortgagee's experienced management team and thought they might be the white knight he needed to slay the Houston dragon. At the end of 1970, Rohnstedt appointed Southeast Region executive vice president George I. Wilson to take over the portfolio consolidation and national loan administration program and ordered it located in Virginia Beach. "He [Rohnstedt] didn't want T. J. Bettes to take over his company," says E. G. Bray, a major participant in the consolidation. "That's what he really feared. That's why he brought in George Wilson."

Although Bray correctly reflects a viewpoint widely held in the early 1970s by the former officers of the T. J. Bettes Company, in fact at a very early date Jess Hay and Rohnstedt privately agreed that, in all probability, Houston would be selected as the site for the company's national loan administration unit. New Haven and Virginia Beach, they understood, were impractical choices. Only Houston had the personnel and the data processing facilities to handle an operation of that size. But it was the pressure from investors complaining about receiving three different sets of records from the same company that made Rohnstedt swallow his antipathy toward Houston and get on with the consolidation. In February 1971, Al Rohnstedt met with E. G. Bray: "Rohnstedt asked me what it would take to do the job here in Houston. I told him I'd need another computer just like the one I had. He said, 'Get it.'" George Wilson immediately drafted a format for each office that provided Houston's data processing operation with the information it needed. By July 1971, L&N's entire servicing portfolio was consolidated on one system in Houston.

"The selection of Houston as a loan administration headquarters," said Wilson in the July 1971 issue of the *Mortgagee*, "is a logical decision. Consolidation will provide our investors simplified and improved reporting methods. The elimination of a multiplicity of records and reporting is also an economic move for L&N.

"The change will centralize service accounting, investor reporting, and related administrative functions. Maintenance of escrow will be provided on a national basis from the Houston location."

Even before the first consolidation ended, a new one had to be incorporated. On March 5, 1971, LNFC's machinery of acquisition lurched forward and purchased Seattle-based Northwest Mortgage, Inc., for over $2 million. The sale included Northwest's $210 million mortgage servicing portfolio and its eight mortgage production offices in the state of Washington. "The addition of Northwest's operations," said Jess Hay at the time of the agreement, "will be a major step forward. It will serve as a base for our market penetration of the Pacific Northwest, a major marketing area not now served by L&N and one which has been a prime target in our expansion plans." Despite Northwest Mortgage's relatively small size (fourth largest in Washington state), the addition of its $210 million portfolio had the distinction of pushing Lomas & Nettleton's servicing portfolio over the $3 billion mark.

Suddenly, we were a monster . . .

A year later, LNFC jumped across the continent and purchased from Philadelphia-based Kardon Investment Company its $550 million mortgage servicing portfolio and other assets for approximately $35 million in cash. The portfolio and assets came from three of Kardon's wholly owned subsidiaries, Peoples Bond & Mortgage Co. in Philadelphia, Murphree Mortgage Co. in Nashville, and Pittsburgh Mortgage Co. This acquisition gave L&N 17 new production offices and entry into major new markets in Ohio, Pennsylvania, Maryland, Delaware, and New Jersey. It also marked another corporate milestone, boosting L&N's servicing portfolio to $4 billion. The Lomas & Nettleton Company now outdistanced the next largest mortgage company by over $2 billion. "We were already by far the biggest [mortgage company] in the country," says Jim Pickup. "Then along comes Northwest and then after that Kardon. Suddenly, we were a monster, and we were having trouble swallowing it all."

It was a monster that required taming at both the national and regional levels. Not surprisingly, George Wilson's interaction with the former Bettes people in Houston was strained. By mid-1971, he had added key personnel from Virginia Beach to help get the job done. One of those closest to Wilson and an indispensable part of his team was James W. Pickup, a hard-nosed mortgage servicing expert whose service in the Royal Canadian Air Force during World War II may have contributed to his no-nonsense approach to management.

Although quite different in temperament, the two men complemented each other perfectly. "George Wilson had a national reputation," says Pickup. "He was a graduate of Wharton, a hell of an accountant, and he knew servicing. George was an organizer. He was not a line man. I'm a line man, a hands-on manager. I was Johnny-on-the-spot, the guy who bitched and screamed and pushed and prodded while George was back in Houston pulling switches."

One of Pickup's most talented proteges was Warren J. Whiteman, who later became senior vice president and manager of hazard administration. Pickup relied on him because "he was a hard worker, well trained, and very knowledgeable. You could count on him all the time. We had a number of good people, but we didn't have that many outstanding people. Warren was outstanding."

The problems in organizing a national servicing operation in Houston were difficult enough. The last thing Wilson and his team needed were regional obstacles. "The bigger we got," says Jim Pickup, "the bigger our problems got. Bray was just going insane trying to program and program and produce and produce. We were cranking out late notices to be mailed nationally and billing notices every month. We didn't need regional headaches. Weaknesses in the regions couldn't be tolerated."

As George Wilson's assistant in loan administration, Jim Pickup was responsible for the orderly transition of new acquisitions into the Lomas & Nettleton system. "We had to go in as the clean-up crew," says Pickup. "Some of the stuff we found didn't sit too well with the company."

Pickup's first assignment was in Seattle, where he spent four weeks converting Northwest Mortgage's servicing to the L&N system. Northwest's loan administration was in pretty good shape and required only one major personnel change: "It was headed by a very weak servicing man. . . . He was the salt-of-the-earth, but he couldn't find his way out of a paper bag, and I had to release him."

The Philadelphia acquisition, on the other hand, had major problems. The difficulties prompting its sale involved the mortgage banking operation, particularly servicing. The root of the problem was the fact that the Kardon Company's primary business was manufacturing, not mortgage banking. When the Kardons received a flurry of complaints about loan originations and servicing from the Department of Housing and Urban Development (HUD) and the Federal National Mortgage Association (FNMA), they decided to sell. It didn't take Jim Pickup long to realize that L&N had inherited migraine-size headaches.

He spent three months in Philadelphia cleaning up what turned out to be one of his most difficult assignments. Lack of management leadership in servicing turned that department into what Pickup described as "an absolute disaster."

"The servicing manager had had a heart attack in his early thirties, and he was scared to death of doing anything, including lifting a pencil. Then, I learned the hard way that one of the top executives was shacked up with the gal who was assistant manager of servicing. I kept running in to him and complaining about this

By mid-1971, key personnel from Virginia Beach were added in Houston to accomplish national objectives. Jim Pickup was among them.

gal. I didn't know he was sleeping with her."

One night while working late, Pickup looked through the desks of a department that had received a large number of complaints from FNMA about delays in processing checks and forms. "I found," says Pickup, "drawers jammed with checks that were weeks old, never been processed. When I complained to the former president who was now regional executive vice president, he said I had no damn business going through desk drawers. I said, 'I have every damn business in the world. You didn't buy us. We bought you. And it's a mess, and I'm going to get it straightened out.'

"In the meantime, I was phoning and sending reports to Jess Hay and Gene Bishop that they couldn't believe. They must have thought I had lost my marbles. They couldn't believe things were as bad as I was saying they were."

It was a discovery made while tracking down another series of complaints that prompted Pickup to take direct control and reorganize the department: "We had gotten an awful lot of complaints from customers about missing checks. They said the checks had been mailed in but never cleared their banks, and our delinquency control department was sending them late notices. One night I dumped all the damned wastebaskets in the cashier's department on the floor. I sat down on my ass and went through the trash and found 29 checks.

"Well, it hit the fan the next day. I called the whole bloody staff in. I said I don't care if you like me or not. I'm not here to win any prizes, but this is what I found last night. I said it ain't never going to happen again, ever! From now on you are going to do exactly what I tell you to do or you're not going to be here.

"To make a long story short, I had to clean house from top to bottom. And that's what I did."

Pickup introduced a series of stringent procedures. He replaced the incompetent loan administrator with strong management in the person of William Glasgow, Jr., whom Pickup had personally trained in Virginia Beach. Finally, he got rid of the "bad eggs and worked like hell to train the ones that were left.

"Once I was able to get it on the straight and narrow and get some reliable management in, and we got our systems going, loan administration began to run more smoothly."

While Houston's centralized loan administration started to function more efficiently, decentralized loan production began to prove its effectiveness. Although L&N's mortgage banking regions had the same production and administrative responsibilities, each one handled them differently. Their autonomy allowed them the flexibility they needed to respond to a variety of market conditions and leadership styles.

The two top-producing regions, for example,

offered a sharp contrast in management philosophies. Jim Wooten structured the Central Region in a way that permitted branch managers to exercise a large amount of autonomy. They had access to bank lines and the authority to decide which loans they would fund. They issued commitments and handled their own personnel. Executive vice president Ernest W. Turnbull's Southeast Region, on the other hand, was closely managed from his Virginia Beach headquarters. "Ernie had tight controls on his branch managers," says Wooten. "He controlled the loan price and the funding check. He was an accountant by background, and he liked to keep track of all the numbers and watch the operation while sitting on his throne. He rarely went into the field. But the bottom line was that his loan volume came very close to mine. So you couldn't argue with what he did. It was just a different style."

That was the whole idea of the regional structure in the first place.

Wooten would be one of the first to acknowledge that Turnbull's ivory-tower approach to management was counterbalanced by the presence of his assistant regional manager, William H. Fantone, Jr. "Bill Fantone was really the hands-on operating officer of the region," says Wooten. "If Ernie wasn't there, Bill was the boss." The complementary management styles worked well.

"That was the whole idea of the regional structure in the first place. If you've got someone who knows what they're doing, and they're bringing you in the cost and the volume that you want, what the hell do you want to start going down there telling them how to do it different for?"

The spirit of autonomy that freed regional managers from many constraints also had a liberating effect on branch managers. They were, for the most part, a dynamic, entrepreneurially oriented breed who pushed loan production to increasingly higher levels.

One of the most enterprising was Lewis C. (Tommy) Thompson, a Southeast Region vice president and branch manager for Winston-Salem, North Carolina. Despite the fact that his region usually came in second behind Wooten's Central Region, Thompson claims the Southeast "was always first in ideas." Thompson's ideas began during a 20-year Navy career. As chief warrant officer on the U.S.S. *Tidewater*, he implemented a training procedure that in 1957 earned him a letter of commendation from Vice Admiral J. L. Holloway, Jr., Chief of Naval Personnel.

Following his naval service, Thompson applied his training skills to mortgage banking, first with United Mortgagee, which he joined in 1961, and then with The Lomas & Nettleton Company. His promotional ideas earned him a reputation as an innovator. Jim Pickup describes Thompson as a "salt-of-the-earth guy who could produce business like gangbusters." Since mortgage loans in the Southeast Region were based primarily on a spot loan market rather than subdivision construction, production depended on real estate agent referrals. Thompson wooed them with a multifaceted campaign of information designed to make their work easier and more successful. He set up seminars for real estate salesmen that Thompson describes as "four-hour sessions on everything the agents needed to know about the mortgage business. We covered down payments, qualifications, and applications. The seminars gave our branches an in with the real estate agents in that community." He followed up the seminars with a weekly newsletter containing helpful real estate information.

One of the most popular handouts was something he called "Tommy Thompson's Ready Reference Guide," an eight-page brochure given to real estate agents as a handout for clients and potential clients. "It gave all the mortgage information a person would want to know," says Thompson. "'What's my monthly payment going to be? What does it take to qualify?' I've had people come back 10 years later and tell me they still use my reference guide. Whenever I gave a seminar, I passed them out and showed the agents how to use them as a sales tool. It was very effective."

Thompson also found ways to avoid the competition in the cities and penetrate the small towns. He built a reliable customer base using instant telephone access: "All they had to do was pick up the telephone. They didn't shop. They looked for Lomas & Nettleton. They'd pick up the phone and say, 'I've got another loan for you.' We called it 'Loans by Phone.' We got all the basic information over the telephone and then forwarded the remainder of what we needed to get in writing." Later, when Thompson took up flying as a hobby, he advertised 'Fly a Loan.' It turned out to be a handy way to deliver loan packages, pick up loan applications, and maintain contact with his production network.

Thompson showed similar ingenuity when he moved to a larger branch office in Winston-Salem. He rented the new space from a store that sold dinnerware. In order to move in more quickly, he bought the retailer's inventory. "I bought all the dishes he had in there . . . and I got them at a real reasonable price and figured I'd use them for a promotion. As soon as we notified the real estate agents about the opening of our new office, we invited them to drop by and pick up a set of dishes. It was very effective. We had a lot of cars backed up to our office and a lot of agents loading them with dishes."

But for sheer salesmanship, Eugene W. Waxman, branch manager for Charlotte and later Nashville, was unique. Tommy Thompson says Waxman "never took no for an answer. If he went in the front door and they threw him out, he'd go in the back door. He pushed until he got a loan." In fact, Waxman's reputation for the brash and unconventional sometimes bordered on the bizarre. Nothing was too offbeat for Waxman to try if it caught the attention of real estate agents and set him apart from his competitors. One technique he used depended first on finding out which agents in an office enjoyed a beer at the end of the day. Then, late in the afternoon just before closing, Waxman dropped by with a cold six-pack.

But the most outrageous ploy was the Reese's Peanut Butter Cup stunt. Just before making a cold call on a new real estate agent, Waxman crumbled a Reese's Peanut Butter Cup on the side of his shoe: "You walk into the agent's office and the first thing you do is put your feet up on his desk and start talking to him. And he gets really upset. Usually, he gets mad and says, 'Here you come barging into my office, you put your feet up on my desk, and you got something on your shoe that looks like dog crap.' That's when I'd reach over and take a big scoop on my finger, eat it, and say, 'Gee, you're right. It is.' That gets his attention, and he realizes it's a joke and starts laughing."

Waxman showed just as much organizational initiative when it came to providing service for the agents he did business with. "I let my real estate agents know," he says, "that I don't get paid until they get paid. So they knew I was pushing the loans through as quickly as possible." In a newspaper interview shortly after he took over the Charlotte office in 1971, Waxman said, "The name of the game here is speed. We're trying to get to the point where we can get our loans processed in 15 [business] days. For most mortgage companies, if they get loans processed in 30 days they're doing well."

An integral part of his branch's prompt service and customer satisfaction was the way he organized his office personnel and turned them into entrepreneurs with an incentive for success. "I paid my employees," says Waxman, "a commission out of my pocket based on total office volume. I think I was the first one who ever did that. I pooled it according to the number of employees. That way we had no weak sisters, and everybody pulled their own weight.

"I made a point of taking my staff out and introducing them to the real estate agents. That way the agents knew my people and weren't just talking to a voice over the phone. My employees were very visible. I made sure they went to all the board of realtor and homebuilder meetings and parties even if I had to pay for it, which I usually did."

Waxman's bold unconventionality lent itself to achieving results quickly. Within 60 days after opening the Charlotte office, loan production passed the $1 million mark. Once he got the operation up to speed, it wasn't unusual for his office to handle 55 or 60 loans a month. When the Southeast Region had production problems in Nashville, they sent Gene Waxman. Six months later, Nashville surpassed Charlotte in loan production and became the second highest regional producer.

Thompson and Waxman were only two among many in the company who took the initiative and helped push L&N loan production beyond what the mortgage industry had ever seen before.

Former executive vice president Fred G. Brunn, Phoenix branch manager and later Southwest regional manager, emphasized relationships with large builders. "He had a great customer relationship among the larger builder-developers in the state of Arizona," says Wooten. "That was his strength. He was very customer-oriented. In fact, he gave them damn near anything they wanted. But it was a well-run, efficient office and very profitable."

The Western Region, under the leadership of former executive vice presidents Norman R. Hall and George E. Francis, opened offices in Torrance, Santa Barbara, Fountain Valley, San Bernardino, Santa Ana, and Las Vegas. The Western Region was also known for insurance production. Former senior vice president Robert L. Helberg ran a low-overhead, high-profit-margin operation. According to George Francis, portfolio insurance sales typically fell in the 5 to 10 percent range. Helberg managed to produce a 35 percent portfolio penetration. Former senior vice president P. Warren Smith, Helberg's boss, understood that kind of initiative. He, too, was a creative, sales-oriented entrepreneur.

Wooten's Central Region added an office in El Paso, and then moved north to open branches in St. Louis and Chicago. Former senior vice president Melvin H. Wilson, who later became assistant regional manager, played an important role in the region's success. Besides opening a number of offices in West Texas, he had a gift for picking good people. "He hired bright, young guys right out of college," says Wooten. "And he trained those guys to do what the customer wanted. He was very good at supervising, motivating, and jazzing them up."

The Western Region expanded under the coleadership of George Francis, above, and Norman Hall.

Hundreds of men and women throughout the country contributed to the pursuit of L&N's publicly stated objective: to become the very best in the mortgage banking industry.

In the late sixties and early seventies, the traditional institutional investor markets that most mortgage companies depended upon to buy single-family residential mortgages began to disappear. Fortunately for the industry, the 1968 Housing Act established the Government National Mortgage Association (GNMA), which enabled lenders to assemble pools of FHA-insured and VA-guaranteed mortgages and issue securities backed by those mortgage pools. The securities were then guaranteed by GNMA for a fee and sold by the vendor into the market.

GNMA -backed securities became the finest, safest investment you could have . . .

The new program was significant because it created an instrument supported by mortgages that was comparable to a government bond. GNMA-backed instruments immediately broadened the market for residential mortgages. State, municipal, union, and corporate pension funds invested heavily in these new securities. They also attracted the attention of credit unions, private trusts, foundations, and even private individuals. "The idea," says former executive vice president David Kelly, Jr., "was to improve the liquidity in the mortgage markets. It's a lot easier to trade a security than it is a bundle of mortgages. If one entity wants to sell a package of mortgages to another entity, then you have to go through the process of recording assignments for each mortgage and the land records and all that kind of stuff."

It also speeded up the commitment process. "You no longer had to send investors loan packages," says Jim Wooten, "and let them look at the pictures and meet with their loan committees and go through the laborious and inefficient process of individual whole loan sales. Investors used to fly in and want to see the houses. I drove them hundreds of miles and wasted days until they became comfortable enough that they didn't need to look.

"GNMA-backed securities became the finest, safest investment you could have, with a yield that traded above treasury yields, so why wouldn't you buy that instead of treasury bonds? And they did. And they do. They've been our principal source of funding for FHA/VA loans."

In 1971, The Lomas & Nettleton Company began pooling mortgages into GNMA-backed securities. The ones issued by L&N were called "fully modified pass-through securities," which meant that the principal and interest on mortgages was paid, or passed through, to investors as monthly mortgage payments accrued. The GNMA guarantee meant investors were paid regardless of what happened to the mortgages in the pool. "During the last six months of fiscal 1971," said Al Rohnstedt in a *Mortgagee* article, "we will have issued $100 million of GNMA mortgage securities. We project $250 million for the next fiscal year."

. . . a Company with a significantly long-term role in American society.

In response to LNFC's status as the largest mortgage company in the country, and in keeping with its corporate objective of building an enterprise based on honor and respect, Jess Hay began to upgrade the company's image.

Since 1969, L&N's annual reports have provided the company with its clearest expression of corporate image and values. That was the year Hay hired Stan Richards, president of The Richards Group, to produce reports with a broader perspective. In the process, L&N broke new ground by moving away from the traditional, narrowly focused report that looked only at the company and its operations. Richards real-

In keeping with important corporate objectives, Jess Hay upgraded the company's image and restated its core values in its annual reports. The cover and double-page spread from the 1969 report typified this dramatic and creative approach to communication.

ized Hay wanted to convey a larger vision. "Jess is a guy with a strong social conscience," says Richards. "He wasn't interested in a nuts-and-bolts annual report that contained only financial information. He saw Lomas & Nettleton as a company with a significant long-term role in America. If you did nothing more than read the theme statements and didn't even bother to look at the photographs, you would get a clear picture of Lomas & Nettleton's relationship to America and to the people of America.

"An annual report . . . is the only thing that the company does during the course of the year that really characterizes the position of the CEO. Everything else is somebody else's product. The annual report is the CEO's product." For 24 years, Richards and his staff have featured Hay's vision in annual reports that consistently win national awards.

In 1972, L&N increased its prestige and public visibility by joining the New York Stock Exchange. Lomas & Nettleton Mortgage Investors was listed on January 24 under the symbol LOM. Lomas & Nettleton Financial Corporation took its place on the big board under the symbol LNF on April 19. "We gained a wider market," says John Sexton. "It was a pretty big stepping stone. We became more and more a broadly based public vehicle. We began banging on the public financial markets a lot more frequently."

It was clear from the beginning of L&N's acquisition program that its corporate headquarters also had to expand. The opportunity came in December 1972 when L&N leased the 35th, 36th, and 37th floors of Trammell Crow's new 40-story office building in downtown Dallas, 2001 Bryan Tower. It was a natural home for Lomas & Nettleton. Besides playing an important role in financing the project, the company had close ties to Trammell Crow, who had by this time resigned from L&N's board in order to pursue a larger business relationship with the company.

Former executive vice president M. D. Wommack supervised the relocation to Bryan Tower. Maxine

On January 24, 1972, L&N joined the New York Stock Exchange. Lomas & Nettleton Mortgage Investors was listed under the symbol LOM. The double-page spread from the Spring 1972 *Mortgagee* celebrates the event.

Tadlock, AISD, the space planner and decorator hired to accomplish the task, was already well acquainted with L&N through her previous design work for the company at their Hartford Building office. It was a massive undertaking that included a two-month buying trip to London and Paris. Described by Wommack as "hard-willed," Tadlock spared no expense or effort to get the design she wanted. Occasionally, that meant tearing out wood paneling or molding that didn't work and starting over. At one point, there were 30 fine-finish carpenters working on the job.

The result was a spectacular mix of exquisite architectural detailing, antique furnishings, and contemporary art. The centerpiece of the project was a free-standing staircase connecting the 36th and 37th floors, highlighted by a Renaissance Venetian chandelier with original hand-blown glass. A feature article in the May 1974 issue of *Interiors* magazine announced: "Maxine Tadlock designs baronial spaces around European architectural elements, fine antiques, and contemporary art works for Lomas & Nettleton in Dallas." The magazine called the finished project a "bravura museum . . . designed with a grand sense of theater and drama."

Most of the drama for Wommack, a CPA with less lavish tastes, came from the realization of what the project cost. When asked by a business associate how the

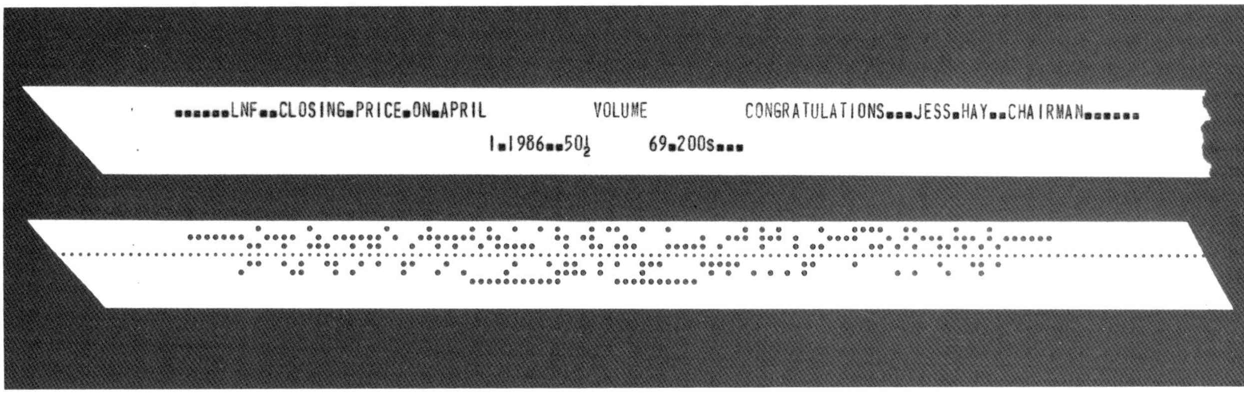

On April 19, 1972, Lomas & Nettleton Financial Corporation took its place on the Big Board under the symbol LNF. The opening day tape congratulates chairman Jess Hay.

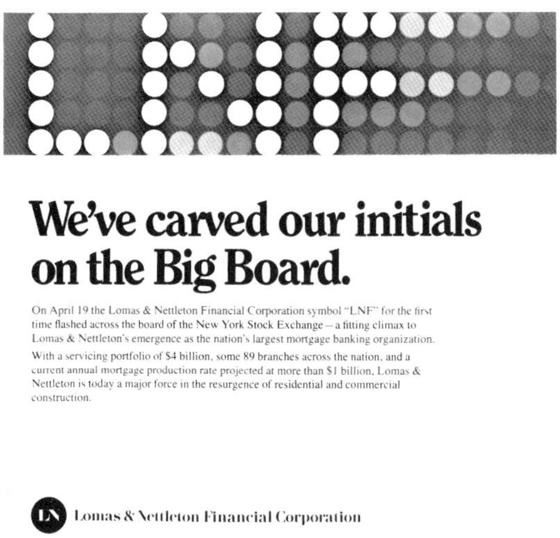

The "We've carved our initials . . ." ad was published nationwide to announce Lomas & Nettleton Financial Corporation's arrival on the New York Stock Exchange.

The Summer 1972 *Mortgagee* featured "LNF—Recognition by the Big Board." From left to right, NYSE President Robert W. Haack welcomes LNFC chairman and chief executive officer Jess Hay and president Gene Bishop to the trading floor the day LNF was listed.

Present at the NYSE occasion were, from left: Tom Chrystie, vice president, Merrill, Lynch, Pierce, Fenner & Smith; Ray Ryan, vice president, The Lomas & Nettleton Company; M. D. Wommack, senior vice president and treasurer, Lomas & Nettleton Financial Corporation; Frank Shedivy, vice president, The Lomas & Nettleton Company; Gene Bishop, president, Lomas & Nettleton Financial Corporation; Merle Wick, vice president, New York Stock Exchange; Jess Hay, chairman of the board and chief executive officer, Lomas & Nettleton Financial Corporation; Al Rohnstedt, vice chairman of the board, The Lomas & Nettleton Company; Gary White, controller, Lomas & Nettleton Financial Corporation.

A

B

C

D

A. Corporate headquarters for L&N expanded into 2001 Bryan Tower in downtown Dallas in December 1972. Courtesy The Trammell Crow Company.

B. The focal point of L&N's reception area was a bronze painted Italian Renaissance chandelier with the original hand-blown glass globes. The sweeping staircase connects the 36th and 37th floors.

C. Small meetings could be accommodated in the elegantly appointed conference room, complete with fireplace and fine wood paneling.

D. The quiet refinement of the executive offices combined antiques with modern art and luxuriant plants.

E. Careful attention was given to creating a pleasant and productive working environment for the entire staff.

F. The mailroom was designed by one of the experts in the field, Dixon Lewis of Houston.

G. File rooms became more attractive when enlivened with bright floors.

E

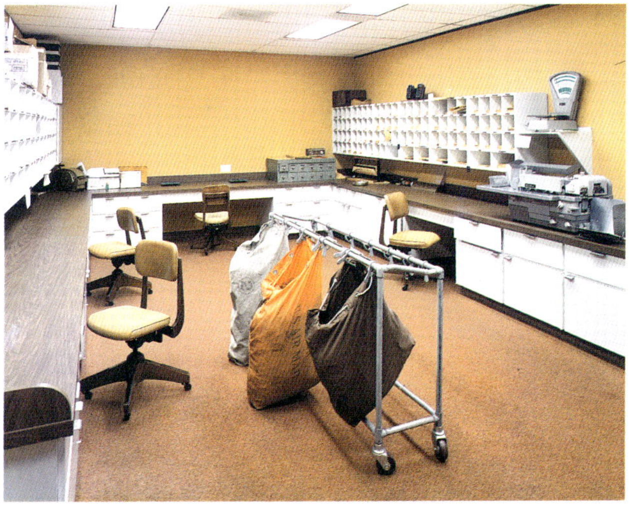

F

G

Eugene M. Locke, U.S. Ambassador to Pakistan, presents his credentials and a letter from President Lyndon B. Johnson to Field Marshal Mohammed Ayub Khan, President of Pakistan. The presentation ceremony was held at President House in Rawalpindi, Thursday, June 9, 1966. On the extreme right is Major General Shaukat Ali Shah, Chief of Protocol, Government of Pakistan. Standing behind the ambassador is the deputy chief of the U.S. mission, Mr. William I. Cargo. Eugene M. Locke Archives.

company created such beautiful surroundings, Jess Hay told him it was based on a simple formula, "M + M"—Maxine and money. Gene Bishop teased the designer by saying, "Maxine Tadlock is the only person I ever gave an unlimited budget to, and she exceeded it."

Eventually, the designer even won over the senior executives whose aesthetics were closely connected to the bottom line. Those who initially flinched at her decorating costs raised their eyebrows in admiration a few years later when the company determined that the value of its antiques and contemporary artwork had appreciated significantly. Maxine Tadlock's fine eye for quality turned L&N's office furnishings into a valuable corporate asset.

Even more important was the contribution the Bryan Tower office made to L&N's enhanced image. That, along with their award-winning annual reports and membership on the New York Stock Exchange,

Eugene Locke's keen interest in politics climaxed with an unsuccessful try for governor of Texas in 1968. At the opening ceremonies of his gubernatorial campaign headquarters in Dallas, candidate Locke is seen with son John at his side. Jess Hay was Locke's campaign finance chairman. Eugene M. Locke Archives.

were key elements in communicating the company's success and growing stature.

There were also financial high points in the early 1970s that represented important milestones in the company's progress. In 1971, stockholder equity moved above $50 million for the first time and the capital base climbed past $100 million. A year later, The Lomas & Nettleton Company produced over $1 billion in mortgages.

In 1972, L&N senior executive vice president Everett Mattson was elected national president of the Mortgage Bankers Association. Mattson was known for his valuable contributions to government relations. He served as a consultant to the National Task Force on Suburbia and as one of the incorporators of the National Housing Partnership, a program designed to provide housing for low-income families.

> *1973*
> now is behind us and few of the L&N family will mourn its passing.

Although few in number, the dark clouds that occasionally appeared during those heady years of expansion were often very personal. The death of Eugene M. Locke on April 28, 1972, was especially painful for Jess Hay. Their friendship represented an important source of support and counsel for both men. It was Locke's interest in real estate and confidence in its growth potential that had brought about the organization of the company and Hay's association with it. Locke had served as the

Jess Hay presented Al Rohnstedt with a bronze sculpture by Harry Jackson on the occasion of his retirement in July 1973. There were some 300 business and personal friends gathered in the ballroom of New York City's Pierre Hotel to pay tribute.

The guiding forces at Lomas & Nettleton, seated, Jess Hay and Gene Bishop, standing, DeWitt Ray and Al Rohnstedt, were not prepared for the events in 1974.

company's first chairman of the board from 1960 to 1963 and as chairman of the executive committee from 1963 to 1966. During the corporate financial crisis, Locke's faith in the business and in Hay's leadership provided a bulwark of strength for the troubled company. Later, Locke's interest in politics led to his appointment first as Ambassador to Pakistan and then as Deputy Ambassador to South Vietnam. At the conclusion of his tenure in Vietnam in 1968, he received America's highest award for public service, the Presidential Medal of Freedom.

Then, in July 1973, the company lost the hands-on leadership of its most experienced mortgage banker when Albert N. Rohnstedt retired as chief operating officer of the mortgage banking division. Fortunately for L&N, this change represented only a partial retirement. Rohnstedt continued to serve as Lomas & Nettleton Financial Corporation vice chairman and to play a leading role at the highest corporate level. The tribute to Al Rohnstedt that appeared in the 1973 annual report acknowledged his 39-year contribution to Lomas & Nettleton and the mortgage banking industry:

> L&N has grown from the small enterprise which Al joined in 1934 to its current position as the nation's largest mortgage banker. In no small measure, this achievement stands as a living tribute to Al Rohnstedt, to his in-depth knowledge of the industry and to his adventuresome and entrepreneurial spirit. . . . The entire L&N family—staff, directors, stockholders, investors and customers—express thanks to Albert N. Rohnstedt for his numerous and lasting contributions to the development of this Company.

It was also in 1973 that the company experienced for the first time since its recovery the difficult reality of a financially troubled economy. Inflation spurred rising interest rates, which resulted in a decline in both loan production and the market value of FHA and VA mortgages. "The year ended June 30, 1973 now is behind us," said Jess Hay in the fall 1973 *Mortgagee,* "and few of the L&N family will mourn its passing."

Despite the sour economic news, L&N continued for the seventh consecutive year to generate more revenue and make more money than ever before. The company's profitability under adverse economic conditions confirmed the advantages of L&N's broad-based approach to financial services. "This performance," Hay said, "is a tribute to the diversity which currently is built into L&N's total operations. . . . L&N enters Fiscal 1974 confident of its ability to sustain its growth even in the current economic environment. Fiscal 1973 proved our capacity to adjust to changing conditions." But, for all Hay's confidence in the company's ability to weather financial squalls, no one was prepared for the fury of the tempest that rocked Lomas & Nettleton Financial Corporation in 1974.

AGNEW OUT

Pleads 'no contest' to income tax evasion

WASHINGTON (AP)—Vice President Spiro T. Agnew resigned Wednesday, his historic decision announced by a weeping staff secretary.

Agnew then pleaded no contest in federal court in Baltimore to a single count of federal income tax evasion.

The vice president, his face drawn, entered the plea before District Court Judge Walter E. Hoffman.

Hoffman told the vice president he considered the no-contest plea the equivalent of an admission of guilt.

Hoffman sentenced Agnew to the maximum $10,000 fine and placed him on probation without supervision for three years.

(Dallas Times Herald Washington correspondent Margaret Mayer said the White House had no immediate comment beyond a White House source saying that President Nixon was advised by the vice president of his intentions on Tuesday night.

(Speculation centered on the likelihood of an imminent appointment of a successor that would be subject to approval by a majority of both houses. Attention has focused in recent weeks on former Texas Gov. John B. Connally as the likely choice.)

Agnew left the courthouse at about 2:40 p.m. stepping into a limousine for an unknown destination. Agnew told

See earlier story on Page 26-A.

newsmen that the Justice Department has not been fully prosecuting witnesses in his case.

Witnesses against him had received either full or partial immunity, Agnew said.

Waving to bystanders, he drove off.

He had attended a hearing in which he and Atty. Gen. Elliot L. Richardson were seated in a courtroom for about 30 minutes.

Agnew's resignation means President Nixon will submit to Congress a nominee to succeed the vice president. The Nixon nominee would take over the vice presidency upon approval by both branches of Congress.

In a statement to the court, Agnew said his decision to resign "rests on my firm belief that the public interest requires swift disposition" of his case.

Agnew entered his plea of no contest to a criminal information filed by U.S. Atty. George Beall.

Agnew said that had not an agreement been reached with the government, and had he been indicted, the case would have dragged on for two or three years and "intense media interest in the case would distract public attention from other matters of national importance."

Richardson announced in the Baltimore courtroom that the Justice Department had recommended Agnew not be imprisoned, on grounds that his resignation and conviction on the tax charge served as sufficient punishment.

The criminal information said Agnew filed a false joint income tax return for 1967 and said he had income of $26,099 and that he owed taxes of $6,416 while in fact his income was $55,599 carrying taxes of $19,967.47.

Richardson told the court that the investigation of kickbacks in Maryland politics during the time Agnew was governor and Baltimore County executive produced evidence which "established a pattern of substantial cash payments to the defendant Agnew during the period when he served as governor of Maryland in return for engineering contracts with the State of Maryland."

Payments by a leading unidentified figure in one large engineering firm began in the early 1960s and continued into 1971, Richardson said.

Agnew also had been under investigation in connection with bribery and extortion accusations.

"I categorically deny assertions of illegal practices on my part by government witnesses," Agnew declared.

THE DALLAS TIMES HERALD

97th Year—No. 283 ★★★★★ • DALLAS, TEXAS, WEDNESDAY EVENING, OCTOBER 10, 1973 Classified: 748-1414 Circulation: 748-6101 Other Depts.: 748-6111 6 Parts Price Ten Cents

MARKETS Pages 9, 10, 11 and 12, Part F

Israeli jets strike Syria, Egypt

By THE ASSOCIATED PRESS

Israel claimed that its warplanes blasted Damascus airport and other strategic targets in the Syrian and Egyptian heartlands today as Iraq announced that its air and ground forces have joined the five-day-old Middle East war.

Syria charged the Israeli jets were hitting civilian targets in the raids on the capital airport, the central industrial city of Homs and Syrian ports on the Mediterranean. The Israeli command qualified the targets as "strategic and military."

Tel Aviv and Damascus reported major aerial engagements also swirled over the Golan Heights battleground and both sides claimed downing large numbers of the other's planes.

The Israeli military command said its raiding jets inflicted "considerable damage" on the Damascus airport. A spokesman said the facility "is no longer a civilian airport but a base for military strikes into Israel."

It was the second reported raid on the Syrian capital. Israeli jets bombed the Defense Ministry and government radio station on the eastern fringes of the city Tuesday. Civilian casualties were reported heavy.

The heavy air battles coincided with indications the ground fighting had tapered off in the Golan Heights and the Sinai peninsula, where Israelis have admitted backing off from their main Suez Canal defense lines against Egyptian forces trying to retake the desert lost to Israel in the 1967 war.

Iraq's announcement that its air and ground forces were playing an active role in the fighting on both fronts formally brought in the Iraquis as the fourth Arab country ranged against Israel in the fourth Arab-Israeli struggle since 1948.

The Beirut newspaper An Nahar reported the Iraqis had committed 18,000 troops and 100 tanks besides air power to support Egyptians in the Sinai and the Syrians in the Golan Heights. These reports were seen as another indication this round of fighting was likely to drag on longer than the lightning six-day Israeli victory of 1967.

With the ground war slowed, the Israeli military command reported its air power blasted installations at Syria's naval base on the Mediterranean, Minat el-Bayda, and fuel installations at Homs, 85 miles north of Damascus.

Homs, an industrial city with oil refineries, was first hit Tuesday by the Israeli raiders.

The Israelis said their pilots reported "accurate hits" in raids on air bases at Khusna and Abu Hammad, west of Ismailia in the Nile Delta, and on a radar station on the Mediterranean coast 60 miles east of Alexandria.

Israeli spokesmen said Israeli planes also flew missions in support of the ground forces facing the Syrians on the Golan Heights and the Egyptians on the east bank of the Suez Canal.

Egypt and Syria said Tuesday that they had beaten back repeated Israeli attacks and were poised for new advances. An Israeli spokesman admitted Tuesday night that Israel's counteroffensive had stalled in both the Sinai Desert and the Golan Heights.

Egyptian officials at the United Nations claimed the Israeli air force also bombed Cairo Tuesday, but the Israelis denied this, and there was no confirmation from the Egyptian capital.

U.S. military analysts told newsmen in Washington they believe the Israelis can drive the Egyptian and Syrian forces back behind the cease-fire lines they crossed last Saturday but only at "a very considerable cost." One official said the Arabs "are doing better this time than they have in the past."

The Pentagon said the amphibious assault ship Guadalcanal, with 2,000 Marines and 30 helicopters on board, was cruising in the eastern Mediterra-

See FIGHTING on Page 20

Israel pressing U.S. for arms

- Israel is pressing the United States to replace military equipment it has lost in the war. (Page 21-A.)
- Lack of Soviet restraint in the new Middle East war causes uneasiness in the Nixon administration although U.S. officials are not willing to publicly charge Moscow with irresponsibility. (Page 28-A.)
- A military affairs analyst says it is perfectly obvious who started the latest Mideast war—the Arabs. (Page 20-A.)
- Jordan, which suffered territorial losses in the 1967 war, intends to stay out of this one if it can. (Page 21-A.)
- Wounded Egyptian soldiers tell how they managed to place bridgeheads across the Suez Canal. (Page 21-A.)

Russia's Malik bolts U.N. talks

By MARTIN G. BERER
Special to Times Herald

UNITED NATIONS—The Soviet ambassador stormed out of the Security Council Tuesday after calling an Israeli air raid on Damascus a "barbaric, gangster act."

It was only one of many expressions of indignation heaped on Israel at U.N. headquarters in response to news reports of Israeli raids on Syria and Egypt, and it came when Israel tried to offer condolences over civilian casualties.

Using some of the most abusive language heard in the council, Jacob Malik of the Soviet Union declared he was "unwilling to hear excuses and condolences from a representative of the murderers and international gangsters." There was scattered applause from the gallery, packed with visitors and diplomats, as Malik left his seat at the council's large horseshoe table.

The outburst came after Josef Tekoah of Israel said his country "expresses its regrets for all the victims — men, women or children — whether Egyptian or Syrian or Israeli or citizens of other states." Tekoah said a large share of the responsibility rested with the Soviet Union for supplying the Arab countries with arms and identifying with their "hatred and barbarity toward Israel." "If not for the Soviet Union, the Middle East might now be in a state of peace," he declared.

Earlier, the ruddy, white-haired Russian referred to unconfirmed wire service accounts of the death of six persons in the Soviet Cultural Center and 30 in the Soviet Embassy and the destruction of 10 embassies in Damascus during Israeli bombing. "Their bloody act is similar to acts of Hitler, when entire cities and villages were destroyed from the earth," Malik said. He called upon Arab countries to unite in a struggle against Israel that is "their sacred and inalienable right." Further, he blamed Israel and world Zionism for "aggression against the entire world," saying that they bore responsibility for keeping the Suez Canal closed and producing worldwide inflation. The Russian launched personal attacks on Israeli Prime Minister Golda Meir and Defense Minister Moshe Dayan, calling both "international criminals" who should be punished for "bloody crimes."

In response to a Syrian denunciation of Israel's action, Tekoah told the council that for the last three days, long-range Syrian missiles had rained fire and death on Israeli civilian villages. Yet, he said, Syria had the audacity to suggest that Israel should not defend itself against military installations in Damascus. He said any civilian losses occurred because they were "in direct proximity" to military targets, which he defined as Syria's army headquarters, air force headquarters and a number of command posts.

Yugoslav Foreign Minister Milos Minic, contending that it was the Arab countries which were engaged in acts of "self-defense," called for sanctions against Israel if it persists in its "ag-

See MALIK on Page 20

—UPI Telephoto

AFTER THE BOMBING—A Syrian civil defense crew reloads equipment onto a truck after fighting fires set in Damascus by Israeli fighter-bombers which struck Tuesday, inflicting considerable damage in the capital.

Court rules pot term cuts illegal

By DAVE MONTGOMERY
Austin Bureau

AUSTIN — The Texas Court of Criminal Appeals Wednesday ruled that persons previously convicted for marijuana possession cannot be resentenced under the state's new drug reform laws.

The court, acting on its first test case under the new statute, ruled that the law's resentencing provision is unconstitutional. The decision does not affect the remainder of the massive statute, which substantially lessens penalties for marijuana possession.

The law went into effect Aug. 27.

In an unrelated decision, the court also reversed the conviction of James R. Wright of Dallas, who was sentenced to a total of four years in prison for possession of marijuana and methamphetamine. The court granted the reversal on the basis of insufficient evidence.

The unanimous opinion on the new drug law — the Texas Controlled Substances Act — upheld a prior ruling by Atty. Gen. John Hill, who earlier declared the resentencing provision unconstitutional.

The provision would have enabled persons convicted of marijuana possession prior to Aug. 27 to petition a district court for possible resentencing under the new law.

The statute reduces possession of less than four ounces of marijuana to a misdemeanor, punishable by a maximum of 180 days in jail and a fine of $1,000. Possession of more than four ounces is a felony, punishable by two to 10 years in prison.

Injustice in justice

Disparity in sentences uncommonly wide here

By RUTH EYRE
Staff Writer

A convicted murderer receives a probated sentence and, in short order, is back on the streets of Dallas.

A young girl, convicted of selling concessions in a theater where an obscene movie is being shown, is sentenced to five years in the women's unit of the Texas State Penitentiary.

ONE IN A SERIES

Two men convicted of kidnaping a Dallas socialite received 5,005-year prison terms—the highest sentences ever handed down by a Dallas jury.

Justice in Dallas County varies widely, depending on the court, the judge, the jury, and the victim.

In recent months, more than a dozen 1,000-year sentences have been returned in Dallas courts and those sentences have put the city in the national spotlight.

But whether the sentences make Dallas look "sick" or whether they have been an effective protest against crime is in question.

"Any juror who sets punishment at 5,000 years is sick and any system that allows it is sick," said Emmett Colvin, a prominent Dallas defense attorney. "It accomplished nothing except to make us the laughing stock of the nation—the world, in fact."

But Dallas County Dist. Atty. Henry Wade said the long sentences "have a good psychological effect" in getting the death penalty restored in Texas.

He said the controversy over sentences as long as 5,005 years now "is a moot question."

"Under the new law the maximum prison terms that can be set are 99 years or life," Wade said.

But the key question —how just is the system of sentencing in Dallas County?—remains.

A Dallas jury gave 50 years to an ex-policeman convicted of assault with intent to rape a young woman who was shot in the head and seriously wounded.

A Dallas federal judge imposed a sentence of 25 years in prison for kidnaping.

A doctor convicted of pushing dangerous drugs, which accidentally could have killed the purchasers, got five

See DALLAS on Page 11

Heat's on fuel

Lower thermostats, Nixon urges

By MARGARET MAYER
Washington Bureau

WASHINGTON — Threats posed by the Arab-Israeli war to America's energy supply gave added impetus Wednesday to a conservation program that President Nixon says could avoid shortages this winter.

While soft-pedaling dangers in the Mideast conflict to the American economy, the White House left no doubt shortages will exist if Saudi Arabia cuts off exports of oil to the western nations.

White House energy adviser John Love said more severe allocations of heating oil than those to be announced later this week will be necessary if the Saudi Arabian supply is curtailed.

Need for 400,000 barrels per day of heating oil in addition to 200,000 now imported via European refineries is anticipated to meet short supplies this winter.

Without referring to the war in the Middle East, President Nixon said Tuesday that more than 400,000 barrels of heating oil per day can be saved if every household will lower its thermostat by four degrees.

Lowering the thermostat was one of the steps recommended in a "citizen action guide to energy conservation" released by a White House Advisory Committee on Environmental Quality Tuesday.

Henry Diamond of New York, spokesman for the group, said one million barrels of oil per day could be saved if only half the American people followed the committee's advice.

"Depend on our self-reliance instead of Arabs for oil," Diamond urged at a White House briefing.

It was one of the few references at the White House to the dangers posed by the conflict in the Middle East.

The administration has developed contingency plans in case its supply of home heating oil from European refineries, using Saudi Arabian crude, is curtailed.

WEATHER REPORT

(National Weather Service Forecast)

Dallas and vicinity: Considerable cloudiness Thursday with chance of thundershowers. Low Wednesday night low 70s. High Thursday low 80s. (See details on Page 4-B.)

WHERE TO FIND

The Middle East conflict between Jews and Arabs erupted on October 6, 1973. The newspaper headline of October 10 shows the developing seriousness of the war, as well as developing problems in the U.S. national government. Reprinted with permission of *The Dallas Morning News*.

CHAPTER VII

A TIME OF TESTING

To a large extent, the economic turmoil of the mid-seventies was a product of the bitter conflict in the Middle East. Antagonism between Arabs and Jews erupted into open hostilities on October 6, 1973, during the festival of Yom Kippur, the holiest day in the Jewish calendar. Despite initial success, the coordinated Egyptian-Syrian attack on Israel ended in failure.

In a display of both solidarity and pique, the Arab OPEC (Organization of Petroleum Exporting Countries) states responded by politicizing oil exports. On October 16, they cut oil production and raised the price 70 percent. On December 23, they raised the price again, this time by 128 percent. Crude oil prices had quadrupled in less than a year.

The abrupt price acceleration overturned accepted Keynesian economic theory and introduced a new economic malady: "stagflation." From a 5.2 percent rate of annual growth with 4.1 percent average inflation, the world moved in 1974 and 1975 to nil or negative growth with an average of 10 to 12 percent inflation. British historian Paul Johnson, among others, considered it the most destructive economic event since World War II.

As Israel's principal ally, the United States suffered the additional burden of an OPEC oil embargo that lasted until March 1974. In an economy dependent on large quantities of inexpensive energy, the crunch came quickly. Thousands of service stations closed on Thanksgiving Day and countless motorists ran out of gas. By early December, New England suppliers of residual oil, which is used by utilities and factories, announced "minimum operable inventories," a dangerous level never before reached in peacetime. On the West Coast, Southern California Gas Co. told 22 of its large corporate customers that their supplies might be interrupted two out of every three days in the coming year. Pacific Gas and Electric Co. curtailed natural gas service to 278 industrial customers for a 24-hour period. The Los Angeles Department of Water and Power warned of possible grid-by-grid blackouts if it could not replenish its sorely depleted supplies of oil and natural gas. In Austin, Texas, a 500-unit apartment complex offered a free keg of beer each month to the tenant using the least electricity. The Milwaukee city council climbed aboard the publicity bandwagon by conducting a meeting by candlelight. In Washington, Interior Secretary Rogers Morton warned that the country might have to endure rolling blackouts, in which certain neighborhoods or towns would be completely without power for limited periods on a rotating basis. The Senate passed an energy emergency bill giving the President near wartime powers over the activities of American citizens and businesses. At Lomas & Nettleton Financial Corporation, Gene Bishop issued a directive that only compact, energy-efficient automobiles would be purchased by the company. A *Mortgagee* article about the energy crunch featured a photograph of George Wilson preparing to throw the switch that would extinguish the neon L&N sign displayed on top of their Houston office building.

Acute fuel shortages and soaring oil prices touched off an inflationary spiral that eroded consumer confidence. By early 1974, a sagging American economy slumped into recession. "In the midst of the horrors of double-digit inflation," a December 1974 *Newsweek* article noted, "recession has now become a bigger problem in the minds of millions of Americans." R. H. Brushkin Associates, a New Jersey market research

Saving energy became a national pastime, and L&N was mindful of its contribution. George Wilson, who headed the Houston servicing office, did his part when he turned out the large neon sign on top of the building, which was a downtown Houston landmark. He also directed that there should be no Christmas tree lights in the offices.

firm, conducted a study that found economic conditions had forced more than 55 percent of American families to make "drastic" changes in their purchasing and living habits. One of the most disturbing statistics from the study indicated that 47 percent of those polled were now buying less food than a year ago.

While most businesses struggled to make it through a harsh business climate, the real estate industry had to deal with widespread devastation. More than most other sectors of the economy, it could lay legitimate claim to depression conditions.

...knocking the hell out of the real estate business.

The industry's problems began when the Federal Reserve Board tried to combat inflation by tightening the money supply and letting interest rates soar. That action triggered a massive outflow of funds from savings institutions. Millions of depositors pulled their cash out of passbook accounts that paid an interest rate of 5¼ percent and bought Treasury bills and bank certificates of deposit that yielded more than 9 percent; and those rates continued to climb. By late 1973, short-term interest rates rose to a record high of 13 percent. Then a normal 2 percent operations fee was added, bringing the real price of money to an astronomical 15 percent. "The severity of the interest rate structure," said James E. Gibbons, president of Sackman-Gilliland Co., a New York-based mortgage brokerage company, "is knocking the hell out of the real estate business. When you're talking about 14, 15, and 16 percent construction money, you know a project can't pay those prices and stay competitive." The annual rate of housing starts plunged from a record high of 2.4 million in 1972 to under one million in 1974.

The mood at the 1974 Mortgage Bankers Association's annual convention was understandably gloomy. "It's not what you call a happy group," said Kent L. Colwell, president of Bankers Mortgage Co. in San Francisco. Attendance declined from the previous year's 5,000 to 3,700. And many of those who attended did so on an austerity budget. First Denver Mortgage Co. sent four people to the convention, the same number as the previous year, but their spouses stayed home. And, for the first time that anyone could recall, the men doubled up, two to a room. According to Alfred M. Mesnick, vice president of the Colonial Group Inc. of Richmond, Virginia, the lack of money wasn't the only problem troubling mortgage bankers. "You can't sell a loan even if you could originate one," the mortgage man complained. "With the soft economy, there aren't any buyers around."

The heaviest blows within the industry fell on real estate development. To some extent, the beating was self-inflicted. The billions of dollars that the REITs had attracted in the early 1970s created a real estate development boom that fed on itself. "The industry," said former LFC executive vice president John F. Sexton, "became overbuilt and oversaturated because there was more product available than demand for it. And there was more product available because there was more money available to make the product . . . a lot of the barriers and disciplines in the real estate lending sector were ignored. Developers and lenders were doing things they normally wouldn't do; they were taking risks they normally wouldn't take. It created a kind of frenzy, and out of that frenzy came the crash."

According to Michael R. Walker, former executive vice president of L&N Management, Inc., the recession was a case of "too much money chasing too little product and too little demand. The Florida market, for example, was horribly overbuilt. The REITs had run out of money. They couldn't afford to finish building, and there wasn't a strong enough market to rent or sell finished condominiums. I remember a trip to Florida in 1974 or 1975 where I saw developers bulldozing condos that were 60 percent complete. That's how overbuilt the market was."

The inflationary environment made survival impossible for many developers. "Investor rates went to 18 percent," said former L&N Management senior executive vice president Buddy Miller, "and the shit really hit the fan. The cost of hanging sheetrock, for example, doubled within a twelve-month period of time. A developer would borrow $3 million for a project, and by the time he got the son-of-a-bitch built, it cost $4 million. . . . Builders began to drop like flies. Those who had deep pockets tried to weather the storm, and some did."

But even large, well-financed developers found themselves scrambling to survive. Many had invested heavily in raw land so they would have a ready inventory for future projects. When the recession hit, they found themselves saddled with a huge land debt that they couldn't carry. "When they write the history of the industry," a troubled Trammell Crow said in 1975, "this period will be described like the 1929 crash."

Jess Hay refused to sugar-coat Lomas & Nettleton Financial Corporation's problems. The first sentence of his stockholders' letter in the 1974 annual report announced the unpleasant reality with what must surely stand as a model of economy and candor: "Fiscal 1974 was a bad year."

We are in a time of testing.

Although it continued to operate profitably, LNFC experienced a significant downturn, producing a net income of $1,597,235 in 1974 as against $7,732,694 in the previous year. Much of the decline was attributed to the company's decision to establish $8 million in additional reserves at year's end. This provision for additional reserves was a precaution against the possibility of future adversity, demonstrating the company's cautious, conservative approach to a recession whose severity was still unknown. "We didn't know where the bottom of that damn thing was," Buddy Miller recalled.

The mortgage banking division took the biggest hit. Its revenues totaled $24,302,772, a substantial decline from $35,404,638 in the previous year. Expenses remained approximately the same at $28,728,895, which resulted in a loss of $4.4 million. "This severe decline," explained the annual report, "is entirely attributable to trading losses and net interest deficits related to the division's warehousing of single-family mortgages."

The trading losses came from the sale of residential mortgages and GNMA securities. "We took," says former Lomas Mortgage USA chairman Jim Wooten, "a large position in 6 and 6¼ percent GNMA securities . . . and held them for what we felt was going to be a reduction in interest rates, and hence a gain in the price of those securities. Well, the short-term rates didn't go the right way, nor did the market. So, we got a double whammy."

With the inversion of long- and short-term interest rates, the short-term money the company used to fund loans until they could be delivered to investors represented a costly interest deficit. In 1973, the company lost about $1 million on its warehousing operations. A year later it showed a loss of $5.6 million. Commercial lending also declined throughout 1974. "For all practical purposes," reported LNFC's 1975 annual report, "commercial and multi-family construction came to an abrupt halt in late 1974." Commercial mortgage loans produced during fiscal 1975 amounted to only $137,769,000, the lowest total since 1967.

Short-term lending in fiscal 1974 contributed $16,742,562 in gross income, an increase of $5.8 million from the previous year. In spite of the trust's strong showing, L&N Management initiated a policy of curtailing its lending activities. "This general policy of constriction," reads the 1974 annual report, "is dictated by current market conditions and will continue until the current deep recession in the real estate indus-

THE DALLAS TIMES HERALD

98th Year—No. 220 • ★★★★ DALLAS, TEXAS, THURSDAY EVENING, AUGUST 8, 1974 4 Parts Price Ten Cents

NIXON TO QUIT

TV address at 8 tonight

By MARGARET MAYER
Times Herald Washington Bureau

WASHINGTON — President Richard Nixon will go on nationwide television Thursday night to tell the people of his decision to resign.

The President called Vice President Gerald Ford to the White House during the morning to notify him of the decision.

The television address is scheduled for 8 p.m. Dallas time.

No man has ever resigned from the presidency.

Press Secretary Ron Ziegler said the President would meet with members of the bipartisan congressional leadership early Thursday night before his television address.

Rep. Olin E. Teague of College Station disclosed Thursday that Nixon has called him to ask him to come by the White House at 7:30 p.m. Thursday.

"He said he wanted to say goodby to his old friends," Teague said, his voice breaking.

Teague, chairman of the House Democratic Caucus, was elected to Congress the same year Nixon was elected; and they are longtime friends.

Teague was Nixon's first choice as successor to Donald Johnson as head of the Veterans Administration earlier this year.

Meanwhile, House Republican Le[illegible] John Rhodes said the President would resign during the day.

Deputy Press Secretary Gerald Warren denied reports from Capitol Hill that Nixon would resign prior to his television address.

He said Nixon would address the nation as the President.

Vice President Gerald Ford was told of Nixon's decision in a 70-minute private meeting in the Oval Office.

Ziegler appeared shortly after the meeting with Ford ended, saying:

"I am aware of the intense interest of the American people concerning developments of the last few days. This has been a difficult time."

He announced the leadership meeting and the television address without elaboration and left the press room before questions could be asked.

Details of the resignation were not immediately known.

White House speech writers were said to have been working throughout the day on the President's speech.

A House Democratic leader said he was told that Nixon's resignation would go to Secretary of State Henry A. Kissinger Friday, and that Ford would be sworn in at 5 p.m. Dallas time Friday as 38th President.

Rep. John McFall, D-Calif., the House Democratic whip, said he got that information from Majority Leader Thomas P. O'Neill.

Other congressional sources said the resignation would be effective at noon Friday.

Ford earlier canceled a scheduled trip to Los Angeles to attend a Republican telethon to be broadcast to West Coast states tonight. The trip was postponed this morning because of the "fast-changing situation in Washington," GOP National Chairman George Bush said in Los Angeles.

Resignation speculation mounted Wednesday night as the presence of the Nixon daughters and their husbands at the White House suggested the convening of a family council where the decision might be made.

A decision had not been reached when three formerly close congressional allies emerged from a 35-minute meeting with Nixon late Wednesday.

Senate Republican Leader Hugh Scott of Pennsylvania, House Republican Leader Rhodes and Sen. Barry Goldwater of Arizona were invited to the White House to give the President an appraisal of his situation in the House and Senate.

Scott told reporters their assessment was "very gloomy . . . very distressing," adding, "I assume he accepted

See PRESIDENT on Page 15

—AP Wirephoto
FORD WAVES—Vice President Gerald Ford gives a friendly wave to photographers as he leaves his home at Alexandria, Va., Thursday.

—UPI Telephoto
PRESIDENT NIXON, trailed by Press Secretary Ron Ziegler, walks to the White House from the Executive Office Building for a meeting with Sens. Hugh Scott and Barry Goldwater and Rep. John Rhodes, congressional Republican leaders summoned by Nixon for consultation.

Resignation rumors fly

By MIKE KELLY
Times Herald Washington Bureau

WASHINGTON — Rumors of an imminent presidential resignation buzzed like persistent flies Wednesday and would not subside despite the best efforts of White House aides to swat them.

The buzzing began on Capitol Hill Wednesday when two newspapers, quoting "informed sources," said Nixon had made an "irrevocable" decision to resign.

The buzzing increased when White House spokesmen at first refused to flatly deny the reports, which appeared in the Providence (R.I.) Journal and the Phoenix Gazette, and a subsequent resignation report by the Westinghouse Broadcasting Corp.

Providence is near the home of Rabbi Baruch Korff, the leader of President Nixon's "grassroots supporters," who left the White House Tuesday afternoon looking shaken.

Korff canceled without explanation Wednesday a series of pro-Nixon radio ads which were to have appeared on the Westinghouse network of radio stations.

The Phoenix Gazette is published in the home state of Sen. Barry Goldwater, whose support is considered essential if President Nixon is to have any hope of acquittal in a Senate trial.

ABC News fueled the rumor mill further about midday Wednesday with a report Goldwater had visited the White House and told the President to resign.

ABC later said the report was wrong.

An angry Goldwater took the Senate floor late Wednesday to deny that he had counseled Nixon to quit.

"I'm forced to do this because of the damned lies that appeared today on ABC and NBC," the Arizonan said. "I have not been in the White House in two weeks. I haven't seen the President since May 5 or 10.

"If American television and the

See PRESS on Page 14

Ford aides establish plans for transition

By DAVID S. BRODER and JULES WITCOVER
The Washington Post

WASHINGTON — Associates of Vice President Gerald R. Ford have been working since Monday night on contingency planning for the transition to a Ford administration, one of them acknowledged Wednesday night.

This planning would have Ford, on assuming the presidency:

—Deliver a brief speech to the American people, calling on the nation to unite behind him, praising the courage of President Nixon for stepping down and asking everyone to put the needs of the country first.

—Ask all Cabinet members and key aides to stay on, with special emphasis on Secretary of State Henry A. Kissinger, whose public popularity is recognized as a source of particular strength for a new administration and President.

—Convert to a Ford team in the White House through gradual transition, and maintain a more open staff operation, in keeping with Ford's own personality and style.

In these and other steps, the clear intent would be to bolster public confidence that the wheels of government will continue to turn, while injecting into the public consciousness Ford's own spirit of good will as he embarks on the presidency.

The planning went forward Wednesday as Ford once again experienced the pressures of what appears to be his certain elevation to the White House. He was riding to Capitol Hill for a breakfast meeting of the Chowder and Marching Society, a House Republican social group, when he got a call to go to the White House.

His car turned and took him to his Executive Office Building suite, where he conferred for about an hour with Alexander M. Haig Jr., President Nixon's chief of staff. Paul Miltich, Ford's press secretary, would say only that the two had "exchanged views about the current situation."

Ford also visited the office of his old friend, House Minority Leader John J. Rhodes of Arizona, and was cheered and applauded by tourists. He conferred in his Dirksen Senate Office Building suite with Senate Assistant

See TRANSITION on Page 15

Wholesale prices jump 3.7% in July

WASHINGTON (AP) Wholesale prices jumped 3.7 per cent last month, the Labor Department reported today.

This works out to a staggering 44.4 per cent on an annual rate.

The monthly increase was the largest since the 6.2 per cent jump last August and compared with an average monthly increase of 1.4 per cent over the first six months of this year.

All figures are arrived at after taking seasonal variations into account.

Since wholesale price increases are usually translated into higher prices for consumers, the report cast a pall over hopes for any slackening in the nation's double-digit inflation.

The biggest wholesale jump was in volatile farm prices. A 6.4 per cent jump in July reversed four straight months of decline.

The Nixon administration had tied falling or at least moderating food prices to its predictions for getting inflation down to a 7 per cent annual rate of increase by year's end. Consumer prices are currently 11 per cent above a year ago.

The wholesale increase in food prices alone was 3.6 per cent on a seasonally adjusted basis, with meat pacing the increase. Processed foods and sugar also posted significant increases. Prices for milk and fresh vegetables declined.

Foreshadowing possible future trouble for meat prices was an even larger rise — 5.5 per cent — for the processed feeds farmers must buy for their livestock.

Auto prices, usually stable at this time of year, also rose. Industrial commodities moved upward, although not as steeply as farm prices. The increase for the industrial commodities was 2.7 per cent, compared to a 2.2 increase the previous month. Wholesale prices have been increasing by more than 2 per cent all year.

See the new Mac Davis Show tonight at 7 on Channel 5. (Adv.)

The Nixon story

- Washingtonians wait in hushed expectancy for history to be made. Page 9-A.
- Rumors of Nixon resignation trigger flood of calls to White House. Page 10-A.
- Nixon told he can count on no more than 15 votes in Senate. Page 10-A.
- If Nixon steps aside, transition to be quick, complete. Page 11-A.
- World leaders assured U.S. policy won't change if Nixon leaves. Page 3-A.

Increase in school tax larger than expected

By ERIC MILLER
Education Writer

Dallas taxpayers will pay an additional 7 cents in school taxes per $100 valuation next year for a $179 million school budget that promises no overall increases in educational programs.

The adoption of the largest budget in the history of the Dallas Independent School District (DISD) by the school board Wednesday came without public comment and increased the school tax rate by 2 cents to the legal limit of $1.50 per $100 valuation with the assessment based on 54 per cent of property values.

The surprise came when the trustees also voted to increase payment on bond debt interest to 37 cents, an increase of 5 cents.

The two increases boost the total school tax rate from $1.80 to $1.87.

As a result, school taxes paid by the owner of a home valued at $20,000 will increase by $7.56 next year—from $194.40 per year to $201.96.

Trustees had indicated an increase of 4 cents had been anticipated—2 cents for the school tax and 2 cents for the interest on the sinking fund.

However, when the board convened at the administration building Wednesday afternoon, reporters were presented with a press package detailing two alternatives, one for a 2 cent sinking fund tax increase and the other for a 5 cent increase.

Without discussion, the board voted 7-1 to approve the 5 cent increase. Trustee Robert Medrano voted against.

Board president Eugene Smith Jr. termed the board's action a "sound move," saying if the board opted for the 2 cent increase, an estimated $1.2 million capital deficit in the interest and sinking fund could damage the DISD's Triple A rating on Wall Street.

Smith later told The Times Herald, in addition to stepping up payment of construction bond indebtedness, the additional 5 cents would cover any losses in security interest or overdrafts as the board continues its search for a treasurer to handle the district's money.

"A triple A rating will, in the long run, save the taxpayer millions," Smith said.

"You don't want to create a situation that will make your bonds less attractive to the investor," DISD controller Charles Hardy said.

The DISD has called for a 1974-75 school operating budget of $125.4 million, the portion which will be financed by local and state funds.

Straws in the wind

Washington is seething with reports of impending resignation of the President, and here are some of the straws in the wind:

* * *

David Eisenhower and Edward Cox, sons-in-law of the President, made the round of the Executive Office Building, and a source said they were saying goodby to old friends, UPI's Helen Thomas reports.

* * *

Gerald Ford's wife Betty said she had given "some thought" about possibly becoming first lady but she is now "living a day-to-day existence. I feel I am just continuing in the same way trying to keep up with the mail," UPI reports.

WEATHER REPORT

(National Weather Service Forecast)

Dallas and vicinity: Partly cloudy through Friday with a 20 per cent chance of thundershowers Thursday night. Low Thursday night lower 70s. High Friday near 90. (See details on Page 12-C.)

Dallas temperatures:

10 pm...78	4 am...74	10 am...76
12 M....77	6 am...74	12 N....78
2 am...75	8 am...73	2 pm...80

Air pollution index: 12 (light).
Herald Square temp., 11 a.m.: 76.

WHERE TO FIND

Arts 5-8B	Horoscope ..11B
Bridge 32C	Jumble 11B
Business ..8-11C	Living 2-4B
Cavalcade ..10B	Metropolitan .1C
Classified 12-31C	Motosport ..11D
Comics 11B	Obituaries ..12C
Crossword ..31C	Owens 10B
Editorials 2C	Seek&Find ..21C
Gallery 1B	Sports ..1-10,12D
Graham 32C	Television ...9B
Health Tips .32C	Theaters ...5,6B

TODAY'S CHUCKLE

Any boy who is anxious to mow the lawn is too young.—(Copyright)

While Lomas & Nettleton was searching for the bottom of its financial problems in 1974, the government in Washington was also searching for the bottom of its political scandals. Reprinted with permission of *The Dallas Morning News*.

try subsides."

Fiscal 1974 fulfilled its billing as a bad year. But one had only to examine the theme from the annual report to find signs of hope. The photograph of three generations of women on the cover provided a glimpse of the indomitable human spirit. Their steady, unflinching gaze suggested deep reserves of strength, competence, and determination. By focusing on the commitment and enduring qualities that link generations of American families, Lomas & Nettleton offered a larger, life-affirming perspective from which to view its present difficulties.

Hay's speeches during this period presented a balanced perspective. Acknowledging the uncertainty of the times, he addressed those fears at general staff meetings:

> Anxiety stands at the very heart of our country today. Our government is in disarray. The stock market reflects gloom and doom. Inflation is eating away at all our resources. Our developer friends are strained at best or broken at worst. Banks are nervous, frustrated, and shell-shocked. And the country itself seems to be grappling aimlessly for direction. . . .
>
> But we are not in a time of crisis . . . for crisis implies a question of survival. That is not a question applicable either to Lomas & Nettleton Financial Corporation or to Lomas & Nettleton Mortgage Investors. . . . Our credit has not been constricted. Our capital has not been impaired. Our portfolio, although weaker in certain respects than in the past, remains relatively liquid and adequately protected by reserves. So the question is not one of survival [but of] whether we can respond reasonably well to adversity and continue as a reasonably profitable institution. . . . We are in a time of testing.

For Jess Hay, the fundamental test involved character rather than credit or capital. "My hope," said Hay

Lomas & Nettleton Financial Corporation 1974 Annual Report

Though fiscal 1974 was a bad year for the company and the whole real estate industry, the theme of the annual report suggested continuity and hope. The cover reflected the indomitable human spirit in a photograph of three generations of women with strong resolve.

at a 1974 staff meeting, "is that we will embrace the future determined to shape it as best we can for our continuing growth, but even more determined to face the future as men and women of integrity—men and women of L&N who recognize that fairness in our dealings with others surely is the one indispensable ingredient of long-term functioning in this or any business."

At the top of the mortgage banking division's agenda was an effort to shut off the heavy losses incurred through warehousing. The Lomas & Nettleton Company attacked the problem on two fronts. First, there was a conscious effort to reduce the total inventory of loans. Then, in July 1974, L&N took a more aggressive step by introducing what they called a "warehousing fee" to help cover a portion of the net cost of carrying residential loans. "We invented the term 'warehousing fee,'" says Jim Wooten, "and tried to sell it to the industry." It was a tough sell. Wooten called it "the cost of doing business" when he spoke at mortgage banking gatherings throughout the country. He explained that mortgage bankers already charged for appraisals, credit reports, and loan originations—a warehousing fee was just one more item that had to be covered. Some were persuaded to add the new fee. Some were not.

. . . g into a survival strategy. . .

Implementing the new policy within L&N itself was no easy matter. Other mortgage bankers didn't hesitate to use the added charge against the company. Angry L&N production personnel flooded Wooten's office with circulars and advertisements from competitors. Printed on each one were the words: NO WAREHOUSE FEE. "There were pockets," says Wooten, "in the Midwest and Northeast that refused to charge a warehousing fee. They collected the same amount of money through a larger discount. We tried to keep that from happening because we wanted to establish an industry standard. About half of the L&N offices adopted the warehousing fee and the other half didn't. Finally, I said the hell with it, just so we get our money."

The corrective measures worked. Instead of a loss, mortgage banking showed a $600,000 gain in its fiscal 1975 warehousing operation.

When interest rates for mortgage loans moved into double digits, L&N's loan production offices scrambled to cut expenses. George E. Francis, who became executive vice president of the Western Region in the summer of 1974, remembers the severe reductions. What had been a 20-office region now found its operations consolidated into nine offices, some with only skeleton crews. "Probably 60 to 70 percent of our total costs," says Francis, "are based on personnel. So the heavy cuts are going to be from the release of people. But that doesn't mean you can't pick up another 10 percent off of travel, expense accounts, and that sort of thing. It was very painful for about a year and a half."

Federal assistance helped ease some of the pain in late 1975. A direct subsidy program run by HUD enabled mortgage bankers to make loans 2 to 3 percent below the market rate. Lining up the actual subsidy commitments, however, took some doing. The government agency's phone lines were jammed with calls from mortgage companies all over the country. In order to get through, Francis assigned a team of employees to do nothing but dial and redial the government telephone numbers eight hours a day. The effort generated $30 million worth of loan commitments "which we used for our builder customers. We made sure we were fair to the people that had been loyal to us. This program enabled us to survive the crunch. Then interest rates started to drop, and we started to expand again." In 1975, the company's savings from reduced production expenses amounted to just under $2 million.

Inflation and high interest rates also took their toll on L&N's commercial lending operation. The 20-office network Fred Morrison had built in the early seventies

The NCR 315 computer system inherited from the T. J. Bettes Company functioned for ten years. The complete magnetic tape system was delivered to the T. J. Bettes Company in April 1963 and was turned over as operational on June 1, 1963. This system consisted of a control processor with 20K memory, six card random access memory units, two high-speed buffered printers, one high-speed card punch with buffer, one 2,000 card per minute reader, and one remote inquiry buffer and six remote inquiry stations. Gene Chandler, a member of the data processing department, is pictured at right.

began to contract under the pressures of recession. "We cut whatever we could in the way of costs and expenses," says former L&N president Fred Morrison, "sloughed off extra personnel, cut office space if a lease came up, and disciplined people in incidental expenses more than usual. In good times, you might not bang a guy if he runs up a big hotel bill, but in bad times you give him hell." It was a mode of operating that for the first time required the division to "retrench, cut back, go into a survival strategy. . . ."

The challenge, according to Charles W. Wingo, who became executive vice president in charge of commercial lending after Fred Morrison left the company in 1976, was in finding new ways of doing business: "We were continuously looking for ways to make something work, like giving equity in joint ventures so that the lenders were part owners. We made deals work that wouldn't work in a normal debt environment." Some of the other business alternatives included foreclosures, property sales, and refinancing. "We were in the fee business," says former L&N senior vice president James C. Brownlow. "Any way we could make a fee, we did it. Consulting, for example. Someone might call and ask us to write a report for $10,000. We'd say, 'Fine, we'll do it.'"

For the resourceful, there was even some commercial loan business available. Jim Brownlow, a commercial loan underwriter at the time, recalls developing new business in what he calls Texas' "second tier cities" such as Tyler, Longview, Austin, and El Paso, which weren't overbuilt like Dallas and Houston: "A number of our investors had available funds, and there was pressure for them to put those funds out. If we could go to a new market and prove there was absorption and good

In May 1972, senior vice president for data processing E. G. Bray recommended the purchase of a Burroughs 6700 computer to replace the NCR 315. It represented the most advanced technology in disk file systems. Charles Babbage Institute, University of Minnesota.

rental rates, they would go there." Brownlow attributes L&N's success in those new markets to concentrating on mainstream bread-and-butter projects that were feasible. "One of the reasons," says Brownlow, "that Chuck [Wingo] and I were so successful is because we didn't waste our time on marginal properties. I knew a lot of mortgage bankers who chased every deal out there. They spent their time working on twenty deals but only one or two of them made sense."

Data processing was the one division in mortgage banking that experienced turmoil and change unrelated to the recession. This upheaval was a product of the decision to change computer systems. The NCR magnetic tape system inherited from the T. J. Bettes Company was seriously outmoded in terms of both technology and capacity. The acceleration of L&N's mortgage banking expansion program in 1970 and 1971 added fresh urgency to what was already a serious problem.

Based on the recommendation of E. G. Bray, the company made a commitment in May 1972 to purchase a Burroughs 6700 computer. It represented the most advanced technology in disk file systems. The disk file capability permitted L&N to place its entire data base on-line for interrogation using any terminal in the system from California to Connecticut. The contrast between the two systems was dramatic. If you needed data at the end of a tape in the older system, it could take ten minutes to access it. "We were the first mortgage company," says Bray, "that ever went to that extent in making data available for interrogation."

Data processing took delivery of its new hardware in the summer of 1973. Bray's division spent the rest of that year setting up a communications network and programming the new system, which required a complete rewrite of existing programs. "1974," says Bray, "was the year we started converting everything from the NCR 315 system to the Burroughs 6700. So we had our hands full and a little bit more. We spent 1975 improving the system. We were busier in 1974 and 1975 than ever before, because we were making a conversion to a new system."

At a cost of just under $2 million, the new system included 23 video disk terminals and ten hard copy terminals that furnished instant data communications between Houston and the company's six mortgage banking regions. A 1974 *Mortgagee* article, titled "The Computer Moves In," noted that Bray and vice presidents James A. May, Jr., and Charles J. Eglinger, Jr., represented a combined total of 65 years of data processing experience.

"How can I compare it with our former system or any other system?" remarked executive vice president of servicing George I. Wilson in that same article. "It's at least three steps ahead, and the future potential is almost unlimited."

When the full impact of the recession shattered

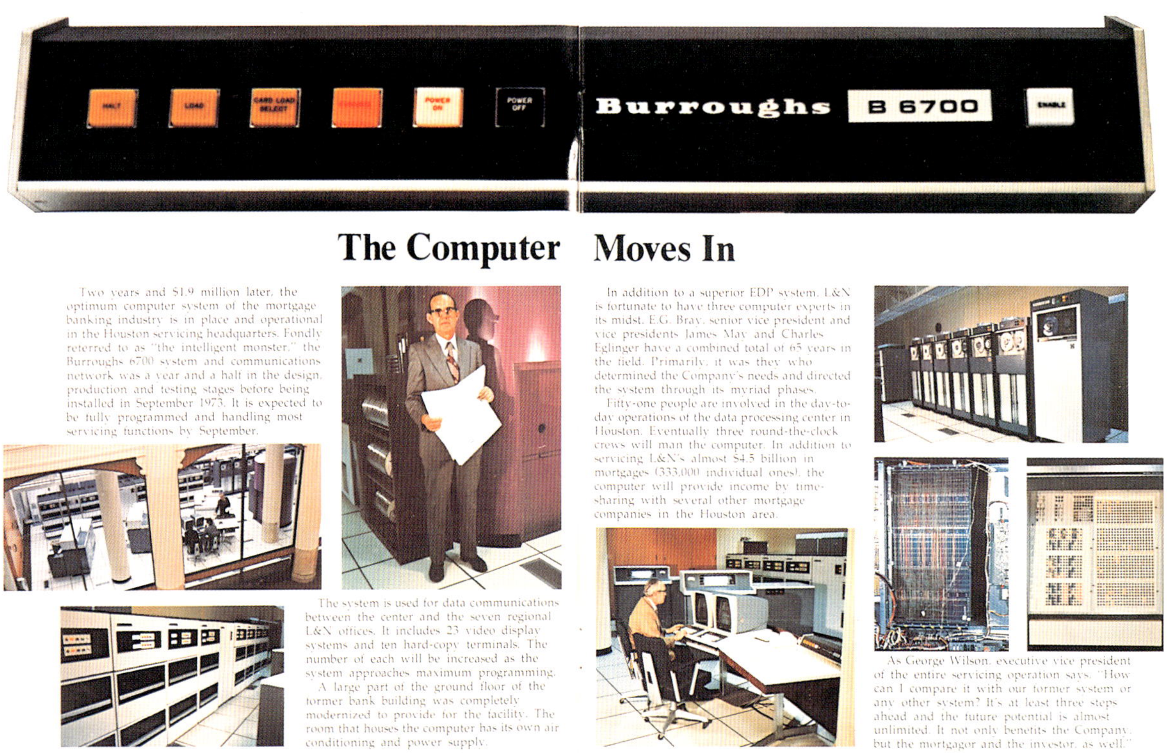

The Computer Moves In

Two years and $1.9 million later, the optimum computer system of the mortgage banking industry is in place and operational in the Houston servicing headquarters. Fondly referred to as "the intelligent monster," the Burroughs 6700 system and communications network was a year and a half in the design, production and testing stages before being installed in September 1973. It is expected to be fully programmed and handling most servicing functions by September.

The system is used for data communications between the center and the seven regional L&N offices. It includes 23 video display systems and ten hard-copy terminals. The number of each will be increased as the system approaches maximum programming.

A large part of the ground floor of the former bank building was completely modernized to provide for the facility. The room that houses the computer has its own air conditioning and power supply.

In addition to a superior EDP system, L&N is fortunate to have three computer experts in its midst. E.G. Bray, senior vice president and vice presidents James May and Charles Eglinger have a combined total of 65 years in the field. Primarily, it was they who determined the Company's needs and directed the system through its myriad phases.

Fifty-one people are involved in the day-to-day operations of the data processing center in Houston. Eventually three round-the-clock crews will man the computer. In addition to servicing L&N's almost $4.5 billion in mortgages (333,000 individual ones), the computer will provide income by time-sharing with several other mortgage companies in the Houston area.

As George Wilson, executive vice president of the entire servicing operation says, "How can I compare it with our former system or any other system? It's at least three steps ahead and the future potential is almost unlimited. It not only benefits the Company, but the mortgagor and the investor, as well."

"Two years and $1.9 million later . . . the computer moves in." The double-page 1974 *Mortgagee* profile referred to it fondly as "the intelligent monster."

With the installation of the Burroughs 6700 computer, the 1974 L&N data processing department had much to smile about. E. G. Bray is third row center.

real estate development in 1974, Lomas & Nettleton Mortgage Investors learned a small lesson in humility. In the early seventies, the trust's highly vaunted lending policies and loan administration procedures encouraged a sense of invulnerability among some of its officers. It was true that LNMI's conservative policies protected the trust from the wholesale devastation that wiped out so many REITs, but they didn't provide the kind of sanctuary many expected. L&N Management discovered how difficult it was to insulate LNMI from the euphoria of the real estate construction boom prior to the recession. The availability of construction money during the boom years increased the pressure on LNMI to step outside its policy guidelines. Many developers refused to do business with lenders who weren't willing to back them through the entire development cycle, beginning with the purchase of land. "We had a stated policy," said former L&N Management senior vice president Robert W. Talkington, an experienced underwriter for the trust during the 1970s, "that said we did not make speculative land loans. The fact of the matter is, we did. Now, in many cases, we rationalized them because they were good customers or because they were going to convert it into a project someday, so maybe it wasn't speculative per se because they planned to flip it. . . . We had land loans all over the place. . . . And they all went bad in 1974 and 1975, totally bad."

We did not believe in quick foreclosures.

The company's close, long-term relationships with developers sometimes made it difficult to ignore special requests. When one of LNMI's proven customers, a high-volume Denver builder, asked the trust to fund a 22-unit condominium project at a ski resort in Copper Mountain, Colorado, the company agreed to make the loan even though recreational loans were clearly outside policy guidelines. "It [was]," says Ted Enloe, "sort of an accommodation deal. Then hard times hit and recreational deals were hit harder than most because of the energy crunch. And we ended up owning them."

According to Enloe, nonpolicy loans represented no more than 10 percent of LNMI's $450 million portfolio. The largest percentage of problems came from loans within the guidelines. For example, management required takeout agreements from third parties before financing hotels. However, Enloe remembers that this offered no protection in the case of four loans because the companies that had issued the takeouts were financially unable to honor their commitments. As a result, LNMI was forced to add four hotels to its growing list of problem assets.

LNMI's emphasis on long-term relationships anchored by trust and integrity contributed to a policy that gave borrowers flexibility. "We did not believe in quick foreclosures," says former L&N Management underwriter Mike Walker. It was a policy that placed considerable faith in a strong customer base of proven professionals. It also made good business sense. Denny Wallace, former senior vice president of real estate at First National Bank of Dallas, had a similar approach to problem loans during the recession: "My theory was if a customer was honest and capable, I didn't want to foreclose because he probably had a greater ability to get rid of the property than I did. After all, the developer has his reputation, his future, his pocketbook, and everything else at stake. If you give capable people time and leave them alone, they will work it out. I didn't bug them for the interest payment every fifteen minutes, either."

Integrity played an important role in foreclosure decisions at Lomas & Nettleton Mortgage Investors. The high standard of honesty the company demanded of itself was expected from those it dealt with. "As long as the developer is honest," says Ted Enloe, "and is capable of dealing with the project, our policy is to stay with him, because it is our feeling that he will do a better job than we will.

"If, however, the developer steals from us and starts taking funds from our project and uses them for his other problems, that's a different story."

It was a period that tested the character of those associated with the real estate development industry. "It separated the wheat from the chaff," said Buddy Miller. "The borrowers with integrity would come in, in advance, and say to us, 'Look, I can't make it. I'm going down the tubes. Let me give you the property back, deed in lieu of,' meaning that the developer agrees to deed the property over to Lomas & Nettleton.

"Developers without integrity denied their problems and fought you all the way. Their tendency was to retreat inwardly. They reminded me of a barroom brawl where it's me against the world, and I get a beer bottle, crack it open, and find a corner. And if you've got guts enough to come after me, then come on.

"If you wanted your money from someone like that, you had to go to the courthouse and use every legal avenue available to collect it. They fought you every step of the way."

A favorite tactic among some developers with their backs to the wall was to use the threat of bankruptcy for leverage or concessions. "I can't tell you," says Ted Enloe, "how many times builders came into my office and threatened me with bankruptcy." One prominent Houston developer demanded the trust pay him $4 million in exchange for not filing for bankruptcy. Enloe had no patience for extortionist threats: "'Wait a minute,' I told him. 'Let me call Robert Price, and we'll drive you to the courthouse right now.' I looked him in the eye and said, 'I'd much rather deal with a bankruptcy judge than a dishonest builder.'

"To make a long story short, he deeded the properties over to us, and we didn't pay him a nickel. We released him from liability, but he was broke anyway so that didn't matter."

The support LNMI extended to borrowers who demonstrated integrity and ability was considerable. "I remember," says Mike Walker, "in meetings with our bankers, Jess was very supportive of the company's quality borrowers. He asked the bankers not to panic and to stay with the people who were honest because they had the entrepreneurial ability to get through the recession if we provided them with the cash to do it."

LNMI customer Ken Good, a Denver developer with an exceptional talent for raw land investments, was an example of how far the company was willing to go to help a borrower survive. "We had," says Ted Enloe, "a lot of land loans with Ken in Denver, Colorado. Then came the recession, along with a severe water crisis. A big water bond was defeated, and the city put a moratorium on development. So we, along with Ken, were left with unzoned, unwatered, unsewered, agricultural land."

"Ken Good," says Walker, "was a case where we just believed in the guy. He was busted. He couldn't cover his overhead. But rather than pull the plug on him, we decided he had the ability to make it if we helped him do it."

Together with Republic National Bank of Dallas, LNMI loaned him new money backed by additional collateral. Because of Good's reputation as a spender and high roller, the trust and the bank took the precaution of carefully allocating the money. "We had Ken on an operating budget," says Enloe, "that included his monthly household money. He had a budget where he could spend *x* amount of dollars per month personally. If he needed more than that, he had to come to me and John Stuart over at Republic Bank to get permission. For Ken, this was a severe restriction because that man could spend more money than anybody could print. He wasn't happy about the restrictions, but he had to have the money to stay alive." Two or three years later, after the Denver economy got back on track, Ken Good struck gold with a land transaction that enabled him to pay off all his creditors, both principal and accrued interest, with enough left over to buy a palatial 22,000 square foot residence in Denver, a house in Vail, and sock ten or so million away in his bank account.

The company also assisted development company giant Lincoln Property. Burdened by a large land debt, it needed working capital to get through the recession. Along with Union Bank of California, another major Lincoln Property lender, L&N Management put together a $27 million "bridge loan," so-called because it bridged the gap between the need for money and the sale of properties. According to Mike Walker, about $6 million of the new funds were used to pay taxes on properties that had not been escrowed during the year because Lincoln had used that money to pay other expenses. L&N participated in another loan to Lincoln Property when the first one proved insufficient. "We did a son of bridge," says Enloe, "a second loan. But it turned out well, and they paid us back. . . . Personally, I'm very proud of our role because we preserved a good company and good customers. Other Lincoln Property lenders were sympathetic about the company's problems but only two, Union Bank and LNFC, were willing to step up and loan new money to keep the organization alive."

Nowhere was L&N's support more forthcoming than for its single most important customer, Trammell Crow. Crow was the largest private real estate developer in the country; when the bottom dropped out of the market, his problems were substantial. By late 1974, his $1.5 billion empire of warehouses, shopping centers, hotels, garden apartments, and condominiums projected an annual negative cash flow of up to $25 million. Fortunately, Crow owned many of the properties he developed. His portfolio of assets, especially large numbers of highly profitable warehouses, was considerable. The sale of those assets became the key to his fight for survival.

Is Trammell Crow going to make it?

The first hurdle to overcome in that struggle was obtaining enough working capital to survive the six to nine months needed to appraise, market, and close a sale. Many lenders refused Crow's requests for a bridge loan. His problems were large and his future uncertain. The help he needed came from two of his most dependable lenders, First National Bank of Dallas and Lomas & Nettleton Financial Corporation.

It wasn't the first time LNFC had helped Crow out of a tough situation. The construction loan for the 40-

The construction loan for Trammell Crow's 40-story Bryan Tower had problems in 1970. LNFC helped Crow out of a difficult situation and the $45 million building was completed in 1972. Courtesy the Trammell Crow Company.

story Bryan Tower hit an unexpected snag in 1970 that almost sank the project. "I had the construction loan worked out with Republic Bank," says Trammell Crow. "But Mr. Aston, who was in charge of the bank, turned it down a week before we were to start building. He said it could only be a one-year loan. Well, you can't build a two-year building with a one-year loan. Jess Hay took me over to Mercantile Bank and within a week I had the loan. Jess is a very, very highly regarded man, and he recommended the loan to J. D. Francis." The incident helped solidify the already strong personal and historical connections between L&N and Trammell Crow.

In mid-1975, First National Bank of Dallas and Lomas & Nettleton Financial Corporation participated jointly in a $25 million line of credit for the Trammell Crow Company. According to former First National Bank senior vice president Denny Wallace, the loan was based on sound lending practices: "It was not a real earth-shaking, flag-waving event. Trammell Crow was the biggest customer we had. We knew his portfolio, and we knew his assets were outstanding. His only problem was cash flow. Lomas & Nettleton, who had been lending to him, was also well informed about his condition. And they, like the bank, were convinced his assets far exceeded his liabilities. We didn't think of ourselves as the sacrificial lamb trying to save our friend Trammell."

The two lenders also used their influence to convince others that Crow was worthy of support. At a LNMI meeting in September 1975 attended by representatives of commercial banks, Jess Hay wrote a memorandum outlining the trust's lending relationship with Trammell Crow, noting that "during the entire six-year period, there has never been, with respect to any of such indebtedness, a material delinquency in the payment of any principal or interest. . . .

"Unlike many in the industry, Trammell Crow has *both the resources and the character to weather the pressures of the current depression in the real estate development industry and he will do so.*"

Overcoming uncertainty among the banking community wasn't easy. An article published by *Forbes* in October 1975 increased apprehension. The story, "Crow Eats Crow," painted a dark picture of the developer at the edge of a precipice, struggling to keep his grip and avoid plunging into a Chapter 11 bankruptcy. A week or two after the article appeared, Denny Wallace attended a Mortgage Bankers Association convention in Chicago. "One day I went to get my mail," Wallace recalls, "and I had a half-inch-thick stack of telephone messages from life insurance companies and bankers wanting to see me. They had read the *Forbes* article, and they were concerned about Trammell Crow. The first person I talked to was a top executive from one of the big East Coast lenders. He asked me point blank, 'Is Trammell Crow going to make it?' I said, 'Yes, sir. No question about it.' Then he asked me why I was so certain. And I looked him right in the eye and said, 'Because we are going to lend him enough money to see that he does.'

"He must have quoted me all over the convention because people came up to me and asked me to confirm the statement I made. When I came home and word about what happened got back to Trammell, he called and said, 'Denny, I wish you'd go to more conventions.'"

Among lenders, the general lack of confidence in real estate investment trusts seemed justified during the recession. Their poor survival rate placed them at the top of the real estate industry's endangered species list. High attrition, even among the largest and most respected REITs, moved LNMI from sixth or seventh in size to the second largest trust in the country. "The banks," says Ted Enloe, "were like most people. They sort of had a herd instinct. . . . We were demonstrably different from other REITs. We never were leveraged to the extent others were. . . . But unfortunately, some banks didn't really differentiate us from them. And as our nonearning assets kept increasing, they became increasingly nervous."

A three-year line of credit with three large national banks that lost confidence in LNMI caused the company a great deal of aggravation. "They were a real pain in the neck," says John Sexton. "They just didn't want to be involved with a REIT because they knew we were going to go broke, too. And if they could get out, great. . . . They were in our offices constantly analyzing what assets were going to go bad next." Despite the fact that the trust was absolutely current in its payments to the three lenders, L&N Management was afraid they would try to find a technical default in the fine print of the loan agreement and call the loan, which would have caused problems the company couldn't afford. "It was a very, very tense time for all of us here," Ted Enloe recalls. "Fortunately, some of our long-standing banking relationships had enough confidence to loan us the money and pay them off."

You need to learn about getting out of a bad situation . . .

The ease with which LNMI arranged the loan to pay off the three problem banks demonstrated the strength of the company's banking relationships. "We had," says John Sexton, "a very strong core of old bank relationships that were just that. They weren't one-shot banking deals; they were real relationships. We had a lot of friends who weren't going to run from us when times got tough."

As L&N Management began to constrict the trust's lending activity, the focus shifted to nonearning assets. According to Enloe, accountability was an important part of the process: "We operated under the theory that if you made the loan you had to collect it. I don't believe in having a separate workout section that does nothing but work on the bad properties while the loan officers are the prima donnas, who just make loans and don't have to worry when they go bad. Besides, you don't learn anything that way. You need to learn about getting out of a bad situation with a broke builder who steals money from you, lies to you, and threatens to file bankruptcy. That's all part of the process."

One procedure for managing the trust's portfolio was to follow the loans more closely and take prompt action before minor difficulties escalated into major problems. Their ability to prevent "tail-ending" demonstrated the strategy's effectiveness. Tail-ending refers to a practice some developers use to finish projects that have run out of money. The builder takes out a second loan for another development and uses a portion of that money to finish the first project. Besides violating loan agreements, it automatically places the second development in jeopardy and forces the developer to take out a third loan for still another project. Although Buddy Miller admitted the company got its "fingers burned on three or four projects," his loan administration division responded quickly with corrective measures. "We monitored our portfolio extremely well," says Mike Walker. "Marvin Sexton, for example, was hired as an auditor to go out and look at the books. It doesn't take long to find out if a builder, instead of paying his subcontractors, is using our money for other projects. All you have to do is ask a subcontractor. He'll let you know pretty quick."

Once it was detected, management controlled the problem by issuing joint payee checks. That meant, for example, that instead of permitting a builder to draw $100,000 in a lump sum, they broke the amount down into joint payee checks and made the checks out to designated subcontractors responsible for supplying sheetrock, lumber, brick, etc. The practice didn't win any popularity contests among the developers forced to live with it. "For the borrowers we felt were tail-ending," said Miller, "we exercised the right to do joint payee checks. Needless to say, many of them squealed like a pig under a gate. They wanted their hands on that money to use at their discretion."

The trust also became adept at liquidating its foreclosures. By early 1975, the sharp increase in nonearning assets prompted management to organize a format for tracking problem loans. The result was a periodically updated document called "The Draft," which listed the trust's substandard loans, including both foreclosed properties and those with severe credit problems. The first installment was printed in March 1975. Underwriters and loan administrators assigned to work on those assets could tell from each entry what a loan's problems were, how they should be corrected, the approximate time required, and the estimated cost. It was a valuable tool for getting a handle on problems that might otherwise have become overwhelming. "The Draft," says Ted Enloe, "helped us break our problems down into very, very small units. . . . Everybody had one or two or three assets that he was working with. . . . We spent long hours in meetings each month deciding who was going to do this and this and this."

"It was like cutting down a redwood tree with an axe," said Miller, "a tree that's so large you can drive a car through it. . . . You look up and it seems impossible, but you cut a piece at a time, slowly chipping away."

The most important step after foreclosing on a partially built development was to finish it. The loan administration staff's strong background in construction gave the company an important advantage. "Because of the in-house expertise we had," said Miller, "most of our projects never lost much momentum." Many competitors who didn't have that ability were left holding half-built developments that remained that way. Miller recalled passing abandoned construction sites where stacks of two-by-four lumber, normally a golden color, had turned black from weathering. "It wasn't unusual to see properties that looked like Berlin after the war. Half complete, just standing."

Company personnel outside the trust also contributed to the liquidation of LNMI's nonearning assets. Management was able to integrate the expertise from its various divisions to help solve problems outside their normal responsibility. Much of the impetus for this came from Jess Hay's strong belief in communal effort. "As individuals," Hay observed in a speech he gave at Southern Methodist University in 1977, "we seldom function effectively in isolation. Rather, we work in community, in relationship with others: pursuing individual tasks to be sure, but doing so in pursuit of common goals and within the frame of shared purpose."

We were one of the few trusts that survived that period.

The Lomas & Nettleton Company with its national mortgage loan operation provided a natural conduit for originating and servicing permanent loans for houses, apartments, and other foreclosed properties the trust needed to sell. Even so, marketing was a challenge. High interest rates and inflation had eroded the economic environment to the point that most real estate transactions were no longer feasible. To compensate for the lack of demand, L&N undertook the task of creating one. "We were pretty aggressive," says Mike Walker, "about trying to provide the financing that was necessary to get the product moved."

Executive vice president Lanelle Latendresse was responsible for tracking loans through the bureaucratic paper maze prior to FNMA approval. Her success made a major contribution to LNMI's survival.

LNMI met the challenge of high interest rates and soft subdivisions by offering permanent loans for single-family houses below the market rate. Special efforts were also made to increase occupancy at trust-owned apartments. With increased occupancy, the company was able to sell the properties by using internal financing with attractive terms and conditions. "We continued to dispose of nonearning assets," said Buddy Miller, "because we offered favorable rates and financing that nobody else could give."

One of the most troublesome and time-consuming problem assets in the portfolio consisted of 40 FHA-insured construction loans. Although the borrowers were generally inexperienced and the projects only marginally viable, the trust's management considered them relatively risk-free because they were government-insured. When several of the loans went bad, the FHA issued unsecured government notes that paid a rate of interest far below the market rate. In order to sell the notes, the company had to discount them and take a substantial loss. The best strategy, as it turned out, was to complete the construction, "get HUD to bless it," and then turn the notes over to FNMA, the permanent lender, for full payment.

Former executive vice president Lanelle Latendresse was responsible for tracking the loans through the tedious bureaucratic maze that was required before FNMA gave its approval. "It is kind of an art form," said Latendresse, "to sell loans to institutions like that. Once you get the hang of what they want you to do, it's not so hard. It's kind of a paperwork nightmare, which was one reason for my involvement. I have always been involved with the paperwork of legal documentation. And we had loan officers stretched so thin trying to liquidate foreclosed property that I sort of got into it by default. Locke, Purnell had a lawyer who once worked for the FHA for several years. He assisted me, and we finally liquidated those loans without large losses. We didn't make a lot of money, but we didn't have any big losses, either. We were one of the few trusts that survived that period."

Not only did LNMI survive, but it did so honorably. Many REITs that had their backs to the wall engaged in what were called "asset swaps." Instead of money, they paid their creditors with foreclosed properties. LNMI steered clear of compromises like that. "If we owed you money," Miller said, "we paid you money when it was due. We have never been in default on a commitment, especially a monetary commitment. We went through some tough times, and we had to scrounge. But if we owed you $10 million, we paid you $10 million. We didn't offer you three apartment projects. We considered that a cop-out."

One indication of just how well LNMI's principled approach to financial obligations was received among the banking community appeared in October 1975. That's when the trust's commercial bank lenders renewed the company's $183 million short-term line of credit at the prime rate. Prime rate borrowing wasn't the only reason for optimism. It looked like the trust's problem loan program was beginning to make some headway. By December 31, 1975, nonearning assets decreased to $65 million from a peak of $83 million. And even though earnings continued to drop in 1975 and 1976 because of LNMI's constricted lending policy, the trust remained profitable. LNMI's conservative lending policies and low leveraging ratio, which many in the real estate industry originally regarded with amusement, had proven their worth under harsh economic conditions.

By the end of fiscal 1976, the worst of the recession was over and a gradual recovery had begun. Inflation eased, and the housing and construction industries improved. The mortgage banking division had its best year ever. Its revenues totaled $43.4 million, a dramatic increase from $31.7 million in the previous year. Mortgage loan production also increased significantly. At year end, the company's mortgage servicing portfolio climbed past the $5 billion mark, totaling $5,298,445,000 in unamortized principal amount. It was an industry record. The servicing fees generated by that portfolio gave the company a large, dependable source of income. "Even in a bad housing year," Jess Hay observed in 1976, "we will have a substantial income from mortgage servicing fees, and that's an important ingredient of our stability."

It is a record of which we are proud.

The good news from mortgage banking was partially offset by a $5.6 million decline in revenues at LNMI. Even so, that kind of balanced fluctuation pointed toward increasing overall stability and equilibrium among the company's operations. "Fiscal 1976," noted the annual report for that year, "attests once again to the significant balance in the Company's total operations, a balance which has been productive of reasonably good consolidated results throughout a sustained period of generally adverse economic conditions since late calendar 1973." As a vote of confidence in the gradually improving economic climate and the company's latest operating results, the board of directors voted in July 1976 to increase the quarterly dividend rate from 10¢ to 12½¢ per share.

Looking back at Lomas & Nettleton Financial Corporation's recessionary ordeal, Jess Hay identified two achievements worthy of special note in his 1976 stockholders' letter: "Profits—admittedly at reduced levels—have continued without interruption throughout the period, and L&N has been steadfast in honoring its commitments, whether to its borrowers, to its banks or to other institutions. It is a record of which we are proud."

When LNFC came face to face with its two most critical tests—financial condition and character—the company met the challenge and prevailed. This accomplishment opened the door to a more secure future. Buddy Miller expressed his thoughts about the ordeal in nautical terms: "If you're a sailor who's been sailing in a calm sea and then you go through a storm, if you make it through that goddamned storm and your boat is still together, you are a lot smarter than when you entered.

"But we did make it, and we made it with such integrity . . . that for the next ten years, anything this company or trust wanted—new issues, capital enhancement, formation of new divisions—Wall Street welcomed us with open arms."

Top-level management in early 1975, when changes and promotions were announced. Seated, left to right, are Ted Enloe, Jess Hay, and Jim Wooten. Standing are Dee DeWitt, Buddy Miller, Daryl Anderson, Everett Mattson, Jim Ludman, John Sexton, DeWayne Wommack, and P. Warren Smith.

CHAPTER VIII

THE GENERAL MOTORS OF MORTGAGE BANKING

Lomas & Nettleton Financial Corporation's successful journey through the recession of the mid-seventies depended to a large extent on the skill of its executive leadership. In February 1975, when LNFC president Gene H. Bishop resigned to become president and chief executive officer of Mercantile National Bank at Dallas, it was a serious loss. "I had very mixed emotions," recalls Jess Hay. "I was delighted for Gene and for the Mercantile Bank, because I believed then and today that it was a tremendous opportunity and that Gene was ideally suited to fill that role. But from a personal standpoint, it was a great loss to me and to the company. He is a tremendously talented man . . . I hated to lose him." A series of promotions following Gene Bishop's resignation underscored Hay's confidence in existing management and in his "no panic" approach to the recession. Ted Enloe replaced Bishop as president of LNFC. Besides this new responsibility, Enloe continued to serve as the chief operating officer of Lomas & Nettleton Mortgage Investors. Jim Wooten was promoted from senior executive vice president of The Lomas & Nettleton Company to vice chairman and chief administrative officer. A year later he became president of the mortgage banking company. John F. Sexton was appointed LNFC executive vice president, finance. The expanded roles of these three officers helped fill the vacuum created by Gene Bishop's departure.

The country's gradually improving economic condition also contributed to the company's return to growth. Lomas & Nettleton Financial Corporation's net income increased 45 percent in 1976 over the 1975 results. The company reported a "near record year" for fiscal 1977, which it attributed to "favorable . . . money

In February 1975, LNFC president Gene Bishop resigned to became president and chief executive officer of Mercantile National Bank at Dallas.

markets, and continuing internal operating efficiencies." Although mortgage banking was the principal contributor, the short-term lending division showed improvement after a three-year constricted loan policy. In May 1977, *American Banker* reported that due to new construction, the servicing of permanent mortgages for investors at the end of 1976 rose $9.8 billion or 11.4 percent over the previous year, the largest percentage gain for servicing since 1972. By fiscal 1978, any doubt about the company's pattern of progress was dispelled, as earnings per share increased by 14 percent or better for the fourth year in a row. Gross revenues totaling $72.5 million this year were the highest in L&N's history. Long-term mortgage production also set a record, as the mortgage servicing portfolio's principal balance increased from $5.6 billion in 1977 to $6.2 billion in 1978. The company's dominance in mortgage banking was overwhelming. By 1978, it was the country's largest in terms of portfolio size, capital resources, geographic distribution, and mortgage production.

Management never lost sight of the connection between productivity and prosperity. Jim Wooten credits much of mortgage banking's success to a skilled, cohesive staff that created "an environment of people that knew what they were doing. We were pretty damn efficient." In a speech Jess Hay gave in 1979, he defined corporate productivity in the following way: "A company that manages to crank out more cars or tennis balls or loaves of bread or single-family mortgages, *without working extra people or extra hours*, is a productive company."

We were pretty damn efficient.

The loan administration office in Houston was responsible for a significant portion of L&N's corporate productivity during this period. Mortgage loan servicing represented the company's largest and most reliable source of income. But with that came the challenge of coordinating an array of clerical-intensive activities that included: collecting and remitting principal and interest payments to investors; maintaining mortgage escrow accounts for payment of real estate taxes, hazard insurance, and mortgage insurance premiums; advising investors about loan delinquencies; assisting in foreclosure proceedings; and performing other loan servicing functions.

Former L&N executive vice president George I. Wilson approached employee productivity with a special sensitivity to the daily administration of loan servicing. Instead of looking at each department from a top-down viewpoint, Wilson began at the lowest level

With the 1975 management changes, Ted Enloe, center, was elected president of the corporation; DeWayne Wommack, left, executive vice president, control, and John Sexton, right, executive vice president, finance. The changes went into effect March 1.

of the operation, looked up, and asked the question: "What do employees need in order to be motivated and highly productive?" For Wilson and other L&N executives, success was a product of individual responsibility and effort within a context of teamwork. He believed productivity depended to a large extent on the efforts of high-quality, first-line supervisors to motivate employees.

Wilson initiated the "BAD Idea" campaign to sharpen productivity: "We had a program we called the 'BAD Idea.' It stands for 'Buck-A-Day.' We asked our employees to come up with ideas that would save their departments a buck a day and write them down on a special form and send them in." Employees who made recommendations received coffee mugs stenciled with "I HAD A BAD IDEA" and the motto "BAD IS BETTER AT L&N." If suggestions from employees were implemented, they became eligible for a grand prize drawing. Lomas Administrative Services vice president

With Gene Bishop's resignation, Ted Enloe, left, became the new president of Lomas & Nettleton Financial Corporation and of L&N Management, Inc. Jim Wooten, right, assumed the office of vice chairman and chief administrative officer of The Lomas & Nettleton Company.

Peggy Hamil, then vice president of Houston personnel and corporate records, remembers the "Wanted" posters that started going up all over the building. Polaroid photographs of department heads and supervisors appeared on the posters along with the caption "Wanted . . . BAD Ideas."

"It went over with a bang," says Wilson, "because the departments began to compete to see who could turn in the most ideas. We got many, many ideas out of it, some of which were developed, some were repeats, and some weren't worth much. But if you get your employees thinking, they will come up with ideas that make a difference."

One idea came from a clerk in the tax department, who suggested changing the filing system for tax bills. Instead of filing the bills according to their expiration dates, the idea was to use the geographic location of the taxing authority. "If somebody, for example, wanted a tax receipt from Delaware County, Pennsylvania," Wilson explains, "the clerk had to also know when the taxes were due. Using the new system, you could look up Delaware County, Pennsylvania, and regardless of the tax date it would be there." A modest refinement. But the cumulative effect of that kind of employee attention to operational efficiency kept L&N at the forefront of the mortgage banking industry.

Senior management also contributed to productivity. The emphasis Jess Hay placed on "working in community in pursuit of common goals" sustained an environment receptive to new ideas. George Wilson and his department managers met once or twice a month for what former L&N executive vice president Jim Pickup called "wild-assed brainstorming sessions." No idea was too farfetched for consideration. Pickup compared their sessions to "GE and their think tanks."

One idea that emerged was a system for tracking the pay habits of homeowners. "We pioneered," says Pickup, "what I call the 'pay habit system.'" It was developed by former data processing executive vice president E. G. Bray, a man Jim Pickup considered "an absolute genius in the field of data processing." In the

Data processing executive E. G. Bray, who developed the "pay habit system," was considered a genius in his field. For the T. J. Bettes Company, he had been chief accountant, 1945–1949; assistant treasurer, 1950–1960; and vice president, 1961–1968. A vice president for Lomas & Nettleton from the acquisition of T. J. Bettes until 1971, he was promoted to senior vice president in 1972, and in the 1980s was made executive vice president.

past, whenever the servicing department needed to determine a mortgagor's pay performance it had to go through the time-consuming process of pulling individual monthly files. Bray developed a way to display a numbered code indicating a 12-month pay performance record on each customer's master record. This was handy toward the end of the year in preparing letters to customers informing them that Christmas was coming and it would be a good idea to get their payments in early. "We could tell the computer," says Wilson, "to only give us the names and addresses of late-paying customers, those with codes of 5 and 6, for example. Don't bother with the 1's and 2's; they pay anyway."

Richard Metcalf, an attorney with Locke, Purnell, Boren, Laney & Neely, assisted John Sexton in designing the collateral trust obligation. Locke Purnell Rain Harrell Archives.

The company's flair for innovation also inspired the addition of new profit centers. One of the most important ventures in the mid-seventies was LNFC's entry into the commercial paper market as an alternative short-term money source for the company's warehousing operation. Normally, short-term money came from bank lines of credit, usually at the prime rate. The cost of commercial paper borrowing was less. It didn't take an advanced business degree to understand the financial advantages. But it took former LNFC executive vice president John F. Sexton, a Harvard M.B.A., to knock down the barriers blocking the mortgage banking industry from participating in that market.

Lomas has always been novel and creative from a financing standpoint.

Typically, only the largest corporations issued commercial paper, companies with a net worth the size of Ford Motor Company or Exxon. Sexton neatly sidestepped that obstacle by coming up with something quite innovative: "I thought we could put a collateral trust together with loans running in and out of it. Then we could sell a piece of paper off of that trust. And because the loans were collateral, the company didn't need a big net worth."

With the help of Richard I. Metcalf, an attorney with Locke, Purnell, Boren, Laney & Neely, John Sexton designed the collateral trust note, later called a collateral trust obligation. The concept was to issue the notes from a pool of liquid mortgages that served as collateral. Since the security of the notes didn't depend on the credit of the issuer, "the company could go broke and disappear" without jeopardizing the noteholders. Their investments were secured by the pool of FHA/VA

Executive vice president David Kelly was part of the team that put together the concept of the collateral trust obligation.

mortgages in the collateral trust. The largest hurdle was persuading rating agencies like Standard & Poor's that L&N's collateral notes deserved a rating. "The frustrating part," says Richard Metcalf, "was educating the rating agencies {about} the mortgage banking industry and how mortgages were originated and sold and how they were valued." Besides Metcalf, Sexton was assisted by L&N president Jim Wooten, executive vice president David Kelly, Jr., and senior vice president Michael Karlak, as well as representatives from Lehman Brothers, the investment banking company responsible for selling the notes. After "six or seven months of intense effort," Standard & Poor's finally agreed to give their highest rating, an A-1, to Lomas & Nettleton. On November 16, 1976, loans valued at $17 million were transferred into the company's collateral trust pool. *American Banker* publicized the event in a front-page news story: "The largest mortgage banking company in the nation is bypassing commercial banks by selling commercial paper to finance its inventory. It is the first use of commercial paper in this form by a mortgage banking firm, industry observers say, and underscores the efforts of mortgage bankers to find cheaper alternatives to bank borrowing."

The article also noted that L&N's entry into this market made the company more competitive with mortgage banking companies affiliated with bank holding companies. Until then, those mortgage bankers enjoyed the advantage of borrowing at lower rates from parent companies that had access to the commercial paper market. "We wish the collateral trust note would disappear," said Harold Flight, senior vice president at the $5.8 billion–deposit First National Bank, Boston, when asked to comment on L&N's accomplishment.

. . . getting a handle on what the hell the problems were.

Collateral trust notes also represented a source of revenue for the company. Since L&N owned the mortgages while they were temporarily warehoused, they collected the interest earned during that time period. The notes gave Lomas & Nettleton one to two percent additional earnings on the loans they held.

"Lomas has always been novel and creative from a financing standpoint," says Richard Metcalf. "They're kind of a wholesaler of money. They borrow from one source and lend it to another source and make money in between. And I think they're always kind of on the cutting edge of the best and most efficient ways to do that. The collateral trust note program was kind of a gigantic step at that time, and it was pretty novel for the industry."

L&N Management's efforts to get out from under LNMI's recession-caused nonearning assets opened the door to an unexpected opportunity. With the exception of raw land, most of LNMI's portfolio of foreclosed properties responded well to the company's liquidation efforts. A new department was organized to deal exclusively with the land problem. This allowed LNMI's loan underwriters to concentrate on selling developed properties and rebuilding the short-term loan portfolio.

The newly created department required specialized outside expertise. Wayne D. Ferguson joined L&N Management in February 1977 as a property analyst. Prior to that he had worked for Bruton Properties, a Dallas development company. The knowledge he gained from their property development program was broad, including experience as both a leasing manager and general manager. L&N recognized Ferguson's ability, and within a year he was promoted to vice president of property management.

The first order of business for Ferguson was "getting a handle on what the hell the problems were." He analyzed the properties and divided them into three categories. The first consisted of properties that had market value and were ready for sale in their existing state. Properties that had market value but required minor development before they could be sold comprised the second group. The third group were what Ferguson called "babysitters": land in remote locations with major development problems and no immediate sale potential. For this last category, Ferguson developed a watch-and-wait approach that included occasional market reviews, meanwhile concentrating his efforts on the first two categories. He aggressively pursued buyers for properties he considered ready for sale, at the same time resolving the minor problems that prevented sales of properties in the second grouping.

After significant progress in liquidating the first two categories, Ferguson turned his attention to the most difficult properties. At that point, he took aggressive steps to direct the market toward L&N's properties. If, for example, a growing municipality planned to extend thoroughfares and utilities, Ferguson and his staff used their considerable sales skills and political savvy to guide the extensions toward L&N-owned land. One way to accomplish this was to organize four or five adjacent landowners and offer the city right-of-way across their land. "Those properties," says Ferguson, "really had no marketability until the city extended its sewer lines and utilities. We worked with the other property owners to make it happen. We just kept pushing the municipalities in order to shorten the time it took to prepare those properties for development." It wasn't long before Ferguson's "make it happen" philosophy became a basic tenet under which L&N's land development division operated.

Mr. Enloe and Mr. Hay and other executives felt there might be an opportunity here.

By 1979, the successful reduction of LNMI's land foreclosures meant the property development department was, as Wayne Ferguson observed, "working its way out of a job." Freed from the burden of nonearning assets, L&N used its entrepreneurial instincts to look at property development as something more than the solution to a problem. "Mr. Enloe and Mr. Hay and the other executives," says Ferguson, "felt that there might be an opportunity here." The arguments for pursuing land development for profit were persuasive. The department had an experienced staff with an established track record. And as far as Dallas and Houston were concerned, Ferguson knew the markets and enjoyed ongoing relationships with important builders. An L&N land development program also increased the likelihood of obtaining builders' short-term and long-term financing.

Initially, the department bought tracts of land adjacent to previously foreclosed properties that L&N had sold to builders who now enjoyed brisk sales. With such a proven market, L&N had no trouble selling the commercial/retail frontage in each property and using that money to develop the rest of the tract. Encouraged by the success of their initial efforts, the company organized L&N Land Corp. in July 1980 and appointed Wayne Ferguson executive vice president and manager. In 1988, the name was changed to Lomas Realty USA.

When land adjacent to existing developments was no longer available, L&N Land Corp. began buying stand-alone properties that had the potential for becoming Class A developments. Ferguson reduced L&N's exposure by implementing risk-reduction procedures. One of the most important was the decision to obtain zoning before purchasing a piece of property. "We are willing to take some engineering and development risks," said Ferguson, "but our philosophy is to avoid political risks. Money can resolve an engineering problem, but it won't resolve a political issue. Maybe the municipality doesn't particularly like this project, or they're mad at the original landowner. Whatever the reason, they can be very subjective and arbitrary." "After all," said former Lomas Realty USA executive vice president J. Stephen Crim, "who wants to take a chance on getting a project blocked just because some guy is mad at some other guy because of what his wife said to the other one's wife three years ago?"

The Land Corp.'s skill in creating quality developments and solving problems also provided a measure of protection against the cyclical nature of the real estate business. Even during a downturn, Ferguson says, Class A developments in good locations with no zoning, engineering, or utility problems "are the last properties that go down, and the the first ones in demand."

One of the first ventures that earned L&N Land Corp. consideration as a major developer was a project called Timber Creek Square. Located northwest of Dallas near the town of Lewisville, the 360-acre tract

In July 1980, the company organized L&N Land Corp. and appointed Wayne Ferguson executive vice president and manager.

A large sign on Interstate Highway 35E proclaimed Timber Creek Square "a planned business and multi-family community." Located northwest of Dallas, the project helped to make L&N Land Corp. a major developer.

At Timber Creek Square, L&N Land Corp. was successful in attracting builders that built a high-quality project. The entire tract had been sold on a predevelopment basis.

had a number of problems despite a sound location. "It was a piece of property," says Wayne Ferguson, "situated between two freeways. It had floodplain problems, some thoroughfare problems, and some utility problems. But we had cut our teeth on problem properties because that's all we had to work on. We understood floodplain, we understood zoning and thoroughfare connections."

Although several developers had been interested enough in the land to option it, no one had bought it. The floodplain was the main obstacle. A 100-acre swath of low-lying land, subject to periodic flooding, ran through the center of the property. Oddly enough, none of the previous prospective buyers had ever conducted a serious engineering study. L&N Land Corp. placed a six-month option on the land and immediately began a hydrological study using complicated computer models. From the study, the company learned that they could reclaim 60 of the 100 acres by moving dirt from the property's two hilltops and filling in part of the floodplain. "We proved," says Steve Crim, "that it would work."

L&N Land Corp. was equally adept at attracting builders to the development. Nine months after it purchased the land, the entire tract had been sold on a predevelopment basis. "We moved through that project very quickly," says Crim. "It was very, very successful."

Ferguson and his staff also demonstrated that cost effectiveness and sensitivity to the environment were not incompatible. On one heavily wooded tract they started a tree farm. The company hired a Texas A&M University agricultural major to select and transplant trees from road right-of-ways and move them to an area set aside for later use. "By removing those trees," says Ferguson, "we probably saved $2 million or $3 million in landscaping costs."

By the early eighties, L&N Land Corp. had proven itself as a reliable profit center with an innovative staff.

"We had a great entrepreneur in Wayne Ferguson," says Jess Hay.

The company also found a profitable outlet for its technology. The data processing division, armed with its state-of-the-art Burroughs 6700 computer, began to flex its electronic muscle in a new direction. Why not, management asked, sell a portion of L&N's computer power and expertise to mortgage banking companies that were unable or unwilling to build their own data processing operation? "Our thought," says Jess Hay, "was that we had a tremendous system for mortgage servicing, and we could reduce our own net cost by making that system available to other mortgage bankers."

> . . . Written for a mortgage company by a mortgage company.

For the first few years, the new venture, called Data Services, was a low-key effort that relied on word-of-mouth marketing. Not surprisingly, customer response was also low-key. The outside client list in the mid-seventies included about a half-dozen Texas "mom-and-pop shops" with an insignificant combined servicing volume. The appointment of Floyd McGlothlin as assistant vice president of Data Services in July 1977 signaled the beginning of a serious effort. A year later, Data Services hired Larry Cornwell as a full-time salesman.

L&N's reputation, by this time, gave it the kind of leverage that contributed to the success of Data Services and other company ventures. Finding new niches didn't hurt either. There were only one or two computer systems with a national capability available to mortgage bankers in 1978, and Lomas had the only one "written for a mortgage company by a mortgage company." It wasn't long after Cornwell started calling on key individuals in the industry that the company began signing up customers. He remembers it as an easy sell: "Everybody knew Lomas. It was the largest [mortgage company] in the nation at that time by a factor of three. My sales pitch was more like the history of Lomas & Nettleton. I probably spent 50 percent of the time explaining how L&N evolved over the years. Most companies thought if it was good for Lomas, it was bound to be pretty good for them. You always had an open door."

The appointment of Floyd McGlothlin as assistant vice president of Data Services in July 1977 was the beginning of a serious effort to sell a portion of L&N's computer power and expertise.

But it was L&N's willingness to use its resources that proved decisive in closing many of the deals. The corporate commitment to Data Services started at the top with Jess Hay, who met many prospective customers when they came to Dallas. At the regional level, the executive vice presidents showed their support by arranging for mortgage bankers to drop by L&N's hospitality suite at national conventions and visit with Data Services representatives.

The breakthrough came in 1978 and 1979 when

Data Services signed computer servicing contracts with the Mason-McDuffie Co. and with Allstate, a subsidiary of Sears. Both were national companies, servicing more than 50,000 loans each. "Allstate wanted a vendor that was willing to support them," says Floyd McGlothlin. "After a couple of trips to California, we brought a number of their folks into Houston and showed what our system could do for them. They had some specific requirements they wanted us to program, and we made the commitment to provide them. They saw we were willing to work with them, whereas our major competitor, CPI, was taking a hard-line approach, 'This is what it is; this is what you get.'

"And the Allstate account helped us get the Mason-McDuffie account. Those two large, nationwide lenders were kind of a turning point."

Compact size and E. G. Bray's aversion to red tape accounted for much of Data Services' flexibility. Approval for customer-requested programming during sales negotiations generally required a single telephone call to Bray. "You didn't have 27 levels of approval," says Cornwell. "If Bray said yes, it was done. If he said no, it wasn't." When outside customers had problems with their internal mortgage banking operation, Data Services didn't hesitate to provide assistance: "If a [customer] had a special problem with insurance or taxes, you could always get somebody from The Lomas & Nettleton Company to help solve it." One of the most dramatic examples of this kind of support occurred shortly after Allstate's conversion to the L&N system. Sears decided to move Allstate's servicing center from California to Chicago, but when those employees confronted the harsh reality of winter in Chicago, many "bailed out and moved back to California. Lomas [responded by] pulling people from its loan administration departments and shipping them to Chicago to work for Allstate until they could hire and train new staff."

Data Services and the entire data processing division had a reputation for lean efficiency. The credit for that belonged to E. G. Bray, who took pride in his ability to run the department on a budgetary shoestring with a minimum of employees. This bare-bones philosophy demanded a higher level of performance from the Data Services staff. It wasn't unusual for Floyd McGlothlin and his crew to work 12- and 15-hour days, seven days a week, on many of the conversions. Limited staffing also meant Larry Cornwell had to spend a week or two with new customers to make sure the system did everything Data Services said it would and to train personnel. Initial problems with the system's performance were rare because each conversion bore Bray's seal of approval. "E. G. Bray personally checked every conversion," says Larry Cornwell. "He checked all the programming. . . . And, during the conversion itself, he personally checked every damn loan and every balance that came out of there. He signed off on each one and said either 'yes, it's balanced' or 'no, it's not.'"

Strong customer support, intense systems scrutiny, and aggressive salesmanship gave L&N a significant share in this new market. Data Services moved from eight outside customers representing approximately 80,000 loans in 1977 to 40 customers with about 400,000 loans in 1981. Revenue during that period rose from $525,000 to $2.4 million.

> *I* saw it and recognized that it was a business we had to get into.

Paul M. Low, one of L&N's most creative executives, added another nugget in 1979 to L&N's growing cache of profitable services, a new venture the company called Master Servicing. Aware of the potential for new business based on changes in federal law, Low's attention was caught by a revision in the tax code. The new law permitted county and city municipalities the right to issue tax-exempt bonds whose proceeds would be used to provide mort-

Paul Low added to L&N's expanding and profitable services in 1979 with a new venture called Master Servicing.

gage money at below market interest rates for low- and moderate-income homebuyers.

The city of Chicago in August 1978 announced the first such transaction. It sold $100 million worth of tax-exempt bonds to fund the purchase of mortgages. Low, who closely followed the progress of that deal, noticed that the city authorized one bank to act as the sole lender to distribute the mortgage funds to homebuyers. "I knew that would not last," says Paul Low, "because politically the lending industry would not permit a city, county, or state to give all the business to one lender. They were going to have to have multiple lenders. And that meant the [governmental bodies] needed someone to watch the activities of the lenders it authorized to make loans on their behalf. And that's what Master Servicing is.

"I saw it and recognized that it was a business we had to get into. It was very clear to me that this was a need that had to be met, and we were equipped to do it. So we were the first to get into that business."

Since the cities and counties had no background in mortgage banking, Low knew that they needed someone to administer and monitor the program for them. That meant approving loans, receiving and disbursing money, monitoring monthly servicing reports from the various lenders, and consolidating that information into one report for the city, county, or state. With characteristic speed, Paul Low organized this monitoring service and called it Master Servicing. He recruited Gary Kell, the senior executive of a bank in Fort Smith, Arkansas, and a former L&N branch manager, to help sell and administer the program.

The fact that L&N was a name virtually unknown among the counties and cities was not a major problem. Low and Kell sold the new service to the financial community, where Lomas & Nettleton was well known and widely respected. It was Wall Street that unlocked the door to over 80 Master Servicing transactions in 20 states within a five-year period.

The investment banking community was receptive to Low's new program because it strengthened their mortgage revenue bond proposals. And L&N benefited because it provided access to customers. When investment bankers such as Goldman Sachs & Co. made presentations before governmental bodies, Master Servicing was often part of their sales pitch.

The company's financial strength and participation in the commercial paper market was particularly helpful when it came to the rating agencies. "It was Paul's idea to go to the rating agencies," says Lomas Mortgage USA executive vice president Gary H. Kell. "We convinced Moody's and Standard & Poor's that because of our expertise we were much more qualified to monitor these deals than a local bank. It got to the point where it became a rating problem for a municipality not to use us." With Master Servicing high on investment bankers' and rating agencies' request list, L&N quickly solidified its position as an authority in the new field. "We became the standard," says Kell, "and everybody tried to copy us."

Word of L&N's highly regarded program spread across the country. When the state of Ohio asked investment bankers for mortgage revenue bond proposals, Goldman Sachs & Co. and L&N made a joint presentation. Despite the fact that Lehman Brothers was ultimately selected, the state insisted that L&N monitor the program.

Master Servicing also earned a reputation for satisfying customers. In Ohio, Gary Kell made a commitment to promote the program throughout the state. He spent six weeks in 22 cities talking to lenders about the program and asking for their participation. The response from both lenders and homebuyers was overwhelming. The lower interest rate offered by the state to first-time homebuyers represented a savings of $150 to $200 a month in the price of a house. In several Ohio cities, people camped in front of lenders' offices for two or three days. The entire $300 million was disbursed to applicants on the first day. By October 1982, the Master Servicing program crossed the $2 billion mark in loans monitored, which produced a revenue stream of about $3 million and a net profit of 50 percent. Paul Low attributes the high rate of return in the first few years to the efficiencies of a small, motivated operation: "When you're entrepreneurial and fearless and you haven't built up this huge institution, it's cheap. Then all of a sudden, you get more sophisticated, and you need more equipment, and you become less profitable."

Earnings weren't the only thing that increased at Lomas & Nettleton Financial Corporation during the late seventies. True, the numbers were good, but equally important was the surge in confidence that declared corporate growth back on track. "Fiscal 1978," concluded the 1978 annual report, "was the best year in L&N's history. All indications are that the current year will be even better, as the Company continues to enjoy the incremental benefits of size, geographic diversification, staff experience and financial strength." The recession and its aftermath no longer consumed management's energy and attention. Infused with renewed optimism, the company began to look outward once more. High on the corporate agenda was the resumption of its mortgage banking acquisition program.

. . . We were under a threat, and the threat was a big one.

Outside the company, however, a growing cloud began to menace L&N's future, and possibly its existence. Saul Steinberg was the name of this unsettling new presence. Backed by the financial clout of Reliance Insurance Company, of which he was chairman, Steinberg began buying LNFC stock, believed by many to be considerably underpriced. This kind of attention from someone else might have been flattering, but from Steinberg it was a cause for concern. His reputation as a wheeler-dealer whiz kid began in the late 1960s when at age 29 he attempted a takeover of Chemical Bank, the sixth largest in the world. Ten years later, a 1978 *Forbes* magazine article observed that the chairman of Reliance had moderated his style, if little else: "Saul Steinberg has a new image. It's not exactly Mr. Nice Guy, but it's a lot mellower than his old image."

Reliance began buying L&N stock at $10 a share. Gradually the insurance company's stock ownership inched upward—from 5 percent to 7, 10, 12, 15, and then past 20 percent. "They just kept buying and buying and buying," says John Sexton. Although Sexton, Jess Hay, and other top executives never believed Steinberg actually wanted to acquire LNFC, that didn't lessen his potential for mischief. "We were under a threat, and the threat was a big one," Sexton remembers. "When someone owns 25 percent of your company, and you don't know what they are going to do with it next, it impedes the progress of the company. It impedes what you are going to acquire and what you are going to expand into. It can be pretty demoralizing."

Despite assurances from Steinberg that his interest in L&N was investment-oriented, his actions suggested otherwise. When Reliance Insurance Company's ownership of L&N stock reached 24.9 percent, senior management met with Steinberg and disclosed that, because of federal regulations, L&N's interest in certain investments would have to be curtailed if his insurance company held more than 25 percent of Lomas & Nettleton. Steinberg assured Hay that he had no intention of buying more stock. Two days later he made another purchase that gave Reliance more than 25 percent ownership. "It became clear at that point," says Ted Enloe, "that he was going to be obstructive to us. He was sending a message that he wasn't going to be a cooperative, passive investor."

L&N immediately offered to buy Steinberg's stock. The transaction was accomplished in a couple of hours by telephone. On September 7, 1978, LNFC's board of directors approved the purchase of 1,687,600 shares of L&N stock from Reliance Insurance Company for about $37 million in notes and cash. "It really recapitalized the company," says Enloe, "because we didn't pay very much cash. Steinberg took subordinated debt . . . [which] did not impair our credit ratings or our ability to borrow money. And, above all, the sale freed us from that uncertainty of what he would do or wouldn't do. It was a very, very big event for the company."

The end of the Steinberg affair, coupled with record earnings in fiscal 1978, gave LNFC the freedom and resources to resume its expansion program. "Mortgage banking was doing well," says Sexton. "The liquidity of the company was increasing, and the credit available to the company was increasing. Consequently, the ability to expand was available to us. And the most logical way to expand was to increase the mortgage banking network."

. . . the most logical way to expand was to increase the mortgage banking network.

Mortgage banking was unquestionably LNFC's core business. It brought in the lion's share of the company's earnings and claimed the dominant position in its industry. L&N's six existing regional offices enjoyed strong geographic coverage in the eastern, western, and south central United States. Conspicuously absent, however, was a strong presence in the Midwest.

On April 17, 1979, the company announced the proposed purchase of Great Lakes Mortgage Corporation, a small, employee-owned mortgage company based in Chicago. Besides the Chicago home office, the transaction included a mortgage servicing portfolio of 18,500 loans totaling $670 million in unamortized principal, and six branch offices in Illinois and Indiana. "The acquisition," said Jess Hay, "will give us, for the first time, a major servicing volume base in the Midwest, will provide our entry into the markets of northern Indiana, and will strengthen our

National Homes Acceptance Corporation, founded in 1947, was a wholly owned subsidiary of National Homes Corporation. The Lafayette, Indiana, company was located in this former factory building at Earl and Wallace streets.

coverage in the Chicago and Illinois markets. This moves us appreciably closer to our frequently stated goal of participation in the total national mortgage market."

Despite its modest size, the Great Lakes acquisition was far from trouble-free. Opposition to the sale from a faction within Great Lakes delayed the closing for several months. Instead of June as expected, the transaction didn't become final until the first of October.

Despite the delay at Great Lakes, L&N was ready when another opportunity presented itself a month later. This time it acquired a significantly larger piece of the mortgage banking pie. On May 29, 1979, the company agreed to purchase National Homes Acceptance Corporation (NHAC), the fifth largest mortgage servicer in the country. The Lafayette, Indiana, company had a portfolio of 160,000 loans with an aggregate unamortized principal balance of $2.8 billion.

Founded in 1947, National Homes Acceptance Corporation was a wholly owned subsidiary of National Homes Corporation, a manufacturer of prefabricated

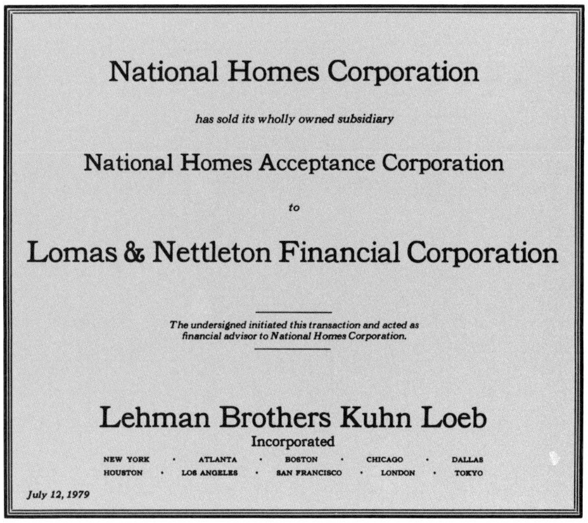
National Homes Corporation

has sold its wholly owned subsidiary

National Homes Acceptance Corporation

to

Lomas & Nettleton Financial Corporation

The undersigned initiated this transaction and acted as financial advisor to National Homes Corporation.

Lehman Brothers Kuhn Loeb
Incorporated

NEW YORK · ATLANTA · BOSTON · CHICAGO · DALLAS
HOUSTON · LOS ANGELES · SAN FRANCISCO · LONDON · TOKYO

July 12, 1979

On May 29, 1979, L&N agreed to purchase National Home Acceptance Corporation. On July 12, 1979, notice was published that Lehman Brothers Kuhn Loeb had successfully completed the transaction. Courtesy J. Robert McGrath.

This NHAC advertisement from the 1960s indicates a shift in corporate strategy. Instead of financing only homes built and sold by the parent company, the mortgage banking subsidiary moved aggressively into the spot loan market.

houses. At first the mortgage banking subsidiary only financed houses manufactured by its parent company. According to one estimate, 98 percent of the houses that left the company's plants in the 1950s were financed by National Homes Acceptance Corporation. That pattern began to change in the early sixties when the parent company's sales began to decline. NHAC responded by shifting into the spot loan market. "Initially," says former NHAC executive vice president J. Robert McGrath, who later became executive vice president for L&N, "we were strongest in the Midwest. The Chicago market was always a good market for us. Illinois, Indiana, and Michigan were strong states." Later, NHAC opened branches in California, Philadelphia, Texas, Florida, and its best producing office in Camp Springs, Maryland, outside of Washington, D.C.

One of the most important contributors to NHAC's growth was its computer system. The data

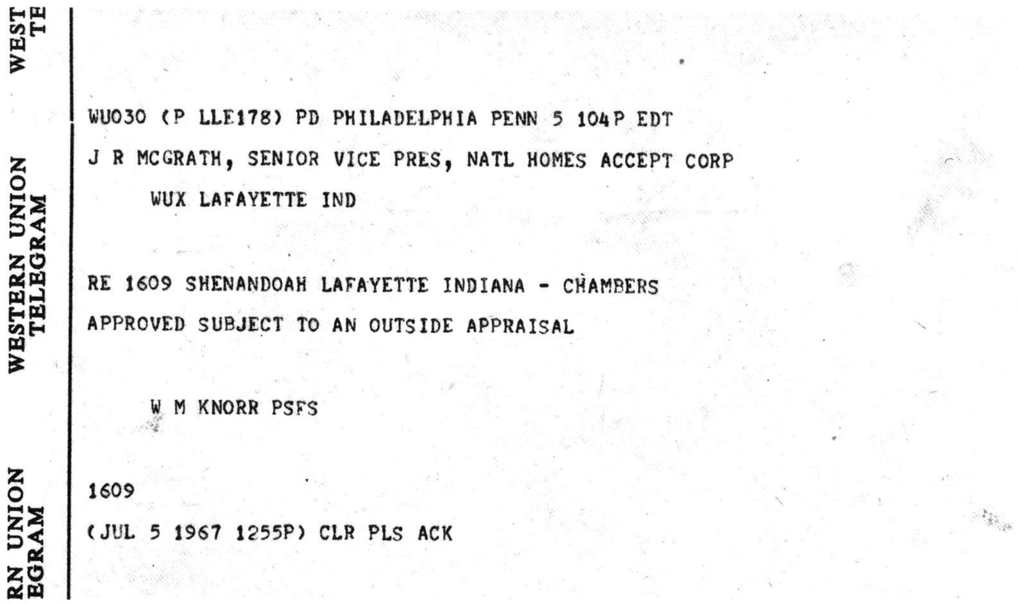
WESTERN UNION TELEGRAM

WU030 (P LLE178) PD PHILADELPHIA PENN 5 104P EDT
J R MCGRATH, SENIOR VICE PRES, NATL HOMES ACCEPT CORP
WUX LAFAYETTE IND

RE 1609 SHENANDOAH LAFAYETTE INDIANA - CHAMBERS
APPROVED SUBJECT TO AN OUTSIDE APPRAISAL

W M KNORR PSFS

1609
(JUL 5 1967 1255P) CLR PLS ACK

This Western Union telegram of July 5, 1967, records the first conventional loan made in Lafayette by National Homes Acceptance Corporation. PSFS in Philadelphia was the largest savings bank in the country at that time. Courtesy J. Robert McGrath.

The value of NHAC and of its senior management was ignored for years by its parent company. The management staff included executive vice president Bob McGrath, seated second from right, and real estate attorney Milton Ecker, standing center, who later moved to Dallas to be with Lomas & Nettleton. Courtesy J. Robert McGrath.

processing requirements of the parent company coupled with those of NHAC made it possible for the two to share a larger, more advanced computer. "I think our computer system," says Bob McGrath, "was better than anyone else's in the mortgage industry. FNMA used to send companies to see how we did things. I remember one time they sent Advance Mortgage down to see how we did our computer work."

The parent company didn't fare as well. By the late seventies, its financial problems had grown. "National Homes Acceptance," says McGrath, "was the only really good, profitable operation that they had. The profits [we] made . . . went to pay the interest on their corporate debt." When creditors insisted on the repayment of a $32 million loan, National Homes Corporation was forced to sell NHAC, its most valuable asset.

Valuable as NHAC might have been, the parent company had ignored it for years. The team of L&N employees sent to Lafayette to help direct the transition were shocked by what they found. "The place we were in," says Bob McGrath, "was a former National Homes factory that had been condemned. When it rained, the water just poured in. . . . We started using plastic wastebaskets because they didn't rust when we used them to catch the leaks. National Homes never spent any money on the building. As far as they were concerned, we were the black sheep of the family. I think they were embarrassed that we were doing so well." L&N's Jim Pickup was amazed by the working conditions he found there: "You had to see it to believe it. It was like a factory, because that's what it was! It was dusty, dirty, and only the computer room and executive offices had air conditioning. When they invited you to lunch, they took you to the truck stop."

For NHAC employees, one of the most onerous links to the company's manufacturing tradition were the time clocks they had to use. Former L&N executive vice president Hugh S. (Dee) DeWitt recalls the reaction of Harold E. Marsh, Jr., L&N vice president, personnel: "When he walked in and saw the time clocks on the wall, Harold said, 'We're going to get rid of those right now.' The employees were delighted with that."

Much of the credit for the relatively smooth transfer of loan files from Lafayette to Houston belonged to the conscientious efforts of former NHAC employees now working for L&N. Despite a strong manufacturing presence in Lafayette, the town and surrounding area were predominantly an agricultural community whose population demonstrated a highly developed work ethic. Jim Pickup discovered, after analyzing the departments, that there were some exceptions to this rule. One of those who didn't survive the transition was the servicing manager, whose work ethic, according to Pickup, was particularly weak: "He thought he was sick when he started to sweat."

Merging the NHAC loans into the L&N system was a massive undertaking. To help make the transfer more manageable, the loan administration staff divided the NHAC portfolio. "We broke it up into three pieces," says former Lomas Mortgage USA vice presi-

On June 28, 1981, L&N's Midwest Regional Headquarters opened in Purdue Research Park in West Lafayette, Indiana. The new office building was designed and built specifically for them.

The leadership of production and marketing for National Homes Acceptance Corporation was headed by Tom Schwartz, left, executive vice president, Bob McGrath, center, and Dick Stadler, right. Courtesy J. Robert McGrath.

dent Sidney L. Kelley. "It worked out to where there was a fairly even amount of loans in each grouping. We moved the private investors first, the FNMA loans next, and the GNMA pools last." In December 1979, Sid Kelley announced the successful transfer of loans in a memo addressed to The Lomas & Nettleton Company staff: "Hooray—the NHAC loans are all on the system! . . . What has been accomplished in the last 60 to 90 days staggers the imagination. Before the year is out . . . we will be servicing 500,000 loans." Jim Pickup also praised the performance of the staff in a memo: "The inherent strength and ability of the Lomas & Nettleton administrative staff is best demonstrated at a time such as this when we are challenged to do something that has never been done before in our industry. No one has ever attempted to move 160,000 mortgage loans from one company to another, certainly not in a relatively short time span."

Jess decided . . . to build a showplace up there.

It wasn't until October 1, 1979, that the issues delaying the sale of Great Lakes Mortgage Corporation to L&N were finally resolved. Originally the company had thought it would build a regional office in Chicago using the Great Lakes operation as its nucleus. Closer inspection of Great Lakes after its acquisition, however, forced L&N to reconsider. "When I first went in there," says Jim Pickup, "I quickly went into shock. The servicing department was a pile of crap . . . tax records missing, hazard insurance missing. The foreclosure department was an absolute shambles. Great Lakes had never purged a single case file, ever. Folders were filed every which way, nothing under a fastener, everything loose." The poor quality of servicing was a reflection of problems at a higher level. "We thought," says Dee DeWitt, "that Great Lakes was an old company with a good reputation, but what we found out when we got there was that it was living on reputation. They had an entire floor in this prestigious Chicago office building with their four top people in corner offices and none of the four spoke to the others. It didn't take long to determine that we didn't have anything there that could be used as a foundation for a regional office."

Although somewhat off the beaten path, the Lafayette operation had the personnel to run a regional office. In late 1979, L&N made it the headquarters for the newly created Midwest Region, the seventh and final addition to the company's national mortgage banking network.

Finding a new office was high on its agenda. Unfortunately, the Lafayette area had nothing available. "We didn't see anything that would suit our needs," says DeWitt. "So it was appropriate to build something that added to the company's reputation. Jess decided . . . to build a showplace up there." The purchase of land at Purdue Research Park in West Lafayette, Indiana, represented a departure from L&N's previous policy of leasing regional office space. Funded by the sale of $2.2 million in principal amount of tax-free economic development bonds, the construction of the 32,000-square-foot two-story building began in mid-1980.

When the employees moved into L&N's new regional headquarters in June 1981, it was an office in which they could take pride. The employee and customer parties celebrating the office opening were as impressive as the new building. The festivities began in the parking lot where a train picked up the guests and delivered them to the front door. "The building," says DeWitt, "was transformed. They got an old lifeboat, filled it with ice, and piled shrimp on top of the ice. There were bars set up everywhere and musicians all over the place." Bob McGrath says there are still people who talk about the event and thank him for inviting them: "The realtors and other people in town . . . still claim that was the best party Lafayette ever had."

Under the leadership of Robert McGrath and then

Jess Hay's appointment to the Board of Regents of The University of Texas System by Governor Dolph Briscoe was an outgrowth of his increasing involvement in politics. Photographed at the December 7, 1979, Board of Regents' meeting in Austin are, from left to right: seated, Jane Blumberg, Dan C. Williams, Thomas H. Law, and Jess Hay; standing, Sterling H. Fly, M.D., Howard N. Richards, James L. Powell, and Jon P. Newton. Jess Hay later served as chairman of the Board of Regents from February 1985 to June 1987. Betty Jo and Jess Hay Archives.

Thomas W. Schwartz, who took over as executive vice president after McGrath left the company in 1982, the new region made a name for itself as one of the company's leading producers. However, it didn't happen right away. Part of the first two years were spent absorbing Great Lakes Mortgage and Great American Funding Corporation, a small production-oriented Chicago mortgage banking operation that L&N bought in March 1980. Then they had to organize branch offices within the nine-state region and train employees on how to price and produce loans according to L&N's specifications. By 1982, the region was stable and prosperous enough to begin expanding into Minneapolis, Madison, Milwaukee, Omaha, Columbus, and the state of North Dakota. "Business started booming," says Tom Schwartz. "The chart was running good, and the offices were doing well. In fiscal 1983, we were probably L&N's second largest producing region."

... the General Motors of mortgage banking ...

The burst of acquisition activity by L&N in 1979 solidified its position as the largest mortgage banking company in the country. With over $10 billion worth of mortgages in its portfolio, L&N was more than twice the size of its next largest competitor. Moreover, the company's long-held goal of national geographic coverage became a reality in 1980. It could point with pride to a marketing presence represented by 142 offices in 39 states.

One consequence of growth and higher visibility was increased attention from the media. *Financial Trend* was one of several publications in the early eighties that "discovered" the L&N phenomenon. In a January 1980 cover story, the magazine had nothing but superlatives for Lomas & Nettleton, the company it called "the General Motors of mortgage banking."

There was, however, little opportunity to savor the accolades. In 1980, Lomas & Nettleton Financial Corporation faced the challenge of an economy beset by spiraling inflation and record-breaking interest rates, and a real estate industry plunging into recession.

By 1982, "For Sale" signs in yards marked the worst depression in the housing industry since the Great Depression.

CHAPTER IX

GROWING PAINS

The effects of unchecked inflation on the housing industry in 1979 triggered the nation's longest postwar housing recession and ended one of our country's most remarkable success stories. For over three decades, the United States held the distinction of being the best housed nation in the world. By the end of the 1970s, almost 70 percent of all U.S. families owned their own homes. The mortgage financing system responsible for that achievement toppled in 1980 when double-digit interest rates stripped homebuyers of easy access to mortgage money. "High housing costs," wrote Herman J. Smith, president of the National Association of Home Builders, in a 1981 article, "plus out-of-reach mortgage interest rates, have dealt a crippling blow to potential home buyers."

In March 1982, *Newsweek* called it "the worst depression in the housing industry since the 1930s. Homeowners who managed to sell their properties lost huge sums because of a sluggish market. The number of housing related jobs has shrunk by 2 million, and the bankruptcy rate among real estate firms and home builders has gone out of sight." In 1981, housing starts declined to an annual rate of one million, half the level of 1978. A year later starts fell to the lowest annual rate since 1945. California, the state that once rode the housing boom's highest waves, found itself beached by the real estate collapse. The state's housing starts fell 50 percent in one year, and West Coast banks were swamped with thousands of bad construction loans and mortgages. The Bank of America in California held 20,000 mortgage loans it could call, but as one analyst asked, "What are they going to do with 20,000 homes?" In Chicago, 35,000 permits were issued for new home construction in 1978. In 1981, that figure plunged to 4,400. Escalating interest rates drove millions of consumers out of the housing market. Larry Stupski, a San Francisco stockbroker trying to sell his house in Marin County, told *Newsweek*: "It's the American dream turned into a nightmare."

. . . *k*issing the conventional, fixed-rate mortgage good-bye.

"The economic conditions in this country today," L&N executive vice president Paul M. Low said at a 1981 IRS public hearing, "are frustrating the middle American and simultaneously destroying the dream every working man and woman has of owning a home. A recent study indicates that fewer than five percent of the American public can afford to purchase a home."

The cost of borrowing money was the villain most responsible for pricing Americans out of the housing market. In 1979, FHA interest rates moved into double digits for the first time in its 45-year history. A year later they went to 14 percent and in 1981 climbed to an unbelievable 17½ percent. The prime rate rose even more dramatically—to a high of 21½ percent in 1981. When asked to describe the interest rate environment in the early 1980s, former Lomas Financial Corporation executive vice president David Kelly, Jr., summarized it in three words: "Welcome to Brazil."

Inflation and inflationary expectations devastated the long-term financial markets. Even safe, high-quality loans lost their allure for investors. Fluctuating interest rates increased the degree of risk inherent in fixed-rate mortgages. For most investors, it made a lot more sense to abandon the long-term market in favor of the higher-yielding short-term market. Small savers, once an important source for low-priced mortgage funds, became more sophisticated in their search for investment opportunities. They withdrew billions of dollars from low-paying savings accounts and began chasing money market mutual funds, six-month certificates, and other short-term investments.

Institutional investors were equally wary of commercial real estate. A March 1980 *New York Times* article reported that the "Bank of America raised its minimum rate on commercial mortgage loans a full percentage point, to 15½ percent, 'which effectively has closed down the market,' says Thomas J. Flynn, Jr., senior vice president, real estate.

"New York Life Insurance Co., another major mortgage lender, 'isn't offering commercial mortgage loans at a fixed rate—period,' says Joseph B. Wilford, senior vice president, real estate."

In order to offset investor disenchantment, developers began offering equity interest on real estate projects. The article noted that Prudential Life Insurance Co. and Equitable had been the insurance industry leaders in joint real estate ventures with developers. Even in Dallas, a city largely unaffected by recession, lender participation was standard operating procedure by 1981. "You can't even discuss a project without equity participation," said Roger Staubach, president of Holloway-Staubach Development Company. "It's mainly because of the instability of interest rates. They could be back up to 22 percent within the next five years. So, investors protect themselves with an equity interest in the project. Anyone lending money right now at the market rate without having a share of the project can get burned down the line. It is a whole different world of investing now."

The world was changing for the single-family mortgage market as well. The fixed-rate mortgage loan, an industry standard for over 40 years, was considered a dinosaur headed for extinction by many in the industry. Among the leaders calling for change was Oakley Hunter, chairman and president of the Federal National Mortgage Association: "The long-term, fixed-rate mortgage must give way to more flexible instruments on which the return, over the life of the mortgage, is tied to the cost of funding it. Last year's

Jess Hay's efforts to structure the company to withstand the cyclical nature of the real estate industry paid off in the early 1980s. The visible, predictable revenues based on fees from the servicing of mortgage loans and the management of financial services insulated L&N from much of the economic havoc in the real estate industry. Despite a sharp decline in residential mortgage production in late 1980, Jess Hay confidently predicted a 25 percent increase in revenues for fiscal 1981. "We've learned," said the CEO, "how to cope with a depressed construction business and inverted money rates."

Allan Oakley Hunter, chairman and president of the Federal National Mortgage Association in Washington, D.C., was one of the leaders who called for a change in fixed-rate mortgage loans.

We perceived that the adjustable rate mortgage was something that was needed and would sell.

It was a lesson that had served them well in October 1978. Anticipating a change in the market, management had arranged a $50 million line of credit at 7 percent in August 1978 and an additional $120 million at a rate equal to prime or one-half percent below the FHA rate, whichever was lower. Obtaining below market rates for L&N's warehousing operation was a product of better-than-average clout with its creditors. The company's biggest bargaining chip in those negotiations was the growth of its escrow funds. In a March 1979 *New York Times* article, Merrill Lynch analyst Thomas J. Kearns said that L&N's "mortgage banking division should not be materially impaired by the current inversion in the rate curve." The prediction was accurate. At year's end of fiscal 1979, the company's warehousing operation contributed $700,000 in net earnings.

The advantages of size were felt in other ways, too. With 142 offices in 39 states, L&N had the flexibility to concentrate its efforts in areas with above-average economic activity. "We are much less vulnerable to a

[1980] performance of portfolio lenders and investors, including Fannie Mae, made it clear that such a transition must occur—and occur quickly—if these institutions are to continue as mortgage money suppliers and new investors are to be attracted to housing." Six months later, in mid-1981, Herman J. Smith gave his assessment of what he called the beginning of a new era: "The solution for the thrift industry has been to bail out of the market for fixed-rate, long-term mortgages. Slowly shaping up on the home loan scene are a proliferation of various variable rate loans passing along the risk of borrowing to the consumer. The experts are already kissing the conventional, fixed-rate mortgage good-bye."

Jim Ludman, L&N executive vice president for the Central Region, considered size an advantage and believed L&N's flexibility made it less vulnerable to an economic downturn.

downturn," said LNFC president Ted Enloe at the time. "In the event that a particular state or states has a downturn in housing, we have an opportunity to make that shortfall up in another state." While most of the country experienced economic hardship, there were geographic pockets untouched by recession. States with a heavy concentration of energy-related industries did especially well.

No one was happier about those circumstances at the time than James L. Ludman, former L&N executive vice president for the Central Region, which included the oil-rich states of Texas, Oklahoma, Louisiana, and Colorado. "The Central Region encompasses states with stronger economies than other L&N regional operations," Ludman said in a 1982 *Mortgagee* article. "Texas, being an energy state, is almost recession proof. There hasn't been a recession in Houston since the 1960s, and there isn't one now. Unemployment in Dallas is only five percent. . . . The economy of the Central Region is strong and people are coming from the North to find jobs. So, the mortgage business is good."

Although interest rates reached record highs in 1979 and 1980, demand for housing remained strong in sections of the Sunbelt. Mortgage loan rates of 12 and 13 percent didn't seem to create undue hardship on those lucky enough to live in the booming oil-based economies. However, there were limits. FHA rates went to 14½ percent in the spring of 1981. Summer was even hotter; interest rates climbed to a sweltering 15½ percent. "We weren't hurt tremendously bad until about mid-1981," says Ludman. "Consumers couldn't qualify at those rates, and builders couldn't sell their houses. We started to go into a real bad period."

Mortgage production in the Central Region went from a torrent to a trickle. Ludman responded to adversity with characteristic Lomas & Nettleton creativity. The beginning of a solution came from an article in *The Wall Street Journal*. A few small mortgage companies, Ludman read, were issuing adjustable rate mortgage (ARM) products that offered lower loan qualifications and payments. Most important of all, the financing source was FNMA. In a meeting with FNMA officials, Ludman confirmed their willingness to buy that kind of new product. Jim Wooten agreed with Ludman that L&N should have its own ARM product. A task force to develop one met in the fall of 1981. "We perceived," says David Kelly, Jr., a member of the task force, "that the adjustable rate mortgage was something that was needed and would sell."

What made the adjustable rate mortgage loan attractive to borrowers was the fact that it offered several years of negative amortization. That meant lower loan qualification requirements and lower monthly payments. Gradually, the borrower's payments increased until they covered the loan's accumulated interest and principal. The interest rate for the loan was based on an index that rose and fell according to changes in the marketplace.

Because there were already a few ARMs available,

the L&N group didn't have to invent the wheel. They channeled their creativity into improving it. "We examined their product," says Ludman, "and then we put together a better product. Their ARMs had payments that went up each year for a five-year period of time. We set up our product so that the initial payment wasn't quite as low, but we held that payment steady for three years and then added a more rapidly increasing payment the fourth and fifth years. There were some other bells and whistles, but that was the main thing." Deciding what to name the new product, Ludman says, wasn't difficult: "We got to talking about what to call it, and it seemed pretty obvious. We called it the 'L&N Plan.'"

The marketing strategy for the L&N Plan was anything but elaborate. The product development committee briefed the senior regional management, who in turn explained the plan to their branch managers. Then the loan production staff from each branch took the new product into the field and offered it to established builders and real estate agents in a one-on-one marketing blitz. Word-of-mouth communication completed the sales job.

. . . the envy of the industry.

FNMA agreed not to disclose details about the L&N Plan for two months. "[The L&N Plan] was unique," says Jim Wooten, "and it was ours for 60 days as far as FNMA was concerned. Then everybody had one. But we were first, and first is very important in any marketing process. It went like gangbusters. Man, did we get the loan business!"

With the interest rate for mortgage loans running at 15 and 16 percent, an adjustable rate mortgage like the L&N Plan that enabled borrowers to qualify at 11⅞ percent was an attractive proposition. It was the only option open for

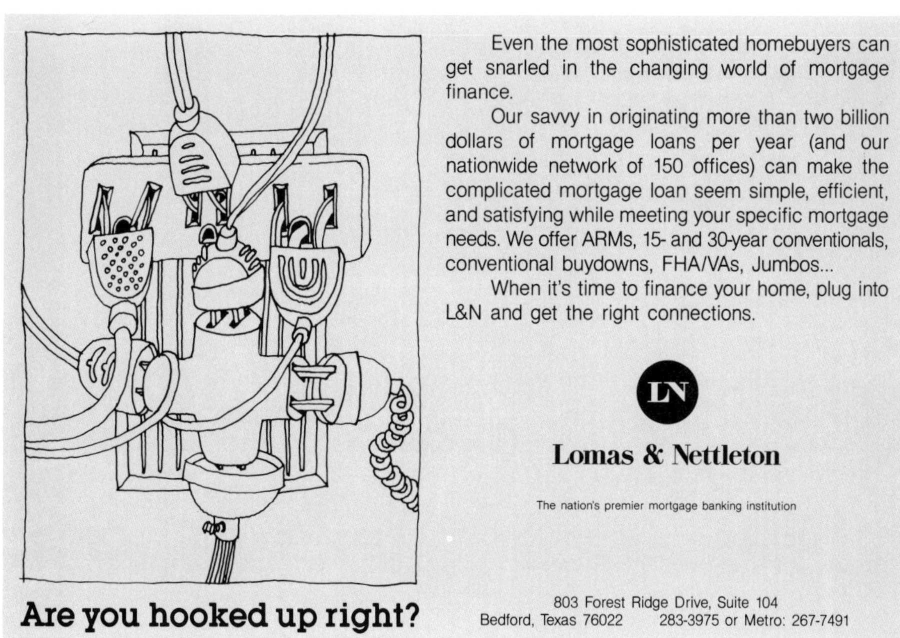

L&N did not invent adjustable rate mortgages. However, as this ad shows, they were creative in their approach to selling the new product.

thousands of prospective homebuyers who wanted to enter the market at that time. Projected annual sales of $200 to $300 million underestimated customer response. Lomas & Nettleton sold its entire $200 million FNMA commitment in two weeks. "And then," says Jim Ludman, "we got another $200 million, and we sold that in three weeks. And before we were through we sold about $1 billion in commitments. In my region alone, Region Three, we sold $500 million."

Speed and market distribution gave L&N a decisive edge. In many parts of the country, the L&N Plan was the only ARM product available. But even among competitors L&N enjoyed a significant lead. "There were a few other companies that had [ARMs]," says Ludman. "But before they could go back and change their product to match ours, we'd already blitzed the country and had most of the customers tied up." The L&N Plan was a prime example of the company's resourcefulness under pressure and the skillful use of its national branch system for marketing.

By the beginning of the decade, the company's reputation for achievement was already well established within mortgage banking circles. But during the recession of the early 1980s LNFC's performance rose to new heights. At the end of fiscal 1981 (June 30, 1981), with FHA interest rates at 15½ percent and the prime rate at 20 percent, the company proudly stated in its annual report that "notwithstanding a severely adverse economic environment, the year produced the best results in L&N's history." Besides producing record revenues and net income, the mortgage servicing portfolio increased by $600 million to a total of $11.6 billion, with mortgage production exceeding $1.4 billion. A year later, still in the midst of a real estate market in disarray, L&N reported the following:

> Fiscal 1982 for Lomas & Nettleton Financial Corporation was another in a series of record years. New highs again were reached in gross revenues, net income, dividends, total resources, and portfolio size. These record results attest to the significant balance in the Company's total operations and to L&N's capacity to function effectively under generally adverse economic conditions.

The company's ability to progress successfully against an unfavorable economic current enhanced its stature among the mortgage banking community. According to Jim Wooten, who had close ties to the Mortgage Bankers Association and its members, L&N was "the envy of the industry" and its products and procedures "widely copied."

The L&N Plan wasn't the only innovative venture that emerged during the economic turbulence of the early 1980s. In fiscal 1981, the company expanded its asset management business by organizing L&N Housing Corp. "The apartment market," says Ted Enloe, "was very tight in 1980 and 1981. Occupancy was excellent. Interest rates had shot up to astronomical levels, 21 percent prime and all that. New starts had trickled off to nothing. Yet the economy in the Southwest was quite good. So we got the idea of forming another real estate investment trust [REIT] that would make participating mortgage loans on newly built apartment rental units with the idea of renting them for several years and then converting them for sale as condominiums. Condo conversions were the rage in the late 1970s and early 1980s. People were making millions of dollars buying old rental units and cutting them up and selling them as condos."

The condominium market got fairly saturated all around the country and demand declined.

Since inflation had priced the average single-family detached home out of reach for most Americans, the

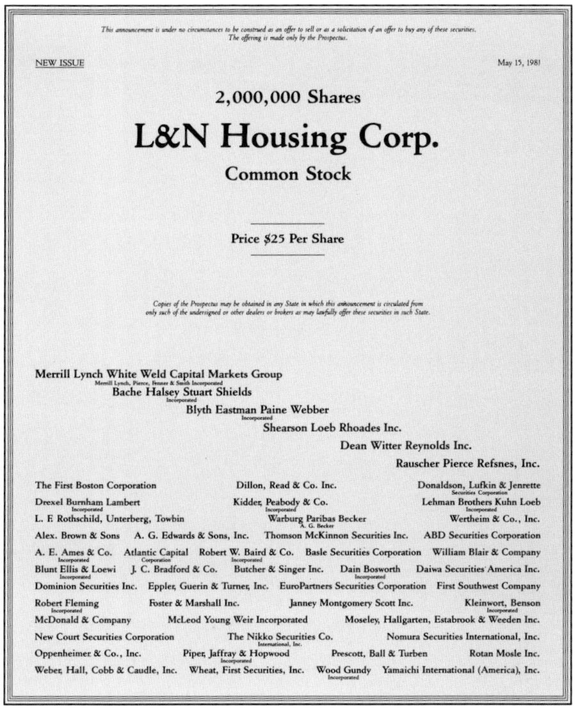

This announcement is under no circumstances to be construed as an offer to sell or as a solicitation of an offer to buy any of these securities. The offering is made only by the Prospectus.

NEW ISSUE

May 15, 1981

2,000,000 Shares

L&N Housing Corp.

Common Stock

Price $25 Per Share

Copies of the Prospectus may be obtained in any State in which this announcement is circulated from only such of the undersigned or other dealers or brokers as may lawfully offer these securities in such State.

Merrill Lynch White Weld Capital Markets Group
Merrill Lynch, Pierce, Fenner & Smith Incorporated
Bache Halsey Stuart Shields
Incorporated
Blyth Eastman Paine Webber
Incorporated
Shearson Loeb Rhoades Inc.
Dean Witter Reynolds Inc.
Rauscher Pierce Refsnes, Inc.

The First Boston Corporation / Dillon, Read & Co. Inc. / Donaldson, Lufkin & Jenrette Securities Corporation
Drexel Burnham Lambert Incorporated / Kidder, Peabody & Co. Incorporated / Lehman Brothers Kuhn Loeb Incorporated
L. F. Rothschild, Unterberg, Towbin / Warburg Paribas Becker A. G. Becker / Wertheim & Co., Inc.
Alex. Brown & Sons / A. G. Edwards & Sons, Inc. / Thomson McKinnon Securities Inc. / ABD Securities Corporation
A. E. Ames & Co. Incorporated / Atlantic Capital Corporation / Robert W. Baird & Co. Incorporated / Basle Securities Corporation / William Blair & Company
Blunt Ellis & Loewi Incorporated / J. C. Bradford & Co. / Butcher & Singer Inc. / Dain Bosworth Incorporated / Daiwa Securities America Inc.
Dominion Securities Inc. / Eppler, Guerin & Turner, Inc. / EuroPartners Securities Corporation / First Southwest Company
Robert Fleming Incorporated / Foster & Marshall Inc. / Janney Montgomery Scott Inc. / Kleinwort, Benson Incorporated
McDonald & Company / McLeod Young Weir Incorporated / Moseley, Hallgarten, Estabrook & Weeden Inc.
New Court Securities Corporation / The Nikko Securities Co. International, Inc. / Nomura Securities International, Inc.
Oppenheimer & Co., Inc. / Piper, Jaffray & Hopwood Incorporated / Prescott, Ball & Turben / Rotan Mosle Inc.
Weber, Hall, Cobb & Caudle, Inc. / Wheat, First Securities, Inc. / Wood Gundy Incorporated / Yamaichi International (America), Inc.

In fiscal 1981, the company expanded its asset management business by organizing L&N Housing Corp. It looked as if raising capital from a public offering would be easy, but the company was forced to restructure its offering downward.

demand for housing, management reasoned, would be met by smaller, less expensive, energy efficient, multi-family units of the type targeted by L&N Housing Corp. Demographic and social patterns also pointed in that direction. The number of persons in households had declined. "These smaller families," observed the 1981 L&N Housing Corp. annual report, "require less space and in many cases prefer to pursue a life style free of the burdens and expenses of caring for larger, more traditional single-family homes."

At first, it looked like raising capital from a public offering would be a piece of cake. The company's earnings and projections were good and REITs had become fashionable again. "Wall Street," says former Lomas attorney James N. Sabin, "wanted to talk to us."

The marketplace, however, was less receptive. The offering that LNFC filed with the Securities and Exchange Commission projected a sale of six million shares of L&N Housing Corp. common stock at $50 per share for a total of $300 million. But the 12 percent return to investors that L&N Housing anticipated lost a lot of its luster in the high interest rate environment of early 1981. "We were swimming upstream in the market," says Ted Enloe. "You're sitting there telling a guy to make an equity investment that will give him a 12 percent return somewhere down the line. And he'd say, 'Why do I want to do that? Why should I take 12 percent from you when I can get 17 percent on a government bond?'" The company was forced to restructure its offering downward. When L&N Housing Corp. began operations on May 26, 1981, 2.2 million shares of common stock had been sold at $25 per share for a net total of $51,500,000.

L&N added its third symbol to the New York Stock Exchange less than a year later. L&N Housing Corp., listed as LHC, made its debut on April 29, 1982. It celebrated the occasion with a national advertising campaign in high-visibility publications that announced the news in a bold type headline—"Lomas & Nettleton just made the Big Board bigger."

Although it was profitable, shifts in the market prevented the new REIT from realizing the degree of success that management had envisioned. "Some of the first projects were very profitable," says former Lomas executive vice president Charles W. Wingo, who was in charge of L&N Housing's national production at the time. "Some were marginally successful. Some of them didn't work out. The condominium market got fairly saturated all around the country and demand declined." It also became apparent over the next few years that despite changes in household demographics, detached, single-family housing was still the lifestyle preference for most Americans.

LNFC discovered in the late 1970s that it had a firmer grip on external economic events than it did on

On April 29, 1982, Lomas & Nettleton added its third symbol to the New York Stock Exchange: LHC, for the L&N Housing Corp. The occasion was celebrated with this notice from the national advertising campaign.

As head of L&N Housing's national production, Chuck Wingo realized some profits, but the market prevented the success management had expected.

the problems associated with internal growth. This was especially evident in the personnel department. Lomas vice president Charles S. Werner, hired in 1976 as manager of employee relations, was one of the first to address the issue. "In looking at the personnel departments," says Werner, "both in Houston and Dallas, I found that there were . . . large, gaping holes. They had no employee handbook, no drafted personnel policies. There was no formalized training department. They had no concept of skills management, which had been around in the personnel world for years. In my estimation, personnel was simply a central record-keeping department."

. . . large, gaping holes.

Research compiled by David Farr, president of TDF Systems, an outside corporate research group that conducted employee surveys for L&N beginning in 1978, confirmed Werner's observations. Employee interviews indicated a need and strong desire for training. The research also revealed a feeling of isolation and lack of unity among large numbers of employees. Many believed L&N's strong, independent regional system built upon the acquisition of formerly autonomous companies was responsible for the problem.

In early 1979 the Human Resources Committee (HRC), made up of about twenty regional and corporate representatives, was organized to address these issues. The name "Human Resources" was itself significant. It indicated a shift away from the old Personnel Department image and toward an increased emphasis on employee development.

After an awkward beginning, the committee formed a bond of friendship and accomplishment that lasted until it completed its mission in 1984. "I can well remember," says former Lomas vice president Betty Watson, a corporate committee representative at the time, "the first Human Resources Committee meeting in January 1979. Everybody was courteous to

Problems associated with internal growth were manifest in the personnel department. Chuck Werner, hired in 1976 as manager of employee relations, was one of the first to address the issue.

each other but not particularly cordial. We all felt a little stiff and formal and uncertain about the task at hand. But that changed very quickly. Pretty soon you realized you had friends in other regions, and you could call on them for most anything."

Aided by the expertise of David Farr and his staff, the HRC developed a five-year plan of objectives. Training headed the list. The first effort was directed at employee orientation. "Chuck Werner and I," says Watson, "went to each region to launch the 'New Employee Orientation Program,' and then we turned it over to the HRC committee members in their respective regions. The reaction in the field was excellent."

Buoyed by the response of L&N employees, they introduced a series of training programs. One of the most ambitious was the Leadership Training Institute (LTI), designed to meet the committee's management training goals. Two groups, each with about 50 L&N management-level employees, participated in LTI's six training sessions beginning in 1981. Besides new skills, the personal interactions and friendships helped build a sense of community that transcended regional differences. "The 100 people who participated," says Betty Watson, "were in a position to make things happen. A lot of links were established. People met people that they previously only talked to on the telephone, or they met people doing a similar job in another region, and that created a feeling of unity."

The Human Resources Committee owed much of its success to strong support from management. The company institutionalized that commitment in 1980 by formally establishing a human resources department. In a speech presented at a general staff meeting that same year, Jess Hay reaffirmed the importance of the people without whom there would be no Lomas & Nettleton.

> Of our many current challenges, none is more important nor, in my opinion, more critical to the future of this company than the careful nurturing of our human resources. . . . This new emphasis on human resources development is mandated by our very nature as a company. To remain at the top of our industry, it is essential that we have the finest personnel—well-trained and intelligently deployed with a clear understanding of who they are and the important part they play in the overall effort.

Personnel matters weren't the only ones that required professionalism and unity. Nowhere was the lack of corporate consistency more visibly apparent than in the variety of materials that displayed the company logo. Each entity had its own idea about how the L&N logo should look on the printed material it used, creating what Jess Hay called a "mishmash." In early 1980, the company asked The Richards Group, who handled many of L&N's design projects, to develop a corporate identity program. Their effort resulted in a revamping of the L&N symbol, logotype, and general trademark, and the distribution of a Corporate

Identification Program manual that outlined how the new standards should be applied to business cards, stationery, forms, advertising, and signage. "The bottom line," says Werner, "was that people were confused about who was what and were they part of an overall group or not. That's when we decided to adopt the tag line 'A member of the Lomas & Nettleton Financial Group,' so that regardless of which entity you were doing business with, you knew it was part of L&N." The new program successfully addressed the goal outlined by Jess Hay: "to strengthen our corporate image by providing a dimension of consistency in all printed materials which are presented by Lomas & Nettleton to its external audiences—regardless of location."

In 1980 the L&N symbol and logotype were redesigned, with examples of usage and standards for application published in a manual. The result was a totally new corporate identity program.

The most serious sign of weakness due to corporate expansion was in the data processing department. There, the strain of growth bordered on breakdown. The transfer of 160,000 loans from NHAC to L&N's servicing system in December 1979 brought a heavily burdened computer system to the brink. Already processing over 300,000 L&N loans and a similar number for outside customers, data processing had little capacity left in its system.

We were not prepared in hardware or software.

It was increasingly difficult for the overtaxed computer to keep up with the file maintenance, an overnight processing procedure. "The capacity of the system was strained," says former Lomas Information Systems senior vice president Milton Gumm. "If anything went wrong operationally, it had a domino effect and took a long time to catch up. The machine was strained. You can only run an engine at redline for so long, and then it breaks."

The core problem was L&N's antiquated hardware. Despite efforts to upgrade equipment over the years,

The data processing department in early 1980 felt the full effect of the transfer of 160,000 loans from NHAC to L&N's servicing system. A serious sign of weakness was outdated hardware. E. G. Bray, third row center, was still head of the department.

the heart of the system was hopelessly outdated. One data processing insider compared it to "driving a 1990 car that gets 40 miles to the gallon and driving a 1970 car that gets 8 miles to the gallon. Both cars can drive from here to California, but the older car is going to cost you a hell of a lot more, and it's a lot more likely to break down along the way."

Heading the department was E. G. Bray, a dominant and respected data processing figure since 1950 when he pioneered the T. J. Bettes Company's entry into computer-automated mortgage banking. He practiced a micromanagement style of leadership that became less effective as the department grew larger. Close, personal control of the organization worked well for a number of years, but when NHAC's portfolio overwhelmed the system, data processing didn't have the depth of management it needed to meet the crisis.

Bray was also known for his reluctance to spend money. Employees who worked for him believed that was a result of working at Bettes, where for many years frugality was an unavoidable fact of life. His passion for running a lean organization created a department some considered anorexic. "Back in those days," says former Lomas Information Systems vice president Jon R. Carter, "data processing worked on a real tight budget . . . the entire budget was $1 million per year. That included salaries, equipment—everything. If you needed something new, it took an act of God to get it."

For many years, the department's lean efficiency worked well. The small, dedicated staff of programmers and operators kept pace with L&N's growing portfolio. But NHAC's avalanche of loans ended that.

"There were times in Houston," says former Lomas Information Systems second vice president Larry Cornwell, "that were really scary. We were way understaffed. Lomas could have been in real jeopardy if a couple of people didn't show up. It was that tight—two people meant the difference between whether or not the system was going to come up in the morning. These were people who never took vacations because they couldn't afford to be gone for a week. Jon Carter would go into the computer room when there was a system failure and would work for 12, 15, 18 hours rerunning tapes and fixing things. When he walked out he looked like a zombie, but the system was back up and current. Nobody knew how the hell he did it. We were pushing people and equipment to their limits."

The memories from that period are still vivid for Jon Carter: "It was a nightmare. We would get behind on Monday and start praying for the weekend just so we could catch up. Data processing was not prepared. We were not prepared in hardware or software." For five years, Carter worked every day "including Saturdays and Sundays. No vacation. No time off." The escalating workload and numbing hours didn't dampen his dedication or that of the other members of Bray's team: "We had a sense of pride in what we were doing." Unfortunately, pride and the heroic efforts of individuals could not solve the problems facing the department.

The pressures on data processing were passed along in turn to the loan administration system it serviced. In the spring of 1980, that strain resulted in what Jim Wooten calls "the hazard insurance policy debacle." The crunch came when the increased demand for overnight data processing created a decline in on-line processing, which eroded the escrow department's ability to update customer files and keep accurate track of their insurance premium payments. For Lomas Insurance Services senior vice president Tom H. Carter that was a cause for real concern: "We are completely tied to the computer. If our terminals aren't working, we may as well go home. We can't answer customer questions or complaints, and we can't get their insurance premiums paid on time. I remember at least once or twice that our terminals were down for a week at a time. And that was when we were processing 2,500 renewals a day. So you can imagine how quickly that backed up when we had five days of straight down time." In addition to the problem of reduced computer access, L&N discovered that much of the insurance information from NHAC was incomplete.

. . . the hazard insurance policy debacle . . .

To meet the influx of homeowner insurance policies from NHAC, the insurance department hired additional staff. Many of the new employees, however, were unqualified. The minimum wage L&N offered turned out to be an economy measure for which the company paid dearly. "We could have done it better," says Lomas Mortgage USA senior vice president Lawrence M. Rogers. "It wasn't as if we didn't know better. We just tried to get off cheap. We didn't hire enough people, and we didn't hire the right quality of people. You don't need a bunch of Rhodes scholars, but you can't hire somebody who has been fired from McDonald's and Jack-in-the-Box twice in the last 90 days because they couldn't get to work.

"We didn't jump in there and work on it hard enough, either. Management and supervisors were going home at five o'clock before I got there."

Some employees reacted to the heavy filing workload by hiding folders behind file cabinets. Later, when an elevator was being repaired, workmen found customer files at the bottom of the elevator shaft. One woman hired by the insurance department to handle incoming mail kept a remarkably clean desk considering the volume of correspondence she was responsible for. According to a supervisor who caught her in the act, she filed the leftover, unopened mail in the wastebasket at the end of the day.

Inadequate computer and employee support had a devastating effect on the hazard insurance department. Its inability to keep up with the workload meant that hundreds of insurance premiums didn't get paid. The already heavy flow of paper became a flood as warning letters and cancellation notices from unpaid insurance companies deluged the Houston office. The cancellations, in turn, set in motion the machinery at L&N that automatically ordered new insurance policies for borrowers. Angry customers barraged the company with still more letters. "Everybody was mad," says Lomas Insurance Services senior executive vice president Ned R. Harris. "Customers were mad. Insurance agents were mad. When Wanda Golemon and I came on board in 1980, L&N was getting complaints out the kazoo. Many of them went directly to the chief executive officer." Jess Hay asked Harris and Golemon to evaluate the problem in Houston. They found the hazard insurance department in disarray. According to their estimate, there were 40,000 letters and notices sitting in cardboard boxes waiting to be answered or acted upon. Jess Hay ordered the formation of a task force to handle the crisis.

Larry Rogers, who helped supervise the task force, remembers his reaction to the enormity of the assignment: "It was like standing behind a 16-yard gravel truck and having it dump around your shoulders." Rogers met his staffing requirements by pulling top people from regional offices and the company's insurance agencies and bringing them to Houston. They spent the summer and part of the fall working two shifts a day, seven days a week for two weeks at a time. At the end of each two-week period, a second team replaced the first.

Organization was the first priority. "I personally identified," says Rogers, "approximately 32,000 insurance files taken from the file room and spread around an entire floor and not identified as to where they were and who had them. The file tracking system we set up was really the salvation of the whole thing. From that point forward, no file went anywhere that I didn't know where it was." The actual work of resolving problems was handled in an assembly line fashion. Some members of the team determined what action was needed for a particular letter, others conducted computer research, and those experienced in answering correspondence dictated letters.

In Dallas, operating under the title of special assistant to the chairman of the board, Wanda Golemon fielded telephone calls and correspondence directed to either Jess Hay or Ted Enloe. "I spent hours on the telephone listening to mortgage customers," says Golemon. "They wanted someone to listen to them vent their frustrations. I had a cauliflower ear for about two years."

By November 1980, Jim Pickup reported at a Midwest Region staff meeting that although "there are still problems to resolve . . . the corner is turned and better days are ahead.

"Our people in Houston, supported by people we brought in from our regional offices, knowledgeable in hazard insurance and customer service, have been working around-the-clock, literally, to correct problems. . . . Our Hazard Insurance [Department] is now current."

The corrective measures, however, were expensive. "We spent a lot of money on customer service," says former executive vice president for loan administration George Wilson. "We put in WATS lines manned by special teams. That cost us a fortune." Pulling experienced employees out of production forced Wilson to hire additional personnel whose inexperience lowered productivity. Management compensated by increasing the numbers of employees and "opening a training school. . . . That all cost money. But when you get in a hole, it costs money to get out of the hole. That's all there is to it."

Even before the temporary disruption of the escrow department in mid-1980, E. G. Bray in Houston and senior management in Dallas understood the necessity for upgrading data processing's performance. "It was

In the spring of 1980, an order was placed with the Burroughs Corporation for two computers.
The 6800, pictured above, was ready for immediate delivery but was a temporary solution.
The larger and more advanced 7800 wouldn't be available until mid-1981.
The Charles Babbage Institute, University of Minnesota.

...a **centralized operation in Dallas.**

clear," says Jess Hay, "that our system, although it had been updated from time to time . . . was driven by outdated architecture. It became an increasingly inefficient operation. . . . In order to produce the desired data, it had to go through perhaps 100 more steps than a reasonably structured system would have to go through. . . . Also, I was very committed to the view that providing data systems work and services to others in our industry held real potential. And along with that we were acquiring portfolios, or proposing to, which greatly increased the volume of business on our computers. So, it was a combination of things that led to the decision to move the Data Center to Dallas."

Consideration of future volume, however, was largely an academic exercise for data processing in 1980 and 1981. The immediate concern was survival. In the spring of 1980, E. G. Bray placed an order with the Burroughs Corporation for two computers. The largest and most advanced of the two was the 7800, which wouldn't be available until mid-1981. The 6800, on the other hand, was ready for immediate delivery. "The 6800," says Bray, "was a stopgap arrangement to handle the excess volume in Houston. . . . We had to get

The Burroughs 7800 was to be housed in a new facility to be built in Dallas. In early 1981, architects presented a model of Lomas & Nettleton Information Systems' Data Center.

Site preparation began on the Data Center in March 1981. Construction of the 60,000-square-foot building was on "a very fast track."

With the Data Center nearing completion by late September, the 7800 computer and support equipment moved into the facility.

November 16, 1981, marked the official opening of the Data Center. In the reception area and atrium, fine craftsmanship and construction materials along with large plants and ficus trees provided a warm greeting.

some more power.

"We crowded the 6800 in beside the 6700. About the only way we could move around was with some pogo sticks."

Although not noted for its customer support, Burroughs responded to L&N's appeal for assistance. "We have cleared the first floor in Houston," Jim Pickup stated at a November 1980 loan administration staff meeting, "to accommodate the local branch office of the Burroughs Corporation. We have seven Burroughs people now working out of our office and we have first call around-the-clock on their services. Burroughs has transferred the Canadian supervisor from Toronto to manage the operation. . . . The presence of the Burroughs people on an around-the-clock basis will provide a consistent monitoring of the system and its components so that proper maintenance can be carried out, reducing the possibility of the disruption of service." Even with this extraordinary effort from Burroughs, the situation didn't improve significantly. Data processing struggled for over a year just to keep its head above water.

Adding loans to the system was no longer an option for L&N. For a corporation whose primary growth strategy was based on acquisitions, the sudden realization that it couldn't do that anymore was disturbing. "Jess Hay woke up one morning," says former senior executive vice president Henry G. Hortenstine, "and found out data processing controlled the company in a way that wasn't very attractive to him. I believe Jess determined he couldn't grow the company any further without a much more sophisticated data processing capability."

The reality of what that meant gave Data Services a sharp jolt in 1981. Larry Cornwell, who had been successfully marketing L&N's computer service to outside customers, was asked to temporarily stop selling: "I was told, 'Don't lose any business if you can help it, but we really don't want you to sign any new business because this thing [data processing] is broke down.' For a year, I wasn't suppose to sign any business. I had several big accounts in the Denver area, close to a closing, and I had to back off, because we couldn't put them on the system."

It was always intended that one day the computer and loan servicing operations would move to Dallas. The time was now right for that process to begin. Besides running out of capacity, the data processing department in Houston had run out of space. A new facility would have to be built if the 7800 computer scheduled for delivery in 1981 was sent to Houston. "Since you had to spend money for a new computer center somewhere," says E. G. Bray, "then for Christ's sake let's move it to Dallas now. That was my recommendation to Jess Hay. If you are going to move the thing, now is the time to do it. And, that already fit into what his thought was all along—to have a centralized operation in Dallas."

With Houston fighting to keep its head above water, speed was an essential consideration in the construction of the Dallas Data Center. Architects were hired and building requirements defined by late 1980. On January 21, 1981, L&N Land Corp. purchased a 5.8-acre site at 1750 Viceroy, eight miles northwest of downtown Dallas with good access to Dallas/Fort Worth International Airport. One specification that had a far-reaching effect on future corporate growth was the decision to design an unobtrusive building that blended well with its surroundings. It was the first structure in what became a cluster of buildings surrounded by landscaped green space. The "Viceroy Campus," as it was later called, represented the company's commitment to growth on a human scale. Not long after the Data Center was completed, L&N Land Corp. bought additional adjacent acreage.

Construction of the 60,000-square-foot building was on what construction coordinator Milton Gumm called "a very fast track." Site preparation began in March 1981. By late September, as the Data Center neared completion, three moving vans containing the 7800 computer and support equipment arrived at the facility. The next couple of months were spent testing programs and making test runs. November 16, 1981, marked the official opening of the Data Center. Its new computer went live the first week of December. "It was a classic event," says Milton Gumm. "On Friday we were in Houston. On Monday we were in Dallas. Besides a new building and computer, the data processing department also had new leadership."

Approaching retirement after a 30-year career in data processing, E. G. Bray had no interest in either leaving Houston or installing a new computer system that someone else would have to take over in a year or two. Henry G. Hortenstine was hired as senior vice president in May 1981 to supervise the installation of the system at the Data Center and then take over the entire operation from Bray. Hortenstine's previous experience included ten years at IBM and four years as the top data processing executive for United Virginia Bank in Richmond, Virginia. It was a resume with the breadth and depth that enabled him to tackle L&N's three data processing priorities: move the operation from Houston to Dallas, upgrade the system's capability, and aggressively market Data Services to outside

The Data Center is located in Dallas on six acres of land near the Brook Hollow Golf Club. When the facility opened, offices accommodated 155 employees, among whom were 33 programmers, 33 data entry operators, 50 people in data services, and eight people in operations.

users. Besides those immediate priorities, there was a larger role that underscored the Data Center's future importance to L&N. "Data processing," says Henry Hortenstine, "was going to be the vanguard of the move to fully centralize the corporation in Dallas."

Shortly after coming on board, Hortenstine changed the name of the data processing department to Lomas & Nettleton Information Systems (LNIS). Besides indicating a new regime, the name change announced the division's expanded role and something about the philosophy of it's new executive: "I felt 'data processing' was an old-fashioned term. Also, I liked the concept of information as opposed to data. Data is the raw material; the finished product is information."

The ordeals suffered by hazard insurance and data processing in 1980 forced management to take a long, hard look at its operations. Servicing procedures that had performed well during the 1970s lost much of their effectiveness in the face of escalating expansion. Strained by the sudden surge in volume from the acquisition of NHAC, loan administration efficiency declined and, as far as the hazard insurance and data processing departments were concerned, temporarily failed. Ted Enloe believed the move toward a new system was a matter of "sheer necessity . . . because the old system was getting dilapidated. It couldn't handle our work any more." The consensus among management at the time, according to former L&N executive vice president Hugh S. DeWitt, was that "it was time we step back and take a look at this thing we've created and see how it can best be managed and how it can best be structured. And what tools do we need to make it efficient and profitable and still build in plenty of room for continued growth."

We have constituted a special task force . . .

Management responded by forming a Task Force on Internal Strategy chaired by DeWitt. "We have constituted a special task force," read a memo from Jess Hay dated January 23, 1981, "to review L&N's entire system structure, with a view to designing a substantially upgraded management and operating system to carry

Along with a new building and computer, the data processing department acquired new leadership in Henry Hortenstine. He changed the name to Lomas & Nettleton Information Systems.

Below: Under Hortenstine's supervision, the Burroughs 7800 computer went into live operation in the first week of December 1981. The Charles Babbage Institute, University of Minnesota.

us through the 1980s." Besides DeWitt, the task force included E. G. Bray, James Pickup, David Buckman, and later Henry Hortenstine, as well as outside assistance from Booz, Allen & Hamilton, an international management consultant company responsible for "organizing the project and providing technological expertise."

Jess Hay had met Booz, Allen vice president Ray Lane in the fall of 1980, when Lane called on Lomas & Nettleton to discuss the findings of a Booz, Allen study about the future direction of banking and mortgage banking. Hay was impressed with Lane and his company's thoughtful approach to future trends in the industry and asked him to join the task force. Besides their organizational ability, the consultant firm offered an objective viewpoint from which to study the company.

Addressing mortgage banking's declining profit margin was an important part of the task force's mandate to upgrade L&N's operating system. Although the company's overall profitability remained strong, deteriorating productivity in LNFC's largest and most important division created concern. The theory of unit price, which served as the basis for many of management's projections, operated on the premise that as L&N increased its loan volume the unit cost of servicing those loans would decrease. In fact, the opposite was occurring.

By mid-1982, the burden of extricating the escrow and data processing departments from their problems had taken its toll. Although fiscal 1982's net income of $20,915,000 was the highest in the company's history, escalating expenses wiped out The Lomas & Nettleton Company's revenue contribution. "Fiscal 1982's performance in certain respects was not entirely satisfactory," Jess Hay stated in a July 23, 1982, report to the board of directors. "Our mortgage banking revenues increased by $9,029,000. And yet, that division's contribution, net of directly related expense, declined by $92,000, indicating that more than 100% of our incremental mortgage banking revenues were consumed in Fiscal 1982 by increased expenses. . . . Our entire staff is concentrating on the task of restoring our mortgage banking division's operating margins. . . . And much of our planning for Fiscal 1983 involves a determination to reverse this discouraging trend."

Outside assistance came to the Task Force on Internal Strategy from Booz, Allen & Hamilton, an international management consultant company. Booz, Allen vice president Ray Lane was invited by Jess Hay to join the task force. Courtesy Booz, Allen & Hamilton, Inc.

A *Mortgagee* article about the task force in May 1981 noted that "the primary goal of the task force is to identify areas where computer resources can assist employees in performing their jobs. . . . By taking advantage of the latest in technical resources L&N will be able to maintain its low servicing cost per loan while the flexibility offered by these changes will enable L&N to expand into new industry areas and ensure its ability to provide a quality service."

The loss of servicing and data processing efficiency wasn't the company's only concern. Loan production and the regional system that drove it also came under scrutiny. The practice of using former CEOs from acquired companies to manage regions created a system of jealously guarded fiefdoms that hindered L&N's ability to execute consistent strategy and control. "We had executive vice presidents," says DeWitt, "in the Northeast, Southeast, Midwest, Los Angeles, and Phoenix, all of whom had run companies. When a guy has been his own boss awhile, it's hard to change his opinion about how he ought to run his business. They were all talented people, but we had to get them moving in unison. There was a feeling that the regions should be operating more uniformly." The fact that many of the regional managers were nearing retirement made the review of L&N's regional structure particularly timely.

...a new Mortgage Loan Servicing System...

Despite their shared goals, the working relationship between the outside consultants and L&N's professionals was strained. Booz, Allen & Hamilton's scholarly perspective irritated mortgage banking veterans like E. G. Bray and Jim Pickup, who viewed task force objectives in terms of hard-nosed practicality, based on years of finding solutions to problems that more often than not defied textbook solutions. "A consultant can come in and give you all kinds of advice," says Bray, who had little patience for what he regarded as Booz, Allen's ivory tower approach, "but they can't implement anything. They tell you what they believe you want to hear. Otherwise, they couldn't stay in business. You wouldn't call them back." The fact that the consultants knew little about the production or servicing of mortgage loans further strained the relationship. "As far as mortgage banking was concerned," says Jim Wooten, "they didn't know their ass from third base." Task force chairman DeWitt's view of the consultant's role was less jaundiced: "The Booz, Allen contribution cannot be overstated—if not for the knowledge and expertise of their professionals, then for their helping us to understand new ways to analyze what we do, why we do it, and how we do it." Their ability to quantify problems and record processes in ways that computer programmers understood was particularly valuable.

By November 1981 the task force, chaired by Dee DeWitt, had completed its analysis and made its recommendations to management.

By November 1981, the task force completed its

analysis of the company's existing systems and recommended ten projects for immediate implementation, which management approved. The projects represented a series of short-term measures designed to upgrade the system where its efficiency was most impaired. In terms of long-term solutions, the task force concluded that the company needed "to develop a new Mortgage Loan Servicing System which would utilize the latest in data base and data communications technology, as well as incorporate many new functional enhancements."

Few of the task force recommendations, however, were fully implemented. A proposal to close a number of loan production offices, for example, met strong opposition. "Jim Wooten," says Ray Lane, "was in charge of residential production. He said, 'Once you close a branch you can't reopen it, and I'm not going to close it because some consultant tells me to close it.' So very few branches got closed. And he's probably right about going in and out of a community. But we wanted to close them because they weren't economically viable and would never be economically viable."

Opposition to task force recommendations revealed a conservatism that was a fundamental cultural characteristic within the mortgage banking division. "Lomas," says Lane, "was an extremely proud organization that had gone from a small Connecticut company to the largest mortgage banker in the industry. And they had done that largely with the management team from T. J. Bettes. They were very proud mortgage bankers who were never going to change. The belief that they were the best overwhelmed the task force results." The resistance of the old guard from T. J. Bettes was an obstacle that impeded mortgage banking's progress for several years.

To meet the task force's long-term goal of developing a comprehensive loan servicing system, L&N organized the Future System project. The program represented a major effort to upgrade data processing in order to meet the company's demand for a more sophisticated system and continued growth. In August 1982, Donald Funkhouser, executive vice president of Symbolics, Inc., a software development company L&N had purchased in July, was asked to manage the project.

The impact of the Symbolics purchase and L&N's agreement, also in July, to acquire another mortgage company escalated the rate of change within the mortgage banking division and throughout the company. However, these were only the latest in a series of changes. In 1980, chairman Jess Hay reflected on the company's rapid growth over the past 15 years: "During that brief period, we have progressed from a relatively small operation, with offices in eight cities, to a nationwide network of 150 offices in 40 states. Our staff has increased from about 200 to more than 2,000, and our financial resources, mortgage production, and servicing portfolio have expanded tenfold."

According to Milt Gumm, who experienced much of that growth firsthand, the impact of those changes forced L&N in the early 1980s "to transition from a large small company to a small large company. Organizationally, it had to have characteristics similar to GM and those kinds of companies. You couldn't run it like a mom and pop shop any more."

The updating of corporate identity, the company's response to human resources issues, the work of the Internal Strategy Task Force, and the relocation of data processing to Dallas were all evidence of this transition's initial progress. But the greatest impetus for centralization came from Southfield, Michigan, when L&N signed a joint venture/acquisition agreement with Advance Mortgage Corporation in July 1982.

Edward Rose, one of Detroit's largest homebuilders, founded Advance Mortgage Corporation in the late 1930s. He had started his career in 1921 and built over 70,000 homes and apartments in 16 states. Rose supported the founding of the National Association of Home Builders. Rose Archives.

CHAPTER X

TRIUMPH AND TURMOIL

Advance Mortgage Corporation, the nation's seventh largest mortgage company, was a worthy addition to Lomas & Nettleton's mortgage banking growth strategy. AMC's hefty 176,000-loan portfolio and its aggregate unamortized principal balance of $4.8 billion increased L&N's mortgage servicing portfolio by 40 percent.

Unlike previous L&N acquisitions, this $42 million purchase was structured as a joint venture for two years under the control and management of the Dallas company. At the end of that period, L&N exercised its option to buy Advance's share of the business. The arrangement served the interests of both parties. Advance Mortgage Corporation was an affiliate of Oppenheimer & Co., which bought Advance from Citicorp in 1979 primarily as a tax shelter. The two-year joint venture permitted Oppenheimer to exhaust the tax benefits derived from the depreciation of its servicing. L&N planned to use the time to further centralize its mortgage banking operation, and the next step required time to execute. It called for the construction of a loan administration office building next to the Dallas Data Center. Upon its completion, L&N planned to transfer Advance's portfolio as well as the loan administration systems in both Detroit and Houston and merge them simultaneously in Dallas.

The glowing praise from L&N inspection reports of Advance's operations and personnel suggested the new acquisition had more to offer than just its servicing portfolio. Known for his exacting standards, executive vice president Jim Pickup observed in an August 18 report: "I was impressed with the Regional staff and systems in Schaumburg [AMC's regional branch in

Irving Rose was 28 years old when he became president of Advance Mortgage Corporation in 1953, and remained head of the organization until it was purchased by Citibank in 1970.

ADVANCE MORTGAGE CORPORATION

On March 25, 1982, L&N and Advance Mortgage Corporation of Detroit, Michigan, an affiliate of Oppenheimer & Co., Inc., announced that the two companies had entered into a joint venture for the eventual merger of Advance's mortgage banking operations into those of L&N. The well-structured corporate logo was symbolic of AMC.

Illinois]. I was further impressed with the staff and systems of AMC at the home office in Southfield. . . . The staff is knowledgeable, well trained and responsive. This is a first class operation."

This is a first class operation.

Advance's superior performance in 1982 had begun in the mid-1970s, part of a dramatic turnaround from problems that had threatened the company's survival. Advance Mortgage Corporation was founded in the late 1930s by Edward Rose, one of Detroit's largest homebuilders. Like T. J. Bettes, Advance was a product of the Depression-era FHA licensing program. It operated as an adjunct to a well-established single-family residential construction business that Rose had begun in 1920. According to family legend, Edward Rose was the only Detroit builder of any consequence "who didn't go broke in 1929." On a reduced scale, Rose continued to build houses throughout the Depression. "My father was always a careful businessman," says Irving Rose, the oldest of Edward's four sons. "He never outreached himself financially." Later in life, the National Association of Home Builders recognized his achievement and longevity in the industry by electing him to their Hall of Fame.

Irving Rose was 28 years old and helping run the family building business in 1953 when Edward asked him to take over as president of Advance Mortgage Corporation. A year later the new president had an opportunity to expand the mortgage business when Edward Rose & Sons began building houses in Dayton, Ohio. "We decided," says Irving Rose, "to see if we could do the mortgage financing. Up till then, our business was strictly local. We did it, but we were concerned about developing good procedures for handling the payments. I remember visiting T. J. Bettes in Houston with our treasurer to see how Bettes processed their California payments."

Left: Bob Mylod, a Citibank executive, helped negotiate the sale of Advance Mortgage to the New York financial institution. He was made president of Advance in 1975 and remained until 1983, when he resigned to become president of the Federal National Mortgage Association (FNMA) in Washington, D.C. Courtesy Michigan National Corporation.

Right: Terry Klein succeeded Bob Mylod as president of Advance on January 1, 1983. Courtesy Sears Mortgage Corporation.

Advance bought an old-line Chicago mortgage company in 1956. That started an expansion program that eventually included more than 20 cities across the country. AMC was considered the nation's third or fourth largest mortgage company at the time of its purchase by Citibank in 1970. By way of explanation for the $30 million sale, Irving Rose says: "They offered us a price we couldn't refuse."

In the late 1960s when New York's Citicorp embarked on an aggressive expansion program, part of their strategy included mortgage banking. A Citibank executive named Robert J. Mylod helped negotiate the sale of Advance to the New York financial giant. Three years later Citibank sent him to Detroit as executive vice president of national production. Walter C. (Terry) Klein, Jr., a protege of Mylod's, was also transferred to Advance in 1973. Klein, a Harvard-educated Marine Corps veteran, had a reputation for a brilliant mind and a dynamic, forceful personality that some colleagues found overbearing and abrasive. When Mylod became president of Advance in 1975, Klein succeeded him as national production manager.

About the time senior management shifted at the top, the company's day-to-day performance declined. Originations and servicing fell to unacceptable levels. A major class action lawsuit in Chicago named AMC as one of several mortgage lenders accused of shoddy originations and unfair foreclosure practices. Problems with the VA in California ended when Advance entered into a consent decree that required the company to pay several hundred thousand dollars in fines and penalties. In another incident, the Department of Housing and

Urban Development (HUD) filed a complaint alleging that Advance did not have an adequate compliance guidebook for its employees in order to ensure that FHA servicing met FHA regulations. HUD and Advance agreed to a consent decree that required Advance to take immediate steps to put into place a compliance guidebook and training procedures that would bring the company's originations and servicing up to federal standards. HUD also placed AMC on probation for six months.

Chastened by these events, Advance implemented corrective measures and began a rebuilding process. "This was a terrible black eye for Citicorp," says Terry Klein, "and the beginning of a revitalization for the company. Citicorp took it all very much to heart, and this brand new president, Bob Mylod, was absolutely hell-bent-for-leather to whip the company into shape.

"Citicorp spent a couple of million dollars a year writing procedure manuals, rebuilding its computer systems, and installing quality assurance and customer service procedures. I believe we were the first national mortgage company to have a toll-free customer service number in 1976."

...the organization through which L&N will enter the package software industry.

Just when the new systems and procedures were largely in place and the company headed toward nominal profits in 1979, Citicorp was forced to sell. It lost on appeal a decision by federal regulators that required Citicorp to divest itself of Advance. Mylod negotiated the sale of Advance to Oppenheimer & Co., who in turn sold it to Lomas two and a half years later.

Although small in comparison to that of Advance, the purchase of Symbolics, Inc., and its subsidiary Symbolics Financial Systems signaled continuing

Gerry Nelson, cofounder and president of Symbolics, Inc., was responsible for market planning, sales, and administration.

Don Funkhouser, the other cofounder and executive vice president of Symbolics, Inc., directed the company's financial, operational, and administrative activities.

changes in data processing that began with the change in leadership and the move from Houston to Dallas. The initiative for the sale in July 1982 came from Henry Hortenstine, the new head of Lomas & Nettleton Information Systems (LNIS). Besides beefing up data processing's computer programming capability, the acquisition was touted as "the organization through which L&N will enter the package software industry." The greatest claim to fame of the small, entrepreneurially aggressive software development company was the automated loan origination system it developed and sold to an impressive client list.

Gerry Nelson and Don Funkhouser, two enterprising computer jocks with backgrounds in software sales and development and corporate management, organized Symbolics in Richardson, Texas. The idea for starting a company grew out of a personal friendship. Informal discussions between the two men while playing tennis and golf together led to the formation of Symbolics in February 1978. Their initial strategy was to identify a new software application that they could develop and market to a generic industry. When a Dallas savings and loan company asked them to produce a loan closing system, Symbolics found its niche. "Nineteen seventy-eight," says Gerry Nelson, "was a golden year for mortgage banking. Business was booming, especially here in Texas. Mortgage bankers couldn't handle the volume of applications, processing, and closings they were getting."

Symbolics developed in 1979 what Nelson refers to as a "full-blown, soup-to-nuts, state of the art" loan production system that the company called the Mortgage Lending Control System (MLCS). It was the first product of its kind to take a loan application and enter it into a computer software system that would prepare all the necessary documentation and track the loan through each operation until the process was concluded at the loan closing. By 1981, Symbolics' success prompted the company to initiate a national advertising campaign whose copy listed an impressive group of clients, including Advance Mortgage Corporation, Citibank, Mason-McDuffie, First Continental Mortgage, American Home Funding, and Cameron Brown.

It became clear in 1982, after discussions between Symbolics and Henry Hortenstine, that L&N's purchase of the company could benefit both organizations.

Headquartered in Richardson, Texas, Symbolics was at the forefront of technological efforts to automate the mortgage loan production process.

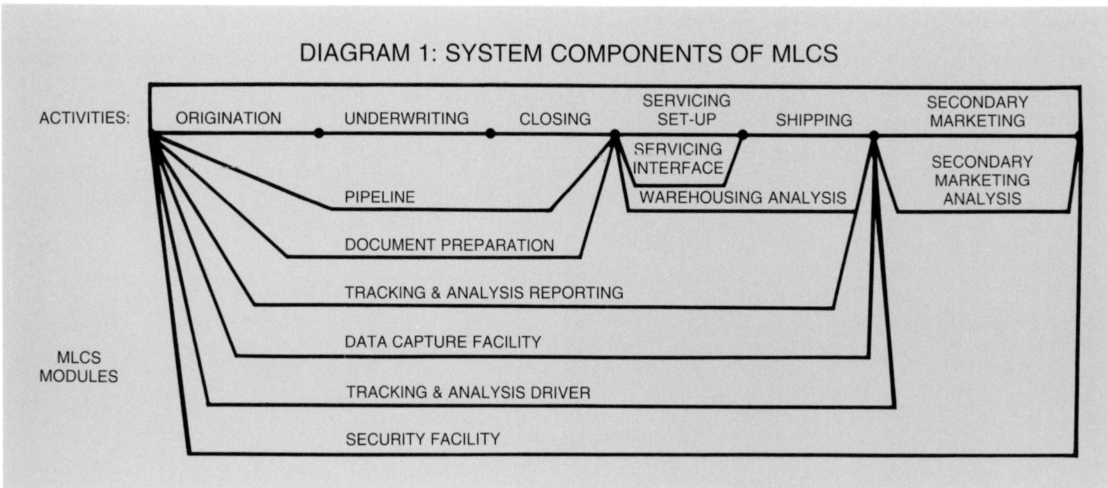

In 1979, Symbolics developed the Mortgage Lending Control System (MLCS), which automated loan origination, tracking, underwriting, production reporting, document preparations, marketing, and getting whatever information a company wanted from its data base. The diagram illustrates the components of MLCS.

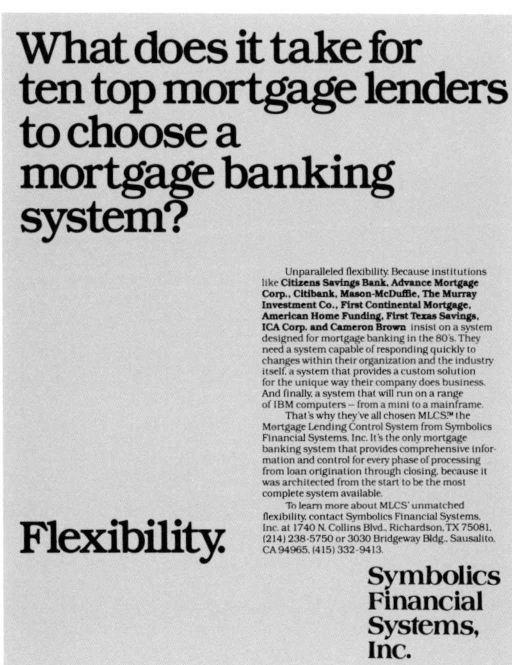

By 1981, Symbolics launched a national advertising campaign stressing the flexibility of the MLCS system.

For LNIS, it helped round out their product line. Already known for servicing mortgage portfolios to outside customers, with the MLCS mortgage loan origination system they now had a proven front-end software product and the potential to develop others. "Part of my vision for LNIS," says Hortenstine, "was to make it a real data processing company that sold both software and service bureau services."

The success of MLCS in the marketplace and the partial development of a secondary marketing system led Nelson and Funkhouser to think of the acquisition in terms of expansion. Symbolics had grown from two to 30 people in four and a half years, funded only by revenues generated from the company. In order to grow significantly larger and capture additional market share, the company needed an infusion of capital. Lomas & Nettleton offered both financial strength and important marketing value as a customer. Hortenstine also assured Symbolics that L&N respected their entrepreneurial spirit and would preserve their independence. "I liked Henry," says Nelson, "and I liked

Lomas. It was a Dallas-based company and the merger made a lot of sense. It was a perfect match."

Almost from the first, however, the two operations failed to mesh. A power struggle within L&N created an atmosphere of antagonism. Opposition from the mortgage banking insiders who resisted the Booz, Allen & Hamilton consultants and the Internal Strategy Task Force report was now directed toward Henry Hortenstine and the subsidiary he championed. "Henry," says Booz, Allen vice president Ray Lane, "was the new kid on the block, and he was breaking into a very tough culture. . . . Dee DeWitt, Jim Pickup, and E. G. Bray all came from the old school and were close friends. They did not trust Henry. They did not trust Henry at all."

. . . trying to explain why Lomas, who had acquired us, wasn't using our product.

Equally glaring were the cultural differences between Symbolics and The Lomas & Nettleton Company. The mortgage company was large, slow-moving, and bureaucratic. Symbolics was led by freewheeling Texas entrepreneurs who latched onto an industry niche and had some success with their software. The easygoing, laid-back lifestyle at Symbolics contributed to the conflict, according to Hortenstine: "A number of people at L&N were probably somewhat jealous of Symbolics. They were a

Lomas & Nettleton Information Systems and Symbolics Financial Systems combined their data processing marketing efforts. This 40-foot exhibit was part of the plan; it was constructed for use in trade shows, lobby displays, and client in-house presentations at L&N's Data Center. The exhibit first appeared in New York City on October 12, 1982, at the National Conference of the Mortgage Bankers Association.

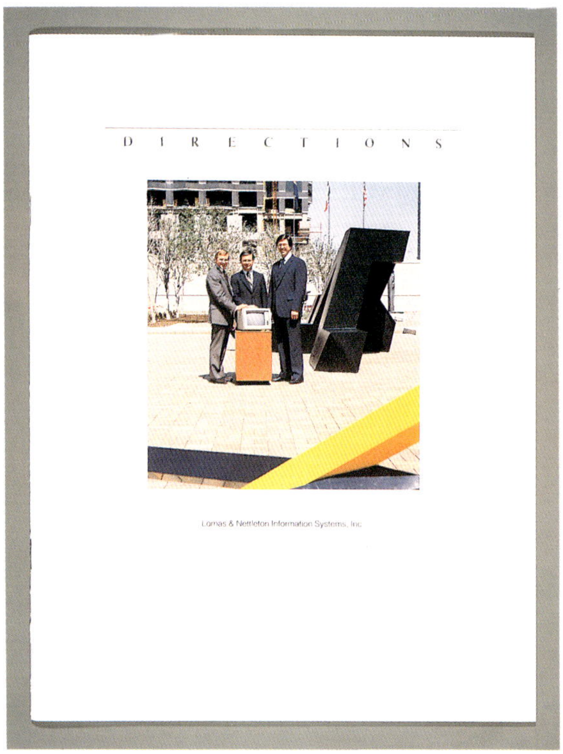

The front cover of *Directions*, a publication of Lomas & Nettleton Information Systems, Inc., ties together art and business. Gerry Nelson, left, president of Symbolics Financial Systems, Don Funkhouser, center, executive vice president, and Jack Nichols, right, product planning director, stand in the sculpture garden of the Dallas Museum of Art. Lomas & Nettleton is a corporate sponsor of the museum and also arranged the financing for the LTV Center, shown in the background.

Symbolics' software systems, created by product development, top photograph, and product planning and control, bottom photograph, were never fully supported by Lomas & Nettleton.

very casual organization. They didn't wear coats and ties. They were out in Richardson by themselves and had a jacuzzi and sauna in their office. They had the kind of lifestyle that almost everybody wants. We were much more disciplined and regimented."

The most significant wedge between the two was L&N's tepid support for Symbolics' product line. Several concerns surfaced during the evaluation of MLCS by the mortgage company. It questioned the software system's ability to handle L&N's large production volume and to process FHA and VA loans, which made up almost 50 percent of L&N's loan portfolio.

Perhaps most damaging was Symbolics' lack of experience in mortgage banking and the belief that they couldn't design a system that would meet L&N's needs. "Shortly after the acquisition," says Don Funkhouser, "The Lomas & Nettleton Company evaluated our loan origination system and said it was probably all right but it needed a lot of additional development to fit into their organization. Our secondary marketing system they totally rejected.

"Lomas was by far the largest mortgage company, and as is often the case with a company like that, they felt their requirements were unique and no generic package would ever fit their needs."

Just how seriously Hortenstine's vision of Symbolics as a software development arm for L&N failed became clear when the mortgage company made the decision to adapt the MLCS product internally through the Future System project. Following its evaluation, the mortgage company took MLCS and used it as the basis for a major redesign in which Symbolics had no involvement. What eventually emerged from the lengthy and expensive enhancement process was called the Automated Production Support system (APS).

The apparent rejection and isolation of Symbolics by L&N was a bitter pill that Funkhouser, for one, never quite digested: "Lomas took our loan origination system and put a lot of people on it to develop and enhance it for their branch operation and never consulted us. There was no communication. And we were the people who knew the product inside and out. They never even consulted us on what they were going to do or how they were going to do it.

"We developed the product and brought it out in less than a year for a total investment of two or three hundred thousand dollars. By the time Lomas installed it, it took about three years and $4 million in development costs."

A bruised ego wasn't the only wound Symbolics sustained. "It was a real problem in the marketplace," says Funkhouser, "trying to explain why Lomas, who had acquired us, wasn't using our product."

MLCS later became part of the Future System project, which resulted in a major redesign of its software. LNIS called the new product the Automated Production Support system (APS).

Symbolics' performance proved disappointing. In hindsight, Hortenstine believes the subsidiary grew too quickly and their management could not handle the complexity of the expanding business. Ironically, L&N's generosity in funding Symbolics' projects contributed to the company's problems. Hortenstine recalls an observation attributed to Dallas attorney Bill Brice about a company with similar difficulties that Brice was asked to evaluate. According to the attorney's assessment, there was nothing wrong with the company that a shortage of money wouldn't cure. "I think a lot of that was true for Symbolics," says Hortenstine. "When they came to Lomas we had deep pockets and could fund all of their projects. We let them grow too fast. From a managerial point of view we didn't manage Symbolics properly. I feel a great deal of personal responsibility for that. Of all the things in my career at Lomas, this was my biggest failure." In 1986, Hortenstine closed the Richardson office and merged Symbolics into LNIS.

There were other LNIS activities that failed to perform according to plan. Contrary to expectations, a new Data Center, a new computer, and new management did not solve L&N's data processing problems. When the Data Center went live in December 1981, LNIS experienced a nightmare instead of nirvana. Miswiring in a major component of the computer and a series of smaller hardware failures once again brought L&N's data processing system to a halt. "Nothing worked," says Henry Hortenstine. "The hardware didn't work. The systems didn't work. It was the biggest debacle I've ever seen." With the assistance of a Burroughs expert flown in from Detroit, the LNIS staff worked day and night to correct the problems. Still, it was several months before the computer functioned at a level that former LIS chief operating officer Matthew S. Jacobs, who was then LNIS operations manager, considered acceptable. Even more disturbing was Jacobs' realization a few months later that "the hardware [7800] which was the latest and greatest Burroughs had to offer and was supposed to last us for seven years barely got us through the first year." In 1983, L&N was forced to install a 7900, Burroughs' newest computer on the market. These experiences fed the company's increasing disenchantment with Burroughs.

Dissatisfaction also played a role in the Future System Steering Committee's 1983 decision to abandon the Internal Strategy recommendation for a "technical rewrite" in favor of building a brand new servicing system. The committee then had to decide whether that system should be Burroughs- or IBM-based. The two-man task force asked to evaluate that question favored IBM. "We were looking at the growth capacity

Among the problems facing Lomas & Nettleton Information Systems was the Burroughs 7800 computer, which was supposed to last for seven years. It only got the company through the first year; in 1983 L&N was forced to acquire a 7900. The Charles Babbage Institute, University of Minnesota.

Left: To support two new software systems, LNIS installed its first IBM computer, the IBM 3083 Processor Complex, in August 1983. International Business Machines Corporation Archives.

Below: Among major disappointments for LNIS was the frequent need for additional hardware. In April 1986, the IBM 3090/200 Processor Complex was installed. International Business Machines Corporation Archives.

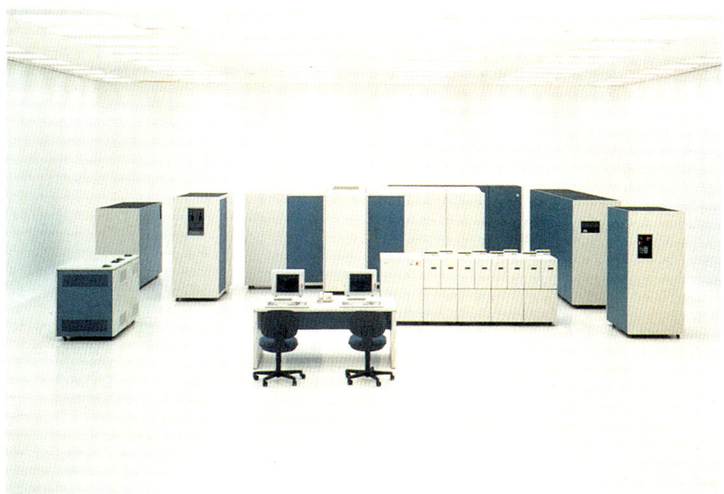

of hardware," says former Booz, Allen consultant David Matthews, who worked on the Future System in 1983. "We were looking at each company's long-range hardware enhancements. We also studied the hardware in terms of speed and the availability of software, data base systems, and communication systems. IBM provided a better package." The fact that IBM dominated the financial software market was another important consideration. "We knew," says Hortenstine, "that if we were going to be in the software marketplace we had to be IBM." LNIS installed its first IBM computer in mid-1983. The new machine supported IBM-based Symbolics and two software systems, general ledger and human resources.

It was optimistically predicted that the Future System project would be completed in 1985 and cost $15 million. As it turned out, those projections fell short by almost six years and, on the basis of capitalized costs, almost $60 million. "The Future System," says Hortenstine, "has been a major disappointment to me. We spent four times plus as much money as we thought we would, and it's taken twice as long to complete as we anticipated. It was bigger than anyone understood, and more complex as well."

There was a we/they problem in the Future System group.

There were other factors working against the project besides size and complexity. The clash of competing cultures made the project all but ungovernable. After only a few months as chairman of the Future System group, Don Funkhouser bowed out and returned to Symbolics. There were several reasons for his decision, but factional strife figured prominently on the list: "I had seen enough to know there was going to be a lot of politics in the decision-making, and I didn't want to be involved in that." From Symbolics executive Gerry Nelson's perspective, "there was a we/they problem in the Future System group." One clique identified itself with long-tenured L&N employees like E. G. Bray, who continued to work as an L&N consultant after his retirement in 1986. Another group supported those new to L&N like Henry Hortenstine and Terry Klein.

Following Funkhouser's departure, Jess Hay asked Dee DeWitt to move the project forward. But "strong-willed, opinionated people like Hortenstine and Terry Klein" blocked his progress. "There wasn't anybody," says DeWitt, "who could tell Terry anything but Jess Hay. By the same token, you weren't about to tell Henry how to run his job, either." On the other hand, Booz, Allen consultant Ray Lane appreciated Hortenstine's position: "Henry was having a hard time getting things done with E. G. still around. When a new guy is hired to come in and take over, he probably doesn't want the old guy hanging around and going to Jess Hay saying he wouldn't have done it that way."

In an effort to bypass the feuding that stalled the Future System's progress, Hay called Booz, Allen and asked Lane to head the project. Lane admits that the word "referee" reflects a large part of the role he assumed. Dee DeWitt also acknowledges that L&N was looking for someone who could act as "an arbitrator between dissenting parties."

Lane hired Ron Stride, a systems design specialist, to manage the project. Stride had just built a large, complicated computer system for Blue Cross/Blue Shield of New York. He was knowledgeable and enthusiastic. It was a hopeful beginning. "Ron Stride's focus," says Lane, "was totally on getting a project team together and doing something. We needed to get on with it. We felt we were a year and a half behind because of infighting between the people who reported to E. G. and the people who reported to Henry. And that stuff had to go away."

Unfortunately, the disunity didn't go away. Conflict ran through the project like a low-grade infection, occasionally flaring to claim four managers over the life of the project. Spencer Haddock and Phillip E. Sellers followed Funkhouser and Stride as project directors. "It may be as simple," says Lane, "as the fact that no one could sit on top of that political quagmire and last." But the company persisted, and the project slogged through to completion.

One of the most unifying factors turned out to be the Future System's fifth and final manager, LIS executive vice president Lynda-Ross Vega (then Lynda-Ross Carter), who took charge in March 1989. Her understanding of the business functions within the system helped heal the rift between technicians and users. Described as a "follow me over the hill, we don't know what we'll find when we get there but whatever it is we'll take care of it" kind of leader, Carter's hands-on style of management inspired confidence and boosted morale. "Lynda-Ross Carter," says Matt Jacobs, "is willing to take risks. She is very intuitive, and she follows her intuition. If something smells like it's right, she'll move forward and do it."

On September 6, 1990, the Future System, now

While problems were being solved and hardware perfected, LNIS mounted an aggressive advertising campaign to market the troubled loan production system. These four ads were published in October 1987 in *Mortgage Banking*, a real estate finance trade publication.

Lynda-Ross Vega, the Future System's fifth project director and a unifying factor, took charge in March 1989.

called Excelis, began servicing loans. Between the lines of the *Lomas Review*'s account of the first phase of the conversion to the new system, one can almost hear reverberating crescendos from the Hallelujah Chorus: "Excelis is officially on-line. After eight years of blood, sweat and tears working on a state-of-the-art mortgage loan servicing system, Lomas Information Systems employees succeeded in enabling the first 5,000-loan portfolio to come on-line this Labor Day weekend." There were still glitches to overcome in the months ahead, and these resulted in an extended conversion process, but Labor Day 1990 proved Excelis' credibility as a viable system.

Acquisition wasn't the only mechanism for achieving L&N's growth objectives. By focusing on business fundamentals, the mortgage company expanded its product line the old-fashioned way—rendering needed services and solving customer problems.

What began as a problem for Gulf Oil Corp., for example, became a profitable venture for L&N because of Jim Wooten's skill in formulating a lucrative solution. Gulf Oil found in 1974 that the procedures for transferring its employees had run aground on the worst housing market in recent memory. A combination of rising interest rates and mortgage institutions short of funds at any price had turned the usually routine transfer of employees into a nightmare. "We'd ask a guy to move," recalls Gulf Oil treasurer Cameron Payne, "but he couldn't find housing, so he'd wind up rotting in some hotel." The relocation of officer-level executives from Pittsburgh to Houston triggered the crisis. Texas' state usury law compounded it by placing a 10 percent interest rate ceiling on mortgage loans.

There was a need, and there was an opportunity.

A Fortune 500 company like Gulf wasn't used to humbling experiences like that. Their frustration, after being turned down for loans by First City Bank in Houston and Republic in Dallas, would soon be felt on the 37th floor of Bryan Tower in Jim Wooten's office.

Gulf's Cameron Payne first learned about Lomas & Nettleton while meeting with Houston's First City Bank. That, too, was a humbling moment. "Cameron," says Jim Wooten, "went over to First City Bank and kind of stormed in and said, 'Look, you guys are turning down loans for my senior officers, and Gulf Oil is your biggest depositor.' The bank representative said, 'Well, Gulf is a tremendously big depositor, and we're very proud of the account, but you're not the biggest.' When Cameron asked who in the hell was larger, they told him it was The Lomas & Nettleton Company."

Not long afterward Payne called on Jim Wooten.

"He was a hell of a good guy," says Wooten. "We struck up a kind of mutual enjoyment session." When Payne asked what it would take to get loans for his people, Wooten told him. Lomas & Nettleton agreed to make 9 percent loans to qualified Gulf employees if Gulf agreed to pay the difference in cost for the higher-priced funds and ensure a profit for L&N. "He went back for confirmation from the personnel department," says Wooten, "and we drew up a simple agreement just between the two of us, no lawyers or anything. Later, when it became more formalized, it was signed by the president of Gulf Oil."

Several months after the deal with Gulf, a front page article in *The Wall Street Journal* under the heading: "Housing Worries Spur Companies to Increase Relocation Benefits" became the basis for additional L&N corporate relocation business. The arrangement between Gulf and L&N figured prominently in the story. "Within a week's time," Wooten remembers, "I heard from everybody, especially the oil companies because the grapevine in the oil business is heavy. Royal Dutch Shell, Phillips 66, Mobil, and Texaco—everybody in the big oil business was calling to find out what we were doing. Then it expanded, and we had about 20 major national and international companies going through the program with us.

"There was a need, and there was an opportunity. It was a beautiful business. We made a lot of money on it."

This new mortgage banking niche owed its success to the company's size and geographic coverage. "I don't think there were that many [mortgage] companies that had the capabilities that we had by virtue of our branch network," says former vice president Dan Stoltje. "The loans flowed right through our regular branch system. It was a perfect adjunct to the business already coming in off the street, and this was good, quality business backed by Gulf and other major corporations."

Although a money-maker, it did not become a self-supporting, stand-alone operation until May 4, 1983, when L&N formed Lomas & Nettleton Securities Corporation (LNSC). The new subsidiary, capitalized at $30 million, "will augment and expand L&N's existing corporate relocation services to major corporate clients," noted the announcement in the *Mortgagee*. "It will also act as a broker/dealer of mortgage and government securities, thus representing L&N's first entry into this arena. The new subsidiary will be headquartered in Stamford, Connecticut."

The concept for LNSC came from its president, Robert Whalen, who had built a successful relocation business at Salomon Brothers, Inc., prior to joining forces with L&N. Whalen's plan called for utilizing L&N's national branch network to originate loans for LNSC's corporate customers. But what had been "extremely profitable at Salomon Brothers" never reached its potential at L&N. "LNSC," says Dee DeWitt, "paid its own way, but it wasn't as profitable as we thought it would be."

A major obstacle was the mortgage company's inability to relate to the high end of the conventional mortgage market, what Whalen calls "the cream of the green."

"The problem," says Whalen, "was that the people in the branch offices weren't able to adapt to change. They had grown up in an FHA/VA environment, and their attitude toward potential borrowers was you're guilty until proven innocent. And we were starting a service for management-level clients. Our attitude was you're innocent until proven guilty.

"When a guy who's vice president of a company and making $200,000 a year calls, he expects to be treated with a certain amount of deference and respect. And these people treated him like he was buying a $65,000 shack."

Whalen found a similar lack of acceptance among the mortgage company's senior management. "Paul Low and Weston Edwards [senior executive vice president, production] and I were always at loggerheads. The guys in Dallas looked at me as this goddamn gunslinger from Wall Street who's trying to tell them how to run a mortgage banking business.

"They kept saying, 'Look, you're just a department in the mortgage company.' And I used to say, 'Screw you. This is a separate business; that's the way it was designed and put together.' I probably could have been more tactful, but if I didn't make waves I never would have gotten anything done."

LNSC performed well for its first two years. But when interest rates declined in 1985, it experienced a surge in business, and, according to Whalen, "the branch system wasn't able to handle it. We had a chance to capture a substantial part of the market, and we blew it. We couldn't deliver the service we said we could."

Servicing problems extended to existing clients as well. Business with AT&T, for example, declined from $50 million to $8 million. In 1986, LNSC tried to correct its problems by bypassing the branch network and originating loans from a central location. But by that time a significant amount of damage had been done. "It just never gelled," says Whalen. "It was two cultures that probably should not have come together."

In April 1983, the Lomas & Nettleton Advisory Group was added by L&N to satisfy the needs of the Teacher Retirement System of Texas. Paul Low directed his talents to satisfying the pension fund's interest in commercial real estate investment.

In April 1983, L&N added the Lomas & Nettleton Advisory Group (later called Lomas Advisors) to its growing list of business activities. Like corporate relocation, it satisfied a particular client's need. In this case, it was the Teacher Retirement System of Texas, an $8 billion pension fund. Paul M. Low, whose talent for developing a string of profitable ventures was already well recognized, now turned his attention toward satisfying the pension fund's interest in commercial real estate investment.

Low learned about their interest through an existing relationship with the trustees, who bought L&N residential pass-through mortgage certificates. "A business opportunity presented itself," says Low, "and I took advantage of it. Lomas had within its bosom certain skills relating to the ability to manage assets for pension funds."

The trustees initiated a nationwide selection process for choosing five investors. L&N was one of the five selected in early 1983. It was a remarkable demonstration of salesmanship, considering the fact that no organization or track record yet existed. "That was quite an accomplishment on Paul Low's part," says former Lomas executive vice president David A. Ridley, "to sell ourselves as asset managers when we didn't even have a department."

Initially, the Advisory Group concentrated on managing the Texas teachers' pension fund. Later the Group added two small, limited partnerships called Lomas Institutional Mortgage Funds I and II, representing about $50 million and 38 clients. But the big management coup occurred in 1987 when Ridley responded to a proposal request from the Pension Reserves Investment and Management Board (PRIM), a group of small Massachusetts pension funds that pooled their money into a $2.5 billion fund. The Advisory Group proposed a program that would generate a good economic return and create badly needed housing for Massachusetts. Impressed by the proposal, PRIM signed a contract with L&N. They were not disappointed with their choice; in the first year PRIM earned 23 percent on their investment dollars, and between 15 and 17 percent in subsequent years.

Compared to other business activities at L&N, the Advisory Group represented a very small piece of the company's bottom line, averaging a net income of about $1 million a year. It was, however, symbolically important because it increased interest in asset management. Particularly appealing was the high profit/asset ratio. "We were not capital intensive," says David Ridley. "We didn't go out and borrow money to make money. Our only overhead was our personnel and our rent. So our return on assets was incredible. We were very profitable."

What worked well for the Advisory Group also worked well for Lomas & Nettleton's real estate investment banking division. The fees paid for placing commercial real estate financing through insurance and savings and loan investors resulted in a record year for 1983. Chuck Wingo reported that the division produced 87 commitments totaling over $427 million, resulting in a fee income of $4,410,844. Of the 12 national branch offices, Dallas, Houston, Denver, Chicago, and Tampa led the division.

> ...an honored place in the financial community.

The company's goal of achieving "profit with honor," first formulated by Jess Hay in 1965 as L&N's central mission, enjoyed a large amount of success in the early 1980s. A string of record years coupled with methodical growth attracted increasing attention and acclaim among business observers. The more subtle side of the equation, "the achievement and maintenance of an hon-

Honors came to Lomas & Nettleton's leaders. Among those honored, Jim Wooten, president of The Lomas & Nettleton Company, was elected president of the Mortgage Bankers Association of America. A two-page ad in the December 1982 *Mortgagee* announced the news.

On October 17, 1983, L&N gave a party when the MBA's convention met in Dallas. The Texas-size invitation poked good-natured fun at itself and promised a welcome that was not exaggerated.

The MBA party guests of Lomas & Nettleton received a greeting printed on a bandana that was pure Texana.

ored place in the financial community," also enjoyed success.

Honor, the accolade earned over time, made its presence felt most visibly among Lomas & Nettleton's leaders. The March 1981 *Mortgagee* announced Jess Hay's nomination to serve on the board of directors of Exxon. Lomas & Nettleton Financial Corporation president Ted Enloe was selected to serve on the board of directors of the Federal Reserve Bank of Dallas beginning in January 1983. And James M. Wooten, president of The Lomas & Nettleton Company, was elected president of the Mortgage Bankers Association of America (MBA) at the organization's 69th annual convention in 1982. A two-page ad in the December 1982 *Mortgagee* announced the news with the headline: "The nation's largest mortgage banking institution just got smaller."

Lomas & Nettleton's pride in the honor bestowed on Jim Wooten culminated one dazzling evening the following year. When the MBA's convention assembled in Dallas in 1983, L&N threw a party. Several thousand Texas-size (25 inch by 10 inch) invitations using a 12-page booklet format invited guests to the "biggest and best party" in the history of the MBA. The theme for this event was Texana pure and simple, as the title of the invitation booklet made clear: "The First & Largest Most Richest Longest & Best Tallest Texas Book." Promotional bluster and boasting aside, it was a spectacle worthy of the country's largest mortgage banker and an unforgettable experience. Former Lomas security officer B. J. (Chili) Clark remembered a replica of an oil derrick in the middle of Market Hall where the party was held "that kind of looked like old Spindletop," surrounded by a dozen bartenders dispensing drinks. "They had every kind of Texas food you can imagine," said Clark. "Mexican street vendors served tacos, quesadillos, and cabrito. Then you'd go a little farther and they had barbecue brisket and sausage. Another place served steaks and another had seafood. If you couldn't find anything you liked, there was something wrong with you."

LFC vice president Kevin McGarry, who was then manager of corporate communications, remembers the occasion as "very grand and innovative. It was like a movie set. It was more than a party; it was a full-scale production that shared a bit of Texana with a lot of people that may never have experienced it before."

The MBA party on October 17 was preceded on October 5 by another upbeat event. Over 600 L&N officers and their spouses gathered in Dallas at the Registry Hotel for the first general staff meeting since 1980. In keeping with the celebratory atmosphere, Jess Hay opened the meeting with highlights of the company's recent accomplishments:

> During the last 10 years our growth has been consistent, predictable, and dramatic. Our revenues have increased from $54 million in 1974 to $206 million in 1983. Our net income has moved from $1.6 million to $27.5 million.
>
> Our annual dividend rate has increased by more than 450 percent, moving from 36 cents in 1974 to $2.00 per share at June 30, 1983—a compound dividend growth rate of 18.71 percent per year—making L&N, according to *Dun's Business Monthly*, one of the 40 best dividend achievers in corporate America. . . .
>
> Finally, and perhaps most important of all, our mortgage servicing portfolio during the last 10 years has expanded fourfold, from $4.6 billion in 1974 to $17.8 billion June 30, 1983. This is a remarkable record of growth.

Division reports and panel discussions from senior executives focused on a company committed to meeting the challenge of increasing growth and change. Central to the success of that effort, noted several speakers, were the people of L&N "who give this Company its definition and drive." The meeting agenda underscored this article of corporate faith at the close of the general staff meeting, first with a speech by Jess Hay and then with an audio-visual slide presentation

The MBA party was preceded on October 5 by the first general staff meeting of Lomas & Nettleton since 1980. Jess Hay hosted the event, assisted by his wife Betty Jo Hay.

extravaganza. One of the goals of the show, according to former director of corporate communications Lou Duggan, was to reach out to employees new to the company, especially those who had worked for Advance Mortgage Corporation and National Homes Acceptance Corporation. "The slide show," says Duggan, "emphasized the things Jess Hay spoke about. It reinforced the importance of integrity and the value of employees. That came through loud and clear."

Over 8,000 slides of 1,100 L&N employees were taken to produce the 22-minute, nine-projector multiscreen presentation. Duggan, who directed the project, recalls the intensity of the effort: "I traveled to 10 major cities in 10 days with a photographer and his assistant. It was really a portrait of L&N. Primarily, we shot employees on location at work so that when the voice-over narrator talked about loan processing, for example, the slides showed loan processing people in their actual work areas. We went to great pains to make the photographs fit the narrative."

. . . an untraditional design solution . . .

Many of the corporate themes and values articulated at the general staff meeting found material expression in the L&N ServiceCenter then under construction. The eight-story steel frame rising beside the LNIS Data Center captured the exuberant spirit of growth, change, and optimism that highlighted the staff meeting. John Sutton, the coordinating consultant who served as liaison between L&N and the architect and contractor, describes it as a project where all the pieces—function, aesthetics, materials, and budget—fit together perfectly. "To me," says Sutton, "the building has enormous integrity."

The decision to build a loan administration service center in Dallas was part of the company's continuing strategy to offer its customers quality service by upgrading and consolidating its operations. Completion of a first-class Data Center in December 1981 marked the first step. Building a comparable facility for L&N's mortgage servicing operations was scheduled next. But it was the merger of Advance in mid-1984 that furnished the target date for completion of the proposed structure. The transfer of the loan administration functions still in Houston was also scheduled for that date. "Advance was up in Michigan," explains Chuck Wingo, "and L&N was down in Houston, and the company wanted to consolidate the two in Dallas."

The merger made speed a critical consideration. "We were on such a short fuse," says Wingo, who headed the ServiceCenter Charter Committee responsible for organizing and supervising the project, "that my role was to make fast decisions. We had to get it done."

To expedite matters, Wingo and the committee hired a familiar and proven architect and general contractor. Architect Harwood K. Smith & Partners (HKS) and contractor H. A. Lott had recently completed an office building project in Houston for L&N and Metropolitan Life Insurance Company. Both HKS and Lott were large companies with the resources to back up their commitments.

The L&N team also included John Sutton, who had served as construction consultant on the Houston project. His contribution as L&N's representative proved invaluable. Wingo's other corporate duties required him to depend heavily on Sutton. "John was there full time, all the time," says Wingo. "I relied on him as the owner's representative on a day-to-day basis for dealing with the technical issues involving the architects and contractors."

The committee, which included John Sutton, began working together in early 1983 on what was the beginning of a very fast track. "Chuck Wingo and I had lunch in January 1983," says Sutton. "Then we met with Jess Hay. Over the next couple of weeks we established a set of principles. We brought in the contractor and invited the architect to present design proposals. Basically, we had the ServiceCenter designed by the end of February. It was a very, very fast job."

In early 1983, the ServiceCenter Charter Committee selected Harwood K. Smith & Partners as architect for the new office building to house L&N's mortgage servicing operations.

The ServiceCenter Charter Committee members included John Sutton of Coordinators Consulting (center, pointing to model); Buddy Miller, executive vice president (seated); and Wayne Ferguson, executive vice president, Bob Cody, senior vice president, Chuck Wingo, executive vice president, REIB, and Sno Flores, vice president (back row, left to right).

Among the written guidelines established by the committee were "to create a quality, functional environment to accommodate the national mortgage loan administration group. . . . The building shall reflect the stable and practical corporate philosophy with an obvious but not overstated air of quality. Locationally, the development shall be sympathetic to the Brookhollow Country Club [Brook Hollow Golf Club]. It shall take advantage of the Dallas city skyline views across the park-like expanse of the golf course. It shall add an interesting but not outspoken profile to the easterly view from Stemmons Freeway. The building shall be sited to stand alone as an entity but also to be a cornerstone of a possible corporate campus development . . . integrating the pre-existing L&N Data Center which abuts the project site to the east. The building shall contain between 240,000 to 250,000 square feet of gross floor area." A data transmission and pedestrian bridge link to the Data Center, a cafeteria, and a child development center were also included in the guidelines.

An internal HKS competition produced three

An internal competition by the architectural firm HKS was won by Julian Tablada's design. The architect's rendering (above) of the ServiceCenter shows how his design takes advantage of the impressive views of nearby Brook Hollow Golf Club and the Dallas skyline beyond (right).

By October 12, 1983, construction progress on the ServiceCenter produced intricate geometric patterns that foretold the building to come.

Jess Hay presided over the topping-out ceremonies at the ServiceCenter on November 23, 1983.

designs for L&N's consideration. The hands-down winner was created by former HKS architect Julian Tablada. What came across most clearly in Tablada's design was his understanding of the importance the company placed on its employees. "Most important," says Tablada, "were the people who were going to work at the ServiceCenter, what they saw as they approached the building and how they felt once they were inside. So human scale was very, very important to me in the design of the building."

What Tablada envisioned was a $30 million building occupying 4.65 acres of land. It included a three-story underground parking garage with room for 750 cars and a three-story skylit atrium lobby. "Energy efficient, bronze insulated glass, framed by concrete spandrels," read a *Mortgagee* article, "will provide views of nearby Brookhollow Country Club [Brook Hollow Golf Club], the Dallas skyline, and open balconies." Commenting in the same article, Julian Tablada explained the concept behind what some employees would later refer to as the "wedding cake" appearance of the building: "In order to take advantage of and be sympathetic to the environment the garage and building are stair-stepped to create a series of terraces that blend the building's base into the sloping terrain. These terraces break up what would otherwise be a large mass of building into smaller elements that relate more closely to the human scale."

H. A. Lott, Inc., vice president Andrew C. Robertson, who worked on the project, describes Tablada's work as "an untraditional design solution that was quite attractive, and was the least obtrusive to the golf course. It just kind of blended into the hillside." For John Sutton, it was love at first sight: "I saw Julian's design before it was presented to L&N, and I knew it was the design that would become the building." It offered a pleasing alternative to the rectangular, glass-encased monoliths that litter the Dallas sky-

The area between the Data Center and ServiceCenter was transformed with a footbridge over land- and waterscape areas.

line. "We could have gone plain vanilla," says former Lomas senior vice president Bob Cody, who kept the account books for the construction project, "and just skinned the sucker in glass and gone straight up. But Jess Hay didn't want that. And I don't blame him. There are too many ugly buildings in Dallas as it is. I think he wanted something semi-unique. Something that would stand out and have some identity."

Attention to the work environment was an integral part of the project. "On the architectural side," says Tablada, "what we hope to achieve is an environment that stimulates a pleasant and invigorating surrounding. If it makes a person feel good to be in a particular space, then we've achieved a great portion of our mission. If the shape of the building and the selection of materials can make an employee feel happy about being in a particular work space, then he or she is going to be more productive and turnover is going to diminish."

One of the most dramatic design elements had nothing to do with the building itself. It focused instead on the weed- and brush-choked creek that ran between the Data Center and the future ServiceCenter. "The property," says Tablada, "was pretty well isolated from the Data Center by the creek, which was just an overgrown ditch. The concept I had was, let's create something that becomes an outdoor focus that the campus can grow around. It was an acknowledgment of the concept of family and the importance of treating members of the company in a humane way and providing amenities that would improve their day." His solution called for a connecting pedestrian bridge that entered the ServiceCenter at the cafeteria and child development center areas. The data links between the two buildings ran underneath the bridge. Above and below the bridge a major land- and waterscape project transformed the snake-infested gully into a parklike setting that included a fountained lake, cascading stream, and forested green space with walkways and outdoor sculpture.

Thoughtful attention was also given to the work space. AMC president Terry Klein, who would later head L&N's loan administration division, helped plan the interior design. One of his and the committee's goals was flexibility. The data cabling system, for example, was connected to a matrix from the Data Center so that every work station and desk in the ServiceCenter had potential access to L&N's mainframe computer system.

Increasing the number of modular offices without disrupting the work environment was another valuable design feature. "A typical 30 foot by 30 foot bay," says H. A. Lott vice president Andy Robertson, "accommodated six work stations. But it was also designed so that it could be expanded to nine work stations without having to go in and tear up the ceiling and pull new electrical cables. In fact, it wasn't long after they occupied the building that they began to increase the density and add work stations. So the built-in flexibility helped them do that without a lot of extra expense."

Former Lomas vice president Linda Frietsch, hired in November 1983 as senior project manager for the completion of the ServiceCenter interior and a direct liaison to Terry Klein, recalls quickly becoming aware of the L&N philosophy that pervaded the project. "Nobody had to explain it to me," says Frietsch. "It was in the air. It was a neat project, and the fact L&N built it for the people who work there made it even better. The company's attitude was, what's going to work best for the employees?"

Sometimes that meant higher costs. "A lot of developers," Frietsch explains, "build the office walls up to the ceiling grid. It's a lot cheaper. We built a deck above for soundproofing. We didn't spare many expenses, but, on the other hand, you can't hear the person in the next office, either."

Planning for maximum productivity, in some cases, meant blazing new trails. One innovation was to raise the partition height of some modular work stations. Frietsch and her staff found that the standard 44-inch height was too noisy for optimum work conditions. L&N asked the manufacturer to increase the height by four inches. Those few inches made a large difference. "We've got," says Frietsch, "over 150 customer service people in an open setting on the second floor, and it's quiet, damn quiet."

But it was necessity that made the interiors group decide to order furniture with a three-inch metal base. "The furniture base," says Frietsch, "is where all the cabling runs, and because we weren't sure what kind of wiring system we would be using, we added an inch. Nobody ever used a three-inch base at that time. They only used two-inch. Today, a three-inch base is standard in the modular furniture business."

The emphasis on corporate values that guided the design of the ServiceCenter also contributed to the success of its construction. Consultant John Sutton was a proponent of those values. His dedication to the project and to the L&N philosophy accounted for much of its success. "He knew exactly what the contractor was doing," says Bob Cody. "He knew why every change order came about, and he researched the cost on each one. He kept Jess Hay informed all the time. He kept Chuck Wingo and Wayne Ferguson informed. He kept me informed. There was no one in the entire project that knew what John Sutton knew, on either side."

> **We transposed the L&N philosophy [to the] building team.**

Monitoring the budget was one of Sutton's principal duties. His close supervision prompted Bob Cody's comment that Sutton "acted like it was his own money." "We established a budget on the front end," says Chuck Wingo, "a very detailed, line item budget, and John Sutton's job was to track that budget and to make certain that the architects and contractors didn't run amuck. John did an outstanding job. Unlike many buildings in that era, we wound up coming in under budget in most areas."

Sutton approached his task guided by the belief that distinctive does not necessarily mean expensive. The decorative use of travertine marble in the ServiceCenter atrium lobby is one example. "We decided," says Sutton, "to use travertine tile instead of large slabs of stone. Big slabs of marble and granite cost about $30 a square foot. The same stone in 12 inch by 12 inch tile form costs about $5 a square foot. We achieved the same effect with the tile and did it within an economical framework."

He also displayed remarkable leadership in building a project team committed to quality and L&N values. He achieved this by appealing to the participants' better instincts. "Contracting," says Sutton, "is often done from a position of power—'You're going to do it right because I hired you and pay you, you son of a bitch'—as opposed to saying, 'I need your help in getting the job done.'

"If you put a piece of string on a table, and you grab one end and try to push it, the string crumples up. But if you pull it, the string follows in a straight line. If you really believe that people want to do a good job you will draw a good job out of them. We transposed the L&N philosophy [to the] building team." Ken Pitcock, electrical superintendent for W. B. Moore Co., was one of the team players who responded to the message L&N and Sutton were sending: "The men got involved in this project. We saw the cafeteria, break rooms, child care center, and we knew that somebody really cares about the people who work here. The building shows that L&N cares about its employees. So we want to leave the job showing it was done right."

Sutton prepared a set of construction objectives and then defined the elements needed to achieve them. Each member of the team recruited to the project made a commitment to fulfill their objectives. Through strict adherence to a schedule of benchmark events, Sutton tracked construction progress and caught potential problems before they became serious.

When Westinghouse Elevator Co., for example, fell a week behind schedule on their shop drawings, John Sutton picked up the phone and called the president in New Jersey to remind him about his company's commitment. The president responded by promising to resolve the problem, which he did. In addition to immediate results, there was a long-term salutary effect to Sutton's action. Five or six months later, a Westinghouse Elevator mechanic working on the ServiceCenter installation stopped Sutton to ask him a question. "'Could you tell me,'" Sutton recalls the man asking, "'why the president of my company is interested in this job? I've worked for Westinghouse for 20 years and I've never had the president personally call and ask me how a job was going.' I said, 'Well, he's interested because he made a personal commitment that this would be a great job, and that's why you're on it.'"

Contractor staffing reflected a similar dedication to excellence and speed. "It was one of the best-staffed jobs I've ever seen in all my years in construction," says Bob Cody, a professional in the business for 36 years. "When they put up the curtain wall, they had almost twice as many people doing it as you normally would. A typical concrete job might call for 30 workers; they used 60. And Lott had three people working on the job, any one of whom could have been a general superintendent for the entire project. They were a-blowing and a-going. It was a hurry-up, kickass job. At one point they were working seven days a week. They made really good time." Evidence of their effectiveness was noted at the October 5, 1983, general staff meeting when Terry Klein, in a report on construction progress, announced that the project was two weeks ahead of schedule. On June 15, 1984, 13 months after the construction team first broke ground, the ServiceCenter received its certificate of occupancy from the city of Dallas.

The finished ServiceCenter was a handsome contrast to the many glass-sheathed office buildings being built at the time. On June 15, 1984, the ServiceCenter received its certificate of occupancy from the city of Dallas.

By whatever criteria you care to judge, the ServiceCenter succeeded. It was on time, within budget, aesthetically attractive, and work-efficient. Guided by the vision of the company's chairman and CEO, it also succeeded as an expression of L&N values. The ServiceCenter's child development facility illustrates the depth of commitment to those principles. Not surprisingly, it also bears the personal imprint of Jess Hay.

...a sense of family.

When corporate child care consultant Peggy Wilks was asked to write a work site child care program for L&N, enthusiasm for the project clearly came from the top. "Mr. Hay," says Wilks, "had very strong ideas about the quality and caliber of the program. He was very direct and straightforward; he wanted it to be the best."

Actually, it was Hay's wife Betty Jo who had first focused on corporate child care 20 years earlier. She says it was the plight of LFC corporate secretary Ramona Taylor that inspired the idea. "I remember," says Mrs. Hay, "when Ramona had those two little kids and Homer died and she had to work. I thought that was awful; she needed some help. That got me thinking about corporate child care, and I lobbied Jess about it for years." It wasn't difficult to sell Jess Hay on the idea, but a scattered employee population made the plan unfeasible. The ServiceCenter changed that. "He came home one night," Ms. Hay recalls, "and said, 'Okay, we're going to do it now.' It was very exciting. I was thrilled to death. I felt like I'd birthed a baby."

Hay and his staff used the lengthy gestation period to determine what kind of facility it should be. By the time Kate Wheeler, former consultant for Highland Park School's Academically Talented Program, was asked to direct the program in early 1984, certain decisions had already been made. "Mr. Hay," says Wheeler, "already knew what he wanted. It would be called The L&N School. He had decided it would be for infants through kindergarten. And he wanted the hours of the school comparable to the working hours of most employees." From there, Wheeler fleshed out the program with a well-paid professional staff, low teacher/student ratios, a full-time registered nurse, library, and parenting program.

Commitment to quality made The L&N School one of the outstanding programs in the country, a fact that was recognized by the National Association for the Education of Young Children in 1986 when The L&N School became one of 19 programs accredited nationwide.

But it is the 20-foot painted steel sculpture at the entrance to the ServiceCenter that most visibly captures the spirit of the building and the human values that lie at the heart of L&N's corporate culture. The abstract representation of three figures portrays a family—mother and father protectively grouped around their child. It is an assertion of humanity and community in its most fundamental form.

Dallas sculptor D. Wallace Dean enhanced the emotional content of his work by facing the figures

The L&N School was designed around generous facilities, with a playground in a landscaped setting.

Kate Wheeler, director of L&N's child care program.

Dallas sculptor D. Wallace Dean created the signature sculpture at the entrance of the ServiceCenter that expresses the company's vision of humanity.

toward the entrance doors of the ServiceCenter: "When you walk out of the building the feeling you get is a sense of friendliness, a sense of caring, a sense of family. Some people have told me that it's exciting to see the little kid looking up in wonderment. That kind of emotion and excitement is what public art is all about."

Like the signature sculpture mounted at its entrance, the ServiceCenter inspired admiration. Expert planning and execution by an outstanding group of professionals created one of L&N's most satisfying achievements. Seven years after it opened, Chuck Wingo admitted: "I can't walk through that building without feeling a lot of pride."

The gleaming new building also heralded the intensification of change in the mortgage banking company. Although most of its clerical staff was new, the deepest changes occurred in leadership. On July 1, 1984, Terry Klein became senior executive vice president, loan administration. Also on that date Weston E. Edwards, a former senior manager at Merrill Lynch, became senior executive vice president, production. With these leaders at the helm, mortgage banking at L&N embarked on a new course.

The *Mortgagee* ad that appeared in the December 1983/January 1984 issue, with its message of "a bridge over troubled water . . . to get from here to there," could have applied to L&N's need to fill key loan administration and production positions to make the changes the company thought were needed.

CHAPTER XI

CHANGE AGENTS

With the decision in 1984 to fill the key loan administration and production positions with outside management, it was clear that the leadership of the parent company saw a need for some basic changes in the mortgage company's way of operating. The organizational structures L&N had inherited from its acquisitions, with the exception of Advance, were not sophisticated enough in terms of management or technology to achieve the kinds of upgraded operations Jess Hay wanted.

The largest acquisition and greatest obstacle to change was the T. J. Bettes Company, which had dominated the loan administration operation in Houston since its purchase by L&N in 1968. As one knowledgeable insider put it, "Lomas really wasn't Lomas. It was Bettes within Lomas. Bettes never gave up their culture. They fought to hold onto it with everything they had."

It was a culture of which they were justifiably proud. Beginning in the Depression, the T. J. Bettes Company had built the largest servicing operation in the country and maintained its dominance for over 30 years. It was regarded throughout the industry as an innovator and was widely copied. The NCR data processing system E. G. Bray had installed at Bettes in the 1960s, for example, represented an important breakthrough in the automation of the mortgage banking industry. But pride in past accomplishments could not obscure the fact that Houston's management had lost its edge. L&N's acquisitions of the 1970s and 1980s took their toll on Houston's previously high level of performance. The systems that worked for the smaller portfolio couldn't support the larger operation.

L&N's loan administration office was located in what had become a seedy part of downtown Houston. Some employees joked about having to step over winos to get inside the front door. The office environment inside was little better. Crowded, open work spaces cluttered with cardboard boxes stacked beside desks contributed to an atmosphere of confusion and inefficiency. The quality of the work force was second- or third-rate at best. Senior vice president Russel D. Young, who was responsible for about 250 of the clerical staff at the time, says L&N was "getting the pits as far as employee quality." Young attributes this to poor recruiting practices, inadequate training, and a location that turned most people off: "We were at the lower end of Main Street, and nobody wanted to come down there to work."

They did not like change.

Lomas Mortgage USA senior vice president Tom H. Carter, who joined L&N loan administration in 1972, claims there was a "Houston syndrome" characterized by resistance to change: "A lot of the people in Houston had been with T. J. Bettes, and a lot of those people did not accept change well. I remember when we installed a new computer system in the 1970s. There was strong resistance to using the new system. I was a fairly fresh manager, and I remember trying to convince people that the old system that had been clunking along wasn't getting the job done and look at all the things the new system can do for us. But they didn't want to see it. They did not like change."

The T. J. Bettes Company featured a bank ambiance and 1960s state-of-the-art data processing equipment, seen between the classical columns.

Carter and others also had to contend with an archaic management style. He remembers the management training books provided by former executive vice president George I. Wilson, who came to L&N from United Mortgagee Servicing Corporation. They were relics from the 1950s, many years older than the textbooks Carter had studied in college. Later, when he took over the tax department, Carter recalls inheriting a female supervisor who had been with Bettes for many years. The woman made a point of informing the new manager that her supervisory duties were limited: "She said she didn't discipline people. She didn't give negative feedback and didn't fire people. She said, 'If someone comes in late, I'll come tell you, and you can go over and chew them out, but I'm not going to do it.' She also told me she left work to get her hair fixed on Wednesday afternoons regardless of what was going on in the office. She left at 2:00 and came back at 4:15. Her rationale was, 'Well, after all, it grows while I'm working.' To me, she was a shining example of the 'Houston syndrome.'"

Frugality was another Houston cultural characteristic that impeded efficiency. "I can remember," says Carter, "trying to get some CRTs for my department because we had people standing in line waiting to use the few we had. It didn't take Albert Einstein to see we were wasting time. But I had to fight tooth and nail to get senior management to come up on the floor and see these people standing there with armloads of work waiting to get to a CRT."

Tom Carter, who joined L&N loan administration and later became Lomas Mortgage USA senior vice president, claims the Bettes culture strongly resisted change.

According to a consultant who worked closely with L&N during the ServiceCenter transition in 1984, maneuvering loan administration out from under Houston's control was an important reason for the consolidation: "The Bettes culture was one of the main things Jess Hay was trying to leave behind [in Houston]. Most of loan administration's key executives at that time had come from Bettes. He knew if he was ever going to change the organization, he had to make a dent in that old, archaic Bettes culture, and that meant making some of the Bettes players less powerful." The move from the Bettes building in Houston to the ServiceCenter in Dallas coupled with Walter C. (Terry) Klein, Jr.'s appointment to head loan administration represented a major step toward reducing the Bettes influence.

Former Lomas executive vice president William Glasgow, Jr., an executive not uncomfortable with change, remembers the transition as an exciting period full of possibility and promise. "The summer of 1984 was very positive," says Glasgow, who was then senior vice president, loan administration. "Everybody was pretty upbeat. They were looking forward to coming into their new home and setting up shop. We had people running around basically trying to create a new company, one that was going to be much different from what Lomas had been over the past 15 or 20 years. It was a company that finally had its corporate and operational centers all located in one city. It was a company that was embarking on a total restructuring of its servicing facilities."

Terry Klein was Citicorp.

Terry Klein was the executive responsible for leading the charge. Lomas senior vice president Patricia A. Gardino, who first worked for Klein in the early 1970s, says: "Terry Klein loves change. He absolutely thrives on change. And that was the challenge here at Lomas." At the time of its purchase by L&N, Advance had one of the lowest servicing unit costs in the industry and a reputation for the best-run servicing organization. "If you could perfect this business," says Gardino, "we had done it at Advance. Loan administration was the team that made that change at Advance. And Terry Klein led that effort."

It is difficult to conceive of an individual more alien to either L&N or Houston's Bettes-dominated loan administration than Klein. His perfectionist, high-energy personality favored regimentation and a tightly controlled, structured work environment. Those traits did not mesh well with the mortgage com-

Terry Klein was responsible for the changes promised in the summer of 1984 at the new Dallas servicing facilities.

pany's relatively undisciplined, laissez-faire management style. There was nothing laid back about the Harvard-educated, six-foot-four former Marine officer. He implemented corporate change much as Lenin forged political change—with a firm, decisive hand. It was a revolutionary approach that flew in the face of L&N's low-key, evolutionary style, but it was effective.

Klein's hard-charging personality was reinforced by the Citicorp business culture in which he grew up. "Terry Klein was Citicorp," says Gardino, who describes her 10-year service under Citicorp management as the finest business education she ever received, "but once you graduate you never want to go back. They are extremely difficult to work for. They are the most demanding organization you'll ever find. They own your soul. A typical day's work for them is seven to seven. That's standard Citicorp. You haven't done your job unless you've been there 12 hours. They tax you that way every day, every month, every year you work for them. They never let up. But that wasn't the mental attitude of the Houston group. I don't think they ever could have adjusted to that pace and style of management."

Evidently, Klein didn't think so either. "They weren't his type of folk," says Gardino. "They didn't think fast. They didn't talk fast. They didn't move fast. Nothing about them gave him the feeling that they would be effective members of his team. In his mind, the Houston people appeared incompetent because they couldn't keep up with him. But that was his problem more than anyone else's."

Soon after looking over L&N's servicing operation, Klein began actively recruiting managers at Advance. Gardino remembers the intensity of his appeals: "He said, 'I've got to have my management team in Dallas.' He had met with the Houston people several times and he said, 'I can't make it work with those people.' He was pretty adamant about trying to get certain people to come with him. He didn't get as many as he wanted, but he got several."

Predictably, negative feelings were reciprocated by many of the Houston personnel who moved to Dallas. "When we first came here," says Gardino, "it was not fun. There were two groups of people. One group was Lomas, and one group was Advance. You didn't socialize. You didn't mingle. There was no camaraderie between the two groups. In fact, there was almost a hatred." The fact that Klein entertained the Advance group at his home on weekends drove the wedge even deeper. Gradually, Gardino developed a "semi-friendship" with a Lomas employee who told her the weekend socializing increased the animosity between the two groups. Gardino stopped going and told Klein why. Over time, he included a few Lomas people in his social gatherings. But it wasn't until Klein left the company that real healing occurred.

Klein's recruiting efforts netted about 25 former Advance employees, while almost 50 L&N employees moved from Houston to Dallas. To make up the loss of clerical personnel, L&N mounted a large-scale recruiting campaign and training program in the spring of 1984.

Klein implemented changes in the personnel system even before hiring began. He asked human resources to put together a compensation and performance appraisal system that measured job requirements and the skills needed to meet them. Prior to the new system, job performance and compensation were handled on a subjective basis. "I told Jess," Klein recalls, "that I couldn't come to Dallas unless I had job grades and salary ranges. I had to have some method of grading the people we hired—so we could determine that this person was a six and that person was an eight, and this job calls for an eight, not a six. At the time, I'd say Lomas had 2,000 or more people with no job grades or salary ranges. For a New York Stock Exchange-listed company, it was in the minority—like the only one."

In the spring of 1984, L&N leased the two-story office building at 1420 Viceroy that became the center of operations for both employment and training.

In the spring of 1984 L&N initiated a recruitment drive and training program to meet the scheduled phase-in of loan administration functions for the new ServiceCenter. The main target was escrow services, which included the large tax processing and hazard insurance departments. About a block from the ServiceCenter, L&N leased a two-story office building at 1420 Viceroy that became the center of operations for both employment and training. LAS vice president Tamara L. Wright was hired in early 1984 as personnel administrator to help organize the recruitment drive. A large advertising campaign developed by the Richards Group featured ads in the two major Dallas newspapers with the bold headlines "NICE JOB" and "CHALLENGE YOURSELF." Besides the print campaign, the advertising agency saturated the airwaves with radio spots that underscored the attractive work environment at the ServiceCenter. For LAS vice president Maureen J. Sando, who was personnel assistant at the time, the unforgettable highlights of those ads were "the birds chirping in the background" and the oft-repeated dialogue line, "Gee, what a nice place it must be to work."

. . . *M*assive training . . .

The campaign generated a large applicant flow. "You could always tell when the radio ad was aired," says Wright, "because of the way the telephones lit up." Besides fielding 300 to 400 telephone calls a day, Sando says their office averaged 75 walk-in applicants "almost from Easter weekend until August." To handle the heavy response, 16 L&N escrow administration supervisors and managers participated in the hiring process. A human resources training seminar on screening and interviewing conducted by Wright and former assistant director of human resources Michael Schwartz provided the fundamentals for fulfilling this temporary personnel role.

The training program L&N prepared for those they hired was also intensive. On May 7, 1984, 13 new escrow administration employees enrolled in the charter class. It marked the beginning of what assistant vice president Rebecca Judd described as a "massive training" program that continued throughout the summer. Although officially called escrow administration training, it was referred to informally as "boot camp." The four-week course was an expanded version of Russel Young's "training-booth program begun in Houston nearly two years ago," according to a description in the June 1984 issue of L&N's employee publication *Pipeline*. "During the month-long session, supervisors who themselves have been trained in effective teaching techniques, take the recruits through the processes involved in their new jobs. Each of the steps is performed on equipment and in an environment similar to the one that will be found at the ServiceCenter."

The *Pipeline* account wasn't strictly accurate, according to Judd, who as training coordinator understood better than anyone the special challenges at the training center: "For some reason there was an invasion of daddy-longlegs spiders. They were everywhere. I know they're harmless, but it didn't go over well with the new employees when they found them in their cubicles. We also had problems with our computer terminals going down. They were Datamax terminals and absolute junk. It meant that the training staff had to become technicians. We carried little mini-screwdrivers so we could go around and fix the terminals."

Hiring and training a loan administration staff of several hundred proved more challenging than anticipated. Although the quality of personnel was higher than what the company had had in Houston, it did not meet Klein's expectations. Judd describes the newly hired staff as a mixed group: "One lesson we learned was that somebody might be a good manager but not necessarily a good judge of who to hire or who not to hire." About halfway through the hazard insurance department's hire-up, for example, lack of proficiency forced the training department to extend the length of boot camp from four to six weeks.

"We had," says Klein, "a bunch of rookies from Houston who were not seasoned managers or interviewers hiring people that looked good but weren't good. So we hired a herd of people that didn't know a lot about mortgage banking. We paid them reasonably well. Gave them a super facility with a child development center and had a very happy group of people that had no idea what was going on. Then we put them through boot camp and thought we could turn out mortgage bankers in five weeks. Wronnng!

"It was too many loans for too many new people. Jess was great. Glasgow worked his brains out, and George Wilson was superb. We underestimated the task."

Despite the fact that Klein began operations with a new staff with a lot to learn in a short time, he successfully implemented changes that improved both productivity and efficiency. Pat Gardino recalls the change in departmental procedure manuals. Those developed in Houston were "too generic. They didn't tell you the things you needed to do your job. It was just, 'Our objective is to process hazard insurance policies as they become due.' Wow! But with Terry, you get it in the door. You date stamp it. And then you go right on down the line. So that anyone who picked up the manual could tell what to do and how to do it."

. . . *a* **breath of fresh air . . .**

Klein also introduced the concept of developing standards by which to measure productivity and efficiency. He viewed servicing much like a manufacturing enterprise. Each department used an assembly line to process financial information that was, in his mind, nothing more than a different kind of widget.

"Everyone had a standard for every job we performed," says Gardino. "He [Klein] made us record how many we got in every day, and how many we processed every day, and how many were left over and then age those items. You could look at one or two pieces of paper and know exactly where you were every hour of the day. He read our weekly reports religiously. He knew exactly where we stood and if our people were working to capacity. If our standard was 100 an hour and we were only doing 60, as a manager we got beat up. His attitude was, 'You get more productivity or you get rid of the people.' So, he brought control to the process and a different way of looking at it than Lomas had before. I believe control was one of Terry's greatest strengths."

The adjustment for many non-Advance employees was difficult. "They thought we were a bunch of idiots who liked to pass paper," says Gardino, recalling the reaction among many of those from Houston. "They didn't understand the value of it. But I think those who survived would agree today that you have to run your business that way."

Then there were those like Tom Carter who welcomed the changes. "When Terry came in, I saw him as a breath of fresh air. His was a totally different approach. One, he held people accountable. Two, he took us from the old, 'Gee, that looks like three or four days' worth of work,' to 'This is exactly *x* days' worth of work.'" Carter, who had been rebuffed in his efforts to introduce work measurement in Houston, found the support he needed in Dallas: "Hazard was the first department in the company to use work measurement. I don't profess to being an expert, but Terry was very supportive. He said, 'I'll get the experts to help you install it.' And he did. We got a couple of consulting guys in here that said, 'OK, here's how to do it.'"

Klein also successfully integrated more efficient technology. One such decision led to the conversion of paper documents in Houston to a computer-activated microfilm system in early 1984. Besides automating loan administration's document system and realizing savings on the cost of expensive floor space, L&N disposed of its paper records in Houston. That was a massive job in itself according to Tom Carter, who participated in the event: "We literally pitched dumpsters full of paper in Houston. We had 3,000 square feet of floor-to-ceiling files just in the hazard department. We put a chute up against the building so we could slide documents from the third floor right into the dumpster. If we had had to haul that stuff down the elevators, it would have taken forever."

Klein's new regime implemented important changes in L&N's branch servicing system. The mandate for a system-wide change came from the 1981 L&N Task Force on Internal Strategy report that suggested the company abandon its decentralized structure. The regional system, according to the report, was cumbersome, expensive, and "dysfunctional" in terms of responsiveness to customer needs. Following the report's publication, the company initiated a gradual move toward centralization. The arrival of Terry Klein and Bill Glasgow, who managed branch servicing, accelerated the process. Glasgow reported a consolidation from seven regional servicing offices and 56 branch offices in 1982 to five regional offices and 22 branches in mid-1984.

Equally significant were the operational changes that strengthened the branches. These included systems upgrades and the redeployment of servicing functions. The impact was dramatic. Branch servicing offices that had been little more than collection offices that funneled information to regional delinquency control now found themselves responsible for a full range of servicing. "This includes," reads an August 1984 report by Glasgow, "payoff and assumptions, customer service, limited cash processing and preparation of government notices required by state and federal regulations. In addition, the branches are responsible for meeting certain corporate standards with regard to unit cost and average loans serviced per person. We intend to reduce our unit cost for servicing by 20 percent and increase our average loans serviced per person by 50 percent."

For Lomas vice president Otha L. Green, Virginia Beach servicing branch manager at the time, it was a welcome change: "It greatly enhanced the branch manager's job. He had many more responsibilities—budgeting, delinquency control, and governmental reporting. He became a manager instead of a collector. It also ended the isolation that had been a feature of the regional system."

"When Terry Klein came in," says Lomas vice president Fredrick G. Zakula, a former Westmont, Illinois, branch manager, "we became part of the Lomas corporation. Prior to that we were pretty much out there in a self-contained world. After Terry took over, we, as branch managers, came to Dallas more often. We really became part of the corporate family. We had a sense of where Lomas was going as a company, and we were encouraged to pass on those corporate goals and ideals to our employees. Prior to that time, that didn't happen."

Automation gave the branch servicing offices an opportunity to achieve the goals envisioned by Klein and Glasgow. The changes, Zakula recalls, were sudden and dramatic: "Prior to Terry coming on board, there were no terminals in the branches, at all. We operated strictly by phone and by paper. Terry gave every employee access to the mainframe computer system, and that was light-years ahead of having a paper folder for everything you dealt with." The mailing capability was one of the more helpful computer-driven aids. Branches went from hand-typing delinquent customer letters to generating thousands of letters "with a few keystrokes."

Customer service, in particular, experienced severe inefficiencies under the old regime. If an L&N customer phoned a branch to ask if his taxes that were due last week had been paid, the employee had to send a written request to Houston for the information. The customer, meanwhile, was told, "We might have the answer for you in two weeks. And most intelligent, assertive customers," says Zakula "didn't like that answer."

When the information became available to branch employees on computer terminals, productivity shot up. Many branch offices doubled and in some cases tripled the number of loans per person they handled. Besides productivity, it gave staff morale a major boost. "We went from being able to get answers in three days to getting answers immediately," says Green. "It was like distributing candy to the staff. They were overjoyed to have all that information at their fingertips."

Ironically, in his drive for efficiency Klein introduced a bureaucracy that overwhelmed the savings he achieved from a more rationally organized operation. To compensate for his lack of confidence in the newly hired staff and the managers from Houston, Klein added management. "I knew all the staff were rookies," says Klein, "and most of the managers were at least one or two levels above where they'd been before the merger, and I thought every so many rookies needed a boss at another level. I layered it with too much management. I threw bodies at it."

> ...We lost track of some of the bigger pieces.

The volume of management information Klein demanded from his senior department heads contributed to the bureaucracy. In some cases senior officers designated one or more employees just to produce the reports Klein required. "Terry had to have all the numbers," says Gardino. "He had to have a graph or chart for everything he did. We used to joke about how he probably kept a chart on how many times he went to the bathroom and how many minutes he spent there. He was a perfectionist. It took three people just to keep his manuals updated and in perfect order. Overcontrol. He thought the more people you had watching over something the better it would be."

While overcontrol cut into productivity on the operational side, lack of attention to financial control cost loan administration even more dearly. "I don't think Terry is a financial wizard," says Gardino. "He was process, process, customer, customer. . . . He could take care of your customer better than anyone, and he could get your process running better than anyone. But the economic or financial side was not within his discipline. We were so busy making widgets that we didn't pay attention to receivables."

For example, if a customer had a shortage in his escrow account, rather than charge the customer's account, loan administration paid the shortage from a corporate fund. The problem, says Gardino, was that no one ever collected those monies and "receivables got way out of hand. As a matter of fact . . . we ended up writing a lot of it off. Our deficit escrows, our red escrows, rose to a point that was almost embarrassing." Although Klein inherited a lax escrow policy, his concern for customers perpetuated the problem. In a dispute between the company and a customer, Klein favored the customer. "He didn't focus as much on the financial side," says Gardino, "because it meant, in many cases, that he couldn't be as customer-oriented as he wanted to be.

"Productivity and efficiency were greatly enhanced and improved under Terry's leadership, but I think in the process we lost track of some of the bigger pieces. His unit cost when he left here was probably twice as high as it is today."

When Terry Klein left L&N in October 1986 to become president of Sears Mortgage Co., Bill Glasgow assumed the leadership of loan administration. His commitment to centralization accelerated a process that had been under way for several years. By 1987 consolidation of the company's regional servicing operation was well advanced. The national servicing structure had been reduced to three large regional offices—Panorama City, California; Virginia Beach, Virginia; and Dallas, Texas. Total centralization in Dallas was achieved when the last remote servicing location at Virginia Beach closed its doors in September 1988. "The consolidation," says Glasgow, "was really focused on one thing. One-stop shopping. All of it here in Dallas. But you couldn't just shut all the regions down and give up all the expertise we had out there. So we

With Terry Klein's departure, Bill Glasgow assumed leadership at L&N loan administration.

Left: Terry Klein, standing at microphone, left L&N in October 1986 to become president of Sears Mortgage Co. His going-away party was celebrated with music, flowers, and a presentation of a memorial album. Courtesy Terry Klein.

staged it to where we closed all the branches and incorporated them into three regional offices. Then, we waited a year or so and folded those into Dallas."

A stronger, national focus was the new management direction for loan production. In July 1984, Weston Edwards was chosen to make those changes.

Just as Klein was hired to change loan administration, the appointment of Weston E. Edwards was an attempt by the parent company to redirect loan production. The original strategy of allowing the companies L&N acquired to operate as autonomous regions was based on the theory that each region knew its geographic area best and would run it more efficiently than Dallas could. The Task Force on Internal Strategy report published in 1981 said that those assumptions were no longer valid. Performance had fallen. It was time, said the report, for a stronger, national focus. A primary recommendation was to hire a senior manager responsible for production.

...a change-agent ...

Weston Edwards was hired in July 1984 as senior executive vice president for production. His credentials were impressive: an M.B.A. and D.B.A. from Harvard; Economic Advisory Board, U.S. Department of Commerce; founder and chairman, Housing Roundtable; and director, Policy Advisory Board of the Joint Center for Housing Studies of Harvard University.

Like Terry Klein, Edwards was an outsider brought in to create change. Other than their intellectual brilliance, the two senior executive vice presidents had little in common. Klein's loud, aggressive personality contrasted sharply with Edwards' gentle demeanor. Both exhibited superior verbal skills. Klein's virtuosity lay in dazzling displays of verbal jousting that often left his targets wounded. "I always thought of Terry Klein as a street fighter, while Weston used soft-spoken logic and quiet reason to get his points across," recalls a former L&N employee who knew both men.

Weston Edwards treated the spoken and written word with devotion, weighing his words carefully. Language was a gift of piety one didn't wish to squander, and Edwards used his to instruct and impart lessons. Several colleagues at L&N attributed Edwards' verbal and personal style to his devout faith as a member of the Church of Jesus Christ of Latter-Day Saints. "Weston," says Lomas executive vice president David L. Chapman II, who worked closely with Edwards, "is a unique individual. I have immense respect for him. He's a Mormon bishop and has 12 kids. His wife is a writer. But he never fit in. He was an outcast. He began production meetings with a prayer. Well, that wasn't normal in the mortgage business. Weston has an air about him that my wife says makes you feel like you're in the presence of God. And people didn't feel comfortable with that."

But Edwards' strong religious convictions and gentle manner were not the whole story. He had a history of solid accomplishments that included the start-up of TICOR Relocation Management, moving it from sixth to first place in its industry, and the development of

Merrill Lynch Realty Associates as a major player in the residential brokerage business. Edwards was a force to be reckoned with. Like Klein, he regarded change as a challenge. "Lomas & Nettleton," said Edwards in a *Mortgagee* interview, "attracted me because it is a leading company on the verge of major change, which I've been a party to for my entire career. At Merrill Lynch for 15 years, I was a change-agent in starting two companies from scratch and making them into leaders in their respective fields."

Edwards' arrival also marked a shift in strategy. Building L&N's loan portfolio with acquisitions presented a twofold problem. Cost was one factor. The purchase of mortgage loans for servicing was relatively inexpensive during the 1970s and early 1980s. That ended when major corporations began buying their way into the mortgage banking business during the mid-1980s.

Another problem was the long-standing complaint from L&N loan administration about the number of inferior loans they had to service. Edwards believed in the company's ability to grow L&N's portfolio by originating superior loans profitably. The key was excellence. "The quality of servicing," says Edwards, "means everything to the bottom line. If you have a mortgage that pays regularly every month, it only costs about $30 a year to process that loan. If the loan goes delinquent once and you have to send a follow-up letter to get it back on track, that costs you an average of $300 a year. If a loan goes into foreclosure, the added effort required averages $1,000 a year. A portfolio that pays every month will make a pile of money."

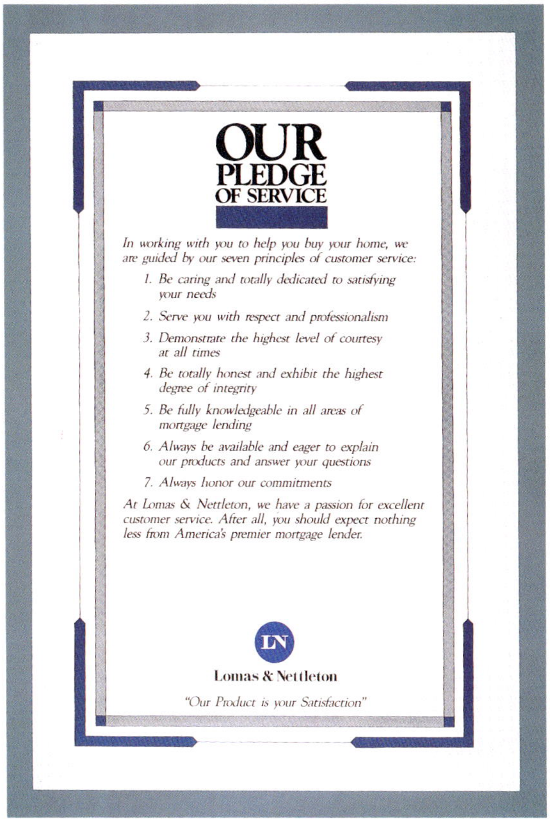

Weston Edwards was influenced by the Tom Peters and Nancy Austin book, *A Passion for Excellence*, when he wrote "Our Pledge of Service," the "seven commandments" of customer service.

Edwards had his work cut out for him. The delinquency rate at L&N was running two and, in some cases, three times what was considered normal for the industry. He attributed part of the problem to an inflexible national pricing system that cost the company quality business. The price L&N charged for loans in California and Philadelphia, Edwards says, was "a good 100 points above the market, and they ended up getting junk. Most of the people that did business with them were those who couldn't get a loan somewhere else. They'd pay the higher rate and get a loan with us, and L&N ended up with the greater delinquencies."

There were no uniform procedures.

Lack of consistency among the regions compounded the problems of national pricing. One of the first things Edwards did was go into the field, visit each region, and talk to L&N personnel and their customers: "I found seven different companies all operating very, very differently. Many of them operated without operating manuals and some had manuals the head office was not even aware of. There were no uniform procedures. There was no manual that everybody operated under to guide their actions. I visited offices that hadn't been visited by anybody from Dallas for 13 years and were rarely visited by regional management. It was very easy to improve the system because there were so many things that could be made to work better.

"Morale was also very low. What had happened, frankly, is the regional leadership had gotten older and lost their interest. That was part of why I was brought in. They had done some wonderful things in the past, but they were tired." The degree to which that leadership had lost touch with their operations was demonstrated to Edwards at one stop on his exploratory tour. An assistant regional manager drove Edwards to visit a branch office located an hour and a half from regional headquarters: "And he got lost. He couldn't find the office. Finally, he called and asked for directions."

"The quality message" heralded by Edwards was the cornerstone of what he called a "major rebirthing and rejuvenation" program projected to triple production in three years. It had several facets, but the one requiring prompt attention was underwriting. "An unacceptably high error rate reported by Corporate Banking and Shipping," Edwards noted in a 1985 report, "excessive exceptions in recent internal audits and quality control reports, persistently high delinquency ratios and growing 1st year defaults all point to a serious loan quality problem that is now receiving top priority attention."

The function of underwriting is to analyze each loan application based on the credit history of the borrower, an appraisal of the property, and an analysis of collateral to determine whether or not the company should make the loan. Unfortunately, the independent watchdog function of underwriting at L&N was subverted by the regional system. Underwriting in each region reported to the regional production manager. It was a classic conflict of interest. Loan production management, whose members were paid an incentive for volume, didn't hesitate to overrule underwriting's objections in cases of borderline loans.

Because each L&N region had its own underwriting manager, consistency was a problem. Each region developed its own forms and standards. "This region over here says these ratios are okay," says David Chapman, recalling the disarray he found when he joined L&N as the head of national underwriting in 1985. "This region over here is off 5 percent from that. This region over here doesn't have any ratios. Their attitude was, if the government will approve it, we'll approve it. It was like looking at seven different companies."

Weston Edwards initiated the intensive search for the key underwriting position that ended with the hiring of Chapman in July 1985. Prior to joining L&N, Chapman had served as the national director of underwriting for General Electric Mortgage Insurance Company and had accumulated almost 30 years in the mortgage business since graduating from college. "We looked for about six or nine months," says Edwards, "before we found the best underwriter in the country and brought him in to establish standards and procedures that would allow us to move ahead vigorously and confidently."

David Chapman was hired in July 1985 to make dramatic changes in the underwriting department.

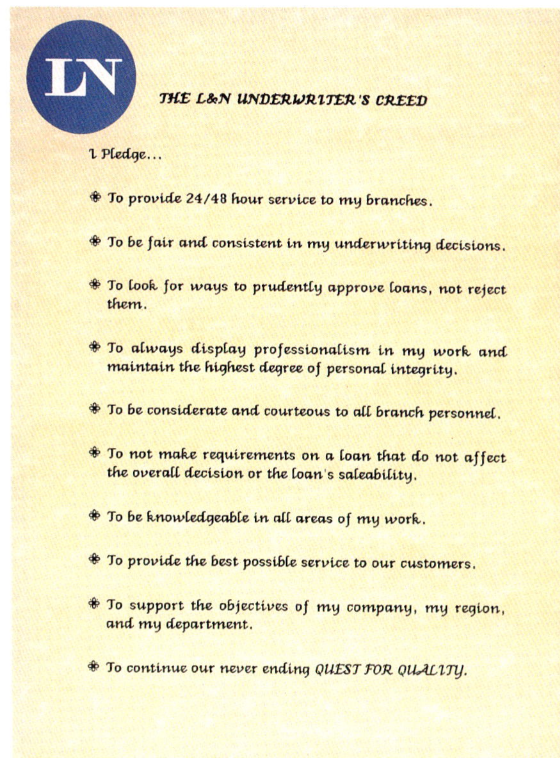

THE L&N UNDERWRITER'S CREED

I Pledge...

- To provide 24/48 hour service to my branches.
- To be fair and consistent in my underwriting decisions.
- To look for ways to prudently approve loans, not reject them.
- To always display professionalism in my work and maintain the highest degree of personal integrity.
- To be considerate and courteous to all branch personnel.
- To not make requirements on a loan that do not affect the overall decision or the loan's saleability.
- To be knowledgeable in all areas of my work.
- To provide the best possible service to our customers.
- To support the objectives of my company, my region, and my department.
- To continue our never ending QUEST FOR QUALITY.

To set forth standards and expectations in his area, David Chapman prepared "The L&N Underwriter's Creed," patterned after Edwards' "Our Pledge of Service."

"I moved to Dallas and started the job July 1, 1985," says Chapman. "After two weeks, I said, 'Oh my God! What have I done?' I knew it was going to be a challenge, but I didn't realize how much of a challenge it would be. Delinquencies were running sky-high."

During Chapman's first week at work, he and Edwards were asked to meet with Mortgage Guaranty Insurance Corporation (MGIC) and explain to them why they should continue to do business with L&N. It was a major crisis. "They were going to cut us off," says Chapman. "Delinquencies on the MGIC portfolio from Lomas were extremely high. And if MGIC cut us off, it would be a disaster for the company. It would signal the industry that the mortgage insurance companies will not deal with Lomas & Nettleton because of their quality." And without mortgage insurance L&N would not be able to meet the legal requirement for insurance coverage for loans above an 80 percent loan-to-value ratio. MGIC responded positively to a "quickie game plan" that Chapman presented, agreeing to give L&N 90 days before meeting again to review the plan's progress.

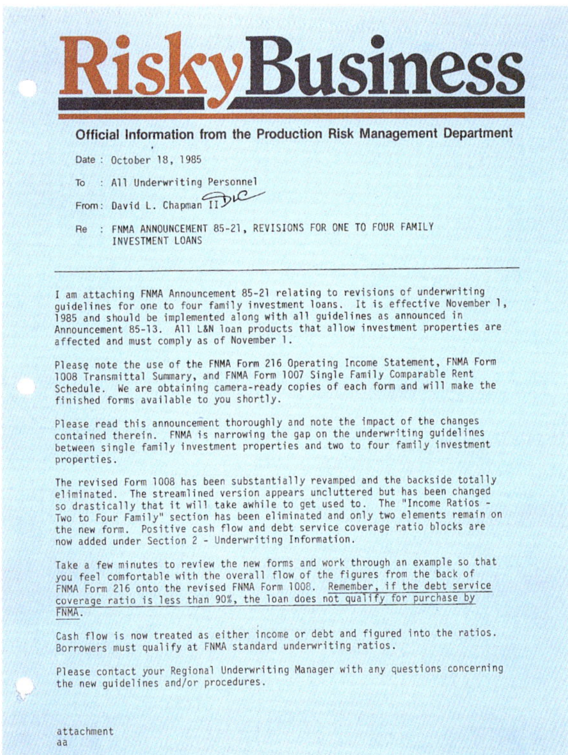

RiskyBusiness

Official Information from the Production Risk Management Department

Date : October 18, 1985

To : All Underwriting Personnel

From: David L. Chapman II

Re : FNMA ANNOUNCEMENT 85-21, REVISIONS FOR ONE TO FOUR FAMILY INVESTMENT LOANS

I am attaching FNMA Announcement 85-21 relating to revisions of underwriting guidelines for one to four family investment loans. It is effective November 1, 1985 and should be implemented along with all guidelines as announced in Announcement 85-13. All L&N loan products that allow investment properties are affected and must comply as of November 1.

Please note the use of the FNMA Form 216 Operating Income Statement, FNMA Form 1008 Transmittal Summary, and FNMA Form 1007 Single Family Comparable Rent Schedule. We are obtaining camera-ready copies of each form and will make the finished forms available to you shortly.

Please read this announcement thoroughly and note the impact of the changes contained therein. FNMA is narrowing the gap on the underwriting guidelines between single family investment properties and two to four family investment properties.

The revised Form 1008 has been substantially revamped and the backside totally eliminated. The streamlined version appears uncluttered but has been changed so drastically that it will take awhile to get used to. The "Income Ratios - Two to Four Family" section has been eliminated and only two elements remain on the new form. Positive cash flow and debt service coverage ratio blocks are now added under Section 2 - Underwriting Information.

Take a few minutes to review the new forms and work through an example so that you feel comfortable with the overall flow of the figures from the back of FNMA Form 216 onto the revised FNMA Form 1008. Remember, if the debt service coverage ratio is less than 90%, the loan does not qualify for purchase by FNMA.

Cash flow is now treated as either income or debt and figured into the ratios. Borrowers must qualify at FNMA standard underwriting ratios.

Please contact your Regional Underwriting Manager with any questions concerning the new guidelines and/or procedures.

attachment
aa

Soon after his arrival, Chapman took underwriting away from the regions and centralized it under his control. On October 18, 1985, Chapman's office published the first issue of *Risky Business*, a newsletter designed to communicate and coordinate the numerous revisions in underwriting guidelines.

Chapman had reason to feel beleaguered, for he found himself caught in a cross fire. Confronting the questions raised by MGIC and other mortgage insurers wasn't easy, but the fire he encountered within the division was heavier and harder to suppress than anything outside the company.

There was no policeman in this organization. I became the policeman.

Chapman opened the campaign by taking underwriting away from the regions and placing it under the control of his department, which was now titled Production Risk Management. The FHA and VA loans that had previously been sent to the government agencies directly from the regions were now routed through Dallas for underwriting approval.

One of the first places to feel the changes was the underwriting department itself. When Chapman discovered that the average turnaround time for loan applications was 10 to 12 days, he established a turnaround goal of 24 to 48 hours. To meet that objective as well as the expected increase in retail production, he increased his staff from about 35 in mid-1985 to 96 in November 1986. It was also an opportunity to upgrade the quality of the staff. "I required a lot of new things from the underwriting staff," says Chapman. "I required they take an accredited appraisal course. Many of them had not had that. Well, that's the key to knowing what kind of collateral you're looking at. If a property is valued at $110,000,

Edwards' flair for inspirational slogans manifested itself throughout the loan production offices with a series of catchphrase buttons and reward ribbons.

you've got to know how it got to $110,000 and whether that appraiser used the correct methodology in getting there."

When risk management introduced standardized forms for loan applications, resistance in the regions escalated. It was the beginning of a very bumpy ride for Chapman: "One of the first things I did was throw away all the old forms. We implemented a new document checklist and said, 'These are the forms. Use them. If you send a loan in using the old form, we'll throw it away and make you get the new one.' You had to be adamant with them.

"Change in the mortgage business is very hard to accept, especially when you've been doing it the other way for 20 years. There was no policeman in this organization. I became the policeman. It was a real growing experience for me. I learned to play hardball like I've never played hardball before. I was the first person who came in and told these people no. And our rejection rate went to almost 50 percent in a matter of six to eight months. I was turning down one out of every two loans. And of course that was when the screaming was loudest."

Chapman was not prepared for the degree of hostility that the regional and branch managers directed toward him. Six months after his arrival Terry Klein noted in a speech that there was only one job he would like to have less than the one he had, and that was Dave

David Chapman's response to Edwards' "Passion for Excellence" was "Quest for Quality." He had buttons made with this motto for the production staff. A year later, he followed up with "Our Quest Continues."

Chapman's. "Maybe I wasn't hated," says Chapman, recalling those difficult months, "but I was vastly disliked. The production people wanted my head. They wanted me out of there, and they made no bones about it. They told me to my face. I had a number of yelling matches on the phone with some of the regional managers. I've never been spoken to the way I was then. The first year was extremely uncomfortable. There were a couple of times when I was ready to throw in the towel." Thanks in large part to the unwavering support from L&N's senior management, Chapman weathered the storm.

The tireless pursuit of quality in the production division was one of the most visible hallmarks of Weston Edwards' administration. He projected that message through speeches, newsletters, memoranda, and reports. Edwards' penchant for slogans and mottos may have been a product of his long association with the Boy Scouts of America, first as a scout himself, then later as a cubmaster and troop committee member. One slogan, borrowed from best-selling authors Tom Peters and Nancy Austin's book *A Passion for Excellence*, became his division's guiding principle. Edwards stated as much in the first sentence of an early memo: "In the Residential Production Division we are dedicated to restoring 'A Passion For Excellence' in all that we do." To secure the slogan's ongoing prominence, he even titled a division newsletter *Our Passion for Excellence*.

> **Tying their pocketbooks to the quality of loans that were coming in.**

David Chapman followed Edwards' lead: "I implemented a slogan that caught on. It was called 'Quest for Quality.' I put it on a button and had several hundred made for the production staff. It was an attention-getter and reminder about what we're here for. Even Jess Hay wore one, and I was very proud to see him do that. Everybody in the division wore that button every day as a reminder that we're going to do quality loans."

Edwards and Chapman, however, did not rely solely on feel-good phrases and motivational homilies to accomplish their goals. No one understood better than they that among L&N's regional and branch management the slogan that carried the most weight was "Money talks; bullshit walks." Lofty rhetoric was one thing, cold cash another. "The only way you can ever get a production person's attention," says Chapman, "is through their billfold. If you're not affecting their income, then they don't care. So, we began tying their pocketbook to the quality of the loans that were coming in. We implemented what we called underwriting report cards and literally graded every loan that came in. And a portion of their incentive compensation was based on those underwriting grades."

Evidence of a shift toward quality loans gradually improved as regional compliance increased. Even so, "pockets of resistance" persisted for some time. Occasionally, a regional loan officer would bypass national underwriting and "walk a loan to FHA." But L&N's computer produced internal reports indicating when this had happened, and underwriting's chief of police issued the kind of warning that produced results: "'Next time it happens you won't get paid.' It all comes down to the almighty dollar. You've got to affect their paycheck. Finally, we got 100 percent compliance. And once we achieved that, it stayed there. It took a year and a half to get that done."

A year after his arrival, Chapman was able to report the following in a memo to the risk management department: "Our quality is up and our delinquencies are down. All the major PMI [private mortgage insurance] companies are now back soliciting our business and we have been reinstated on FNMA's preferred pricing list. Our Passion for Excellence and Quest for Quality has indeed shown fantastic results." First-year loan delinquencies dropped from 6.95 percent in 1985 to 1.96 percent in May 1987.

Loan quality continued to improve as changes in the underwriting department gathered momentum. In April 1989 Standard & Poor's published a Mortgage Origination and Servicing Report that rated L&N's loan underwriting above average. A report from Lovett, Mitchell, Webb & Garrison, Inc., noted that the mortgage banking division "is enjoying the lowest composite delinquency rate in the last 10 years."

Edwards also tied monetary incentives to quality control in the branches. A quality assurance group was established to review loan documentation and verify underwriting information. A report from Edwards indicated that in April 1985 quality control became "an important criterion upon which the quarterly cash payments of Branch Managers were based."

Standardizing national production required the development of a training department to teach the new procedures. In 1986 Gloria D. Brown, who had been hired the year before to write a procedures manual and who later became an L&N vice president, was asked by Edwards to coordinate training for the production division. The actual training would still be conducted in the regions, but now it would be supervised and directed from the Dallas office. A primary reason for the training program was the anticipated roll-out of the much-delayed Automated Production Support system (APS). Its success depended on well-trained personnel and uniform procedures. Change was difficult here, too. The reaction Brown heard most frequently in the regions when she initiated national training was, "We don't do it that way."

As the importance of consistency became more evident, management revised the quality control audit to take the new procedures into account. As with the underwriting report card, those who failed to follow the new guidelines received lower scores. "Branch manager compensation," says Brown, "was tied to their performance—their quality performance. If they didn't perform, then they didn't get the money they used to get."

APS presented another difficult hurdle. It was designed to fully automate what had been a manual process, thereby reducing errors and standardizing procedures. Resistance to the new system was widespread. The transition from a manual to a computerized, automated environment was difficult enough, but the APS system made matters worse by acquiring a reputation for user-unfriendliness. "I lost five of my best people because they refused to use that kind of system," says Lomas senior vice president Thomas D. (Sandy) Tolbert, branch manager for San Antonio at the time. "It was very slow. You could take an application by

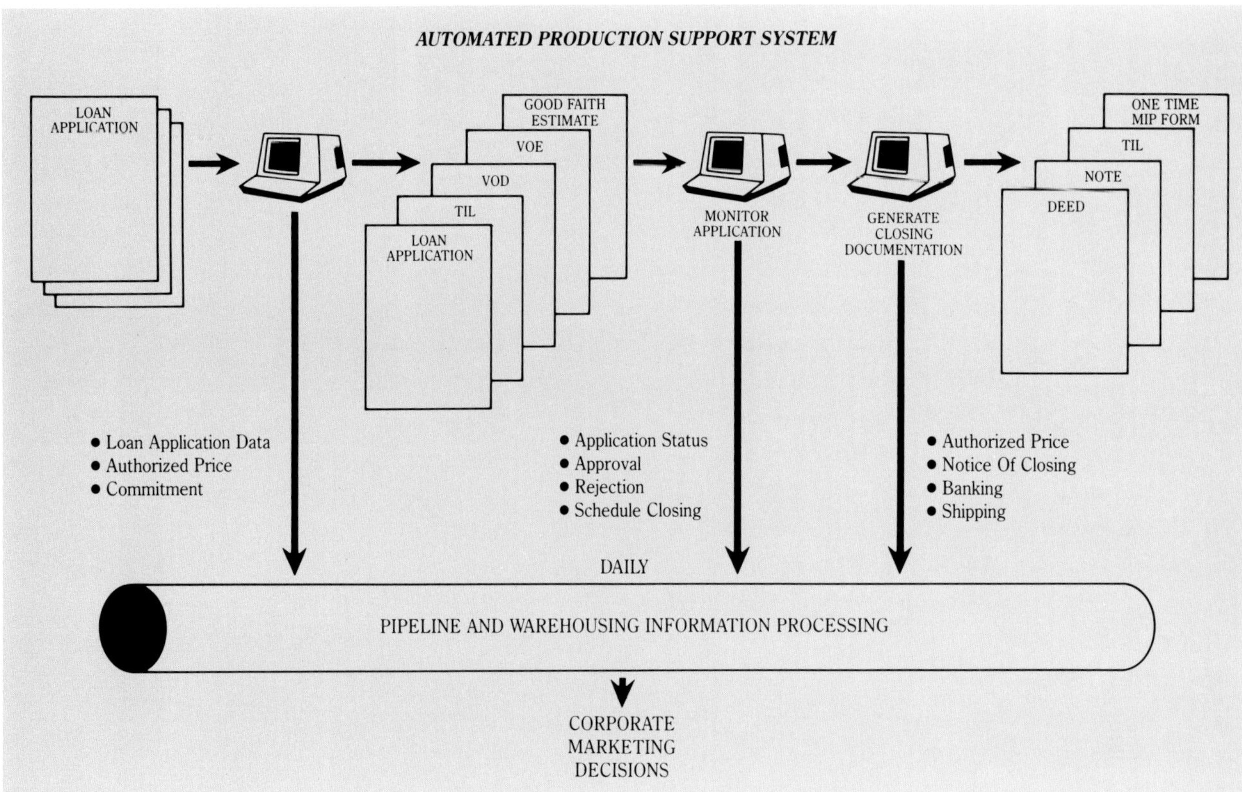

This diagram illustrates how the Automated Production Support system (APS) operated. The system automated loan origination procedures.

hand in 22 minutes. It took over an hour on the APS system, and you couldn't keep a customer waiting that long." Despite the system's drawbacks, proponents like Brown thought automation was the only thing that made sense: "APS was the way to do it for the future. And many of the people in the regions didn't want to do it that way. It took time to learn how to use the system. It took time to do things differently. Of course you can write a loan application faster manually if you've been doing it that way for five years, but you can also make typographical and mathematical errors."

One of the most effective implementations of APS into a branch was former L&N vice president Tessia L. Van Curen's method. According to Brown, Van Curen took all the office typewriters and locked them in a closet. "It was either do or die," says Brown. "That's what it came down to. She said it was the only way she could get them to use the computer."

The new technology carried a large price tag. The computer equipment and sophisticated telephone lines that the branches required represented a costly investment that Brown, for one, found difficult to justify: "I never thought, for the amount of money and support APS required, that it ever really paid for itself. It cost so much money to develop, to install, and to keep it going."

Although the development of APS predated Weston Edwards, the introduction of the high-tech system during his tenure complemented his plan to upgrade the division's operations and to triple originations. The production goal was based on a strategy that emphasized larger branches and a shift toward higher-quality conventional loans with larger loan balances instead of the smaller FHA and VA loans that had dominated L&N production for years.

. . . Maybe there should have been more restraint.

The new strategy and requisite face lift coincided with a shift in L&N's public posture. For the first time in 17 years, The Lomas & Nettleton Company lost its position as the nation's largest mortgage banker. In 1985 GMAC Mortgage Co., with a servicing portfolio of $20.4 billion, edged ahead of L&N's $19.7 billion. GMAC's takeover of first place in the industry was part of a growing trend of well-capitalized corporate giants buying their way into the mortgage banking industry in the mid-1980s. A 1986 article in *The Washington Post* noted that mortgage servicing, traditionally dominated by savings and loans and mortgage companies, "has exploded into one of the most sought-after financial products for banks, insurance companies, department store chains and even auto makers vying to become full-fledged financial-service providers. Companies as diverse as GM, Sears, Roebuck & Co., Ford Motor Co., Chrysler Corp. and American Can Co. have jumped into the mortgage business in the past two years." *American Banker* in May 1986 reported that only one of the top six mortgage servicers in 1985, Lomas & Nettleton, was a veteran of the business.

Weston Edwards acknowledged the change in status in a staff memo, noting that the company was now "substituting 'premier' for 'largest' in our public statements of corporate goals." The focus on "premier"

The Premier Originators

"Consistent!" "Competitive!" "Profitable!"

Volume 1, Number 1

Who We Are, Or Are Committed To Being

Having watched the tape of the recent Chairman's Circle Meeting and read my memo that accompanied it, you should be fully aware that we truly understand the difficulties you are facing, and that we are doing all in our power to support and sustain you. L&N is a great company and we are going to be here long after many of our competitors have disappeared. Let me assure you that our company is totally honest in all of our business dealings and that we do care about each other and our customers.

Now is a time when we need to repeat these truths and feelings to each other and really believe them. We need to show our customers the kind of people we are made of — the right stuff! We are a strong company and when we show them that we are encouraged and dedicated to serving them in an excellent and superior manner, they will come back to us and we will be even more respected than before.

It would be nice for me to be able to assure you that we will quickly move back into an easy-to-make-money environment, but I cannot do so. You are always assured of my honesty and my best guess is that the next six to nine months will be extremely volatile and fiercely competitive. We are determined to do a lot better than our competitor.

If you are not already an L&N stockholder, my encouragement to you is that you buy some stock even if it is just a handful of shares. It is good for us all to think of ourselves both as employees and stockholders.

We have worked hard this year on improving the quality of our operations. Much has been accomplished for which we should all be proud

Continued on Page 9

By Weston Edwards senior executive vice president - residential production

By Paul M. Low senior executive vice president - marketing & business development

Production Marketing

Integrity Caring Excellence

Our Premier Issue

This month you will see a new publication cross your desk, *The Premier Originators* which will be replacing *Our Passion for Excellence.*

The change goes further than just a new name and a new design, it is a change in philosophy. This newsletter demonstrates our commitment to a stronger sense of teamwork and partnership between production and marketing.

The incorporation of the triangle into the masthead design is a reminder of three basic principles which are the foundation of what we do: "Integrity," "Caring" and " Excellence."

Highlighted at the top of page are our battle cries: "Consistent!" "Competitive!" and "Profitable!"

Our Vow: The Best Price The Market Will Allow

Recent events in the capital markets once again have shown us that residential mortgage lending is, indeed, a very risky business. This spring in a period of less than two months, the average interest rate on a conforming conventional loan went from 9⅝ percent to 11 percent and during the same period the VA rate went from 8½ percent to 10 percent.

These interest rate spikes certainly don't make running our business very comfortable. However, there is a positive side. Everything that does go up must come down, including interest rates. And, as in the past, we probably will see a return to lower interest rates or, at the very least, no significant increases in the foreseeable future.

Given that we now know about the perils of the mortgage market, a restatement of our company goal and pricing policy seems to be in order. The goal and objective of the Company and the rationale of our pricing policy is to achieve a nominal trading gain on all of our production equal to ⅓ of 1 percent of the total volume resulting in the creation of a cushion to meet the minimum gain objectives of the Company, and to partially compensate for the basic risks inherent in the mortgage banking business.

The implementation of part of the strategy occurs by setting the authorized price of the loans to the branch office off the price at which the loans can be delivered into the secondary market. Other factors, besides rate, that are considered include loan amount, date of delivery, and volume.

In other words, we are compelled to price according to the price for which the product can be sold. The extent to which the interest

Continued on Page 10

The Premier Originators replaced the publication *Our Passion for Excellence.* More than a new name and design, it was a change in philosophy. The newsletter demonstrated a commitment "to a stronger sense of teamwork and partnership between production and marketing."

struck a responsive chord in Edwards, whose "aristocratic" manner served as a role model for the production division. Lomas executive vice president Sidney E. Leake was one of the branch managers who responded to the image Edwards projected: "He brought a kind of charisma and presence that made me want to elevate my image. He was real Madison Avenueish and real polished. His memos were perfections of etiquette. He created an environment that made you want to step up a notch. Like we are the premier company. I found myself getting another suit and dressing up a little bit more and emphasizing polish more than before."

But the price of "polish" was expensive, and Edwards' costly strategy to expand production failed to produce profitable originations. "Weston," says Brown, "used to harp on the fact that Lomas & Nettleton was the premier mortgage banker. That everything was the best when Lomas did it. Then there was the feeling that Lomas had a lot of money, too. And maybe Weston himself had that perception and didn't realize that he needed to keep a closer eye on what it was costing. It should have been made clear to Weston sooner that maybe there should have been more restraint."

The emphasis on originations and a lack of concern for costs was codified in the division's incentive plan. "The compensation plan that Edwards introduced," says Leake, "was strictly production driven. All of a sudden you didn't even really have to consider your expenses. The emphasis was on production, and expenses got out of control."

The operating overhead of the larger "hub" branches that Edwards introduced was high. Expensive long-term leases, new furniture, and advertising campaigns to create visibility in a new market replaced what had been a lean, low-budget operation. Edwards also placed a priority on upgrading branch management, which required "huge salaries."

Theoretically, the larger fees from the higher loan balances and the increase in production volume would more than make up for the costs. The reality was otherwise. "We did more volume," says Chapman, "but we also kept adding people and the new volume didn't offset it. I mean, you've got to do a lot of volume to negate hiring a $25,000-a-year processor. And that never happened. From my perspective, I don't think Weston addressed the cost factors."

The closest loan production came to supporting the burden of its fixed costs was during the refinance craze that swept the country in 1986. For the first time in seven years interest rates fell to about 10 percent, and homeowners raced to get out from under mortgages on which they were paying as much as 17 percent. The strain on the system staggered and in many cases overwhelmed the mortgage banking industry. Lyle E. Gramley, chief economist of the Mortgage Bankers Association, called it an "avalanche," and *Business Week* referred to the phenomenon as a "stampede" in an April 1986 article. The article went on: "The mortgage industry is working overtime. 'We can hardly man the phones,' complains James M. Wooten, president of Dallas-based mortgage banker Lomas & Nettleton Co. He has beefed up his staff by 400 people to handle the record $40 million of mortgages that Lomas is making each day, half of them refinancings."

Refi mania was a nightmare.

"Refi mania was a nightmare," says Brown. "We took too many loans with too few personnel. Then it got bogged down in getting credit reports and appraisals, and that's when commitments started running out. It was crazy.

"When you're that far behind and you hire up, you don't get ahead because people are still coming through the door. You're lucky to get anything out, period. It's just overwhelming. Every phase backed up except the loan officers who were taking applications. They didn't have any sense. They were like sharks feeding."

The stream of refinance customers that flooded Sid Leake's Corpus Christi branch forced him to arrive at work by 6:00 a.m. in order to catch up on essential paperwork. "Once the doors opened at 8:00 a.m.," says Leake, "I didn't have time to go to the bathroom." David Chapman had to hire contract underwriters to get out from under the boxes of loan files that came in every day: "I'd load up two or three boxes of files and drop them off at their houses every evening so they could help us underwrite. We were no better than anybody else trying to keep up with it. We had massive backlogs."

One management exception to the refi madness was Winston-Salem branch manager and vice president Lewis C. (Tommy) Thompson. "He is the only branch manager I know of," says Brown, "that actually shut down his production and told his loan officers that the branch didn't have the staff or the ability to handle this, so we're not going to take any more refi applications for *x* number of days. It was unbelievable. Thompson had a wonderful, wonderful reputation in his area. And when refi mania was over with, he still had a lot of production because his real estate customers appreciated what he did."

Edwards' ambivalence between pushing for production and pulling in the reins to prevent chaos was evident even five years after the fact: "I think if I had it to do all over again we would have turned more business away. We did have some document problems. And in the areas it got out of control we had to go in and provide teams, SWAT teams we called them, to help branches get caught up. I remember Virginia Beach just exploded. But it was hard to be too critical because they were making so much money. They made more money than anybody else."

The lack of profitability in the production division became glaringly apparent after the refinance frenzy subsided. Former L&N vice president Benjamin A. Cotharin, Jr., remembers the concern he heard expressed at the time: "People kept saying, when refinance goes away you're going to have all these offices sitting out there with nothing to do. Then refinance went away, and the offices had nothing to do." The fixed cost of branch operations went up and the volume moved down. "When business fell off as it did after refi mania," says former Lomas executive vice president David A. Buckman, "that's when we saw the net cost of producing a loan in the branches go way up."

The production division's failure to produce profitable originations cost Weston Edwards his job in July 1988. "You have to be P&L driven," says Sandy Tolbert. "You have to make money. I can go out and get all the production you want, but what do I pay to get it? I think the bottom line was that Edwards just didn't make money for the company."

Although the strategies Terry Klein and Weston Edwards employed were controversial and the results they achieved mixed, it is hard to challenge their ability as agents of change. Their leadership provided the catalyst for accelerated change that led to more sophisticated servicing and production. Turning L&N's mortgage banking juggernaut in a new direction was not easy, but Klein and Edwards met the challenge with energy and determination.

Change also occurred in other parts of the company during the mid-1980s. The most significant was an expansion program that reshaped Lomas & Nettleton Financial Corporation and tested its ability to grow in new directions.

Paul Low became senior executive vice president for marketing and product development in 1984.

CHAPTER XII

BOLD MOVES

Responsibility for adding profit centers at the mortgage company fell to Paul M. Low, who in 1984 became senior executive vice president for marketing and product development and the third member of L&N's new management team. His counterparts, Terry Klein and Weston Edwards, were fresh faces charged with the task of breaking new ground. Low, on the other hand, was a familiar face responsible for nourishing an old and respected corporate tradition. Although other executives at L&N had similar skills, Low's entrepreneurial ability was unrivaled. Preferring to work alone or with a few like-minded individuals, he had built a well-deserved reputation for putting together successful, innovative ventures since his association with the company in the early 1960s. His appointment to head the marketing division formalized what had previously been an unstructured, low-profile role and underscored the value of his contribution to the company.

Nine months after his new appointment, Low reported on the progress of his division's "campaign to nurture new financial services." One early success involved a joint venture with USAA, a Texas-based insurance company. The relationship spawned a unique direct marketing program for L&N that later became known as Premium Programs.

It focused on what was called "affinity groups" marketing—identifying organizations that represent large groups of individuals connected by a common interest and then soliciting those individuals for mortgage loans. In the eyes of L&N's marketing division, the untapped potential of USAA's gold-plated membership glittered especially bright.

An early success for Low was a joint venture with USAA , a Texas-based insurance company, headquartered in San Antonio. Courtesy USAA.

Former USAA vice president Larry James knew that his company's unfamiliarity with mortgage banking meant it would have to think in terms of a partnership. Courtesy USAA.

The San Antonio insurance company catered to active and retired military officers and their families. "There is nothing like USAA," says former USAA vice president Lawrence E. James. "The average age of its members is mid-forties. The average income is $46,000. The average home mortgage at the time I left was $96,000. The percentage with college degrees is very high. You're talking about upscale people. These are people that have a lot of discretionary income."

...a very nice piece of business.

In the spring of 1984 USAA decided to offer its 1.4 million members mortgage products through its newly chartered federal savings bank. The company's unfamiliarity with mortgage banking forced it to think in terms of a partnership with an organization capable of originating and servicing mortgage loans for its membership nationwide.

Even at this early stage, L&N's reputation and dominant presence in the industry began to be felt. Lomas senior vice president Sandy Tolbert, production branch manager and one of the most prominent members of the mortgage banking community in South Texas, received a phone call from USAA: "It was suggested by one of their board members who was a friend of mine that USAA come talk to us." Tolbert got the ball rolling by setting up an unofficial meeting with L&N executive vice president Gary H. Kell, a key marketing executive. Kell, in turn, got Paul Low involved.

When it came time to submit a proposal to USAA, Low was ready. The agreement centered on fee sharing for both originations and servicing. Most important from L&N's standpoint, USAA brought its membership and considerable marketing skills to the table. It agreed to provide the direct mail and telemarketing needed to promote the mortgage products being offered. Besides L&N's extensive branch network and national servicing capability, USAA was impressed with the cooperation among Low, Klein, and Edwards during the bidding process and after. This was a large part of the reason why it selected L&N. "We had all three senior executive vice presidents interested in this project," says former executive vice president David A. Buckman. "They recognized that it was something bold and unique to the industry, and they paid a lot of attention to it."

"I think Lomas put as much energy into the USAA project as any company possibly could," says Lawrence James. "We got all kinds of support from Low, Edwards, and Klein. Everybody was pulling together trying to make the USAA alliance work. Lomas & Nettleton was committed to the relationship and you could tell it."

That was the kind of commitment the San Antonio company was looking for. USAA's phenomenal growth had been built on price and customer service. "I'd never seen a company so focused on service," says Buckman. "In the ranking of insurance companies, they consistently scored the highest for service and attention to their customers."

Early on in the discussions with USAA, L&N understood the importance of service to the San Antonio company and developed a strategy that helped calm its fears about turning the servicing of its customers over to anyone but USAA employees.

One idea L&N incorporated into its proposal that later became a reality was the development of an 800 number counseling service in Dallas exclusively for USAA members. Known as the USAA Support Group, this telemarketing unit was trained to counsel USAA customers about loan programs and to prequalify applicants.

Terry Klein developed a similar unit on the servic-

USAA decided to offer its 1.4 million members mortgage products through its newly chartered USAA Federal Savings Bank, located in this building. Courtesy USAA.

L&N executive vice president Gary Kell was a key marketing person and got Paul Low involved in the USAA project.

ing side. It was made up of loan administration professionals who handled escrow and delinquency problems for USAA customers.

The teamwork and ingenuity that L&N displayed contrasted sharply with several of the other major players active in the negotiations. USAA's Lawrence James recalls, for example, the poor impression Sears made: "It was obvious they weren't going to get anywhere. The Dean Witter people didn't know the Sears guys. It was incredible. They didn't know what the hell they were doing. They showed up with five guys, and all these guys worked for the same company but nobody knew one another. Low, on the other hand, came down with the servicing guys and the origination guys. They came down organized and ready to go. Low knew what the hell he was doing. There was really no question about who we'd pick." USAA and L&N signed a contract on November 2, 1984.

The USAA Support Group was led by former L&N vice president and navy ensign Brian M. Burback. Weston Edwards recruited him from L&N's Salt Lake City production office because of his membership in USAA and his mortgage banking expertise. It was a difficult assignment. The USAA membership displayed what Burback calls an "officer mentality, where you demand results and you get results. They don't take no for an answer. And if you come up with a 'no,' you'd better have it justified as to why, seven days from Sunday." It was a style of customer service with which L&N and most of the mortgage banking industry had little familiarity. But it didn't take Burback's support group long to get its sea legs. "Brian Burback and his staff," says James, "just killed themselves trying to do a good job. The people that worked for Lomas busted their butt to provide good service to the USAA members."

"It was very challenging," says Weston Edwards, "because their members are very demanding. They're used to good service. And we had to train our people to respond in an exceedingly thoughtful way. They had to get used to calling people by their military rank when they wanted it that way, which was most often."

Weston Edwards described Premium Programs as "a very nice piece of business." However, the teamwork demonstrated among L&N's three mortgage banking divisions was never repeated. Courtesy Weston Edwards & Associates.

USAA became an excellent source for profitable loan production. Using that relationship as the prototype, L&N organized a department called Direct Marketing Services to sign up other affinity groups. By 1988, the program was called Premium Programs, with a membership that included the Pentagon Federal Credit Union, Unisys Federal Credit Union, and two IBM credit unions. "It proved to be an economically efficient way to originate mortgages," says former Lomas executive vice president John L. Sly, Jr. "When you're able to do a large volume out of only one brick-and-mortar location, you can be pretty cost-effective. Also, we weren't paying traditional loan officer commissions."

The October 1985 general staff meeting coincided with the twenty-fifth anniversary of Wallace Properties, the predecessor to LNFC. At the meeting, Jess Hay emphasized his corporate vision of teamwork.

Weston Edwards described Premium Programs as "a very nice piece of business." "It was a good product," says Gary Kell. "We probably produced about a billion dollars in loans, $500 million with USAA and about $500 million from the credit unions. A significant amount of our production volume came from Premium Programs."

As it turned out, cooperation among L&N's three mortgage banking divisions proved to be the exception rather than the rule. The teamwork demonstrated so successfully for the USAA venture was never repeated. David Buckman believes that the antipathy among the division heads stemmed from the three very different personalities, each with "a healthy respect for himself" and the belief that he had the ability to manage the other divisions. "Also, they were very proud individuals," says Buckman, "and when you add that all up, you don't get a lot of cooperation or communication."

As a result, the senior executive officers tended to go in three different directions. That kind of divisiveness was destructive of good results and of Jess Hay's corporate vision, an issue Hay addressed at the October 1985 general staff meeting. "Hay expanded upon the concept of teamwork," the November issue of *Pipeline* reported, "by reminding everyone that the 1985 General Staff Meeting was 'not a miscellaneous gathering of some 400 oddly assembled individuals' nor 'several groups of isolated fiefdoms or divisions, but rather members of one team. . . . Try it if you will,' Hay proffered. 'You will find that as you reach out to others they normally will respond; and in the process you will discover that together you can accomplish infinitely more than as individuals working alone or pulling against one another.'"

Hay's appeal, however, failed to end the rivalry among the mortgage banking leadership. "I think they [Edwards, Klein, and Low] all shared Mr. Hay's common goal," observes Lomas senior vice president Pat Gardino, "but they all disliked one another so greatly that they refused to work together to reach that goal. Each one wanted the others to do it his way."

Among the successes of these years was the addition of another Lomas acronym to the New York Stock Exchange. "When the opening bell sounded at 10 a.m. Sept. 13," reads a story in the October 1985 *Pipeline*, "eight of the many L&N officers and spouses who helped bring about Lomas Mortgage Corporation stood ready to watch the LMC symbol flash across the electronic ticker tape." Lomas Mortgage Corporation, the third real estate investment trust (REIT) affiliated with LNFC and the fourth member of The Lomas & Nettleton Financial Group to be listed on the New York Stock Exchange, was another marketing coup for Paul Low.

. . . One more of the profitable businesses that we got into without investing capital. . .

The idea for this venture began when Low, at Hay's request, focused on finding a consistent market for the high-balance loans the mortgage company originated. Single-family jumbo residential loans exceeded the limits for loan amounts prescribed by FNMA or FHLMC. Although there was a ready mar-

Standing on the floor of the NYSE when the opening bell rang at 10 a.m. on September 13, 1985, five L&N officers who helped bring about Lomas Mortgage Corporation watched the symbol LMC light up the electronic ticker tape. Shown here are, left to right, Gary White, senior vice president, control; Gary Kell, senior vice president, marketing and business development; Randy Weldon, husband of Joy Weldon, assistant vice president, investor relations; Jim Wooten, president, and his wife, Marjorie; Paul Low, senior executive vice president and LMC director, and his wife, Nedda.

ket for FHA, VA, and most conventional single-family loans, jumbo loans were difficult to place. "There was not a consistently stable market for jumbo loans," says Low. "Sometimes it was there, and sometimes it wasn't. LMC provided a capital base to provide constancy to a product." After brainstorming with his staff and with representatives of Merrill Lynch, Low's solution was to create a publicly owned REIT that gave L&N a place to sell its nonconforming jumbo loans and also earned a management fee for LNFC. Under the management of Lomas Mortgage Managers, Inc. (later called Capstead Advisers, Inc.), the new company offered investors the opportunity to participate in the income generated from "a portfolio of long-term, non-conforming, high-quality, high-balance, first-mortgage loans."

When Lomas Mortgage Corporation began operations on September 13, 1985, it received net proceeds of $111,102,000 from the successful offering of 5,990,000 shares of common stock. It took most of that money and immediately bought $101,435,000 principal amount of first-mortgage single-family residential loans from L&N. Emphasis on a high-quality portfolio was an important part of LMC's strategy. "To establish a basis for investor confidence, we established a basic set of rules," says Low. "The loan-to-value ratios couldn't exceed *x*, and they would be on single-family properties only. The second piece was a diligent review of applications from originators who wanted to sell loans to the REIT to make sure we were doing business with good originators. In addition to that, in order to add more credit, virtually all of the purchased mortgages were insured by the major mortgage insurers. It's a very sound portfolio."

Former Capstead Advisers president Ronn K. Lytle, an L&N senior vice president at the time, was chosen to manage LMC's investments. His background in mortgage inventory management and directing trades in mortgages and securities for the mortgage company had already earned him a reputation as "a brilliant strategist."

LMC had two primary revenue sources. One was

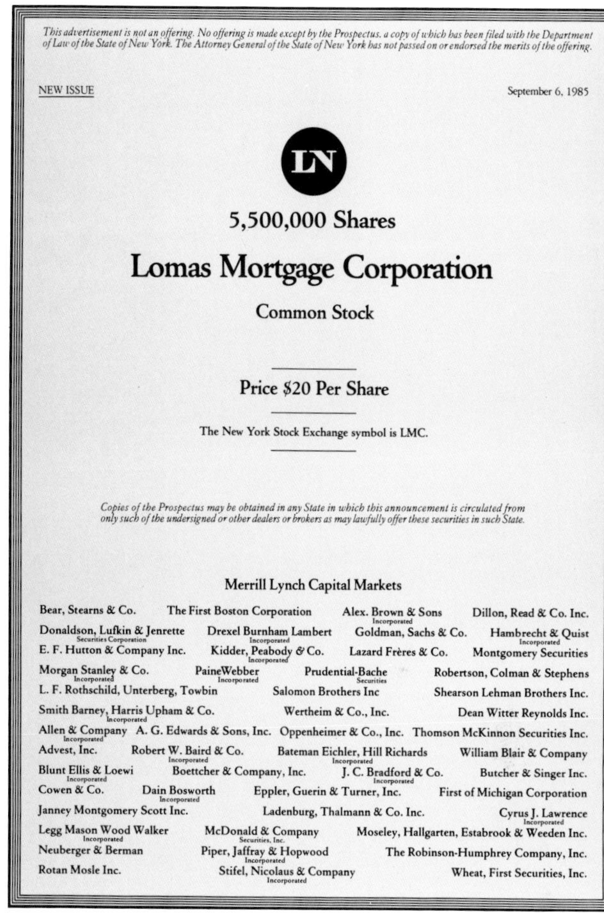

This advertisement is not an offering. No offering is made except by the Prospectus, a copy of which has been filed with the Department of Law of the State of New York. The Attorney General of the State of New York has not passed on or endorsed the merits of the offering.

NEW ISSUE

September 6, 1985

5,500,000 Shares

Lomas Mortgage Corporation

Common Stock

Price $20 Per Share

The New York Stock Exchange symbol is LMC.

Copies of the Prospectus may be obtained in any State in which this announcement is circulated from only such of the undersigned or other dealers or brokers as may lawfully offer these securities in such State.

Merrill Lynch Capital Markets

Bear, Stearns & Co. The First Boston Corporation Alex. Brown & Sons Incorporated Dillon, Read & Co. Inc.
Donaldson, Lufkin & Jenrette Securities Corporation Drexel Burnham Lambert Incorporated Goldman, Sachs & Co. Hambrecht & Quist Incorporated
E. F. Hutton & Company Inc. Kidder, Peabody & Co. Incorporated Lazard Frères & Co. Montgomery Securities
Morgan Stanley & Co. Incorporated PaineWebber Incorporated Prudential-Bache Securities Robertson, Colman & Stephens
L. F. Rothschild, Unterberg, Towbin Salomon Brothers Inc Shearson Lehman Brothers Inc.
Smith Barney, Harris Upham & Co. Incorporated Wertheim & Co., Inc. Dean Witter Reynolds Inc.
Allen & Company Incorporated A. G. Edwards & Sons, Inc. Oppenheimer & Co., Inc. Thomson McKinnon Securities Inc.
Advest, Inc. Robert W. Baird & Co. Incorporated Bateman Eichler, Hill Richards Incorporated William Blair & Company
Blunt Ellis & Loewi Incorporated Boettcher & Company, Inc. J. C. Bradford & Co. Incorporated Butcher & Singer Inc.
Cowen & Co. Dain Bosworth Incorporated Eppler, Guerin & Turner, Inc. First of Michigan Corporation
Janney Montgomery Scott Inc. Ladenburg, Thalmann & Co. Inc. Cyrus J. Lawrence Incorporated
Legg Mason Wood Walker Incorporated McDonald & Company Securities, Inc. Moseley, Hallgarten, Estabrook & Weeden Inc.
Neuberger & Berman Piper, Jaffray & Hopwood Incorporated The Robinson-Humphrey Company, Inc.
Rotan Mosle Inc. Stifel, Nicolaus & Company Incorporated Wheat, First Securities, Inc.

Paul Low and his staff with representatives of Merrill Lynch created the publicly owned REIT Lomas Mortgage Corporation from the successful offering of shares of common stock.

Lomas Mortgage Corporation bought first-mortgage single-family residential loans and developed printed materials to support the program.

the interest yields on the single-family residential loans purchased by the REIT. This was further enhanced by using bank lines and commercial paper to buy additional mortgages and earn a spread on the cost of funds and the higher interest rate on the purchased mortgages. But the principal source of revenue came from collateralized mortgage obligations (CMOs). By pooling the mortgages in the portfolio and pledging them as collateral, LMC could create CMO mortgage-backed securities with variable maturity rates. The variable maturity rates were particularly attractive to investors who required more flexibility than that offered by 30-year GNMA mortgage-backed securities. "By taking a pool of mortgages," Lytle explains, "and carving them up into securities with two-year, five-year, 10-year, and 20-year maturities, you can broaden the market for those who want to buy mortgage-backed securities." LMC, as the issuer of the securities, retained a residual investment in the CMO, usually of 2 percent. A CMO issued for $100 million, for example, gave LMC an investment of $2,000,000 and earned $400,000 on a 20 percent return. LMC issued its first CMO in November 1986. The reception, according to Lytle, "was not great, but it got sold." CMOs were a relatively new product and it took time to build a market for them.

LMC's earnings, on the other hand, were anything but slow. The REIT produced a net income of almost $3.4 million in the first three and a half months of operation and paid an initial quarterly dividend of 50¢ per share on December 23, 1985. Less than two years after its formation, Lomas Mortgage Corporation sold 2,700,000 additional shares of its common stock and added proceeds of $65,861,000 to its working capital.

It also performed well as a profit center. The dollar amount it earned in management fees was not large,

L&N senior vice president Ronn Lytle was chosen to manage LMC's investments.

but that $1.5 million to $2.5 million figure represented, according to former vice president Mark Nieberlein, a 50 percent profit margin. "When you considered the number of employees and our expenses," says Nieberlein, "the return was really incredible. We became very efficient at managing large dollar assets with very few people."

From Paul Low's perspective, Lomas Mortgage Corporation was "one more of the profitable businesses that we got into without investing capital, . . . [utilizing] the internal resources we had to build an income stream through management fees." LMC was one of a growing string of successful asset management ventures. Just how important those had become was noted in the October 1985 issue of *Pipeline*: "LMC's successful offering now puts the capital and credit resources managed by Lomas & Nettleton Financial Corporation at more than $1 billion."

LNFC's progression toward a larger array of financial services led to the formation of the real estate development division. Before its formal organization in 1979, it had operated "as a two-person shop to help L&N 'work out' and liquidate nonperforming tracts of land burdened with problems such as zoning snarls or inadequate utilities." The new division shifted gears and began buying and developing land for sale to investors and single-family homebuilders, primarily in metropolitan Dallas and Houston. By 1984, the real estate group had purchased more than 6,500 acres of land, developed 5,000 single-family lots, and "generated over $107 million in real estate sales and $24 million in gains," which represented approximately 14 percent of the company's net operating profit.

Success encouraged the group to expand operations in 1984. Under the leadership of Wayne D. Ferguson, who later became president of the division, real estate adopted a strategy designed to increase its low inventory base with larger-size projects. "The real estate group," says former executive vice president M. DeWayne Wommack, who was chief control officer for the division, "had reached a point where their inventory was being sold out every year and they had nothing on which to base their continuing growth. It was determined at that time to get into some larger projects that would give the group a basis on which to increase sales volume and still have something left to sell."

The real estate division adopted a conservative acquisition philosophy. The strategy called for buying land in developing growth corridors near urban centers with significant economic strength. "We believe in adhering to the basics," Wayne Ferguson wrote in a 1987 report, "and feel that real value is created through the development process, not through speculation, and to that end, we attempt to purchase tracts that are ready for immediate development from the original or long-term owners. We contract for properties with extended feasibility periods in order to give us time to identify and quantify all political, engineering, and marketing risks. And we only acquire properties when all of these items are satisfactorily resolved."

The real estate group implemented their new strategy with land purchases in Houston, Dallas, and Tampa. According to a National Planning Association study, those locations ranked first, fifth, and twelfth nationally in terms of population and job growth at that time. L&N began buying tracts of land 24 miles north of downtown Houston in late 1983 for a development project it called Northgate Crossing. By May 1986, the group had purchased 880 acres from 65 sellers for a total of $28.7 million. The development plan envisioned by L&N included garden offices, corporate headquarters, midrise multifamily housing, and retail.

We believe in adhering to the basics . . .

The 585 acres in the Tampa/St. Petersburg metropolitan area, purchased from 15 sellers in 1986 for $23.5 million, was the group's first major project outside of Texas. It marked the beginning of a strategy to diversify their geographic markets. Development plans for Gateway Centre, as the Florida project was named, called for an office park for commercial, retail, light industrial, and two hotel sites. It was the largest planned-development business park in the St. Petersburg area.

The largest and most impressive in terms of development amenities and projected sales revenue was Vista Ridge, a 972-acre tract located in Lewisville, 25 miles from downtown Dallas and 10 miles from Dallas/Fort Worth International Airport. "The driver of that area, and really the whole metroplex, is the D/FW Airport," says former real estate executive vice president J. Stephen Crim, referring to the sprawling economic complex that claims a daily, on-premise employment of 34,000. "It is the second busiest airport in the country and the single most important economic generator in the state of Texas." The land for Vista Ridge was purchased in September 1984 from five sellers for $25.2 million. The development's master plan called for a business park and residential community; the amenities included jogging trails, lakes, canals, an amphitheater, an athletic club, and extensive landscaping.

If it were not for a venerable Texas business tradition, the first and largest tract, over 600 acres owned by H. R. (Bum) Bright, would not have been acquired and there wouldn't have been a Vista Ridge. The purchase was what Crim calls "a handshake deal." This custom has little legal meaning, relying only on the integrity of the parties involved, but that was enough to make it work. When Bright decided to sell the property he contacted Ferguson, who had expressed interest in the land for several years. A deal was quickly negotiated. True to Bright's business style, the two men, says Crim, shook hands and walked away. No contract.

Later, when one of Bright's associates pressured him to revoke the deal and accept another offer for $5 million more than L&N had agreed to pay, Bright refused. Ferguson remembers one meeting where he observed Bright's reaction firsthand: "The business associate said, 'This deal is not under contract, we don't have any obligation to them. They knew the risk.' And Bright replied, 'You don't understand. We shook this man's hand, and we are going to damn well do what we said we would do.'

"If it hadn't been for Mr. Bright sticking to his word, the deal would never have happened."

"Since 1965," reads a 1987 LNFC report, "Lomas & Nettleton gradually has been evolving into a diversified financial services company. The pace of that evolutionary process has quickened since 1984." One reason for the acceleration was the realization that L&N's growing loan portfolio held a vein of untapped value waiting to be mined. In the past, the company had looked at its portfolio and seen mortgage loans. In the early 1980s, it saw retail customers. "As we grew," says John Sexton, "we focused more on the customer base. It was 400,000. Then it was 500,000 and growing. And

An L&N publication touted the real estate group's Northgate Crossing project 24 miles north of downtown Houston, which included garden offices, corporate headquarters, midrise multifamily housing, and retail.

Left: Gateway Centre, in the Tampa/St. Petersburg area, was the real estate group's first major project outside Texas.

Below: The largest and most impressive development was Vista Ridge, 25 miles from downtown Dallas. The promotional material graphically dramatized its sweeping concepts.

"A diversified financial services company" found its visual representation in this cartoon-style illustration on the cover of *The Mortgagee.*

as we got the mortgage base up to a certain size, a bell went off and we started asking, 'What else can we do with this customer base? What other businesses should we be in?'"

The Task Force on Internal Strategy in 1981 provided the focus needed to help answer those questions. It was now technologically practical to create a customer-oriented data base. "The task force," says Ted Enloe, "led us to believe that we could create a whole different type of system, one that related to the customer base instead of the mortgage, which would enable us to sell more products. Our previous system was designed to only process the servicing of a mortgage. Once a person paid a mortgage off, he disappeared from the system. We wanted to create a system where the servicing of the mortgage was ancillary to all the other financial data on the borrower, so that even when the mortgage paid off, we could continue to solicit that individual for other products and services."

. . . a **bigger and more diversified revenue base.**

When the Future System Group reported on its progress at the 1983 general staff meeting, the commitment to finding ways to turn borrowers into consumers had begun. "We are organizing our data base and servicing around the customer, not the loan," said then LNIS executive vice president Henry Hortenstine. The component for that part of the Future System was called the Customer Information System. "This system," a newsletter article explained, "acts as a central repository of all customers' data, allowing users to see the entire L&N relationship with a customer as mortgagor . . . or potential buyer of other services." The best visual depiction of where L&N was headed appeared on the February/March 1984 cover of the *Mortgagee.* The *New Yorker*–style cartoon showed a Lomas & Nettleton retail department store offering a smorgasbord of financial services.

At the general staff meeting in 1985, Enloe predicted that by identifying existing L&N customers as customers for additional products and services, L&N had the potential of becoming "the nation's premier financial services company." What made the projected new services different from previous ones was the fact that they weren't related to mortgage banking. By diversifying the company's income stream, the new businesses could act as a protective hedge against the real estate market's recessionary cycles.

Growing competitive pressure was another and even more pressing motivation. The mortgage industry was increasingly dominated by GMAC, Citicorp, and other financial giants. Added to that, national demographic studies projected fewer family units, which meant reduced demand for mortgage financing. The prospect of stronger forces competing for a declining market suggested to L&N's senior management that it might be a good idea to shift toward "a bigger and more diversified revenue base."

A strong capital base gave L&N the ability to pursue that strategy. In fiscal 1985 the company sold $100 million principal amount of 9 percent convertible subordinated debentures. "As a result of this offering and of earnings retained during the year," said the 1985 annual report, "the Company's capital base . . . increased from $286 million at June 30, 1984 to $402 million at the end of Fiscal 1985." The next year L&N sold $145 million principal amount of its subordinated 9 percent liquid yield option notes and $172 million principal amount of its 7 percent convertible subordinated debentures due in 2011. By June 30, 1986, the company's total capital base exceeded $750 million.

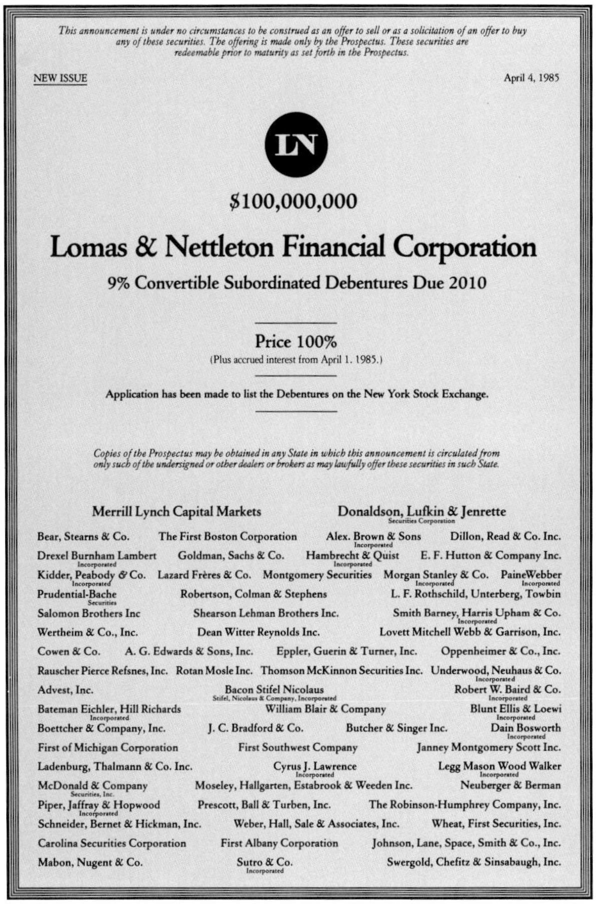

This announcement is under no circumstances to be construed as an offer to sell or as a solicitation of an offer to buy any of these securities. The offering is made only by the Prospectus. These securities are redeemable prior to maturity as set forth in the Prospectus.

NEW ISSUE

April 4, 1985

LN

$100,000,000

Lomas & Nettleton Financial Corporation

9% Convertible Subordinated Debentures Due 2010

Price 100%

(Plus accrued interest from April 1, 1985.)

Application has been made to list the Debentures on the New York Stock Exchange.

Copies of the Prospectus may be obtained in any State in which this announcement is circulated from only such of the undersigned or other dealers or brokers as may lawfully offer these securities in such State.

Merrill Lynch Capital Markets
Donaldson, Lufkin & Jenrette Securities Corporation

Bear, Stearns & Co. | The First Boston Corporation | Alex. Brown & Sons Incorporated | Dillon, Read & Co. Inc.
Drexel Burnham Lambert Incorporated | Goldman, Sachs & Co. | Hambrecht & Quist Incorporated | E. F. Hutton & Company Inc.
Kidder, Peabody & Co. Incorporated | Lazard Frères & Co. | Montgomery Securities | Morgan Stanley & Co. Incorporated | PaineWebber Incorporated
Prudential-Bache Securities | Robertson, Colman & Stephens | L. F. Rothschild, Unterberg, Towbin
Salomon Brothers Inc | Shearson Lehman Brothers Inc. | Smith Barney, Harris Upham & Co. Incorporated
Wertheim & Co., Inc. | Dean Witter Reynolds Inc. | Lovett Mitchell Webb & Garrison, Inc.
Cowen & Co. | A. G. Edwards & Sons, Inc. | Eppler, Guerin & Turner, Inc. | Oppenheimer & Co., Inc.
Rauscher Pierce Refsnes, Inc. | Rotan Mosle Inc. | Thomson McKinnon Securities Inc. | Underwood, Neuhaus & Co. Incorporated
Advest, Inc. | Bacon Stifel Nicolaus Stifel, Nicolaus & Company, Incorporated | Robert W. Baird & Co. Incorporated
Bateman Eichler, Hill Richards Incorporated | William Blair & Company | Blunt Ellis & Loewi Incorporated
Boettcher & Company, Inc. | J. C. Bradford & Co. | Butcher & Singer Inc. | Dain Bosworth Incorporated
First of Michigan Corporation | First Southwest Company | Janney Montgomery Scott Inc.
Ladenburg, Thalmann & Co. Inc. | Cyrus J. Lawrence Incorporated | Legg Mason Wood Walker Incorporated
McDonald & Company Securities, Inc. | Moseley, Hallgarten, Estabrook & Weeden Inc. | Neuberger & Berman
Piper, Jaffray & Hopwood Incorporated | Prescott, Ball & Turben, Inc. | The Robinson-Humphrey Company, Inc.
Schneider, Bernet & Hickman, Inc. | Weber, Hall, Sale & Associates, Inc. | Wheat, First Securities, Inc.
Carolina Securities Corporation | First Albany Corporation | Johnson, Lane, Space, Smith & Co., Inc.
Mabon, Nugent & Co. | Sutro & Co. Incorporated | Swergold, Chefitz & Sinsabaugh, Inc.

To build and increase a strong capital base, Lomas & Nettleton Financial Corporation in fiscal 1985 sold $100 million principal amount of 9 percent convertible subordinated debentures.

True to the company's entrepreneurial style, Lomas & Nettleton Financial Corporation pursued its objective without preconceptions about what it would buy. The absence of a formalized process stemmed from the belief among management that when you make a decision to buy a particular business you probably pay too much. "We just sort of waited for things to appear," Enloe explains. "We tend to be opportunistic," says Jess Hay. "We are always interested in the market and ready to respond to opportunities that seem to be good fits for us."

One opportunity that had been germinating for several years was life insurance. The acquisition of National Homes Acceptance Corporation in 1979 included a small, wholly owned life insurance company called Mayflower National. L&N acquired a second small life insurance company when it signed an agreement to buy Advance in 1982. L&N immediately changed the name from Lakeland Assurance to Lomas Financial Security In-surance Corporation. Two years later Mayflower National was consolidated into LFSIC.

He **asked me if we'd be interested in acquiring a life insurance company.**

L&N's flirtation with the life insurance business became more passionate in 1984 and 1985 when senior management decided it was a good business in its own right for the company to be in. "It's solid, stable, and it's something we think we can manage," says Enloe. "And the stability of the insurance income would be good for us, because it would diversify us away from mortgage banking." The idea of selling insurance products to the mortgage company's customer base enhanced its appeal. Jess Hay referred to it as "a natural add-on."

Kenneth W. Phillips was hired as president of L&N's two life insurance subsidiaries in April 1984 to provide the leadership needed to grow the business. He had been associated with the life insurance industry since his graduation from The University of Texas at Austin in 1964. Most recently he had served as executive vice president and treasurer of American Income

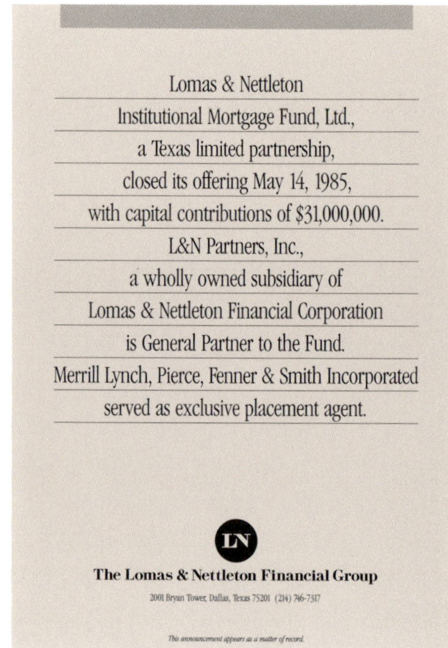
Lomas & Nettleton
Institutional Mortgage Fund, Ltd.,
a Texas limited partnership,
closed its offering May 14, 1985,
with capital contributions of $31,000,000.
L&N Partners, Inc.,
a wholly owned subsidiary of
Lomas & Nettleton Financial Corporation
is General Partner to the Fund.
Merrill Lynch, Pierce, Fenner & Smith Incorporated
served as exclusive placement agent.
The Lomas & Nettleton Financial Group
2001 Bryan Tower, Dallas, Texas 75201 (214) 746-7317
This announcement appears as a matter of record.

At the time the general capital base was expanding, there was capital expansion in other areas as well. Lomas & Nettleton Institutional Mortgage Fund, Ltd., was increasing its fund for specifically related real estate investments.

In April 1984, Ken Phillips was hired as president of L&N's two life insurance subsidiaries.

Life Insurance Company.

Phillips realized early on that building a meaningful life insurance division was a major challenge. "We were a life insurance company in name only," says the former life insurance group president. "We really didn't have a back office administration capability, and we didn't have a marketing organization. It was obvious to me that an acquisition was the way to get into the business very quickly."

Phillips did not have long to wait for an opportunity. An investment banker from E. F. Hutton made a cold call to Phillips in early 1985: "He asked me if we'd be interested in acquiring a life insurance company. And his call hit me at the time when I was exploring that as a possible strategy for Lomas." The offer was for Jefferson National Life Insurance Company, a company well regarded by those in the industry. An on-site visit by Phillips to Jefferson National's corporate headquarters in Indianapolis confirmed the company's high quality. "It was indeed a fine organization," Phillips reported after his initial inspection. "It had been very conservatively managed. It had a clean balance sheet and an excellent reputation in the business."

If L&N was serious about entering the life insurance business on a larger scale, Jefferson National offered an outstanding opportunity. "I remember my comment to Jess when we talked about buying Jefferson National," says Enloe. "I told him we either need to get into life insurance or get out of it. The two small life companies we owned weren't big enough to give us any kind of critical mass. I said we either need to get out of it, or we need to buy one that is a going company, a large company with a good portfolio and strong management. Something that we can grow. And that led to our deciding to go forward and pursue Jefferson."

Principally owned by the McKinney family since its founding in 1937, the Indianapolis-based company, says Phillips, had established itself as "a prominent name in the industry, with an excellent track record of growth and stability." E. Kirk McKinney, Jr., had

Jefferson National Life Insurance Company, with corporate headquarters in Indianapolis, Indiana, offered an opportunity for L&N to become a major player in the life insurance business.

In 1936, E. Kirk McKinney and a small group of Indiana citizens founded a life insurance company in Indianapolis. The first policy was issued in 1939 to E. Kirk McKinney, Jr., son of the founder.

E. Kirk McKinney, Jr., right, at the time of the sale was chairman of the board and chief executive officer of Jefferson National Life. Bernard S. Lyon, left, was president and chief operating officer.

played an active role in the management of the company, progressing from assistant treasurer in 1949 to chairman and chief executive officer at the time of the sale.

Long, difficult negotiations ended in October 1985 with an agreement by L&N to purchase Jefferson National Life Insurance Company (JNL) and its $4.6 billion life insurance in force for $86.5 million in cash. Following the acquisition, Lomas Financial Security Insurance Company was consolidated into Jefferson, creating combined annual premiums in excess of $70 million and life insurance in force of about $6.4 billion. The negotiated agreement also called for the appointment of McKinney to L&N's board of directors, which was ratified by that body on January 17, 1986. "As a result of the acquisition," L&N's 1986 annual report stated, "the Company now is positioned to provide an enhanced array of financial services to its homeowner-customers."

Opportunity bred opportunity. After the Jefferson National acquisition, L&N became known as "a player," says Phillips, "and once you get that reputation you get lots of calls." The most interesting call came from Hunt Financial Corporation in mid-1986 when their subsidiary Union Life Insurance Company of Little Rock became available for sale. L&N liked Union Life because it was the oldest legal reserve life insurance company in Arkansas and it enjoyed a good reputation. From a marketing perspective Jefferson and Union Life made a good fit, because the products they sold were similar but their geographic markets for the most part were complementary. Lomas & Nettleton Financial Corporation announced the acquisition of Union Life Insurance Company for $52.5 million in cash on

Protracted negotiations ended in October 1985 with an agreement by L&N to purchase Jefferson National Life. Appearing together in the 1985 Jefferson National annual report are Kirk McKinney, Jr., left, of Jefferson National and Ken Phillips, right, president and chief operating officer of Lomas Financial Security Insurance Company.

November 12, 1986. In a statement released at the time, Jess Hay noted: "The addition of Union's insurance in force to that of Jefferson National will increase L&N's total insurance in force to approximately $13.5 billion, its policyholders to some 300,000, its consolidated insurance and policy reserves to more than $343 million and its premium volume to more than $112 million per year. As a result, L&N's insurance operations, in terms of size, will rank in the top 10 percent of all insurance companies in the United States."

A third insurance acquisition followed in September 1987 when LNFC bought First Continental Life Group, Inc., for $50 million in cash. Although the purchase increased L&N's total life insurance in force to $14.5 billion, its policyholders to 722,000, and its premium volume to more than $150 million per year, the principal reason for the acquisition was operational efficiency. Except for a small credit life company in Texas, First Continental did not have a marketing organization. This gave Phillips the opportunity to realize expense savings by closing down First Continental's main office in Salt Lake City and filling the excess administrative capacities that existed within Union Life and Jefferson National. Further efficiencies were realized in late 1989 when Phillips closed the Little Rock office and merged its operations into those at Indianapolis.

The steady, consistent profits L&N predicted for its life insurance acquisitions were realized, with operating profits of $12.8 million in 1986, $18.7 million in 1987, and $24.7 million in 1988. By 1987 revenues from the life insurance division represented about 20 percent of the company's total revenue.

The credit card business was one financial service product that L&N thought about starting from scratch. Research indicated, however, that a successful operation required an organization with a certain amount of volume and personnel in place. As serendipity would have it, that kind of organization appeared on L&N's doorstep in 1986. A slumping economy in the Southwest forced numbers of banks strapped for cash to sell their credit card accounts. The largest of these to go on the block was MCorp's MNet, a wholly owned financial services subsidiary. Considering the close friendship between MCorp's chairman and CEO Gene H. Bishop and LNFC's Jess Hay, it isn't surprising that Lomas & Nettleton learned about MCorp's intention to sell

. . . *a* single bold move.

With the acquisition of MBank USA, a banking organization that provided credit card services, L&N gained high visibility and moved toward the corporate goal of diversification.

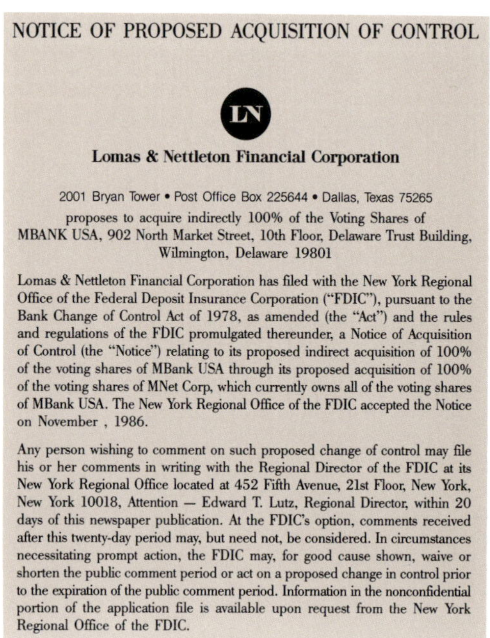

NOTICE OF PROPOSED ACQUISITION OF CONTROL

Lomas & Nettleton Financial Corporation

2001 Bryan Tower • Post Office Box 225644 • Dallas, Texas 75265
proposes to acquire indirectly 100% of the Voting Shares of
MBANK USA, 902 North Market Street, 10th Floor, Delaware Trust Building, Wilmington, Delaware 19801

Lomas & Nettleton Financial Corporation has filed with the New York Regional Office of the Federal Deposit Insurance Corporation ("FDIC"), pursuant to the Bank Change of Control Act of 1978, as amended (the "Act") and the rules and regulations of the FDIC promulgated thereunder, a Notice of Acquisition of Control (the "Notice") relating to its proposed indirect acquisition of 100% of the voting shares of MBank USA through its proposed acquisition of 100% of the voting shares of MNet Corp, which currently owns all of the voting shares of MBank USA. The New York Regional Office of the FDIC accepted the Notice on November , 1986.

Any person wishing to comment on such proposed change of control may file his or her comments in writing with the Regional Director of the FDIC at its New York Regional Office located at 452 Fifth Avenue, 21st Floor, New York, New York 10018, Attention — Edward T. Lutz, Regional Director, within 20 days of this newspaper publication. At the FDIC's option, comments received after this twenty-day period may, but need not, be considered. In circumstances necessitating prompt action, the FDIC may, for good cause shown, waive or shorten the public comment period or act on a proposed change in control prior to the expiration of the public comment period. Information in the nonconfidential portion of the application file is available upon request from the New York Regional Office of the FDIC.

LNFC published a "Notice of Proposed Acquisition of Control" for MNet on November 17, 1986. MNet's principal subsidiary was MBank USA.

MNet at an opportune time. "MCorp," says Enloe, "was actually going to put MNet on the market and sell it through First Boston. Jess happened to be visiting with Gene Bishop when he learned about the intended sale. And Jess said we would like to buy it. It was as simple as that. So, MCorp held First Boston off and told them not to send their packages out and literally within two or three days we negotiated a price and agreed to buy it. It never really got to the marketplace. That's opportunistic."

L&N announced the acquisition of MNet on November 17, 1986, for $300 million in cash, stock, and notes. MNet's principal subsidiary was MBank USA, "an independently operated and self-funded Delaware banking organization which provides credit card services to some 700,000 currently active customers." Other financial services offered by MNet to 575 correspondent banks included a discount broker business, credit life and accident and health coverages, investment advisory services, telemarketing, and travel services.

A *Dallas Morning News* business article acknowledged the importance of the acquisition with the headline: "L&N Takes Giant Step to Diversification." The article went on to say that "with the purchase earlier this week of MNet, the financial services subsidiary of Dallas-based MCorp, Lomas moved from a snail's pace to fulfilling a long-held corporate ambition in a single bold move." Besides a thriving credit card operation and a customer base of 700,000, L&N looked at MNet as the vehicle for marketing the company's financial service products to its growing customer base. "The acquisition of MNet and MBank USA," said Hay, "is another in a series of steps aimed at positioning Lomas & Nettleton to provide more efficient and more comprehensive financial services to its existing and future customers. MNet will become an integral part of our strategic plan for continuing growth in the future."

Acquisition of Equitable Life Leasing Corporation, announced on May 11, 1987, was something of a departure from L&N's full-speed-ahead financial services strategy. Although the $263.3 million purchase made sense in terms of diversifying away from mortgage banking and generating revenue and profits, it did little to broaden the company's cross-marketing financial services strategy. Based in San Diego, the 25-year-old company specialized in buying, leasing, and reselling mainframe computers and other office automation and advanced technology equipment. "The acquisition of the leasing company, which reported revenues of $242.3 million in 1986," an article in *Pipeline* noted, "is expected to supply L&N with a reliable and growing income stream that will contribute positively to future earnings growth."

"The leasing business is a different kind of a cat," says John Sexton. "The fit for L&N is that we know something about money and what you need to do to operate a leasing business. The spread you work in is similar to other businesses. We don't know anything about residuals, which is the core of that business, but

Lomas & Nettleton Financial Corporation

has acquired

Equitable Life Leasing Corporation

a subsidiary of

The Equitable Life Assurance Society of the United States

We acted as financial advisor to Lomas & Nettleton Financial Corporation in this transaction.

Merrill Lynch Capital Markets

June 30, 1987

In its pursuit of diversification, LNFC's acquisition of Equitable Life Leasing Corporation, which bought, leased, and resold mainframe computers, was a departure from its financial services strategy.

With acquisitions and diversification, the name "Lomas & Nettleton," with its variations, became difficult to work with. "Lomas" became the new corporate name, as revealed in this dramatic announcement.

we hired that when we bought the company. We bought the most conservative of the best. It was a very good acquisition at the time and also built up the equity base of the company."

Refocusing L&N's corporate image even before the flurry of acquisition activity ended was a primary concern by early 1987. L&N asked Richards/Gravelle, a Dallas advertising agency specializing in financial services, to look at the situation and develop a strategy. In the first phase of the process, a study conducted among L&N employees by David Gravelle revealed that even within L&N, the corporate identity was diffused because of the inconsistent use of names and initials. Some entities used "Lomas & Nettleton," others "L&N," and still others "Lomas." The fact that shorter names had higher retention and recognition tied in nicely with Gravelle's discovery that most employees on an informal basis referred to the company as Lomas. "Employees felt that the name should change," says Gravelle. "The name Lomas & Nettleton with all its various permutations was far too cumbersome to work with. We found out that in an effort to simplify the name people were calling the company Lomas." Hay agreed with the recommendation that "Lomas" should become the company's new common name. The next phase in the process required the selection of a logo from about 70 choices developed by the Richards, Brock, Miller, Mitchell, and Associates design group. Gravelle describes the logo Hay selected as "an elegant design. It's very classical. Even the modified Roman typeface is classical. It appealed to Mr. Hay, I believe, because it is a straightforward presentation of the name. We kept the same color blue as a way of saying, 'Yeah, we're changing the name, but we're not really changing it.'"

Our name will be Lomas.

To inaugurate the mortgage company's name change, Paul Low had Lomas Mortgage USA flags made. On June 30, 1988, the eve of the new fiscal year, with instructions from Low, David Chapman saw that some 2,000 flags with letters were on the desks to greet each Lomas Mortgage USA employee the next day. On another occasion during Operation Desert Storm, U.S. flags with yellow ribbons were distributed to show Lomas' support of the military action.

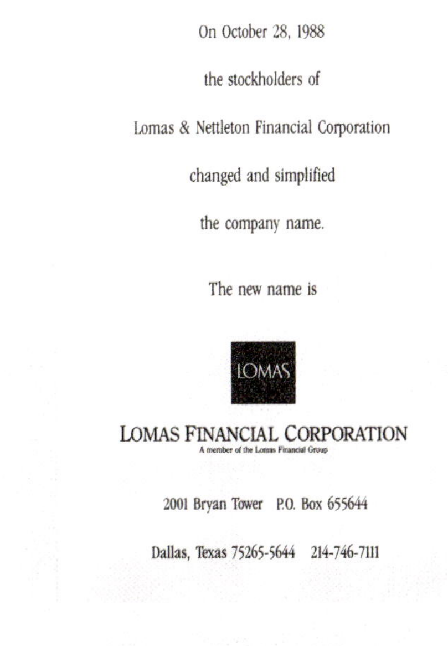

On October 28, 1988
the stockholders of
Lomas & Nettleton Financial Corporation
changed and simplified
the company name.

The new name is

LOMAS

LOMAS FINANCIAL CORPORATION

2001 Bryan Tower P.O. Box 655644
Dallas, Texas 75265-5644 214-746-7111

In a formal announcement, senior management gave notice that the stockholders on October 28, 1988, had changed the company name.

A brochure widely distributed throughout the company in March 1988 announced the change: "Our name will be Lomas. It is a unifying name that preserves much of the valuable equity we have in Lomas & Nettleton. It is simple, memorable, strong, and uniquely ours." The last two pages of the brochure listed the changes and a 16-month schedule for implementing them. Among the new designations, the parent company became Lomas Financial Corporation, the mortgage company was now Lomas Mortgage USA, the real estate group became Lomas Realty USA, MNet changed to Lomas Bankers Corp, and MBank USA to Lomas Bank USA. The names of the life insurance companies remained unchanged because of long-standing recognition within their industry. They were, however, referred to collectively as the Lomas Life Group.

The quest for unity that the new name and logo symbolized addressed two critical issues. From the standpoint of marketing, "a new common name" applied consistently to the company's various businesses

"One word . . ." expressed the hope that the new name would contribute to cultural unity within the company.

was essential, especially as it moved to sell its products on a broader basis. It was also thought that the new name would contribute to cultural unity within the company. "In the past," Hay wrote in the March 1988 brochure, "you may have considered yourself part of Lomas & Nettleton, Equitable Life Leasing, or MBank USA, or another of our businesses. Lomas will bring us closer together not simply in the public eye, but in our own minds as well, and that increase in fellowship will itself be a worthy achievement."

There is, however, little evidence to suggest that the name "Lomas" achieved the kind of fellowship and unity senior management envisioned. The company found itself dealing with a familiar problem: the fundamental conflict between competing corporate values. Lomas' collective vision of each member of its corporate family pulling together to meet a common goal clashed head-on with the high value Lomas placed on the entrepreneurial performance of divisions. The impulse toward divisional autonomy and initiative blocked the long-term corporate strategies based on integrated effort. This classic Lomas conflict found its latest expression in the company's attempt to implement its cross-marketing strategy.

By the end of 1986 it looked like L&N's diversified financial services strategy would coalesce around MNet and its potent credit card subsidiary MBank USA. That purchase more than any other gave L&N the marketing wherewithal to put together what Wall Street analysts said had "the earmarks of a formidable financial services operation."

Seemingly, all the company had to do was hitch its diversified products wagon to the extraordinary marketing success of MNet chairman and CEO (later Lomas Bankers Corp chairman and CEO) John C. Tolleson. As MNet's leader since its formation in August 1984, Tolleson soon made a name for himself

PIPELINE

July 1987

Mouth watering

Cafe staff members are cooking up specials to tempt the palates of campus employees . . . . Page 2

Analysts' questions answered

Wall Street takes stock of L&N's future plans

Financial analysts can be the lifeblood of a public company. Theirs is the job of studying and scrutinizing these companies and determining their growth and earnings potential.

Analysts, working out of research departments of brokerage firms, investment companies, bank trust departments, insurance companies or other organizations that analyze markets and securities, often focus on particular stocks, commodities and specific industries.

Others forecast movements of the market as a whole. Thus, an analyst whose advice is followed by many investors can have a major impact on the prices of individual securities.

Often analysts watch and carefully study a company for years; so when a public company makes a new acquisition or experiences a change in revenues, dividends or management, a red flag goes up. The analysts stop, ask questions. They want to know why.

Not surprisingly, the dramatic growth of L&N during the last four years has unfurled a few red flags. In and of themselves, the acquisitions of Jefferson National, Union Life, MNet and the recently approved purchase of Equitable Life Leasing probably raised a few eyebrows. But, the additional announcement this spring of the third quarter loss due to the large reserves set aside for foreclosures, coupled with a large increase in dividends, made the analysts stand up and take notice.

The analysts began asking questions such as "How will the acquisition of Equitable Life Leasing affect the capital structure of L&N? How will it affect the overall income base? How will it change the overall structure of the company?" And, they are keenly probing for answers about the company's earnings potential.

In an effort to answer those and other questions, senior management invited analysts from across the country to attend a comprehensive briefing June 2 and 3 in Dallas. During the meeting, representatives from all of L&N's subsidiaries and divisions presented an in-depth review of current operations as well as projected revenues and net income for the future.

"This is the first time we have had a briefing of this size that went into such detail on projected earnings," said John Sexton of LNFC finance.

"We have 30 million shares represented out there and this was a good time to relate what the changes mean in view of the Equitable acquisition."

Sexton explained that simply issuing news releases on earnings or sending out a quarterly report to interested analysts just isn't enough anymore. "You have to work at it every single day. Jess (Hay), Ted (Enloe) and I spend a lot of time speaking to the analysts, but it is almost impossible to talk to everyone. We felt the briefing would be a better way to reach as many of the analysts as possible.

"Our timing was good," Sexton said of the briefing that predated the June 29 stockholder meeting and vote on the Equitable acquisition. "It brought the analysts up-to-date and gave them a clear understanding of our future directions."

In answer to many of the analysts questions, Hay gave an overview of L&N's plans and recounted the reasoning behind the board's decision to set aside the

continued on page 4

MNet and L&N
A profitable combination

When L&N acquired MNet last December, Wall Street analysts generally viewed the move as beneficial for both companies. L&N was allowed to diversify its product line and, when considering MNet's profit projections, LNFC's earnings per share would also be substantially enhanced.

Today, seven months later, the move looks even better than originally anticipated. MNet has seen significant growth within the past several months and the future looks just as promising.

John C. Tolleson, chairman and chief executive officer of MNet, said the marriage of MNet and L&N "works extremely well" and sees the business growing at a steady and rapid pace.

"From the onset of the acquisition, MNet operations have gone on without interruption," Tolleson said. "We have received an overwhelming amount of support from employees and officers of L&N. And, most importantly, the capital resources have already allowed for continued growth."

The last seven months have been productive for MNet. A sampling of the highlights so far this year points to the purchase of 300,000 credit card accounts with portfolio values totaling $249.7 million and the pending acquisition of Texas First Brokerage Services, Inc., a Houston-based discount brokerage operation. In addition, a revolving home equity line of credit has also been implemented by MNet with funding provided through MBank USA.

See Related Story Page 2

"The home equity loans complement other Lomas & Nettleton products," Tolleson said. "We're one of the first to offer this type of credit on a nationwide basis. Competing companies are offering the product principally in their local markets. We have the advantage of utilizing L&N's branch system throughout the United States as well as cross-marketing to the existing Lomas customer base."

John C. Tolleson of MNet

Home equity lines of credit are floating rate loans with interest which is tax deductible for qualified homeowners. The optional credit card utilized for accessing the equity funds works like a regular MasterCard/VISA, except that the items charged — from home improvement materials to cars — are secured by existing equity in the customer's home. The interest, as well as being tax deductible, is available at rates much lower in comparison to other bank credit cards.

"Home equity lending is a major business for us. We expect to see $50

continued on page 2

Equitable acquisition approved

June 29 the stockholders of Lomas & Nettleton Financial Corporation, by a majority vote, approved the purchase of Equitable Life Leasing from Equitable Investment Corporation, a wholly owned subsidiary of The Equitable Life Assurance Society of the United States.

The consideration to be paid by L&N for Equitable Life Leasing will consist of $1 million in cash, 1,500,000 shares of L&N's new Series C preferred stock and $8.944 million principal amount of L&N's 9 percent Senior Notes due 1994.

'We think it (the acquisition) will contribute materially to the company's continuing capacity to generate growth.' *—Jess Hay*

The market value of the total consideration is approximately $263.3 million.

"We're pleased with the demonstration of stockholder support for this acquisition, which marks an important step in our diversification strategy," said Jess Hay, chairman and chief executive officer.

"This is the third of our three major acquisitions of fiscal 1987, which have equipped our company to compete effectively in the rapidly changing financial servies marketplace. We think it will contribute materially to the company's continuing capacity to generate growth."

A 25-year-old company, based in San Diego, Equitable Life Leasing specializes in buying, leasing and reselling computers and other office-automation, electronic-communication and advanced technology equipment.

The acquisition of the leasing company, which reported revenues of $242.3 million in 1986, is expected to supply L&N with a reliable and growing income stream that will contribute positively to future earnings growth.

Equitable employs more than 300 people and has 27 sales offices nationwide.

United Way campaign kicks off in July

The children of today will be the leaders of tomorrow; but to assume those rightful roles, many of today's future leaders will need a helping hand. And, Lomas & Nettleton employees in Dallas, through this year's United Way program, have a chance to help build a better tomorrow for our future leaders.

In addition to giving sanctuary to the poor, battered and homeless through its many organizations, the United Way has programs designed specifically to benefit youths. Organizations such as Big Brothers and Big Sisters, Scouting, Camp Fire Inc., and Girls and Boys Clubs — all affiliates of United Way — give children an opportunity to interact with all segments of the community.

Other examples include Dallas Children and Youth Project, which provides community-clinic medical care for young people up to the age of 18, and the South Collin County Infant Program, providing therapeutic and educational services for developmentally delayed children ranging in age from infant to 3.

"Building Our Future Together" is L&N's theme for the annual campaign. As a pacesetter corporation, L&N's activities are seen as an incentive and inspiration for the Dallas community and will be used as an example for other area corporations during the general campaign that takes place in the fall.

The volunteer board of directors for the Dallas United Way has set an area-wide goal of $35,626,777. That figure, officials say, is the minimum needed to support the 100 United Way affiliates in 1988.

L&N's goal is $200,000, a pledge that is easily within reach if each employee donates his "fair share." The United Way's suggested guide for giving a "fair share" is one hour's pay per month for those with a annual income of up to $25,000. Individuals with a salary of more than $25,000 are asked to consider donating one percent of their annual income.

To kick off the campaign, a United Way film will be shown to employees of Bryan Tower and the Corporate Campus in mid-July. Following each film a volunteer from one of the affiliate agencies served by United Way will answer questions.

Those employees especially interested in a particular organization can specify that their contributions be directed to one of the 100 agencies affiliated with United Way of Metropolitan Dallas Inc.

United Way

'Building our future together'

Pledge cards will be passed out by supervisors during July and at that time employees can specify if they want their funds to go to a particular agency or for the United Way general fund.

Pledges can be honored with a lump-sum payment or through monthly automatic payroll deductions that will begin in January 1988.

United Way has served the Dallas area for 26 years through a network of affiliated agencies providing direct assistance, information, referral, education and counseling to approximately 1.8 million residents of the 19-county area around Dallas.

Every gift or pledge makes a difference to the agency it serves. Listed below are some of the ways contributions can help.

- *A gift of $15 can provide transportation to a radiation treatment center for a cancer patient.*
- *A gift of $40 can purchase two hours of legal interpreting for a deaf senior citizen who needs a will.*
- *A gift of $125 can provide school clothing and shoes for a needy child.*
- *A gift of $150 can provide training for 10 instructors to teach arthritis patients to cope with their disease.*
- *A gift of $200 can provide a scholarship to train a person to become a home health aide.*
- *A gift of $450 can provide Red Cross services to a family whose home has been destroyed by fire.*
- *A gift of $500 can provide a six-week employment preparation course for a person who has seizures.*

"Some of the programs offered by local health, youth-agency, rehabilitation and family service organizations couldn't have continued without the volunteerism and money from the United Way," said a spokesman for the United Way.

MNet chairman and CEO John Tolleson (in the two *Pipeline* photographs) guided MBank USA in acquiring eight new portfolio additions that made it "the nation's twelfth largest MasterCard/Visa issuer."

and the retail products and marketing subsidiary he headed. MNet became the Southwest's first bank holding company to consolidate retail banking divisions into one company and aggressively market its products and services on both a wholesale and retail basis. His decision in 1985 to move the credit card bank to Delaware and become competitive nationally projected the company to another level. Since receiving its charter, a September 1987 MNet publication reported that "MBank USA has grown 115%, has added 400,000 new customers, and has grown from a staff of 280 to 480." The article also noted that eight portfolio acquisitions made MBank USA "the nation's twelfth largest MasterCard/VISA issuer." The portfolio acquisitions increased the number of accounts to 1.6 million and the number of agent banks from 700 to 1,000, making MNet's the largest agent bank program in the United States. MNet's meteoric rise also attracted industry attention. L&N's June 1987 *Pipeline* reported Tolleson's election to the board of directors of MasterCard International.

It was not one for all and all for one.

One major obstacle Lomas encountered in its pursuit of synergy came from the fact, according to former Lomas Bank USA president Richard W. Vague, that "you have companies with separate bottom lines that are really focused on achieving their own results." The strength of that reality tended to overwhelm the spirit of cooperation Hay tried to nurture. Lomas Life Group senior vice president Sam A. Butler, Jr., was hired in December 1985 by Ken Phillips to market insurance products to the Lomas customer base. Although Butler enthusiastically pursued the cross-marketing strategy, the resistance he encountered left him angry and frustrated: "MNet seemed like a real opportunity for us, but it really became no opportunity at all, because they were a separate company and they had a separate mar-

The brochure "There is no substitute for gold" was part of an advertising campaign created to sell the MasterCard/Visa program.

keting philosophy. They had a bottom line profit objective that they were driven by, and if it cost them some money to do business internally they were not obliged to do that."

When Butler approached Lomas Bankers about consolidating their small credit life operation into one company in the life group that would handle credit life for everyone, they said no. "They never were interested in having anything to do with the life insurance companies we had," says Butler. "In fact, they competed directly against us and tried to take accounts away from us in Texas."

Butler met similar resistance when he tried to obtain customer lists from Lomas Bank in order to initiate direct marketing for life insurance. The bank made it clear after several meetings that their principal concern was the earnings they made from selling the lists rather than to whom they sold them. "In all my meetings," says Butler, "their attitude was, 'We're going for the best deal. If you guys don't pay the highest, you don't get the business.' So, we never marketed anything [to their customer base] to my knowledge."

Particularly galling to Butler was the lack of reciprocity. "They quickly took the ball and ran with it as far as marketing into our portfolio. We allowed them to market the mortgage company file with their MasterCard without charging them. But when it came time to give any of us access to their customers it was like, 'What is the best deal? Who is going to pay the most?'

"It was not one for all and all for one. Their attitude was, 'We're doing our deal, and we're going to have our earnings. You guys do your deal and you have your earnings, and we'll see who does the best.' There was no real love between the life insurance company and the credit card operation."

Other Lomas companies experienced similar difficulties. Lomas Mortgage senior vice president Rex E. Masterman came from Advance in January 1983 to set up a second mortgage department. It was one of the mortgage company's first successful cross-marketing efforts. Prior to Masterman's arrival, Lomas customers who wanted a home equity loan were forced to find another lender. That, in turn, opened the door for customers to pay off their first mortgage. By cross-selling second mortgage home equity loans to Lomas customers, the second mortgage department added another mortgage product and helped prevent servicing runoff.

In January 1983, Rex Masterman came to Lomas Mortgage from Advance to organize a second mortgage department.

In 1987, however, when Masterman wanted to market other customer bases, he did not get far. "We were supposed to be able to sell Lomas products to insurance customers," says Masterman. "We never got the opportunity to do that. It never happened. They never gave us the list to cross-sell there. We wanted to take the Union [Life] portfolio and cross-sell for first and second mortgages, but it never happened. We wanted to cross-sell the Lomas Bank card portfolio, and that never happened."

Senior management responded cautiously to the challenge of integrating entities. Each of the new divisions in fiscal 1988 performed remarkably well. Their net operating contributions exceeded initial forecasts, with $41.9 million by the credit card unit, $35.6 million by the commercial leasing division, and $24.7 million by the life insurance group. Forging the subsidiaries into a united financial institution without impairing corporate earnings required a delicate sense of balance.

On December 28, 1987, Jess Hay prepared a memorandum that addressed the lack of unity and failure to implement corporate goals. It called for the formation of an ad hoc committee composed of senior executives from each division under the chairmanship of John Tolleson. Leading Hay's agenda was a call for actions that would "move L&N away from its current status as a loose confederation of operating divisions toward a more cohesive, comprehensive financial institution." A second objective focused on resolving problems associated with cross-selling. A third agenda item called for strategies that would accomplish "full integration of our customer outreaches within the next three years."

The ad hoc committee recommended in February 1988 the formation of a permanent Executive Management Committee that "will function as the senior advisory group to the Chief Executive Officer." It also called for the formation of an Executive Marketing Committee "that has the responsibility to coordinate, monitor and facilitate the cross-selling efforts of L&N." Hay approved the recommendations. The committee approach was a departure from the direct, hands-on management style the CEO typically used. He was confident, however, that unity would evolve over a three-to-four-year period without disrupting the demonstrated profitability of the new operating divisions. Unfortunately, as it turned out there wasn't enough time to test this strategy.

Initially, the attempt to coordinate marketing through a high-level committee accomplished little. The Executive Marketing Committee's most memorable success was the development of four statement stuffers to help cross-sell various Lomas products. The stuffers were linked by an 800 number to Lomas Telemarketing, a department originally created by Tolleson as a vehicle for selling MNet bank products and services. In 1988, Telemarketing shifted its focus toward the retail products at Lomas. Former Lomas Bankers Corp vice president Susan Sumner, who managed Lomas Telemarketing, remembers the training program as a "screaming nightmare." Teaching her staff the components of 18 different products was challenging enough. Compounding the difficulty was the fact that "there was no one directly responsible for communicating information back to us from any of the companies.

"The reality of the situation," says Sumner, "was there were too many chiefs. There was no clear direction, and the communication lines were foggy. My perception was there were four different companies, and they didn't blend."

The inability to blend was, in fact, the Marketing Committee's greatest failure. Lomas executive vice president David H. Farr, an expert on corporate development and human interaction, closely followed the events of that period. According to Farr, the marketing committee lacked the kind of leadership that had the power and authority to unify different groups. Instead, it was organized "the way you organize a church committee: 'You all get together and work it out.' You can't have integrative leadership if you are pushing your own agenda. It requires corporate leadership that is relatively 'agendaless' except on behalf of the whole. They were a good group. There wasn't anybody on the committee that wasn't a good person. But they couldn't provide the leadership to pull the group together. They were all scrambling for power, and that left a leadership vacuum."

There wasn't anybody sitting on top . . .

Viewed from the top, the committee's lack of progress made a similar impression on former Lomas board member Kirk McKinney: "They didn't meld, because there wasn't anybody in charge. There wasn't a concerted effort by one individual with a strong hand who had the authority to bang heads and put those things together. The mortgage company was going this way, the bank card company was going that way, and the life insurance company was going another way. There wasn't anybody sitting on top saying let's get this thing organized to go. And as a result nothing went."

Whether or not Lomas Financial Corporation could have attained a reasonable amount of cooperation among its subsidiaries and achieved its cross-marketing goals will never be known. Economic conditions within the company made that a moot point by 1988 and 1989. "The financial situation changed," says Richard Vague. "Pennies started being pinched. So the whole [cross-selling] effort didn't have any length of time to mature."

The financial situation changed . . .

The winds of change that forced LFC to abandon its course blew from an inhospitable direction. Fueled by an increasingly turbulent real estate market, they turned stormy. And when the full fury of the tempest struck Lomas, the company found that many of the pillars supporting its mortgage banking and real estate businesses had been swept away.

pipeline

Hay named by *Financial World* magazine as one of the nation's best CEOs

Jess Hay, chairman and chief executive officer, has been named by *Financial World* magazine as one of the 10 best CEOs in the country.

For the past 12 years, *Financial World*, a monthly magazine that claims to be America's fastest-growing business and financial publication, has sponsored a competition to determine a CEO of the Year.

To arrive at a list of candidates, the magazine annually asks several hundred securities analysts to vote for the chief executive officer they consider to be the best in each of 42 major-industry categories. This year, *Financial World* also sent ballots to more than 2,300 CEOs, asking them to cast their votes for their competitors within their own industries.

Those who rise to the top in the first stage of the selection process become bronze medal winners. Among the 42 first-place finishers on this year's bronze honor roll were Chrysler Corp.'s Lee Iacocca and John Akers from IBM Corp.

A panel of senior securities analysts and research directors — namely, the people who follow companies and calculate their potential on behalf of brokerage houses or the investment departments of financial institutions — then narrows the field to 10 silver medalists. Each of these is thereby a candidate for the magazine's Gold Medal Award.

According to *Financial World*, "The judges did not have an easy time coming up with the winner" because the competition was "so fierce." Evidentally, each of the 10 finalists fared well when put to the acid test that measured standards such as return on capital, net income and management of debt as well as the CEO's "sense of innovation" to inspire and motivate his work force.

Although Sam M. Walton from Wal-Mart Stores Inc. was ultimately proclaimed CEO of the Year, the magazine paid a near-equal tribute to the other finalists when it said, "It's no secret that all great CEOs share certain traits. More than just exhibiting self-confidence and a winner's mentality, they have an almost mystical ability to inspire confidence and trust in those around them."

The following article, written by *Financial World* staff writer Catherine Stevens, recounts some of the reasons why Hay was accorded silver medalist honors.

Doing Another Deal

Asked to define the type of company he is building, Jess Hay responds in his slow-drawling, Texas style, "Oh, I don't really know, and that's part of the fun of it. We don't know what we ultimately will be." Though his open-ended business strategy may seem more suitable to an untested entrepreneur than to a seasoned mortgage banker, no one can argue with Hay's consistent success as chairman and chief executive officer of Dallas-based Lomas & Nettleton Financial Corp.

"Since Jess Hay became president (and

continued on page 2

Stan Shellstrom vows to live his retirement to the fullest

Company gives him a gift that 'Sits him to a tee'

The whole Shellstrom family seems to like Stan's retirement gift. Shellstrom's daughter-in-law, Kathy (left); his wife, Betty; Stan and his son, Alan; try out his new golf cart from L&N at his retirement party.

Claiming he'll live his "retirement to the limit," Stan Shellstrom left L&N on March 31 after 36 years with the company.

You can make book that when he says he intends to "live it up," he really means it. Indeed, Shellstrom has penned a portfolio of plans — among them, reading the Bible from cover to cover and tracing art history back to the Renaissance — that would rival those that some people try to tackle in an entire lifetime.

But that's Shellstrom's style. Friends say he has an enviable track record of setting, then meeting, goals. Some of these, though, had humble beginnings. Although he retired as vice president of administration with L&N Management Inc., Shellstrom began his career in mortgage banking in 1950 as a supervisor of the night crew in the T.J. Bettes cash department in Houston. Labelling it "tough work," Shellstrom recalls he earned $1.10 an hour and "worked every night from 6 often until 2 or 3 in the morning. It was detailed — taking out checks from envelopes, checking off amounts on loan cards and sending checks to investors."

After four years Shellstrom became a cashier only to be named seven months later as manager of the cash department. He was promoted to vice president and head of the banking department in Houston in 1969. Two years later Shellstrom moved to Dallas and in 1980 assumed his most recent assignment.

Shellstrom said the growth in the company since his start has been unbelievable. "But one thing that hasn't been altered," he says, "is the quality service our employees offer in their daily duties and to their customers. There's a healthy, caring attitude L&N

continued on page 3

Symbolics names new board member

John Richardson has been named to the board of directors of Symbolics Financial Systems Inc.

The appointment was announced by Gerry Nelson, president of L&N's software subsidiary that is based in Richardson, Texas.

Senior vice president with The Lomas & Nettleton Company in Dallas, Richardson works in secondary marketing sales for the marketing and product development division of L&N.

Before joining L&N, Richardson was with Wells Fargo Mortgage Company in Santa Rosa, Calif., where he served as vice president and director of the secondary marketing activities.

Symbolics Financial Systems Inc. is a wholly owned subsidiary of Lomas & Nettleton. SFS develops and markets computer software for the mortgage lending industry. Products under the Mortgage Lending Control System include MLCS-Loan Production and MLCS-Secondary Marketing. MLCS operates on a range of IBM computer equipment from personal computers to large mainframe computers. ■

Pipeline carried the news that Jess Hay was honored in the April 1986 issue of *Financial World* magazine as one of the 10 best CEOs in the country.

CHAPTER XIII

STORM CLOUDS

In early 1986 the coming cataclysm seemed remote. One of the most pleasant notes that spring came from *Financial World* magazine when it announced in its April 1986 issue that Jess Hay had been selected one of the 10 best CEOs in the country by a panel of senior security analysts and research directors. It was a singular honor and clearly a laurel for Hay's leadership and the company's consistent growth for 20 years. The benefits that Hay predicted would accrue to an organization that subscribed to integrity as its cornerstone principle were confirmed. The award underscored Lomas Financial Corporation's long-held commitment to "profit with honor" and its successful efforts to achieve "an honored place in the financial community."

But even as Hay accepted the honor for leadership and corporate achievement, the economic forces that meant future trauma for the company gathered momentum. By the time Hay wrote the shareholders' letter for the 1986 annual report on August 29, 1986, the probability of a difficult year in fiscal 1987 was already evident.

> We are mindful that the year ahead well may be the most difficult one to confront L&N since the mid-1970s. Various storm clouds indeed do appear on the horizon. The overall economy is sluggish. The national deficit is chronic and seemingly beyond the reach of any real remedy, and many of our major markets today are plagued by very real and very deep economic disruptions. These conditions, coupled admittedly with some excesses from the past, have produced historically unprecedented delinquency and foreclosure rates and flat-to-

Hay's letter to the shareholders in the 1986 annual report anticipated a difficult year in fiscal 1987.

> declining real estate values in many areas of the country. . . . Thus, the environment, as we enter Fiscal 1987, is not as attractive as one might wish.

The tone of the letter suggests that the problems beginning to manifest themselves were cause for concern rather than alarm. After all, the company had a long history of negotiating the ups and downs of real estate cycles. What Lomas wasn't prepared to confront was a series of economic events that had no previous historical basis. How does one prepare for the unimaginable? But all too quickly for Lomas and others in the real estate industry, the unimaginable became a reality.

The series of events responsible for shattering the Texas economy and that of other oil-producing states during the 1980s was unique. "It was a confluence of forces," says economist Dr. M. Ray Perryman, "as unexpected and unprecedented as the mutual alignment of nine planets."

...a **confluence of forces.**

It began with a boom. The euphoria of rising oil prices in the late 1970s and early 1980s inspired a boomtown psychology that radiated a rosy glow of unbridled optimism. The Sunbelt was on a roll in the early 1980s. Chamber of commerce types referred to Texas as the golden buckle on the Sunbelt. While most of the country experienced recession in 1980 and 1981, one Texas newspaper article described the Dallas/Fort Worth economic outlook as "cloudless." "Recession-proof" was a term often applied to Texas. The prospect for future growth seemed boundless. And why not? The average price of crude oil pushed above $32 a barrel in July 1980. By the spring of 1981 the price reached an all-time high of $35.53 a barrel. Even when the price of oil began to dip later that year and then stabilize at about $30 a barrel, the confident optimism continued. The population of Texas grew by more than 11 percent between 1980 and 1984, compared with an increase of less than 5 percent nationwide. Unemployment in Texas was 6.9 percent in 1982, far below the national rate of 9.7 percent.

Despite the beginning of an oil glut in 1982, prosperity from the boom continued in a new direction. Banks that had prospered from energy lending searched for new areas to generate profitable loans. "They found their answer," says Perryman in his book about the Texas economy during the 1980s, *Survive and*

Conquer, "in a burgeoning real estate market buoyed by new tax laws that encouraged development almost irrespective of the health of the underlying economy. The savings and loans, flush with the excitement of the resulting runaway real estate spree and endowed with expanded lending capacity and powers courtesy of deregulation, were jumping into commercial ventures like there was no tomorrow. But there was, and we're still paying for it."

In the summer of 1983, *The Dallas Morning News* ran a story entitled "Lenders Rush Back to Real Estate." And rush they did. The three-year period of 1983–1985 was what Perryman calls "an all-out real estate frenzy." Driven by new tax incentives and wholesale deregulation, enormous amounts of capital created an environment ripe for excessive real estate investment. "There was just so much money available," says former LFC president Ted Enloe. "And developers will always build a project if they can get the money. They convince themselves that their project is going to be the best project. Everybody got bitten by the bug, and it wasn't just the S&Ls. The banks did it in a big way, too. It was a craze. It led to overbuilding and overfinancing. And a lot of the projects just made no economic sense."

People began to refer affectionately to the construction cranes that silhouetted the skylines of Dallas, Austin, San Antonio, and Houston as the state tree of Texas. At one point there was more square footage under construction in downtown Austin than there was existing office space. By the end of 1987, there was more empty office space in the Dallas market area than there was total office space in the central business district of Boston.

Paul Z. Pilzer, author of *Other People's Money*, writes that the new owners of S&Ls in Texas "were like cowboys out on a drunken spree after a dusty trail drive. The industry's new speculators poured tens of billions of dollars into ventures that had nothing to do with the thrift industry's traditional role, financing homes for people. One Texas thrift, Lamar Savings, announced plans to open a branch on the moon. Another opened a chain of barbecue stands. A third backed a speculative residential development that would have required

New tax incentives and wholesale deregulation helped create an environment for excessive real estate investment. A forest of construction cranes dotted the Dallas skyline. Courtesy the Trammell Crow Company.

building a bridge over a ten-lane Interstate highway."

The newly deregulated S&Ls had no commercial real estate qualifications. "They were grossly inexperienced," said former Lomas senior executive vice president Buddy Miller. "They had the ability to evaluate whether or not my credit was adequate to buy a house, but they didn't know shit from wild honey about a shopping center or an office building."

Among the new S&L owners in Texas who bought their way into the industry following deregulation in 1980, business practices were notoriously casual. According to Pilzer, it wasn't unusual for Edwin "Fast Eddie" McBirney of Sunbelt Savings, a Dallas S&L, to sketch out the broad outline of a loan on a tablecloth over lunch at Jason's Steak House and then turn the tablecloth over to Sunbelt lawyers with instructions to "paper the deal." Accounting and control procedures were also lax at Independent American Savings and Loan Association in Irving. One former executive quoted by *Business Week* magazine recalled walking through Independent American's offices collecting loose checks from desktops; by the time he completed his stroll, he had over $20 million in his hand.

The real estate binge came to an abrupt end in 1986 when oil prices fell below $10 a barrel and Congress eliminated the tax advantages on real estate investments. "The combination of falling oil prices and changes in the tax law," says Pilzer, "turned the real estate boom into a bust almost overnight. Before long, Texas bankruptcy courts would be playing host to such well-known figures as the Hunt brothers, heart surgeon Denton Cooley of Houston, and former Texas governor and treasury secretary John Connally." Before May of 1986, unemployment rates above 9 percent were unknown in Texas. Later that year they climbed to 11.1 percent. "It takes nerves of steel to be in this market," was the comment from one Austin real estate player according to a March 1987 issue of *U.S. Housing Markets*. "Market collapsed after mid-year," continues the report. "Sfd [single-family dwelling] inventory is so large no one has a handle. Low-end houses are discounted 5–6%; some throw in a Yugo. In $200–300 [thousand] range, some discount 25%. In one high-end northwest Austin subdivision half the houses are foreclosed. Almost no builder made money in 1986."

The news was even worse a year later, when *U.S. Housing Markets* reported the Dallas/Fort Worth "overbuilt market glutted with REO [real estate owned]. Companies stuck with houses bail out for any offer." In Houston, a first-time-buyer market for new homes was nonexistent. From Denver the news was equally dismal: "Bottom fell out of housing market in mid-'86 and is still dropping. FHA runs 8 pages of ads for HUD homes in Sunday papers. . . ."

The housing market continued to drop, and then the fall gradually spread to other parts of the country. By 1991, some realtors were grasping at the unlikeliest straws. *The Dallas Times Herald* business section reported the following news item on November 3:

> IF IT WON'T SELL, TRY PRAYING: Dallas real estate agents anxious to resurrect the area's wayward housing market can take faith. Literally. A California company is offering divine assistance in the form of a plastic statue of St. Joseph, the patron saint of family and household needs. Buried six inches deep near the "For Sale" sign, with his feet toward heaven and facing the street, the icon is said to ensure a speedy sale. . . . The tradition dates back to the 18th century when Spanish nuns took up the practice to acquire more land for convents. It's been revived on the East Coast, and the husband-and-wife team who started the company say they've sold more than 5,000 statues already.

The collapse of the real estate market in Texas and throughout the Sunbelt devastated Lomas Financial Corporation's investment in raw land. As it turned out, the decision to expand the company's real estate inventory in 1984, 1985, and 1986 was ill-timed. "Everybody in the real estate group, including me, thought that these were excellent, excellent projects,"

DeWayne Wommack, along with others in the real estate group, thought that expansion of the company's real estate inventory in 1984, 1985, and 1986 was a good idea. It wasn't.

The Lomas & Nettleton real estate division was slow in recognizing the depth of the problem.

says former executive vice president M. DeWayne Wommack. "And based on the market conditions at that time, they were. It just so happened that the timing was such that by the time we bought them and got the zoning approved and developed them the market had gone away from us, and we had spent millions of dollars getting to that point. The timing was absolutely abominable."

The timing was absolutely abominable.

The real estate division's recognition of the depth of the problem was gradual. "We were too optimistic from the standpoint of how short we thought the downturn in real estate would be," says Wommack. "We kept thinking that real estate would come back up in two or three years. But that didn't happen. It appeared to me we kept saying it's going to be another two years, and the two years kept getting extended." Lack of perception about the magnitude of the collapse wasn't limited to Lomas. "Everyone anticipated it was going to be a short-lived downturn," says economist Dr. M. Ray Perryman. "No one believed it would be as severe or long-lasting as it was. For that reason, it made sense for experienced developers to ride it out. That was the strategy that history would dictate. Had it been a cycle like the cycle in the 1970s, Lomas could have come out of it in very good shape. But the values just kept falling and falling. Liquidity dried up . . . so there was no one to buy the properties, which drove prices down even further."

The company's original strategy to grow its investment in land to about $300 million collapsed as completely as the economy. Instead of the quick sales and rapid turnover of property that the division enjoyed in the early 1980s, the real estate group suddenly found itself becalmed in a sea of land. Its inventory eventually grew to $600 million. As the market fell apart, so did large numbers of transactions already made. When land values fell dramatically many buyers walked away from their deals, and the land reverted to Lomas. The same thing happened even when land values held reasonably well: many of those buyers lost the ability to continue carrying their Lomas projects because of financial pressures from other real estate investments. "Why did we invest $600 million in real estate?" asks Ted Enloe. "The answer is we never intended to. About $280 million of our current inventory was a result of having to foreclose and in effect reacquire previously sold inventory. That's what caused the balloon. If we could have foreseen what has happened in Texas and now on a national basis, we certainly wouldn't have bought the land. Unfortunately, we were not clairvoyant."

The debt obligations associated with the properties owned by Lomas became a significant burden. Advances from LFC to the real estate division, Enloe says, amounted to almost $400 million. The parent company also arranged for the financing of another $200 million that the real estate group carried on its books. "And what does $600 million cost us?" asked Buddy Miller. "If our cost of funds is 10 percent, that's $60 million a year. And where does that money come from? It comes from borrowed money—debt."

The failure of the economy also devastated Lomas Mortgage USA (LMUSA). This was the second of LFC's businesses that experienced losses rather than gains, but here the losses went beyond dollars. Mortgage banking was the company's core business, the spiritual and financial center from which its other businesses evolved. For almost 20 years, its consistently profitable growth fueled the financial giant that Lomas Financial Corporation had become. It was difficult to acknowledge the fact that the business with which the company was most familiar was now faring so poorly. The external forces that hurt Lomas Mortgage revealed internal weaknesses as well. Fortunately, LMUSA had the talented and dedicated personnel to confront their problems, and by the end of the ordeal it had learned, in the words of LMUSA chairman Jim Wooten, how to "run the damn thing tight and right."

Retail loan production was particularly hard hit by the economic downturn. Weston Edwards' program for increasing both loan volume and loan quality rested on an expensive production network. "The mortgage banking business changed," says Ted Enloe. "Huge production networks were no longer profitable, because you couldn't deal with the wide swings in volume. If you build a network that's supposed to produce $4 billion with an infrastructure designed for $4 billion and then all of a sudden it's only producing $1.8 billion, your costs go through the roof. It became impossible to match revenues with expenses." Former vice president Ben Cotharin, who worked closely with Edwards when the housing market fell, characterized production expenses as "gruesome."

In order to reduce its losses, retail production began to downsize its operation—from over 100 branches in 1987 to 34 in early 1989. The reduction in branches and personnel, however, failed to stem expenses sufficiently. The net cost of originating single-family mortgage loans in 1988 exceeded 200 basis points, which was more than the price of servicing acquired in bulk from a growing number of dependable sources. "We couldn't afford to pay 2.5 percent for servicing," says Wooten, "when we could buy it all over town for 1.5 and 1.75. And that's what eventually led to the decision to quit producing mortgages on a retail basis. We let our costs get out of hand, and we couldn't seem to get them back."

The gradual reduction strategy was expensive. Executive vice president David Stephens estimates that the production operation cost the company about $14 million a year. One reason for the reluctance to kill retail production quickly and mercifully, as several senior executives recommended, was because the branch system was the marketing network through which Lomas had planned to implement its cross-selling strategy. By 1989, however, the shift in priorities

Changing with the times

Fort Worth Star-Telegram / CAROLYN BAUMAN

Jess Hay says Lomas has "achieved enough diversification to remain competitive in any economic environment.'

Lomas tries to recapture prominence

BY MITCHELL SCHNURMAN
Fort Worth Star-Telegram Dallas Bureau

DALLAS — Jess Hay, who has made a national name in mortgage banking and Democratic politics, is fond of saying, "Today is not forever."

That longer view is especially helpful now, as Hay tries to return his company, Lomas Financial Corp., to the kind of prominence — and profits — it once enjoyed.

Hay already has directed a major makeover at the $1.2 billion company. He has turned what was once the country's largest mortgage-banking firm into a diversified company with revenues from commercial leasing and credit card processing that surpass its former core business.

But Hay's efforts, including a painful downsizing of Lomas' mortgage banking operation 10 months ago, haven't bowled over Wall Street.

Since September, the Dallas company's stock price has fallen roughly 40 percent, and investors still seem concerned about higher interest rates, Texas foreclosures and Lomas' ability to manage its newly diverse operations.

"It's clear we haven't recovered as rapidly as we'd hoped," said Hay, Lomas' chairman and chief executive officer. "But we've come a long way in the past four years. We've achieved enough diversification to remain competitive in any economic environment."

Lomas' evolution is notable because the company elected to de-emphasize the core business — mortgage banking — that had spurred it to 22 straight years of profits and consistent double-digit growth rates.

The profit streak ended this year, when soaring foreclosure and bankruptcy rates saddled Lomas with a net loss of $56.3 million.

In light of the Southwest's real estate troubles, Lomas' decision to diversify seems a simple one. But the company began looking at ways to spread its bets in 1981, long before Texas real estate started to sour.

Lomas accelerated its strategy in late 1985, because large, deep-pocketed competitors such as Citicorp and General Motors Corp. had targeted the mortgage banking business in a big way.

Citicorp Mortgage now holds the No. 1 position in the industry, with a portfolio almost twice as large as that of Lomas. And GMAC Mortgage Co., a GM unit, has leapfrogged past Lomas by acquiring a host of other mortgage banking firms.

"We couldn't isolate ourselves with just one product," said Hay, a former practicing lawyer who has headed Lomas for 24 years. "These new competitors could have hurt us very quickly and very badly."

So from Dec. 30, 1985, to June 30, 1987, Lomas acquired a commercial leasing company in San Diego, a credit card services firm in Dallas and life insurance companies in Little Rock, Ark., and Indianapolis.

The total price tag: $700 million in stock and cash.

The result: "Lomas is no longer just a mortgage banking company," said Frank Anderson, an analyst at Stephens Inc., a brokerage in Little Rock. "It's a financial services company now. It's like a stool with six legs — and four of them are doing pretty well."

Lomas' strong operations are commercial leasing; retail banking (largely credit card servicing); short-term loans, primarily for construction; and its life insurance business.

The laggers are Lomas' real estate development arm, which has about 65 percent of its assets in Texas, and the company's traditional mortgage banking business.

Mortgage bankers, including Lomas, typically earn income from servicing home loans. They lend money for individual mortgages, sell the notes in the secondary mortgage market and then earn a small percentage for collecting and processing the loan payments.

The fees add up, especially when the portfolio is as large as Lomas', which totaled $23.5 billion on Oct. 31.

Hay said Lomas currently isn't losing money in mortgage banking — unlike fiscal 1988, when the business reported operating losses of $111.6 million for the 12 months that ended June 30.

But with foreclosures and delinquencies still high, and home sales dragging, the mortgage banking business is generating about half the income Hay expected at this time of the year — roughly $4 million to $6 million a month, he said.

A few years ago, such disappointing results would have devastated Lomas' bottom line. Not so today.

Mortgage banking now accounts for 21.5 percent of Lomas' revenues. Three years ago, mortgage banking accounted for 69.7 percent of revenues.

The change is not the result of falling sales; in fact, Lomas' mortgage banking revenue grew by more than a quarter in the last three years.

But the earnings and revenue from commercial leasing, life insurance and retail banking have helped to significantly offset losses tied to real estate, and they've given the company a counterweight to real estate's volatile cycles, analysts said.

Together, leasing, retail banking and insurance accounted for more than two-thirds of Lomas' $1.2 billion in revenues in fiscal 1988. Three years earlier, Lomas had no operations in leasing or retail banking, and the insurance sector accounted for just 6.3 percent of revenue.

In hindsight, with a clear view of the Southwest's real estate problems, analysts

(More on LOMAS on Page 2)

Lomas Financial Corp.

Business — One of country's largest mortgage banking firms, with major interests in commercial leasing, retail banking and life insurance.
Headquarters — Dallas.
Employees — 4,751 nationwide; 2,461 in Dallas area.
Top executive — Jess Hay, chairman and chief executive officer.
Revenues — $1.2 billion for the 12 months ended June 30, compared with $632.4 million for the previous year.
Earnings — Net loss of $56.4 million for 12 months ended June 30, compared with net profit of $45.4 million for previous year.

SOURCE: Lomas Financial Corp.

Fort Worth Star-Telegram

A new look

Since 1985, Lomas Financial Corp. has diversified beyond mortgage banking, which used to dominate its business.

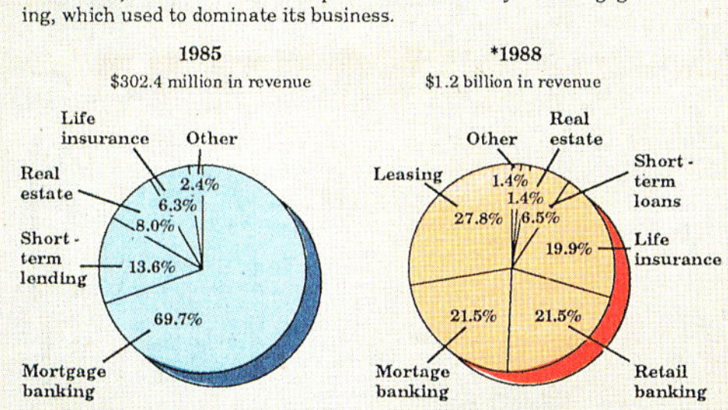

SOURCE: Lomas Financial Corp.

*For the 12 months ending June 30

Fort Worth Star-Telegram / DON COOK

The front page of the *Fort Worth Star-Telegram* business section for Sunday, January 1, 1989, reflected that Lomas was "Changing with the times" with a change to a smaller, scaled-back production network. Reprinted with permission of the *Fort Worth Star-Telegram*.

Henry Hortenstine, along with David Stephens, met privately with Jess Hay to present their views about why the scaled-back production network was not working.

was such that cross-marketing was no longer a viable option for the company.

There were other reasons as well. Proud of a mortgage banking tradition that included retail production since 1894, the company found it difficult to admit failure. The fact that many senior executives had built highly successful careers in mortgage production didn't make the task any easier. "Lomas was one of the first in the [mortgage banking] business," says Stephens. "We had a system we had built over many, many years which has been emulated by many others, and we were reluctant to get out completely. Our mortgage business was oriented toward production. The leaders of the firm had always been production people."

By early 1989 it was apparent that the smaller, scaled-back production network was not working. Senior executives attended a series of meetings in the spring of 1989 to resolve the problem. Paul Low and Gary Kell favored maintaining a production presence. Jim Wooten wanted one, too, but wasn't fighting for it because he knew it wasn't working. Henry Hortenstine and David Stephens were convinced by this time that they couldn't make it work and wanted to get out. "We had these meetings," says Stephens, "and we all agreed that this wasn't working and that wasn't working, but then Low brought up some side issue and we would leave not making a decision. That happened two or three times." Finally, the day before another meeting, Hortenstine and Stephens met privately with Jess Hay and persuasively presented their views. The next morning about 30 minutes into the meeting Low brought up "some side issue and it looked like we were going to get nowhere," says Stephens. "Then Jess suddenly asked, 'Well, is there anybody who wants to stay in the retail origination business?' That's the way he put it. 'Is there anybody who wants to stay in?' And no one said anything. Then Hay said, 'Okay, we're getting out.' Just like that. Final."

"After unsuccessfully attempting in fiscal 1989 (through the rationalization and streamlining of its retail system) to reduce the net cost of single-family mortgage loan originations," reads a 1990 company report, "Lomas Mortgage closed its network of retail mortgage origination offices in June 1989."

Damage to the loan administration side of mortgage banking was also severe. Widespread unemployment coupled with declining real estate values delivered a one-two punch that left LMUSA stunned. In the past, thanks to inflation and the appreciation of real estate, delinquencies and foreclosures had been a minimal part of the mortgage banking business. But when the value of property dropped below mortgage balances, the number of loan defaults increased sharply. "It was easy for somebody to walk away from a house when its value fell below the mortgage balance," says Ben

Cotharin. "Even though the loans were insured and guaranteed, the expenses associated with the foreclosure process were tremendous. The private mortgage insurance companies and VA changed their claims settlement practices, and we got stuck with the houses. Nothing worked to our benefit. The company was taking losses all over the place."

The FHA responded to the avalanche of foreclosures by issuing new regulations about the amount of counseling and loan restructuring a servicer had to perform. This, in turn, further slowed the foreclosure process and escalated costs for mortgage companies.

To make matters worse, Lomas wasn't prepared for this unprecedented turn of events. "Part of it was our fault," says Enloe. "We got behind, and we had stacks of loans down there that we weren't really handling expeditiously. It was costing us money, but we couldn't pass that on to the investor because it was our fault. We couldn't charge him for our dereliction in servicing. We found that on FHA loans instead of losing $1,800 for each one [on the foreclosure process], we were losing $3,400."

Losses from Lomas' VA portfolio were even worse. "The most damaging development," Wooten explained in a 1988 speech, "has been the change made by the VA, in contradiction to a policy of some 40 years, of turning the foreclosed VA loan property over to the lender instead of paying the loan balance and the accrued interest claims. This is the so-called VA No-Bid. The VA has awarded the property to the lender in over 45 percent of the foreclosures." More often than not, the value of the property plus the guaranty paid by the VA failed to cover the debt. "As a result of the VA no-bids," says executive vice president Bryard Poer, "mortgage bankers were stuck with REOs. Lomas lost between $20,000 and $30,000 on each property they sold."

The traumatic effect of these events was expressed in a company report:

> The years 1985 through 1987 produced a staggering 1.4 million bankruptcies in this country, of which 91,000 were in Texas and the balance disproportionately concentrated in the nation's other oil producing states. The economic conditions reflected by these bankruptcies also produced the highest rate of single-family mortgage foreclosures in the history of modern mortgage banking.
>
> The wave of foreclosures began in 1986 and peaked in 1987, overwhelming the administrative systems and personnel of the VA, the FHA, private mortgage insurance companies and mortgage bankers throughout the country. Lomas was no exception, and as a consequence, the division's operating results were adversely affected in Fiscal 1987, devastated in Fiscal 1988, and again negatively affected in Fiscal 1989.

The company's failure to respond quickly and decisively to the mortgage division's problems proved costly. "Bottom line, the process got away from us," says former executive vice president William Glasgow, Jr., whose role as the top servicing administrator at Lomas Mortgage gave him an ideal vantage point on the events of the period. "We lost control. And that was not tied to any one individual's contribution or lack thereof. It was tied to a company that lost the focus on its core business. As great a company as it was, there was a breakdown in a lot of areas." Lomas Mortgage's long preeminence contributed to its lack of focus. Like other large, dominant institutions, LMUSA had become sluggish and complacent, and that led to a loss of accountability.

> ... there was a breakdown in a lot of areas.

One of the most destructive and deep-rooted problems in the corporate culture was the casual attitude toward financial control. Former senior executive vice

In March 1987, the company became serious about control and hired David Stephens as its first professional auditor.

Jim Pickup demanded accountability from the mortgage division's servicing system during the early 1980s. He exercised strong control while he was in charge of regional coordination.

president Terry Klein's emphasis on customer satisfaction contributed to the disregard for fiscal responsibility. "There was no discipline in the financial area," says senior vice president Patricia A. Gardino. "Terry was so customer-oriented that he did not want to tighten up the escrow analysis system because that would cause the customer to be unhappy. Terry was very lax about enforcing our escrow policies. His first priority wasn't making money; it was making customers happy."

Leniency on money matters, however, predated Klein. After almost two decades of routine profitability and an abundance of cash, monetary concerns for the most part were not a high priority. "Excess money takes away the discipline of real bottom line management," says Wooten. "It gives you an opportunity if you use it right, but it can also lead you down the wrong path. We got very sloppy in managing our cash. This company decided that the escrow funds we advanced to pay mortgagors' taxes wasn't any big thing. We've got plenty of money. So, let's give them four years to pay us back the $1,000 we had to advance. The first thing you know, we look around and we've got $40 million of the company's money out on a nonearning basis."

Terry Klein recalls an example of his colleagues' relaxed attitude at an audit committee meeting he attended before his departure in 1986: "It seems that the Central Region had gotten an unacceptable rating in the banking and shipping area for the fourth consecutive audit. I suggested that the audit be circulated, not as a public pillorying but as a way of saying, 'Gentlemen, we need to correct this.' And I was told, 'No. We never publish audits. We file them.' That was indicative of the company's laissez-faire attitude towards control. And that cost Lomas a lot of money."

The company became more serious about control in March 1987 when it hired its first professional auditor, David C. Stephens. Prior to that, auditors "were people that had been in the production operation," says Stephens. "The company just anointed them 'auditors' and told them to check the other production guys."

The mortgage division's rapid growth during the

1980s also contributed to a loss of accountability. Executive vice president Bryard D. Poer recalls the high level of oversight that former executive vice president Jim Pickup had exercised over a smaller portfolio when he was in charge of regional coordination. On a monthly basis, Pickup questioned regional managers about delinquent status report loans—loans that had five or more payments due and were not in foreclosure. "The regional managers had to be prepared to answer any question about any loan on that report," says Poer. "You had to be able to tell Jim Pickup why a particular loan was not in foreclosure. He remembered what you told him, and he might pick the same loan a month later to see if your story changed. When Jim Pickup retired, that kind of accountability walked out the door with him."

The budgeting process also increased the company's difficulties. Profit goals came from senior management. When things were going well, division budgets met their targets. But when the economy soured, the servicing departments that couldn't hit their assigned goals constricted operations. This impaired the quality of service they provided at a time when outside pressures demanded an operations expansion. These events, according to one LMUSA executive, weakened loan administration's systems and "created long-term damage in order to solve a short-term problem." Pat Gardino says there were a few servicing managers who identified their escalating problems but failed to attract senior management's attention: "There was no real understanding or even an attempt to get an understanding. We were told, 'Here's the bottom line number we want. Make it happen.' No one took the time to understand why it couldn't be that number."

Corporate growth also reduced the effectiveness of Jess Hay's management. When Lomas was smaller, Hay's direct, hands-on style was particularly effective. But as the company expanded, those tight reins loosened somewhat. "When Weston Edwards came in to run retail loan production, he reported to Jess," says former executive vice president Donald Funkhouser. "Terry Klein reported to Jess. The marketing organization reported to Jess. So there really wasn't one person running the mortgage company other than Jess. And that was at the same time he was doing the acquisitions. So, even though he worked seven days a week, 18 hours a day, he was stretched pretty thin."

Bill Glasgow, who spent 20 years with the company, also believes it was a difficult assignment for one individual: "Jess Hay is one of the most honorable, respected men I have met or will ever likely meet, but he needs to delegate authority to people who will be respected in their own right. One single human being cannot control and should not even attempt to control every major decision that takes place in a company like Lomas."

Lomas may have had little control over the rising wave of foreclosures and REOs, but its failure to perceive the trend and respond more quickly was lamentable. Much depended on the vigilance of the company's accounting and control functions. Although Hay doesn't "fault our accounting people" and suggests instead that "all of us should have been more inquiring and picked up on it sooner than we did," others are less charitable. Even the company's chief financial control officer, former executive vice president David Kelly, Jr., admits that there were "rough spots and gaps" in the link between servicing information and general ledger accounting information. "They are two separate systems," says Kelly, "that didn't always communicate accurately." Pat Gardino is more blunt: "We didn't have the right bean counters in place. There's no excuse why accounting didn't recognize the problems and take them to Mr. Hay. Why didn't our internal auditors catch it? The

Nobody was minding the store from an accounting standpoint.

The company's chief financial control officer, David Kelly, admitted that there was a lack of accountability between servicing information and general ledger accounting information.

Bill Glasgow brought the problem of insufficient reserves to the attention of senior management at a luncheon meeting with Jess Hay in early 1987.

foreclosure receivables should never have been allowed to get that high, nor should the red escrows have been allowed to get that high. But nobody was minding the store from an accounting standpoint."

Bryard Poer, who served as a regional servicing manager and then regional servicing coordinator during this period, agrees that there was poor coordination between the general ledger and servicing system. He points out, however, that all the status reports, portfolio summaries, and statistics needed to confirm the growing trend were available: "Nobody was paying attention to the damn dollars. It was as simple as that." Former loan administration manager Bill Glasgow concurs. The trends occurring in the mortgage company, he says, were "pretty much in full view."

It was Glasgow, in fact, who brought the problem to the attention of senior management, an act requiring no small amount of courage according to former executive vice president David Farr: "People at Lomas are very reluctant to take bad news to Jess Hay. And around this issue, they really were." Glasgow had little such reluctance. "I have a lot of respect for Bill," says senior vice president Tom H. Carter, "because of his knowledge of our business and because of his tenacity to get things done. He isn't one of these aloof managers that stays back at arm's length. If there's a problem, he's willing to roll up his sleeves and dig into it. His intensity was unbelievable. If a problem came to the surface, he'd stay on it until he was sure it was either dead or fixed." That kind of intensity served Glasgow well in solving servicing problems, but his incendiary personality alienated people. One former colleague claims, "He had an ego he couldn't live with, nor could anyone else. He always had to win—highly competitive and extremely aggressive." "Bill was very confrontational," says Pat Gardino. "Everything Bill did involved conflict. He made everything a battle."

For 20 years Glasgow had wound his way up through the ranks of L&N's loan administration division. Glasgow was the heir apparent to head loan administration after Terry Klein's departure in October 1986, but before his official appointment in July 1987, he first served an "apprenticeship" for eight months. Alarmed at the escalating numbers he saw, Glasgow tried to calculate the potential losses from foreclosures and REOs and what that might mean in terms of setting reserves for the company. "One didn't necessarily branch out and start dabbling in accounting matters," says Glasgow about his attempt to get a handle on the company's growing problem. "I wasn't trained to do it, I wasn't expected to do it, but I sat down after Terry left and said, 'Let me see if I can come up with an estimate.' And I came up with about $18 million."

Bryard Poer, who worked closely with him, remembers this departure from Glasgow's normal servicing responsibilities: "Bill Glasgow was the man that put a pencil to the reserves and made the recommendation to Jess Hay to increase the reserves in order to cover the losses that were coming down the road. I didn't think about it at the time, but I've thought about it since then. Why should Glasgow be the one that had to convince Jess that the reserves were insufficient? It should have been the accounting folks that were convincing Jess."

Glasgow took the opportunity to persuade Hay at a meeting in February or March of 1987. It was the kind of small, "state-of-the-union" meeting for which Hay is famous, says David Farr. Farr attended the informal session along with senior vice president and secretary Ramona Taylor. They met at the ServiceCenter in what had been Terry Klein's large corner office on the fourth floor, now occupied by Glasgow. The open-ended, how-are-things-going luncheon discussion gave Glasgow the opportunity to drop his bombshell: "Jess was sitting in my office having lunch with Ramona Taylor. I'll never forget it, because I thought it was time to shoot the messenger. According to my rough calculations, our loan loss reserve for that year could easily come in at around $18 million, and we were not reserving anywhere close to that. So, I broke the news to Jess. We went back and forth, assessing the potential impact on the company, and Jess was prudent enough to go back and get people like David Kelly to take a closer look at the situation. And so we posted an additional reserve."

Although Farr's knowledge of loan administration was limited, his impressions about the meeting were vivid. The friendship and close professional association with Hay gave him a unique perspective. "Bill started telling Jess about the REO and foreclosure issues," says Farr, "and all of a sudden I noticed Jess turned deathly white, and I'd never seen Jess do that before. My impression at the time was this information should have been reported far, far earlier. Jess' reaction was one of shock. He got very, very quiet. The tone of the meeting changed. And my memory is that the meeting sort of ended. And Jess said, 'Well, we've got a major problem. I'll get back to you on that.' I wasn't even following the content of the conversation. I just knew something horrible had happened. And subsequent to that, apparently David Kelly was asked to verify the information. That was the first major signal that the mortgage company was in crisis."

It's not a wheel squeaking anymore. The train was off the track.

Unfortunately, the report Kelly prepared for Hay failed to sound the proper alarm. Although Kelly's confidential memorandum indisputably confirmed Glasgow's fears about losses and the inadequacy of the mortgage company's reserves, it didn't go far enough, and it wrapped the bad news with an optimistic ribbon that undercut what should have been a stronger message of concern. The seriousness of the $18 million reserve recommended in the report was diluted by the prediction that "the worst is behind us." Entirely missing from the memorandum was any mention of the perilously high red escrow balance. The reserves the company posted soon after were later characterized by Hay as "grossly inadequate."

On April 20, 1987, Lomas announced a $25 million charge against earnings, $18 million of that amount to cover foreclosure losses. This resulted in a third quarter net loss of $4.4 million, down from net income of $14.5 million reported for the same quarter in the previous year. It was the company's first quarterly net operating loss in more than 13 years. The setback, however, was seen as a temporary interruption and LNFC's board voted to increase the quarterly dividend from 28¢ to 35¢ per share.

It was clear by the end of fiscal 1987 that the third quarter reserves earmarked for foreclosures were insufficient. Net income for fiscal 1987 declined to $45.4 million from $54.5 million in fiscal 1986. It was the first net earnings decline for a year since 1974 and only the second decline since Hay had assumed management of the company in 1965. LNFC's 1987 annual report attributed it to the $25 million reserve and "to increases in single-family foreclosure rates, which continued to worsen universally in the mortgage banking industry throughout Fiscal 1987." A Standard & Poor's report on Lomas Mortgage USA noted that "the foreclosure rate increased from 1.04% in June, 1986 to 1.86% in June, 1987. The numbers of loans in the process of foreclosure went from 6,500 to 12,000. The firm was overwhelmed by the sheer numbers that jump entailed." "It crept up on us," says Hay, "at a very rapid rate."

It wasn't until the problems afflicting the mort-

The cover of the 1987 Lomas & Nettleton Financial Corporation annual report showed a man calmly reflecting on a tranquil setting with a soothing beverage. The information inside and the "Net Income" financial chart stood in contrast. The foreclosure rate had increased alarmingly.

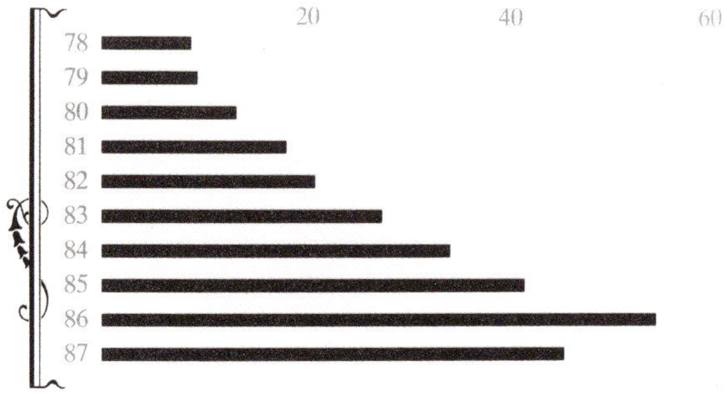

NET INCOME (millions of dollars)

gage company loomed very large that senior management shifted gears and introduced two dramatic initiatives. David Farr says that kind of "crisis management" represents the way Lomas responds to many problems: "This company has always been short on developing the structure and administrative staff they need until they have to. There is a procrastination about developing those things until the outside pressures are overwhelming." Those pressures were abundant by mid-1987. "It's not a wheel squeaking anymore," says former vice president Sidney L. Kelley, recalling the condition of the division at the time. "The train was off the track."

One major change was in leadership. On July 23, 1987, Paul M. Low was promoted to president of the mortgage banking division. Senior executive vice president Henry G. Hortenstine assumed responsibility for the mortgage company's administrative services, which included servicing. Bill Glasgow became the manager of loan administration. Robert E. (Bert) Byerley, Jr., was designated principal control officer for the division and Hal Hillman became its principal administrative officer. Former L&N president James M. Wooten was promoted to chairman and chief policy officer. Low, Hortenstine, and Glasgow directed their attention to the mortgage company's bloated production and management structure. Meanwhile, Jess Hay attacked the servicing problems through the creation of a special task force headed by David Stephens.

... the formation of a task force which we called Project Recovery.

The appointment of Stephens may have seemed a curious choice at the time. After all, he had been with the company less than four months and knew little or nothing about mortgage banking. Hay relied on Stephens' strong accounting, auditing, and organizational skills to uncover the problems and formulate a solution. The CEO chose very well.

Vice president Sid Kelley remembers the pressures of mid-1987.

Stephens discovered that it wasn't simply a matter of large foreclosure, REO, and red escrow volumes. There were also operational problems due to budget constraints and the centralization of servicing functions. He found the foreclosure department "woefully understaffed." Thousands of bankruptcies and foreclosure cases were in backlogs awaiting various legal and clerical actions. In some cases, delinquencies could be measured in years rather than months. "We had 3,000 loans a month coming into foreclosure and only 800 going out," says Stephens. "The 18,000 loans in foreclosure had been building for $1\frac{1}{2}$ years. We ended up having over $100 million in losses related to foreclosures."

The depth of internal disruption at Lomas was indicative of the massive turmoil that the mortgage industry was experiencing. Hay discussed these events in subsequent annual reports: "Along with the rest of

When Russel Young started the escrow administration part of Project Recovery with Tom Carter (not shown), they found that some accounts had not been analyzed for years.

the mortgage finance industry, our mortgage banking division since 1985 has had to cope with record rates of delinquencies, bankruptcies and foreclosures. The years 1985-87 produced a staggering 1.4 million bankruptcies in this country, of which 91,000 were in Texas and the balance of which were disproportionately concentrated in the nation's other oil producing states. The economic conditions reflected by these bankruptcies also have produced the highest rates of single-family foreclosures in the history of modern mortgage banking."

The escrow department also lost effective control over red escrows, the corporate money Lomas paid for taxes and insurance that was the mortgagors' responsibility. "Escrow balances were being overdrawn by leaps and bounds," says Tom Carter. "When Russel Young and I started the escrow administration part of Project Recovery we found accounts that hadn't been analyzed in four, five, six, and eight years. There was a red escrow report produced by our data system. Russel and I found out no one knew about the report. We asked, 'Where's your red escrow list?' And they said, 'Huh?' They weren't using the reports produced by the system. The person who managed the escrow analysis department didn't even know the red escrow list existed."

The REO department experienced similar problems. "Our REO inventory was growing monthly," says Stephens, "and we didn't even have a list of all the properties we owned. Some of the houses that had been in the department for over a year hadn't even been listed for sale."

The difficulties confronting the mortgage division were immense, according to Stephens' report to Hay: "The mortgage company had big problems, and we needed a lot of people to work this because it's a giant." Armed with the information provided by Stephens, Hay initiated the formation of a task force. "We were confronted with a fairly substantial problem," says Hay, "way beyond anything we had imagined. We saw the problem accelerating and growing and we intervened rather dramatically in July or August 1987 with the formation of a task force which we called Project Recovery. It was designed to address the growing foreclosure problems and to accelerate the liquidation of foreclosed properties. It was also designed to reduce the frightening growth of the company's investment in foreclosure receivables and in red escrows."

David Stephens may have coordinated Project Recovery, but it was the task force's creator, Jess Hay, who imbued it with the energy and commitment that ensured its success. "It was a very effective move on Jess' part," says Bill Glasgow. "It sensitized everyone very quickly to the severity of our problems. It created the first team of people to deal with the hemorrhaging of the mortgage company. All the stops were pulled out. Where we needed resources we got resources. It sensitized the entire company to the fact that this was something we all had to be committed to and work together on. And if anyone gets credit for that, it is Jess Hay."

Hay and Wooten drew up a list of individuals to staff the five designated teams. The group they selected represented the company's outstanding mortgage banking personnel. "The task force was peopled with our most talented and experienced people," says Hay. "The mortgage banking talent assigned to Project Recovery was about as good as we could bring to bear, and it was designed to be that way."

It required two years of intense effort on the part of the teams before the balances in the various accounts declined to normal levels. In the process, new operational procedures were developed that enabled the mortgage company to recapture control of its servicing problems.

Senior vice presidents Russel D. Young and Lawrence M. Rogers, as co-leaders of the escrow analysis team, developed stronger accountability and controls for this area. Escrow analysis on each loan was performed on a regular basis, and if a higher payment was required the team aggressively pursued it. "We designed a whole system of informing homeowners on a monthly basis that their escrow account had turned red," says Young, "and they needed to send us so much additional money. That eventually led to the decision to go to monthly billing."

Buddy Miller was brought over from short-term lending to head the REO team. Here, too, aggressive guidelines were implemented. Within 24 hours of acquisition the team performed a detailed property valuation and recommended a marketing strategy. Regional sales teams were responsible for listing agreements with brokers, insurance coverage, and property inspection. By April 1988, future REO manager and executive vice president Sidney E. Leake explained in a memorandum to Bill Glasgow why the REO team was able to sell Lomas properties *above* fair market value. "We are quite 'picky' about cleanliness and proper maintenance," Leake reported. "Trash and debris must be hauled off. The property must be swept, the carpet cleaned or vacuumed and the landscaping maintained on a regular basis. Curb appeal is very important. If putting a few shrubs in the yard or flower bed enhances the showing, we do it.

"By being more demanding we get more money from our sales, therefore, helping our recovery and minimizing our losses. We are always looking for ways to expand on this concept." In fiscal 1988 the REO team sold $55 million in property, and $21 million in the first half of 1989. The group's success prompted LMUSA to begin marketing its REO services to investors and other mortgage servicers in 1988.

Larry Rogers and Russel Young were co-leaders of Project Recovery's escrow analysis team.

The foreclosure problem carried with it the largest

volumes and the greatest financial exposure. Two task force teams were assigned to this area: the foreclosure submissions team focused its attention on streamlining the process for getting delinquent loans into foreclosure, while the foreclosure team applied its expertise to processing foreclosures with all deliberate speed.

Bill Rudluff made a contribution to Lomas which should never be forgotten.

Former senior vice president William H. Rudluff worked in both areas. Colleagues say his performance was exceptional. Former vice president Gus W. Voelkel, who worked closely with Rudluff during that period, says simply: "He got the train back on the track. Let's put it that way." Bill Glasgow remembers Rudluff's unwavering commitment. "Bill Rudluff took the responsibility that was given to him, and he managed it from sunup to sundown," says Glasgow. "He had good people working with him, and he knew how to manage those people as well as the process. He is a remarkable person. Bill Rudluff made a contribution to Lomas which should never be forgotten. He contributed more to Lomas in 1988 and 1989 than any one human being in the entire company, including Jess Hay."

Bryard Poer recalls the complaints about Rudluff over foreclosure submissions from the regional managers who reported to Poer. "If you spend any time around Bill Rudluff you'll know how persistent that sucker can be," says Poer. "He and Gus Voelkel drove the regions crazy, and they needed to be driven crazy. Rudluff and Voelkel were the most persistent members of the team. They discovered all kinds of stuff out there in the regions that the regional managers should never have let get by them."

Bill Rudluff was hailed by colleagues for making major contributions in 1988 and 1989.

Rudluff's reorganization of the foreclosure department, which he took over in October 1987, was his most considerable achievement. Working his way through a complicated matrix of legal and clerical procedures, Rudluff established standard time frames for accomplishing each event governing the foreclosure process for each of the 50 states. "I said it should be accomplished within this period of time," Rudluff recalls, "and it was possible to do it within that period of time. It was probably an ideal standard and my staff might miss it occasionally, but I held them to it as close as possible."

He eliminated competing priorities among the various tasks by placing the process on an assembly line basis. Staff members were responsible for a specific task. The department quickly realized benefits in terms of increased volume and less time required to perform each function. "We perfected the time frames," says

Gus Voelkel, an old guard employee from T. J. Bettes in Houston, worked closely with Bill Rudluff to reorganize the foreclosure department.

Rudluff, "and things just started flowing the way they should flow. We reduced the age of a loan in foreclosure from something in excess of 20 months to an average age of seven months. It reduced our loss from roughly $4,500 per loan to its present $2,300 per loan. When you're foreclosing 1,000 loans per month, that's a tremendous savings."

Rudluff also corrected the slow movement of loans associated with bankruptcies. The attorneys representing Lomas lacked the aggressive spirit Rudluff thought they needed to move the cases through the bankruptcy courts. He hired a law firm to supervise the Lomas attorney network. "This reduced the average life of the loan in bankruptcy from 18 months to nine months," says Rudluff. "This alone resulted in a savings of more than $4.5 million in P&I {principal and interest} advances."

One of the most creative responses to the crisis was the organization of a small, proactive unit called Operation Opportunity under the leadership of Bryard Poer. This department directed its efforts toward pre-

Lomas absorbs a pretax loss of $202 million for fiscal year

"It (abandonment of mortgage originations, plus the sale of subsidiaries) is a step to firmer ground, from which we will be able to move more effectively and positively into the future."

— Jess Hay
chairman, Lomas Financial Corp.

By Dan Piller
Fort Worth Star-Telegram

Lomas Financial Corp. of Dallas, once the nation's largest mortgage banker, said it will report a pretax loss of $202 million for the year that ended yesterday, primarily because of a $253 million reserve set aside to cover real estate losses.

The loss is more than double last year's loss of $63.9 million, which was the company's first in its 24-year history.

Lomas has been hit hard by the real estate recession in Texas.

Earlier this year, it announced the sale of its credit card subsidiary, Lomas Bankers, to Merrill Lynch Capital Partners for $435 million. In 1988, it laid off more than 500 workers nationwide and cut its network of 60 offices in half.

In a letter to shareholders yesterday, Chairman Jess Hay gave details of the company's reorganization of its debt and operations.

Hay said Lomas proposes to reduce its consolidated debt of $5.6 billion by 62 percent by applying $435 million from the sale of Lomas Bankers, and the proceeds from the expected sale of its leasing subsidiary, Equitable Lomas Leasing.

The company has asked its principal bank lenders for a waiver of 90 days for compliance with various net worth requirements. During that period, Hay said, Lomas will revise its long- and short-term senior credit facilities.

Lomas' debt also will be reduced because the company no longer needs to borrow extensively to support its now-closed mortgage origination business, Hay said. The company announced in April that it would stop originating mortgages.

Instead, Lomas will concentrate on mortgage servicing, which is the process of receiving monthly payments, accounting for mortgage balances and interest costs, paying taxes and insurance, and maintaining escrow accounts on mortgages owned by others.

Servicing companies receive a fee amounting to about 1 percent of the principal value of the mortgage for such work.

"The servicing end of the business has always been more profitable than the origination," Hay said yesterday. "We simply got to the point where originations had become too expensive."

Hay said that Lomas' mortgage origination unit lost money at the rate of $4 million per quarter in the quarter ending last Sept. 30.

"This reality, coupled with rising interest rates and the related decline in mortgage originations, mandated the decision to discontinue the activity."

Lomas for years was the nation's largest mortgage banker, and it does about 65 percent of its business in Texas. With the slowdown in the Texas real estate economy in recent years, Lomas had closed several offices, reduced its work force and in the process dropped to number three in the industry.

It was not known yesterday where Lomas will rank after the restructuring.

Hay said Lomas is expected to return to profitability in 1990. When completed, the consolidation of the company and reorganization of its debt will reduce the ratio of senior debt to shareholder equity from the current 943 percent to 502 percent, and senior debt to total capital from the current 402 percent to 140 percent.

Hay acknowledged that the abandonment of mortgage originations, plus the sale of subsidiaries, "represents a strategic retreat." But, he said,

(More on LOMAS on Page 2)

Even though there were some savings from Project Recovery and Operation Opportunity, the mortgage company sustained large losses, as reported in the *Fort Worth Star-Telegram* on July 1, 1989. Reprinted with permission of the *Fort Worth Star-Telegram*.

venting loans from becoming REO property by modifying loan agreements favorably for Lomas mortgagors. Relief measures principally involved interest rate reductions. The unit also helped Lomas customers obtain second mortgages to reinstate loans that had fallen into foreclosure. Mortgagors found it difficult to believe when Operation Opportunity loan counselors called to tell them the company wanted to reduce their interest rates from 14 and 15 percent to 12 percent. "Many of our customers thought it was too good to be true," says Poer. "But they didn't understand the big picture. We weren't giving away anything. We were avoiding a tremendous liability on down the road. We targeted FHA and especially VA loans above 12 percent, and we kept enough loans out of foreclosure and the REO department to save the company $5 million in a two-year period."

Despite some savings from Project Recovery and Operation Opportunity, the mortgage company sustained large losses. Estimates are that the retail production unit lost $14 million for each of its last three years until it closed in June 1989. Exiting from retail production cost an additional $25 million. On the servicing side, foreclosure losses cost $21 million in 1987, $100 million in 1988, and $24 million in 1989.

Against this bleak financial landscape, Project Recovery offered an oasis of accomplishment. The task force demonstrated the company's ability to respond successfully to an unexpected crisis. Even more important for the long-term health of LMUSA, the project laid the foundation for a strengthened loan administration system by developing and integrating new operational guidelines. Those procedures became the backbone of a revitalized mortgage servicing operation, the core business around which the company would later reorganize.

Paul Low, eight days after assuming the mortgage company's presidency, initiated sweeping changes within the division.

CHAPTER XIV

"WE HAVE LANDED IN A DITCH"

While Project Recovery addressed the operational problems associated with a devastated real estate market, LMUSA's Low, Hortenstine, and Glasgow responded to the losses by radically restructuring the mortgage company. It was a sobering experience for the institution and many of the individuals associated with it.

Eight days after assuming the mortgage company's presidency, Paul M. Low addressed division executives with a memorandum that read in part: "Lomas & Nettleton's mortgage banking division has experienced lower earnings, and as a result, it is necessary to reduce the division's work force." The memo's matter-of-fact tone understated the sweeping changes it signaled in the division's focus as well as in its corporate culture. For a company that tended to protect its people in both good and bad times, the need for a work force reduction was an alarming admission. The high value Lomas traditionally placed on tenure, some claimed at the expense of usefulness, was one of the first cultural characteristics to fall. During the affluent 1960s, 1970s, and early 1980s, says former executive vice president David Farr, performance was not a singular focus: "Then the [economy] died, and we started looking at performance. The fact that you could now terminate employees on that basis was a norm-breaker for Lomas."

Coincidentally, the purchase of Equitable Life Leasing Corporation (later called Equitable Lomas Leasing Corporation) on June 29 had brought the total number of Lomas employees to just over 5,000. Too brief to celebrate, this high water mark of corporate growth quietly receded with LMUSA's August staff reductions. It was a small but definitive moment in the company's history. Lomas & Nettleton Financial Corporation crossed a threshold in the summer of 1987 as its focus began to shift from growth and expansion to retrenchment and consolidation.

Vice president Charles S. Werner believes that the speed and decisiveness with which the new leadership acted was the product of "a fairly intense budget meeting over a long weekend." It was clear from the income projections that "a number of steps needed to be taken urgently, and they needed to be dramatic steps." Declining revenue and a disproportionately large mortgage banking staff and structure gave management few options. "Downsize" and "restructure" became the two most important words in LMUSA's new lexicon.

It really turned this place upside down.

Henry Hortenstine and Bill Glasgow guided the process. The teamwork they displayed was largely a product of Hortenstine's ability to forge collaborative relationships. He was also intellectually strong. Senior vice president Tom Carter recalls Hortenstine's quick grasp of essential data. "He could sit down and listen to you talk about something he knew absolutely nothing about," says Carter, "and within a few hours glean a tremendous amount of high-level information from you. Then he'd come back to you two weeks later with some pretty damn good suggestions."

Both men also displayed a tough-minded management style essential for accomplishing the difficult goals they faced. "Henry was very instrumental in making some very tough decisions which led to gaining efficiency throughout the mortgage company," says Glasgow. "His focus was not just on servicing. It was on the total mortgage company." Glasgow also held an uncompromising attitude toward performance. In Bryard Poer's estimation, it represented a significant departure from that of previous servicing managers: "It was do or die. If you didn't succeed in your job, Bill Glasgow wasn't going to make a position in order to keep you." The former servicing executive also had the ability to unify his managers around the organizational changes that needed to be made.

Glasgow remembers his last two years at Lomas as one long struggle to cut costs. "If you look at the company starting about June 1987, it was a situation where we were trying to find additional ways to save the company from financial crisis. Henry Hortenstine and I, along with a lot of other people, worked day to day trying to figure out ways to reduce costs. From June of 1987 to October 1989, when I left Lomas, it was a process of downsizing and trying to figure out ways to reduce our expenses."

Two relatively minor changes in policy gave employees a glimpse into the future and management's shifting priorities. On August 6, 1987, Russel Young announced in a memorandum that the 37½-hour work week, a mortgage company tradition for over 20 years, had officially ended. All employees were now required to work a 40-hour week for which they were already being paid. Instead of working from 8:30 to 5:00, employees now had to begin work at 8:00. Former Lomas Administrative Services vice president Darlene Winchester (now Darlene Thimmig) remembers the complaints from many of her friends who had to fight the heavy Dallas rush-hour traffic for the first time. Resistance to the new policy, however, was minimal. The new president initiated the practice of walking through the departments at 8 a.m. to greet the staff. "Paul started walking the floors at 8:00 just to see who was coming in and who wasn't coming in," says Winchester. "As soon as he got off the elevator, the phones started ringing and everybody knew he was on the way. Never underestimate the power of the grapevine." Winchester also recalls the absence of a Christmas bonus later that year, another Lomas tradition that fell by the way. Employees found these changes jarring, but their feelings turned to fear when they realized that the shakiest ground of all was job security.

It was called a "reduction in force," RIF for short, and it became the phrase of choice for layoffs among corporations forced to downsize their operations in the 1980s. Clearly it was a euphemism, a public relations term designed to avoid something more offensively explicit. "I think layoff is a very hard term," says Russel Young, who as a human resources executive was deeply involved in the RIF program at Lomas. "None of us like to say layoff. Nor termination. Reduction in force does essentially the same thing, but it's softer. Lomas tried to convey the bad news as softly and compassionately as we could."

Although a compassionate termination is something of an oxymoron, David Farr believes LMUSA's straightforward RIF strategy was less devastating than a more emotional approach: "It was a rational process. We gave people lots of notice. There were no lies. No rhetorical meetings, 'Oh, we're so sorry we have to do this—blah, blah, blah.' It was very straightforward. We said we will work with you. We will help you. But this is it. And that tone got established here." Generous severance and early retirement packages also played a part in alleviating some of the pain.

The first RIF lasted from August 3 to October 31. An early retirement program began on August 3 and ended on September 30. The goal was to achieve a 20 percent staff reduction. Branch production clerical staff were the primary targets, although servicing also felt the effects.

Shattering Lomas' myth of invincibility and the protective environment it supported created genuine fear. Morale plummeted. "It was a very dark time," says Young, who uses the term "womb to tomb" to describe the nurturing corporate culture that existed prior to 1987. Layoffs "were contrary to the Lomas culture. There had been a family feeling, and although mutual caring and support would remain one of the company's fundamental values, many protective aspects of that commitment were going to change. It was very, very hard for us to do this and for me personally because a lot of my staff was going to go."

"It really turned this place upside down," Chuck Werner recalls. "We had no history of anything like this. As a matter of fact, the image that the organization had internally of itself was exactly the opposite. [Staff reductions] really flew in the face of that." When Tom Carter found out Lomas was going to lay off personnel he was amazed: "I said to myself, 'This is unbelievable.' I'd been with Lomas for 15 years, and I had been insulated from some of the problems other companies were having. That was the first realization I had about what was going on in the real business world. There was a lot of shock among the tenured employees in the company. I know I said goodbye to a lot of people that had worked for me or I had worked with for 12 or 15 years. It was pretty tough." "It was very scary," says Darlene Winchester, "because Lomas was known for mortgage banking. We couldn't believe this was happening. Lomas was such a powerhouse, and we had been making all this money. There were signs this was coming, but nobody really believed it was going to happen until the first RIF."

It was apparent that the kind of restructuring the mortgage division needed wasn't going to be accomplished with one RIF. In fact, the October 31 deadline became meaningless as reductions continued to shrink LMUSA on a more or less continuous basis. "A lot of people realized that this [the first RIF] was not going to get it done," says Werner. "There were going to have to be significantly more reductions. Central funding was hit pretty quickly after the first one. You could always find a pocket somewhere where someone was being affected. We had three and four and five amendments to the reduction in force plan. We just kept extending it. It sort of set up a feeling that there is no end to this. There was a lot of fear on the part of many people, even at fairly senior levels."

Despite the pain and dislocation created by the process, making a smaller, more centralized mortgage company was essential to LMUSA's survival. The task required two years to complete. Bryard Poer believes much of the credit belongs to Henry Hortenstine. "The most visible thing that Henry brought to the loan administration area," says Poer, "was delayering the organization. He was a big believer in no secretaries. He skinnied the staff down as far as you can to decrease unit costs and increase loans serviced per head. Henry had a good feel for the big picture. He was relentless at attaining goals." At the end of the skinnying process, the mortgage banking division had been restructured into a lean operation totally centralized in Dallas.

Senior vice president Pat Gardino was approached by Bill Glasgow to organize and manage national customer service, loan administration's weakest link.

Centralization provided the opportunity to strengthen loan administration's weakest link—customer service. It was the forgotten stepchild of Lomas' regional servicing system. Most branch managers considered customer service an annoyance, because it interfered with the branch's ability to improve its bottom line. This long-festering problem received little attention until the arrival of Terry Klein, and he made little headway in addressing the situation comprehensively before his departure from Lomas. Jess Hay focused his attention on the issue in the spring of 1987. "I've always believed," says Hay, "that service to your customers is at the heart of any business, and I also felt that the quality of our customer service had deteriorated. So we made a major effort to upgrade the quality of our service." There was also a long-term strategic reason for upgrading the department. Because of diversification, Lomas was committed to becoming a supplier of multiple services to its customer base, which at its peak totaled about 3.2 million.

. . . the premier provider of customer service for the mortgage banking industry.

When Bill Glasgow first approached senior vice president Patricia A. Gardino about organizing and managing national customer service she rejected the offer. She was skeptical about the company's commitment to the project. "Everyone says they want to deliver good customer service, but no one is willing to put their money where their mouth is," says Gardino. "When Bill Glasgow came to me and started talking about Lomas becoming the premier provider of customer service for the mortgage banking industry, I can remember chuckling and thinking to myself, 'I've heard that story before.'" But a month or two later when Gardino learned the company was willing to spend a half million dollars on a technologically sophisticated telephone system, she realized the effort was serious and accepted the position.

Others who worked closely with Gardino also understood that the company was serious about the changes it wanted to make. "I think there was corporate recognition that they were going to have to do something very, very radical," says former vice president Dana A. Call. "And they did. They didn't want the old Lomas thinking. They wanted a new way of thinking—a more professional approach."

It would be difficult to find a candidate more suited for the job than Gardino. Professionally nurtured in the rigorous Citicorp corporate culture at Advance, she was far removed from the old Lomas thinking. "[Gardino] is very methodical, very detailed, and very strong willed," says Call. "She's got a very strong personality but in a quiet way." Gardino's first encounter with Terry Klein at Advance illustrates the strength, confidence, and integrity upon which she built her professional career. The incident took place in the early 1970s, not long after Klein began working at Advance as a branch servicing manager. Gardino, in the course of her duties as a servicing vice president, wrote a report tracking the errors Klein's branch made in setting up new loans. When Klein saw the report, the six-foot-four ex-Marine stormed into Gardino's office, threw it on her desk and demanded she change it. "He said, 'I don't like your report, and I don't like the job you're doing,'" says Gardino, recalling the incident. "'This goes to my boss. How dare you. I want you [to look up the loans in the report] and prove every single error that you claim my branch committed.' And I said, 'Big boy, see that Lektriever [mechanized file system] over there? If you want them, you go find them.'"

Later, when Gardino moved to Dallas in 1984 to work for Lomas as one of Klein's senior managers, she demonstrated similar determination in overcoming an uncomfortable sexist situation. A couple of individuals in the division's male-dominated, good-old-boy mortgage banking executive network refused to recognize her presence. "When we got together as a group with the senior management, they'd go around and shake hands and greet people. They acknowledged everyone except me. I was the only woman in the room." For an experienced manager with a proven track record, she found the behavior insulting and unacceptable. Gardino devised her own affirmative action program. "I went directly up to those individuals, threw my hand out in front of them and said, 'Hi, Mr. so and so,' and forced them to deal with me."

That kind of tenacity stood her in good stead for managing customer service. Gardino established a sharply focused, well-communicated agenda that emphasized extremely high standards. What she wanted to achieve rested on a foundation of technology and personnel.

It took almost three months to find a phone system that could do the job. Gardino systematically viewed all the top vendors and visited various sites to see how each one worked before choosing ASPECT. One reason for its selection was that system's ability to recognize preprogrammed 800 numbers and alert customer service personnel with identifying prerecorded messages. As a cross-marketing tool, this was an invaluable feature.

A premier operation also needed a superior staff. High-school-level personnel filled customer service positions under the regional system. Gardino had the opportunity to hire a new staff and she used it: "Initially, we set very high criteria for our positions, not just a college graduate. We wanted individuals with 3.5 grade point averages and above. We wanted the movers and shakers, the go-getters." As it turned out, those criteria overshot the mark. The hirees' performance was outstanding, but they didn't stay long. "We went after the type of individual that we could not keep happy for more than three to six months," says Gardino. "They gave us more than we expected, but the high turnover was killing us. We had to readjust our hiring practices."

National customer service began operation on September 1, 1987, using a temporary telephone system. One month later, the new ASPECT system was installed and operational. Between September and the end of December customer service consolidated the mortgage banking portfolio and closed the branch system. Besides telephone customer service, the department also answered correspondence and queries from walk-in customers.

The money and commitment to quality paid off. "We completely cleaned house and started over from scratch," says David Farr, who helped screen applicants and train new customer service employees. "Under Pat Gardino's leadership the quality of the department changed in six weeks' time. The quality improved 100 percent from what it had been over the past 20 years, or even further if you take it back through Bettes."

A report on LMUSA by Standard & Poor's in early 1989 lauded the customer service group. "The firm's emphasis on quality service is reflected in the sophistication of the customer inquiry section where as many as 100,000 calls/month have been answered," the S&P report noted. "The unit's success can be measured in that recently the number of calls has fallen to 75,000/month. This emphasis on service is expected to pay off in reduced costs in the future."

Declining revenue bred introspection at the parent company as well. Lomas Financial Corporation undertook a self-examination and identified the general services provided by the company as an area where lack of supervision resulted in wasted corporate resources. This area was the last remaining bastion of the old decentralized Lomas. While the company was smaller and more prosperous, the financial impact had been small. Corporate expansion and declining revenue, however, altered its significance. The millions of dollars those activities cost now became very relevant.

Lomas was a very lavish company.

A relaxed attitude toward spending was a longstanding feature of Lomas' corporate culture. Years of financial success produced an environment largely unconcerned about the cost of doing business. "Lomas was a very lavish company," says former director of corporate communications Lou Duggan. "That was part of the culture that I walked into when I arrived in 1979. Whenever Lomas did anything they went first class, and that mentality permeated the organization to the lowest level, so that anytime anyone bought anything it was relatively expensive."

On January 14, 1988, Jess Hay announced the formation of a new subsidiary called Lomas Administrative Services, Inc. (LAS). Its purpose was to centralize the company's diverse services, rationally administer their operation, and curb the freewheeling spending practices of the past. Hay listed some immediate goals for the new unit in a memorandum:

> The elimination of wasteful duplication. The control of all capital expenditures.
>
> The establishment of an enlightened system for contract negotiations and administration, which should include reasonable requirements for review and approval by the Company's general counsel.
>
> Conversion of purchasing attitude to one aimed at obtaining goods and services from outside vendors at the best available price.

The establishment of this new entity was the company's first step in applying the brakes to uncontrolled spending. LAS "was part of an attempt to watch the money," says Jim Wooten, "to manage some of those things that had just been left to Charlie Brown or whoever. There was a need to manage the cash and our assets better. The idea was to build a structure under this [general services], have a cost center, and put it out on the right basis . . . to really see what we're paying for a telephone or for putting a new plug in the wall."

"Jess realized that we did not have control over the general services portion of the company," said former LAS president Buddy Miller. "Everybody was buying their own pencils. Everybody had their own copiers. There was no organization. That's what LAS accomplished."

Hay's memo announced Miller's selection as president of LAS and leader of the effort to control general services expenses. It was a good appointment. Miller's passionate commitment to Lomas over the course of his 18-year tenure with the company was well known. "Buddy Miller was 100 percent company," says former executive vice president Jim E. Nichols, who worked closely with Miller. "Everything he did was for the betterment of the company. It was always Lomas first."

Miller already had a reputation for careful scrutiny of loan performance as the manager of the loan administration department for short-term lending. "Buddy monitored all the construction loans," says Lomas Insurance Services senior executive vice president Ned R. Harris. "And he was really good at it. He always said he knew how the damn contractors could screw you, because he used to be one." Colleagues also claim Miller had a gift for detecting potential problems. "Buddy had incredible instincts," says Ted Enloe. "I always listened to him in loan committee [meetings], because when he smelled trouble with a borrower there almost certainly was a problem." Another Lomas executive put it more bluntly: "Buddy Miller could spot bullshit coming a mile off." As president of LAS, that kind of watchdog mentality served him well in supervising the administrative services necessary for the day-to-day operations of the company. Those included purchasing, payroll, building maintenance, mailroom operations, security, audio-visual support, and management of The L&N School.

Despite the intense efforts of Project Recovery, in early 1988 the mortgage company discovered, to its dismay, that the magnitude of the foreclosure problem

Buddy Miller was selected by Jess Hay to serve as president of Lomas Administrative Services, Inc.

Miller, center, had a reputation for close scrutiny of loan performance as manager of the loan administration department for short-term lending's construction loans.

had not been fully understood or quantified. "Our mortgage banking division was confronted with some heavy trauma," says Jess Hay. "It was reflective of what I call the deferred impact of the highest rates of single-family foreclosures and personal bankruptcies in the history of the country, which appears to have crescendoed in December of 1987. Then we had the unpleasant task of providing financially the reserves required to get the problem behind us." In mid-February 1988, Hay announced the results of an in-depth review of the mortgage banking division by its senior management: "They reluctantly have concluded that the only means through which the division might be restored immediately to profitability will involve a second major restructuring and downsizing of its operating units." A press release issued a day later explained that "the magnitude of the problems has been greater and the pace of that progress has been slower than had been anticipated. . . . Restructure of the Company's mortgage banking division and cessation of its homebuilding operations are expected to produce a nonrecurring charge of approximately $93 million to net income for the quarter ending March 31, 1988. This is expected to result in a net loss of approximately $69 million for the nine months ending on March 31 and projected net loss of some $55 million for the fiscal year ending June 30, 1988." The restructure resulted in a 20 percent staff cut, which decreased the number of LMUSA employees from a high of 3,600 in 1987 to 2,180, an overall reduction of 40 percent.

I think there was a reluctance to admit we really had a problem.

The board of directors that approved the reserves for losses was an overwhelmingly homogeneous group of successful Texas businessmen noted for their strong ties of friendship and long association with Jess Hay. "There was a feeling on the board that we were all in this together," says former board member Jon Newton. "We thought there were some events beyond Jess' and the company's control that were affecting the accuracy of the company's projections. There was not a finger pointing toward Jess or anything like that on the part of the board. I think we were all frustrated with the performance of the company and frustrated with the economy of Texas. But no one thought it was any individual's fault."

Jon Newton was a member of the board of directors that approved the reserves for losses in February 1988. The board realized that there were events beyond Jess Hay's control that were affecting the company's financial position.

The publications assembled into a package for members attending the Lomas Financial Group's national staff meeting held March 2–4, 1988, were the last collected evidence of "The Grand Lomas."

News of the restructure and additional reserves put a damper on the general staff meeting that the company held March 2–4, 1988. Past gatherings had been upbeat, unity-building affairs. Recent events, however, ruled out that kind of good feeling. It was an event rife with contradictions. Although the company's recent acquisitions were doing extremely well, the mortgage banking and real estate divisions were not. There was talk of expansion and cross-marketing the customer base, while what had been LFC's largest subsidiary focused its attention on survival. Paul Low laid out the situation in an apologetic yet defiant speech delivered on March 3:

The news has been bad. The mortgage banking business is a war zone. The battle is fierce, and there are many casualties. We are experiencing unprecedented foreclosure levels far and above my imagination. A challenge that the industry and our company simply was not prepared for. . . . It has been a very painful experience. It is not easy to endure the realization that 1,200 of your fellow employees and colleagues are no longer with us. It is not easy to acknowledge that we have slipped from our lofty position in the mortgage banking industry. It is not easy to take the financial losses that we have sustained because of current business

Jess Hay's ideas were reflected in a corporate advertising campaign in the spring of 1988, at the time of the national staff meeting. The positive record of the company's previous ten years, the bright future, and America always wanting to build its dreams were the threads running through the ads at a time when something positive needed to be said. The copy line under the logotype reads: "The nation's premier mortgage banking institution."

conditions.

In a word, we are under siege. But let me tell you something, we are not giving up on this business, and we are in it for the long haul. . . . We have set the stage for placing our company back in the lead. . . . We have started to build this company back into the highly profitable industry leader it can, it should, and it will be.

For those in the audience from the mortgage company, like Tom Carter, the contradictions were particularly glaring: "I recall the upbeat stuff, but I was discounting most of it, saying, 'This is b.s. We're not doing well. I've seen the numbers, and we're just not doing that well. And I don't understand why we're having this party.' They used to distribute financial statements for all the divisions, and I'd get a copy from Bill [Glasgow]. Production was losing a million a month or better. And I recall the return on investment at LIS was something like 3.5 percent. And I said to myself, 'Why in the world would I ever put my money in LIS?' I could go to the credit union and put it in a savings account and come out with a better return on my investment. I think there was a reluctance to admit that we really had a problem."

One large disappointment for those attending the meeting occurred on the last day at the closing luncheon in the Fairmont Hotel's Regency Ballroom. For a program finale, the company featured a film produced by The Richards Group titled "The Tapestry of Lomas," an elaborate 35 mm production of image, light, and sound. It was skillfully crafted to highlight the Lomas corporate family and leave the audience with a warm feeling of community and purpose. Expectations ran high, then collapsed as Stan Richards stood before an empty, white screen and explained that an electrical problem prevented the film's screening. The power failure that derailed the high profile spectacle was a depressing portent for the future. In fact, as events unfolded over the next few months, the tapestry that made up the Lomas family of companies began to unravel.

James Bray, vice president of Moody's Investors Service, coordinated his company's evaluations of Lomas.

The company discovered that its foreclosure and REO losses contributed to a loss of credibility with the outside world. Past assurances by Lomas that it had "fully assessed the magnitude of the foreclosure problem" rang hollow in the face of the large reserves taken by the company in February 1988.

It was a significant downgrade.

Moody's Investors Service, the well-regarded rating agency, was the first outside entity to publicly confront this issue and question Lomas' financial strength. One area of concern that Moody's had raised in discussions with Lomas in 1987 centered on increased losses due to the high rates of delinquency and foreclosure. A September 1987 summary report by vice president (now senior vice president) and treasurer Bert Byerley, following a meeting with the agency, indicates the company's high degree of confidence about the way it was addressing its mortgage banking problems. "They [Moody's] are particularly focused on the foreclosure and REO situations," Byerley wrote. "They need to understand that we have fully analyzed the situation, and have made adjustments to our earnings forecasts to cover losses which may arise due to working out these problem areas." News about the February reserves released on February 17, 1988, undermined the company's earlier claims and increased the skepticism among the rating agency's analysts. Moody's responded with a news release on February 18, 1988, announcing "that it has placed the credit ratings of Lomas & Nettleton Financial Corporation . . . under review for possible downgrade."

The blow fell on May 4, 1988. "Effective today," the announcement from the rating agency read, "Moody's Investors Service downgraded the senior debt ratings of Lomas & Nettleton Financial Corporation (LNFC) and its subsidiary, Equitable Life Leasing Corp.

(ELLCO). At the same time, Lomas & Nettleton Financial Corp.'s rating for commercial paper was lowered from Prime-2 to Prime-3."

"It was a significant downgrade," says Jan Konstanty, assistant vice president for Moody's at the time the release was issued under his name. "It reflected the stress the company was going through and was going to be going through." Former Moody's vice president James N. Bray, who led his company's relationship with Lomas prior to his retirement in early 1988, says the downgrade was one of several major signals to the financial community that companies that invested in real estate faced serious problems. A self-described financial conservative, Bray remembers thinking that management's pursuit of bold growth strategies had created serious concerns. "What stands out in my memory about Lomas," says Bray, "was I felt they were aggressive. It struck me at the time that we'd been in an up cycle in the economy, particularly for real estate, since 1982, and this was now five years later and the cycles tended to last about five or six years. And here we are going full blast with all the furnaces stoked up and the leverage going up. It just struck me that maybe this was not the time to pour more fuel on the fire. I think some of our reverses in recent years have been good for people. It reminds them that the world really hasn't changed. What goes up, generally, will come down."

Bert Byerley, who participated in discussions with the rating agencies, remembers the May 1988 downgrade by Moody's as a disappointment but not necessarily a surprise. "At the time, our mortgage banking division was having problems with foreclosures and REOs. So that was a concern to them. And our real estate was in the beginning of a very illiquid market. They felt like our overall borrowing and our leverage was too high. That was a concern of theirs and rightly so. With regard to debtholder protection, they were probably looking at our stockholders' equity, which decreased $93 million after we took the large reserves in February. Also, in this same time period, we saw our interest rates rise rapidly, which caused our cost of short-term funding to go up. So that was a concern of theirs as well. Moody's downgrade was clearly another signal from the external world that we had problems, and that was disappointing. But facts were facts. We did have problems."

On May 5, the day after the ratings downgrade, Hay announced to an assembled group of executives: "Together we have landed in a ditch; and together we need to pull ourselves out . . . cost savings are to be targeted throughout our system, and every employee is responsible for minimizing the Company's expenses." It was one of the first internal public statements from senior management acknowledging the severity of the situation. It also suggested that those problems had grown deeper and spread throughout the company. Previous measures had been confined to the mortgage banking company. These new policy changes applied to the parent company and eight of its subsidiaries. Only the recent acquisitions were excluded.

The tone and content of the announcement were uncharacteristically strong for Lomas. Two months before, at the general staff meeting, Hay had delivered a similar message in loftier terms, using a parable from the New Testament: "And so I want to hold before you with all the passion I can command my concern that we enhance our understanding of ourselves as stewards. This will mean that we take seriously that we are responsible, that we are accountable for what we do. . . . Stewardship is inextricably a part of sound management. As a practical matter, it is impossible to manage effectively without fully embracing the responsibility to be a good and effective steward of the resources placed in our care." Thanks in large part to the reserves taken in February, responsibility for good stewardship of corporate resources was becoming more urgent and less voluntary in May. "Accountability," Jess Hay stated, "would be enforced through periodic audits by the internal audit division."

Items both large and small were targeted for cost savings. Everything mattered. The company imposed a

Gary White became a "steward of the resources" in Hay's revised policies program, which targeted company expenses both large and small.

freeze on senior officers' salaries, limited increases for other employees, restricted corporate travel, and authorized no new hires "unless approved in advance and in writing by Jess Hay." The new policies also curtailed "the prior practice permitting liberal usage of [country] clubs," as well as eliminating the executive dining room, executive automobiles, car telephones, and parking spaces for Bryan Tower-based employees. Surplus company-owned tickets to athletic and entertainment events that had previously been given away would now be made available for purchase by employees. It seemed that wherever senior management focused on expense reduction it found vestiges of past excesses, including an oversubscription problem: "Subscriptions to newspapers, periodicals, etc. are out of control. No renewals for such items are to be made for the Company's account without Gary White's prior written approval. No reimbursement for any unauthorized renewal or new subscription will be made."

For Lomas, these were draconian measures. The new policy changes represented more than the curtailment of extravagances. They overturned long-held cultural values. Acceptance of these and other wrenching changes, all within a matter of months, was difficult for many employees. Their psychological dislocation was as profound as Dorothy's when she stepped from her storm-shattered house, gazed in amazement at an otherworldly Oz, and said, "Toto . . . I have a feeling we're not in Kansas anymore."

The world had turned for Lomas in other ways as well. The large reserves it took in early 1988 triggered deep concern among banks with credit relationships to the company. "Everybody saw the reserves we had taken in February," says Byerley. "That's when a lot of banks started asking questions and wanting more information about what was happening at Lomas." That, in itself, was evidence of a serious problem. "In the past, the banks didn't have to understand Lomas, because we made money every year," says vice president and assistant treasurer Paul D. Fletcher. "So who cares what we do. Now we're losing money, and they've got to explain to their management why we're having problems."

We had banks that said they wanted out of the credit.

Lomas could ill afford that kind of negative attention. The company depended heavily on its ability to maintain low-cost borrowing in order to fund the daily operations of most of its businesses. It was no exaggeration when John Sexton characterized the company's lines of credit secured by banks as "the lifeblood of our business." Over the years, Sexton's relationship-driven philosophy had built strong ties to those lending insti-

John Sexton's strong connections to large lending institutions secured Lomas' most important lines of credit.

tutions.

The strongest historical connections were to four of Texas' largest banks. InterFirst, Republic National Bank (later FirstRepublic), MCorp, and First City National Bank, Houston, were LFC's earliest and most reliable sources of bank credit. When Lomas faced a liquidity crisis in the 1970s, the financial strength of those lending institutions almost single-handedly sustained the company. Lomas, in turn, became their largest credit and deposit customer. When the energy and real estate markets collapsed in the 1980s, however, the effect on those banks was devastating. MCorp, for example, reported a net loss of $258.3 million in 1987. "The company's results reflected deteriorating asset quality during the first three quarters of 1987," that year's annual report noted. "These results are symptomatic of the economic recession in the Southwest and the effects of MCorp's credit exposure to the real estate and energy sectors of the regional economy." FirstRepublic and First City National Bank failed in 1988. MCorp filed for Chapter 11 in the spring of 1989. The demise of those once proud Texas institutions seriously hurt Lomas in 1989 when it once again faced a liquidity crisis.

The Linebankers Meeting that Lomas hosted annually in Dallas underscored the importance of its banking relationships. The last such meeting to receive front-page prominence in *Pipeline*, the Lomas corporate newsletter, took place on October 5 and 6, 1986. More than 125 representatives attended the event from 55 commercial lending institutions that maintained Lomas' $3 billion in credit lines. As the company's principal liaison with the banks, Sexton noted in the newsletter that "this year's meeting was especially important. It afforded a timely opportunity to demonstrate that, unlike many financial concerns headquartered in the Southwest, L&N has not been adversely impacted by the downturn in oil and the slowdown in the area's economy." One year later, Lomas could no longer make that claim. Two years later, the line banks lost that perception as well.

That change in attitude represented a potentially devastating threat to the company's carefully nurtured credit structure. Lomas initiated a campaign to reassure the banks and hold the credit together. "There was a lot of education," says Fletcher, who estimates he spent 90 percent of his time on the effort along with John Sexton and Bert Byerley. "We spent a lot of time explaining our projections, a lot of time explaining what the reserve meant. The information we put out was not doomsday. We said we had a bad year. We've corrected it, and we're coming back. So there was hope of Lomas bouncing back relatively quickly, but it took a lot of effort to keep the bank group together. A lot of effort."

Even so, the company's explanations failed to reassure a number of banks. Many of those wanted either to reduce their credit exposure or exit entirely. "We had banks that said they wanted out of the credit," says Fletcher. "They couldn't exit the credit until October, but they damn well were ready to exit as soon as they could get out of there. The number of banks that left

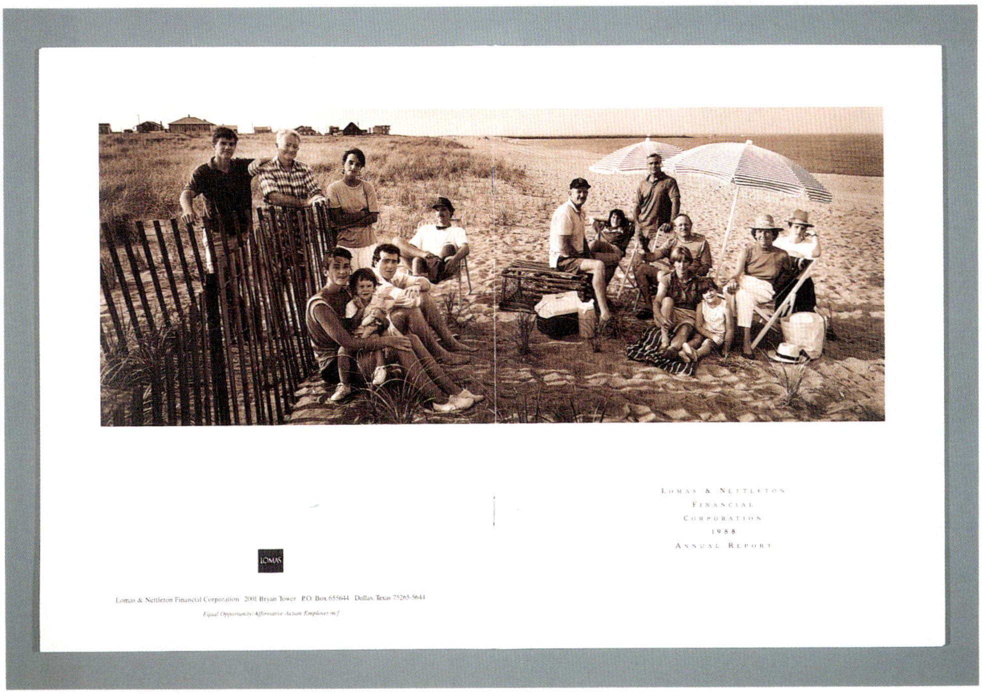

The somber tones of the 1988 annual report cover were a prelude to the bad news inside, which revealed the Lomas & Nettleton Financial Corporation's first net operating loss since 1965.

was a minority, but there was clearly concern in the total group." Although Lomas expended much of the goodwill it had built up over the years, Fletcher believes it gave the company an edge in getting through the "1988 time frame." However, the pace of deteriorating credit confidence quickened over the next year. From October 1988 to September 1989, LFC lost almost $900 million from lines of credit totaling just under $1.4 billion.

Predictably, Lomas' 1988 annual report contained little good news. Consistent with the institution's commitment to integrity, the most important and difficult news of the year appeared in the first paragraph of the shareholders' report:

> Fiscal 1988, for Lomas & Nettleton Financial Corporation, was a bad year and one productive of the Company's first net operating loss since 1965. During the year the Company established and charged to income $141 million in reserves, principally to cover projected single-family foreclosure losses and the estimated cost of restructuring and downsizing its mortgage banking division. As a consequence of this provision, operations during the year ended June 30, 1988 resulted in a net loss of $56.4 million, or $1.65 per share.

Management seized on the fourth quarter net income of $13.6 million to declare that the company's

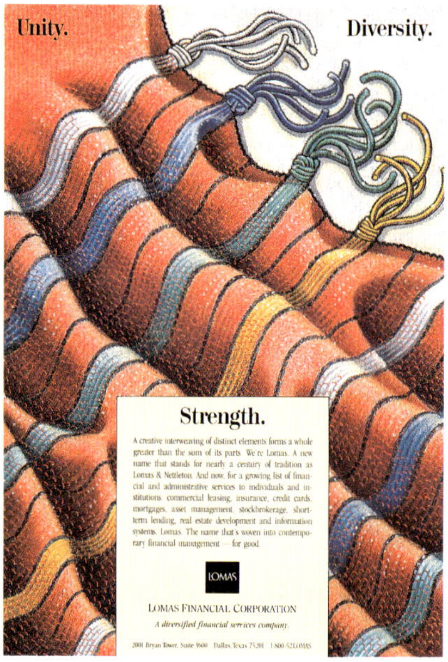

As the company's financial condition was deteriorating in the fall of 1988, it simplified its corporate name to Lomas and restructured its identity, dropping "Nettleton." To publish the new name, a series of ads emphasized the qualities of "Unity" and "Diversity," along with "Strength," "Harmony," and "Completion."

worst days were behind it. In *The Dallas Times Herald* of July 29, 1988, Jess Hay was quoted as saying, "We believe that the recovery will be sustained and that the fourth quarter's results clearly evidence the reasonable prospect of a good fiscal 1989."

Hay's annual report predictions for the coming year had been a reliable economic indicator for 21 years. But confidence in Hay's crystal ball began to falter in 1988. His 1987 prediction missed the mark considerably when he forecast mortgage banking's return to a normal level of profitability in the second half of 1988 and consolidated net operating profits that "will be at least the second best in the Company's history." In the 1988 annual report Hay estimated that net income for the next year would exceed $62 million. That prediction was lowered in October to between $46 million and $60 million. Even this proved overly optimistic. Corporate earnings for the first three quarters in 1989 totaled only $6 million. A February 7, 1989, article in *Financial World* claimed that Lomas Financial Corporation had landed in "Credibility Gulch." Hay admitted in the article that his 1988 annual report predictions may have been too optimistic.

Repercussions from Hay's soothsaying and the company's deteriorating financial condition appeared as early as October 1988 when investment banker Bruce Garrison, then of Lovett, Mitchell, Webb & Garrison, wrote: "The low predictability of Lomas & Nettleton Mortgage's [LMUSA's] earnings increases the short-term risk in the stock [LFC] and accordingly, we have placed it in the sell category." Caution and pessimism infected other apples in the Lomas barrel. "LNMI, which specializes in short-term lending to the real estate industry, is encountering an increase in non-earning assets," Garrison wrote in the same report. "We now rank the stock as a sell due to the lower predictability of eroding fundamentals."

The pressures being brought to bear on Lomas demanded radical remedies, and in late 1988 the company responded. "It was an overall feeling," Bert Byerley recalls. "We looked at the financial performance of the company. We looked at the foreclosure and REO debacle. We looked at the illiquidity in real estate. We looked at the rising interest rates. All those things didn't happen in one day. It takes time to assimilate all that. But over the course of time we realized we did have problems, and that eventually led, in November 1988, to our 'Vision' memo."

. . . a **strategic retreat . . .**

First drafted by Jess Hay on November 12, 1988, the document bore the title "A Vision for Discussion." It was highly confidential, with limited distribution among only the most senior Lomas executives. It established the seriousness of the situation in no uncertain terms, with the admission that the "remedial actions taken in March 1988 have not yet restored the mortgage banking division to a reasonable earnings base" and that "the net operating loss incurred in Fiscal 1988 and the related $100 million reduction in our stockholders' equity account have materially increased our cost of funding . . . and have resulted in a reduction of ratings on our debt securities to marginally acceptable levels."

The most radical measures that the memorandum "proposed for immediate implementation" included the sale of a 50 percent interest in 10 of Lomas Realty USA's current projects for $153.3 million. Also under consideration was the sale of a 50 percent interest in the Campus and West Campus properties for $85 million. Most extreme of all was the fourth proposal: "Sell Division VI [Equitable Lomas Leasing Corporation] and Apply Net Proceeds of Sale Principally to Reduce Corporate Debt. Reluctantly, we have concluded that this step provides the only means through which LFC's credit rating might be restored quickly to A or A+ at S&P and Moody's. Restoration of the ratings is significant to our long-term capacity to function competitively in the financial services industry." Reduction of corporate debt and restoration of the company's credit ratings took precedence over Lomas' diversification strategy. The measures in this memorandum pointed toward a company whose vision now focused on survival.

The "Vision" memo, however, remained an abstraction. Investment interest in Texas real estate was nonexistent, and initial indications of interest in the purchase of ELLCO reached no conclusion and then fizzled out.

By March 27, 1989, "The Current Perspective" (title of a memorandum from Hay on that date) was dismal. Hay admitted that LFC was in "a strategic retreat." The document concluded that "current operating pressures coupled with the prevailing interest rate environment make it clear that Lomas must reduce its debt, which at December 31, 1988, totaled $5.5 billion.

"The only way (i) to achieve significant reduction in our total debt and (ii) provide the earnings required in Fiscal 1989 to enable a major restructuring of our mortgage banking division is to sell our commercial leasing and retail banking divisions." The proposals in this document as well as earlier efforts eventually led to a comprehensive plan for restructuring the company's operations. Also on March 27, Lomas advised Moody's and Standard & Poor's about its proposed restructuring and the company's intention to reduce consolidated debt by 27 percent and general corporate debt by 30 percent. During this period, Lomas and Moody's reached an understanding that the rating agency would not initiate a downgrade before June 30, by which time the company would have completed its restructuring plan and informed Moody's about its contents.

Advisories and agreements notwithstanding, pressure on the company escalated. Standard & Poor's issued a credit watch on LFC's debt on March 20 that said in part: "Lomas Financial continues to suffer from depressed earnings, illiquidity in real estate markets, and an aggressively leveraged balance sheet." Then on April 4, Moody's Investors Service announced that it had placed the debt and commercial paper ratings of LFC "under review for possible downgrade." In late March, in order to maintain shareholders' equity at $500 million or above in accordance with bank loan covenants, Lomas was forced to sell 40,000 shares of newly issued preferred stock to Merrill Lynch on "onerous terms," according to an article in *Forbes*.

A May 1, 1989, news release from the company announced a third quarter net loss of $12.4 million. "External pressures are continuing in our real estate development division which lost $19.5 million during the first nine months of Fiscal 1989," Hay explained. "These general pressures have been compounded by the 390 basis point increase since March 1988 in the Company's cost of short-term borrowings, which

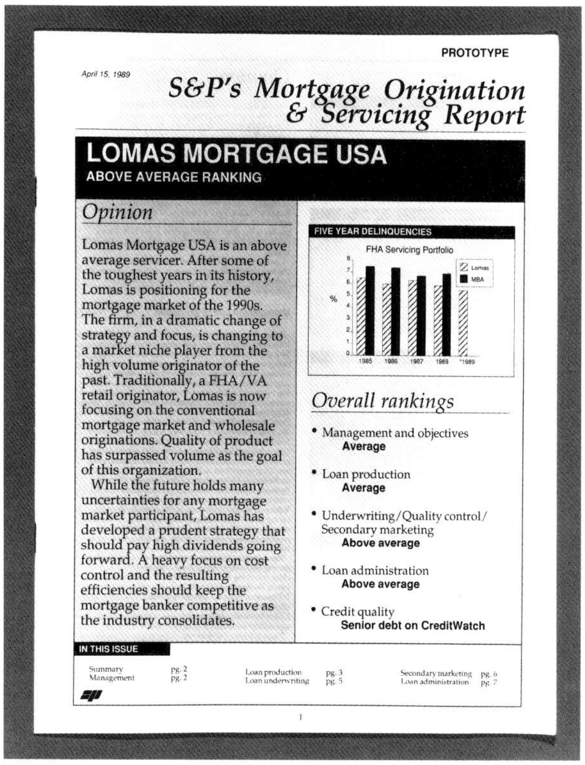
PROTOTYPE

April 15, 1989

S&P's Mortgage Origination & Servicing Report

LOMAS MORTGAGE USA

ABOVE AVERAGE RANKING

Opinion

Lomas Mortgage USA is an above average servicer. After some of the toughest years in its history, Lomas is positioning for the mortgage market of the 1990s. The firm, in a dramatic change of strategy and focus, is changing to a market niche player from the high volume originator of the past. Traditionally, a FHA/VA retail originator, Lomas is now focusing on the conventional mortgage market and wholesale originations. Quality of product has surpassed volume as the goal of this organization.

While the future holds many uncertainties for any mortgage market participant, Lomas has developed a prudent strategy that should pay high dividends going forward. A heavy focus on cost control and the resulting efficiencies should keep the mortgage banker competitive as the industry consolidates.

FIVE YEAR DELINQUENCIES

Overall rankings

- Management and objectives
  Average
- Loan production
  Average
- Underwriting/Quality control/ Secondary marketing
  Above average
- Loan administration
  Above average
- Credit quality
  Senior debt on CreditWatch

IN THIS ISSUE

Summary	pg. 2	Loan production	pg. 3	Secondary marketing	pg. 6
Management	pg. 2	Loan underwriting	pg. 5	Loan administration	pg. 7

1

Pressure escalated on April 15, 1989, when Standard & Poor's Rating Group issued a Mortgage Origination & Servicing Report on Lomas Mortgage USA that placed the mortgage company's senior debt on credit watch. Reprinted with permission of Standard & Poor's Corporation.

increased cost of funding . . . and negatively impacted operating results in the March quarter of our retail banking, commercial leasing, short-term lending and mortgage banking divisions." "We weren't seeing an improving scenario," was the way Bert Byerley later recalled the company's growing problems. The board of directors accelerated the pace of retreat by voting to reduce the quarterly dividend rate, from 35¢ to 18¢ per share.

The single bright spot in an otherwise gloomy picture was the announced agreement in early May to sell the company's credit card operations. It represented the first positive step Lomas could claim in its efforts to implement the restructuring strategy initiated by Hay in November 1988. A group led by Merrill Lynch Capital Partners, Inc., agreed to purchase Lomas Bankers Corp for $435 million in cash and $65 million in preferred stock. The sale reduced the company's consolidated debt by a hefty 32 percent. Despite its size and importance, however, the proposed transaction failed to halt the momentum that carried Lomas toward its ultimate crisis.

Negative perceptions from the outside world increased as the problems within Lomas mounted. A June 12, 1989, article by *Forbes* titled "The Last Roundup?" derisively presented LFC's litany of woes. It also dubbed the company's restructuring efforts a "disorderly retreat." This characterization proved either prophetic or self-fulfilling within 24 hours. The downgrade actions by Moody's on June 13 fired the shot that turned Lomas' "strategic retreat" into a stampede.

. . . another nail in the company's coffin.

"On June 13, about 5:30 in the afternoon, Moody's called me and said, 'We are downgrading you today,'" Lomas treasurer Bert Byerley recalls. "My first question was, 'What happened to our June 30th time frame?' As unbelievable as it sounds, they said, 'Our vacation schedules over the next six weeks make it impossible to convene a full credit committee meeting which we would need in order to make a decision about Lomas. Therefore we had to go ahead and do something today.' And I said, 'You mean to tell me that our life is hanging in the balance and whether we live or die depends upon the whims of your vacation schedule?'" They also told him that LFC's commercial paper was lowered to a non-investment grade category, from Prime-3 to Not Prime.

Byerley asked the Moody's representative to temporarily hold their press release. Senior officers from Lomas would fly to New York that night and meet with Moody's analysts in the morning to discuss the company's restructuring plan so that the rating agency could make a more informed decision. "They said, 'Well, we're sorry, but we've already issued the press release.' About that time, one of my staff walked in with a fax and said, 'You're not going to believe this.' And I said, 'Yes I am!'"

In addition to the commercial paper downgrade, the agency also lowered LFC's term debt and the credit ratings of three of its subsidiaries, Lomas Mortgage USA, Lomas Bank USA, and Equitable Lomas Leasing Company. One of the principal reasons cited for Moody's actions was "LFC's exposure to Texas real estate."

"As I recall," says Moody's analyst Jan Konstanty, "the residential, commercial, and speculative development markets in Texas continued to spiral down. People kept telling us that we've hit bottom, and then six months later it was clear that wasn't the bottom. Asset values needed a downward adjustment, and even a downward adjustment could need a future downward adjustment. We learned that predicting the bottom is fraught with difficulty."

In fact, exposure to real estate was the major reason for LFC's financial problems, and was the single greatest source of concern among the rating agencies and the banks. The decline in real estate values that had begun in 1986 continued. Real estate projects lost their viability and land previously sold by Lomas "started coming back in droves." "The build-up of our inventory of developed and undeveloped real estate reached a peak approaching $700 million," says Jess Hay. "It was the single factor that really brought the whole thing down. It turned out to be $700 million that was for all practical purposes frozen. Sales got very close to zero, so it was a non–income producing and totally illiquid investment."

As real estate values continued to drop, the rating agencies and banks became increasingly disenchanted with LFC's financial condition. Moody's Not Prime rating meant that the quality of LFC's commercial paper now fell below investment grade. Buddy Miller called the event "another nail in the company's coffin." Two weeks later Standard & Poor's drove in a larger nail when it downgraded the company's ratings and forced Lomas Financial Corporation to withdraw from the commercial paper market. "That's when it became clear that the orderly reduction of our debt was no longer a possibility," Byerley recalls. "Everything kind of changed in June."

After graduating from Texas Tech University in 1982, Bert Byerley was hired by Lomas as an analyst for the financial control group of the mortgage company.

CHAPTER XV

RUNNING ON EMPTY

Moody's downgrade of LFC's securities to non-investment grade forced Lomas senior vice president and treasurer Robert E. (Bert) Byerley, Jr., to confront the nightmare of corporate illiquidity. Certain that Standard & Poor's would soon follow Moody's example and force the company out of the commercial paper market, he responded decisively: "I began the process of drawing down every one of our bank lines with a view to retiring all of our commercial paper borrowings. I knew that several hundred million dollars of commercial paper would mature over the next several weeks and that we, therefore, would need every available dollar to cover those maturities.

"I also knew that any failure to cover commercial paper maturities would produce catastrophic results which would have a negative impact on every component of the company's operations. For that reason, treasury's singular focus during this period was on the task of generating sufficient liquidity to assure our ability to meet the scheduled maturities."

According to Byerley, pressure was intense, anxiety was constant and nerves frequently were frayed: "We were a young group suddenly faced with a huge challenge and an awesome responsibility. Adrenalin flowed from dawn to dark, and we did the best we could under the circumstances.

"To be perfectly honest, several banks were not happy about what I did in the last two weeks of June 1989. But if I had it to do over, I would not hesitate one second to do the exact same thing again."

That kind of brash, self-confident response to a crisis was one of the reasons for the 29-year-old Byerley's rapid rise at Lomas. Like Jess Hay, Byerley is a product of small-town Texas, having grown up in Sudan, a small, windswept community located on the high plains of far West Texas. "It has a population of a little over 900," says Chamber of Commerce president Jonelle Bandy. "The main businesses are the high school, Sudan Livestock and Feeding Company, Central Compress, and the Farmers' Co-Op Gin. We have one grocery store, one full-service filling station, and two places that sell gasoline. We're a small town, but we're a proud town." Bert Byerley remembers Sudan as "a good place to grow up in. It has a lot of community spirit. Everybody knows you and cares about you."

Bert was the fair-haired boy.

Byerley's strong work ethic came from his stepfather, whom Bert describes as having been "a hard worker first and foremost," but the convivial personality was his own. "I grew up working," says Byerley, "whether it was mowing yards or whatever. I worked in the grocery store my father managed from the time I was 12 or 13, and I loved it. I had a blast. I did everything from working in the meat market, to checking, to sacking, to stocking the vegetable and produce section. I liked being around all the people. I loved talking to everybody. And this probably sounds cocky, but everybody liked me too. It was fun."

Sociability and a thirst for accomplishment highlighted his school years as well. "I enjoyed growing up in a smaller school," says Byerley, "because you got to do everything." To play class A high school football or any of the other activities that Sudan High School offered its 130 students, says principal Buddy Lowrance, "all you need is desire." And Bert had plenty of that: "I did just about everything. I played football. I ran track every year from seventh grade on. I played basketball through my sophomore year. I was in the marching band and stage band from seventh grade on. I was involved in student government my last four years in high school, and I was elected student body president my senior year."

Lowrance, who also advised the student council, remembers Bert as "polite, well-mannered, hard working, and respected by his peers." He also lauds Byerley for reinstating the practice of electing a homecoming queen. "We're still doing it exactly the same way. The procedure is identical to what we set up that first year, and it's been real successful."

Bert developed an interest in business and finance while attending Texas Tech University in Lubbock. But it was his charismatic personality that made the deepest impression on former Lomas assistant vice president Pat Quinn, who attended business school with Byerley and lived across the hall from him in a campus dormitory. "Bert was a very popular person in college. He was good at meeting people. He had tremendous social skills. If I had to pick a profession for him back then, I would have said sales."

After graduating from college in 1982, Byerley was hired by Lomas as an analyst for the financial control group of the mortgage company. Legend has it that he was the person who figured out how to work the very first personal computer that Lomas ever bought. With it he set up spread sheets and produced a series of reports that broadened the scope of corporate financial analysis.

It was Byerley's attitude as much as his aptitude that caught the attention of the man he worked for, former senior vice president Eric Booth: "Bert had a can-do attitude. He never took no for an answer. Totally open and honest and willing to try anything. If something needed to be done, Bert would step in and do it, even if it wasn't his area."

One of the reasons vice president D. Scott Holtz joined Lomas in 1984 was because of Byerley. "I was fresh out of school," says Holtz, "and I didn't know that much about the business world. I was real impressed with Bert and the way he handled himself. He was very professional and efficient but at the same

Vice president Scott Holtz joined Lomas in 1984 because he was impressed with Byerley's professional but personable business attitude.

Former LAS president Hal Hillman formed a personal friendship with Byerley when they worked together.

time very personable and down-to-earth."

About a month after Holtz began work at Lomas, he had a firsthand opportunity to observe Byerley in action. Bert was responsible for putting together a major financial report for senior management: "We worked on that project all night until we finished at 6:30 in the morning. I'll never forget that night. We had five or six people up there [at Bryan Tower] and Bert was running around with his shoes off ordering pizza and trying to keep everybody working and everybody happy even though we were dog-tired.

"That's Bert in a nutshell. He leads by example. He's in there with his sleeves rolled up doing it with you. He makes it fun. You might be working your butt off until late at night, but you're having a good time. He's got an incredible amount of energy and drive. And once he sets his sights on something, he's going to get it done."

It wasn't long before that kind of energy and ability attracted the attention of Jess Hay. "Mr. Hay would wander into our offices," says Holtz, "and stop to talk to Bert, who worked on budgeting back then. I think Mr. Hay realized that Bert was the one doing most of the work." From time to time, the CEO asked Byerley to handle special projects for him. The bond between the two men deepened into a mentor relationship not unlike the one that had developed between Jess Hay and Eugene Locke 30 years before. Within four years of Byerley's arrival at Lomas as a rookie analyst, he had clearly won Hay's confidence. "Bert was the fair-haired boy," says former LAS president Hal Hillman, who formed a personal friendship with Byerley when the two worked for Eric Booth.

Beyond ability and a can-do attitude, Byerley possessed another attribute that made him particularly valuable to Jess Hay. "Bert is the only person I know of in the company that comes closest to thinking like Jess," says Hillman. Senior vice president and general counsel James L. Crowson says that Hay and Byerley share "a similarity of styles in terms of the way they deal with numbers. They write about financial data in a way that is nontabular and flows with a narrative. They can weave numbers and a story in a way that makes good sense, as opposed to just [listing] a bunch of cold numbers. Jess relies on Bert a great deal." The degree of trust and confidence became evident in the spring of 1988 when Hay named Byerley treasurer. With characteristic enthusiasm, the new appointee organized a treasury department staffed by young, aggressive financial specialists. Those dedicated men and women made an outstanding contribution to the company through their defense of its cash resources during the financial crisis.

Although the company had drawn down about $500 million from its bank lines to reduce its commercial paper borrowings, it wasn't enough. The problem was that a portion of LFC's commercial paper debt was backed by credit lines that the banks could cancel at any time. When that began to happen, the company's credit resources were insufficient to meet its commercial paper maturities.

... *t*he snowball is starting to roll.

It was part of what former executive vice president John F. Sexton refers to as "the liquidity snowball. It starts with the rating agencies, and then it infects the banks. Things you could normally do by picking up a telephone you can't do, because all of a sudden you've got this stigma on you. The rating agencies downgraded us because they analyzed that the company is not worth what we say it's worth. Then the banks that have to absorb that [commercial paper] debt begin to say the same thing. Now, all of a sudden, red flags are going up everywhere, and the snowball is starting to roll."

One red flag that went up came from the criticism of an LFC bank credit by federal bank examiners. Other lenders within the credit were notified about the unfavorable classification, and that ended the availability of future credit from those banks. "The bank criticism changed the status of our loan," says Byerley. "The biggest implication was that the loan was now a substandard credit, and in a lot of cases that pushed it into a workout area. It signaled a change in the relationship between the banks and Lomas."

Spurred by an atmosphere of negative perceptions, a half-dozen banks resisted the funding of committed bank lines. "Technically, they could not say no to us," says vice president and assistant treasurer Paul D. Fletcher. "They had a liability to fund, because we weren't in default. We had bad ratings, but they still had to fund us. The ones that resisted their commitment did anything and everything they could not to fund. They asked for information and reports, and they made us sign certifications about the company's financial condition."

Although those few banks did grumble about funding their firmly committed lines, all but one finally advanced 100 percent of the principal amount of their respective commitments to the company. This was a tribute both to the character of the participating banks and to the strength of the documentation supporting those credit arrangements.

The restructuring plan that LFC revealed at the end of June confirmed the fact that the company was in headlong retreat. Seriously overburdened by debt, Lomas planned to shrink itself back to profitability by returning to its mortgage banking roots. "Mortgage banking," read the news release, "will continue to be the principal system through which Lomas intends to drive its growth." There was, however, one major difference. The company's exit from retail mortgage production underscored its concentration on the more profitable servicing side of the business.

The plan's targeted 64 percent reduction in consolidated debt ended LFC's efforts to become a moderately diversified financial services company. That dream died with the upcoming sale of Lomas Bankers Corp, the intended sale of ELLCO, and possible sale of other major assets.

"Establishment of Reserves" was the part of the reorganization that made the headline of an article in *The Wall Street Journal*: "Lomas Financial Plans to Take Massive Charge." The $202 million pretax loss for 1989, more than three times LFC's 1988 loss of $56.4 million, dealt the company a crippling blow. The size of the loss was unexpected. Some analysts claimed that LFC's credibility suffered "because of continued negative surprises."

But it was the reduction in stockholders' equity to $263 million that triggered the company's most immediate problem—a technical default of bank credit agreements that required Lomas to maintain $500 million in net worth. The covenant violation required waivers from the banks to remove the default.

By the end of June 1989, the struggle for survival had shifted to the banks. The curtailment of access to funding brought the viability of Lomas' continuing operations into question regardless of how they were restructured. "The Company intends . . . to revise its long- and short-term senior credit facilities," said a special stockholders' report dated June 30, 1989, "to assure the continued availability to the Company of sufficient financing for its restructured operations. . . . The Company is optimistic that in the future the Company will be accorded the continuing support of those banks."

The first opportunity to gauge bank support, however, indicated that LFC's optimism may have been misplaced. The company asked its banks to attend a meeting in Dallas on June 29 where it planned to explain its reorganization, obtain waivers, and revise its long- and short-term credit. One of the reasons for LFC's difficulties had to do with changes in the banking world. "One of the biggest problems Lomas had," says former Chase Manhattan vice president Richard Hay (no relation to Jess Hay), "was the absence of its traditional friends, the Texas banks. They were all gone. The banks in Texas that they historically turned to when they had problems were not there anymore. They were all being run by the federal government."

Nobody signed a waiver that day.

"Back in the old days," says Paul Fletcher, "the company had several very powerful Dallas banks that would do virtually anything Lomas wanted to do. There are no Dallas banks anymore." The company's rapid expansion forced another change. In order to increase its access to credit, LFC began to do more business with New York and foreign banks. "And for the most part, those banks are not relationship-driven," says Fletcher. "They're transaction-oriented. They haven't been with Lomas for 25 years. They haven't known Mr. Hay and Mr. Sexton for 25 years. The bank relationship environment changed."

To accomplish its objectives, Lomas enlisted the support of two major banks, Chase Manhattan and Bank of New York. "Jess asked us to step up and lead the charge," says Dick Hay. "Of course, we didn't have a lot of lead time, and we didn't really understand the magnitude of the problem. Our role was to try to encourage the banks to look at this as a short-term problem. We took what we thought was a mature approach. We said, 'We've got a problem. We've got to work it out, and it's better to work it out on a friendly basis.' Other people were just trying to cut and run." According to Dick Hay, the Lomas bank meeting divided into two groups. About 25 percent were angry. They had had no idea Lomas was in trouble, and they demanded immediate payment. About 75 percent of the banks wanted to work something out with the company. Paul Fletcher recalls the surprise among many of the bank representatives "that we were in that bad shape liquidity-wise."

Lomas failed to accomplish its objectives. "I think Lomas pretty much expected everybody to agree to sign on that day, because that's the way the banks had always treated them before," says Dick Hay. "But that didn't happen. Nobody signed a waiver that day."

"They definitely weren't agreeing to sign anything," says Fletcher. "The banks were trying to figure out what had happened. Initially, there wasn't any approval of any sort. This was all thrown on them very quickly. It took a lot more education. There was a lot of scrambling by people to talk to each other and try to find out, 'What do you think? What does he think?' They all went different ways. Some met in rooms. Some left. Some tried to get more information from management. It was a mess."

The only unpleasant incident occurred in a smaller meeting that Byerley called at the conclusion of the main meeting. "The other problem that was staring us in the face was a $120 million term loan in the mortgage company which was maturing on July 1," says Byerley. "And because we had been forced out of the commercial paper market, we had no way to pay it." The purpose of Byerley's meeting was to persuade the banks in that credit to sign waivers and extend the maturity date of the loan until the first of August when the retail banking division sale was scheduled to close and funds would be available for repayment. The meeting immediately turned confrontational. "Connecticut Bank and Trust [CBT] sent three new people that we had never seen before," Byerley recalls, "and they really got ugly in this smaller meeting. They said, 'We don't care what anybody else in this room is going to do. We are not going to extend the maturity. We are not going to give you a waiver. And we are going to call you in default and accelerate the debt if you don't pay us out.'" The woman who acted as spokesperson for the CBT delegation left a decidedly unpleasant taste in Byerley's mouth: "She was not a very nice person at all. She stood up and jabbed her finger at me the whole time. Anyway, I finally ended the meeting and said, 'Ladies and gentlemen, there is no point in us continuing this meeting like we are right now. I thought we could talk about this in a reasonable manner but obviously there are some people who don't want to do that. We will contact each one of you on a one-to-one basis and will work out whatever we can.'

"Things went from bad to worse with Connecticut Bank and Trust. Little did I know when we walked out of the room that there was an urgent phone call waiting for me from Lomas Securities Corporation [a secondary marketing unit] in Stamford, Connecticut, which funded all its loans through CBT. And although Connecticut Bank and Trust hadn't bothered to tell us, they instructed all their offices not to give a dime of money to Lomas anymore. So all of a sudden Lomas Securities had 20 loans to fund that day that totaled about $3 million, and they had no way to fund them."

LFC scheduled a meeting with CBT's bank meeting representatives that afternoon. This time Jess Hay led the Lomas delegation. "If there was ever a time that I've seen Mr. Hay get upset, it was that afternoon," says Byerley. "He told them in no uncertain terms that they were acting in the most unprofessional way that he had ever seen a bank act. He went on and on and on, and then walked out." Later that same day Lomas Financial Corporation wired the money for the loans from its account in Dallas and ended its relationship with Connecticut Bank and Trust.

Disappointment by Lomas' lack of success at the June 29 bank meeting turned to dismay four days later. The company's strategy for overcoming its liquidity problems was to put together a bridge loan that would meet its financial needs until the sale of the retail banking division. But first, and even more immediately, Lomas needed a smaller bridge loan to cover the time it would take to put together the main bridge loan. The company had an important commercial paper maturity on July 3 and others due soon after that. "There was a piece of commercial paper coming due which we could not pay," says general counsel Jim Crowson. "Had it not been paid, it would have been a significant event on Wall Street. You just don't default on commercial paper and remain ongoing. It would have been very, very bad."

We kept struggling, struggling, struggling to get the necessary signatures.

Jess Hay and other senior executives arrived at Chase Manhattan Bank on Monday morning, July 3, believing the company could borrow the requisite $60 million in plenty of time to meet the maturity deadline that afternoon at 3 o'clock. But as the negotiations stalled, it was clear that despite a close relationship between Lomas and Chase that spanned several decades, there were limits to friendship. "It looked as if Lomas was going to get a loan," says Davis Polk & Wardwell attorney Robert J. Levine, who represented Lomas, "and then all of a sudden, the Chase people went and caucused with their management, changed their minds, and said, 'We won't give you a loan.'"

In retrospect, Dick Hay believes Lomas' expectations were somewhat unrealistic. "Initially, they came in looking for a loan," says the former Chase vice president, who met with LFC management that day. "Then it became clear that the bank was not going to grant a loan, because they didn't want to have a further unsecured position based on what they believed to be the uncertainty of LFC's ability to execute its plan. Ted Enloe, John Sexton, and Jess would get up and say, 'This is what we're going to do, and these are the assets we're going to sell, and this is what it's going to look like.' Well, that's fine. Except, what if it doesn't happen?

"You're dealing with a company that had never been told 'no' by a bank before. They were used to walking into institutions and pretty much getting anything they needed. And this was over the last 25 years. I believe it was a combination of naivete on their part and a fundamental change in the way banks were looking at credits."

Then, in a last-minute effort to make something work, the two parties negotiated a sale. Chase agreed to buy $6 billion worth of servicing for $90 million, $60 million to be paid immediately. Lomas had the right to repurchase the assets within 60 days, which it intended to do after the sale of Lomas Bankers Corp.

"We had approximately 20 minutes to discuss the offer, write a contract, and sign it," says Bob Levine. "We ended up signing a one-page contract. Three sentences scribbled on a piece of yellow paper. That contract should be in the Lomas Hall of Fame. It's probably the shortest contract ever written for a $6 billion sale.

"It was written in pencil. Their lawyer scribbled two sentences and then someone said, 'You left out the ability to buy it back.' So I added another sentence that we had the ability to buy it back. Then Jess Hay signed it in pencil, and I made him sign it again in ink. So it had two signatures on it. And that's how the first financing was done."

This sale bought LFC only a handful of precious days. Survival now hinged on a $375 million bridge loan that would give Lomas the money required to meet its commercial paper maturities and other cash needs until the retail bank was sold. Chase Manhattan, Bank of New York, Barclay's Bank, and Bank One–Texas agreed to make the loan. It was secured with short-term loan assets from LFC and a pledge to repay the loan from the proceeds of the retail bank sale. But the loan couldn't be consummated until Lomas cleared its default by obtaining waivers from a two-

July 5, 1989

Lomas Mortgage USA ("Seller") hereby sells, transfers and assigns to The Chase Manhattan Bank, N.A ("Chase") all of Seller's right, title and interest in and to the Assets described on Exhibit A hereto. Seller agrees to immediately execute and deliver to Chase any and all bills of sale and other instruments of transfer with respect to such assets as Chase shall, in its sole discretion, require. The purchase price for such assets shall be $80,000,000, with $60,000,000 having been paid by Chase on the date hereof, with the balance to be paid upon Chase's review and approval of 3 such assets and upon the approval by any independent auditor engaged by Chase of such assets.

LOMAS MORTGAGE USA

By

Seller shall have the right to repurchase the Assets at any time within 60 days after the date hereof for a repurchase price equal to the amount paid by Chase plus an amount equal to interest thereon computed at a rate equal to Chase's prime rate plus 1% per annum

With a 20-minute deadline fast approaching, Lomas transacted a $6 billion sale to Chase Manhattan Bank.

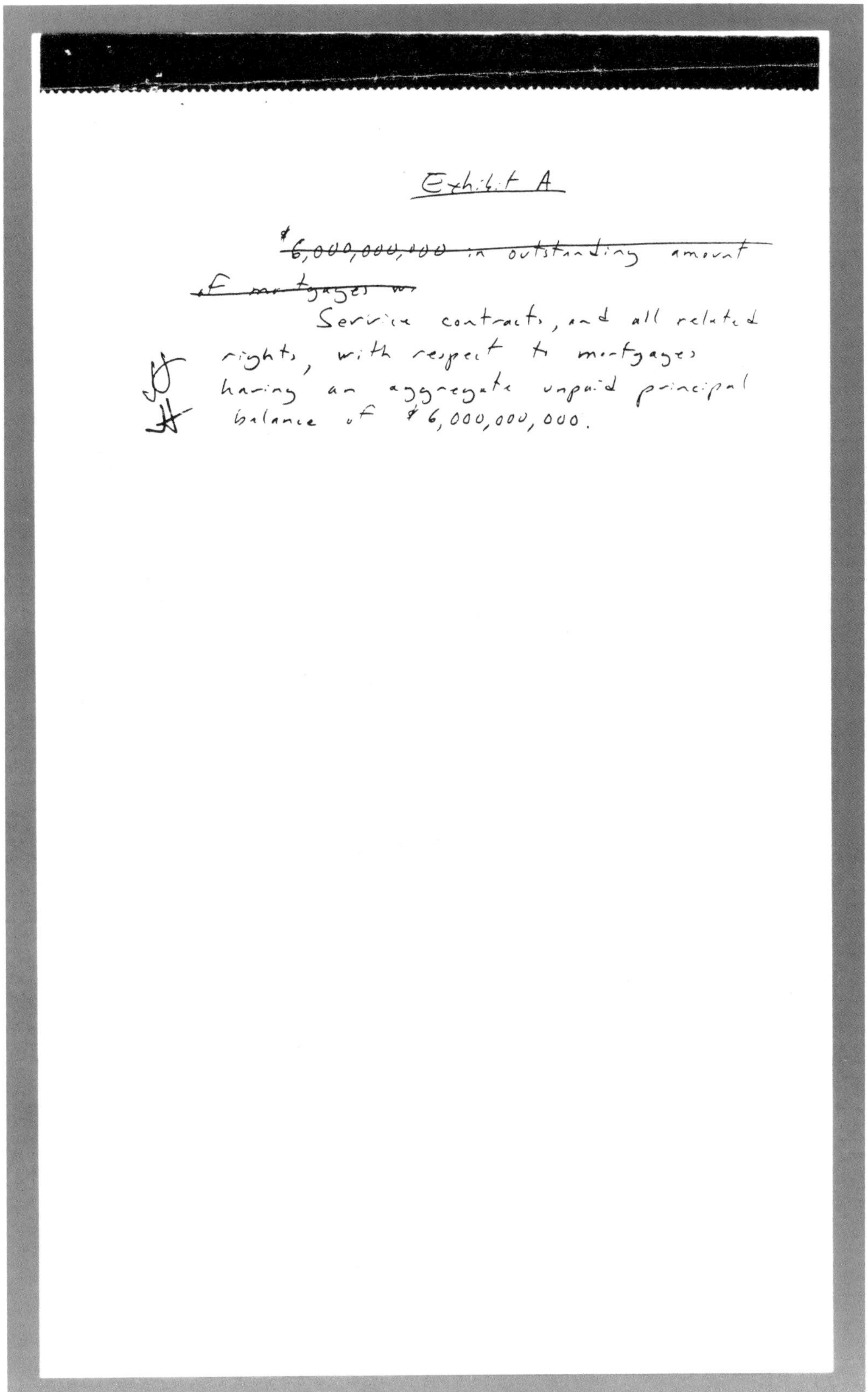

Exhibit A

~~$6,000,000,000 in outstanding amount of mortgages w~~

Service contracts, and all related rights, with respect to mortgages having an aggregate unpaid principal balance of $6,000,000,000.

The contract contained three sentences scribbled in pencil on a yellow pad.

thirds majority of its creditors.

"We were sweating, trying to get that loan closed," says Bob Levine. "We kept struggling, struggling, struggling to get the necessary signatures. The Japanese banks were difficult, and there was a Dutch bank, I believe, that was a problem. A lot of them said, 'We'll only go if everybody else goes.' And some said, 'Well, maybe we will and maybe we won't.' Or, 'This guy is going to sign the waiver, but we've got to find him.' And then they couldn't find him." John Sexton says one Italian bank refused to sign a waiver because the other Italian bank in the credit hadn't signed one. And neither wanted to sign until the other one signed first. "There was all kinds of bullshit going on," Sexton recalls.

Jim Crowson theorizes that the difficulty with the Japanese banks was cultural: "They listened to us and then said they had to go think, and they'd be back. But it never happened. Apparently, in their culture no decision doesn't get you in any trouble. We were chasing those guys at really strange hours our time and fairly strange hours their time." Finally, on July 13, LFC announced "the completion of a secured short-term bank facility to provide liquidity pending the previously announced sale of its Lomas Bankers Corp subsidiary."

LFC president Ted Enloe was a major contributor in helping the company through a summer of financial crises.

LFC president Ted Enloe played a major role in helping the company clear many of the hurdles blocking its path that summer. One of the most critical occurred in early August. The sale of Lomas Bankers Corp, on which the future of the company now depended, got hung up over federal regulatory issues. As the company experienced a series of frustrating delays and postponements, Hay asked Enloe, who was off fighting on another front, to come in and help get it done. "I'll never forget the final day," says Enloe. "It was about 11 o'clock in the morning and Hay says, 'I can't stand this. I've got to get out of here.' And I said, 'Take off. I guarantee you that I'll get this closed this afternoon. It's going to close. Don't worry about it.' I was afraid he was going to have a heart attack he was so upset. His face was flushed, and he was sort of trembling. So he and Ramona took off. They drove around for four or five hours. They may have driven to Oklahoma, I don't know. He called me twice on the car phone. He called about 2 o'clock and asked how it was going. I said, 'It hasn't closed, but don't worry about it. I promise you it's going to close.' Then he called about 4 o'clock from the car, still driving. And I told him, 'It closed.' That was tense."

Even with the infusion of money from the bridge loan and the sale of Lomas Bankers Corp, it required heroic efforts on the part of the treasury department to keep the company solvent. "Our department was under a significant amount of pressure," says Byerley. "I spent a lot of sleepless nights wondering if we were going to have enough money to fund this massive organization called Lomas. Things were tighter and things were delayed a bit, but we managed to squeak by. We met our payroll, and we paid our vendors. I am extremely proud of the company and the treasury group that we were able to manage the cash that tightly."

The realization that the company's existence was on the line drove the treasury staff beyond the call of duty. "I think in times of stress you tend to cram five times as much learning into a shorter time period than it would normally take," says Byerley, "because you don't have any choice. You just do it. I noticed an increase in the maturity level and commitment to the company from my staff. As a group, we were working on the average 12 to 16 hours a day. It was not uncommon to find us still in the office at 10 or 12 o'clock at night. One night I stayed until 5:30 in the morning, went home and took a shower and was back at the office by 7:30."

The tireless efforts by the treasury department produced results. Careful management of the cash flows within Lomas provided the funding needed to survive the critical months of July, August, and September. "One division's cash flow funded another division," says Paul Fletcher. "Each division had cash requirements, and we had to satisfy everyone with a finite amount of cash. It was a very stressful period."

There may have been a deficit of cash at LFC, but there was no shortage of humanity when personal tragedy struck Bert Byerley the first week of July. A phone call from Sudan one evening informed him that his parents had been involved in a head-on highway collision. The accident killed his stepfather. It took over an hour to extract his mother from the wrecked car and rush her unconscious to a hospital. Distraught with grief, all Byerley wanted was to get back home as soon as possible. Unfortunately, there were no more flights to Lubbock that night. "In desperation," says Byerley, "I called Mr. Sexton and said, 'I don't know what to do. I can't get home.' And he said, 'Just go to Lomas' hangar. I'll find you a plane.'" The two planes the company owned were unavailable at the time. However, when Byerley arrived at the airport later that evening, a private airplane owned by Lincoln Property chairman Mack Pogue was fueled and waiting.

Byerley also placed a call to Jess Hay who was vacationing in Acapulco to tell him the news and cancel a business meeting the next day. Minutes later, while Byerley was packing, Hay called back: "He said, 'Bert, I just want you to know how heartsick I am. Now, I want you to put this in your back pocket. I hope you don't need it, but if you do, I have already contacted The University of Texas Southwestern Medical Center, which has one of the best trauma centers in the United States. They are standing by ready to accept your mother should you need to bring her to Dallas.'" Fortunately, Byerley didn't have to use that option. His mother's injuries, though serious, were not critical.

The actions John Sexton and Jess Hay took that night made a deep and lasting impression on Byerley: "You can say whatever you want about . . . the business world not caring personally about people, but that is not Lomas. That is not Lomas."

With the bridge loan in place and its covenant defaults removed, Lomas Financial Corporation resumed negotiations to arrange a long-term credit facility with 44 banks. To represent Lomas at those proceedings, Jess Hay turned to Davis Polk & Wardwell, a venerable Wall Street law firm whose continuous history dates from 1849. His confidence evolved from a 30-year relationship that began with Wallace Properties, Inc. When Wallace made its initial public offering in 1960, Davis Polk represented Harriman Ripley, the investment banker handling the sale. Later, in the early 1970s, when the company needed a law firm to represent it in New York, Hay asked Davis Polk. "In many ways, the practice of law is a business of trusting people," says Davis Polk partner Jeffrey Small, who led the firm's relationship with Lomas. "And there is a trust that comes from getting things done successfully. Jess was pleased. Ted Enloe was pleased. So the relationship sort of flourished." That bond deepened when LFC began negotiating with the banks. "It became a crisis pretty quickly," says Small. "Jess came up for what looked like a brief stay. It ended up with him pretty much living here for awhile. We spent a lot of very late nights at Davis Polk trying to patch together a banking arrangement."

We spent a lot of very late nights at Davis Polk trying to patch together a banking arrangement.

In essence, Lomas' restructuring proposal asked the banks to provide long-term credit for the company so that it could operate until it was profitable and able to pay off its debt. In exchange for the credit, LFC agreed to secure the banks with collateral from assets in the company. The time constraint hanging like a noose around Lomas' neck was $145 million of senior public debt that matured on September 1. The funds to meet that obligation would be provided for in the new credit facility if it could be closed prior to September 1. It was an uphill battle. "We had a very disorganized banking group with a lot of different constituencies," says attorney Jeff Small. "You would have a bank officer make a deal with you, and then he'd come back later and say his superiors overruled him. Then you had to start over again. When you finally got a deal that that bank could live with, they'd tell you they couldn't sell it to the banking group. Ultimately, the banks couldn't agree among themselves."

Crowson remembers spending "lots of seven-day weeks in New York," much of that time holed up in one of Davis Polk's conference rooms. He estimates they prepared at least 50 drafts of the restructuring agreement. Each proposal they sent to the banks for review came back considerably altered. "It wouldn't bear any resemblance to the draft we sent out," says Crowson, "and we'd have to start all over again. In retrospect, it was probably Pollyannish to think we could ever get it done."

Jeffrey Small, of the Wall Street law firm Davis Polk & Wardwell, led his company's relationship with Lomas as they tried to negotiate a long-term credit facility. Courtesy Davis Polk & Wardwell.

Even Hay's skill as an arbitrator and consensus builder couldn't overcome the differences within the bank group. "Jess is a great conciliator," says Small, "and also a great optimist. I believe he thought that justice and reason would prevail. The problem with the banks is that it isn't always a question of what's fair. Often it's a question of whether another bank is getting something that they think is better than what they're getting, even if what they're getting is fine."

Lomas general counsel Jim Crowson remembers seven-day weeks in Davis Polk's conference rooms in New York, with the credit restructuring agreement going through at least 50 drafts.

Bob Levine, a Davis Polk partner who specializes in banking transactions, was a key player in the credit negotiations. Courtesy Davis Polk & Wardwell.

The complicated, exhausting discussions made sufficient progress by the end of August for Lomas to issue a news release. On Thursday, August 24, the company drafted a statement that said progress had been made and that it "hoped to have an agreement in principle from substantially all holders of senior debt by September 1, 1989." That evening, says Bob Levine, Lomas read the release to the two lead banks, Chase and Bank of New York, who registered their approval. "The next morning," says Levine, "we sent out the press release and within an hour we received a fax of a letter from Bank of New York disavowing the draft proposal and saying it had not been approved. Needless to say, everybody was upset."

"Bank of New York dropped a bombshell on us Friday," said Bert Byerley at the time of the event. "They said, 'We changed our minds.'" It was a major setback. Lomas and its attorneys frantically worked over the weekend to persuade Bank of New York to reconsider, but were unable to make adequate progress. On Monday, August 28, Lomas was forced to issue another news release stating that "agreement has not yet been reached. As a result, LFC does not expect that this restructure will be completed by Friday, September 1, 1989, the date on which approximately $145 million principal amount of senior debt matures." That same day Moody's announced a further downgrade of LFC and several subsidiaries, which included ELLCO's commercial paper rating dropping from Prime-3 to Not Prime.

Embarrassment about having to write a retraction was the least of Lomas' concerns, says public relations consultant Michael Sitrick, president of Sitrick And Company, who was hired by LFC a week after this event: "One moment they thought they had a deal and the next moment they didn't have a deal. I think that was more upsetting than the public perception. It was also pretty representative of the way those negotiations went. When you have [44] different banks involved in a group and each with its own agenda, you have a very difficult time getting agreement on anything."

Although outwardly optimistic and focused, Jess Hay was exhausted both mentally and physically in the summer of 1989.

As predicted, Lomas was unable to meet the public notes maturity on September 1. It was the culmination of the liquidity crisis that had been developing since June and "finally exceeded the Company's coping capacity on September 1," as Jess Hay wrote in a letter to stockholders later that month. It was also the first monetary default in the company's history. As it turned out, the event had little practical effect. Lomas and the banks still felt they had a shot at making a deal. And the trustees of the public notes agreed not to accelerate their debt when Lomas told them that credit restructuring talks were continuing and that restructuring would include full payment for them.

Senior vice president and secretary Ramona Taylor, a career-long business associate of Hay, knew that he was more troubled than at other times.

No one experienced the agony of events more keenly than Jess Hay. Although he was outwardly optimistic and focused on the business at hand, those closest to him believe the events that summer exacted a heavy cost. "I know he's exhausted both mentally and physically," Byerley stated in August 1989. "He lives with this 24 hours a day, and it's been hard on him. He's drained from it. Even so, he's still the eternal optimist today, which is good. We all need that to keep our spir-

It was a hellish period.

its up, and he's good at that. But it's been tough on him." Judy Justice, a former member of Hay's staff responsible for special projects, recalled her reaction to events and their effect on the CEO:

> I remember when the negotiations started with the banks. Mr. Hay in his usual fashion wanted the lawyers to jump on things and get everything settled right away. I believe he expected a conclusion within a few weeks. The weeks dragged on, first with minor glitches, then major glitches, numerous trips to New York, and heated conference-call discussions between Dallas and New York. The feeling in the office was one of frustration and impending disaster. Mr. Hay always maintained his sense of humor, but we knew things were wearing him down. We were concerned about Mr. Hay and the constant stress he had been under for such a long time. I never heard him talk about how he felt except to say in a staff meeting that the last three months had been the most difficult of his life.

Described by those who know him best as "an intensely private person," Hay reacted to the stress by retreating inward. Ramona Taylor recalls one example during those pressure-filled days: "He was more troubled than at other times. When we went to lunch, he always wanted to get away from downtown and Bryan Tower. Then, when we got through eating, he'd say, 'Let's drive around.' We drove. I can't tell you how many miles we drove. We drove through the entire metroplex over that period of time. We drove to Forney, where he was born. We drove to McKinney. We drove through Vista Ridge many times. Usually, I was just sitting there driving. It wasn't as though we were in these deep discussions or anything. I mean if he wanted to talk, of course we talked. I knew that he needed quiet. He needed no phones. He needed no one bringing anything else to him. I don't know how he endured the stress." Occasionally, after the drives, Hay went home to take a nap. Taylor feared that the long, silent drives and late afternoon naps meant Hay was in "a deep depression. Everything he worked so hard for all these years seemed to be crumbling around him. It was a horrible, horrible time."

If Hay lapsed into depression during those difficult days, it was a temporary condition. The core values that held his world together and gave it meaning were very much intact. According to vice president Wallace E. Chappell, whose friendship with Hay dates from the late 1950s, a personal incident brought Hay's priorities sharply into focus, reaffirmed his faith, and lifted his spirits. Chappell believes it was a "breakthrough moment" for the leader of Lomas. Aware of the pressures Hay endured, Chappell says, "It was a hellish period. I wondered what was keeping him up." He learned the answer one day in July or August at a luncheon meeting attended by Chappell, David Farr, Buddy Miller, and Ramona Taylor in Hay's office: "It was an interesting meeting. We had sandwiches brought in, and he was elated. It was as though the burden was lifted." Hay told his assembled friends that a moment of awareness had come during a bank negotiation meeting in New York. The discussion was not going well. Then, while the lawyers were wrangling over some technicality, Hay stood up and walked across the room to a window that overlooked Wall Street, Manhattan, and beyond. Ramona Taylor, who was with Hay, remembered the moment and wondered half-jokingly at the time if he was thinking about jumping. Nothing was further from the truth. "Hay found himself thinking about his family, his wife, his daughters, his grandchildren, his home—all the things that meant the most to him," says Chappell. "That life was good regardless of what happened to Lomas. That whatever happened would be okay, because he still had his family."

"What it meant to me," says former executive vice president David Farr, "was that his reason for living has always been his family. That he had been so preoccupied with saving Lomas that he got his priorities out of order. Jess has always had a philosophy that family was first, friends and community second, and work third. He realized that all the madness of dealing with the creditors really didn't matter. I think I understand that because I've been there several times myself. When you are facing a massive crisis like that, you have to get into prioritization very quickly or you lose it. And getting your priorities straight gives you the strength to do the crazy stuff. And that's all there was to the meeting. He was trying to tell us that his family was the most important priority in his life."

It became apparent after September 1 that the concessions demanded by the banks made the proposed credit agreement less viable for Lomas. "Bob {Levine} and I became concerned that we just were not going to work it out with the banks," says Jeff Small. "The banks' terms were too onerous. And even if LFC wanted to accept them at the end of the day, they were not going to work. The company would end up bankrupt in six or nine months with the banks fully collateralized, and the game would be over. All the banks wanted to do was get collateral. They really didn't want to help the company get out of trouble. Those of us involved in the day-to-day negotiations became persuaded that the banks were not really interested in the company recovering."

We wanted to preserve Lomas.

From Jim Crowson's perspective, the banks' proposal began to look like a liquidation instead of a restructuring: "There was some pressure to push us toward a liquidation mode. The banks wouldn't explicitly say they viewed it as a liquidation, but they acted as though they viewed it as a liquidation because of the way they wanted to force us to operate."

Filing for Chapter 11 under the federal bankruptcy code was anathema to all at Lomas, but to no one more than Jess Hay. "He was adamant that we were not going to go into Chapter 11," recalls Ramona Taylor. "I think they {the Davis Polk attorneys} had been . . . talking about it for a long time before they got up enough nerve to really talk directly to Jess about it. They knew he would resist it to the very end."

There were good reasons for opposing the Chapter 11 option. First, it was an expensive proceeding. And there was the fear that the stigma attached to the process could cause the company's business to deteriorate and make growth all but impossible. As a financial services company, that was no small concern. Worried customers, after all, can go elsewhere. Then there was a concern about selling assets in Chapter 11 at distressed prices. Also, the question of interference loomed very large. How much control over its business operations would Lomas lose because of creditor and court supervision? And to what degree would the bankruptcy process disrupt the ability to conduct normal business?

There was, however, one paramount consideration that swayed Jess Hay toward the bankruptcy option: his commitment to Lomas, its employees, and its shareholders. "I think the realization had come to all of us," says Taylor, "that there wasn't anything else we could do to preserve the company. And that was everyone's goal. We wanted to preserve Lomas."

"I think he finally pushed himself over the line," says Jeff Small, about Hay's decision to file for bankruptcy sometime in September. "He's a very strong individual with great internal conviction and a great sense of right and wrong. I think at that point he concluded that the only way to protect Lomas and not see it dismantled by the creditors, who cared nothing about the institution or its employees, was to file for Chapter 11."

Although negotiations with the banks continued after September 1, the possibility that Lomas would be forced to seek bankruptcy protection became more likely. Prudently, the company pursued dual paths. The most noticeable shift toward preparation for filing centered on the retention of outside professionals and consultants with solid expertise in the Chapter 11 process.

Lazard Frères & Co. was hired by Lomas to act as the company's financial advisor. General partner Tom Haack was the primary contact for the relationship. Courtesy Lazard Frères & Co.

Consultant John Grigsby, president of John Grigsby and Associates, was hired because of his business skills and knowledge about the bewildering labyrinth of Chapter 11.

Lomas hired Lazard Frères & Co. to act as the company's financial advisor. Thomas R. Haack, a Lazard general partner, was the primary contact for that relationship. The company hired the accounting firm of Ernst & Young in early September to provide management consulting and the accounting services associated with Chapter 11. Restructuring and reorganization specialist Alan D. Bell led that relationship. The big six firm, however, was no stranger to Lomas. Its association with the company dated from 1962, when it first provided tax and audit services. Consultant John T. Grigsby, Jr., president of John Grigsby and Associates, Inc., was hired because of his blend of business skills and proven ability to lead companies "through each facet of the Chapter 11 process." The highly specialized world of Chapter 11 communications was assigned to Sitrick And Company, a public relations firm that had assisted over 50 troubled companies. Its task throughout the process was to provide a clear and consistent message for the company's internal and external communications. While one team of Davis Polk attorneys pursued negotiations, a second group headed by Don Bernstein and Laureen Bedell began planning a legal strategy for Chapter 11. Much of their early efforts focused on the preparation of documents required for filing. They also recommended filing the case in New York rather than Texas. A New York jurisdiction had several advantages. The judges there were used to large cases and tended to be generous toward debtors when it came to investing available cash in orderly growth and employee benefits. New York was also a more practical location. Most of the company's large creditors and professional advisors for both sides worked there.

Don Bernstein, left, and Laureen Bedell, right, headed a second group of attorneys from Davis Polk to plan legal strategy for Chapter 11. Courtesy Davis Polk & Wardwell.

Lomas Financial Corporation's board of directors held a special meeting on September 15, 1989, to grapple with the options facing it. The atmosphere was tense. The discussions that day, however, did not lead to a decision. "There were some {board} members who thought it was time to file," says Jeff Small, "and there were others who said they thought it was worth another try. They decided to adjourn for one week and see if they could get the banks to come up with a package that would be more acceptable to the board. I think everyone felt it was a long shot." To help them evaluate the bank proposal, the board asked Tom Haack of Lazard Frères & Co. for an independent assessment.

At the end of the day, it was a unanimous judgment . . .

The atmosphere in the office that week, says former assistant vice president Jeanne M. McDonald, felt like "there was a huge cloud of gloom hovering overhead, ready to descend." Ramona Taylor called together a group of Bryan Tower co-workers and asked them to block off the coming weekend. They needed to be available to work all day Saturday and Sunday. "At which point," says former assistant secretary Lorraine Grant, "we knew that we would probably be filing for Chapter 11."

The board of directors reconvened at 3:00 p.m. on Friday, September 22, 1989. It was a difficult meeting for Jess Hay. "My recollection was that Jess was very distraught," says Tom Haack. "He looked pale. He looked shaken. I think it was the most significant emotional item that he's ever faced in his life. He took it hard.

"He led the meeting, but not to the extent that I've seen him in other meetings. At that point, he became resigned to the inevitability that he was probably going to file for bankruptcy." It appeared to Haack that the other members of the board seemed equally resigned.

Haack's presentation concluded that the bank

restructuring proposal was "overly aggressive" and that its terms, if accepted, represented "a significant risk" to the company. Then the board met in executive session with its attorneys. "Not enough progress had been made for us to conclude that we could cut a deal with the banks in anything close to a period of time that would salvage the company," says Small. "Although he regretted it, Jess finally and irrevocably concluded that filing for Chapter 11 was the only responsible decision for the company. At the end of the day, and in response to Jess' recommendation, it was a unanimous judgment by the company's financial advisors, lawyers, directors, and management."

"After a full discussion and consultation with its attorneys," read the minutes from that meeting, "the Board voted unanimously to file for reorganization under Chapter 11 of the United States Bankruptcy Code in the Southern District of New York."

Jeanne McDonald first learned about the decision when Bert Byerley slipped away from the meeting before it adjourned. He looked drained and appeared to be in a state of shock: "He came out and said, 'Well, we're going to file.' I thought, 'Okay, we're going to file.' But it seemed sort of unreal. It was hard to believe we were really doing that."

"I stayed at the office until the meeting broke up, about 6:30," says Judy Justice. "Ramona came back from where the meeting was held and told me the decision. I knew it was coming but the full impact and finality of the news didn't hit me until then, and I was very emotional. At the time, I knew very little about Chapter 11, and it seemed like a dark alternative to working things out with the banks. It was a sad feeling to know that we were going into Chapter 11. When I was attending boarding school in the ninth grade, my mother called me one night to say that there had been a fire, and the family business burned down. I felt a lot like I did that night—very sad and very unsure as to what the future held."

Outside professional Amy Goldberg, vice president at Sitrick And Company, witnessed the events of that day and for several days following. She was impressed with the response from LFC's administrative staff: "I sensed a kind of sadness. It was as if something had happened to your family. But people knew that work had to be done. I was struck by the professionalism that everybody in Mr. Hay's office displayed. Often, by the time a company files for Chapter 11, the employees are cynical and may be planning to leave. I had a sense of real commitment from Lomas' employees. That they were going to stick with Lomas and see it through. They took a personal pride in the company. That's very unusual. That really impressed us. It's a shame the Chapter 11s we've worked on subsequent to that were not like Lomas."

The opportunity for reflection by the staff was brief. Led by Sitrick And Company, they quickly mobilized to implement a massive communications strategy. To ensure the best coverage from LFC's standpoint, Lomas agreed to Mike Sitrick's suggestion that the company file on a weekend. "You have a much better opportunity to control the story," says Amy Goldberg. "The weekend [newspaper] staff pretty much has to take your story and go with what you're telling them. You own the story the first day. You can control the story, and you have time to prepare your employees.

...a communications effort on several fronts.

"It was a communications effort on several fronts. And the way that is handled at the beginning can be critical for a successful outcome. During a filing, one of the greatest problems companies run into is the rumor mill and a lot of confusion. When Braniff filed for Chapter 11 the first time, there was no communications effort and the company was literally paralyzed for the first days after the filing. Employees thought the company was immediately going out of business. They didn't show up for work.

"If your message is not clear and consistent then you're going to feed that rumor mill, and that can have a snowball effect and create tremendous problems. What you do at the starting gate can set the tone for the entire process." The core message that Lomas established early on said Chapter 11 was not a liquidation. It was a reorganization, a way for the company to solve its financial problems and then go forward. Other parts of the communication were adapted to fit Lomas' various constituencies. Beginning early Friday morning on September 22, the team from Sitrick began producing written materials for the press, shareholders, employees, vendors, customers, and homeowners. Ramona Taylor, Joy Weldon, Jeanne McDonald, and Jess Hay reviewed and revised the copy. The company's administrative staff spent Saturday organizing the printed material for distribution. It was a massive undertaking. Judy Justice described the day's events in a written account she prepared in early 1990:

> When we arrived on Saturday, we quickly assessed the situation at hand and everyone went to work on their various tasks. Some put labels on envelopes to be sent to stockholders; some made out Federal Express labels for packages to be sent to the Board of Directors for each of the five Boards; some had information printed by a confidential printing facility for procedure packets regarding how to respond to outside vendors. . . . Mr. Hay and Ramona were the core and everything written, as always, was personally done by Mr. Hay, or at least contained his revisions, thoughts and direction. Press releases were prepared and ads for the various newspapers were finalized.
>
> One of the pages of the press release contained a minor typographical error. Ramona made the decision to replace the defective page. We refused to lower our standards, even though it meant 15 or more people working a couple of [extra] hours in an already too short day to make the correction. I think that incident was very telling. The standards in the Chairman's office are higher than any I have ever known, and that did not change.
>
> As a staff, we had done projects of this intensity . . . a hundred times before. This is what we did best. In a way it was a great relief once we got started. Instead of waiting and worrying, we could move forward with purpose and action. We put the agony of indecision behind and came together in a unified effort. We didn't know what the future held, but we knew what we had to do that weekend to begin dealing with our new status.

The Sunday afternoon drive that Lomas general counsel Jim Crowson took with Davis Polk attorneys Laureen Bedell and Don Bernstein on September 24, 1989, was no lighthearted weekend jaunt. Their destination was suburban Westchester County and the home of U.S. bankruptcy court clerk Cecelia M. Lewis. Their purpose was protection from Lomas Financial Corporation's creditors. Lewis had agreed earlier in the week to handle the filing in the event it proved necessary. "We went to Cecelia's house," says Bedell, "and she stamped our petitions . . . using her little kitchen clock. So, at 3:08 p.m. on Sunday we were officially filed."

Now, we could start the process of healing.

The summary petition that Lomas delivered that afternoon explained its objectives:

> The Debtors believe that under the aegis of the Bankruptcy Court and through the financial reorganization provisions of Chapter 11, they will be able to formulate and propose a plan or plans of reorganization that both will realize more for creditors and equity security holders than would a liq-

uidation and be consistent with their capacity to perform. The Debtors intend that such a plan or plans of reorganization will provide for the equitable treatment of all parties in interest while permitting the Debtors to emerge as viable and successful Businesses.

From the clerk's house, Crowson and the other attorneys drove to Judge Howard Bushman's residence, also in Westchester. Judge Bushman agreed to act on an emergency basis to approve a series of special court orders permitting the continued operation of the company's payroll and cash management. Seated at his kitchen table, wearing a kick-back flannel shirt, he questioned Crowson about the first-day order requests. "He asked whether our debt was secured or unsecured," says Crowson. "I told him that because we failed to do the restructure it was largely unsecured. He said, 'Then you've got a chance,' and signed our first-day orders."

Once it had filed, Lomas Financial Corporation issued a news release. Also that afternoon Hay met with business journalists and bureau chiefs for *The New York Times*, *The Wall Street Journal*, *The Dallas Times Herald*, and *The Dallas Morning News* for previously arranged one-on-one interviews. Senior management first broke the news to its officers at a meeting held that evening in LFC's 36th floor Bryan Tower auditorium. Just prior to the meeting Jess Hay telephoned Dick Hay. "I got a call on Sunday night at about 8 o'clock," says the former vice president for Chase Manhattan Bank. "I was surprised, and I think sort of numb. He said something about the board voted to file, and we fought the good fight, and we'll move on from here. I didn't have a whole lot to say at that point. I was very depressed. I thought we had a vehicle to get the thing done. One hundred eighty percent of my energies had been spent on this since probably June 29. So, I was pretty well burned out."

"When the meeting began at 7 p.m. there wasn't an empty chair in the 36th floor auditorium," reads an account of the officers' meeting that appeared in the first issue of *Lomas Review*, a new corporate publication. "It was Jess Hay, Chairman and CEO, who stepped to the podium and announced what nearly everyone had by then guessed, Lomas Financial Corporation had filed for voluntary protection from its creditors under Chapter 11 of the U.S. Bankruptcy Code."

From Michael Sitrick's perspective, the meeting was a positive, effective communication: "The fire bell rang, and the horses came charging out of the barn." It included a comprehensive explanation of the sequence of events that led to the filing. And that made a difference, according to LFC records manager Carol Forsberg: "Mr. Hay explained what happened, and that helped bring everything into clearer focus. He was reassuring. He said, 'This is what happened. This is what we're going to do. This is approximately how long we're going to be in Chapter 11, and this is what I need from you.' Overall, the tone was upbeat. He didn't go overboard, but it was encouraging. He was blunt, straightforward, yet reassuring. And we needed that."

"The meeting was quiet and very supportive of Jess," says David Farr. "My memory of it was that there was no panic. There was relief. It brought clarity to our situation. Most of management realized that Chapter 11 was going to be a solution rather than a problem, because it was going to buy the company time."

Lorraine Grant also appreciated the end of ambiguity that Chapter 11 represented: "We were relieved, because there was no question anymore about where we were. Now, we could start the process of healing." Grant also observed a difference in Jess Hay. She noticed the previous day that he "looked horrible. Then on Sunday I sensed a feeling of relief. The stress I saw Saturday was gone. It was like he said, 'I embrace this decision, and now I go forward.' And that's what he's done ever since that day. He accepted the challenge that was before him, and we accepted it with him."

FREE FOR ALL: A SAMPLING OF NEW FEATURES, COLUMNS. PAGE 9A.

The Dallas Morning News

Texas' Leading Newspaper ©1989, The Dallas Morning News — Dallas, Texas, Monday, September 25, 1989 — 6 Sections — B — ••• 25 Cents

Lomas Financial files for Chapter 11

Texas ties unduly hurt company, chairman says

By David LaGesse
Staff Writer of The Dallas Morning News

To hear Jess Hay tell it, the day Lomas Financial Corp. filed for bankruptcy, guilt by association had felled the huge company.

The Lomas chairman appeared calm Sunday as he sat for an interview in the opulent executive offices on the 36th floor of Bryan Tower in downtown Dallas.

Affable, businesslike and characteristically optimistic, Mr. Hay nonetheless displayed frustration at the key credit analysts who he said blackballed Lomas because of its Texas connections.

Lomas remains fundamentally sound, he said — just strapped for cash because it lost access to short-term, unsecured borrowings.

Bank examiners, for example, had focused on the company's Texas properties and forced lenders to consider it a troubled company, Mr. Hay said.

"I think there is a knee-jerk reaction that is unnecessarily committed to the view that we are down for a long time," Mr. Hay said of his home

Please see TEXAS on Page 6A.

Jess Hay . . . says the company decided that "time had run out" on negotiations.

Bankruptcy is one of nation's largest; no major staff reductions expected

By David LaGesse
Staff Writer of The Dallas Morning News

Lomas Financial Corp., in one of the largest bankruptcies in the nation, on Sunday filed for protection from creditors in a New York court.

After three months of a liquidity crisis, the company decided that "time had run out" on negotiations to restructure some of its debt, chairman Jess Hay said.

With more than $6 billion in assets, Lomas is believed to be the second-largest bankruptcy in Dallas history — behind the 1986 collapse of LTV Corp. — and the sixth-largest nationally. The company, with operations in mortgage banking and real estate finance, on Friday decided to terminate discussions with its bank lenders.

The company then sought protection under Chapter 11 of the U.S. bankruptcy code. Only the parent company and some land development subsidiaries filed for bankruptcy, freezing payments on a total of $2.1 billion in debt.

Other subsidiaries, including Lomas' mortgage banking, life insurance, and leasing companies, did not seek bankruptcy protection, the company said.

Mr. Hay said that Lomas' continuing operations should remain largely unaffected and that the filing should not cause any "material staff reductions." Lomas employs about 2,600 people in the Dallas-Fort Worth area.

He said he remains confident that Lomas can emerge from its problems as a strong company. "Nobody has seriously questioned the company's solvency," he said.

"Our problem is liquidity."

Mr. Hay predicted a "relatively

Please see LOMAS on Page 6A.

Here To Stay

Immigration act gives family brighter future

Second in a series
By Frank Trejo
Staff Writer of The Dallas Morning News

HOUSTON — Dreams of a happy future have replaced more ominous thoughts in the minds of Juan and Marta Aguilar and their family.

"I used to have nightmares all the time," Mrs. Aguilar said. "They were dreams of him (her husband) on the other side, and me on this side, trying to reach him, but I couldn't. I would not tell him about these dreams because of my superstition that if you talk about something, it might come true."

AMNESTY'S SECOND PHASE
Impact on families
■ Enforcement problems. 8A
■ Workplace discrimination. 8A

What separated the couple in Mrs. Aguilar's nightmare was the U.S.-Mexico border. And until two years ago, Mr. Aguilar knew that the nightmare could come true. At that time, the Aguilars and three of their six children were illegal immigrants living in Dallas, constantly on guard and fearful that the lives they had built for more than a decade could be forever disrupted in an instant, if one of them was caught by U.S. immigration authorities.

But instead of coming between them, the U.S. government came to their aid. The Aguilars benefited from the sweeping Immigration Reform and Control Act of 1986, which was intended to reduce the flow of illegal immigration and legalize millions of immigrants already in the country.

Under the act, illegal immigrants who could prove they had entered the United States before Jan. 1, 1982, and had been living here continuously since then could qualify for general amnesty if they met certain other criteria. Nearly 1.8 million aliens applied for general amnesty during the yearlong application period that began May 1987, with more than 1.5 million getting it, 80,000 being refused and nearly 144,000 ap-

Please see FOR SOME on Page 8A.

Redskins beat Cowboys, 30-7

The Dallas Morning News: Gary Kanadjian

Washington's Markus Koch (No. 74) and Darryl Grant (No. 77) celebrate after sacking quarterback Troy Aikman in the Cowboys' home opener. A fumble return gave Dallas its only touchdown Sunday. (Stories on Pages 13A, 1B.)

Hugo victims beset by food, water shortages

From Wire Reports

CHARLESTON, S.C. — Victims of Hurricane Hugo scrambled to meet life's basic needs Sunday, fretting over shortages of food, fresh water, cash and electricity. Unable to cook or boil water, people stood in line for blocks waiting for hot meals.

"There's no bread; there's no meat," said Harold Washington, 21, at a supermarket that had doughnuts and peanut butter but lacked staples. "You can't survive like that. Things just aren't working fast enough."

Mr. Washington, who lives with his mother and four siblings, said the family was burning candles at night and washing clothes by hand. They worried that the water they were using to brush their teeth was contaminated.

HURRICANE HUGO'S AFTERMATH
■ St. Croix recovering. 3A
■ Hurricane counseling 16A

National Guardsmen with M-16 rifles patrolled the streets of the battered city of 65,000 people, guarding against looters and keeping order at locations where residents lugged coolers and plastic jugs to get fresh water.

By Sunday night, 27 people had been charged with looting in Charleston, with all the arrests made before Sunday. About a dozen others had been arrested and charged with such offenses as disorderly conduct, violating the curfew

Please see FOOD on Page 4A.

Democrats' fears eased

New chairman plays down ties to Jackson, works on fund raising

By Carl P. Leubsdorf
Washington Bureau of The Dallas Morning News

WASHINGTON — For nearly an hour the other morning, Ronald Brown picked at his eggs Benedict and fielded questions ranging from the future of Rep. Barney Frank to the Democratic Party's problems in countering President Bush.

Finally, a reporter asked him about the political plans of the Rev. Jesse Jackson.

"I thought this would be the first one where I haven't gotten a Jesse Jackson question," quipped the Democratic national chairman, who managed Mr. Jackson's 1988 convention operations.

Still, the questioning dwelt only briefly on the subject that often dominated such sessions after Mr. Brown in February became the first black to head a major U.S. political party.

"I think it's fading away as an issue for me because I've proven to my party that I'm my own man," Mr. Brown said. "And as I've projected that, there are fewer and fewer ques-

Please see DEMOCRATS on Page 4A.

Ronald Brown . . . the transition has been difficult.

Anti-drug efforts take new direction in Peru

U.S. aid aimed at countering Shining Path rebels

By Gustavo Gorriti
Special Contributor to The Dallas Morning News

SANTA LUCIA, Peru — Here at the starting point of the world's cocaine pipeline, the United States and Peru have built a fortress that takes President Bush's war on drugs in a deadly new direction.

The base is defended by minefields, layers of barbed wire, a sandbagged perimeter, underground bunkers and watchtowers equipped with heavy machine guns. It is staffed by a dozen or so U.S. Drug Enforcement Administration and contract personnel and about 100 Peruvian police officers.

Santa Lucia sits on the hub of the world's coca heartland, the Upper Huallaga Valley, where the Shining Path — a ruthless Maoist guerrilla organization — rules with a mixture of discipline and terror.

The base here and President Bush's $70 million anti-drug assistance package to Peru are visible signs that the U.S. coca-eradication program is evolving into counterinsurgency warfare against the Shining Path.

The $70 million involves $40 million for the army, $26 million for the

Please see PERU on Page 7A.

COLOMBIA
ECUADOR
BRAZIL
Santa Lucia
Pacific Ocean
PERU
BOLIVIA
Area detailed
The Dallas Morning News

Mattox disputes News story on alcoholism, campaign

Austin Bureau of The Dallas Morning News

AUSTIN — Attorney General Jim Mattox said Sunday that although he considers alcoholism and drug abuse issues in the 1990 gubernatorial campaign, he does not intend to single out his opponent in the Democratic primary, state Treasurer Ann Richards, as a recovering alcoholic.

Mrs. Richards acknowledges that she sought treatment for alcoholism nine years ago and says that she has not had a drink since then.

In a statement Sunday, Mattox campaign press secretary Steve Levine said Mr. Mattox's comments in a *Dallas Morning News* story Sunday about the ability of a recovering alcoholic to govern the state were taken out of context.

"*The News* took his words out of context when he was talking about the effect of drug and alcohol abuse on his family and friends, and strung his words together to create a personal attack on Ann Richards, which did not take place.

"Jim Mattox has not made an issue out of her alcoholism, thus far

Please see MATTOX on Page 6A.

INSIDE

Accident clues

Townspeople and investigators gather at the scene of a bus accident in Alton, Texas, trying through science and gut reaction to make sense of the tragedy that killed 20 schoolchildren.

Page 19B.

Ann Landers	2C	Metropolitan	13-16A
The Arts	5C	Movies	6C
Bridge	8C	Obituaries	16A
Business	1-6D,8D	School Quiz	19B
Classified	Sec. E	Sports	Sec. B
Comics	9-11C	Television	7C
Crossword	8C	Texas & S'west	19B
Dear Abby	8C	Today	Sec. C
Discoveries	6-7D	Viewpoints	11A
Editorials	10A		
Free for All	9A		

Weather on Page 8D.

On Monday morning, September 25, 1989, *The Dallas Morning News'* front-page headline said it all. Reprinted with permission of *The Dallas Morning News*.

CHAPTER XVI

THE END OF THE BEGINNING

Sitrick And Company's communications game plan picked up momentum on Monday, September 25. An article in the *Lomas Review* described its implementation:

> Before dawn the next day, officers and managers began arriving at their desks, getting an early start on the critical task at hand: placing phone calls to customers and other vital constituents of Lomas. The goal was simple but critically important, explain to these key people exactly what Chapter 11 would—and would not—mean. At his desk Hay began phoning a long list of bankers and others close to Lomas. On the same floor down the hall, Ted Enloe, president, was working on his own list of key contacts.
>
> The message was the same. Lomas needed time to continue the business restructuring plan begun in June. Chapter 11 would provide that time.

The public relations professionals skillfully orchestrated news of the event. That coverage contained most of the key points in the company's news releases, even to the extent of using similar phrasing and similar quotes from Jess Hay. LFC's filing captured the front-page headlines in Dallas' two dailies. As *The Dallas Morning News* noted in its headline story, bankruptcy filings don't get much bigger than this, in Texas or anywhere else: "With more than $6 billion in assets, Lomas is believed to be the second-largest bankruptcy in Dallas history—behind the 1986 collapse of LTV Corp.—and the sixth-largest nationally."

Mike Sitrick took time out from his schedule Monday for a bit of public relations morale boosting

Sitrick And Company confidently mobilized Lomas for a massive communications strategy. Seated, left to right, Steve Stern, Mike Sitrick, and Rivian Bell. Standing, Ross Palmer and Amy Goldberg.

aimed at Lomas' chairman and CEO. He found a print shop that specialized in gag newspaper headlines and printed one that prophesied an upbeat end to the process, handing it to Jess Hay that afternoon. In large, bold print, it announced: "LOMAS EMERGES FROM CHAPTER 11. A great success story of the '90s."

On Tuesday, the company dominated coverage of the event by running full-page ads in *The Wall Street Journal*, *The New York Times*, *The Dallas Times Herald*, and *The Dallas Morning News*. Addressed to "the friends of Lomas Financial," the ads explained why Lomas had entered Chapter 11 and what it expected to achieve. They also clarified the fact that the filing included only Lomas Financial Corporation and Lomas Realty USA and its subsidiaries.

Telephone calls flooded the company's switchboard. Much of the burden fell on assistant vice president for stockholder relations Joy T. Weldon, the treasury department, and Hay's office. "The whole world was calling about the Chapter 11," says Byerley. "Banks, stockholders, bondholders, analysts, newspaper reporters, magazine writers— it seemed like everybody in the world was calling. On Monday, the day after we filed, I got over 600 phone calls. Most of the people I spoke to were nice, and some were angry." Then there were the callers who weren't satisfied with the information they got and called back—repeatedly. One of these was a stockholder who owned 50,000 shares. "He called five or six times a day, and

The whole world was calling about the Chapter 11.

To the friends of Lomas Financial

By now you probably are aware of the news: Lomas Financial Corporation (LFC) has voluntarily filed a petition for reorganization under Chapter 11 of the federal Bankruptcy Code. You probably are less aware, however, of the circumstances – some negative, some positive – surrounding our difficult decision to begin Chapter 11 proceedings. As a friend of our company, you deserve to know the reasons why we took this step, the events leading up to it and the results we expect it to achieve.

Who the filing includes.

Many companies carry either the Lomas name or a well-known association with Lomas. Of greatest concern today is the inevitable confusion over precisely which of these companies LFC's filing includes. The answer, fortunately, is simple and brief. Lomas Financial Corporation, Lomas Realty USA and its subsidiaries, including principally Lomas Land, and Roosevelt Office Center, Inc. are the only companies included in the filing.

Who the filing does not include.

LFC's action should have no material impact on our operating subsidiaries:

Lomas Mortgage USA
Lomas Advisors
Lomas Corporate Services
Lomas Information Systems
Lomas Management
Lomas Administrative Services
Equitable Lomas Leasing
Jefferson National Life Insurance Company
Union Life Insurance Company
First Continental Life & Accident Insurance Company

Nor will it materially affect four affiliated companies which, despite the similarity in name, are independently owned and separately listed on the New York Stock Exchange. These are:

Lomas Mortgage Corporation
Lomas & Nettleton Mortgage Investors
Lomas Mortgage Securities Fund
L&N Housing Corp.

How we got here.

For LFC, Chapter 11 is neither an end nor a beginning. Rather, filing for Chapter 11 protection affords us the time to continue a course begun some months ago, a financial restructuring which brought promising accomplishments until the constraints proved impossible to overcome.

LFC's national and local markets have been in turmoil, with personal bankruptcies and home foreclosures reaching record highs last year. At the same time, national demand for home mortgages was falling.

In Texas, where more than half of LFC's real estate investments are concentrated, the real estate depression was deepening. Interest rates were rising for the short-term borrowing LFC needed to bridge the crisis.

Then, in June, federal bank examiners criticized LFC's credit; and major rating agencies downgraded the company's debt securities.

With business in a downturn and short-term credit choked off, LFC undertook a restructuring which within two months was already showing dramatic signs of success. Largely through the sale of our retail banking division, we reduced general corporate debt by approximately $475 million and cut consolidated debt by more than $1.9 billion, from $5.7 billion at the end of June to $3.8 billion by the end of August. The sale of our leasing unit within the next few months was expected to retire another $1.5 billion of consolidated debt. Our major lenders already had agreed in principle with our restructuring plan and seemed to share our belief that LFC would return to profitability and, in time, to leadership in the industry.

Yet, despite the progress and the promise, LFC and the private lenders were unable to reach a fully documented agreement before September 1, when notes totaling $145 million matured. As the complex restructuring negotiations and disputes among creditors dragged on, time simply ran out. Left with no reasonable alternative, LFC filed for Chapter 11 protection.

How we intend to proceed.

Under Chapter 11 LFC will have time to complete the restructuring program to the benefit of all our constituencies – creditors, stockholders, customers and employees.

We will continue to operate in the ordinary course of our businesses. Customers should notice no change in our operations.

We will not decimate the organization. Our restructuring plan includes the strategic positioning of our mortgage banking, funds management, real estate finance and information systems businesses to help them compete most effectively in the future. We intend to continue every operation which can return us to profitability.

We plan no further cuts in employment. Reductions appropriate to our planned restructure already have been made. Until very recently, LFC was at the top of its industry. No one is better equipped than our employees to help us regain that position.

We will repay our debts. Already we have reduced our consolidated debt dramatically. Operating under Chapter 11, we expect to accomplish the divestitures in our original restructuring plan. Thus, as we emerge as a reorganized company, our consolidated debt will be significantly reduced and related financial ratios will be improved.

We have great faith in the employees of our company, the viability of our businesses and the markets in which we operate. We strongly believe that the company will be strengthened and value enhanced through the actions we are taking.

We are confident that all of our constituencies will benefit and that LFC will be able to reestablish its preeminence as a provider of financial and administrative services to the real estate and mortgage finance industries.

LOMAS

LOMAS FINANCIAL CORPORATION, 2001 BRYAN TOWER, DALLAS, TEXAS

As seen in *The New York Times*, Tuesday, September 26, 1989

Lomas demonstrated that it was on top of the event, controlling the coverage with a full-page ad addressed to its "friends."

The company's switchboard was inundated with telephone calls from concerned investors. Joy Weldon, assistant vice president for stockholder relations, was there to answer their questions in her calm and knowing way.

The *Lomas Review* was edited by Kevin McGarry, for an audience that included the Lomas work force as well as members of the creditors and equityholders committees.

asked the same questions," says Byerley. In an attempt to extract additional or different information, the shareholder resorted to impersonating the treasurer of TRW. It took Byerley two phone calls to determine his true identity.

In shareholder relations, Joy Weldon and her staff "literally sat at their desks 12 hours a day for the rest of the week, just answering and returning phone calls," says Byerley. "I think Joy Weldon did an absolutely great job. I don't know how she kept her sanity." Sitrick And Company helped fill the breach by fielding many of the media and shareholder calls.

The primary source of information for Lomas employees came from the *Lomas Review*, the corporate newsletter whose first issue appeared on October 9, 1989. Written for the most part by Sitrick's staff, the copy reinforced the Lomas message about Chapter 11. Vice president and publication editor Kevin G. McGarry compiled a two-page "family tree" that identified the various business areas of the Lomas family of companies. The most popular front-page feature was one titled "A Message from the Chairman." It was a personal column from Jess Hay, and it provided an important source of direction, inspiration, and hope throughout the Chapter 11 proceedings. The column showcased Hay's charismatic ability to articulate the company's values and goals and motivate the staff toward their accomplishment.

It was a serious newsletter. Most of the early issues contained profiles about the professionals associated with the Chapter 11 proceedings and in-depth articles that featured the divisions and key departments within Lomas. The *Lomas Review*'s audience also included the members of the creditors and equityholders committees. Word filtered back that they were among the newsletter's most avid readers. Chapter 11 consultant John Grigsby claimed that the creditors committee, in particular, "devoured" each issue, cover to cover.

Prominent displays of magazine and newspaper articles on office bulletin boards helped enhance communication. The outside professionals retained by

LOMAS REVIEW

VOLUME I, NUMBER I OCTOBER 9, 1989

A MESSAGE FROM THE CHAIRMAN

The decision to file for reorganization under Chapter 11 was a difficult yet necessary one. It has cleared the cloud of uncertainty that has been hanging over us and will allow us to move forward with the fundamental restructuring of our businesses.

We can function effectively and productively in this environment if we embrace the belief that today is neither the beginning nor the end. Rather, it is a new stage in a restructuring process begun some months ago.

It is our task to reach out and demonstrate to the outside world that Lomas' operations will not be substantially impacted by the actions we have taken and will, in fact, be strengthened.

Our core business, mortgage banking, has every expectation of generating substantial operating cash flow this year. It is strong both operationally and financially. The same can be said for our life insurance and information systems divisions, which are essentially debt-free and functioning according to plan.

Although our short-term lending unit, for a while, will be constricted, its portfolio of investments is as sound as any in our industry and its staff is of the highest conceivable quality. Challenges confronting the division recently have been intense, as both Lomas & Nettleton Mortgage Investors and Lomas Financial Corporation have shared liquidity pressures and related funding capacity limitations. But even in the context of limited resources, our loan and administrative officers will continue to execute their mission professionally and, just as was the case in the late 1970s, they will emerge as premier providers of financial services to the real estate development industry.

Our commercial leasing division also has experienced liquidity pressures due to the lowering of its credit ratings. Negotiations are in progress to finalize the restructuring of its debt, so that its superb staff of professionals can concentrate its efforts on the efficient execution of the division's business.

As I said in my letter to you last week, we would have preferred to implement our restructuring program outside the confines of a Chapter 11 proceeding. However, we were left with no reasonable alternative. Despite substantial progress in restructuring our business, exhaustive negotiations with our lenders over a three-month period did not produce timely closure of a satisfactory debt restructure. As the complex negotiations and disputes among creditors dragged on, time simply ran out.

I know how difficult this period has been for you, but the uncertainty is now behind us. Our goal is to emerge from Chapter 11 in a relatively short period of time, and I am confident that we will do so.

My conviction in this regard stems in no small measure from my devotion to and confidence in you, the people of Lomas. It is our job, working together as a team, to bring the Company out of Chapter 11 as a viable, fully restructured operation, with our equity intact and all of our constituencies — creditors, stockholders and employees — fully provided for.

During this critical period, as in every period, the Company's strength derives primarily from its people. In crisis, you have performed remarkably well. For that I thank you, and want you to know personally how important your dedication and support have been and will continue to be during the weeks and months ahead. Together we will prevail.

Hay, Enloe, Others on Phone at Dawn Monday Explaining Reasons

Most Units Unaffected by Chapter 11; Filing Gets Consistent, Wide Coverage

The news reached the 36th floor of Bryan Tower just after 2 p.m. Sunday, Sept. 24. Lawyers for Lomas had succeeded in filing the papers necessary to start Chapter 11 proceedings. Now the assembled task force could start the phone calls that would summon senior officers and managers to a meeting to be held early that evening. The group had worked feverishly all weekend, preparing reams of materials that would be needed once the filing had been accomplished.

Included were letters to managers, employees, stockholders, bondholders, and various customers as well as press releases and other materials.

When the meeting began at 7 p.m. there wasn't an empty chair in the 36th floor auditorium. It was Jess Hay, chairman and CEO, who stepped to the podium and announced what nearly everyone had by then guessed, Lomas Financial Corporation had filed for voluntary protection from its creditors under Chapter 11 of the U.S. Bankruptcy Code.

Before dawn the next day, those same officers and managers began arriving at their desks, getting an early start on the critical task at hand: placing phone calls to customers and other vital constituents of Lomas. The goal was simple but critically important, explain to these key people exactly what Chapter 11 would — and would not — mean. At his desk Hay began phoning a long list of bankers and others close to Lomas. On the same floor down the hall, Ted Enloe, president, was working on his own list of key contacts.

Their message was the same. Lomas needed time to continue the business restructuring plan begun in June. Chapter 11 would provide that time.

Later in the week both Hay and Enloe would fly to New York to carry that important message personally to key Lomas lenders.

In other circles, reaction to the filings was widespread. Among employees, a common sentiment was reflected in the comment from one who said, "I feel like a big weight has been lifted with the removal of the uncertainty of our situation. It was the uncertainty that was so hard to deal with."

Media interest in the announcement was equally widespread. Both Dallas daily newspapers carried accounts as did the New York Times and the Wall Street Journal. Stories also appeared in many other newspapers around the state and country, and radio and TV stations gave the story prominence.

On its front page of Monday, Sept. 25 the Wall Street Journal summarized the filing thus: "Lomas Financial filed for bankruptcy-court protection. The chairman predicted the company would emerge from Chapter 11 relatively quickly with a plan that will provide 100 percent payment for creditors."

Jess Hay echoed that assessment in an interview in the Dallas Morning

continued on page 4

Commonly Asked Questions, Answers to Those Questions

The following information is designed to help you sort through the complexity of the Chapter 11 proceedings and answer questions you may encounter as a member of the Lomas team.

Q. WHAT DOES CHAPTER 11 MEAN?

A. It means Lomas Financial Corporation has taken the initiative to seek the protection of the United States Bankruptcy Court in order to work out a plan that will allow us the necessary time to implement our restructuring program and redirect Lomas so that it is positioned for a viable future.

Q. WHY DID LOMAS FILE CHAPTER 11?

A. When the Company began negotiations with its lenders three months ago, management believed there was sufficient time to implement an out-of-court plan it had developed as a solution to the Company's difficulties. The Company is now past that point. Thus, after an intensive review of the Company and its current liquidity pressures, the board of directors concluded that prompt and decisive action must be taken to preserve the Company. Accordingly, we filed voluntary petitions for relief under Chapter 11 of the federal Bankruptcy Code for Lomas Financial Corporation, Lomas Realty USA and its subsidiaries, including principally Lomas Land, and Roosevelt Office Center in the United States Bankruptcy Court in New York City, where many of our principal creditors are located.

continued on page 4

The Lomas Review debuts today as a newsletter designed to communicate with all Lomas employees during the Chapter 11 reorganization period and beyond. It will initially appear every other week, with publication frequency later to be determined by the amount of new information available.

"It is important that we do all we can to ensure that employees have access to the most up-to-date information available," said Ted Enloe, president of Lomas Financial Corporation.

In addition to the newsletter, other communication vehicles are being developed to increase the flow of information. For example, bulletin boards throughout the company are now displaying newspaper and magazine clippings related to Lomas. They will be updated as news unfolds.

It is important to emphasize that any calls from the media should immediately be referred to our public relations counsel, Sitrick And Company, either through (214) 746-7106 in Bryan Tower or through its headquarters in Los Angeles at (213) 208-1108.

Factual information for Lomas employees came from the *Lomas Review*. The first issue appeared on October 9, 1989.

Lomas provided another source of information about Chapter 11 and how to function in it. "Within the first few days of filing," says Ernst & Young Chapter 11 consultant Alan Bell, "I made presentations to the accounting and treasury departments. 'This is what Chapter 11 is. Here's what's going to happen, and these are some of the terms you're going to hear. If someone calls you a DIP, for example, don't take it personally. It just means debtor-in-possession, which is what you call a company that files a Chapter 11 petition.'"

Sessions like Bell's offered reassurance. "The first thing you want to do is stabilize the organization," says Grigsby, "because bankruptcy is a scary word to the organization and to its customers. We spent a lot of time early on meeting with people throughout the company, explaining what the Chapter 11 process was all about and trying to reassure them that it didn't mean the end of Lomas."

Following Lomas' Chapter 11 filing, Ernst & Young was retained to offer management consulting and accounting services associated with the reorganization. Seated, Tracie Klein and Gary Keiser. Standing, left to right, Jon O'Sullivan, Alan Bell, Tom Haid, and Rob Caire.

The professionals, with the advantage of prior bankruptcy experience, were optimistic about a successful outcome. In terms of litigation, Davis Polk attorney Laureen Bedell considered Lomas "boring." To her, it looked like a workout that ran out of time, and seemed to offer little opportunity for major litigation. Grigsby called it a "traditional financial restructuring." The company needed to restructure its balance sheet, restructure its businesses, and negotiate with its creditors. "Typically, the first problem I have to deal with is how to stop the bleeding from companies hemorrhaging money. That wasn't the case at Lomas. It was fun for me. It was the first time in a long time that I was dealing with a company that clearly had a very good business and a very bright future."

I had the authority to protect our investors by taking over LMUSA's GNMA portfolio.

That's not to say there weren't immediate problems to overcome. The two most serious involved cash and confidence. By the end of September the treasury department had all but exhausted its ability to perform magic with the company's declining cash supply. "On the Sunday that we filed, we were very, very short of cash," says Byerley. "We hardly had enough to keep our operations shoestrung together on a daily basis. We knew we had to get some cash into the system to even survive the first two or three weeks in Chapter 11." In fact, it was during the filing weekend that Byerley met with The CIT Group, a company that specializes in debtor-in-possession (DIP) financing. Lomas obtained a $50 million facility. The DIP credit, however, lost its importance as the company's mortgage banking and short-term lending divisions demonstrated their ability to generate cash. "It seems to me that the most we ever drew on that line of credit was $39 million, and that was only for maybe a week," says Byerley. "We got the [DIP] financing sometime in October, and we borrowed periodically on it through December and never used it again after December."

Ironically, the filing that protected Lomas from its creditors threatened to destroy the company's mortgage banking division—described in corporate reports as "the principal system through which Lomas intends to drive its growth." The threat came from the Government National Mortgage Association (GNMA), for whom the mortgage company was a major servicer. Almost half of LMUSA's $22 billion servicing portfolio fell under the terms of the GNMA Guaranty Agreement. Under that agreement, LFC's filing could be interpreted as a "material change in business status" and the basis for an immediate default. Once in default, GNMA had the right to seize the mortgage company's GNMA portfolio without compensation. Jim Wooten believed that that would have been the first in a series of very destructive falling dominoes: "There goes GNMA. Then, there goes FHA, VA, and even servicing contracts from individual privately owned institutions.

"We had plenty of net worth, and we followed all the rules. But our parent was in bankruptcy. Now, what do you do as a bureaucrat?"

Fortunately for Lomas, U.S. Department of Housing and Urban Development special advisor Arthur J. Hill was no ordinary bureaucrat. He was, in fact, a successful Miami banker who had arrived in Washington, D.C., one month before LFC filed for Chapter 11. His principal concern focused on LMUSA's financial and operational performance. There was little question that he would have pulled the plug at the slightest sign of impropriety from either the debtor or the creditors. "I had the authority to protect our investors by taking over Lomas Mortgage USA's GNMA portfolio," says Hill. "If the creditors [or debtor] did anything that caused me to feel uncomfortable, then we would have stepped in and executed our rights under the GNMA Agreement."

There was no shortage of comfort from Lomas

The treasury department had the unenviable task of supplying cash and confidence at a time when both were in short supply. Bert Byerley, left, Deborah Nesbitt, and Steve Hall.

From left to right, treasury's Todd Hunnicutt, Robert Kane, Lauri Rothballer, and Joan Holmes.

Standing, left to right, Paul Fletcher, Warren Caldwell, Jr., and Shelley Krause. Seated, Scott Holtz.

HUD special advisor Arthur Hill's principal concern focused on LMUSA's financial and operational performance. He had the authority to protect his investors by taking over LMUSA's GNMA portfolio. Courtesy U.S. Department of Housing and Urban Development.

management. Special advisor Hill found himself enveloped in a cocoon of reassuring phone calls, meetings, and financial data. The competence and calm, low-key demeanor of LMUSA's financial officer, executive vice president David Stephens, made a particularly good impression. In briefings, Hill found Stephens "very competent and very responsive. He had the answers to most of my questions on the spot. And if he didn't, he got them."

The input from Lomas was helpful, but it wasn't enough. Hill proved a hands-on administrator who observed a judicious concern for multiple constituencies. He decided he couldn't "sit in an office in Washington and make a decision. First and foremost I wanted to perform my duties under the charter of GNMA and protect our investors. Secondly, there were a lot of people who had jobs at Lomas. Families depended on this entity for their livelihood, and I didn't want to make a decision without a firsthand look. So I got up out of my chair, and I took a flight." It was an important trip. Scrutiny by Hill and his staff went a long way in satisfying agency uncertainties. "I found very strong management," says Hill, "and a clean and efficient high-tech operation. Our investigation reaffirmed our initial view that the ongoing viability of LMUSA was not in jeopardy."

Hill found the company's commitment to integrity equally compelling. When Hill asked a friend of his who was also the chairman and CEO of a major Florida bank about Paul Low, the banker told him that LMUSA's president was an "honorable man who can be trusted." That information corresponded with what Hill calls "an intuitive feeling about the character of [LMUSA's] management." Integrity coupled with the mortgage company's willingness to provide both solicited and unsolicited information won the support of this critically important federal agency.

Evidence of GNMA's confidence in LMUSA went beyond the decision not to place it in default. The November 1989 issue of the *Lomas Review* reported that LMUSA "began subservicing 1,200 loans for GNMA in October." This small but not unimportant morale-boosting event demonstrated to both Lomas employees and the industry that LMUSA had the capacity to survive the injury to its parent.

Jess had a plan.

Two and a half weeks after LFC filed for Chapter 11, the CEO prepared a four-page internal memorandum outlining his vision of the future. He called it "A Preliminary Direction." It pointed to an old and valued formulation for Lomas and for Jess Hay: profit with honor. "Lomas Financial Corporation's primary objective is to emerge from

Chapter 11 on or before June 30, 1991, as a restructured, fully viable and profitable institution. . . . In the context of its primary objective, the Company also is committed to honoring its responsibilities to:

- its employees,
- its customers,
- its creditors and
- its stockholders."

According to the memorandum, the "financially strong enterprise" that emerged from Chapter 11 would be structured around five continuing operations. Those included mortgage banking, funds management, short-term real estate lending, information systems, and real estate development. "As envisioned," read the document, "the mortgage banking, funds management and information systems units will be cast in a growth mode; the short-term real estate lending division will be moderately restricted at least initially; and the real estate unit will continue in a liquidation mode."

Despite the subsidiary's excellent record, Lomas Advisors failed to overcome the stigma of Chapter 11. Left to right, Jim Trowbridge, David Farmer, David Ridley, Barbara Childers, and Paul Michaels.

John Grigsby was impressed by the memorandum and Hay's vision of what the company would look like at the end of the process. Strategic planning was usually one of the roles he assumed for the companies he advised. That wasn't necessary at Lomas. "In terms of strategic planning, there wasn't an awful lot to be done," says Grigsby. "Jess had a plan. He knew what the company should look like going forward. For someone who had never been through the process before, his memo was amazingly well done. It was astonishing to see how many ideas from it ended up being conceptually embodied in the plan of reorganization."

Efforts by management to stabilize the company's businesses were, for the most part, successful. As John Grigsby predicted, after a couple of months' adjustment it was "business as usual." Lomas Information Systems (LIS), however, was one of several exceptions. Sales and marketing took the biggest hit. Doors slammed shut on executive vice president Floyd L. McGlothlin's efforts to add clients to LIS' outside servicing bureau roster. New business prospects told McGlothlin and his staff that their boards of directors wouldn't permit them even to talk to Lomas representatives. The "growth mode" senior management envisioned was further hampered by continuing delays and added expenditures for LIS' Future System, a highly automated mortgage loan servicing system. Failure to bring this product to market on schedule seriously undermined the division's growth objectives.

The Chapter 11 environment was particularly harsh for the company's funds and asset management businesses. Although the circumstances in each case differed, the company could not sustain its connection to Lomas Advisors, a wholly owned subsidiary, and the four affiliated companies Lomas managed—Lomas & Nettleton Mortgage Investors (LNMI), L&N Housing Corp., Lomas Mortgage Corporation (LMC), and Lomas Mortgage Securities Fund. Even so, senior management implemented strategies that minimized the discomfort and maximized the value of each entity.

Lomas Advisors, which acted as a broker and advisor to pension funds that invested in income-producing real estate, failed to overcome the stigma attached to Chapter 11. Despite its excellent record as a profitable, middle-size investor, pension funds managers treated the advisory group like an infectious disease. "We were a fiduciary for pension funds," says former executive vice president David A. Ridley, who managed Lomas Advisors. "We invested their real estate dollars. And when your parent company is in bankruptcy no one is willing to give you dollars to invest." Besides the drought in new business, Lomas Advisors' two largest clients began to question their continued association with it. Rather than watch the advisory group disintegrate, Ridley and others urged senior management to "realize value now while we still had a good track record and money under management. That made sense to Jess Hay, and he agreed to sell it." On April 20, 1990, Invesco Capital Management, Inc., acquired Lomas Advisors. The company earned $5.2 million in total proceeds from the transaction.

The strategic decision by Lomas to liquidate the assets of LNMI's short-term lending portfolio was a course of action imposed by the marketplace. Faced with the inability to borrow money at favorable rates and a recessionary construction market, the business no longer made economic sense.

L&N Housing Corp. was least affected by Chapter 11. It was designed as an investment vehicle for an inflationary economic climate, a premise that had changed by the late 1980s. "It was clear even before we went into Chapter 11 that we probably either needed to liquidate L&N Housing or find a new home for it," says Hay. "Ultimately, we found a new home for it."

The strategy for Lomas Mortgage Corporation had a happier result. Lomas' management group, Lomas Mortgage Managers, contributed significantly to the publicly traded company's success. Beginning in June 1989, the collateralized mortgage obligation (CMO) securities that LMC sold became less desirable because of their affiliation with Lomas Financial Corporation and its credit problems. Lomas Mortgage Managers, led by Ronn K. Lytle, responded with the acquisition in November 1989 of Strategic Mortgage Investments, Inc., a similar but smaller funds management group. The purchase added badly needed capital at a time when it would have been difficult, if not impossible, to raise in the marketplace. It also provided an opportunity for LMC to distance itself from its Lomas affiliation.

With the shareholders' vote on the acquisition went a proposal to change the company's name to Capstead Mortgage Corporation. "LMC's Board of Directors believes that the new name will underscore LMC's separate identity and will allow name recognition independent of Lomas Financial Corporation," read the explanation in LMC's proxy statement. "The Board of Directors of LMC believes this recognition will enhance LMC's long-term prospects and enable it to more effectively implement its business strategy." The change may have been a good business decision, but it made depressing news for others in the Lomas family of companies. No amount of corporate spin control could finesse the feeling that the name "Lomas," in late 1989, appeared to be a liability rather than an asset.

The Lomas management group for Capstead, now called Capstead Advisers, Inc., successfully addressed another problem unrelated to the bankruptcy. LMUSA's exit from the retail mortgage loan origination market in mid-1989 left Capstead without a source for the jumbo loans it marketed. The management organization began the task of developing systems and a large customer base that initiated a period of dramatic growth. Their efforts had major assistance from the marketplace: as banks, S&Ls, and insurance companies decided to get out of the jumbo loan business, they left the market wide open for conduits like Capstead. "Today, we're doing about $500 million of loans each month, compared to $300 million a year when we relied on Lomas' retail production," Capstead president Lytle said in early 1992. "The loans are coming in at a very fast clip from over 200 financial insti-

With the reorientation of the company by Capstead Advisers and positive business events, the cover of the 1990 Capstead annual report reflected an upbeat mood.

tutions."

The Lomas management organization met its challenges with determination. Two months after LFC filed for Chapter 11, Lytle projected that spirit despite a setback: "We'd planned to get another fund started through Merrill Lynch, but we're not going to get that done. We know we've been turned down because of the bankruptcy. But that doesn't mean we'll be turned down the next time we go back. And we're not going to quit going back. I don't accept any limitations on what our group can accomplish—period."

Although net income dropped from $21.1 million in 1988 to $16.3 million in 1989, the reorientation of the company by Capstead Advisers coupled with an exploding jumbo loan market produced impressive results over the next two years. Net income climbed to $29.1 million in 1990 and to $33.7 million in 1991. The cover of Capstead's 1990 annual report—a photograph of a family framed in happy pastels—reflected the good news.

Besides Capstead, Lytle's group also managed Lomas Mortgage Securities Fund, a mutual fund organized by Lomas in 1988 that invested in mortgage-backed securities. Senior management decided that this affiliate should also undergo a name change. On February 19, 1991, it became Tyler Cabot Mortgage Securities Fund.

One of the first steps in the Chapter 11 proceedings was the appointment of two committees by the court's United States Trustee. The 15-member creditors committee was made up of representatives who held either senior or subordinated debt obligations. The equityholders committee consisted of representatives of Lomas' common and preferred stockholders. As senior debtholders, the banks tended to dominate the creditors committee, although consensual agreement among all parties was a requirement for any final settlement. Among the largest and most influential banks were Chase Manhattan Bank, Bank of New York, Chemical Bank, First National Bank of Chicago, and First Interstate Bank of California. The creditors elected Chase to chair their committee. William A. Teitelbaum served as chairman of the equityholders committee.

I want to disrupt your focus on numbers . . .

In mid-November 1989, the management of LFC met with the creditors committee in Dallas for a two-day review of Lomas. Hay used the opportunity to define the company and its core beliefs. The ultimate source of corporate value, he pointed out in his opening speech to the committee, resided in the staff and its ability to meet the challenge of fulfilling customers' needs. His message was unambiguous. The scope of this Chapter 11 proceeding would include people, and Jess Hay was their advocate:

> Numbers say a lot. And numbers, in the context of your responsibilities, represent the bottom line. But those numbers do not derive from computers or calculators or accountants or lawyers. Those numbers derive from successful, caring outreach to customers. We are in the service business. And our revenues derive from our successful interface with customers. Our numbers derive from providing customers services that they need. And for that reason I want to disrupt your focus on numbers for five minutes to try to put flesh and bone and blood into your thought process as you try to envision what the mortgage banking business as we have redefined it is really all about. We have a five minute film that features people on the firing line interfacing with customers who need help. . . . If you will pardon the disruption of numbers for just five minutes, I'd like for you to sense what the mortgage servicing business is really all about.

Hay's opening remarks included his conviction that the road LFC now traveled would eventually lead to profitability. He believed that the creditors, over time, would share his optimism: "I persevere in the hope that ultimately we will emerge from our current environment with our creditors comfortable with the balance of the debt which will have to be liquidated over time, and with their having confidence in the fact that Lomas Financial Corporation and its continuing operations are viable and that going into the future will be profitable."

Jess Hay was selling trust. But trust, especially in this context, did not come easily. His hopeful outcome fell on skeptical ears. For the most part, it was an audience of workout bankers. "The workout banker's mindset is unique," says Grigsby. "They are, for all intents and purposes, bill collectors. That's what they do. They tend to blame. They tend to say, 'This company screwed us. They borrowed money from us, and they're not paying us back.' Typically, the creditors committee is adversarial to start with because that's who they are. They're workout guys."

"There was an initial period of hostility," says senior vice president and general counsel Jim Crowson, which led to suspicion of wrongdoing. "'How did you get into this horrible mess? There must have been mismanagement, perhaps even fraud. You guys are a bunch of jerks, otherwise you wouldn't be in this kind of shape.' Those were the kinds of things openly discussed by creditors committee representatives." Former Chase Manhattan vice president Dick Hay admitted the group was unhappy: "How can you be happy when you have a large, outstanding debt collecting no interest?"

> We're here to storm the place, because you people are out of control.

The creditors committee hired Price Waterhouse (PW) as its accounting professional. PW's duties included a comprehensive understanding of Lomas so it could advise the committee about corporate reorganization, cash accumulation, and debt load. Unfortunately, the PW people created considerable friction by adopting an aggressive, accusatory attitude in their interaction with the Lomas staff. Crowson says their inquiries about the company carried with them "the tone of an investigation." Ernst & Young's Alan Bell recalls a similar impression beginning with PW's accountants' arrival at Bryan Tower. "The lead partner from Price Waterhouse shows up with seven people," says Bell. "The signal that sent was less than friendly. To me that said, 'We're here to storm the place, because you people are out of control.'"

From that inauspicious beginning the relationship deteriorated. Rather than request appointments and discuss what information they needed, the PW staff showed up at offices and expected Lomas employees to drop what they were doing to serve them. Byerley, who had numerous run-ins with Price Waterhouse, says they displayed "a pushy, New York attitude. They acted like assholes most of the time."

Alan Bell recalls the "hallway comments" that PW made in front of Lomas employees and the poisonous effect they had on the relationship: "They said things like, 'We ought to fire this guy. We ought to get rid of that guy. This place is mismanaged. Nobody knows what they're doing. It's ridiculous to have a company this size with a treasurer only 29 years old. No wonder they are in bankruptcy. We ought to fire everybody and start from scratch.'

"One of the purposes of the bankruptcy process is conciliation. Oftentimes when we [Ernst & Young] work for a creditors committee, we end up getting along very well with the debtor, and in a number of cases the debtor calls us for advice. Well, I assure you nobody at Lomas would call Price Waterhouse for the time of day, the feelings were so bad."

Because of senior vice president Ramona Taylor's 30-year association with Jess Hay and her understanding of the value he placed on integrity, she found the creditors and their professionals' manner deeply offensive. "They treated us like we were criminals and had done something sinister and shady," says Taylor. "They wanted to see every inch of office space—as though we were hiding something. Their attitude made me angry, because all of our people have a lot of integrity, especially Mr. Hay. It was a real eye-opener for me. I didn't realize professionals behaved that way."

Although nettlesome and unpleasant, PW's rude behavior posed no threat to Lomas. The same, however, could not be said about PW's information-gathering techniques. "They [PW] knew they were getting paid for every hour that they spent," says Lazard Frères outside professional Tom Haack. "So they didn't have any incentive to perform on an efficient, intelligent basis. Consequently, they just threw bodies at us. When the creditors, for example, wanted to know about LIS, PW was down there talking to Lynda-Ross Vega and Matt Jacobs all the time. They were there two or three days a week and Lomas people were getting a little bit pissed off at them because they couldn't get any work done. PW did the same thing with the real estate area. They spent an incredible number of hours bugging them under the guise of being 'thorough and professional.'"

Lomas tried to protect the company's operations through a system of special procedures. "You try to protect the ongoing business as much as you can," says Crowson. "You set up structures and you have somebody like a Bert Byerley or me or Louis Gregory [vice president and associate general counsel] take the brunt of those questions, and you use your outside accounting firm as a buffer as much as possible."

Cash was the focal point of the tension between creditors and debtor. The creditors wanted the company to accumulate as much cash as possible for distribution at the end of the process. The company, on the other hand, intended to use a portion of the available cash to reorganize its operations and enhance its viability. LIS became a major battlefield upon which those competing interests fought.

Price Waterhouse decided they needed to know more about MLS.

Presentations to the creditors about LIS did not create the reassurance management hoped for. The successful development of the Future System project on which LIS hung its future was far

The Future System project began in 1983, after L&N acquired Symbolics, Inc., and decided to replace the company's Burroughs system with an IBM-based system. This 1983 ad urges potential clients to use these "three systems that let you pick the brains of Lomas & Nettleton." Seven years later, the viability of Lomas Information Systems and of Excelis was still in question.

from clear. The venture had begun in 1983 following a decision to replace the company's Burroughs system with an IBM-based system "designed to support our mortgage loan servicing needs into the twenty-first century." Upon completion, the project, named Excelis in 1990, would provide support for all phases of the loan servicing business.

Concern about the viability of LIS and Excelis was not without foundation. Although the company claimed that the project was nearing completion, this was far from evident to the creditors committee. "This is the largest development project outside of the government arena in the Southwest," wrote executive vice president Lynda-Ross Vega in a 1989 report, the same year she was promoted to director of systems development. "Historically, less than 10% of the projects this size in the private sector reach completion." Large cost overruns became another concern when the creditors learned that the company had spent about $120 million on a project originally estimated to cost $50 million. "The creditors committee was not at all sure that the company ought to be putting substantially more money into the project," says Crowson. "To put it in candid terms, the creditors and Price Waterhouse thought it might be a black hole." In late November, when Lomas asked that a cash management order include $15 million in mortgage loan servicing (MLS) development costs, the creditors balked. Through a compromise Lomas received $12 million and, if required, could obtain an additional $3 million with the consent of the creditors.

Shortly after the debtor and the creditors held their first meeting in November, the creditors committee and their professionals targeted the project for a comprehensive review. Lomas received a request from PW for Future System documentation. Now it was Lomas' turn to balk. "Price Waterhouse decided they needed to know more about MLS," says Vega. "They requested a whole series of documentation to be sent to their office in New York. It was things like design specifications, programs, and data base structures. And I said, 'No.' That's $100 million worth of documentation. It's proprietary and confidential. If they wanted to come and view it here that's fine, but we're not sending this stuff out tripping around the country." Vega also believed that the kind of information requested wasn't relevant to the task of making sound business recommendations to the creditors. "I thought, Oh, no! Here we go again with another group of people that is going to tell us that they don't like the way we've integrated the data base or something," says Vega. "And that was not what we needed to hear. In fact, I had a brief discussion with Mr. Hay about it. I said, 'This is no longer a democracy. The time for voting is over. We've got what we've got, and we're going to make it work.' Mr. Hay laughed. He has a tendency to laugh at my comments a lot. I haven't decided whether that's good or bad yet."

Lomas and PW agreed to meet at Bryan Tower in mid-December for a detailed presentation about the project. It was the first in a series of meetings that turned out to be some of the most acrimonious of the entire process. Vega's keen observations and wry commentary paint an interesting picture of those events. She notes with particular amusement the heavy involvement of outside professional handlers and what creditors committee representative Dick Hay describes as "enormous posturing on both sides, by professional posturers." He suggests two reasons for PW's aggressive style: "The people at Price Waterhouse didn't really understand the system they were looking at. They were also getting pressured by the committee to get information. Lomas was giving them information. They just felt they weren't getting the proper information. A lot of the people on the committee thought this was a black hole."

Before LIS representatives could meet with PW, they first had to go through a series of pre-meetings with Lomas' professionals from Ernst & Young. "One of the things I found most entertaining about this whole process is that you could never have just one meeting," says Vega. "You have a pre-meeting for the pre-meeting. Then you have the pre-meeting, and then you have the meeting. It's like you need to practice what you're going to practice, and then practice, and then do it. So, we walked through the content with E&Y. And we discussed ad nauseam what it is that PW might really be looking for versus what they were actually asking for."

Lomas and PW crossed swords at the first meeting even before it began. According to prior agreement, the presentation was for Price Waterhouse. But when PW arrived, their entourage included committee professionals from Prudential-Bache and Gregory Bauer, a creditor representative from Bank of New York. "They show up with all these other people," says Vega, "and it plays out like a movie. There's all this eye contact between the knowing people. Everybody polarizes and goes to their appropriate room to call their lawyers to find out whether or not to continue. Alan Bell, John Grigsby, and Bert Byerley scramble out of the room—casually scramble—and call Davis Polk. They decide to go ahead with the meeting, but first we chastise PW for breaking the rules." Surprise attender Greg Bauer did little to calm the waters. During the introductions before the meeting opened, he identified himself and the bank he represented, then added belligerently, "and I'm here to get my money back."

Vega observed during the meeting that several creditor representatives appeared less than attentive: "During several presentations Bauer visibly worked on other things. He went through his briefcase, pulled out stuff and worked on files. I don't know what he was paying attention to, but it wasn't the presentations. The industry expert from Prudential-Bache slept through Floyd McGlothlin's report on what the system does. Literally slept. I sat there and watched him. His eyes were closed. I gave Floyd a sleep score.

"Grigsby was incredible. He never moved. He blended into the background. I think that's what makes his observation skills so good. Bert sat in the back of the room with Scott Holtz. He was the one that spoke up when they asked for something that was out of line. They constantly asked for information that pertained to our five-year plan. They wanted detailed financial information. Bert would interrupt and answer the question. It was like answer number 27—'We've got preliminaries. We're going through the internal process of validating it, and as soon as we have something that we believe is totally representative we will give it to you.' Bert must have explained that four or five times. It was pretty entertaining."

A few days later, Lomas learned that PW wanted another meeting because they didn't get enough detail. A second meeting was scheduled the next week. In order to give PW easier access to requested documentation, Lomas agreed to meet in a conference room at LIS on the Lomas campus. PW representatives were even more persistent in asking for financial data. "We had to do a lot of 'I'm sorry but that's part of the financial information that we will be sharing with you later, but I'm not prepared to release it today,'" says Vega. "Keith Maib [of Price Waterhouse] was there again. He got kind of hostile and would say, 'Am I to assume from that answer that you have something to hide?' That was one of his standard lines. Another thing that irritated them was the fact I refused to furnish them with information from previous systems. Again, Keith asked if I had something to hide. I said, 'No. The point is you are here to evaluate MLS, and the previous systems have nothing to do with MLS.' They decided that I must be hiding something really big. I found out afterwards they said I was uncooperative."

Matt Jacobs, on right with Henry Hortenstine, was upset by Price Waterhouse's "creative approach" to due diligence.

Later that day, an LIS account representative took a call from a customer who told him about a strange telephone conversation. Someone claiming to be from Lomas called and asked all kinds of unusual questions. He left a telephone number that turned out to be the number for Price Waterhouse. Former LIS chief operating officer Matthew S. Jacobs and Bert Byerley couldn't believe it when they heard about PW's "creative approach" to due diligence. First, they corroborated the incident. "We verified that we had all of our facts right," says Vega. "Then, Bert got a security guard and escorted Price Waterhouse off campus. He told them that there had been a serious breach in the ethical protocol of the Chapter 11 proceedings, and he would contact them later to let them know if the meeting would resume.

"When Bert contacted the head of the creditors committee to explain what happened, his initial reaction was disbelief. He said, 'Nobody in their right mind would contact one of your clients.' A couple of hours later he called back and said, 'Well, I guess they did. Actually, they contacted three of your customers.'"

"The first time Bert talked to Chase Manhattan vice president Bob Sacks to report the incident, Sacks, in effect, said that was bullshit, and we were overreacting," says Crowson. "Bob Sacks called back later and apologized. He said we were correct, and that the committee would take corrective action with regard to Price Waterhouse."

Despite the ruffled feathers, Lomas agreed to finish the meeting the next day. Afterward, PW claimed that it still didn't have enough information and wanted to meet again in January. Meanwhile, in late December, LFC president Ted Enloe asked the creditors committee to increase LIS' cash advance from $12 million to $15 million. It took at least two more meetings with PW and the creditors before the committee agreed in February to advance the $3 million.

The committee's approval of the cash advance was not a vote of confidence. At that point, they had little choice. "The creditors saw it as a gigantic waste of money that was not being controlled," says Ernst & Young's Alan Bell. "They saw the losses and heard the old refrain justifying additional expenses—'Well, we're just about there. We just need another 10 million bucks.' The creditors agreed, but they agreed because the alternative didn't make a very pretty picture. You've already got all this money in the project. If you pull the plug now, then it's for sure not worth anything. But if you roll the dice one more time and put a little more money into it, then maybe it will work."

It is very unusual to be growing your company in Chapter 11.

LIS wasn't without its supporters. The strongest endorsement came from IBM in February 1990. The *Lomas Review* trumpeted the news in its February 26 issue:

A strong endorsement came from IBM when it named Lomas Information Systems an Industry Application Specialist and IBM Business Partner, allowing its logo to be incorporated into LIS' advertisements.

> In a move that acknowledges Lomas Information Systems' leading role in providing applications solutions to the mortgage lending industry, International Business Machines Corporation has named Lomas Information Systems an Industry Application Specialist and IBM Business Partner. . . .
>
> Lomas Information Systems' Chief Operating Officer, Matt Jacobs, negotiated the partnership with IBM for more than a year. Jacobs said that the designation of Industry Application Specialist moves LIS one step closer to its vision of becoming the leading provider of information systems products and services to the mortgage lending industry.

The Business Partnership enabled LIS and IBM to make joint sales calls and LIS to receive a revenue share of any hardware sold by IBM as a result of a customer buying LIS software. It also gave LIS permission to incorporate the IBM Business Partner logo into its advertisements and marketing materials.

The designation Industry Application Specialist was even more important. It represented a powerful endorsement of LIS' Future System. "It was a major coup," says Vega. "From an industry standpoint, it gave us a definite leg up on our competitors." "It has given us more credibility than we had back in November," said Jacobs at the time. "So, that's been a big change in the way people are viewing us, not only outside the company but also within the company."

The news from IBM was the first in a string of successes for Lomas. With each announcement there was a boost in credibility and morale. The most spectacular announcement came in April when Lomas reported it would acquire Bright Mortgage Company's $3.5 billion mortgage servicing portfolio, adding 94,000 loans to LMUSA's servicing portfolio. According to loan administration executive vice president Terry J. Deyoe, who engineered the transaction, it "represents an 18 percent portfolio increase, and reflects not only the viability and quality of our mortgage servicing operation, but also Lomas Mortgage USA's commitment to future growth."

The acquisition marked a first in mortgage banking history. It was the first portfolio sale by the Resolution Trust Corporation, the government entity charged with selling the assets accumulated from failing S&Ls. Ironically, because of Lomas' ability to amass cash in the Chapter 11 environment, it was one of a very small number of companies that could take advantage of the buyer's market for servicing following the S&L debacle. Even the cash-conscious creditors recognized the unique business opportunity the sale represented. With little opposition, they approved the $33 million purchase. "It is very unusual to be growing your company in Chapter 11," says Laureen Bedell. "Normally, you can stabilize it, but capital expenditures are very hard to get. The creditors committee agreed with Jess that servicing was a sensible thing to buy. They didn't like the idea that it was their cash, in effect. They'd rather have the cash up front. But they had to acknowledge that he was right—that the market was very good, that it was the right time to buy servicing, and that servicing was the one business around which the company should reorganize."

The company reaffirmed its commitment to portfolio growth a month later, announcing on May 30 the signing of an agreement to acquire a $600 million portfolio from Ameriway Mortgage Corporation of Houston. "The acquisition . . . will increase Lomas Mortgage USA's mortgage servicing portfolio to $24.7 billion—a figure that surpasses its previous high of $23.5 billion posted in June 1988," an article in the *Lomas Review* noted. "The transaction also will add 10,000 loans to Lomas Mortgage USA's servicing portfolio, bringing the total loans serviced to approximately 625,000."

On April 26, 1990, LMUSA benefited from another coup. Its ever-resourceful president, Paul M. Low, devised a way to turn a portion of what were affectionately called "turkey loans" into $55 million of ready cash. The "turkeys" were about $100 million worth of loans with missing documents, no insurance, or whose loan-to-value ratios exceeded the permissible limit.

In April 1990, LMUSA's Paul Low devised a method to turn "turkey" loans into ready cash.

Those deficiencies prevented their sale into the secondary market. "Paul Low came up with an idea," says former LAS president Hal Hillman. "He and Dave Chapman figured out a way to securitize the loans that had good payment histories and sell them to Freddie Mac [Federal Home Loan Mortgage Corporation]." Besides the collateral of seasoned loans with good payment histories, Low added a cash reserve that the buyer could draw on in the event of a default.

"We approached Freddie Mac with the proposal," says senior vice president David L. Chapman II. "They took a look at the deal for about a week and then they came back and said they'd do it. It was an innovative idea that was not difficult to organize even though it had never been done before. Freddie Mac loved it, and we were able to get rid of a ton of loans." In exchange for the loans, Freddie Mac issued the company $55 million in marketable securities that Lomas turned into cash.

Besides the blossoming of LMUSA, there were other events that brightened Lomas' spring in 1990. On April 1, LFC reached an agreement to sell ELLCO to General Electric Capital Corp. for $161 million in cash and the assumption of $1.0009 billion of debt and $30.6 million of preferred stock. The transaction received a mixed review. On the up side, it removed a large amount of debt and moved the company closer to achieving its restructuring goals. The bad news was that Lomas took a beating on price. When LFC put the subsidiary on the market in early 1989, management believed a price somewhere in the $400 million range was not unrealistic. "The main reason for the [low price] was because the leasing business was starting to deteriorate," says Lazard's Tom Haack, who found the buyer and helped negotiate the sale. "Quite honestly, the business at that point hadn't been functioning as well as it had when the company bought it. Also, people knew that Lomas had to sell it. The buyers we approached knew we didn't have any choice. They knew our debt was in default. If we didn't sell it, we were going to have to file bankruptcy for ELLCO—which would have affected the Lomas bankruptcy, which would have been a real mess."

Jess took the high road . . .

The sale of ELLCO was followed by the July 10 announcement of an agreement to sell its life insurance group to Conseco Capital Partners for approximately $140 million in cash and $25 million in securities. The sale of those two assets represented a major step toward streamlining the company's operations and focusing on its core business. "By concentrating our business in fewer areas," said Jess Hay in a news release at the time, "we are better able to identify opportunities for growth and ultimately to maximize profitability."

The divestitures and LMUSA's servicing portfolio acquisitions demonstrated a commitment to a business-based approach to Chapter 11. Lomas chose a path that led toward fairness for all parties. Partisan advantage at the expense of corporate honor, in Jess Hay's estimation, was a poor trade and unworthy of the company's heritage. "Jess Hay took the high road, and that gained him a lot of credibility in the end," says Davis Polk attorney Laureen Bedell. "He never made decisions that weren't business-based. He never did things for sheer bankruptcy strategic purposes. He could have held the insurance business hostage, but instead he said, 'It isn't related to the core business. We intended to sell it, and we're going to sell it now.'"

When the sale of the Lomas Life Group went before the equity committee for approval, there was strong opposition initially. According to Bedell, the members of that committee had good legal grounds for objecting: "They could have stopped that sale. Jess persuaded them that they would be benefited by the company reorganizing around the mortgage company. They believed in Jess. He was very credible to them, and they accepted that he was trying to do his best to maximize value. The equity committee accepted Jess' arguments and backed off. They did not object to the sale."

One black cloud darkened an otherwise pleasant spring. On May 7, Lomas announced the worst news yet relative to reserves. "Firm Admits Its Portfolio of Real Estate Is Shakier Than Earlier Estimated," read the headline to a *Wall Street Journal* article. "Lomas Financial Corp., admitting that its real-estate portfolio is far shakier than it had previously estimated, said it took a $505.5 million special charge in its fiscal third quarter ended March 31, resulting in a $500 million loss for the period.

"The big financial-services and real-estate concern said about $286 million of the reserve, or 56%, stems from its real-estate holdings, while an additional $74 million reflects a write-down of the company's short-term construction and development loans." The story also reported a $49 million charge based on the estimated cost of completing the company's new mortgage loan servicing system and related write-offs.

The Five-Year Consolidated Business Plan (BP) that Lomas presented to the creditors committee on June 28 and the equity committee on July 10 increased the company's credibility. Lazard's Sandra Lamb, who served on Lomas' Business Plan Task Force, wrote in a memorandum that the BP "is the cornerstone of the reorganization process. . . . [It] permits creditors to determine how and over what period they will be repaid from operating cash flows."

The business plan was certainly Jess' baby.

"If I had to oversimplify it, the business plan is what we have done, what we are doing, and what we intend to do," says vice president and associate general counsel Louis Gregory. "And in order to communicate that you need to tell a little bit about the company, the people, and the products. The business plan includes five-year financial projections for each division. In a nutshell, the business plan determines how we reorganize the company. It takes all of our assets and projects what they're going to earn for five years, and that information will be plugged into how we reorganize our debt, how we pay it off, and under what terms."

The six-month project captured Jess Hay's full attention. And for good reason. It was the first, and perhaps only, opportunity Lomas had to define its business and its vision of the future. Hay's August 23 *Lomas Review* column revealed his commitment to the BP and all that it represented:

> The plan represents infinitely more than formal compliance with a requirement imposed by the Company's Chapter 11 proceedings. It is a blueprint, a guide and reference base which is intended to drive us into the future and to serve as a measurement of our operating performance in subsequent periods. As always, the Company's future depends on the people of Lomas, on their hard work and on the depth of their commitment, dedication and determination. As you embrace the future, I encourage you to think of yourselves as professionals engaged as a team in the execution of a challenging, invigorating and fun assignment: the task of rebuilding a great company and restoring it to its prior position of preeminence in its industry.

"Infinitely more than formal compliance," indeed. There was an aura of spirituality surrounding the business plan that elevated its importance to the level of corporate Holy Writ. Some viewed it as a gospel from whose pages would spring forth Lomas Financial Corporation's resurrection and salvation. And those that would lay hold of it, cleave to it, and embrace its challenge would be among the elect embarked on a great crusade.

"I've known Jess a long time," says LFC director Gene H. Bishop, "and if you can get his attention, there is no one better to have [working] on a critical issue or problem. The bankruptcy had his attention. The business plan certainly was Jess' baby. He spent a tremendous amount of time and energy on it. He's extremely good on something like that if he puts his mind to it. And he did."

Production of the plan involved "tens of thousands of man-hours in the assembly, coordination, and presentation of the data." As a participant, Hal Hillman recalls the staggering amount of work required: "We spent weeks, night after night, at 1820 Regal Row in the conference room. I'd finish my regular job, and then I'd go over there about 7 o'clock and join Jess, Ramona, Bert, and all of Jess' staff. Normally, Jess came out sometime during the day and stayed until 7, some nights until 9 or 10. Then he'd be back early in the morning reading what everybody put together the night before. Then he'd come back and work all day Saturday and Sunday. It was a pretty intense effort." At a luncheon commemorating the plan's completion, Bert Byerley, Ramona Taylor, assistant secretary Lorraine Grant, and vice president Kevin McGarry were singled out for special recognition.

By almost any standard, the Five-Year Consolidated Business Plan was a remarkable document. It contained 1,975 pages divided into seven volumes. The plan also got good marks from Lomas' outside professionals, with one exception. In their scrutiny of its contents, the financial advisors from Lazard raised questions about one of the company's most troublesome divisions—Lomas Realty USA. "It was very optimistic," says Haack. "Even at the time, everybody thought it was very optimistic. Lomas Realty planned to sell $60 or $70 million of land in the first year. Well, obviously that didn't happen. They ended up selling probably $10 million of properties the first year."

LIS was another trouble spot. Haack recalled that the business plan from LIS gave the impression that the MLS system was on schedule for completion. It failed, however, to meet its projected deadline. In fact, the process degenerated into a lengthy, protracted, and very rocky conversion that wreaked substantial havoc on the division's five-year plan.

"Apart from the fact that real estate was too optimistic and nobody could understand, even people within the company, that the LIS thing was too optimistic as far as their timing, the general reaction to the BP was extremely favorable," says Haack. "It was a very good plan. The company did a terrific job in putting it together. At the close of an all-day presentation of the BP to the equity committee, their lawyer, who has been in the business for decades, got up at the end of the meeting and said he thought it was the best business plan he'd ever seen. That was quite a compliment coming from the equity committee." The attorney later repeated the accolade to Judge Lifland in open court.

The five-year business plan represented a major milestone for Lomas. By "demonstrating the profitability and dynamic potential of the Company's continuing operations," Lomas abandoned its defensive posture of the previous nine months and took the initiative. Publication of the plan marked a shift in the bankruptcy proceedings. The creditors were forced to respond to Lomas' vision of the future. The struggle was far from over, but a corner had been turned. In that context, the hopeful words of Winston Churchill following the British victory at El Alamein had special significance for the beleaguered company: "This is not the end. It is not even the beginning of the end. But it is, perhaps, the end of the beginning."

The decision by the creditors committee not to replace Jess Hay was nothing less than remarkable.

CHAPTER XVII

EXIT

The favorable reception of the business plan by the creditors and equityholders committees coincided with a similar feeling about Jess Hay. Although developed as a bottom-up plan, the final draft bore Hay's heavy editorial imprint. He reviewed all of it, and rewrote much of it. Then, at the company's presentation of the document to the committees, he publicly established personal ownership. "Jess really came out from cover and did a phenomenal presentation," says Alan Bell. "Jess is impressive when he gives a speech. It's pretty awesome when he gets fired up."

The enthusiasm projected by Hay struck a responsive chord among the creditors. Their interest in a viable future for Lomas was almost as great as the company's. "There was only so much cash to go around," says Grigsby. "There was a recognition that they [the creditors] were going to get some paper along with some cash. They were going to get a lot of paper. And if those securities were going to have real value and pay what you expected to get from them, then you had to have a good company that was performing well. The creditors began to show greater interest in what was going to happen after bankruptcy."

Consideration of life at Lomas after Chapter 11 led to what LFC director Gene H. Bishop identifies as one of the most remarkable events of the proceeding—the survival of Jess Hay as CEO: "It's one of the few times in a major bankruptcy where the previous CEO survived. I wouldn't have bet two cents on his staying." Bishop believes the five-year business plan and Hay's close association with it gave him a leg up with the creditors. "He developed it," says Bishop, "and he was an integral part of its execution. The creditors concluded that Hay was the logical guy to execute the plan."

"The Bank of New York and Chase, to the extent that they could control the process, wanted Mr. Hay to survive the process," says Jim Crowson. "I think they concluded that the events that forced the company into Chapter 11 were not Jess' fault. I think their perception was that Jess was a good CEO and would continue to be a good CEO."

There were ways, of course, to enhance the chances of Hay's survival, and the outside professionals at Lomas adopted a strategy for that purpose. It wasn't complicated. The plan came straight out of Survival 101 under the heading "It's the whale who comes to the surface that gets harpooned." John Grigsby and the attorneys at Davis Polk recommended a low profile for the CEO. "The best chance he had of surviving," says Grigsby, "was to keep him out of the fray. We knew we would have fights with the creditors, and they were going to get upset. We didn't want to put Jess out front where he'd get his head chopped off. We made a conscious decision to keep Jess out of the process, and he bought off on that." The numerous day-in and day-out meetings between Lomas and the creditors were conducted by Ted Enloe and Jim Crowson.

Physical absence notwithstanding, Hay's presence was very visible on the front page of each *Lomas Review*, where his leadership and gifted communication skills were displayed to best advantage. "All you have to do is go through those *Lomas Reviews* and read his messages and you get a great understanding of Jess," says Grigsby. "Those went to all the creditors. They read all those messages, and Jess Hay began to come across to them. I think they began to get a real sense of who he was and how much he meant to this organization. Jess is unique, and that began to come across. They began to understand Jess' vision for Lomas as well, and it made sense to them."

The decision not to replace Hay was no less remarkable for at least one of the committee representatives. "I remember having dinner with one of the leaders of the creditors committee toward the end of the case," says Grigsby. "And he said, 'I am amazed at how I feel. I am amazed that I don't want to replace Jess Hay. To the contrary, I believe that this company needs Jess. And that surprises me. This is the guy that brought us into Chapter 11, but I feel like we need him, and I don't want him to leave.'"

"Lomas Information Systems Unveils Excelis," announced the headline from the August 23, 1990, *Lomas Review*. It was an unveiling as grandiose as the occasion demanded. After seven long years of development costing tens of millions of dollars, LIS was ready to celebrate completion of its Future System with a naming at its annual division meeting. Manager of media services Rene D. Rodriguez and media consultant Chip Hardy were the multimedia gurus who put together the high-tech, nine-projector slide show that delivered the name to the division at the Loews Anatole Hotel auditorium on July 17.

It became very obvious that we couldn't convert the Lomas portfolio in December.

Theirs was the unenviable assignment of trying to satisfy years of pent-up anticipation. Rodriguez and Hardy pulled out all the stops for the seven-minute extravaganza. Although most expected a big bang from the event, the audience of 300 wasn't prepared for the multi-megaton explosion of sight and sound. As the lights in the auditorium dimmed, a wave of music from 38 speakers washed over the audience creating a Dolby-like effect that Rodriguez called "surround sound." Then from left to right across a 10-foot by 30-foot screen flashed the words LOMAS IS EXCELLENCE. The letters dissolved into a fast-paced photographic collage of LIS employees. A crescendo of sound signaled the finale as the name EXCELIS in dazzling chrome filled the screen. "There was an eruption of emotion," says Rodriguez.

This 1984 ad anticipated an investment of $22 million and operational date of 1987 for the Future System. Both missed the mark.

"They just roared." The reaction was especially gratifying to Rodriguez, who describes the LIS audience as "cerebral and sedentary, less likely to get emotionally involved." "It was very dramatic," says Matt Jacobs. "Everybody was sort of rocking-and-rolling by the time the letters formed the Excelis logo at the end." Lee Ballard, director of The Naming Center, a division of The Richards Group, explained that the name was chosen because it blended the idea of excellence and motion with the division's initials.

Enthusiasm was heightened at the division meeting when management unfurled the advertising slogan "Crossing The Finish Line," which it planned to introduce at the Mortgage Bankers Association's national convention in October. As it turned out, the analogy with auto racing proved a poor choice. For Excelis, the finish line defied crossing.

It was clear even in July that a "coming out party for the product in October" was premature. Conversion of LMUSA's portfolio, originally scheduled for the Labor Day weekend, was postponed until December. "The conversion program and the system weren't ready," says Jacobs. "And yet we felt we had to do something." LIS set its sights on an easier target—the conversion of 5,000 loans from the mortgage company's 650,000-loan portfolio. Even the achievement of that modest goal required an inordinate amount of effort. The *Lomas Review* heralded news of the event with the headline "Excelis Launched During Labor Day Conversion Marathon." Despite effusive testimonials praising the conversion, the article closed with a cautionary quote from Lynda-Ross Vega: "To tell you the truth, I won't really celebrate the accomplishment until we complete Lomas Mortgage USA in December. Then, for me, the fireworks will start." Unfortunately for Vega and Lomas, those fireworks were connected to a long and maddeningly slow fuse that stretched well past December. "There was still optimism even at that point [October, when LIS added 10,000 loans to Excelis from the Ameriway portfolio] that the conversion for Lomas would take place in December," says Jacobs. "But it was a very unrealistic optimism, because the system wasn't performing well. It was taking too long to process 15,000 loans—650,000 loans never would have gotten processed. The system was eating up more computer resources than it should have, and there were serious problems with the programs. The bottom line was we had to do some performance tuning and fix some problems with the programs. It became very obvious that we couldn't convert the Lomas portfolio in December. I think deep down, if you can get anybody to admit it, the people on the project knew it before Labor Day. Everybody was scared to death to pull the trigger on the big conversion."

Maintaining credibility with the creditors was difficult. Each delay required more funding and an explanation for the latest setback. The creditors imposed a series of benchmarks that the system had to meet in January, February, and March. "We met them," says Jacobs, "but quite frankly, it was not very scientific. Some of the advisors to the creditors took exception to the way they were done, and they had some valid points. When the actual conversion took place in June a lot of the things they said would happen did happen."

Labor Day was also a time of special sadness for Lomas Financial Corporation. The death of Buddy Miller was a painful loss for many at the company, especially Jess Hay. "September, Labor Day 1990," Hay wrote in the *Lomas Review*. "The day the Company lost a distinguished leader. The day the Lomas family lost one of its own. The day I lost a dear friend. The day H. H. (Buddy) Miller died.

"Buddy Miller served Lomas faithfully and exceedingly well throughout his 21-year tenure. . . . He loved the Company and he loved the people of Lomas."

I felt that maybe I could be helpful to him.

Miller's loyalty to Lomas and to his own moral code remained steadfast even after his physical condition deteriorated in the months before his death. He wasn't too weak to squelch talk about increasing his disability payment beyond what he thought he was entitled to. Dave Stephens recalled Miller's emphatic refusal: "Buddy said, 'No! Let's do the company plan. That's what I want. I don't want to get preferential treatment because I'm Buddy Miller.'"

Not long after Miller's death, LFC announced the upcoming retirement of LMUSA president Paul M. Low and the arrival of long-time board member Gene H. Bishop as vice chairman, LFC chief financial officer, and LMUSA president and chief operating officer after Low's departure. The former MCorp chairman and CEO's decision to return to Lomas management, where he had served as president of the company from 1969 to 1975, was based more on personal friendship with Jess Hay than career considerations: "I felt that maybe I could be helpful to him. And I think it turned out that way. Jess spent a lot of time on the bankruptcy, and I spent most of my time on the mortgage company and the computer company." Bishop brought with him the full confidence of Jess Hay and the unquestioned authority to act decisively.

His first priority was the infusion of badly needed leadership at LMUSA. "People were looking for decisions, looking for direction, looking for guidance, looking for action," says Bishop. "Leadership at the mortgage company was missing, and Jess didn't have the time to devote to it. It was never really Paul Low's bag. Paul was very strong in certain areas, but day-to-day management of a business enterprise was not his cup of tea."

It was, however, very much Bishop's. He had a quick, clear eye for administrative detail and decisive action that translated into increased efficiency and overhead reductions. Those traits served him well when he noticed accounting duplications spread throughout Lomas' seven companies. "He got a quick intuition," says Stephens, "that that didn't make sense." In December 1990, Bishop restructured the general accounting functions into Lomas Accounting, a single, consolidated department. Senior (now executive) vice president Thomas J. Clooney headed the new unit, vice president (now senior vice president) Mary Ann Brown managed the new general accounting section, and LIS vice president (now senior vice president at INTELLIFILE) Flavio Daibert led the group that converted Lomas' general accounting to a new and enhanced data system. The centralization of accounting wasn't a new idea to Lomas management, but Bishop managed to pull it off without the delays and emotional upheavals associated with other consolidations.

The loss of Buddy Miller was felt far and wide, as illustrated by the marquee of the Davenport Hotel in Spokane, Washington. Miller and Lomas Management saved this structure from destruction. It was later sold to an international hotel chain.

Bishop's presence was particularly reassuring when Jess Hay learned in October that he had a heart condition that required bypass surgery. The medical procedure was successful, and after seven weeks of convalescence Lomas' CEO returned to the office and gradually increased his work load. Best of all, from the standpoint of long-term health, Hay gave up cigarettes. "He had to stop, and did stop," says Stephens. "Cold turkey."

When Dick Hay retired from Chase Manhattan Bank in September, LFC lost a strong supporter of a rational, reasonable bankruptcy process. His absence gave Chase vice president Robert T. Sacks a freer hand to exercise a more aggressive, adversarial leadership. "Bob Sacks is a tough collection guy," says John

In December 1990, Gene Bishop restructured the general accounting functions into a new department, Lomas Accounting. Left to right, Melinda Vandenberg, Peggy Gibbs, Brian Griffin, Ginny Wrape, and Mary Ann Brown.

Other members of the accounting group included, standing: Julie Hanrahan, Flavio Daibert, and Joann Timberlake. Seated: Joe Clooney and Monique Willoughby.

There is an aura of domination here that I find disconcerting.

Grigsby. "He has a very controlling, domineering personality." "Sacks was very adversarial with everybody," says Tom Haack. "He was an autocrat."

The heavy hand of Bob Sacks landed on Lomas on October 10, 1990, when the company presented a plan of reorganization (POR) to the creditors committee. The plan determined the capital and debt structure of the reorganized company, as well as the allocation of consideration among the various constituencies. It was commonly understood that the debtor's initial POR proposal was simply a first offer—an invitation to negotiate. Sacks and other like-minded senior creditor representatives treated it as a declaration of war, and promptly blew apart the proposal with a very large bomb. The senior creditors led by Sacks brushed aside the plan and voted to oppose Lomas' right to exclusivity at an upcoming bankruptcy court hearing, so that the committee could file its own POR. The force of the explosion may have been impressive, but a "smart" bomb it was not. Casualties included members of the committee. The 12–3 vote to oppose debtor exclusivity reflected unanimous opposition from the three members of the committee who represented the subordinated debtholders. In a proceeding that depended on coalition and consensus for its ultimate success, the senior creditors crippled the effectiveness of their committee with a self-inflicted wound.

There was little objection to the structure of the plan, according to Tom Haack. The distribution of the proceeds provoked the angry response: "The fundamental architecture of the October 10 plan basically survived all the way to the end. The senior lenders didn't like the fact that the company started out by offering them 80 cents on the dollar. They rejected the proposal and said, 'We want a hundred cents on the dollar.' And they stayed with that demand for quite a long period of time. Their philosophy of negotiation was always be a hard-ass. Always take an extreme position and sustain that position as long as possible."

The senior creditors' highhanded refusal to negotiate and their attempt to terminate the company's exclusive right to file a POR rubbed many people the wrong way. At the October 23 hearing on exclusivity, opposition to the senior creditors included the subordinated debtholders, the equity committee, the debtor, and, last but certainly not least, the Honorable Burton R. Lifland. "I think Bob [Sacks] wanted to control the process," says Grigsby. "Rather than negotiate off of our plan, he wanted to negotiate off of his plan. It was, frankly, a very stupid thing for him to do. Coming out of the hearing, the judge clearly had strong negative feelings about what the senior lenders tried to do and strong negative feelings toward, among others, Bob Sacks who testified at the hearing."

Inflexibility on the part of the senior lenders made a particularly poor impression on Judge Lifland: "It appears to be that you [Joel B. Zweibel, counsel for the creditors committee] or your committee has found reasons, either tactically or substantively, to treat a proposal with a high degree of obduracy: 'That's it. We ain't heard what we want, and we ain't gonna deal any more.' That's not the dynamics and the tensions that are expected when there has been a first advance of a first submission."

Later in the hearing, the appearance of Bob Sacks as a witness further rattled the judge's cage: "I am somewhat disturbed over the witness' role in the affairs of the debtors. . . . There is an aura of domination that I find disconcerting." The court ruled in favor of continued exclusivity for Lomas.

Hay's view of Sacks and the members of the creditors committee was more benign. His perspective was long-range and admittedly at variance with most of those who worked for Lomas: "I see it a little differently than the guys that were in the trenches. Although Bob Sacks was often volatile and short-tempered, he ultimately was a constructive force. His relationship with me remained reasonably good throughout the process, and we always were able to discuss problems in a constructive way."

Hay also maintained that for the most part the proceedings were civil and nonconfrontational. He believed this underlying civility made a major contribution to the ultimate success of the company's reorganization. According to Hay, the creditors committee, on balance, was tough but fair: "Each member in his own way contributed to the final and favorable outcome, and we are grateful to each for his cooperative spirit throughout the 21-month process."

The judge's admonishment to the creditors committee about its refusal to negotiate with the debtor failed to move the committee to action. Quite the opposite; the committee fully embraced obduracy. "There was really no negotiation process," says Haack. "It just stopped. I think the internal divisions within the committee were the main problem. The subordinated people liked [Lomas'] plan. The senior lenders didn't like it. A lot of the negotiations during the blackout were negotiations within the committee. They had a whole series of issues that they had to resolve among themselves. The senior lenders didn't want to talk to the company unless the company agreed to talk to them about 100 percent recovery. Consequently, nothing happened for months."

"The creditors committee would not meet with us," says Crowson. "We were in a blackout. The senior creditors, in their view, claimed that the POR we put on the table in October too richly rewarded the subdebt and the equity at their expense. We kept requesting a response and meetings, and they kept saying no."

For Lomas, exiting Chapter 11 at the earliest possible date was a priority, and the company marshalled its forces to persuade the creditors to resume negotiations. "We were under a lot of pressure, particularly from Jess, to move the process, because he wanted to get out of bankruptcy by June 30, 1991," says Grigsby. "We came up with a dual strategy. 'If the senior lenders won't talk to us, let's see if we can strike a deal with the sub-debt and with the equity.' An agreement with the sub-debt in particular meant the senior lenders couldn't cut a separate deal with them and gang up on us. The other part of the strategy was, 'Okay, if you're going to make us sit here in Chapter 11 then we're going to make it very expensive for you. And we're going to do that by asking the court to authorize us to spend more money to buy servicing.' So we filed a motion asking the court to authorize us to spend $120 million to purchase additional servicing rights. And frankly, I believe that's what broke the log jam.

We came up with a dual strategy.

"Laureen Bedell and I sat down with Gordon Harriss, who is Davis Polk's bankruptcy strategy guru, and asked ourselves what the creditors committee's biggest fear was. Their biggest fear was that the judge lets all the cash go out the door before a POR can be circulated and voted on. And we related that to the mortgage company's need to grow its servicing portfolio. So that's when we adopted a plan to ask the creditors committee for a real aggressive amount of cash."

As expected, the creditors filed an objection that led to a hearing before Judge Lifland on December 13, 1990. In Crowson's view, the hearing that day was "the biggest, toughest, single-issue negotiation we had while we were in Chapter 11." Early in the hearing Lifland indicated that he was receptive to the idea of growing the company's mortgage loan portfolio. Rather than throw themselves upon the mercy of that particular court, the creditors suggested that the two parties withdraw to another room and negotiate a compromise. Lomas agreed. The resulting compromise authorized the company to advance $81 million to LMUSA to finance bulk purchases of mortgage servicing. Grigsby later learned through the grapevine that Sacks couldn't believe Lomas would attempt a maneuver like that and called it "Machiavellian."

The resumption of talks on March 12, 1991, between the creditors committee and the company marked the beginning of lengthy, tedious discussions. "The negotiations were always slow," says Haack. "We dealt with a negotiating committee which ended up having a lot of people on it. Also, Bob Sacks couldn't deal with more than one issue at a time. The way you normally negotiate is to list all your issues on a pad of paper and then go through them and state your position on each one and then trade them back and forth. Sacks couldn't do that. He had to do things in a very sequential way, which made it difficult because you hated to give in on something not knowing what else was on his list."

Much of the early discussion focused on the levels of recovery for the senior and subordinated creditors and the equity as well as the forms of recovery. Another major concern was how much debt the company would carry and where and at what interest rate. "And then we embarked on a whole series of negotiations that related to the nitty-gritty detail of the forms of the covenants and collateral," says Grigsby. "It was incredibly detailed. And the scriveners or notetakers became very important in disputes over what had actually been agreed to. We had negotiations that involved Tom Rohan from First Chicago saying, for example, 'My notes say this.' And I'd say, 'Well, Tom, my notes say this.' We had long discussions about our understanding of agreements."

Inspired by the Gulf War then in progress, Hay

Lomas files proposal for reorganization

By Steve Brown
Real Estate Editor of The Dallas Morning News

Almost two years after seeking bankruptcy protection, Dallas' Lomas Financial Corp. filed a reorganization plan Tuesday that if approved would give creditors ownership of the company. It also would spin off Lomas' real estate subsidiary into a new company to be owned primarily by Lomas Financial's current stockholders.

Lomas Financial, one of the country's largest mortgage servicing firms, presented the restructuring plan to the U.S. Bankruptcy Court for the Southern District of New York.

Lomas filed for Chapter 11 bankruptcy protection in September 1989, after it was unable to meet payments on debt accumulated in acquiring other companies and building a portfolio of large-scale real estate developments.

A majority of Lomas creditors must approve the company's reorganization plan. Lomas has until Aug. 19 to prepare a disclosure statement on its plan for the bankruptcy court, after which

Jess Hay . . . optimistic that creditors will support plan.

creditors and stockholders will vote.

A financial adviser to the equity holders' committee said Tuesday that while the reorganization plan represents some progress, it doesn't meet all of the equity holders' needs.

Wilbur L. Ross Jr., a senior managing director at New York investment banker Rothschild Inc., said the Lomas restructuring plan "is a step in the right direction, but not the final answer."

Lomas Financial chairman and chief executive officer Jess Hay

Please see LOMAS on Page 2D.

Lomas Financial files reorganization plan

Continued from Page 1D.

said in a statement that the creditors committee has not yet taken a position on Lomas' reorganization plan. However, Mr. Hay said he is optimistic that the creditors will support Lomas Financial's proposal.

"The Lomas that will emerge from Chapter 11 is a stronger, leaner, more focused company," he said. "The company is, in effect, returning to its roots.

"Our core business will be our existing mortgage banking and information system business," Mr. Hay said.

Lomas Mortgage USA, the largest operating subsidiary of Lomas Financial, handles payment and escrow services for more than 600,000 U.S. home loans. At the end of 1990, Lomas Mortgage had servicing contracts for almost $26 billion in home loans.

Senior creditors would fare the best under the reorganization, recouping about 90 percent of their claims in cash, notes and a 52 percent share of the reorganized company.

If the bankruptcy plan is put in place, Lomas Financial's vast real estate holdings — which includes the 1,000-acre Vista Ridge development in Lewisville — will be spun off in a new company, Lomas Realty USA.

Lomas Financial will get a 19 percent stake in Lomas Realty. The rest of the real estate company's ownership will go to Lomas' current stockholders.

When Lomas Financial filed for bankruptcy protection, Lomas Realty USA owned a portfolio of major real estate developments stretching from California to Florida. About 50 Lomas Realty's properties were in Texas, including developments in Dallas, Houston, Austin, Corpus Christi and San Antonio.

About one fourth of Lomas Financial's total debt at the time of bankruptcy was on the Lomas Realty properties.

"The plan filed today provides a fair and equitable settlement of the claims and interests of all classes of creditors and equity holders, while insuring that the company has the resources necessary to succeed in the future," Mr. Hay said in the announcement.

Mr. Ross said the equity holders' committee is still studying the proposal.

"It is a considerably better plan from our point of view than their earlier plans," he said. "We think that the recovery to the equity holders is a good deal better than what they put on the table previously.

"However, we feel it still falls short of what the equity holders need," Mr. Ross said. "We are hopeful that they will be able to find a way to improve it more."

LOMAS FINANCIAL REORGANIZATION PLAN

Filed for Chapter 11 bankruptcy protection on Sept. 24, 1989, in U.S. Bankruptcy Court for the Southern District of New York.

Under terms of the reorganization plan announced Tuesday:

- **SENIOR CREDITORS** would receive: $337.3 million in cash, $68.9 million of convertible notes, $236.2 million of secured notes, $319.3 million in Lomas Mortgage USA notes, $127.9 million in Lomas Realty USA notes and 52 percent of Lomas common equity.
- **GENERAL UNSECURED CREDITORS** would receive: $5.7 million in cash, $2.2 million of convertible notes, $3.8 million of secured notes, $5.2 million of Lomas Mortgage USA notes, $2.1 million of Lomas Realty USA notes and 1.6 percent of Lomas common equity.
- **SUBORDINATED DEBTHOLDERS** would receive: $17 million in cash, $68.9 million in convertible notes, $5.5 million of Lomas Mortgage USA notes and 43.4 percent of Lomas common equity.
- **PREFERRED STOCKHOLDERS** would receive: 1.3 percent of Lomas common equity, 30 percent of the common equity of Lomas Realty USA and warrants to purchase approximately 880,000 shares of Lomas stock.
- **COMMON STOCKHOLDERS** would receive: 1.7 percent of Lomas common equity, 70 percent of the common equity in Lomas Realty USA and warrants to purchase approximately 3.52 million squares of Lomas common stock.

The Dallas Morning News

On July 15, 1991, almost two years after seeking bankruptcy protection, a newspaper article announced that Lomas had filed a proposal for reorganization. Reprinted with permission of *The Dallas Morning News*.

painted a jingoistic picture of Lomas' Chapter 11 strategy at an executive meeting on February 25, 1991: "Our strategy is like the air campaign against Iraq. First, demolish their models and arguments and then sell them on ours." On March 11 at another meeting for executives, Hay moderated his enthusiasm and cautioned against the idea of a blitzkrieg-like resolution of issues: "We don't foresee any fast-breaking events in the near future." Dissatisfaction with the progress of negotiations mounted on May 20. "Chapter 11 is progressing at a snail's pace," lamented the CEO. "Everybody is reluctant to sign off on agreements. The process demands an inordinate amount of time. We have a formal agreement in principle between the subordinated and senior creditors. Next, we get into intense negotiations about defining the terms of various debt and covenants." A month later Hay reported that agreement among the constituencies "is very, very close. It's hard to get all the pieces nailed down at one time. You can get one of them nailed down, but then they say, 'We're not ready to sign off until we see what the other guy gets.' It takes a lot of coordinated tweaking. And none of them trusts the others, and I doubt, down deep, that they trust us. So that doesn't make for a particularly tranquil negotiation process."

Lomas filed a POR on July 15, 1991, that Crowson described as "98 percent consensual. It should be 100 percent consensual, but we got into issues that don't have a lot to do with economics. We're dealing with who's-the-biggest-and-toughest-kid-on-the-block kind of issues right now." Negotiations ground on throughout the summer. "Unfortunately, I have very little news of significance to share with you," said Hay at a meeting for Lomas executives on August 20. "The negotiations with the creditors committee are still on track, but it's a very, very slow pace. Hopefully, the matter will be concluded some time this week or next. The way things have gone, I would have to bet on next week."

At long last, in early September, a smiling and much-relieved Jess Hay announced news of an agreement to Lomas executives:

> Ladies and gentlemen. After any number of these sessions where we have said accord is very close on the horizon, it is a great pleasure to report to you that, at least for the time being, there is accord with the Creditors Committee and the Equity Committee. And we did, in fact, last week file an amended Plan Of Reorganization. The Plan as refiled is very similar to the one filed in July. We also filed last week our Disclosure Statement which is a document containing 400 to 500 pages. It includes a full description of the Company and its recent history and its affairs projected three years into the future. I would like to hold up for special acclaim five individuals who devoted literally countless hours to the effort, including many 20-hour days to get the job done within the permitted time. Jim Crowson, Bert Byerley, Gary White, Robert Kane, and Tsu Tan.

Despite Hay's impatience with the glacial pace of negotiations, they could have taken far longer. Jess Hay's and Jim Crowson's determination to keep the process moving helped Lomas sail over rough spots that could easily have snagged the proceedings. "Jess' approach and Jim Crowson's approach," says Grigsby, "was very much a straightforward kind of thing, 'Look, let's try to find some common ground.' There were times, for example, that Jim would make a new proposal to the creditors or give something away and Laureen Bedell, Bob Levine, Tom Haack, and I would say, 'No, Jim. Don't give that yet.' And Jim would say, 'Look, I want to show some movement here, because I want to keep the process going.' There's a reason that Jim Crowson and Jess Hay are so close. And a lot of it has to do with the similarities in their philosophy and personal styles. They share the belief that reasonable men can always find a rational basis for compromise and for settlement."

Like Hay, Crowson engendered trust. "Jim made a perfect first lieutenant on the firing line," says Laureen Bedell. "He's a mediator. He's excellent at negotiations. People are impressed with him, and they like him. He spent a lot of years as vice chancellor and general counsel of The University of Texas System. He knew how to deal with multiparty negotiations. He understood the concept of a limited pool, and was very good at balancing people's interests. That made an enormous difference. He and Jess made a good negotiating team."

"Crowson was fabulous," says Haack, who also worked closely with Lomas' general counsel. "He is intelligent and has a very good sense of negotiation and a good sense of posture and positions to take. He is also extremely hard working and persevering. He stayed with it. Even when Jim was frustrated with Bob Sacks, he never threw up his hands and said, 'Sacks, you're an idiot. I'm never going to talk to you again.' He could have. I'm sure he felt like doing that. But he bit his tongue and stayed with it."

The reorganized Lomas Financial Corporation as envisioned by the POR was a company that lost all claim to its former status as a "moderately diversified financial services enterprise." Although significant, the loss of Lomas' bank card, life insurance, and leasing operations could be viewed with a certain amount of equanimity. After all, those divisions had no close ties to the company's historic real estate-associated businesses. The same could not be said, however, for the abandonment of short-term lending. Its loss, for the sake of future corporate viability, was a blow.

Lomas' initial strategy of constricting short-term construction lending until happier times could not be supported. Unfavorable interest rates and a recessionary construction market ended the business' viability for the near future, and the company lacked the financial resources to maintain the franchise until happier times, principally its established relationships with developers and homebuilders throughout the country. Under the terms of the POR, a secured debt of $240 million was placed on the division, which was to be paid off through the orderly liquidation of the short-term lending portfolio. Notwithstanding this constrictive direction, the company's talented short-term lending staff, under the leadership of Lomas Management president Carey B. Wickland, remained and performed its responsibilities with remarkable dedication and success.

> Real estate just kept getting worse.

The real estate development market was even less promising. "Real estate," says Ted Enloe, "just kept getting worse." The financial advisors from Lazard agreed. "It was pretty clear to us that Lomas Realty USA had some real problems," says Haack. "There was no market, and there was no financing from the banks. So it was frozen. The only way to generate cash was to sell property, and those properties weren't going to be sold." Even if they were sold, it would be at a significant loss. "The lack of capital and financing sources has created illiquidity in the marketplace which has resulted in much lower market values of land," reads a description of the real estate business environment from the November 6, 1991, disclosure statement. "The value of LRUSA's properties have declined dramatically. As of June 30, 1991 the aggregate net realizable value of the properties was approximately $184.7 million. LRUSA's cost basis in its projects totaled approximately $572.1 million."

Lomas made the determination soon after filing for Chapter 11 that a principal objective was to find a way to divest its real estate development division. Haack agreed that the company had a better chance for a positive outcome if it wasn't tainted by real estate. He believed, as did the company, that the business world would judge Lomas on the basis of its "lowest common denominator rather than its highest common denominator." The POR neatly sidestepped that potential pitfall by spinning off the real estate division as a separate company. The new entity would carry $130 million in debt. This arrangement severed LRUSA's historic dependence upon Lomas for funds, as the disclosure statement made painstakingly clear: "Reorganized LRUSA will operate as a separate legal entity from Reorganized Lomas and will not have access to funds from Reorganized Lomas. Reorganized Lomas will not guarantee any of Reorganized LRUSA's or its subsidiaries' obligations. Accordingly, creditors of Reorganized LRUSA will have no direct or indirect recourse to Reorganized Lomas with respect to obligations of Reorganized LRUSA."

Other pieces in the reorganized capital structure included $140 million of debt for LFC and $330 million for LMUSA. Lomas also agreed to distribute among its creditors a cash payment of $360 million.

> ...a once-in-a-lifetime opportunity to acquire servicing at unreal prices.

The ultimate liquidation of short-term lending and the loss of real estate development (except for a 19 percent stock ownership in the new company) sharpened LFC's focus on LMUSA and LIS. They were the divisions on which the new Lomas staked its future.

LMUSA's strategy was not complex. Grow the servicing portfolio and leverage its profitability through economies of scale and increased servicing efficiency from the Excelis system. The problem was obtaining additional mortgage loan servicing. The company lost its traditional source for loans when it shut down single-family loan production in June 1989. As loans were paid off, the servicing portfolio—which stood at $21.5 billion in 1989—began to shrink at the rate of about $200 million a month. In less than a year, the portfolio was down by a billion dollars. There were those within the industry that had already written Lomas Mortgage's obituary. The reports were premature, however. The pessimists had underestimated the company's capacity for innovation. LMUSA responded to the crisis by building a multifaceted gathering system that acquired the servicing rights to loans originated by others. Among the half-dozen methods used to replenish the portfolio, the most explosive growth came from the Bulk Acquisitions Department, which purchased servicing portfolios from other financial institutions.

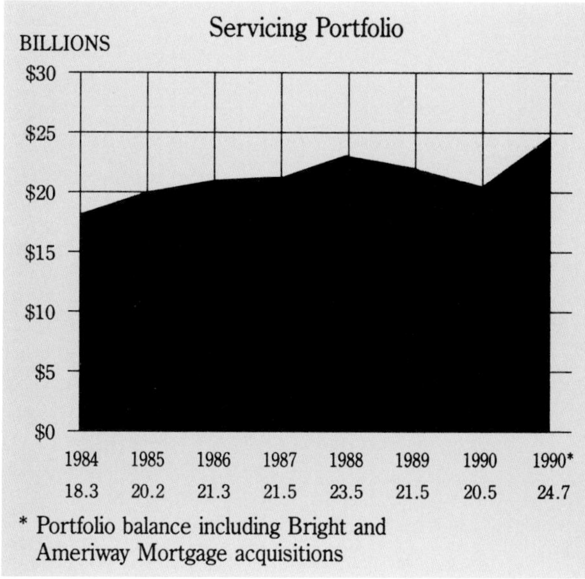

After Lomas purchased the servicing portfolios of Bright Banc and Ameriway, its portfolio balance showed a dramatic increase.

Lomas jumped into the Resolution Trust Corporation (RTC) buyers' market when it purchased Bright Banc's $3.5 billion servicing portfolio in April 1990. It wasn't until the Ameriway portfolio purchase in May, however, that senior vice president Richard K. Magel, who headed the department, fully appreciated the market's profit potential. "When the dust settled," says Magel, "we took a long, hard look at it [the Ameriway portfolio] and saw that the yields were astronomical. Lomas was going to make an incredible amount of money from the transaction."

Soon there was a flood of servicing acquired from RTC-operated thrifts that were dropping their mortgage servicing on the market to generate cash. The two key figures at LMUSA responsible for mining the growing bonanza were executive vice president Terry J. Deyoe and his assistant and protege Richard Magel. They were supported by senior management. Gene Bishop, in particular, provided critical leadership for the aggressive pursuit of portfolio acquisitions. "Gene Bishop had the vision to see what was going on in the market," says Magel. "He understood it was a once-in-a-lifetime opportunity to acquire servicing at unreal prices. He and Terry and Dave Stephens were working with Jess, fighting to get cash from the creditors." The approval of $81 million from the creditors for the purchase of servicing in January 1991 coincided with a market glutted with mortgage loan portfolios.

LMUSA spent the money wisely. By playing to the mortgage company's strengths, management maximized the rate of return on its investments. "As we moved into 1991," recalls Magel, "we said, 'We're not going to just blow through this money. We're going to make this the most profitable time in the history of Lomas' acquisition of mortgage servicing.' We tightened our yield requirements and put out more bids. We became a niche player in some of the dirtier portfolios. We had the wonderful Lomas loan administration machine that could take a portfolio and clean it up in

Terry Deyoe, LMUSA executive vice president, loan administration, was a key person in the acquisition of mortgage servicing from RTC-operated thrifts.

Richard Magel, far right, and the Bulk Acquisitions Department were instrumental in these profitable acquisitions. From left: Alan Ray, Roger Stotts, and Brenda Cockerham.

short order and double the value of the asset. The new entrepreneurs wanted to buy clean portfolios. They were still getting a good deal, but Lomas was making a steal on the portfolios that most buyers weren't looking at.

"It was unbelievably profitable. Never in the history of mortgage banking have transactions been done at the level Lomas did them over the last two years. We blew away all expectations in regard to yield. We were, at a minimum, six points higher on our expected internal rate of return. In some cases, we doubled what the creditor and equity committees expected us to make."

LMUSA's reputation for excellence and reliability climbed as dramatically as its portfolio. "The Lomas image and reputation went through the roof in the marketplace," says Magel. "The brokers across the country knew that if Lomas said we'd pay *x*, we paid *x*. And if we said we'd close at the end of the month, that's when we closed.

"There was a lot of game playing in the market. Entrepreneurs were trying to buy servicing packages at a low price, but they couldn't perform. One transaction in Houston took 18 months to negotiate. About that same time, we did a transaction in three weeks with a New Jersey brokerage house. There wasn't another firm in the industry that could perform that way. We were willing to jump through hoops to make it happen. Our reputation went way up and that helped roll us forward from transaction to transaction. We never busted out of a deal. If Lomas put a bid on the table, Lomas would do the deal."

Bulk Acquisitions' concentrated burst of activity paid off. From July 1990 to mid-1991, the department added approximately $8.7 billion to LMUSA's portfolio. By August 1, 1991, the loan servicing portfolio had grown to more than $29 billion, representing a 41 percent increase despite run-off.

The contrast between the two divisions responsible for growth under Lomas' five-year business plan was dramatic. While LMUSA surged forward, LIS sank under the weight of problems that crippled both confidence and performance. Jim Crowson claimed it was the single most difficult issue he had to deal with in the Chapter 11 negotiations, and the one that created the most credibility problems.

The whole thing absolutely frightened me to death.

Not long after Gene Bishop's arrival, Jess Hay asked him to evaluate Lomas Information Systems and Excelis. The range of problems Bishop discovered included management and the design and complexity of the system. "The whole thing absolutely frightened me to death," says Bishop. "But you're in the middle of the stream. You don't have many choices. About all you can do is try as best you can to get the system in place and get it operating. And that's the decision we made. There was nothing else you could do but move ahead, complete the system, and get it installed even though it was a very high-risk, very traumatic, very costly experience for the company."

Gene Bishop rejoined LFC shortly after Buddy Miller's death. Jess Hay asked Bishop to evaluate Lomas Information Systems and Excelis.

Reluctantly, the creditors committee agreed. "The problem with systems like that is you don't know if they're going to work until they're finished," says former Chase vice president Dick Hay. "You don't want to take the $150 million that you have already invested and throw it away when you're at the finish line. That was the argument that the company was making, and most of the creditors would make the same argument. You've got too much money invested in it not to spend another $20 million or whatever it takes to get it finished."

During the bankruptcy, the creditors committee

approved the approximately $71 million that LIS said it needed to complete the development phase of the project and to fund the conversion of LMUSA's portfolio and those of its other customers. But the committee's patience was wearing thin. The pattern of postponements and delays that characterized much of the development and conversion process provoked the creditors to set a series of benchmarks that LIS had to meet. LIS scheduled LMUSA's conversion for no later than June 1, 1991, and the committee held them to it. "It was presented in the manner of, 'You better do this or else,'" says Lynda-Ross Vega. "But I had about five or six of those. The reality of it was that each of the milestones carried with it a pretty heavy penalty for failure. It was somewhat like a sword of Damocles. The creditors committee and their advisors doubted our capability in doing the work, and therefore if you missed a milestone it was fodder for the gristmill of why we should be closed down."

"Basically," says executive vice president Floyd L. McGlothlin, "the creditors committee was saying, 'If you don't make this date we'll probably just pull the plug on the whole project.' So there was a lot of pressure to make that date and continue the conversion of service bureau customers. Those conversions probably should have been stopped, but because of the pressure from the creditors committee we kept on trucking."

On May 1, 1991, one month before the LMUSA conversion, Mitchell Mortgage Co. became the first LIS service bureau customer to convert to Excelis. By testing the system with another small portfolio, LIS hoped to identify and prevent problems in June. The strategy failed because it took a couple of months before the problems at Mitchell manifested themselves.

Working in 24-hour shifts, the LIS team converted Mitchell's 12,000-loan portfolio in three days. Once on the system, Excelis performed well in some areas and badly in others. "The new system caused a lot of problems," says Mitchell Mortgage site administrator Trish Maxie. "For example, we had 30 REO loans, but according to Excelis we had over 500 REOs. So we had to figure out what caused those loans to fall into that status. We also had some bank accounts that were pretty messed up. Investor accounting took a long time to straighten out. The reports weren't correct. The reports said one thing and the on-line system said something different.

"It really is a good system, but it's very complex. We knew it was going to be difficult. Lomas knew it was going to be difficult, and they prepared us. It was nothing we didn't expect. It's just that once it hits you, even though you know it's coming, it still kind of slaps you in the face. It was more than we expected."

LIS responded to Mitchell's problems and those of the customers that followed as if their concerns were a matter of life and death, which, in fact, they probably were. The computer company spared no expense in its efforts to clean up and retune the programs in the system until they performed as advertised. That kind of customer satisfaction was expensive. Besides the costly human resources required to make the technological changes, LIS waived many of the fees it normally charged. It also reimbursed customers for the extraordinary conversion expenses that they incurred. But the loyalty of customers like Trish Maxie, almost a year and a half after Mitchell Mortgage's difficult conversion, underscored the policy's success: "Lomas' product support is fantastic. You can call LIS and say, 'Hey, I'm having a problem with such-and-such. Am I doing it wrong, or is there something wrong with the system?' They get right on it, and they get it fixed. They never leave you high and dry. Lomas is always there. They'll turn around and get you an answer—right now."

The nightmare of the conversion is going to stick with me forever.

Problems also followed the conversion of LMUSA's 641,000-loan portfolio on June 1. They

Lomas Mortgage USA and Lomas Information Systems made history when they implemented the largest computer system conversion in the history of mortgage banking. Lynda-Ross Vega holds a bonsai tree presented to her by Terry Deyoe, left, and Gene Bishop on behalf of Lomas Mortgage USA.

Jess Hay stands with Lynda-Ross Vega at the June 1991 conversion of the LMUSA servicing portfolio.

weren't unexpected. Jess Hay prepared Lomas executives at a March 25 meeting for the upcoming challenge: "I hope you will embrace a difficult transition period as we move toward the future, a future that places Lomas in the forefront of mortgage banking technology."

Still, the transition was more troubled than expected. "Once we got the loans on the system, they didn't run very efficiently even though all the models we had done to make the benchmarks for the creditors showed that they should have run efficiently," says Jacobs. "A lot of the programs didn't operate the way they were supposed to. So there was a lot of going back and fixing things. There was also a lot of data contention. The data that was supposed to be there wasn't, and the data that was there wasn't the right data. Name a problem. It existed in one form or another."

No one appreciated the need for prompt corrective action more than Terry Deyoe, who sometimes punctuates conversations with the non sequitur "Time is *so* precious." "The heartbeat of the mortgage company's loan administration area has a very rapid pulse," said Deyoe in a report he gave to executives on August 20. "We're working desperately with the new system, Excelis-MLS, and with Matt and his folks to work through the problems that we currently have so he'll have a system he can sell.

"There are pieces of the system that are working very, very well. But there are parts of the system that are not working well. And, unfortunately, part of the system that is not working well is our investor reporting. There have been some enhancements made this week that have improved that somewhat, but there are a number of our investors who have not been successful in getting their reports or their money.

"As Matt indicated, he's got the burners turned up full throttle to correct these issues, and we're talking to investors and looking them in the eye to assure them that the problems will be corrected."

Concern over investor accounting was well founded. The end-of-month reports and cash transfers that LMUSA sent to its investors had to be both accurate and timely. Initially, they were neither. "Investor reporting was much, much worse than we thought it would be," says McGlothlin. "Making the monthly reports accurate and getting them done in time was a real challenge. Major investors were hacked off at us. We had weekly conferences with FNMA over those issues. Some private investors came to see Lomas Mortgage and told them that if they didn't get the problems straightened out soon they would pull their servicing."

Telephone calls from irate investors came in faster than LMUSA employees could answer them. At one point, Deyoe counted 60 an hour to his office alone. "'I'm not going to put up with this. I'm going to pull our servicing' was pretty typical," says senior vice president, investor services, Tommy R. Harris, who fielded more angry investor calls than he cares to remember. "Other investors asked, 'Why in the hell did you convert to a system without first testing it for these types of errors? Can you put me back on the old system?' We had some pretty upset investors who we were in heavy contact with all the way through November."

At the urging of Deyoe and Harris, a two-member task force was organized to travel around and meet with dissatisfied investors. Senior vice president Sandy Tolbert and senior vice president Ray L. Ryan were asked to handle that responsibility because of their well-regarded ability to work with people. They offered reassurance that investors' problems were being addressed, and that bought Lomas the time it needed to make the necessary corrections to the system. "It was amazing what a personal visit would do to increase a company's patience level," says Harris.

The most challenging investor Harris' department worked with was First Security Bank of Utah. The dose of comfort Ryan's September visit gave that institution was exhausted by December. "They were basically ready to pull their servicing because they couldn't get their account to balance," says Harris. "And we said, 'Listen, it can be balanced.' And they said, 'It's impossible. If you think it can be done, then come up here and do it.' So, we said, 'Okay, we're coming.'"

A team made up of vice president Douglas J. Gressett, supervisor Regina Sapp, and portfolio specialist Rita Sefah made the trip. "The first couple of days were difficult," says Harris, "because First Security's attitude was, 'You'll never do it. It's impossible. You're wasting your time. Just pull it.' But after a few days when some of it began to balance, they said, 'These guys may actually have a shot at it.' And they started cooperating with us. It took the Lomas team a week working from sunup to sundown, but they balanced the account—to the penny."

"They were very happy and surprised," says Gressett, "and said we had performed a great service for Lomas because they fully expected that they would have to pull their servicing. Rita and Regina saved the company a lot of money."

That was one example of the kind of dedication LMUSA and LIS employees displayed during the stabilization of Excelis. Harris recalls the long hours that effort required: "There's no telling how many hours were put in by the employees. We got to the point that we were almost numb. Sixty-hour work weeks were standard for extended periods of time. The nightmare of the conversion is going to stick with me forever. There's no doubt about that. I spent lots of nights here in my office sleeping on that couch."

Although it took longer and cost more than expected, the conversion to Excelis succeeded. LMUSA survived the largest conversion in the history of the industry without losing a single customer. And once stabilization was accomplished, the system outperformed its competitors. Despite the problems that ravaged his department, Tommy Harris conceded in mid-1992 that LIS "came out with what I believe is the premier servicing system in the country."

The difficult conversion and initial poor performance of Excelis dashed any immediate hopes LIS had of marketing the new system. "When the horror stories started getting out in the public," says Jacobs, "everything slowed down. People started getting concerned. I don't know of any new business being signed after August 1991." Says McGlothlin, "We took a big black eye in the market. No question about it."

Equally disheartening was the loss of several existing service bureau customers who rejected the new system. They were, for the most part, customers with small portfolios who concluded that Excelis was not particularly user-friendly. "Technologically, I don't think there is a better system, but it's overly complex," says Jacobs. "It's so complex that the average mortgage company can't relate to it. That's what ran off the small companies. They decided they would be taking a major step backward if they went on the new system. They didn't want the complexity. Many of the smaller companies make a lot of money because they keep it simple."

While LIS and LMUSA struggled to stabilize the new system, the Chapter 11 negotiations entered their final round. One of the last issues discussed was corporate governance. Typically, in a bankruptcy the creditors remove the old board and senior management and replace them with individuals that have no connection to the events that led to the company's difficulties. "If you go into the ditch like we did," says Crowson, "the creditors usually go in and clean house." Despite this, Lomas and its advisors managed to extract significant concessions. Most unusual of all was the retention of Jess Hay as chairman and CEO of Lomas Financial Corporation. The creditors also agreed to permit Lomas to keep four serving board members as well as the right to approve new directors. They insisted, however, that a majority of new directors make up the new board. "The existing board was Jess Hay's board," says John Grigsby. "That was the reality of it. It had been his board for awhile, and they were close to him and they liked him and respected him. The creditors wanted a new board made up of a majority of individuals that they had, in effect, cleared as being acceptable to them. They had the perception that a new board would hold senior management more accountable than the existing board would."

*I*f you go into the ditch like we did, the creditors usually go in and clean house.

By November, LFC's 12-person board included seven new members: James R. Adams, president and chief executive officer of Southwestern Bell Telephone Company; Robert G. Boucher, former chairman and chief executive officer of United Mortgage Company; Robert V. Lindsay, former president and director of J. P. Morgan & Co., Incorporated; Dr. Diana Natalicio, president of The University of Texas at El Paso; Hugh G. Robinson, chairman and chief executive officer of The Tetra Group; Harvey M. Schuster, president of California Investment Counsel, Inc.; and Paul T. Walker, an independent financial consultant and former executive vice president and senior credit policy officer at The Chase Manhattan Bank. Later, the board voted to add two additional members: Rod Dammeyer, president and chief executive officer of Itel Corporation; and Douglas L. Rock, chairman, president, and chief executive officer of Smith International, Inc. As finally constituted, the new board thus included five continuing members and nine additions jointly selected by the creditors committee and the company.

Surprisingly little blood was shed among the ranks of management under Jess Hay. The one exception was the real estate development subsidiary, which reported to LFC president Ted Enloe. It was the division perceived as most responsible for taking the company into Chapter 11, and those responsible for its management had to pay a price. "There was a strong desire among the creditors to clean house in real estate," says

Crowson. "Those were the guys who took a hit." Enloe announced his resignation as president and member of the board of directors of LFC on September 4, 1991. Lomas Realty USA president Wayne D. Ferguson and executive vice president J. Stephen Crim resigned from the company effective December 31, 1991.

Another major management change that fall had nothing to do with Chapter 11. Lomas announced on October 14 that Gene Bishop would resign from his positions as LFC chief financial officer and president and chief operating officer of LMUSA to become the chairman and chief executive officer of Life Partners Group, Inc. Bishop remained a member of Lomas' board of directors.

Two days later Lomas Financial Corporation announced the appointment of Michael E. Patrick as chief financial officer of LFC and president and chief operating officer of Lomas Mortgage USA. As executive vice chancellor for asset management for The University of Texas System, Patrick was responsible for the management of more than $4 billion in assets and $900 million of outstanding debt. Prior to joining The University of Texas System, he had served as treasurer of Superior Oil Company and held senior executive positions with Southwest Bancshares, Inc.

"Michael Patrick is a very talented executive with both strong business and people skills," said Hay in the news release announcing the appointment. "He not only understands the numbers side of business, but the people side as well. He has done an outstanding job at The University of Texas System. I am confident that he will do an equally outstanding job here." Hay's confidence came from firsthand experience. When Hay served as chairman of The University of Texas System's board of regents from 1985 to 1987, Patrick reported directly to him. Patrick's asset management work also required a close working relationship with Jim Crowson when Crowson was vice chancellor and general counsel for the university system. Their association developed into a warm, personal friendship. Patrick's relationships with Hay and Crowson were persuasive factors in his decision to join Lomas.

On October 16, 1991, Lomas Financial Corporation announced the appointment of Mike Patrick as chief financial officer of LFC and president and chief operating officer of Lomas Mortgage USA.

As part of the Chapter 11 process, the creditors committee looked at the company's expenses and made a list of cost-cutting measures it thought Lomas should make. The committee strongly suggested that Lomas sell the airplane it owned. "An airplane, as I understand it," says Crowson, "is a big signal. You just don't go through one of these and get to keep a corporate airplane."

Less well received was the suggestion that Lomas move its corporate headquarters from Bryan Tower to the Lomas campus. It was a rational recommendation, and one that the company had previously considered. The strongest proponent, before his death in 1990, was

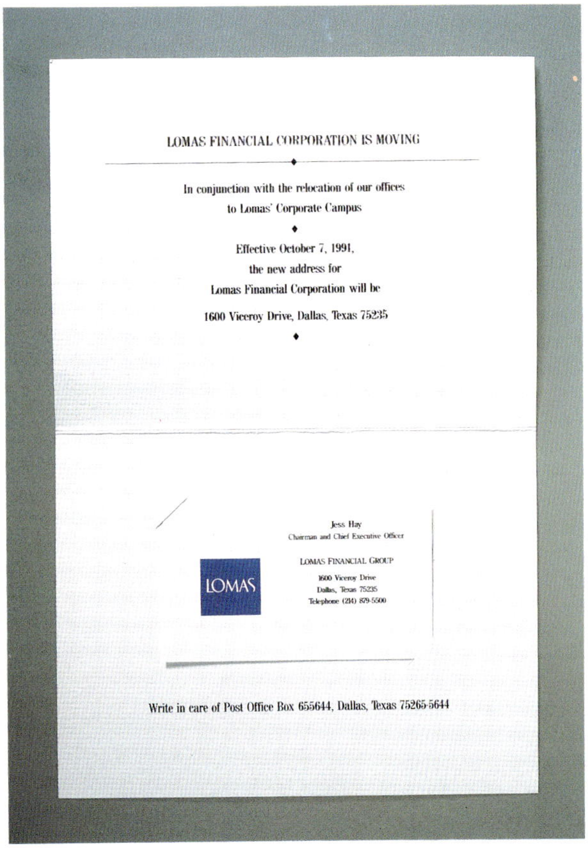
LOMAS FINANCIAL CORPORATION IS MOVING

In conjunction with the relocation of our offices
to Lomas' Corporate Campus

Effective October 7, 1991,
the new address for
Lomas Financial Corporation will be
1600 Viceroy Drive, Dallas, Texas 75235

Jess Hay
Chairman and Chief Executive Officer

LOMAS FINANCIAL GROUP
1600 Viceroy Drive
Dallas, Texas 75235
Telephone (214) 879-5500

Write in care of Post Office Box 655644, Dallas, Texas 75265-5644

In early 1991, LFC made the decision to move its corporate headquarters from downtown Dallas to the Lomas campus. Formal announcements of the relocation went out in the fall.

Buddy Miller. As early as the fall of 1987 he had lobbied hard for a reduced presence at Bryan Tower, with the idea of eventually abandoning that location entirely in favor of the Lomas campus. Hay agreed to a reduction but felt strongly about maintaining a downtown presence. Leased space at the expensive office building dropped from fourteen floors to seven, then five, and finally by the spring of 1990 to three. Relentless in his pursuit of savings for the company, Miller continued to press for a complete move to the campus. "You have to ask yourself, is it really necessary for a particular function of the company to sit in these opulent quarters," Miller said in an interview five months before he died. "And the answer is no. In fact, it could probably function better in a less expensive environment at our campus. My ultimate goal is for Lomas to get out of Bryan Tower. But that's not going to happen. I will not prevail in this. I've tried and tried and tried. I'm reasonably convinced that as long as Mr. Hay is CEO, we're going to be at Bryan Tower, and we're going to be downtown, and we're going to sit on these three floors.

"And I'm not bitching. Don't misunderstand. My ass likes $150-a-square-foot tenant improvement, because it just seems to fit real good. My daddy didn't raise no fool."

Acceptance of Miller's goal had made significant progress by the end of 1990. A smaller, more narrowly focused Lomas, extremely concerned about cost reductions, inevitably gravitated toward the campus property it owned. At an executive staff meeting on November 12, Hay acknowledged that management was studying "relocating to the campus. We don't want to congest the campus, but it is feasible to move more operations out there. It costs about $750,000 per year per floor in Bryan Tower." LFC made the decision to move its corporate office to the Lomas campus in early 1991. Formal notification announcing the relocation went out that fall: "Effective October 7, 1991, the new address for Lomas Financial Corporation will be 1600 Viceroy Drive, Dallas, Texas 75235." A single floor at Bryan Tower remained leased to Lomas. Capstead Advisers, Inc., occupied most of that space.

The move from Bryan Tower was particularly difficult for Jess Hay and Ramona Taylor. They were products of the Dallas business culture of the 1950s, where status was measured by the office height of downtown skyscrapers. For almost 20 years, the 36th floor of Bryan Tower filled that need. "Personally, I was upset to leave Bryan Tower," says Taylor. "But from an absolute company point of view it was a good idea for us to move out to the campus. It was good for employee morale, and it was good from the standpoint of hands-on management.

"It wasn't easy for Mr. Hay. He has a strong sense of tradition. I hate to use the word sentimental, but I think he is sort of sentimental. And to give up everything we had at Bryan Tower wasn't easy. Bryan Tower was a symbol. It was symbolic of everything that he had worked so hard for, for so many years."

The consummation was nothing but a big closing.

The war ended on November 6, 1991. All the battles had been fought, and peace was finally concluded with the publication on that date of the first amended disclosure statement and the second amended joint plan of reorganization. On page one, in boldface, upper case letters, were the three paragraphs signaling consensus, the essential requirement for a satisfactory conclusion to the Chapter 11 process:

> . . . THE DEBTORS BELIEVE THAT CONFIRMATION OF THE PLAN IS IN THE BEST INTERESTS OF CREDITORS AND EQUITY SECURITY HOLDERS AND RECOMMEND THAT YOU VOTE TO ACCEPT THE PLAN.
>
> THE OFFICIAL COMMITTEE OF UNSECURED CREDITORS ENDORSES THE PLAN AND RECOMMENDS THAT UNSECURED CREDITORS VOTE TO ACCEPT THE PLAN.
>
> THE OFFICIAL COMMITTEE OF EQUITY SECURITY HOLDERS ENDORSES THE PLAN AND RECOMMENDS THAT EQUITY SECURITY HOLDERS VOTE TO ACCEPT THE PLAN.

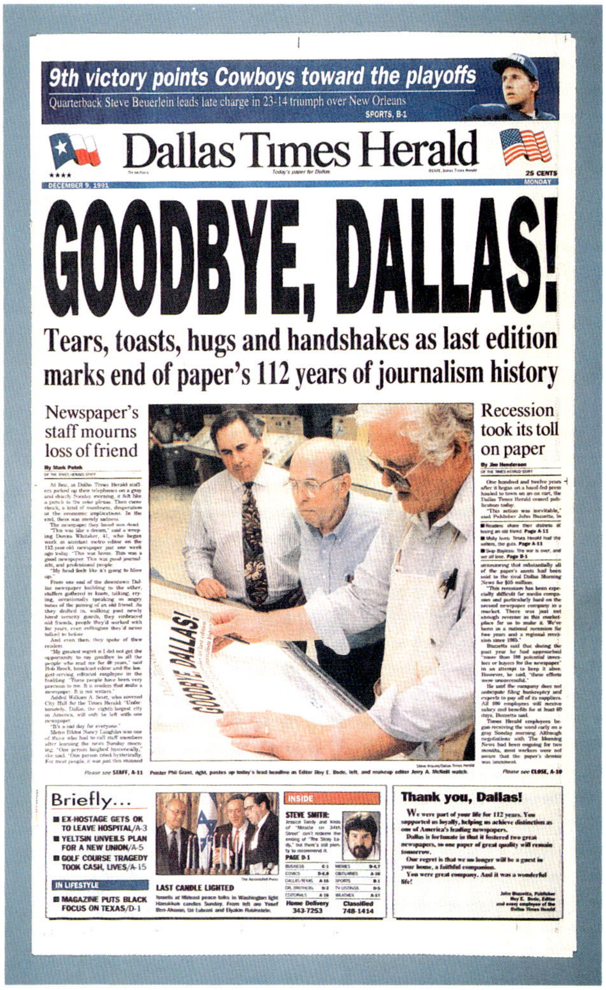

Shortly after Lomas left Bryan Tower, *The Dallas Times Herald* announced its closing. The company and the newspaper, giants in their respective fields, were both victims of the recession. Reprinted with permission of *The Dallas Morning News*.

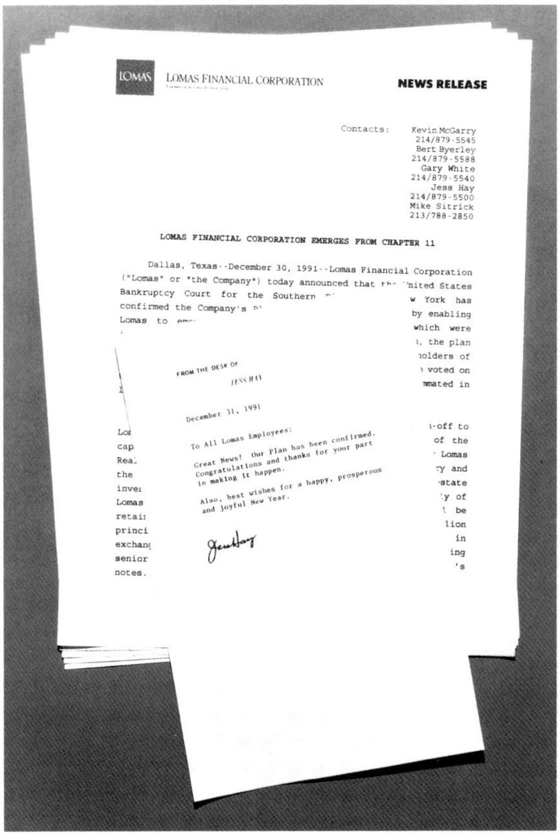

The good news of the emergence from Chapter 11 was received by each member of the Lomas family in a news release on December 31.

The acceptance of a consensual plan of reorganization by the various constituencies is usually a foregone conclusion. The vote in Lomas' case was no exception. When assistant vice president and bankruptcy claims manager Pat Turner tallied the final votes on December 23, 1991, at 11:30 p.m., members of the official committees, stockholders, and bondholders had voted overwhelmingly in favor of the agreement.

The two remaining events before Lomas Financial Corporation freed itself from Chapter 11 were the confirmation hearing and the consummation. At the former, the judge confirms the results of the balloting and grants a discharge. The consummation is where the plan of reorganization is actually implemented and the cash and securities physically distributed.

The confirmation hearing was held on December 30, 1991, at 2:00 p.m. in the Bankruptcy Court of Southern New York. Significance notwithstanding, it was a low-key affair. Crowson testified that all the conditions for confirmation had been met and nothing would preclude the plan from being consummated. The hearing itself was a procedural event totally lacking in fireworks, or even sparks. Afterward, interaction among the former adversaries was congratulatory. "It was very pleasant," says Crowson. "At that point everybody was pretty lovey. 'I know I called you an asshole but I really didn't mean it' kind of stuff. Everybody was happy it was over."

For Pat Turner, who attended the hearing in case he had to testify about the balloting, the routine ending was unexpected. "When December 30th hit, it was the culmination of long nights, weekends, and no time off. So, you fly to New York and say to yourself, 'Boy, this is going to be great. It's celebration time!' Instead, everybody walked out of the courtroom, said good-bye, and went their own way. It was kind of like—nothing. Very anticlimactic."

Jess Hay's spirits, on the other hand, were high. The dinner party he gave that evening at the Regency Hotel for Lomas' Chapter 11 team failed to match his ebullience. "Jess Hay was a happy camper," says Grigsby. "In fact, he took everybody to dinner that night. The big problem was everybody was absolutely exhausted. Some people had been working for 72 hours straight. People were passing out at the table. They wanted to sleep, not eat." "Sleep," says Crowson, about the days prior to confirmation, "was something you caught somewhere on a couch in a rumpled suit."

Employees were among the first to learn the good

Business Tuesday

Weather
Texas & Southwest

Tuesday, December 31, 1991 © 1991, The Dallas Morning News **The Dallas Morning News** Section D

DIGEST

TODAY'S NEWS

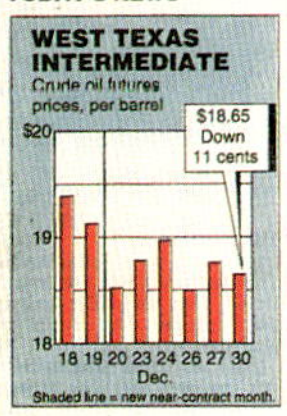

■ **Zale Corp. said** it will close 400 jewelry stores — 20 percent of all its outlets — and will freeze debt payments in a bid to survive. 1A

DOW AVG.
Up 62.39
Close:
3163.91

■ **Records again were** shattered as money poured into Wall Street. The Dow Jones industrial average was just one of many indexes that leaped to new highs for the third consecutive trading day. The Dow index of blue chip stocks added 62.39 points or 2 percent to close at 3163.91, its high for the day. 1D

■ **The lowest** mortgage rates in 14 years are helping end a summer slump in sales of existing homes, but a separate survey released Monday showed that Americans remained deeply apprehensive in December about their economic future. 1D

■ **It's a cold** Tuesday morning and a few stragglers are still sipping coffee and trading the latest bits of gossip at Bino's Cafe near the Trinity Meadows racetrack. But come back on race days — Thursday through Sunday — and Bino's bustles, especially at lunchtime. Over a hamburger or the daily blue-plate special, customers scan tip sheets purchased at the Quarter Pole Handicapping Center next door and swap stories about the fastest ponies and the best jockeys racing that day.
UPDATE 1D

■ **More than two** years after filing bankruptcy to escape the crush of almost $6 billion in debt, Dallas-based Lomas Financial Corp. has received final court approval of its reorganization. The federal bankruptcy court ruling clears the way for Lomas to formally emerge from Chapter 11 next month as a much smaller, less diversified company with a dramatically reduced debt load. 1D

■ **New York's bankrupt** *Daily News* has enough cash to operate through February without the help of a buyer, the paper's editor told creditors Monday. 3D

■ **Just in time for** the visit by President Bush and his entourage of auto executives, the Japanese government has made plans to introduce subsidies to encourage Japanese to buy more foreign cars, a Japanese newspaper said. 3D

■ **Southwest Airlines Co.** and its flight attendants have agreed to scrap the airline's three pay scales for the workers and put them all on a single salary plan. The three-tier plan, implemented in the 1980s as Southwest was trying to control labor costs, mimicked similar plans at other carriers that paid newer employees less than more senior workers. 4D

■ **Carolco Pictures** Inc. said it faces a cash crisis that may force it to suspend some film projects, and analysts said the once-powerful studio may be headed for bankruptcy. 5D

■ **A General Dynamics-led** team that saw its A-12 U.S. Navy stealth attack plane project canceled in January has received a $20 million contract to compete for the Navy's next-generation AX aircraft, General Dynamics said. 6D

TODAY'S COLUMN

■ **Financial freedom** seldom appears on shopping lists. If you want to be out of debt, financial freedom has got to be on your shopping list. It has to be right up there with food, clothing, auto maintenance and entertainment. It has to be as real to you as a new TV set, a new couch or whatever *thing* you have your heart set on getting. The way to start is with a budget. Put "financial freedom" at the top of that list.
SCOTT BURNS 1D

■ **Robert Miller** is on vacation.

FINANCIAL

Confidence sags; home sales rise

Associated Press

WASHINGTON — The lowest mortgage rates in 14 years are helping end a summer slump in sales of existing homes, but a separate survey released Monday showed that Americans remained deeply apprehensive in December about their economic future.

Home sales jumped 5.4 percent in November to a seasonally adjusted annual rate of 3.33 million homes, the National Association of Realtors said. It was the second consecutive monthly increase and the biggest rise in six months.

Separately, the monthly Consumer Confidence Index, released in New York by the Conference Board business research group, suggested Americans are still pessimistic about the economy, despite lower interest rates.

The index reading, based on a 1985 scale of 100, read 52.4 in December, about the same as the November figure of 52.7.

Dorcas T. Helfant, president of the real estate trade group, said falling interest rates are bringing first-time home buyers back to the market.

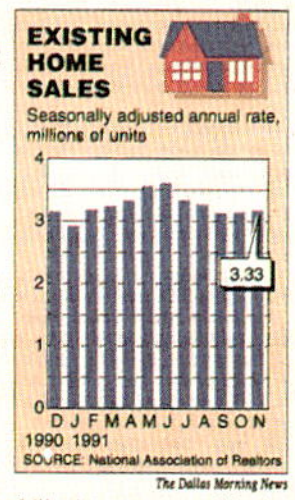

The Dallas Morning News

However, "move-up buyers" — those who must sell a home in order to buy a better one — are "sitting tight until the economic picture improves," she said.

The November resale rate was 5.7 percent above the year-ago rate of 3.15 million units.

Home-buying activity was heaviest in the lower-cost areas of the nation, the association said.

While November was a strong month for nationwide existing home sales, the opposite was true

Please see HOME on Page 2D.

Wall Street continuing ride into record territory

Stock market closes up 2% in heavy trading

By Joe Simnacher
Staff Writer of The Dallas Morning News

Records again were shattered Monday as money poured into Wall Street.

The Dow Jones industrial average was just one of many indexes that leaped to new highs for the

■ Dollar ends mixed. 2D

third consecutive trading day. The Dow index of blue chip stocks added 62.39 points or 2 percent to close at 3163.91, its high for the day.

Some market watchers said the year-end rally is evidence of a reversal of investor confidence. Others say stocks have leaped ahead in a buying pandemonium, while still others were at a loss for words to explain the new enthusiasm for equities.

Before the new trading week began, the Bank of Japan unexpectedly lowered its discount rate to 4.5 percent from 5 percent.

Analysts said that lent new impetus to downward trends in U.S. interest rates, and held out the promise of stronger demand in the Japanese economy.

World markets reacted strongly to the Japanese reduction, with rallies on markets in London, Tokyo and Frankfurt, Germany. In Japan, the market ended the year up 546.45 points or 2.44 percent to 22,983.77, before trading began in New York.

A. Marshall Acuff Jr., portfolio

Please see STOCK on Page 6D.

MONDAY'S BIGGEST GAINERS
Top five gainers Monday on the New York and NASDAQ stock exchanges.

New York Stock Exchange		
First City Bancorp Texas Preferred B	+45.5%	to $2.00
Cineplex Odeon	+37.5%	to $2.75
Russ Togs	+37.5%	to $1.375
Equimark Corp. Preferred	+25.0%	to $7.50
Republic Gypsum	+24.1%	to $4.50

NASDAQ National Market		
Jean Philippe Warrants	+61.4%	to $2.875
First Citizens Financial Corp.	+60.0%	to $1.00
Gencor Industries	+55.6%	to $5.25
ACOI Inc.	+42.9%	to $1.25
Security Savings Bank	+40.0%	to $7.00

SOURCE: Associated Press
The Dallas Morning News

Trinity Meadows' boom just a hoofbeat away

N. Texas racetrack a long bet awaiting its full potential

By Kathryn Jones
Special Contributor to The Dallas Morning News

WILLOW PARK, Texas — It's a cold Tuesday morning and a few stragglers are still sipping coffee and trading the latest bits of gossip at Bino's Cafe near the Trinity Meadows racetrack. But come back

UPDATE

on race days — Thursday through Sunday — and Bino's bustles, especially at lunchtime.

Over a hamburger or the daily blue-plate special, customers scan tip sheets purchased at the Quarter Pole Handicapping Center next door and swap stories about the fastest ponies and the best jockeys racing that day.

Bino's owner Sharon Suarez, who's also the town's mayor, says her lunch business has tripled since the new pari-mutuel horse racing track opened in late May. She hired two additional employees to keep up with the race day crowds, expanded the cafe's menu to include popular Mexican dishes and began serving breakfast.

"We're a lot busier during the day now," Ms. Suarez says.

Other business owners say Trinity Meadows also has brought them additional customers. But as the racetrack nears the end of its inaugural season Dec. 31, Willow Park still awaits the boom that many townsfolk expected and some even feared.

Bino's remains the only sit-down restaurant in the community of about 2,300 residents. Willow Park still doesn't have any hotels, forcing out-of-town racing fans to stay in Fort Worth about 9 miles to the east or in Weatherford to the west.

Such retail businesses want to come into Willow Park, but the big holdup is the lack of a sewer system, says Paul Noe, president of the local Chamber of Commerce. Willow Park, formerly part of a ranch before it became a town, still uses septic tanks for its waste.

"Without the sewer, we just can't grow," says Mr. Noe, who owns an auto parts store in the same strip shopping center as Bino's and the Quarter Pole. "Because of that, development of this area has been throttled back. Until we get it, development can't occur because we can't put in hotels and restaurants."

Many analysts are watching Trinity Meadows since it's the first pari-mutuel racetrack in North Texas in about 50 years. Other communities want to lure racetracks as a way to boost local economies.

That development has yet to occur in Willow Park. Vacant parcels of land for sale line both sides of I-20 near the medium-size — or Class 2 — track. The main commer-

Please see AS on Page 4D.

Paul Noe (left), owner of Willow Park Auto Parts, at his store with his wife, who is a mutual teller at Trinity Meadows racetrack. Sharon Suarez (below) is owner of Bino's Cafe.

The Dallas Morning News: Erich Schlegel

Lomas gets reorganization plan approved

By Steve Brown
Real Estate Editor of The Dallas Morning News

More than two years after filing bankruptcy to escape the crush of almost $6 billion in debt, Dallas-based Lomas Financial Corp. has received final court approval of its reorganization.

The federal bankruptcy court ruling clears the way for Lomas to formally emerge from Chapter 11 next month as a much smaller, less diversified company with a dramatically reduced debt load.

"We are a very lean and efficient operation as we exit Chapter 11," said Lomas chairman and chief executive Jess Hay.

Lomas Financial — one of the country's largest residential loan servicing companies — now focuses on three primary lines of business: mortgage banking, information services and short-term real estate lending.

LOMAS FINANCIAL CORP.

BEFORE BANKRUPTCY: (June 30, 1989)		AFTER BANKRUPTCY: (January 1992)	
■ Total debt:	$5.7 billion	■ Total debt:	$900 million
■ Stockholders' equity:	$210 million	■ Stockholders' equity:	$341 million*
■ Total employees:	3,754	■ Total employees:	2,303
■ Principal businesses: Mortgage banking, information system services, short-term lending, real estate development, life insurance, commercial leasing, retail credit card operation.		■ Principal businesses: Mortgage banking, information system services and short-term lending.	

* As part of the reorganization, Lomas shareholders received 81 percent of the capital stock of Vista Properties Inc., formerly the company's real estate development subsidiary, which was spun off into a separate firm.

SOURCE: Lomas Financial Corp.
The Dallas Morning News

Before filing for Chapter 11 protection in September 1989, Lomas subsidiaries also were active in real estate development, life insurance, commercial leasing and consumer credit-card operations.

"The (reorganization) plan provides a fair recovery for the company's creditors and stockholders and concurrently enhances enterprise value by providing a capital structure which will enable Lomas to maintain its position as a leader in the mortgage banking industry," Mr. Hay said.

Lomas sold its life insurance, leasing and credit-card divisions. And the commercial real estate subsidiary is being spun off into a separate company as part of the reorganization plan.

Sales of the subsidiaries and reorganization of the company's balance sheet will leave Lomas with a total debt load of about $900 million. That compares with a peak of

Please see LOMAS on Page 4D.

Put financial freedom on shopping list

SCOTT BURNS

Q. You're always offering advice to people who have money. But can you help someone who lives from check to check? Unlike many of your readers, we don't have CDs, mutual funds, stocks, annuities, etc., that value into the tens of thousands of dollars. Here's our situation.

I am 28; my husband is 31. We have two children, ages 5 and 7. I don't work outside the home. My husband earns

Please see THOSE on Page 5D.

On December 31, 1991, the reorganization news was made official to the world on the first page of the business section of *The Dallas Morning News*. Reprinted with permission of *The Dallas Morning News*.

Business

Texas & Southwest

Friday, January 31, 1992 — © 1992, The Dallas Morning News — The Dallas Morning News — Section D

DIGEST

TODAY'S NEWS

WEST TEXAS INTERMEDIATE
Crude oil futures prices, per barrel
$18.94 Up 5 cents
$20 / 19 / 18 / 17
21 22 23 24 27 28 29 30 Jan.
Shaded line = new near-contract month.

Officials at Wallace Co. forgot something important after winning the coveted Malcolm Baldrige National Quality Award in 1990 — how to run a profitable business. The family-owned pipe and valve distribution company based in Houston filed for Chapter 11 bankruptcy protection earlier this week, strapped for cash amid dwindling inventories. 1D

Pan Am Corp. sued Delta Air Lines Inc. for at least $2.5 billion Thursday, alleging that Delta killed Pan Am by breaching a contract to finance a revitalized Pan Am. 1D

After stacks of legal papers get signed Friday, Lomas Financial Corp. will exit the real estate business for the first time — and probably for good. 1D

Ten weeks before it opens east of Paris, Euro Disneyland is coming under increasing fire from Frenchmen miffed at what they view as American imperialism and Uncle Scrooge-like management practices. 1D

An increase in home sales helped Dallas-based Centex Corp. record a 22 percent improvement in earnings during its most recent quarter. 2D

DOW AVG. Up 19.90 Close: 3244.86

The stock market put together a mild rally, steadying after Wednesday's late drop. Analysts said the market drew support from hopes for a renewed decline in interest rates and a smattering of upbeat corporate earnings reports. 4D

The Bank of Tokyo, ignoring flash-point tensions between the United States and Japan, will open a banking office in Dallas. 11D

Rep. Charles Wilson of Lufkin vowed to block the export of East Texas wood chips to Japan. 11D

Texas Instruments Inc. has elected Gloria McDermith Shatto as the 13th member of its board of directors. 11D

Fina Inc. reported net income of $21.8 million for the fourth quarter of 1991, up 14 percent from the similar period last year. Fourth-quarter revenues were $859.1 million, down 28 percent from a year ago. 12D

REAL ESTATE

With record high vacancy rates in cities around the country, building owners are looking for a way out of the most overbuilt office market on record. A growing number of office landlords are considering residential conversions as a potential for new profits.
REAL ESTATE REPORT 1D

The Atrium at Collin Ridge office building in Plano has been purchased by an investment group lead by Pacific Partners Inc., a Dallas real estate firm.
BUILDING SPECS 2D

TODAY'S COLUMNS

Mortgage holders who were sitting on the fence waiting for lower interest rates have gotten a nasty surprise during the last couple of weeks. Responding to political moves, the interest rates on long-term loans have scooted up since early January, causing a panic among the thousands of home owners who are hoping to refinance at lower rates.
STEVE BROWN 2D

Be prepared to enjoy an evening of recognition for some of our top civic leaders. Be prepared to pay homage to the Boy Scout movement. Be prepared to rub shoulders with others as dedicated as you. You've probably guessed by now the above references are to the local observance of the 82nd anniversary of the Boy Scout movement in America on Tuesday evening at the Apparel Mart.
ROBERT MILLER 3D

FINANCIAL

WHAT NYSE DID	4-5D
FUTURES PRICES	4D
WHAT AMEX DID	6D
OTC STOCKS	6-8D

Pan Am sues Delta for calling off deal

Bankrupt airline seeks $2.5 billion

By Terry Maxon
Staff Writer of The Dallas Morning News

Pan Am Corp. sued Delta Air Lines Inc. for at least $2.5 billion Thursday, alleging that Delta killed Pan Am by breaching a contract to finance a revitalized Pan Am.

The action, filed in New York, also asks that Delta not be repaid $115 million it had loaned Pan Am or other claims Delta has against Pan Am. The lawsuit is similar to an action filed Dec. 8 by Pan Am creditors who are also seeking $2.5 billion or more from Delta.

Delta responded Thursday that it did nothing improper when it backed out of its deal to help fund a new Pan Am. Delta said it would vigorously fight the lawsuit.

Please see PAN AM on Page 2D.

DURABLE GOODS
New orders, in billions of dollars, seasonally adjusted
Dec. 1991: $117.7 billion
132 / 128 / 124 / 120 / 116 / 112 / 108 / 0
J F M A M J J A S O N D
1991
SOURCE: U.S. Department of Commerce
The Dallas Morning News

Durable-goods orders plunge

Reuters

WASHINGTON — Orders for big-ticket durable goods fell sharply in December, and new claims for jobless benefits rose in mid-January, the government said Thursday in reports that showed a stagnant economy and gave no hints of recovery.

"There is no way you can look at the (reports) and see any signs of life in the economy," said Stephen Slifer, economist at Lehman Government Securities.

The 5 percent plunge in orders for durable goods ranging from planes to refrigerators was the biggest decline in more than a year and far worse than economists' expectations of a 0.7 percent decrease.

For all of 1991, durable goods orders — considered a good gauge of

Please see DURABLE on Page 3D.

REAL ESTATE REPORT

Filling a vacancy

Office glut leads developers to try apartment redos

By Steve Brown
Real Estate Editor of The Dallas Morning News

When Dallas architect Mark Humphreys was hired to come up with a renovation plan for a suburban Washington, D.C., office building, he knew the owners wanted a creative solution.

Built in the 1960s, the six-story brick office complex was outdated and only 30 percent occupied.

A glut of new buildings in the area made the project an unlikely competitor for new business tenants.

The solution: remodel the office building for another type of tenant — apartment renters.

With record high vacancy rates in cities around the country, building owners are looking for a way out of the most overbuilt office market on record.

A growing number of office landlords are considering residential conversions as a potential for new profits.

"We have all these buildings, all this space," Mr. Humphreys said. "What we need are occupants.

"I think that in this decade, creative, adaptive re-use is what it's all about," he said.

Along with the Fairfax, Va., project — which is currently out for construction bids — Humphreys & Partners Achitects has plans for similar residential redevelopments in the Dallas area.

Residential use of empty office buildings recently came into the spotlight in Dallas when preservationists suggested converting the historic downtown Cotton Exchange building into apartments.

"These older buildings have taken it on the chin as far as their rental and occupancy rates," Mr. Humphreys said. "The building we did in Fairfax was in a very good area, but had a very low occupancy.

"But rental housing in that area is in short supply," he said.

"A 100 percent occupied apartment tower at top rates performs a whole lot better than a 30 percent occupied office tower at the lowest rates."

Humphreys & Partners redesigned the exterior of the building with balconies and a new roofline, and added landscaping and recreation facilities on what had been part of the surface parking lot.

"We have looked at properties in Dallas to do the same thing with," he said.

While those projects are in the central city, Mr. Humphreys said suburban conversions are also viable.

"A California firm contacted us recently about a much newer building out in the Galleria area they are considering turning into apartments," he said. "If you can purchase a foreclosed building for $15 to $20 per square foot and put $20 to $25 in additional finish-out inside, then you are in the project at a price that makes sense."

For some of these empty office buildings, residential re-use may be the only alternative to the wrecking ball, said Brent Byers of Dallas' Corgan Associates Architects.

"We can't see the office demand for these projects coming back quickly," Mr. Byers said. "It's

Please see OFFICE on Page 2D.

The Dallas Morning News: Paula Nelson

Preservationists have suggested converting the historic downtown Cotton Exchange building into apartments.

Lomas making shift as bankruptcy ends

Firm leaving real estate development

By David LaGesse
Staff Writer of The Dallas Morning News

After stacks of legal papers get signed Friday, Lomas Financial Corp. will exit the real estate business for the first time — and probably for good.

Lomas emerges from a two-year bankruptcy as a mortgage company amid growing investor interest in its stock. Friday's signing party at a New York law firm completes a shift the Dallas-based company started in 1960, when Lomas first loaned money for mortgages as part of its property development activities.

"We've always been — always have been until tomorrow, at least — involved in real estate," Lomas chairman Jess Hay said Thursday.

"I don't foresee that this company again will be involved in real estate development."

That's little surprise. Real estate investments crippled the company in 1989. Lomas filed for Chapter 11 protection from creditors after the value of Texas properties collapsed, causing a liquidity crisis.

Lomas is a much different company than it was in the late 1980s. Besides its real estate, now to be held in a separate company largely owned by Lomas' former shareholders, Lomas has shed units that issued credit cards, life insurance and financed commercial leases. Lomas bought those companies in the mid-1980s as it sought to diversify outside the mortgage business.

Forced to find cash, Lomas sold those subsidiaries for a profit, Mr. Hay said.

"They were not the problem. Real estate was the problem."

Somewhat surprising, perhaps, is investor attention that Lomas has gained as it prepares to emerge from court protection.

The company's new common stock, officially available Friday, has traded for several weeks on a

Please see LOMAS on Page 3D.

Jess Hay

Baldrige winner Wallace Co. seeks Chapter 11 protection

Reuters

HOUSTON — Officials at Wallace Co. seemingly forgot something important after winning the coveted Malcolm Baldrige National Quality Award in 1990.

How to run a profitable business.

The family-owned pipe and valve distribution company based in Houston filed for Chapter 11 bankruptcy protection earlier this week, strapped for cash amid dwindling inventories.

Wallace won the prestigious award for its success in adapting Japanese management methods.

But while the company was gaining distinction from the award, it was losing $300,000 a month, according to a consultant brought in to turn the company around.

"The company had officials that just let it get out of hand," said Gail Cooper, chairman of Cooper Consulting in Dallas. "They got so wrapped up in the award."

When Mr. Cooper came to the company in July at the request of the board of directors, he found a firm that saw operating costs rise by $2 million from 1988 to 1990 while sales remained flat.

Please see WALLACE on Page 2D.

E-Systems sales, earnings reach record in '91

By Gregg Jones
Staff Writer of The Dallas Morning News

Bucking the national defense industry blues, Dallas-based defense electronics manufacturer E-Systems Inc. on Thursday reported record 1991 sales and earnings.

E-Systems chairman E. Gene Keiffer also offered a bright forecast for the immediate outlook for the highly secretive manufacturer of electronic intelligence, reconnaissance and surveillance systems. In a statement, Mr. Keiffer said that none of E-Systems' programs will be affected by the $50 billion in defense budget cuts proposed Tuesday by President Bush in his State of the Union address.

In one indicator of the company's financial strength, E-Systems finished 1991 with a record business backlog of unfilled orders, totaling $2.509 billion. A company spokesman said he expects local employment at E-Systems to rise slightly this year above the current figure of 10,000 jobs.

Please see E-SYSTEMS on Page 12D.

E. Gene Keiffer

The magic fiefdom?

French unions chafe under Euro Disney restrictions

Associated Press

PARIS — The Seven Dwarfs sang as they strode to work, cheerful toilers one and all. But as Walt Disney's heirs scramble to finish Europe's biggest theme park, they can only wish they had it so good.

Ten weeks before it opens east of Paris, Euro Disneyland is coming under increasing fire from Frenchmen miffed at what they view as American imperialism and Uncle Scrooge-like management practices.

"France has always had a love-hate relationship with the United States," said Euro Disneyland's president, Robert Fitzpatrick. "At some level, there's just a little bit of jealousy."

Much of the problem involves differing French and American conceptions of culture and labor.

UPDATE

As workers labor overtime to ensure that Euro Disneyland's 30 attractions and 5,200 hotel rooms will open on schedule April 12, Disney faces even bigger headaches.

Unions have accused Disney management of trying to suppress French individualism with an employee dress code that prohibits facial hair on men and heavy makeup or jewelry on women.

In addition, 16 contractors have banded together to demand that Disney pay $157 million in claimed cost overruns. Disney has said it only will pay the best documented claims and says it will refer the rest to arbitration.

Newspapers have echoed the outcry with headlines reading: "Euro Disneyland No Longer Amuses Anyone" and "Hue and Cry Over Uncle Scrooge" — the miserly uncle of Donald Duck. Some even have made puns on

Please see FRENCH on Page 12D.

On January 31, 1992, the date of Lomas' Chapter 11 consummation, *The Dallas Morning News* reported the company's announcement that it was leaving the real estate business. Reprinted with permission of *The Dallas Morning News*.

news. Each member of the Lomas family received a news release on December 31 with the headline they'd been waiting for: "Lomas Financial Corporation Emerges From Chapter 11." Covering each release was a personal note of appreciation from Jess Hay: "Great News! Our Plan has been confirmed. Congratulations and thanks for your part in making it happen. Also, best wishes for a happy, prosperous and joyful New Year."

The consummation took place on January 31, 1992. "It's just like a transaction closing," says Crowson. "Documents get signed and notes and stocks get delivered. The judge is not there, just lawyers and business people. The consummation is nothing but a big closing." The operative word, in this case, was "big." It certainly marked a milestone for Lomas' Chapter 11 counsel, Davis Polk & Wardwell. The New York law firm had never participated in a larger closing transaction in its 150-year history. "Just the display of the closing documents alone will require four large conference rooms at Davis Polk & Wardwell," Crowson wrote in the January 21 issue of the *Lomas Review*. "Lomas' legal staff is spending lots of late-night hours, as are Bert Byerley's treasury team, Joe Clooney's accounting staff, Gary White in Corporate Control, and Tricia Zimmerman in Stockholder Relations." To put the magnitude of their task in perspective, Crowson noted that the consummation included the distribution of three issues of new debt totaling $710 million, 20 million new shares of Lomas Financial Corporation common stock, warrants to purchase seven million shares of new Lomas Financial Corporation common stock, and the transfer of almost $400 million in cash.

Once again, management's response to the conclusion of this event failed to meet Pat Turner's expectations: "Everything was going at an incredible pace, and then it just quit and died. I was looking for balloons and streamers and 'Let's pop the champagne corks and make a toast.' That never happened. The mood was very quiet.

"I was looking at it from my standpoint as a worker bee. I wanted to celebrate doing a good job. Looking at it from management's standpoint, the bankruptcy phase was nothing to be proud of, nothing to brag about, and nothing to highlight except that it was an obstacle that we overcame."

Monday, February 3, 1992 The Dallas Morning News 3 D

A New Beginning For Lomas Financial

This Monday morning, Lomas Financial Corporation opened its doors to a new and exciting period in its history, emerging from 28 months of operation under Chapter 11 of the Federal Bankruptcy Code. The Company's confirmed Plan of Reorganization was consummated last Friday, January 31.

While you may have read some of the reports of Lomas' emergence from Chapter 11 — most of which have been reasonably accurate and generally favorable — we feel it important to provide a more complete picture of the Company which today affirms its position as a strong and innovative competitor in the mortgage banking field.

First, A Word of Thanks

From the outset, the threefold aim of our restructuring effort was to preserve the institution, to protect the people of Lomas and to maximize recoveries for each of the Company's constituencies. Twenty-eight months ago, even the most optimistic observer would scarcely have predicted the civility, dispatch and good faith with which this goal was accomplished.

The Company owes a great debt of gratitude to all those who weathered this challenging period with us:

- To our thousands of customers who never wavered and who faithfully stuck with us throughout the process;
- To the people of Lomas for their fidelity, tenacity and cheerful willingness to shoulder any task;
- To our Directors for their calm, steady and strong leadership;
- To our Creditors' and Equityholders' Committees for their cooperative spirit and constructive attitude;
- To our professional advisers for their creativity and enlightened counsel;
- And to Judge Burton R. Lifland for his judicially responsible, fair and decisive administration of our Chapter 11 proceedings.

Thanks to all of their efforts, Lomas has accomplished a strategic return to firmer ground and may now move positively into the future.

Mortgage Banking: The Core of Our Continuing Operations

Far from being consumed with matters relating only to its restructuring, Lomas has remained a force in the marketplace. It emerges as a company sharply focused on its core business, which since 1965 has been mortgage banking and which today features:

- A $28.5 billion primary mortgage servicing portfolio;
- A $7 billion master servicing portfolio;
- An $800 million subservicing portfolio;
- Extensive insurance agency and field services operations;
- An investment advisory group which manages two affiliates (Capstead Mortgage Corporation and Tyler Cabot Mortgage Securities Fund) with combined assets of more than $4 billion, which is more than double the combined total one year ago and which continues to grow at a rapid rate;
- And finally, a correspondent production or gathering system which now draws mortgage product from hundreds of originators and which in December added $543 million to the Company's primary servicing portfolio.

The production strength of the Company's mortgage banking operation is a factor which has been overlooked by a few who erroneously have concluded that the current mortgage market is unfavorable to the Company's mortgage banking operations.

Specifically, some have suggested that the current level of mortgage refinancing in this country inevitably will erode Lomas' portfolio.

Although it is true that the current refinancing fever has increased the Company's portfolio runoff rate, it also is absolutely clear that this same phenomenon and the generally increased activity in the mortgage market have increased to an even greater extent the rate of additions to the Company's portfolio. Specifically, during the month of December the Company's primary servicing portfolio performed as follows (in millions):

Beginning balance	$28,335
Amortization, sales and satisfactions (15.3% annual rate)	(360)
Additions (23% annual rate)	543
Ending balance	$28,518
Portfolio gain during the month	$183

At its December 31, 1991 balance of $28.5 billion, the Company's primary servicing portfolio already is $900 million higher than the total projected for June 30, 1992 in the Company's November 6, 1991 Disclosure Statement.

Thus, our mortgage banking operations in fact are doing very well in the current environment. Lomas Mortgage USA, the Company's mortgage banking subsidiary, during the six months ended December 31, 1991, produced net pretax income of $11.5 million, which is $2.2 million higher than anticipated. We see no reason why that level of contribution will not be maintained throughout the balance of the year, in which case the mortgage banking contribution to the Company's fiscal 1992 operating results clearly should exceed earlier expectations.

Other Continuing Activities

The Company's continuing operations, in addition to mortgage banking, also include the activities of Lomas Information Systems, Inc. ("LIS"), a wholly owned subsidiary which provides a broad array of products designed to serve the management information systems and data processing needs of the mortgage finance industry. One or more of LIS' products currently are used by 126 commercial banks, savings and loan associations and mortgage banking companies. Its data processing service bureau now provides data services related to mortgage servicing portfolios which include more than 1.9 million loans with an unamortized principal balance of more than $93 billion.

LIS recently introduced a new and innovative mortgage loan servicing system which is believed to be the most technologically and functionally advanced system available to the industry today. In the years ahead, we expect the increased automation of the new system, first, to enhance the efficiency of our own mortgage servicing operations, and second, to attract many new customers to LIS and its Excelis line of mortgage related products.

The Company also continues to hold other investments from which it receives recurring dividend, interest and other income.

Short-term Lending

Although the Company has discontinued its short-term real estate lending business, it retains and currently is liquidating:

- Earning short-term real estate loans which at December 31, 1991, totaled $212.9 million in principal amount;
- $18 million in earning real estate which previously was acquired through foreclosure; and
- Non-performing assets which (net of $54 million in reserves) are carried in the Company's consolidated accounts at approximately $105 million.

These investments and approximately $30 million of cash are held by ST Lending, Inc. ("STL"), a wholly owned and single purpose subsidiary. In due course, STL will liquidate this remnant of the Company's discontinued short-term lending operation and will apply the proceeds thereof, to the extent required, to retire $240 million principal amount of STL's notes which were issued as part of the consummation of the Company's Plan of Reorganization. We expect the liquidation of STL's debt to be completed in orderly increments during the next three and one-half years, after which the balance of STL's assets will revert to Lomas Financial Corporation..

What About Real Estate?

In the more focused approach which Lomas is now taking, direct investments in real estate remain only as vestiges of past operations. In the future, the Company's direct exposure to risks related to the real estate development business will be substantially eliminated. As part of the completed reorganization, real estate development assets have been distributed to stockholders through a spin-off of 81 percent of the common stock of Vista Properties, Inc. Although Lomas retains a 19 percent interest in Vista, the retained interest is carried in the Company's accounts at only $3.8 million.

A Word About the Company's Capitalization

Lomas emerges from Chapter 11 with a relatively strong capitalization which is carefully tailored to the Company's continuing operations and which includes the following (in millions):

Short-term warehouse debt (self liquidating)	$217
Consolidated term debt (various issues)	754
Stockholders' equity	330
Total capitalization	$1,301

Ratios:

Lomas Financial Corporation debt-to-equity	42%
Consolidated term debt-to-equity	229%
Consolidated term debt as a percentage of total capitalization	58%

In short, the restructured Lomas is well positioned operationally and financially to participate profitably and creatively in the challenging, exciting and ever-changing world of mortgage banking.

Guided By Strong Hands: Our New Board of Directors

Our confidence today is all the greater because of the extraordinary individuals who form the new Board of Directors of Lomas Financial Corporation:

James R. Adams
President and CEO, Southwestern Bell Telephone Company

Gene H. Bishop
Chairman and CEO, Life Partners Group, Inc.

Robert G. Boucher
Chairman (retired), United Mortgage Company

Dolph Briscoe
Banker and rancher, former Governor of Texas

Rod Dammeyer
President and COO, Itel Corporation

Jess Hay
Chairman and CEO, Lomas Financial Corporation

Robert V. Lindsay
Former President and Director, J.P. Morgan & Co., Incorporated

Dr. Diana Natalicio
President, The University of Texas at El Paso

Jon Newton
Partner, Clark, Thomas, Winters & Newton

Hugh G. Robinson
Chairman and CEO, The Tetra Group

Douglas L. Rock
Chairman and CEO, Smith International, Inc.

Harvey M. Schuster
President, California Investment Counsel, Inc.

Paul T. Walker
Financial consultant, former Executive Vice President and Senior Credit Policy Officer, Chase Manhattan Bank

W. Ray Wallace
President and CEO, Trinity Industries, Inc.

We have great faith in these leaders, in the people of Lomas and in the markets in which we operate. It is with an optimism exceeded only by our gratitude to our friends and associates that we embark today on our new beginning.

LOMAS

LOMAS FINANCIAL CORPORATION

For additional information about the new Lomas, contact Kevin McGarry at 214/879-5545 or write 1600 Viceroy Drive, Dallas, Texas 75235

At the end of the Chapter 11 ordeal, a full-page newspaper ad celebrated the company's survival and its "retreat to firmer ground."

CHAPTER XVIII

A NEW BEGINNING

Reluctance to celebrate the end of its ordeal did not dampen the company's public optimism about the future. Full-page ads in *The Wall Street Journal* and *The New York Times* greeted business page readers on February 3, 1992, with the headline "A NEW BEGINNING FOR LOMAS FINANCIAL." The bulk of the ad presented an updated portrait of the new Lomas. Mortgage banking, the company's core business, dominated the picture. Lomas Information Systems, Inc., was the other, smaller piece of its continuing operations. ST Lending, Inc., a wholly owned single-purpose subsidiary, was dedicated to liquidating the remnant of its loan portfolio and retiring the division's $240 million debt. The ad also reassured the public that Lomas' sharper focus did not include real estate investments. Former real estate assets were now part of Vista Properties, Inc., a separate corporation in which Lomas retained a 19 percent interest.

The response to Lomas' optimism was mixed. A *National Mortgage News* article published February 17 reported that LFC's and LMUSA's newly issued debt received "poor ratings" from Standard & Poor's. The Single-B and Double-B ratings, S&P said, "reflect non-investment-grade capitalization, weak financial flexibility and the lack of an established track record." The article ended with a cautionary note: "At this early stage of LFC's new life, it is unclear just how strong the company will become and how robust an earnings stream will develop." A January 20 article in *Forbes* offered cautious optimism: "Back from bankruptcy, Lomas Financial Corp. looks like a promising company again."

Public optimism notwithstanding, Lomas' senior management had few illusions about the company's

Chapter 11 didn't close the book on Lomas

BY MITCHELL SCHNURMAN
Fort Worth Star-Telegram Dallas Bureau

DALLAS — For three decades, Jess Hay built one of the nation's top mortgage banking companies. For the past 2½ years, he's been resurrecting it.

Steering Lomas Financial Corp. through bankruptcy was not Hay's idea of a legacy. But it may prove to be his lasting one, depending on how Lomas recovers — and whether Wall Street embraces the company again.

So far, stock buyers have been wary, despite upbeat talk about Lomas' "textbook restructuring."

Lomas' stock price has fallen steadily since its new issues began trading two months ago. And short sellers are still ripping the company, questioning its prospects and quietly suggesting that Hay should go.

That Hay and Lomas are getting mixed reviews is not surprising.

Hay was the toast of his industry for years, as Lomas pushed its way to the head of the mortgage banking class.

Then, in the 1980s, Lomas spent $744 million to diversify into other businesses and hundreds of millions more to develop raw land. Hay hoped that those tacks would insulate Lomas from the ups and downs in mortgage banking. But the strategy fell short, overwhelmed by the collapse in Texas real estate.

Now, a month after emerging from Chapter 11, Lomas is less than half its peak size, and competitors have surged ahead.

But the bankruptcy hasn't been all bad news. It forced Lomas to return to its roots — earning fees from servicing home mortgages — and it let the company cut away nearly $4 billion in debt.

Moreover, Lomas' core business actually grew sharply during Chapter 11, a reflection of how well the reorganization went.

"We always regretted having to file Chapter 11," said Hay, who has been Lomas chairman and chief executive officer since 1965. "But now we feel like we're a leaner, more efficient operation."

The numbers tell part of the story: Lomas' revenues for fiscal 1991, ended June 30, were $269.9 million, down from $1.2 billion three years earlier. Total employment was 2,138, compared with 4,016 in 1989. And the drop in consolidated debt was the most dramatic: from $5.7 billion two years ago to $971 million today.

Several experts are calling the Lomas case a model restructuring. Lomas' bankruptcy was one of the five largest in U.S. history, but despite its size and complexity, there were no major court fights or high-profile showdowns.

Management and creditor groups built up some trust early, negotiators say, and each gave ground as the process advanced. In the end, management agreed to sell off key assets to increase payouts to creditors, and creditors approved funds to build up the mortgage banking business — and give Lomas a shot at a strong future.

"It sounds Pollyanna, but this was a classic restructuring," said Laureen Bedell, a veteran bankruptcy lawyer who represented Lomas for the New York law firm of Davis Polk & Wardwell. "The company reorganized around a viable business, and management stayed in place. That's how Chapter 11 is supposed to work, but usually it doesn't."

Among the surprising results, at least to many analysts: Hay, 61, is still at the helm.

Often in bankruptcies, management becomes a lightning rod for creditors and stockholders. They're eager to fix blame for their losses, and many believe that executives who led the company into a mess shouldn't be the ones to get it out.

It was Hay, for instance, who loaded Lomas up on debt to diversify. And he approved the real estate buildup that ended with nearly $450 million of write-downs that wiped out Lomas' equity.

But Hay's tenure never became a major issue, all sides say.

Like creditors, Hay personally lost millions when Lomas' stock cratered from a high of $39.25 in 1987 to about $1 a share two years later. That's not why Hay won over creditors, though; he succeeded by striking a balance among competing interests, sources familiar with the Lomas restructuring say.

Creditors cite Hay's attitude about

(More on LOMAS on Page 2)

"It sounds Pollyanna, but this was a classic restructuring. The company reorganized around a viable business, and management stayed in place. That's how Chapter 11 is supposed to work, but usually it doesn't."

— Laureen Bedell
bankruptcy lawyer

Fort Worth Star-Telegram / DALE BLACKWELL

Jess Hay, chairman and CEO, led Lomas through a textbook Chapter 11.

Reorganization chart

Key moves Lomas made to emerge from bankruptcy in 28 months:

- **Shrinking the company:** Revenues fell 78 percent from 1988 peak and, in two years, expenses were slashed 43 percent and employment cut from 4,016 to 2,138.
- **Selling assets to raise cash:** Lomas sold its retail banking operation, commercial leasing business and three life insurance companies for $826 million.
- **Growing the core business:** Lomas' mortgage servicing portfolio — the key to its future — grew from $21.6 billion to $29 billion in two years.
- **Slashing corporate debt:** Through asset sales and Chapter 11 proceedings, Lomas cut total debt from $5.7 billion to $971 million.
- **Spinning off real estate:** Lomas spun off 81 percent of its real estate development operation to stockholders, putting some distance between the company and the volatile business that pushed it to bankruptcy.
- **Keeping Jess Hay in charge:** Hay, the company's longtime chairman and chief executive, held on to his job and forged a quick, amicable resolution.

On March 8, 1992, a month after Lomas emerged from Chapter 11, the *Fort Worth Star-Telegram* printed a feature article about the event. Reprinted with permission of the *Fort Worth Star-Telegram*.

status in the financial markets. "I never expected a big, warm welcome on Wall Street," says Jess Hay. "We exited from Chapter 11 knowing that we probably had to experience two or three years of penance."

"It was one thing to say you came out of Chapter 11 in good standing and you were on firm ground again," says Bert Byerley. "But talk is cheap. There were a lot of questions about the health of the company that had nothing to do with the capital structure we exited with. We needed to get several quarters behind us in order to show that we were making money, that we were able to overcome our information systems problems, and that we were able to cope with the heavy refinancing going on within the mortgage banking company. We needed time to prove we were back from the 'semi-dead,' because that's what some people chose to believe we were."

In fact, the "strategic retreat to firmer ground" had soft spots in both of the remaining operating divisions. The Excelis-MLS system at LIS continued to plague the division with performance problems and an unremitting stream of red ink. The mortgage company, on the other hand, had to contend with a drop in interest rates that triggered a refinance frenzy.

At Lomas Information Systems, the road to stabi-

ployees through June 15.
The two plants have produced Haggar

That shutdown was also attributed to the influx of imported goods.

depending upon the season, between 2,000 and 3,000 outside the country.

Lomas Mortgage plans to skip June interest payment

By David LaGesse
Staff Writer of The Dallas Morning News

Facing a cash crunch next year, Lomas Mortgage Investors Corp. said it plans on skipping an interest payment due on $100 million in debt in June.

The Dallas-based investment trust also said it retained Bear, Stearns & Co., a New York-based investment firm, to advise the company on restructuring its debt.

If Lomas Mortgage Investors skips the interest payment in June, noteholders could force it into bankruptcy. But the company hopes to complete an out-of-court transaction, president Ted Enloe said.

"It's a way to force everybody to the table to begin discussions," Mr. Enloe said of skipping the payment.

Lomas Mortgage Investors is one of the affiliates of Lomas Financial Corp. that didn't go through its parent's bankruptcy proceedings. Lomas Financial recently emerged from Chapter 11 protection from creditors after more than two years working to restructure its debt.

An investment trust that made construction and development loans, Lomas Mortgage quit extending new credit soon after its parent filed for bankruptcy in 1989. The trust has been shrinking as the construction loans are paid and Lomas Mortgage, in turn, retires its corporate debt.

But the company faces a showdown next year, when all of its outstanding debt comes due. Lomas Mortgage owes $149.6 million to a group of senior creditors and another $100 million to holders of its subordinated notes.

Lomas Mortgage and its lenders are close to an agreement on restructuring the senior debt.

LFC had demonstrated resiliency in overcoming its Chapter 11 crisis. However, on April 9, 1992, *The Dallas Morning News* reported that Lomas & Nettleton Mortgage Investors had a cash crisis of its own, and planned to skip its June interest payment. Reprinted with permission of *The Dallas Morning News*.

lization for Excelis-MLS was difficult and expensive. Only gradually did LIS sort out the long list of enhancements the new system required. "We had a significant need to get the system stabilized," says Michael Patrick, who became president of LIS in early 1992. "As late as February or March, MLS was not stabilized by any rational standard. It was functioning well in some areas and chaotically in other areas. It was getting better, but it wasn't where it needed to be."

...We were spouting red ink.

But it was the inability of LIS' management to get a handle on operating losses and cash deficits that brought the subsidiary to a point of crisis. Hay pressured management to come up with a plan that decisively addressed those problems. He increased the pressure in February 1992 by appointing Patrick as president of LIS. The news from former chief operating officer Matt Jacobs, however, indicated that the division had not found a new direction. LIS' projected cash requirement for fiscal 1992 was about $30 million, and for fiscal 1993 Jacobs' projection ranged from $30 million to as much as $50 million.

One result of creditor dissatisfaction with LIS' performance during Chapter 11 was a covenant that provided greater scrutiny and accountability from the board of directors. Additional funding for LIS now required the approval of a LIS subcommittee of the board of directors and an independent LIS Technical Advisory Board made up of five outside industry experts.

On April 21, 1992, the Information Systems Committee and Technical Advisory Board met to consider a request for additional LIS funding. They learned at the meeting that LIS' projected cash deficit from April 1992 to the end of fiscal 1993 was between $24 million and $30 million. LIS also projected a net operating loss in fiscal 1993 as high as $23 million. The

The benchmark 30-year FHA rate is 7.5 percent.

Lomas posts loss in year, 4th quarter

By Steve Brown
Real Estate Editor of The Dallas Morning News

FINANCIAL PERFORMANCE
LOMAS FINANCIAL

Operating results for fiscal year ended June 30. All numbers in thousands. There are no year-ago comparables due to reorganization:

Continuing operations	
Mortgage banking	$25,941
Info. services	-$18,063
Other	$16,532
Total	$24,410
Operating profit	
Before reorg. cost	$20,344
Loss from continuing operations	$-7,765
Net loss	-$40,585

SOURCE: Lomas Financial Corp.

Lomas Financial Inc., which emerged from bankruptcy in January, reported a loss of $18.2 million or 19 cents a share for its fourth quarter ended June 30.

From continuing operations, the Dallas financial services firm had a $3.2 million profit for the period.

Lomas ended its fiscal year with a $40.6 million net loss. The company generated 1992 operating profits of $24.4 million, which were offset by reorganization expenses, costs associated with discontinued operations and administrative expenses. From continuing operations, Lomas had a $7.8 million loss for the year.

Lomas Financial's biggest profit center this year was its core mortgage banking division, which had $25.9 million in operating income for the year ended June 30, the company said.

Lomas treasurer Robert Byerley Jr. said the company increased the size of its mortgage servicing portfolio by 25 percent during fiscal 1992, despite the loss of almost $6 billion in loan servicing due to the high volume of mortgage refinancings. "We were able to keep pace with the runoff in our portfolio and actually grow," Mr. Byerley said.

He said the company doesn't anticipate that the current mortgage refinancing boom will result in a decline in Lomas' loan servicing portfolio. At the end of June, Lomas had a $39.4 billion loan servicing portfolio.

Changes in the technology that Lomas uses to service those loans have been costly. In fiscal 1992, Lomas' information systems division lost $18 million associated with the installation of its new computerized loan servicing system.

Lomas began converting to its new Excelis computer system last year and expects to complete the process during the next 10 months. But the company said that segment of the company won't have a positive cash flow until the end of calendar year 1994.

Some of the information systems expense will be offset by savings Lomas expects to gain in interest payments in fiscal 1993 and 1994 because of a $375 million reverse interest rate swap in July. The company said that the swap will result in $9 million in savings in 1993 and $10 million annually thereafter.

BUSINESS NOTES

Despite the focused response of Hay and Patrick, it was reported in *The Dallas Morning News* on August 21, 1992, that LIS had lost $18 million associated with the installation of and conversion to Excelis. Reprinted with permission of *The Dallas Morning News*.

2 F The Dallas Morning News Saturday, November 14, 1992 A

Lomas earns $4.4 million

By Steve Brown
Real Estate Editor of The Dallas Morning News

Lomas Financial Inc., which 10 months ago emerged from bankruptcy protection, reported net profit of $4.4 million or 22 cents a share for the quarter ended Sept. 30.

Jess Hay

The Dallas mortgage and financial services firm reported a $5.7 million profit from continuing operations for the period.

Revenue for the quarter totaled $76.5 million. Year-ago numbers aren't comparable because Lomas was under Chapter 11 protection.

During the last quarter, Lomas earned $8.6 million from its mortgage banking division.

Lomas Financial's income from the company's core mortgage services division were depressed by a sharp increase in payoffs of home loans. Mortgage rates at 20-year lows prompted many home owners to pay off their old mortgages by refinancing during the last few months.

In September alone, Lomas' loan prepayments totaled about $922 million. And for the quarter, Lomas estimates that $2.175 billion of its home mortgages were paid off. That equals an annualized rate of 29 percent of Lomas' total loan services portfolio.

In the year ended June 30, Lomas lost almost $6 billion in loan servicing due to the high volume of mortgage refinancings.

The early loan payments, or runoff, in the latest quarter cost Lomas' mortgage banking division $3.6 million.

While that was partially offset by interest-rate hedging and the sale of equipment to affiliate Capstead Mortgage, the outlook for additional mortgage prepayments prompted Lomas to predict decreased income during the next three quarters.

"Unless portfolio runoff rates decline, the net operating contribution of the mortgage banking division will be lower in the final three quarters (of the company's current 1993 fiscal year) than in the first," Lomas chairman Jess Hay said in a statement. "General corporate income will also be lower.

Even with the prepayments caused by refinancing, Lomas combined loan servicing portfolios grew by $1.8 billion during the last quarter to a total of $41.2 billion at the end of September.

Lomas' information systems division continued to suffer during the quarter, contributing an operating loss of $3.8 million.

On November 14, 1992, it was reported that Lomas had earned $4.4 million for the quarter, but LIS continued to lose, resulting in an operating loss of $3.8 million. Reprinted with permission of *The Dallas Morning News*.

committee approved an expenditure of not more than $12.5 million through September 1992, with the agreement by management that it would explore "alternatives with regard to dealing with the situation."

According to this latest information, LIS still hadn't found a way to avoid large cash deficits and operating losses. Jess Hay opted for direct intervention. Six days later, he completed an eight-page memorandum that outlined a new direction for LIS. It was not an operating plan or projection but rather a "blueprint to radically change LIS' prospects in the year ahead." It began with a ringing disavowal of LIS' recent projections as "unacceptable." Hay's minimum objectives included: (1) reducing total cash expenditures in fiscal

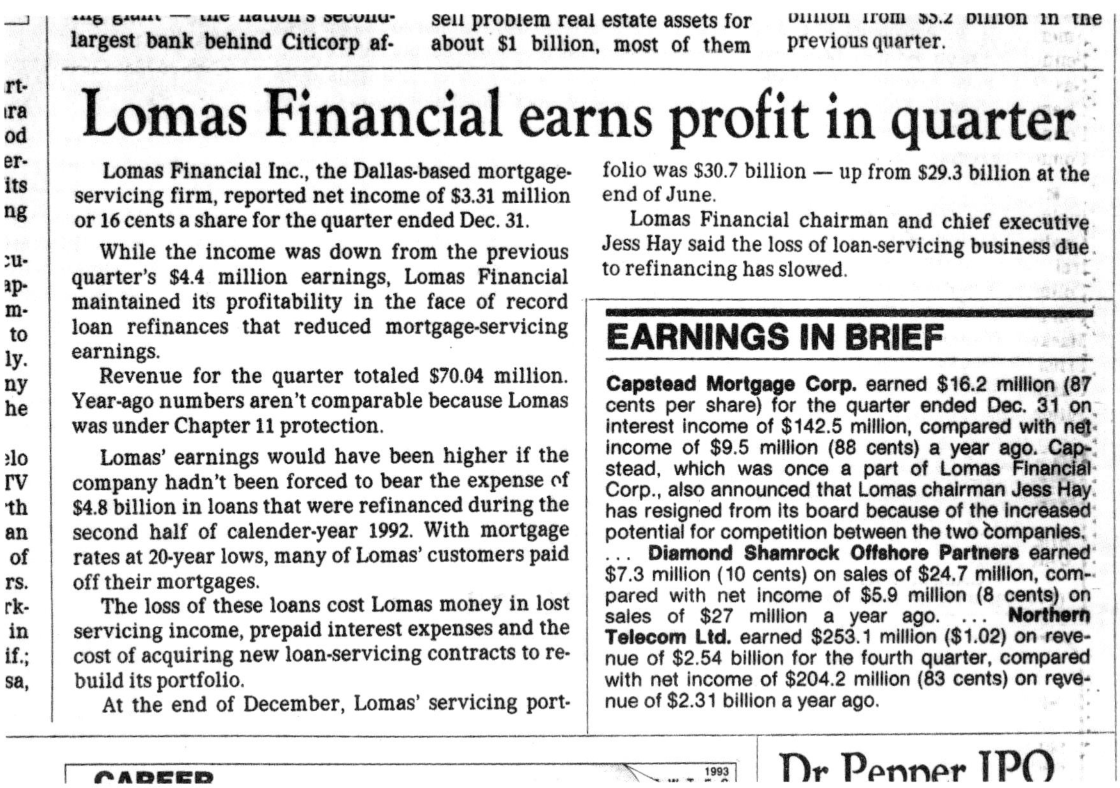

largest bank behind Citicorp af- | sell problem real estate assets for about $1 billion, most of them | previous quarter.

Lomas Financial earns profit in quarter

Lomas Financial Inc., the Dallas-based mortgage-servicing firm, reported net income of $3.31 million or 16 cents a share for the quarter ended Dec. 31.

While the income was down from the previous quarter's $4.4 million earnings, Lomas Financial maintained its profitability in the face of record loan refinances that reduced mortgage-servicing earnings.

Revenue for the quarter totaled $70.04 million. Year-ago numbers aren't comparable because Lomas was under Chapter 11 protection.

Lomas' earnings would have been higher if the company hadn't been forced to bear the expense of $4.8 billion in loans that were refinanced during the second half of calender-year 1992. With mortgage rates at 20-year lows, many of Lomas' customers paid off their mortgages.

The loss of these loans cost Lomas money in lost servicing income, prepaid interest expenses and the cost of acquiring new loan-servicing contracts to rebuild its portfolio.

At the end of December, Lomas' servicing portfolio was $30.7 billion — up from $29.3 billion at the end of June.

Lomas Financial chairman and chief executive Jess Hay said the loss of loan-servicing business due to refinancing has slowed.

EARNINGS IN BRIEF

Capstead Mortgage Corp. earned $16.2 million (87 cents per share) for the quarter ended Dec. 31 on interest income of $142.5 million, compared with net income of $9.5 million (88 cents) a year ago. Capstead, which was once a part of Lomas Financial Corp., also announced that Lomas chairman Jess Hay has resigned from its board because of the increased potential for competition between the two companies. ... **Diamond Shamrock Offshore Partners** earned $7.3 million (10 cents) on sales of $24.7 million, compared with net income of $5.9 million (8 cents) on sales of $27 million a year ago. ... **Northern Telecom Ltd.** earned $253.1 million ($1.02) on revenue of $2.54 billion for the fourth quarter, compared with net income of $204.2 million (83 cents) on revenue of $2.31 billion a year ago.

For the quarter that ended December 31, 1992, Lomas posted a profit, although less than the previous quarter's. Earnings would have been higher if the company had not been forced to bear the expense of refinanced loans during the second half of calendar year 1992. Reprinted with permission of *The Dallas Morning News*.

1993 to no more than $54 million; (2) increasing fiscal 1993 revenues by 8 percent through aggressive marketing; (3) holding to a cash requirement in fiscal 1993 of no more than $18 million and an operating loss of no more than $12 million. To meet those objectives the memo targeted specific cost reductions.

As has often been the case under Hay's leadership, the memorandum represented more than the announcement of a change in direction. It was a charismatic call to action that captured the spirit of change as well as the dimensions. In a letter accompanying the memorandum that was sent to the members of the board of directors on May 7, Hay emphasized that approach: "The enclosed memorandum presents a broadly stated portrait of what the final product of our current remedial work at LIS may be. It is not a plan; rather it is intended to serve as a catalyst to encourage the development of a reasonably acceptable plan for fiscal 1993."

Hay underscored the company's determination "to make fiscal 1993 LIS' year of transition to profitability" by also announcing in the letter "major management changes at LIS." The most significant was the resignation of chief operating officer Matt Jacobs and his replacement by Mike Patrick. "They were good individuals," says Patrick, "but they had been there during the high-stress development period of the system, and they had gotten kind of arthritic in their approach to things. There was not, in my view, the level of teamwork or cohesion within the organization that would give them a chance to be successful. All this time, of course, we were spouting red ink."

Hay's and Patrick's focused responses produced results. By June 23, they reported a cash subsidy reduction for fiscal 1993 of $8.3 million, a reduction of LIS' projected fiscal 1993 loss by almost $9 million, and the promise of more to come. The anticipated shutdown of the old UNISYS system in fiscal 1994 would save another $3 million to $4 million in known costs.

The effort to control expenses coincided with a shift toward stabilization of the Excelis-MLS system in April, May, and June. "Only in April did everyone start getting happy about MLS," says executive vice president David Stephens. "The system was working on a day-to-day basis, which was a pleasant change." "The system just got better and better and better," says Patrick. "All of a sudden I could see that people were starting to smile in the mortgage company." Behind the good feelings stood solid performance. By midsummer Terry Deyoe claimed a 100 loans per person increase in efficiency for the loan administration division over the past year, and he attributed 75 percent of that increase to Excelis. Jess Hay confirmed the new system's progress in a report about Lomas' June 30, 1992, results: "The recent performance of the system, specifically with respect to its ability to increase the productivity of large mortgage servicing operations, such as Lomas', has been particularly encouraging."

Confidence in Excelis increased when Terry Deyoe attributed 75 percent of the loan administration division's rise in efficiency to the Excelis system.

Still more encouraging was the decision by Sears Mortgage Company in September 1992 to convert its $28 billion portfolio to Excelis. Although Sears had been an external service bureau customer on Lomas' UNISYS system, the company made it clear that it would select a vendor only after careful scrutiny of Excelis and its competitors. "Sears made it painfully clear to us that we did not have their business," says Patrick. "And the only way we could get their business was by earning it. They told us we were going to be in competition with the other leading systems, and if we won, fine, and if we didn't, too bad.

"The good news is we won. The competition was intense. We spent five full days in Chicago demonstrating. We took our modules to every single primary servicing unit in Sears, and they went exhaustively through the system. It was not a casual event.

"But at the end of the day, Sears added it all up and said, 'Lomas, your system is the best, period.' We subsequently had that confirmed by two other parties."

Throughout the summer there was increasing evidence of greater and more enthusiastic acceptance of Excelis. Unsolicited praise for the system from LMUSA employees who stopped Patrick in the hall or cafeteria was one indication. "If I ask someone, of course they'll tell me the system is doing great," says Patrick. "But when I don't ask and they make a point of speaking out, that's significant." More praise came from Houston-based Mitchell Mortgage's Trish Maxie. "Excelis is a fantastic system," says Maxie. "In fact, a woman who worked here recently left to work for a mortgage company that uses CPI {Computer Power Incorporated, LIS' chief competitor}. She came by to visit the other day and said, 'CPI is a joke. You don't really appreciate the full extent of what Lomas has until you actually go and work on another system.'"

Although not included in the Chapter 11 filing, LIS emerged at the end of the process battered and bleeding red ink. Lomas Mortgage USA, on the other hand, was clearly a winner. "The mortgage company accomplished almost unbelievable results," says Terry Deyoe. "It went from $21 billion to $29 billion and outran significant portfolio run-off at the same time. It conquered its computer conversion. It became profitable, and it changed its industry perception. At the same time morale was enhanced. I was pleased and proud of the management staff that made all that happen."

Everybody told me that the mortgage business was volatile . . .

Unfortunately, the economy brought the spectacular climb in portfolio growth to an abrupt end. A significant drop in interest rates in late 1991 kicked off a wave of mortgage refinancing by homeowners. As mortgage loans poured off LMUSA's servicing portfolio, they took with them important revenues from the mortgage company's largest and most profitable source of income. And now that LMUSA no longer had large amounts of cash to spend on bulk acquisitions, some in the industry questioned the company's ability to survive. They failed to take into account the other components of LMUSA's production gathering system. "People don't give Lomas enough credit for its ability to generate new mortgages," Salomon Brothers analyst Bruce Harting observed in an article.

"It is probably the most unique way of building a servicing portfolio in the industry," says senior vice president Richard Magel. "You've got all these creative people out there finding creative ways of bringing in servicing and building the portfolio." The components of the gathering system included Capstead and the Flow Purchases, CalPERS, Bond Administration, Subservicing, and Second Mortgage and Refinance departments.

"The key is flexibility," says Magel. "We can move anywhere in the market we want. We don't have any branch offices or employees. If we want to get out of a market, we stop buying loans there. We buy them someplace else. If the market changes in an area, we can react to those changes in seconds."

Record additions to the servicing portfolio were matched by record portfolio run-off from "refi mania." The extended duration of this particular bout of mortgage refinance had no historical precedent. Its arrival just prior to LFC's exit from Chapter 11 and continuation for another 12 months hobbled what Lomas had hoped would be a fast break out of the chute. "The unexpectedly high rates of servicing portfolio runoff and additions during the March quarter were in substantial balance," the first quarterly report noted on May 13. "As a result, LMUSA's mortgage servicing portfolio declined by only $46 million during the three months." Lomas reported $1.839 billion in portfolio run-off and $1.793 billion in portfolio additions for the quarter. The news on June 30 was essentially the same. With astronomical run-off of $3.72 billion and an equally phenomenal $3.78 billion in added new servicing for the six-month period, the two numbers "were in substantial balance." The company's primary servicing

Half a year after Chapter 11, the Lomas 1992 annual report noted with disappointment that LMUSA's primary servicing portfolio balance of $29 billion had only gained $65 million. Some observers took satisfaction that things were improving; others did not share that view.

portfolio balance of $29.274 billion on December 31, 1991, had moved to $29.339 billion six months later. The 1992 annual report noted the minuscule $65 million increase with disappointment. Optimists like Lomas investor Mark Feldman, president of Cold Spring Management, Inc., took satisfaction in the fact that "the spigot is filling the tub faster than the tub is draining." Steve Eisman, an analyst at Oppenheimer & Co., was less impressed: "The best they {Lomas} can do in this environment is tread water."

LMUSA president Patrick wasn't prepared for the ride on the refinance roller coaster: "The pace of business has been frantic. We've had to run very, very hard throughout the company just to stay even with our portfolio. We managed to keep the portfolio even, and grow it somewhat. But it's like a treadmill. You run like crazy just to stay in place. We're adding servicing at rates that we've never experienced, and we're losing servicing at rates we've never experienced. So, if you put them together, we're not going anywhere. We're growing, but slowly. Everybody told me that the mortgage business was volatile, but all it's ever been since I arrived {January 1992} is just madness."

Net growth, although small, continued to inch upward. Lomas' primary servicing portfolio reached a historic milestone when it passed the $30 billion mark on December 31. In October, an ad composed by Fannie Mae and appearing in *The Wall Street Journal* during the Mortgage Bankers Association's national convention read in part: "Hats off to you Lomas Mortgage USA. After difficult economic times, you've made a remarkable comeback with an impressive $1 billion commitment with Fannie Mae." The ad sent a signal to the industry that Lomas was alive and well as

On October 26, 1992, Fannie Mae placed an ad in *The Wall Street Journal* congratulating Lomas Mortgage USA on its remarkable comeback.

both a servicer and producer of mortgage loans. "We got a lot of publicity from it," says executive vice president Gary Kell, one of the key architects of LMUSA's production system, who attended the convention. "The comments I heard most often were, 'God, how did you do that?' and 'Where did you get your loans?'"

Lomas lost its affiliated company, Capstead Mortgage Corporation, to success. As Capstead's mortgage production, capital resources, and revenues and income continued to climb, pressure increased for it to move toward an independent status. By 1992, the company had grown to a point where it could no longer be managed economically by its outside manager, Capstead Advisers, Inc., a wholly owned subsidiary of LMUSA. Lomas and Capstead resolved the issue with a phased transition that Jess Hay referred to as "a royal-type divorce." Concurrent with the move toward independence, Tyler Cabot Mortgage Securities Fund, Inc., another affiliated company managed by a wholly owned subsidiary of LMUSA, agreed to merge with and into Capstead.

Lomas and Capstead agreed to a 4½-year transition involving scheduled increments of compensation. The 1992 annual report's statement of consolidated operations described the arrangement as follows:

> In June 1992, the Company negotiated an agreement to revise its management contract with Capstead. The agreement, which is subject to approval by Capstead shareholders, extended the management contract to December 31, 1996. Under the terms of the agreement, management fees would be reduced to an amount equal to the Company's operating costs plus a predetermined profit aggregating $14.5 million during the term of the extended agreement. At the end of the term of the management agreement it is anticipated that Capstead will move to a self-administered status.

The company also reached an agreement "to sell certain computer systems currently used in the operations of Capstead" to Capstead for additional compensation. Capstead Advisers, Inc. president Ronn K. Lytle's contract of employment was terminated by mutual consent on July 31. Lytle became a full-time employee of Capstead, serving as the chairman of the board and chief executive officer, on August 1, 1992.

Consistent with the company's corporate reorganization, which deemphasized asset management and discontinued short-term lending, Lomas moved to sell the stock it owned in L&N Housing Corp. On February 6, 1992, Lomas announced that it had reached an agreement in principle to sell its 352,000 shares of common stock to EastGroup Properties, a Maryland real estate investment trust, and Walker Investments, L.P., a Mississippi limited partnership, for $3,344,000.

Even more important from a cash standpoint was the sale of common and preferred stock that Lomas had acquired from the sale of its credit card operation to First USA in 1989. Lomas was still in bankruptcy in the summer of 1991 when First USA approached the company about buying the stock back. The agreement they reached generated $32 million in cash for Lomas in 1991 and $33 million the following year.

Capstead, Tyler Cabot to merge

By David LaGesse
Staff Writer of The Dallas Morning News

A pair of companies started by Lomas Financial Corp. said Wednesday they will merge through a stock swap.

Capstead Mortgage Corp. said it will buy Tyler Cabot Mortgage Securities Fund Inc. Both Dallas companies were started in the 1980s, trade mortgage securities and are currently managed by Lomas Financial, the Dallas mortgage company that recently emerged from bankruptcy protection.

The combination with Tyler Cabot will help the companies operate more efficiently and increase the capital available to Capstead Mortgage, Capstead president Ronn K. Lytle said.

Merging the companies in a stock swap takes advantage of the high trading value of Capstead Mortgage's stock, Mr. Lytle said. The company's stock closed Wednesday at $31.50, or more than 150 percent of the company's book value of $20 per share.

Buying Tyler Cabot will increase capital at Capstead Mortgage to $635 million from $315 million, Mr. Lytle said.

That will allow Capstead Mortgage to buy more loans for resale to investors. Lomas Financial originally established the independent company as a buyer for large mortgages that Lomas Financial wrote.

Faced with financial problems in the late '80s, Lomas Financial left the business of making mortgages. Lomas Financial filed later for bankruptcy protection in proceedings completed in January and has emerged as a servicer of mortgage loans.

On its own, Capstead Mortgage continued to grow by buying mortgages on the wholesale market and now holds assets of $6 billion.

Tyler Cabot is a mutual fund that primarily invests in mortgage securities.

If approved by shareholders, the agreement would make Mr. Lytle the first full-time chairman of Capstead Mortgage, which was formed in 1985. He will replace Jess Hay, chairman of Lomas Financial, who will remain a director at Capstead Mortgage.

Capstead Mortgage also negotiated a new contract with a management subsidiary of Lomas Financial. The agreement extends the contract to the end of 1996 but lowers the rates paid by Capstead Mortgage, which also agreed to buy computer software from Lomas Financial as part of the agreement.

Jess Hay . . . will remain a director at Capstead Mortgage.

On June 18, 1992, *The Dallas Morning News* reported the merger of Capstead and Tyler Cabot, and Lomas' new negotiated contract. Reprinted with permission of *The Dallas Morning News*.

It was a very successful transaction.

The stalled progress of its operating divisions didn't prevent the company from advancing in another important arena. Two transactions in particular demonstrated that Lomas had lost none of its flair for financial maneuvering. LMUSA responded to an opportunity in mid-1992 to increase the yield on the fiduciary funds it held in escrow for mortgagors, and it took it. "The strategy," says vice president Paul D. Fletcher, "was to create more value from the escrows without taking undue risk. The swap is a way to take escrows that are earning a 30-day rate and have them earn a five-year rate without putting them in a five-year instrument." "On July

21, 1992, LMUSA . . . entered into a $375 million reverse interest rate swap . . . with Lehman Brothers Special Financing Inc.," read the Lomas news release. "Under the terms of the swap, Lehman will pay Lomas a fixed annual interest rate of 6.0025 percent and Lomas will pay Lehman a floating annual interest rate based upon the 30-day average A1/P1 commercial paper rate."

The transaction was particularly clever in the way it eliminated Lomas' exposure to negative cash flow in the event that short-term interest rates climbed above the 6 percent fixed rate Lomas earned. As the short-term rate rose, so would the earnings on the escrow balances Lomas held, each offsetting the other. The company expected the transaction to earn $9 million in fiscal 1993 and $10 million in subsequent years through fiscal 1997.

Lomas proved no less adept at eliminating potential interest rate expenses. The $330 million in long-term debt that the creditors placed on LMUSA carried an escalating interest rate schedule. "Our incentive was to get out from under that thing," says Fletcher, "because it was going to be expensive going forward. We ended up hiring Goldman Sachs as the lead underwriter in the offering that was going to raise money that would pay the old issue off. It was a very successful transaction." Through a public offering in October, LMUSA issued and sold $340 million principal amount senior notes that enabled the mortgage company to retire the $330 million debt to its creditors.

The sale of new notes was one of several positive signals that made a favorable impression on the banking industry. Over the course of 1992, Lomas moved from pariah to prospect. It was a major turnaround that boded well for a business that depended heavily on credit to finance its operations.

Fletcher attributed the change in perception to Lomas' successful exit from Chapter 11, LMUSA's ability to sell long-term debt, and the consistency of LMUSA's earnings in the first three quarters of 1992—$6.4 million, $8 million, and $8.6 million, respectively. Although not dramatic, the numbers indicated a consistent trend of profitability that pleased lenders.

Acceptance of LMUSA as a borrower gained momentum toward the end of 1992. Credit for LMUSA's warehouse operation became the object of active pursuit by lending institutions. "We now have banks calling us and viewing us as potential customers," said Fletcher in November 1992. "The mortgage company is starting to get a lot of interest from banks for its warehouse. We're also looking at a commercial paper program for LMUSA that would function as a warehouse credit. Banks are willing to lend money to Lomas Mortgage USA. That's significant, because a leveraged company like Lomas needs credit."

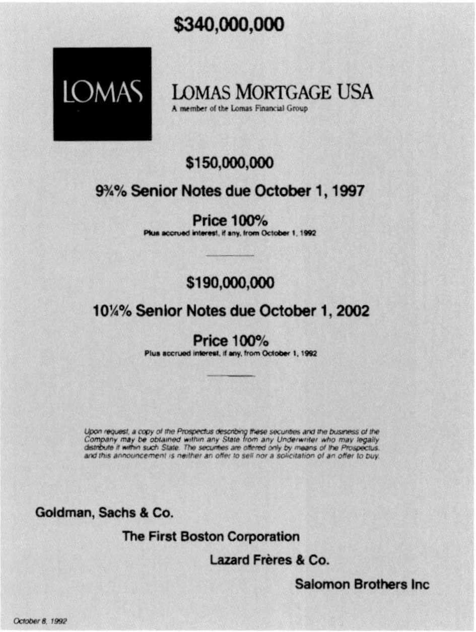
$340,000,000

LOMAS

LOMAS MORTGAGE USA
A member of the Lomas Financial Group

$150,000,000

9¾% Senior Notes due October 1, 1997

Price 100%
Plus accrued interest, if any, from October 1, 1992

$190,000,000

10¼% Senior Notes due October 1, 2002

Price 100%
Plus accrued interest, if any, from October 1, 1992

Upon request, a copy of the Prospectus describing these securities and the business of the Company may be obtained within any State from any Underwriter who may legally distribute it within such State. The securities are offered only by means of the Prospectus, and this announcement is neither an offer to sell nor a solicitation of an offer to buy.

Goldman, Sachs & Co.

The First Boston Corporation

Lazard Frères & Co.

Salomon Brothers Inc

October 8, 1992

This tombstone notice appeared in *The Wall Street Journal* and other papers to announce the issuance of $340 million in Lomas Mortgage USA notes.

To combat the onslaught of portfolio run-off, Lomas added another weapon to its gathering system arsenal. Marching orders were issued to executive vice president David L. Chapman II in early 1992. The message from Patrick, Chapman recalls, was brief: "Mike said, 'I want you to get wholesale up and running.'" With that declaration, the mortgage company reentered the wholesale origination arena. Even as Lomas exited the retail and wholesale markets in 1989, management vowed to return one day to its traditional loan-gathering sources. The timing for a wholesale (also called correspondent lending) operation appeared opportune. An industry-wide transition from large retail branch networks to small- and medium-size mortgage brokers influenced the decision. Competition among those low-cost suppliers drove down the price of loans. Attractive market conditions coupled with Lomas' ability to start up a flexible, low-overhead centralized operation at its Dallas headquarters gave the company a rational basis for reentering the market.

... I want you to get wholesale up and running.

The timing for a reentry into the wholesale market seemed right, and David Chapman was appointed to head the new operation.

Chapman was a good choice to head the new business. Quality has been a prominent feature of his professional career. This became evident at Lomas with the turnaround he performed on the mortgage company's underwriting department in the mid-1980s. Besides careful attention to detail and organization, Chapman also projected an infectious enthusiasm and flair for marketing. Even so, he didn't allow optimism to overwhelm good judgment. He believed the way to proceed successfully in a crowded field of competitors was first to stop and listen to prospective customers. A survey of mortgage brokers that he commissioned turned up surprising results. Price was not their overriding concern; reliability was. Brokers wanted a lender they could depend on every day. Second in importance was customer service. Chapman structured the operation around that information. "We're always going to be competitive on price," says Chapman, "but we're not going to be the leader. As long as we're in the marketplace, and we're there everyday, and we give good service, we'll get a lot of business." With a commitment to staying in the marketplace as a given, Chapman devoted much of his energy to developing what he calls the "spirit of customer service."

"Customer service is our number one thing," says Chapman. "When someone calls us, he's going to think he's our only customer. We'll hand-walk his loan all the way through and he'll get his money so promptly that he'll come back a second time. We're going to say to brokers, 'Give us one loan, and see how we handle it. If

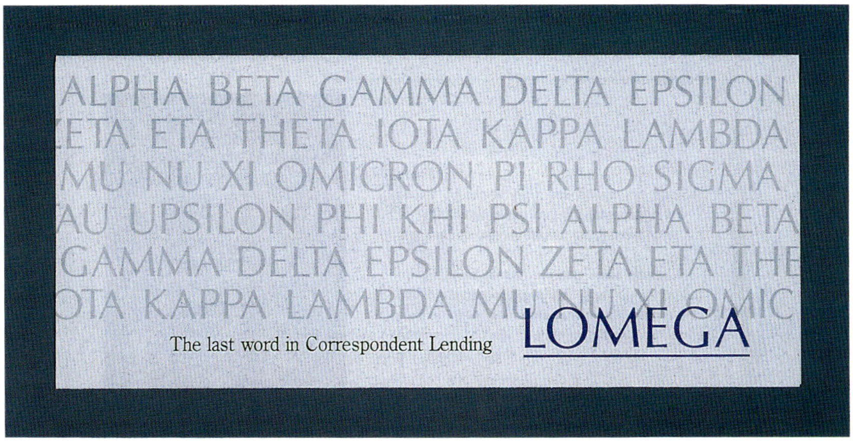

The last letter in the Greek alphabet, omega, was the basis for the name of the new wholesale marketing unit.

we do it well, then give us two loans next time.' I believe we can develop customer loyalty by delivering outstanding service."

By fall, the new unit revealed its name in a brochure with a catchy lead-in: "The first name in mortgage banking, Lomas Mortgage USA, proudly announces the last word in correspondent lending . . . LOMEGA." After three difficult years, the advertising piece reflected Chapman's confidence in the new venture's association with the name Lomas. Senior vice president David C. Stewart, hired by Chapman in November 1992 to manage the correspondent lending operation, shared Chapman's confidence. "The Lomas name means something, and I'm talking as an outsider looking in," says Stewart, whose executive management background includes 17 years of experience in mortgage banking and nine years in correspondent lending. "If Lomas says it, you can believe it. That's just the way it's always been."

Automation would play a key role in LOMEGA's march toward what Stewart described as "market dominance." He predicted that LOMEGA would reap an important efficiency advantage by using a proven LIS product called the Loan Production System (LPS). The sophisticated loan-tracking system was adapted to handle wholesale originations. It gave LOMEGA an important competitive advantage by streamlining the lending operation and increasing its ability to deliver superior customer service.

Both Chapman and Stewart believed that a high-performance operation emphasizing quality and service would build significant volumes for LOMEGA. Stewart predicted originations of $500 million a month by the end of calendar 1993. Chapman, noting the enormous $9 billion quarterly production of a correspondent lending competitor, was less specific but equally optimistic: "The sky's the limit."

Correspondent lending was the first step in Patrick's expansion of the gathering system. Finding new sources of growth for the mortgage company's principal portfolio required looking at all options, including retail. "We will go back to retail," said Patrick in early 1993. "I don't think our future is grand without retail."

Building the kind of "money machine" that LMUSA's president envisioned meant harnessing new

LOMEGA employees, left to right, Adrienne LaCava, Ken Karant, Sue Denny, Scott Holtz, David Stewart, and Julie Maddux.

and larger horses to what was already in place. "[Retail] isn't a rejection of what we've been doing. It would supplement what we've been doing and make us stronger. It's another product line and another way to do business. You just don't do one thing. If you only do one thing, you put yourself at risk when the business climate changes.

"Our gathering system is substantially a system that purchases loans. We can talk about it all we want, and we can take the facts and figures and squirrel them to where people don't know what in the hell is going on. But basically, we're buying everything."

Dependence on bulk purchases to supplement volumes in the face of portfolio run-off also raised what Patrick called the "quality issue." "I'm not against bulk purchases," Patrick states, "but every time you buy bulk, you're buying somebody else's idea of what was acceptable quality. My view of the industry is that quality has been inconsistent at best. Maybe the lion's share of what we buy, 85 or 90 percent, is fine. It's that last 10 percent that is rife with nightmares and drives our servicing organization berserk. Can we sift and sort and chase documents? Of course we can. But it's a tough way to make a living."

Patrick understood that LMUSA maximized profits when the loan administration department operated smoothly on an assembly line basis. The key to processing larger volumes of servicing more efficiently, Patrick said, would come from internally controlled retail and wholesale production.

The single most important advantage Lomas enjoyed following its exit from Chapter 11 was cultural. The core belief that corporate value came from the creativity of its staff fostered a consistently entrepreneurial approach toward the marketplace. One of the newest and most fervent practitioners was Mike Patrick. He first encountered Lomas innovation in 1981. As treasurer of Superior Oil Company, he was asked to find a "mortgage solution" for the relocation of corporate personnel. Patrick discovered that Lomas was the only mortgage company he talked to that was willing to adapt its business practices to solve Superior Oil's problem. That made a lasting impression on him and influenced his decision to join Lomas in January 1992.

It's one of the hallmarks of the company.

"It's one of the hallmarks of the company," says Patrick. "Lomas will figure out a way to adapt a solution to the marketplace rather than say, 'This is what I do, and I hope you like it.' I suspect that it stems from Jess Hay's personality. By virtue of who he is and the way he thinks about the world, he has attracted people who are problem solvers."

Patrick cites Lomas Field Services as a "crisp example" of entrepreneurial problem solving. In 1986 Lomas became disenchanted with the performance of the outside companies it contracted to inspect and preserve its troubled real estate. LMUSA management, under the leadership of Bill Glasgow, decided the company could increase the level of service by hiring its own field representatives. It worked. A year later management turned it into a business venture by selling the service to other mortgage companies. "Lomas was willing to invest the money needed to get Lomas Field Services up and running," says Patrick. "And presto! We have a business that is producing a profit of $1.5 million a year."

Another, more recent example was what LMUSA called its one-third partnership. That relationship helped solve the problem of how the mortgage company could expand bulk acquisitions despite limited capital resources. It was clear by the second half of calendar 1991 that capital constraints would impede Lomas Mortgage's growth. The court-approved cash allotment that LMUSA used for bulk acquisitions would soon be exhausted. That fact, along with the prospect of restrictive creditor covenants and reduced borrowing capacity once the company emerged from Chapter 11, limited the company's plans for portfolio production. It was the kind of financial challenge that appealed to executive vice president David Stephens, who explored various "capital raising concepts" beginning in mid-1991. Logistical problems and activities associated with the conclusion of the bankruptcy hampered progress on that front. Then a business acquaintance of Stephens' who worked for J. P. Morgan called in late October to tell him about two companies that were looking for a third party to form a partnership to buy servicing. "When I got the call, I pursued it," says Stephens. "It was an easy pursuit. They were looking for somebody, too. Their objectives were very similar to ours."

The interested parties were Dana Corporation, an automotive equipment manufacturer, and a large New Jersey public utility. The limited partnership that emerged from their discussions was structured so that each participant became a one-third investor. Each partner agreed to put up $10 million in equity and then borrow additional money in the partnership's name to buy servicing.

"It turned out to be a fairly elegant deal," says Stephens, whose understated personal style conceals considerable financial acumen. "By virtue of this being a partnership investment, it qualifies for something called 'equity accounting.' All we do is record our investment in a partnership on the balance sheet, but no debt appears on LMUSA's balance sheet. This is attractive to us because it doesn't hurt us in any of our debt covenant calculations, and therefore it increases the amount of servicing we can acquire.

"We're making fees from our direct investment and a lesser amount as subservicer of the partnership's portfolio. And if the partnership exceeds a certain earnings return on equity, we earn an additional 3 percent incentive compensation."

The partnership began operations in June 1992. Six months later Stephens allowed that it was "off to a flying start, I guess you'd say." If extravagant figures of speech don't exactly come tripping off his tongue, the relevant numbers do. By December, the partnership portfolio was over $2 billion, with yields easily exceeding previously set targets. Looking toward the end of calendar 1993, Stephens projected "conservatively" that the relationship would earn $2 million in net income for Lomas on an investment of $5 million.

David Chapman's entrepreneurial instincts took a new turn in early 1992. His appreciation of LMUSA's technologically advanced laser disk image processing system began in 1991 when he assumed responsibility for records administration. The paper-intensive department had first used laser disk technology in 1987. "It helped us, tremendously," says Chapman. "We gradually spent more and more money and increased our commitment to an optical disk records storage environment.

. . . there was a business opportunity surrounding imaging services.

"It's like a compact disk that you put in your car—only it's 12 inches in diameter. One disk holds 150,000 pages or 1,600 mortgage files, which translates into 40 file drawers." The reaction of assistant vice president Pat Turner, who learned about image processing and what it can do at a briefing by Chapman in 1992, was typical: "It's kind of like printing the Bible on the head of a pin."

Information is actually placed on a disk through a scanning process that converts documents into electronic images that are stored on optical disks. A retrieval code gives an authorized user the ability to access the information within seconds via a personal computer monitor, facsimile machine, or laser printer.

When Lomas applied the technology to one of its mortgage banking departments, the results were impressive. "Central payoff is an intensely paper-sensitive area," says Chapman. "After we implemented optical disk imaging, we immediately reduced our staff by 25 percent. The cost savings were tremendous. Other departments saw how well it worked and said they wanted to be next.

"We did it internally only. Then I went to Jess in early 1992 and said, 'We've become experts in this. We've got almost $5 million worth of equipment sitting over here, and we're only using one shift, eight hours a day. We could run this sucker 24 hours a day and sell the service to other people. We've got a window of opportunity here.' He said, 'I want you to pursue it. Let's do it.'" Nine months later, INTELLIFILE opened for business. Senior vice president Russel Young managed the operations and administration. Senior vice president Thomas J. Clancy, hired by Lomas in late 1992, directed sales, marketing, and product development.

INTELLIFILE was added to the marketing mix at Lomas in 1992. Its executive team includes, from left to right, Flavio Daibert; David Chapman, president; Rick Smith; Russel Young; and Scott Wenning.

"As early as February-March [1992], David [Chapman] presented me with a memorandum about the fact there was a business opportunity surrounding imaging services," says Patrick. "Not every company would have said, 'David, go put something together. Let's see what it is.' David, in effect, was encouraged to be a complete entrepreneur within Lomas. That is part of the Lomas culture. There's a willingness and openness to let somebody start up a business and see if they can make a go of it. And the economics looked very attractive. INTELLIFILE could turn out to be a very substantial business for us."

Just how substantial? If the new department's business plan was an accurate indicator, potential "revenues and profits are seemingly gigantic." That level of

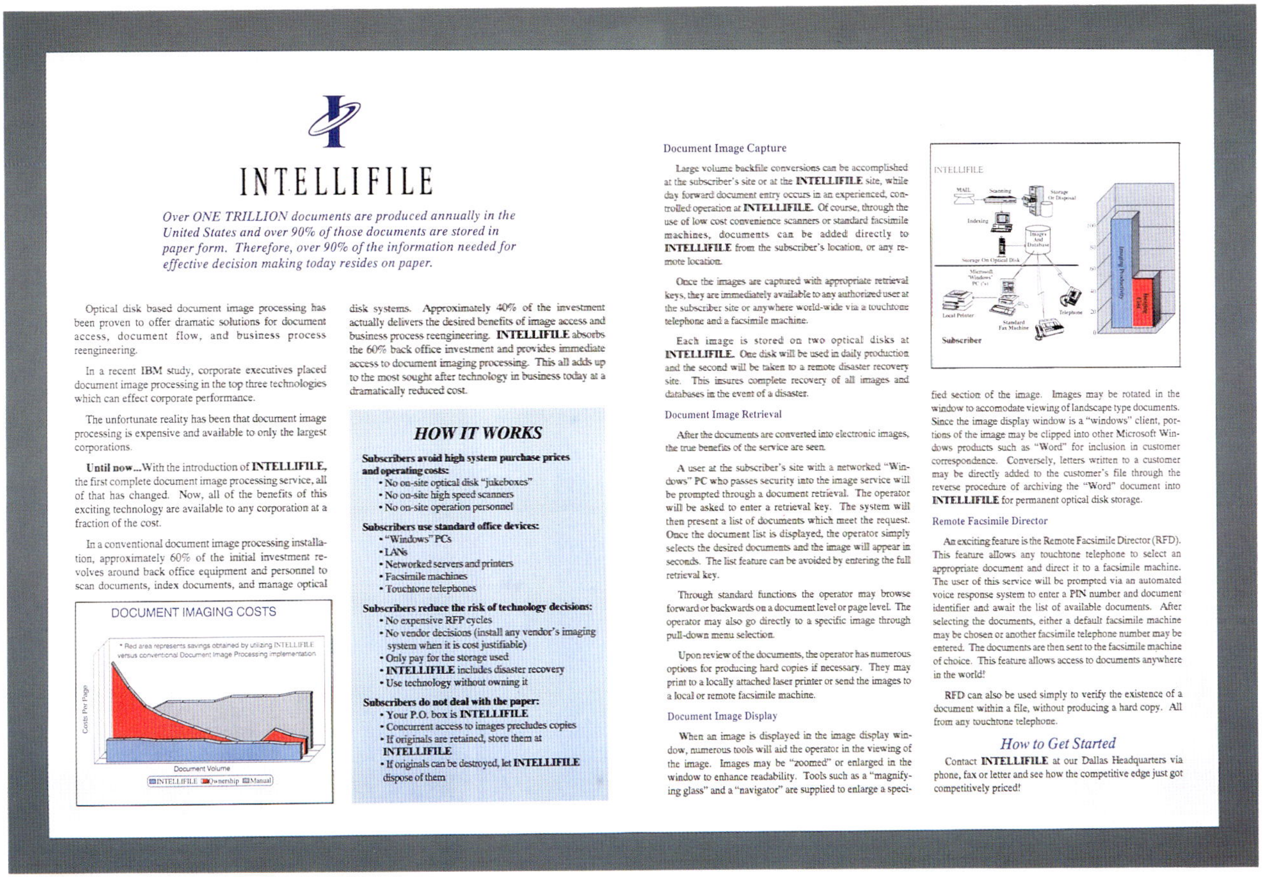

INTELLIFILE

Over ONE TRILLION documents are produced annually in the United States and over 90% of those documents are stored in paper form. Therefore, over 90% of the information needed for effective decision making today resides on paper.

Optical disk based document image processing has been proven to offer dramatic solutions for document access, document flow, and business process reengineering.

In a recent IBM study, corporate executives placed document image processing in the top three technologies which can effect corporate performance.

The unfortunate reality has been that document image processing is expensive and available to only the largest corporations.

Until now... With the introduction of **INTELLIFILE,** the first complete document image processing service, all of that has changed. Now, all of the benefits of this exciting technology are available to any corporation at a fraction of the cost.

In a conventional document image processing installation, approximately 60% of the initial investment revolves around back office equipment and personnel to scan documents, index documents, and manage optical disk systems. Approximately 40% of the investment actually delivers the desired benefits of image access and business process reengineering. **INTELLIFILE** absorbs the 60% back office investment and provides immediate access to document imaging processing. This all adds up to the most sought after technology in business today at a dramatically reduced cost.

HOW IT WORKS

Subscribers avoid high system purchase prices and operating costs:
- No on-site optical disk "jukeboxes"
- No on-site high speed scanners
- No on-site operation personnel

Subscribers use standard office devices:
- "Windows" PCs
- LANs
- Networked servers and printers
- Facsimile machines
- Touchtone telephones

Subscribers reduce the risk of technology decisions:
- No expensive RFP cycles
- No vendor decisions (install any vendor's imaging system when it is cost justifiable)
- Only pay for the storage used
- **INTELLIFILE** includes disaster recovery
- Use technology without owning it

Subscribers do not deal with the paper:
- Your P.O. box is **INTELLIFILE**
- Concurrent access to images precludes copies
- If originals are retained, store them at **INTELLIFILE**
- If originals can be destroyed, let **INTELLIFILE** dispose of them

Document Image Capture

Large volume backfile conversions can be accomplished at the subscriber's site or at the **INTELLIFILE** site, while day forward document entry occurs in an experienced, controlled operation at **INTELLIFILE**. Of course, through the use of low cost convenience scanners or standard facsimile machines, documents can be added directly to **INTELLIFILE** from the subscriber's location, or any remote location.

Once the images are captured with appropriate retrieval keys, they are immediately available to any authorized user at the subscriber site or anywhere world-wide via a touchtone telephone and a facsimile machine.

Each image is stored on two optical disks at **INTELLIFILE**. One disk will be used in daily production and the second will be taken to a remote disaster recovery site. This insures complete recovery of all images and databases in the event of a disaster.

Document Image Retrieval

After the documents are converted into electronic images, the true benefits of the service are seen.

A user at the subscriber's site with a networked "Windows" PC who passes security into the image service will be prompted through a document retrieval. The operator will be asked to enter a retrieval key. The system will then present a list of documents which meet the request. Once the document list is displayed, the operator simply selects the desired documents and the image will appear in seconds. The list feature can be avoided by entering the full retrieval key.

Through standard functions the operator may browse forward or backwards on a document level or page level. The operator may also go directly to a specific image through pull-down menu selection.

Upon review of the documents, the operator has numerous options for producing hard copies if necessary. They may print to a locally attached laser printer or send the images to a local or remote facsimile machine.

Document Image Display

When an image is displayed in the image display window, numerous tools will aid the operator in the viewing of the image. Images may be "zoomed" or enlarged in the window to enhance readability. Tools such as a "magnifying glass" and a "navigator" are supplied to enlarge a specified section of the image. Images may be rotated in the window to accomodate viewing of landscape type documents. Since the image display window is a "windows" client, portions of the image may be clipped into other Microsoft Windows products such as "Word" for inclusion in customer correspondence. Conversely, letters written to a customer may be directly added to the customer's file through the reverse procedure of archiving the "Word" document into **INTELLIFILE** for permanent optical disk storage.

Remote Facsimile Director

An exciting feature is the Remote Facsimile Director (RFD). This feature allows any touchtone telephone to select an appropriate document and direct it to a facsimile machine. The user of this service will be prompted via an automated voice response system to enter a PIN number and document identifier and await the list of available documents. After selecting the documents, either a default facsimile machine may be chosen or another facsimile telephone number may be entered. The documents are then sent to the facsimile machine of choice. This feature allows access to documents anywhere in the world!

RFD can also be used simply to verify the existence of a document within a file, without producing a hard copy. All from any touchtone telephone.

How to Get Started

Contact **INTELLIFILE** at our Dallas Headquarters via phone, fax or letter and see how the competitive edge just got competitively priced!

INTELLIFILE published a brochure explaining how the optical disk image processing system worked.

optimism came from Chapman's "yellow pages" perception of the market: "Open the yellow pages and go down the businesses and ask yourself, 'Who operates with paper and needs to store and retrieve it?' It's, 'Yes . . . yes . . . yes.' Almost everybody. I want to make this a line item on every company's budget. Just like Federal Express. No one dreamed Federal Express would become that important 10 years ago. Today, it's a line item on every budget. Optical imaging can achieve the same thing.

"An article in *Time* magazine said that by 1996 revenues from image processing would total $12 billion. We think INTELLIFILE is going to be a huge profit maker. In four years, we anticipate $60 million in revenues and about $25 million in profits."

Profitability at Lomas Information Systems remained elusive. Scrambling to generate revenue, Patrick adopted a "broader vision" for the troubled subsidiary. The original vision had run aground. At least three problems impeded the progress of Excelis-MLS, the system designed to take the servicing of mortgage loans into the twenty-first century.

One obstacle was the long period of instability that plagued the new system. Even allowing for the fact that it takes time to work out the bugs from any new system, many within the industry thought the 12 months that LIS took was excessive. As late as the spring of 1992, the division announced the suspension of all conversions to the new system for three months in order to concentrate on increasing its functionality. The postponement worked, but the legacy of delays and the perception of instability undermined the product's acceptance in the marketplace.

Do we have other capabilities that we can exploit?

Another marketing problem was the unavailability of a large, sophisticated outside customer to use as a reference. Although LMUSA certainly had a large, sophisticated operation, it could hardly be characterized as a disinterested third party. Patrick believed the problem would resolve itself in April 1993 when Sears Mortgage Co. was scheduled to convert to Excelis-MLS.

The division's financial condition also impeded progress. Four straight years of losses did not inspire confidence among potential customers. "We had a major prospect in Austin who had known us for years and thought our system was better than the competition," says McGlothlin. "But the chairman of the board had trouble giving us approval because of our financials. 'What guarantee do I have that you will be here next year?' and 'What do I do if you're not?' were some of the questions he asked."

Shortly after taking over the management of LIS, Patrick confronted the reality of "real slow sales" for Excelis-MLS. He concluded that the rate of progress the division would make given its limited market was not financially satisfactory: "And so the question became, 'Do we have other capabilities that we can exploit?'

"Our goal is to rapidly move the business to a cash-positive position. We are moving aggressively to reposition LIS so that it is more than the premier software provider to the mortgage banking industry. We also want to take advantage of the other things that we do well."

One of the things it did well was develop software. LIS believed it could sell the software development

ELECTIONS '92 SPECIAL REPORT: PAGES 15-19A, 1-12K.

The Dallas Morning News

Clinton triumphs

'The people have spoken,' Bush concedes

Perot finishes 3rd, wishes Democrat well

Women's wins signal big changes

Experts say economy swayed voters most

Williamson easily beats Guerrero

Bush carries adopted home state

Clinton runs close 2nd; Perot takes 3rd place

Rug importer kills brother, himself; 2 others wounded

November 1992 was a season of triumphs and hopes for both the Democratic Party and Lomas. Bill Clinton, the new leader of the Democratic Party, was elected President, reflecting the economic discontent that ended 12 years of Republican administration. The triumphs for Lomas after Chapter 11 were slow in coming, but there was optimism both at Lomas and the nation. Reprinted with permission of *The Dallas Morning News*.

skills it had acquired building Excelis to other companies. Of particular value was its expertise in customizing software.

The quality of its Data Center was another lucrative offshoot LIS chose to exploit. Excess computer capacity and the ability to run dedicated computers for individual customers who required that service became the basis of the new venture. LIS hoped to cash in on a growing trend toward "outsourcing" computer services. According to Patrick: "Businesses were increasingly saying, 'Why should I run a data center when I can outsource that? Why don't I hire someone whose full-time business is computers and let him worry about that? Then I can manage my core business and use data as a tool rather than another line of business.'"

LIS scored its first success in November 1992 with First American Tax Services, a company that provides homeowner tax information to mortgage companies. When the company decided to relocate to Dallas, it intended to build a data center to run its highly automated operation. LIS approached the company and sug-

LIS' first outsourcing computer services success came from First American Tax Services in November 1992. Lomas provided this building at the Lomas campus for a tape distribution center.

After inspecting LIS' facility, which is one of the largest data processing centers in the Southwest, First American decided that it would be cost-effective to have LIS run a discrete computer with their programs.

gested using LIS' Data Center instead. After touring the facilities, First American agreed that it would be cost-effective to let LIS run a discrete computer with their programs and also provide a building at the Lomas campus for a tape distribution center. The contract First American Tax Services signed with LIS in late November added $3 million in annual revenue to the division's bottom line.

Patrick believed that the revenues LIS generated from First American and customers like it could make a dramatic difference if the cards fell right: "It's something that could be low-key and low-grade and slowly build revenues, or it's something that could hit a grand slam home run."

Guarded optimism made a sensible forecast. The floor of LIS' executive suite was littered with fragments from the rose-colored glasses that others had worn. "LIS is a tough knot to untie," says Patrick. "It has been a very difficult piece of business for Lomas. It's getting better, but it just never gets as far down the road as we'd like it to go."

A year and a half after Chapter 11, the difficult knots at LIS and throughout the company were beginning to loosen. "We are pleased with the Company's progress since its emergence in January 1992 from its Chapter 11 proceedings," Jess Hay wrote in the 1992 annual report, "and we are committed to the task of creating a steadily expanding horizon for the enterprise in the years ahead."

. . . the spirit of Lomas

As Lomas Financial Corporation moves toward that horizon, it is evident that many of the forces that shaped its past continue to influence its future. Prominent among those is entrepreneurship, a fundamental corporate value that Patrick identifies as "the spirit of Lomas—the willingness to let people within the organization go to bat and swing." There is nothing new about that. People at Lomas have been stepping up to the plate and swinging throughout its history. The company has always valued what Franklin Roosevelt called "bold, persistent experimentation." Many of the milestones in Lomas' 100-year history highlight that trait:

- Undaunted by the recent failure of his furniture store, John E. Lomas opened an office in New Haven, Connecticut, in September 1894 and offered customers mortgage loans and other financial services.
- Six years later, Lomas invited Edward L. Nettleton, a childhood friend, to become his partner. Nettleton left the security of an established family grocery business and accepted the offer.
- When the Great Depression threatened to sink Lomas & Nettleton's mortgage loan business, the company shifted business directions. Sydney W. Gould introduced cutting-edge technology by leasing IBM keypunch machines that enabled the company to track its growing property management business.
- Following the initiative of Al Rohnstedt in the 1950s, Lomas & Nettleton opened a branch office in California and met the challenge of an expanding business 3,000 miles from its Connecticut base of operations.
- Meanwhile, in Houston, the energetic entrepreneurship of Torrey James Bettes and John Austin laid the foundation for the T. J. Bettes Company, the country's largest mortgage banker.
- Then, in 1965, under the leadership of Jess Hay, Lomas launched what became the company's greatest period of growth.

These and hundreds of other defining moments make up the long and successful heritage of the enterprise called Lomas. As the company prepares to celebrate its centennial, responsiveness to change remains one of the crucial characteristics from the past that continues to direct its future.

Another legacy of the past thirty years has been

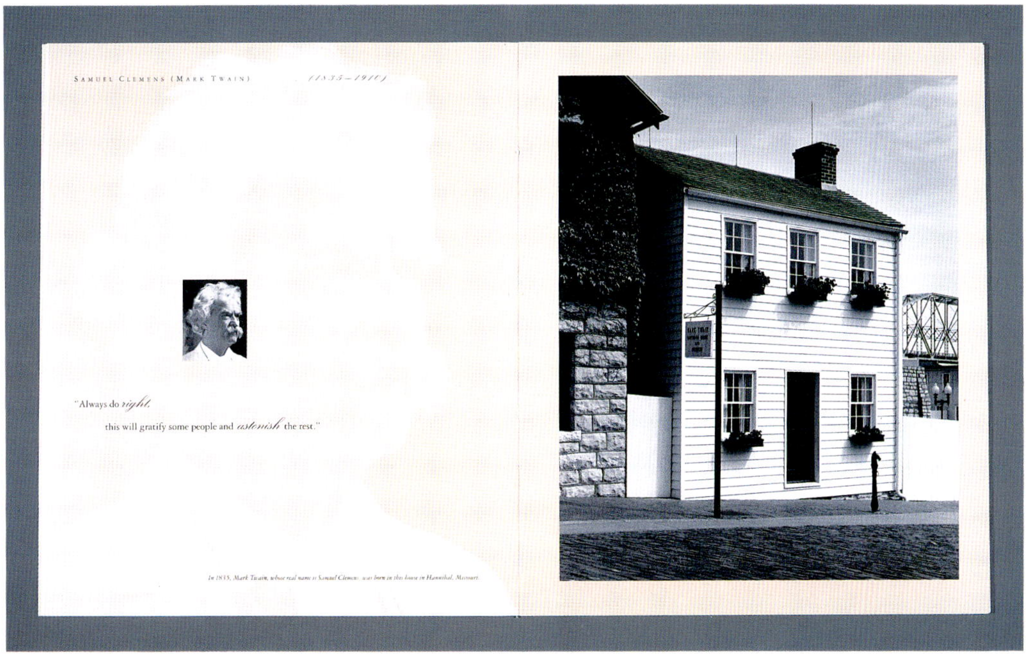

Jess Hay's commitment to the corporate legacy of profit with honor was well expressed in the Lomas 1992 annual report with a quote from Mark Twain: "Always do right, this will gratify some people and astonish the rest."

Jess Hay's unswerving commitment to integrity. That ideal has served the company well. Guided by Hay's moral compass, Lomas steered clear of the classic misbeliefs that have bedeviled much of corporate America's pursuit of money and power—that success is preferable to excellence, that wealth is the equivalent of honor, that strength is superior to reason, that rules are the same as ethics, and that profits are more important than standards.

Profit with honor, the corporate mission statement announced by Hay in 1965, remains the core belief driving Lomas toward the future. "Finally and most fundamentally, we value and remain committed to integrity," Hay wrote in 1988. "Integrity, consistently applied in the nurturing of all of our relationships in the execution of our corporate mission, produces trust and confidence: and that trust, in turn, is what holds us together and enables continuing progress. It is the catalyst which expands the Company's horizons. . . .

"Although the Lomas of tomorrow in fact is different from the L&N of the past, in a fundamental sense it has not changed."

"We value integrity."

This was the concluding idea to a speech written and delivered by Jess Hay.

David Chapman responded to the message by adapting the last paragraphs of the speech

for distribution at a national meeting and within the company.

❖ WE VALUE INTEGRITY. ❖

We believe that honesty and integrity are the hallmark of character, and essential components of long-term functioning in this or any other society. ❖ Integrity involves a lot more than just not lying. It involves being true to yourself, and being truly yourself in dealing with others. ❖ It involves 'being you,' but not in the hedonistic sense of 'doing your own thing' without regard to the needs of others. 'Being you' is to be true to your own values, your own convictions, your own potential, your own responsibilities without inordinate or overriding concern for reward, pleasure or penalty in any given moment. ❖ The antithesis of integrity and of character is the tendency to do, in response to every situation, that which is easiest and least demanding of you as a person. Integrity is keeping your head, your own sense of history, your own sense of purpose and direction, your own sense of conscience, of right and wrong, your own perspective (rooted deeply in the whole of our life) even as all those around you are pushing you in conflicting and contradictory directions. Integrity recognizes the imperfection of every person, and a person of integrity recognizes and accepts his own imperfection. He, therefore, is slow to judge, quick to forgive and anxious to redeem, and he also is open to forgiveness and to redemption when it is offered to him by others. When he errs, he does not seek the momentary and illusory comfort of pretense or escape. ❖ Rather he faces his error squarely, resolves to make amends, hears and accepts God's word of perpetual grace, and proceeds with the task and joy of living in honest relationship with others.

❖ The person of integrity accepts responsibility for his words and for his actions. He does not try to shift that responsibility if things go wrong. A person of integrity is a man or a woman endowed by God's creative hand with the determination to be a fully functioning responsible human being, a contributor, a participant, a risk taker, a doer, a lover and, in his relationship with others, a compassionate outreach and extension of God's love. ❖

EPILOGUE

The pace of change at Lomas quickened following the conclusion of this book's final chapter in early 1993. During the first six months of fiscal 1994, the mortgage refinancing wave of the early 1990s peaked and produced an annualized portfolio run-off rate of more than 45 percent, by far the highest ever experienced by Lomas. Fortunately, mortgage production exceeded run-off by a slight margin, thereby avoiding any net portfolio erosion; however, the related investment required to achieve that result was substantial and, for the first time, exceeded Lomas' internally generated cash flow. It became clear that mortgage banking in the future would be more capital intensive than ever before and that productive response to emerging opportunities probably would require capital augmentation from one external source or another.

To meet these new challenges, Lomas retained Salomon Brothers Inc in March 1994 to help evaluate various strategic options, including the possibility of merging with or being acquired by another institution. "We feel the current situation in our industry provides unique additional possibilities for growth," said Jess Hay, chairman and chief executive officer of Lomas. "While Lomas has demonstrated that it is capable of maintaining the size of its portfolio in the face of unprecedented high prepayment rates, it nevertheless is true that with additional capital resources our mortgage and computer businesses would flourish, thereby potentially increasing value for our stockholders and concurrently serving the best interests of our operating businesses, our customers and our employees. What we are doing is making sure that all such possibilities are explored. Regardless of our course from this point forward, we are very optimistic about the future and we are confident that, one way or another and as they have throughout the last 100 years, the people of Lomas will continue making significant and creative contributions to the evolving nature of our industry."

DIRECTORS OF LOMAS FINANCIAL CORPORATION

Name	*Tenure*
James R. Adams	1992–1992
John F. Austin, Jr.	1960–1963
Henry C. Beck, Jr.	1960–1964
Gene H. Bishop	1969–
Robert G. Boucher	1992–
L. D. Brinkman	1979–1992
Dolph Briscoe	1979–
A. B. Cass, Jr.	1960–1968
William H. Cothrum	1963–1964
Frank M. Crossen	1965–1992
Jerome K. Crossman	1960–1969
Trammell Crow	1960–1961
	1965–1971
James L. Crowson	1994–
James M. Cumby	1963–1964
Rod Dammeyer	1992–
R. Ted Enloe III	1970–1991
Mark M. Feldman	1993–
Osborne Fernald	1960–1973
J. D. Francis	1966–1977
Felix Harris	1960–1960
Jess Hay	1960–
George Heftler	1964–1978
Edmund M. Hoffman	1960–1976
Joe B. Hutchison	1960–1964
Woodward Kingman	1976–1984
James J. Laney	1960–1964
Robert LeBuhn	1993–
Robert V. Lindsay	1992–
Tom Lively	1960–1965
Eugene M. Locke	1960–1966
H. Neil Mallon	1960–1974
E. Kirk McKinney, Jr.	1986–1992
Bill O. Mead	1976–1992
John B. Mills	1964–1974
Fred B. Morrison	1967–1976
Reid Nagle	1993–
Diana Natalicio	1992–
Jon Newton	1983–1993
Michael E. Patrick	1992–1994
Maurice E. Purnell, Sr.	1972–1972
DeWitt T. Ray, Sr.	1965–1987
Hugh G. Robinson	1992–
Douglas L. Rock	1992–
Nat S. Rogers	1976–1992
Albert N. Rohnstedt	1964–1987
Ira Rupley	1960–1960
Harvey M. Schuster	1992–
John F. Sexton	1987–1992
Stuart Silloway	1960–1964
L. R. Strickland	1968–1971
George Underwood, Jr.	1975–1976
Paul T. Walker	1992–
E. E. Wallace, Jr.	1960–1964
W. Ray Wallace	1966–
Richard M. Wartes	1964–1965
Paul S. Wolansky	1993–
James M. Wooten	1976–1992

DIRECTORS OF LOMAS MORTGAGE USA, INC.

Name	*Tenure*
George Bender	1963–1964
Gene H. Bishop	1970–1975
	1990–1991
David L. Chapman II	1994–
James L. Crowson	1989–
James M. Cumby	1964–1964
Minott A. Davis	1938–1948
Terry J. Deyoe	1992–
R. Ted Enloe III	1977–1989
F. Peter Gaffey	1971–1977
Alex L. Gleckler	1961–1963
Sydney W. Gould	1923–1952
Jess Hay	1964–
Gary H. Kell	1994–
David Kelly, Jr.	1968–1989
John E. Lomas	1894–1930*
John W. Lomas	1947–1963
Russell E. Lomas	1916–1932
Paul M. Low	1989–1990
Everett Mattson	1977–1984
Thomas J. Melody	1961–1963
Fred M. Morrison	1967–1975
Donald E. Nettleton	1923–1966
Edward L. Nettleton	1900–1928*
Kenneth E. Nettleton	1911–1946
Michael E. Patrick	1992–1994
DeWitt T. Ray, Sr.	1965–1977
Irving L. Rhodes	1943–1963
	1966–1971
Albert N. Rohnstedt	1946–1977
Remore B. Ross	1938–1968
John F. Sexton	1985–1989
David C. Stephens	1992–1994
Edmund L. Stoddard	1946–1963
E. E. Wallace, Jr.	1963–1964
Richard M. Wartes	1964–1965
Harold E. Whitcher	1943–1963
Gary White	1990–
M. D. Wommack	1963–1977
James M. Wooten	1975–1993

**Includes service as General Partner prior to the Company's incorporation in 1917.*

HONOR ROLL

Among the thousands who have contributed to the Lomas Financial Group during its first 100 years, the following is an incomplete listing of those who have served with distinction as officers and/or directors of Lomas and/or its affiliates:

Name	*Tenure (circa)*
Raymond G. Abide, Jr.	1993–
Charles A. Abright	1952–1973
David G. Adams	1982–1986
Donald K. Adams	1987–1989
James R. Adams	1992–1992
Rebecca A. Aduddell	1989–
Bentura Albizo	1992–
Van C. Alexander	1972–1987
James B. Alleman	1994–
Noline C. Allen	1961–
Robert B. Allen	1987–
William H. Allen	1974–1974
W. Meredith Alliston	1980–1989
Daryl Anderson	1971–1976
Elena Anderson	1987–1989
Mary A. Anderson	1974–
Thomas W. Anderson	1974–1989
Gail D. Andrews	1987–
Jerry D. Angerman	1989–1989
Robert L. Appel	1990–1993
Janis L. Aramburu	1989–
David Armato	1986–
Cynthia Armstrong	1988–1993
Vickie L. Atteberry	1980–
John F. Austin, Jr.	1960–1963
Richard A. Ayers	1970–1989
Mary Jo Babcock	1981–1990
Deborah A. Bacon	1983–1989
Arthur E. Bailey, Jr.	1968–1979
Donna R. Baker	1987–
Perry L. Ball	1987–
William Ballew	1992–
William S. Banowsky	1987–1993
F. Charles Bantuelle	1964–1982
William F. Barbish	1954–1987
Charles B. Barefoot	1969–
David T. Barenbrugge	1976–1982
	1985–1987
Janet M. Barnes	1985–
Roger F. Barney	1971–1973
Frederick J. Bastel	1980–
Don Batchelor	1965–
Carl Bauer	1960–1988
Will M. Beale	1952–1969
James V. Beaman	1989–
Kathleen M. Beaudette	1972–
Henry C. Beck, Jr.	1960–1964
Charles W. Becker	1986–
Elizabeth Joan Becker	1992–
Michael L. Becky	1982–1987
Lydia J. Bedell	1980–
David A. Bell	1983–
Jamie L. Bell	1972–
Doris E. Belle-Isle	1955–1987
George Bender	1962–1964
Drake C. Bennett	1986–
Gwen M. Bennett	1982–
Russell L. Bennett	1958–1967
	1971–1976
George H. Bergdoll	1971–1977
William L. Best	1992–
Robert H. Beuttas, Jr.	1977–1990
James N. Bibb	1985–1993
Darrell Bidwell	1981–1984

David D. Billingsley	1968–1980
Gene H. Bishop	1969–
J. Phil Bishop	1973–1989
Daniel E. Black	1987–1989
Larry J. Blair	1977–1986
Richard J. Blake, Jr.	1985–1986
Gary Blend	1982–
Judy Bliss	1989–
Howard Blizzard	1993–
Joseph C. Blum	1988–1989
Sarah Boggus	1991–
Steven D. Boice	1983–
Victoria S. Boice	1984–
Kevin L. Boltz	1989–
Richard A. Bondie	1971–1983
Lynne G. Bondy	1984–1990
Russ Bones	1973–1977
Eric D. Booth	1979–1985
June J. Bottema	1984–
Robert G. Boucher	1992–
Patrick D. Bouldin	1994–
Elvis Bowens	1991–
Robert A. Bowie II	1987–1989
Richard W. Bowman	1987–1988
Paulette Bradshaw	1982–1988
Richard H. Bramblett	1967–1974
Beth A. Brannan	1988–
E. G. Bray	1945–1986
N. Preston Breed	1969–1990
B. A. Breeding	1989–
James A. Breeze	1993–
Mattie Brian	1958–1978
David W. Bridewell	1988–1989
Eloise B. Briley	1957–1986
L. D. Brinkman	1979–1992
Dolph Briscoe	1979–
Sharon K. Brock	1987–
Ronald J. Brodt	1987–1989
B. Saunders Brook	1967–1967
Cotton Brown	1970–1985
Gloria D. Brown	1985–1988
Mary Ann Brown	1988–
Michael L. Brown	1987–1993
James C. Brownlow	1972–1980
Fred G. Brunn	1955–1983
William R. Bryan	1992–1993
Alexander L. Buck	1983–1991
Edmund L. Buckley III	1980–1983
Patricia D. Buckley	1987–1988
David A. Buckman	1980–1991
Michael R. Buda	1988–
Carolyn A. Edwards Bullock	1983–
Brian M. Burback	1984–1988
David A. Burdette	1985–1988
Robert R. Burdt	1991–1994
Willie E. Burgess II	1991–
Anne-Marie Burgett	1986–
Jerri D. Burkhart	1982–
L. Keith Burkhart	1982–1986
Mary F. Burnette	1989–
Ron Burnette	1992–1993
Eugene Buss	1987–
James L. Busselle	1968–1977
Len A. Bussey	1987–1987
John R. Butler	1941–1977
Sam A. Butler, Jr.	1985–
Bradley S. Buttermore	1980–
Debra A. Buttermore	1988–
Robert E. Byerley, Jr.	1982–
Lisa L. Caire	1986–
Robert D. Caire	1993–1993
Michael C. Caldwell	1989–1989
Warren F. Caldwell	1965–1989
Dana A. Call	1987–1993
James Callery	1969–1993
Eugene F. Cammarota	1988–1988
Carol A. Campellone	1971–1988
Michael J. Carlson	1987–1989
Richard H. Carnevale	1961–1987
Robin A. Carr	1989–1991
Susan L. Carroll	1992–
Jon R. Carter	1974–1991

Tom H. Carter	1972–
William L. Carter, Jr.	1973–1978
Eilene Sandra Caruso	1976–1994
James E. Cary	1972–1974
Daniel Casey	1985–1988
A. B. Cass, Jr.	1960–1968
Joseph G. Cervini	1970–1973
James E. Chambless	1987–
Pamela R. Chance	1987–
David L. Chapman II	1985–
Wallace E. Chappell	1989–1991
	1992–
Chris R. Chase	1986–1989
Patricia A. Chase	1982–1988
Bettinna M. Chatham	1973–
Vicki L. Chenault	1992–
Robert R. Chilton	1969–1969
Richard Choffel	1987–1988
Anthony J. Cifelli	1975–1987
C. J. Cimino	1952–1979
Alan J. Cizdziel	1986–
Thomas J. Clancy	1992–1994
C. Willis Clark	1963–1978
Michelle A. Cline	1985–1990
Thomas J. Clooney	1987–
Bob Cody	1972–1989
Louis R. Coffman	1987–1989
Kathleen M. Cole	1993–
Alan B. Coleman	1981–1992
Patricia L. Coletti	1974–
Vincent Coletti	1939–1987
G. Wade Compton	1987–1989
Frank Comroe	1946–1985
Morton L. Comroe	1950–1985
William P. Comroy	1972–1972
Thomas Cone	1973–1982
Fred P. Connor	1963–1985
Ralph D. Cook	1971–1985
Clinton J. Cope	1988–
Howard Cordray	1960–1964
John H. Cornish	1987–1988

J. Michael Cornwall	1992–1993
Benjamin A. Cotharin, Jr.	1975–1987
William H. Cothrum	1963–1964
Ronald L. Cowan	1980–1991
James M. Crafton	1986–1990
William Cravens	1975–1978
John Cregar	1971–1971
John H. Crew	1938–1969
J. Stephen Crim	1979–1991
John Crone	1971–1982
Kendall C. Crook	1986–1987
Frank M. Crossen	1965–1992
Harold S. Crossen	1960–1963
Jerome K. Crossman	1960–1969
Trammell Crow	1960–1961
	1965–1971
James L. Crowson	1987–
Richard D. Cruise	1988–1989
James M. Cumby	1963–1964
James P. Cunningham	1961–1973
Dean P. Cuplin	1987–1989
David J. Curtis	1987–1988
Denise E. Daft	1990–
Flavio Daibert	1989–
Charles A. Dale	1987–1989
John H. Dalton	1985–1992
Frank D'Ambra, Jr.	1987–1989
Rod Dammeyer	1992–
Edward R. Daniel	1988–
Richard E. Danley	1966–1972
N. Anthony Dann	1975–1976
James H. Daughdrill III	1992–1992
Deborah Davis	1988–1991
Dennis J. Davis	1989–1993
John R. Davis	1972–1974
Mark Davis	1993–
Minott A. Davis	1934–1948
Barbara R. Deborah	1992–
James P. DelVecchio	1980–1985
	1989–1989
James De Nicholas	1962–1963

Omar L. Dennis	1979–1984
Patrick L. Dennis	1982–1992
Paula S. Denny	1976–
Robert R. Denton	1978–1985
John Detzel	1993–
Jan Nanning de Vries	1987–1988
Hugh S. DeWitt	1953–1987
Tim E. DeWitt	1988–
Terry J. Deyoe	1989–
Pravin K. Dhingra	1986–
Ken Dickenson	1986–1989
Jon N. Dickerson, Sr.	1989–
Byron Todd Dillard	1989–
Joy Dillon	1984–1989
Kenneth C. Dippel	1973–1978
Patricia J. Disbrow	1981–
Tom Dodds	1975–1981
Thomas P. Dohney	1950–1981
Eric L. Donowho	1984–
Brian E. Doran	1988–1991
Randy J. Dorman	1989–
David E. Doss	1987–1988
Randall Dotson	1982–1989
Forrest B. Dowdy	1972–1977
Victor G. Draper	1988–
Jim Dryden	1987–1989
Joseph O. Dryer	1969–1976
	1988–1988
Dorothy Autrey Dunne	1984–1993
Henry H. DuPre, Jr.	1943–1982
W. John Dziadul, Jr.	1983–1987
Michael G. Eagan	1985–
Patrick Eagle	1987–1988
Robert R. Earl	1987–1988
Donald E. Earnhart	1976–1989
Felicia M. Eastman	1991–1993
John F. Eastman	1965–1989
Donald M. Eaton	1978–1983
Robert F. Ebach	1970–1987
Steve Eberhardt	1978–1983
Kelly W. Eckels	1984–
Milton E. Ecker	1958–1989
Scott A. Eckert	1986–1993
James O. Edwards	1991
Marshall B. Edwards	1975–1976
Robert L. Edwards	1988–1989
Weston E. Edwards	1984–1988
Charles J. Eglinger, Jr.	1965–1984
M. Sue Elfving	1980–1988
Delta A. Emerson	1982–1994
F. Charles Emery	1985–1992
R. Ted Enloe III	1969–1991
Thomas D. Enneking	1986–
Patricia R. Entesari	1991–1994
Rhonda Esquivel	1984–
John E. Ewing, Jr.	1975–1987
Dave Facka	1975–1979
Bruce M. Fahsel	1990–1991
George F. Fairbanks	1981–1988
Robert E. Falco	1981–
Edward R. Fancher	1917–1920
William H. Fantone, Jr.	1965–1987
David N. Farmer	1987–1990
David H. Farr	1986–1991
James A. Farr	1991–
Stephen W. Faulkner	1990–
Mark M. Feldman	1993–
John F. Ferguson, Jr.	1987–
Wayne D. Ferguson	1977–1991
Pamela M. Ferguson-Gaines	1988–
Osborne Fernald	1960–1973
Walter A. Fernandes	1985–1986
Charles H. Finn, Jr.	1986–1988
William N. Fisher	1969–1974
James M. Fleming	1961–1978
Perce Fleming	1971–1971
Diane Monroe Fletcher	1983–
Paul D. Fletcher	1987–
Suzanne Fletcher	1986–
Lewis Thomas Flint	1965–1976
Senovio Flores	1978–1990
Michael W. Forbes	1988–1991

Stephen Ford	1982–1986
Mick Forde	1991–1994
Bruce Forney	1986–
Carol A. Forsberg	1986–
Carole Foster	1987–
Rosalind C. Foster	1987–
Thomas J. Fourmy	1951–1985
David G. Fox	1985–1993
Ross C. Fox	1956–1971
W. Theodore Fraebel	1986–1987
George E. Francis	1956–1987
J. D. Francis	1966–1990
Richard Frazer	1975–1976
Shannon D. Frazier	1987–
Bruce L. French	1980–1990
R. Bruce Frey	1984–1984
Gloria F. Friant	1969–1986
Linda A. Frietsch	1983–1990
Charlotte Fritchie	1983–1984
W. Lewis Frye, Jr.	1974–1977
Donald D. Funkhouser	1978–1989
Jody S. A. Furtney	1990–
F. Peter Gaffey	1952–1986
James W. Gaines, Jr.	1980–
Robert M. Galisin	1972–1987
Pamela Jean Gallahar	1989–
Charles O. Galvin	1976–1993
Mario Garcia	1986–
Patricia A. Gardino	1970–1994
James B. Gardner	1981–1992
Dennis M. Gartin	1976–
Leonard W. Gasperin	1989–1993
Donna W. Geel	1972–1989
Carl F. Geiser, Jr.	1957–1976
E. Ted Geistweidt	1979–1993
Howard S. Geltman	1985–1987
Theodore A. Genetti	1980–1988
Mary Lynn Genovesi	1987–
John N. Geyer	1982–1983
Robert W. Gibbs	1964–1966
Darlene Gibson	1988–
Frank E. Giglio	1980–1986
Thomas L. Gilbert	1986–1987
Vicki J. Gilhooly	1985–1990
E. John Giliam	1986–
Norman C. Gillespie	1991–1991
Karen M. Glasgow	1974–1989
William Glasgow, Jr.	1969–1989
Alex L. Gleckler	1952–1978
Richard J. Glynn	1946–1976
Robert A. Golden	1987–1989
Wanda Golemon	1980–1989
Leon M. Golinski	1985–1987
Gary Pat Goodwin	1983–1986
Larry Gore	1983–1991
Norman Gould	1986–1988
Sydney W. Gould	1922–1952
Jim C. Goyen	1960–1965
Joseph E. Grady	1986–1987
Lorraine Grant	1985–1992
Kathleen M. Gray	1987–1989
Michael R. Gray	1976–1976
Otha L. Green	1970–
Mark Gregor-Pearse	1984–1989
Louis P. Gregory	1988–
Cynthia L. Gressett	1990–
Douglas J. Gressett	1990–
James Griffey	1988–1989
Brian J. Griffin	1987–
Steven R. Grundon	1987–1989
Milton Gumm	1979–1990
Allen C. Gunter, Jr.	1978–1987
Milton Gunther	1985–1987
Anita L. Haddy	1983–1993
Curtis Haire	1984–1990
Michael G. Haley	1976–1978
Norman R. Hall	1965–1975
R. Steven Hall	1987–
Keith Hamby	1985–
Peggy R. Hamil	1959–1989
Marcus Berry Hamilton	1982–1990
L. Howard Hamlin	1986–1987

Julie Lynn Hanrahan	1989–
John E. Hanson	1986–1990
Paul A. Harber	1971–1991
David B. Hardin	1972–1973
James J. Hardy	1975–1980
Jackie R. Hargrove	1983–
George S. Harkins	1964–1967
O. Riddick Harrell	1977–1982
Felix Harris	1960–1960
James M. Harris	1986–
Jeannie Harris	1988–
Lynn Wyler Harris	1984–
Ned R. Harris	1980–
Tommy R. Harris	1987–
Susan P. Hartman	1992–
Maurice D. Hawbaker	1961–1980
Jess Hay	1960–
Bert P. Headden	1992–
Patsy Heaton	1985–1989
George Heftler	1964–1978
Charles M. Hegarty	1987–1989
John S. Heine	1985–1993
Robert L. Helberg	1962–1986
Jim Hendry	1970–1976
Edward R. Herman	1987–1989
Michael F. Herman	1987–1989
Polly Hershey	1986–
Ann P. Hill	1973–
Cloressa Hill	1971–1989
James Hill	1987–
Kenneth E. Hill	1988–1989
Kim S. Hill	1984–
Philip J. Hill	1987–
Hal Hillman	1983–1993
Gretchen Hobbs	1990–1994
Gilbert H. Hockeborn	1985–1986
Diana L. Hodson	1986–
Edmund M. Hoffman	1960–1976
Brenda K. Hoffpauir	1974–
Ronald O. Hogue	1987–1989
Barbara A. Holland	1973–
Thomas W. Holland	1985–1986
Susan E. Holliday	1986–
John D. Hollister	1979–1988
Roy L. Holloway	1987–1989
Joan C. Holmes	1986–
Thomas J. Holmsley, Jr.	1953–1985
Michael A. Holt	1984–1990
D. Scott Holtz	1984–
Henry G. Hortenstine	1981–1990
Kim Horton	1982–1988
Suzanne Hosch	1988–
Francie L. Howard	1981–
Martha W. Howard	1982–
Kevin M. Hoyt	1977–1988
Thomas J. Hruska	1980–1988
Jay Nell Hubbuch	1978–1991
Dennis E. Huber	1967–1987
William E. Hughes	1986–1989
	1993–
Glenn L. Human	1987–1988
Todd L. Hunnicutt	1988–
Medford B. Hunt	1972–1973
Randall L. Hunter	1984–1985
Robert B. Hurd	1948–1987
Joe B. Hutchison	1960–1964
Kay Bailey Hutchison	1986–1991
Harry M. Huter	1964–1967
Roger D. Innes	1987–1989
Jeanette M. Isaacs	1975–1984
Patricia D. Isken	1987–1989
C. Robert Jackson	1986–1990
Ronald L. Jackson	1986–1990
Andrew F. Jacobs	1988–1993
Matthew S. Jacobs	1981–1992
Alvin W. Jaetzold	1951–1980
Deborah James	1983–
Gary Michael James	1968–1983
Gary R. Janko	1974–1988
James H. Janssen	1987–1989
Scott E. Jefferies	1985–1990
	1991–1994

Melvin E. Jefferson	1987–1988
Alan S. Johansson	1978–1988
Lawrence A. Johnes	1987–1989
Gary B. Johnsen	1987–1989
Charles R. Johnson	1972–1987
Dianc R. Johnson	1975–1988
Esther Johnson	1932–1987
Helmer O. Johnson	1969–1989
Joseph A. Johnson	1993–
Phillip E. Johnson	1971–1974
Robert E. Johnson	1978–1989
Whitaker M. Johnson	1987–
David L. Johnston	1973–1978
James L. Johnston	1978–1982
Gordon E. Joiner	1984–
Hays Jones	1936–1974
James H. Jones	1969–1972
Leon E. Jordan	1985–1987
Rebecca Judd	1979–
James Judge	1982–1992
John Jumonville	1984–1988
Paul M. Jurkoic	1987–1989
Judy Justice	1985–1990
Scott A. Kahl	1993–1994
Kenneth F. Kalka	1968–
Kenneth M. Karant	1985–
Michael Karlak	1962–1986
Timothy C. Kay	1985–1991
Leslie D. Keefe	1984–
Gary H. Kell	1969–1976
	1979–
Richard J. Kelleher	1987–1990
Sidney L. Kelley	1948–1987
David Kelly, Jr.	1962–1989
Patrick Kelly	1977–1983
Stanley Z. Kelts	1987–1989
Judith P. Kent	1984–1986
Judy A. Kernea	1983–
Michael L. Kerr	1983–
Craig Kimray	1979–1993
Billy Wayne King	1968–1977
Francis P. King	1980–1987
Stephen E. King	1988–1994
Woodward Kingman	1976–1984
Robert L. Kinney	1964–1969
James Kirby	1971–1973
J. Colin Kirkham	1986–
Barbara J. Klatt	1989–
Walter C. Klein, Jr.	1969–1986
James E. Kleitches	1990–
Kenneth A. Klusewitz	1982–
Nelson E. Knapp	1946–1963
Michael A. Knudsen	1988–1993
Mary Patricia Knuffke-Dietz	1988–
Joni M. Koch	1981–
Deborah E. Kohls	1985–
Marcie J. Kolb	1988–
Pamela Kolb	1975–1989
Ken Kolodziej	1967–1978
Patricia S. Koning	1988–1992
Sharon W. Koplan	1991–
Janice E. Kozumplik	1981–
Howard Krollfeifer	1987–1988
Joseph Krupka	1984–1986
Adrienne LaCava	1985–
William H. Laird	1946–1973
Mark A. Lambert	1980–
Marjorie G. Land	1993–
Brett L. Landes	1984–1989
Richard L. Lane	1958–
James J. Laney	1960–1964
James E. Langhurst	1986–
Hiram G. Langley III	1988–1988
Richard F. Langston	1969–1972
Wayne T. Larroque	1985–1988
John H. Larson	1983–
Henny Lasley	1990–1992
Lanelle Latendresse	1960–1989
David M. Law	1984–1988
Janetta P. Lea	1988–1991
Sidney E. Leake	1966–
Robert LeBuhn	1993–

D. Jack Lee	1971–1973
Jack L. Lee	1969–1972
Robert E. Lee	1977–1987
Robyn S. Lee	1992–
Louis M. Leimbach, Jr.	1969–1976
Calvin E. Lemmon	1977–1977
Marvin R. Leventhal	1972–1976
Lawrence I. Levy	1972–1976
Charles W. Lewis	1969–1989
Roger J. Lincer	1988–1990
Henry H. Lindner, Jr.	1972–1987
Robert V. Lindsay	1992–
Albert N. Lindstrom III	1986–1988
Lorraine E. Link	1988–1989
Richard O. Linsert	1965–1984
	1992–
Norris Lipscomb	1967–1972
L. Lloyd Little, Jr.	1973–1979
Tom Lively	1960–1965
David Livingston, Jr.	1980–1980
Norman P. Lober	1961–1977
Eugene M. Locke	1960–1966
John Locke	1973–1980
John E. Lomas	1894–1930
John W. Lomas	1945–1974
Russell E. Lomas	1914–1932
Mark W. Long	1981–1987
O. William Long	1987–1987
Gordon E. Longacre	1969–1969
Paul M. Low	1958–1991
Steven D. Lowe	1986–1987
James L. Ludman	1964–1985
Robert J. Lynch	1966–1984
Maurice F. Lytle, Jr.	1972–1977
Ronn K. Lytle	1977–1983
	1985–1992
Matt G. Maberry	1980–
Marion L. Maciejeski	1950–1977
Phyllis Maclachlan	1983–
Daniel P. MacLean	1963–1979
Donald J. MacMaster	1970–1970
Mary J. Macy	1969–1984
Julie Maddux	1984–
Stacey L. Magee	1986–
Richard K. Magel	1989–1994
Thomas J. Maher	1970–1980
Sam J. Mainord	1990–1993
George A. Maler	1987–1988
H. Neil Mallon	1960–1974
Terry W. Malone	1978–1983
Angela D. Maloney	1982–
Robert M. Maloney	1976–1980
Bobbie R. Mandell	1987–
Gary R. Manion	1985–1987
Sam Marcus	1963–1963
Mike J. Markovich, Jr.	1972–1988
Harold E. Marsh, Jr.	1955–1983
Jacquelyn Marsh	1986–
Thomas L. Marsh	1974–1989
J. William Marshall	1985–1987
Richard J. Marshall	1956–1989
Barbara H. Martin	1986–1988
Kelli Lane Martin	1988–
Leigh Martin	1986–
Raymond C. Martin	1971–1974
Joe G. Martinez, Jr.	1990–
Julia Martinez	1977–
Nancy Massenburg	1986–
Rex E. Masterman	1981–
Valerie Masters	1989–
Beth S. Mathews	1993–
John L. Matthews, Jr.	1973–1987
Everett Mattson	1945–1984
James A. May, Jr.	1971–1973
Garry G. Mayo	1990–
Paul C. McAllister	1970–
Leigh McBride-Ross	1986–1987
Mona L. McBryde	1976–1987
Cindy McCafferty	1987–
Jeffrey A. McCalmon	1979–1986
E. L. McClennahan, Jr.	1975–1976
Stephen L. McCord	1975–1979

Julia G. McCormack	1988–
Donald K. McCortney	1988–1992
Joseph B. McDade	1972–1972
Bryan Drew McDonald	1988–
Jeanne M. McDonald	1976–1991
Kevin McGarry	1983–
Richard L. McGhee	1973–1987
Floyd L. McGlothlin	1973–
J. Robert McGrath	1953–1982
James R. McKay	1978–1980
Jan McKenney	1987–1989
E. Kirk McKinney, Jr.	1986–1992
Michelle A. McKinney	1992–
Robert H. McKinney	1986–1990
D. Steven McLaughlin	1986–
John E. McLemore	1987–
Stewart Ronald McLeod	1986–1990
O. Dale McPherson	1980–
Jo Anna McWilliams	1991–
Bill O. Mead	1976–1992
William Measures	1989–
Kevin P. Meehan	1988–1989
R. Jon Meier	1981–1986
Daniel J. Mekemson	1978–1983
Leslie J. Melcher	1988–1989
Thomas J. Melody	1958–1965
Robert A. Meloy	1981–1985
John Meyerhoffer	1985–1988
Paul S. Michaels	1982–1990
Harriett E. Miers	1988–1993
James W. Mignogna	1987–1989
Forrest W. Miller, Jr.	1978–1987
Henry S. Miller, Jr.	1969–1991
H. H. Miller, Jr.	1970–1990
Minor S. Miller	1977–1982
Ronald L. Miller	1974–1983
	1988–1990
John B. Mills	1964–1974
Edward M. Mirick	1952–1987
Kathleen R. Misch	1979–
Dennis E. Mitchell	1984–1994
Joseph A. Monahan	1985–1987
Dinah L. Monger	1985–1990
Lori J. Moody	1984–1988
	1990–
Joyce Moore	1973–1986
Julie A. Moore	1988–1993
Christopher J. Morell	1987–1989
Robert J. Moretti	1989–1990
Cynthia D. Morgan	1985–
Porter E. Morris	1946–1981
Dana S. Morrison	1987–
Fred B. Morrison	1967–1976
John R. Morrison	1975–1987
B. Paul Morsani	1971–1980
Stephen H. Morse	1971–1979
Michael E. Mox	1987–1989
G. Lee Mulder	1936–1984
Jim C. Mulford	1987–1990
Mary M. Mullen	1988–1992
Dianna C. Mullinax	1986–1994
Charles B. Mullins	1988–1993
Charles A. Munoz	1987–
Joseph E. Murphy	1969–1970
Russell C. Murphy	1972–1978
Donald W. Murray	1963–
Billy B. Musgrave	1985–1992
Jim Myckleby	1986–1989
Reid Nagle	1993–
Clinton D. Narmore	1972–1978
Diana Natalicio	1992–
J. Bradley Nease	1992–1993
Frank L. Nedney	1987–1989
Gerry C. Nelson	1978–1986
Karen R. Nelson	1990–
James R. Nettles	1988–
Donald E. Nettleton	1919–1966
Edward L. Nettleton	1900–1928
Kenneth E. Nettleton	1912–1946
Robert E. Nettleton	1954–1976
Jon Newton	1983–1993
Jim E. Nichols	1977–1991

John Nichols	1982–1989
F. Russ Nicholson	1987–
Mark Nieberlein	1985–1993
Krista K. Nix	1987–
Michael E. Norris	1986–1991
James R. Nowicki	1984–1989
Antonio A. Nunes, Jr.	1988–
Barbara F. Nye	1988–
Timothy O'Connor	1986–1993
James E. Odem	1954–1974
Kimberly Ogles	1983–
J. William Oldenburg	1962–1972
Ray Olds	1975–1977
Marc Olins	1970–1977
Catherine D. Olson	1990–
Jeri E. Oman	1965–1986
Barbara L. O'Neal	1988–1991
Elaine M. Orchard	1981–
James K. O'Reilly	1987–1990
William A. Orton	1984–1989
Erik G. Ostebo	1987–1989
Harry D. Pallick	1978–1991
Rhonda E. Parker	1970–
Sendai Parker	1988–1994
Thomas C. Parker	1986–1990
Richard A. Parkins	1982–1987
Betty J. Parsons	1956–1983
Michael E. Patrick	1992–1994
Patrick F. Patrick	1964–1976
Pamela H. Patsley	1987–1989
Dennis P. Patton	1976–1988
Marshall B. Payne	1992–1993
Thomas D. Pearson	1985–1987
Amy Carnes Peck	1986–
Robert J. Pelletier	1968–1977
John J. Pembroke	1984–1986
Antonio F. Pena	1971–1973
Joe L. Penland	1988–
Shirley Bird Perry	1988–1993
Timothy L. Perser	1987–
George Persons	1991–
Lester C. Persson	1961–1962
Michael A. Peters	1990–
Gary M. Petro	1961–1988
H. D. Petty	1964–1965
Arthur H. Pfeifer	1990–
Ben R. Phillips	1985–
Kenneth W. Phillips	1986–1990
James W. Pickup	1965–1986
Terry L. Pierson	1988–
Paul Pirok	1987–1989
John L. Plunkett	1987–1989
Wayne Plunkett	1988–1993
Bryard D. Poer	1978–
Thomas R. Poitevent	1963–1989
Scott E. Pollock	1987–1989
Kim Poole	1987–1994
Cynthia Porter	1983–1987
Gregory D. Powalski	1988–1989
William G. Powell III	1981–1991
John C. Prendergast	1968–1987
Glenn L. Prettyman	1991–
Robert E. Price	1961–1988
Richard G. Prosser	1969–1969
Debbie S. Pruett	1988–1992
Maurice E. Purnell, Sr.	1972–1972
James Rae	1954–1993
Raymond C. Ralph	1950–1985
Troy G. Rampy	1990–1993
Becky H. Raudebaugh	1983–
Pamela J. Rawlins	1983–1984
DeWitt T. Ray, Sr.	1965–1987
C. David Redmon	1980–1988
Susan D. Reece	1985–
Jerry Reed	1990–
Rebecca Reed	1990–1991
Steven P. Reed	1988–
Linda L. Reid	1973–1983
Nona L. Reid	1986–1991
	1993–
Randall S. Reid	1987–1992
Dan Reiff	1993–

Joseph F. Reilly	1960–1981
Phillip A. Reinsch	1993–1993
Sharon L. Reitzell	1988–1989
Roger A. Revell	1987–1989
Robert D. Reynolds	1973–1974
Irving L. Rhodes	1933–1971
Dennis B. Rich	1983–1993
E. Ann Richardson	1986–
John B. Richardson	1985–1987
David A. Ridley	1983–1990
N. Gary Rinehart	1971–1985
Richard M. Ringering	1983–
Wanda J. Rivera	1984–
Andrew H. Roberts	1948–1977
Mary A. Roberts	1986–1986
Maureen Roberts	1986–
Hugh G. Robinson	1988–
Richard H. Robinson	1987–1989
Douglas L. Rock	1992–
Donald D. Rodgers	1959–1977
Gordon R. Rogers	1988–1989
James A. Rogers	1972–1972
Lawrence M. Rogers	1966–1994
Mack L. Rogers	1976–
Nat S. Rogers	1976–1992
Robin L. Rohmer	1987–
Albert N. Rohnstedt	1934–1987
Fred C. Rohrbacker, Jr.	1966–1989
Ralph D. Rolen	1987–1988
M. Robert Roofner	1983–
Michael B. Roosth	1984–1987
Edward W. Rose III	1992–1993
Michael L. Rose	1987–1989
Joseph C. Ross	1984–1989
Remore B. Ross	1936–1971
Weda Ross-Branch	1987–
Donald C. Rosselli	1979–1988
Lauri S. Rothballer	1988–
Claude T. Rowe	1971–1972
Michael K. Rubin	1987–1989
William H. Rudluff	1963–1993
James S. Rudnick	1980–1983
Robert T. Rudy	1979–1987
Samuel R. Runco	1972–1972
Ira Rupley	1960–1960
John L. Rusie	1987–1989
Cynthia B. Russell	1982–1987
David L. Russell	1993–
Robert C. Rustigian	1986–1987
Ray L. Ryan	1959–1987
A. Dale Ryle	1985–1993
Gayle Saathoff	1986–
James N. Sabin	1978–1989
Jeffrey J. Sanders	1988–
Maureen J. Sando	1983–
Steven Scarbrough	1983–
W. A. Scarbrough	1960–1968
Jeffrey G. Schadt	1987–
Margaret E. Scherer	1955–1985
Stephen R. Schiffer	1973–1983
Karen Schlund	1986–
Jay W. Schmoll	1987–1990
Gary L. Schneider	1972–
Robert H. Schorn	1983–1993
Carol Finley Schuler	1989–
Jack Schure	1985–1988
Harvey M. Schuster	1992–
Thomas W. Schwartz	1965–1987
Kenneth C. Scott	1987–1989
Sandra L. Scott	1986–
Edward R. Scully	1988–1989
Jenifer M. Sebastian	1984–
Narinder S. Seera	1993–1993
Natalie J. Sekel	1984–
Phillip E. Sellers	1984–1992
John F. Sexton	1960–1992
J. Marvin Sexton	1974–1989
Paul Sexton	1962–
Richard W. Sharry	1973–1973
G. Frank Shedivy	1971–1979
Cindy L. Shellhorse	1987–1989
Stanley L. Shellstrom	1950–1986

Valorie L. Shelton	1988–
Carl L. Shepherd	1986–1990
Gary R. Shobe	1986–1986
James K. Short	1987–1989
Ronald E. Shults	1987–1989
Richard C. Sibert	1969–1974
D. Christopher Sieber	1987–1993
Sandra C. Silkey	1986–1987
Stuart Silloway	1960–1964
Doris M. Sims	1987–
Gordon L. Sims	1986–1990
Shellie M. Sims	1985–1990
Wade Sirmons	1990–
Christa C. Sladden	1974–
John M. Sladden	1973–1989
Janet Slaton	1993–
Helen Sloan	1930–1977
John L. Sly, Jr.	1981–1989
Nita Smiley	1984–
Alfred F. Smith	1966–1981
David E. Smith	1990–1993
Elizabeth Smith	1984–1990
Gary Smith	1984–1986
Goodhue W. Smith III	1992–1992
H. James Smith	1987–1987
Jerry L. Smith	1982–1984
Judy S. Smith	1982–
Karen R. Smith	1975–1989
P. Warren Smith	1971–1982
Rick W. Smith	1992–
Stephen W. Smith	1987–1989
Todd A. Smith	1987–1993
Wendy L. Smith	1987–
William R. Smith	1992–1993
Michael A. Sole	1969–1993
George J. Solibakke	1962–1973
Webb Sowden	1989–1990
James E. Sowell	1992–1993
Meyer Specter	1972–1972
Leland R. Speed	1991–1992
William D. Speed	1986–1994
Bruce Spencer	1981–1986
Jon P. Sprinkle	1986–
Carol J. Spruiell	1990–
Gene Sprung	1969–1976
James R. Stanley	1961–1964
William R. Starkey	1970–1989
Ashley Stephens	1983–
David C. Stephens	1987–1994
John P. Stevens	1987–1988
David C. Stewart	1992–
Robert C. Stewart	1985–
Homer E. Stine	1987–1989
Edmund L. Stoddard	1946–1969
Daniel B. Stoltje	1954–1987
Roger D. Stotts	1986–1993
L. R. Strickland	1968–1971
J. Robert Stringer	1988–1989
R. A. Struglia	1973–1978
John T. Stuart III	1981–1992
Cynthia Stynchula	1994–
Duoen Janis Su	1992–1994
Audrey E. Suehs	1981–1989
Barry F. Sullivan	1990–
David B. Sullivan	1981–1987
John L. Sullivan	1988–
Timothy H. Sullivan	1981–1984
Tom Summers	1987–
Susan Sumner	1987–1989
Laura Murillo Sutherland	1986–
Nita Swafford	1978–
Carol Swaner	1972–1991
Lewis T. Sweet, Jr.	1986–1993
Mary L. Symes	1987–1989
William C. Tagau	1989–1989
Della Talbert	1960–1964
Robert W. Talkington	1971–1989
Tsu Tan	1985–
Thomas L. Tanner, Jr.	1986–1992
James N. Tardy	1963–1964
Cathy Tarver	1989–1990
Wayne R. Tate	1986–1988

J. Austin Tatum	1951–1971
Keith L. Taylor	1983–
Ramona Taylor	1965–
Scott A. Taylor	1987–1990
Hugh H. Tebault	1964–1970
Ben Tellez	1987–
Betty C. Temple	1982–
James J. Terrell	1988–1988
Joel L. Terry	1973–1985
John M. Teutsch, Jr.	1966–1972
Darlene Winchester Thimmig	1985–1993
Gay M. Thomas	1986–
Kenneth R. Thomas	1954–1985
L. Lanay Thomas	1987–1989
Omar E. Thomas, Jr.	1967–1976
W. Tack Thomas	1981–1992
Lewis C. Thompson	1961–1987
Julie A. Thorpe	1985–
Virgil Mike Throne	1985–1989
Thomas Thurman, Jr.	1957–1987
Joel D. Tibbott	1986–1990
Henry Y. Tileston	1987–1988
Bruce F. Tingle	1971–1972
Elaine M. Toal	1990–
David M. Toepp	1983–1989
Sandy D. Tolbert	1968–
John C. Tolleson	1987–1989
Catherine A. Tomasz	1982–1989
Henry C. Tong	1920–1937
Dawn E. Traverse	1988–
Calvin C. Trim	1986–
James W. Trowbridge	1989–1990
Jean A. Tuffield	1979–
Monte L. Tullos	1991–
David Turek	1978–1982
Ernest W. Turnbull	1961–1985
Burl E. Turner	1983–1986
Pat Turner	1989–
Robert J. Twitty	1977–1987
Martin Tycher	1986–1993
John G. Umdenstock	1969–1980
Connie A. Underwood	1970–
George Underwood, Jr.	1975–1976
James Unger	1980–1980
Jack W. Upton	1967–1987
John G. Urban	1987–1989
Christi L. Urbanovsky	1973–
Gabe Utz	1987–
Richard W. Vague	1987–1989
Bill D. Vance	1971–1983
Byron E. Vance	1987–1989
Tessia L. Van Curen	1979–1989
Melinda A. Vanderberg	1990–
Karen Vandiver	1985–
Catherine R. Van Hest	1987–1989
Roger D. Van Scoy	1987–1989
Edgar VanSlyke	1977–1981
Rick G. Vaughan	1988–1989
Robert R. Veach	1980–1983
Lynda-Ross Vega	1983–
Ricardo Alberto Vega	1993–
Dennis C. Veit	1986–1987
Capi E. Vellinga	1977–1989
Angelia M. Venker	1988–
Meredith Vertrees	1987–1993
Stanley Vickhouse	1971–1974
Reagan K. Vidal	1987–1992
Richard P. Viviano	1987–1989
Gus W. Voelkel	1958–1987
Mary H. Vu	1989–
James C. Wadkins	1980–1989
James E. Walicek	1985–1991
Michael R. Walker	1972–1982
Paul T. Walker	1992–
Wade Walker	1986–1993
Evelyn V. Walla	1954–1985
E. E. Wallace, Jr.	1960–1964
W. Ray Wallace	1966–
Thomas A. Walsh	1972–1972
Frederick D. Wampler	1988–1989
Bruce Ward	1983–1987
Whitney O. Ward	1982–1987

Shirley Warren	1986–
Stephen J. Warren	1987–1987
Richard M. Wartes	1964–1965
Randall G. Waters	1985–1993
Betty Watson	1963–1989
Marlene Weed	1991–
Robert F. Weissman	1973–1978
Joy T. Weldon	1975–1991
Paul S. Wenning	1993–
Thomas K. Werder	1990–
Charles S. Werner	1976–
Martin J. Wertheim	1985–
George Westmoreland III	1982–
Kate Wheeler	1984–
Harold E. Whitcher	1927–1972
Gary White	1969–
Karen L. White	1988–
Sally White	1975–
William C. White	1987–1988
Warren J. Whiteman	1960–
Albert A. Whitesell	1961–1987
Jeffrey D. Whitlatch	1985–1989
Jo Karen Whitlock	1986–1989
Morton K. Whittaker	1951–1974
Carey B. Wickland	1982–
Eugene Wilhelm	1982–1990
Mary Yvonne Wilkerson	1985–1991
Dennis C. Williams	1987–
Mel L. Williams	1984–
P. Gregory Williams	1986–1990
René Williams	1987–
Susan C. Williams	1991–
David M. Williamson	1993–
Brent Willmott	1987–
Benjamin R. Wills	1986–
Diane Files Wilson	1987–1993
George I. Wilson	1961–1985
Jimmie G. Wilson	1986–
Larry L. Wilson	1969–1974
Lawrence A. Wilson	1981–1992
Melvin H. Wilson	1953–1985
Teresa Wimberly	1978–
J. Gregory Winchester	1983–
Charles W. Wingo	1969–1991
Henry P. Winkler	1946–1981
Robert J. Winnick	1978–1987
Robert Jay Wisdom	1985–
Adrian G. Wnukowski	1986–
Paul S. Wolansky	1993–
Ruth A. Womack	1983–1992
M. D. Wommack	1960–1979
	1984–1991
Thomas K. Woodruff	1970–1992
James M. Wooten	1946–1994
Alyson S. Wright	1987–
Cindy J. Wright	1990–
James P. Wright	1982–1988
Kimberly A. Wright	1986–
Paul J. Wright	1989–
Tamara LaMotte Wright	1984–
G. Michael Wueste	1977–1985
Willie D. Yarbrough	1990–
George R. Yates	1987–1989
Julie Fenton Young	1983–1988
Russel D. Young	1973–
Timothy C. Young	1983–
William C. Young	1982–1987
Frederick G. Zakula	1980–
Tricia M. Zimmerman	1980–
Louis A. Zola	1980–

INDEX

LOMAS: THE FIRST ONE HUNDRED YEARS

was designed, produced, and set in 11 on 14 Garamond 3
with initial caps in Garamond 3 italic, on
Macintosh IIci, in QuarkXPress 3.2.
Subheads set in Helvetica Black with initial caps
in New Baskerville italic.
This book is printed on 140 gsm Espel paper
in a first edition of 5,000 copies.
The binding fabric on standard hardbound books
is Brillianta.
The cover material for special edition books is
Cromwell "Sederra" binder's leather.

EDITED BY MATTHEW ABBATE
DESIGN AND PRODUCTION BY JAMES A. LEDBETTER
SPECIAL PHOTOGRAPHY BY WILLIAM K. SACCO
COVER AND FRONTISPIECE PHOTOGRAPHY BY RAY HAND
PRINTED AND BOUND BY SOUTH CHINA PRINTING CO.,
SHATIN, NEW TERRITORIES, HONG KONG